ALSO BY MARGOT PETERS

Charlotte Brontë: Style in the Novel

Unquiet Soul: A Biography of Charlotte Brontë

Bernard Shaw and the Actresses

Mrs. Pat: The Life of Mrs. Patrick Campbell

The House of Barrymore

MAY SARTON

MAY SARTON

A BIOGRAPHY

MARGOT PETERS

FAWCETT COLUMBINE
THE BALLANTINE PUBLISHING GROUP • NEW YORK

A FAWCETT COLUMBINE BOOK
PUBLISHED BY THE BALLANTINE PUBLISHING GROUP

Copyright © 1997 by Margot Peters

All rights reserved under International and Pan-
American Copyright Conventions. Published in the
United States by The Ballantine Publishing Group, a
division of Random House, Inc., New York,
and simultaneously in Canada by Random House of
Canada Limited, Toronto.

http://www.randomhouse.com

Library of Congress Catalog Card Number: 98-96017

ISBN: 0-449-90798-8

Cover design by David Stevenson
Cover photographs courtesy of Margot Peters

This edition published by arrangement with Alfred
A. Knopf, Inc.

Manufactured in the United States of America

First Ballantine Books Edition: July 1998
10 9 8 7 6 5 4 3 2 1

FOR P.R.J.

Contents

Contents

Acknowledgments

The bulk of May Sarton's papers are in the Berg Collection of the New York Public Library. My thanks to Philip Milito, technical assistant at the Berg, for his assistance over the years. I also worked with a considerable archive of material at Sarton's home in York, Maine, much of which will go to the Berg Collection and to Westbrook College in Portland. I am also grateful for the assistance of Elizabeth Joffrion, archivist at the Archives of American Art, Smithsonian Institution; John Lancaster, curator of special collections, Amherst College Library; Patricia C. Willis, curator of American literature, and Alfred Mueller, public services assistant, the Beinecke Rare Book and Manuscript Library, Yale University; Cathy Henderson, research librarian, the Harry Ransom Humanities Research Center, the University of Texas at Austin; Patricia J. Albright, assistant archives librarian, Mount Holyoke College Library; Carolyn A. Davis, reader services librarian, Syracuse University Library; and Leo M. Dolenski, Mariam Coffin Canaday Library, Bryn Mawr.

For their kind permission to quote from letters, very special thanks to Eric Dubois (Eugénie Dubois), Professor Carolyn G. Heilbrun (Carolyn G. Heilbrun), Francis Huxley (Sir Julian and Lady Huxley), Mrs. Robert Woods Kennedy (Edith Forbes Kennedy), Jean T. Kroeber and Graham R. Taylor Jr. (Katharine Taylor), Elena Levin (Harry T. Levin), Margot Lieberman (Jean Clark Lieberman), Ruth Limmer (Louise Bogan), Morgan Mead (Morgan Mead), Eric F. Menoyo, Palmer & Dodge (Professor Cora DuBois), William Rukeyser (Muriel Rukeyser), Helen Sheehy (Eva Le Gallienne), Joy Greene Sweet (Katrine Greene), Eric Swenson (Eric Swenson), Timothy Matlack Warren (Judith Matlack), and Mrs. D. Bradford Wetherell Jr. (Anne Thorp).

I am grateful for the invaluable help of May Sarton's many friends, acquaintances, associates, and others: Page Ackerman, Molly Howe (Mrs. Faneuil) Adams, Theodore Adams, Joanna Hawthorne Amick, Abigail Avery, Charlotte Bouton Barnaby, Barbara Barton, Professor Walter Jackson

Bate, Professor Brian Beck, Dr. Eric Berger, Alan Best, the late Eleanor Blair, Lee Blair, Claire Bolder, William Theo Brown, Mrs. Lillian Budd, Jean P. Burden, Horace Colpitts, Honor Conklin, Helen Storm Corsa, Catherine D. David, Linda H. Davis, Bradford Dudley Daziel, Eric M. and Denise Dubois, Amanda (Mrs. Philip) Dunne, William B. Ewert, Hermann and Kate Field, Christine Fisher, Vincent Frazzetta, Dean and Sylvia Frieze, Dr. James Gilroy III, Laura Graham, Professor Ray Griffith, Doris Grumbach, Jeannette S. Guildford, Edythe Haddaway, Beverly Hallam, George R. Hanna, Judith Harrison, Sir William Hawthorne, Linda Herbert, Marcie Hershman, J. Parker Huber, Constance Hunting, John Hurley, Eleanor Newman Hutchens, Francis Huxley, Professor S. Jackman, Beulah E. Jenkins, Nancy P. Jordan, Mary B. (Mrs. Robert Woods) Kennedy, Professor Karl and Jean Taylor Kroeber, Ethel Kurland, Jane P. Leonard, Elena (Mrs. Harry T.) Levin, Jacqueline Limbosch, Norman Lloyd, Dr. Patricia Locuratolo, Evangeline Maginnis, Charlotte Mandel, Jerre Mangione, Janet Mann, Morgan Mead, Hugh S. Moorhead, Victoria T. Murphy, Professor Andrea Musher, Jack Nelson, Janice Oberacker, Deborah Pease, Margaret W. Pepperdene, Eleanor Perkins, Richard Pipe, Naomi Pritchard, Charlotte Radintz, Lucy Barry Robe, Helene J. Rodar, Margaret Roets, Karen Saum, David G. Selover, Susan Sherman, Judi Siegfried, Morris Simon, Mary-Leigh Smart, Polly Thayer (Mrs. Donald) Starr, Joy Greene Sweet, Eric Swenson, Graham R. Taylor Jr., Professor Michel and Huguette Thiery, Margaret Vaughan, Dorothy Wallace, Frances (Mrs. D. Bradford) Wetherell Jr., Martha Wheelock, Anne Woodson, Warren Keith Wright, and Marilyn J. Ziffrin. My gratitude as well to "Dinah," "Elspeth," and "Monica."

Very special thanks to Timothy Matlack Warren, Judith Matlack's nephew and May Sarton's personal representative, and to Phyllis Warren for their generous help; to Carolyn G. Heilbrun, May Sarton's literary executor, for her encouragement and collegiality; and to Margaret Whalen and Barbara Martin, whose hospitality, assistance, and friendship assisted so materially in the writing of this biography.

I am very grateful to Professor Rebecca Hogan, the University of Wisconsin–Whitewater, who read the entire biography in manuscript and offered detailed comments and insights.

Loving thanks to Peter Ridgway Jordan and Elsie McCullough for their scrupulous reading of the manuscript.

To Victoria Wilson, my editor, warm thanks for her wise and friendly support. Many thanks, too, to her assistant, Lee Buttala, for his good care.

Finally, my best thanks to May Sarton, who authorized me as her biographer. Like most famous people, I suspect, May both desired and feared a biography. Yet, though far from well, she entered into the project whole-heartedly, not only corresponding with me, sending me her books, and providing introductions to friends, but granting me more than fifty hours of interviews over the last four years of her life as well as permission to quote freely from her published and unpublished writing. I treasure the fact that she looked forward to our talks, which became increasingly frank, despite my warning that the biography would be "warts and all." She was, *au fond,* a woman of spirit and fortitude. I am glad to have known her.

MAY SARTON

Prologue

May Sarton—poet, novelist, journal writer, feminist, and lesbian—is speaking on campus, any campus during the 1970s, anywhere in the United States. Electricity charges the air. For the first time since the feminist movements of the nineteenth century, women are listening to other women—not to men—talk about themselves. For her frankness and intimacy, Sarton has won more fans than perhaps any other contemporary American woman writer.

She is a striking woman in her sixties: short, curly white hair; strong, classic face; black horn-rims emphasizing the pallor of unlined skin; bright lipstick. Rather portly, but the weight is attractive. She is probably wearing a deep purple suit from Gertrude Singer, her favorite shop in Harvard Square, or, for a formal reading, an elegant black pantsuit. She favors suede flats; like Harriet Hatfield, one of her fictional characters, she's vain about her small feet.

Her voice is a strong, clear contralto; as she reminds admirers, she was trained in the theatre by Eva Le Gallienne. But it's immediately obvious that she is a performer, used to mesmerizing audiences. These audiences are, and have always been, largely female. Some are lesbians, but the majority are not—a statistic that Sarton, who hopes her writing has universal appeal, enjoys.

At a local feminist bookstore near campus, young women gather, surrounded by recent feminist biographies of Charlotte Brontë, Mary Wollstonecraft, and Zelda Fitzgerald, as well as by the books that have made May Sarton a heroine of feminists and the woman on the street: *Mrs.*

Stevens Hears the Mermaids Singing, Plant Dreaming Deep, Journal of a Soli-tude, and *As We Are Now.* Sarton seats herself on a low stool, the women on the floor at her feet in a semicircle. For the majority it is their first encounter with a writer who speaks directly about the problems of being a writer in a literary establishment dominated by men. The questions spill out: "What made you become a writer?" "How do you *do* it?" "What's it like, being a role model for women?"

Sarton has a gift for getting down to cases. "I write because I must. That's the only way anyone's going to become a published writer. I write three hours a day, every day, five pages of a novel; I'm proud of that disci-pline in my life. It's tough, but I'm not exactly breaking stones for a living—it's what I want to do. The problem is, my readers write me! I never get out from under the letters that pour in. Yet the letters save my life, because they show me how I've saved other lives. That's a great gift to me."

"Your journals seem so open," says a young woman. "Have you always been that honest?"

"No. It takes time to grow into honesty. I didn't come out as a lesbian until *Mrs. Stevens,* when I was in my forties. I didn't want to be labeled too soon, set off like Radclyffe Hall. More important, I waited until my par-ents were dead. I didn't start living alone until then, either. You shouldn't live alone until you've lived a lot. You have to be enormously disciplined; you have to have something physical to do—in my case it's gardening. Contacts are important, but they dissipate the intensity of living, and it's the intensity that makes the work of art."

A young woman in a sweatshirt and jeans raises her hand. "How can a married woman with children ever achieve that kind of intensity?" she asks. "A thousand things distract me every moment of the day."

"Perhaps the women's liberation movement will make it possible for mothers to be literary creators. It can be done, but it's terribly difficult. You don't have to work ten hours a day, but as I say, it's the quality of time around the working hours. Look at the great women writers—Austen, Eliot, the Brontës, Woolf. None of them were mothers. But marriages are changing. The thing is, in America we want everything, and the creative life costs something. But too much literature has been written by women like me who are not wives and mothers. We need to hear from women who are. And the first task is to make the kind of love women feel for each other clear. Because women have something to give each other which very rarely men can give. Not necessarily sexual, but a love and a trust. Feeling. Americans are terribly afraid of feeling. Sex is all right as long as you don't feel. That's why men hate women poets; women's feelings make them squirm. It's the last thing they want to hear about."

"Are you writing poetry now?"

"Yes. Because I have a Muse again, which is amazing when you're sixty-five. Poetry is a gift; you can't make it on will. With me it's the Muse who causes poetry by focussing the world. It doesn't matter whether I go to bed with her or not. With me, it's been half and half." She expels a gust of laughter. "Perhaps because I couldn't persuade the other half!"

After a dozen more questions, Sarton lights a cigarette and glances at her watch: she has a poetry reading on campus in half an hour. The women crowd round, offering books for signing. "I didn't say faithful love isn't possible," says Sarton around her cigarette, autographing a copy of *Mrs. Stevens.* "It is, as long as people go on growing. What's hell is having to pretend that love is faithful to death when that love is dead. When it's no longer nourishing."

They follow her out into the crisp October night, reluctant to let her go, though the poetry reading is ahead. She is a myth made material, a palpable charge of inspiration. Her courage gives them courage. For that precious moment, she is sister, mother, lover, mentor, and friend.

May Sarton's gift for inspiring others was perhaps her greatest achievement. But no public figure levels completely with an audience—and Sarton was a performer above all. As I would discover to my dismay, her real life, as opposed to the myth she created, was turbulent, guilt-ridden, full of pain and disappointment—and just plain messy. I am tempted to post a warning: THIS BIOGRAPHY STRONG MEDICINE. NOT TO BE TAKEN INTERNALLY BY SARTON FANS. Yet perhaps the real May Sarton will be more lasting inspiration than the myth, a phoenix risen from the ashes of fires hotter than anyone guessed.

CHAPTER I

Wondelgem: 1911–1914

For May Sarton, the house in Belgium where she was born would always be a lost paradise.

It stood in flat countryside about five kilometers north of the Flemish city of Ghent in the ancient village of Wondelgem, beautiful in its simplicity and harmony of line. A red tile roof overhung two stucco stories opened to the air and sun by large casements flanked by shutters. Glass entrance doors sheltered a roofed porch with benches inside, English church style. Green lattices enticed climbing roses and vines.

Inside, the house blended utility and art. A large kitchen with red-tiled floor, a generous laundry room, a large master bedroom, and sturdy dumb-waiters satisfied practicality. But it was the exquisitely stitched muslin curtains and linen tablecloths, the hand-crafted and -painted cupboards, beds, and tables of bird's-eye maple and walnut, the heavy, dark Flemish bahut, the books lining the walls, and the vases of bright flowers perfuming the air that lent the house its distinctive charm.

Secluded from the cobbled streets, the grounds too combined art and utility. Oaks made a park of the long sweep of green lawn; formal beds bloomed with columbine, sweet peas, poppies, peonies, and larkspur. Behind the house a small orchard yielded plums and apples for pies and preserves; there were strawberry beds and gooseberry bushes, cold frames for lettuces and cucumbers, and a large *potager* bursting with leeks, turnips, beans, radishes, and Brussels sprouts.

In the house lived George Sarton, a young scholar intent on making an international name as a historian of science. The sale of his father's wine cellar had made possible the purchase and remodeling of the Wondelgem house, which did not much interest him. Mabel Elwes Sarton, his wife, was six years older, a willowy Englishwoman with wistful blue eyes. She was an artist of nervous sensibility, neurotically plagued by illnesses both real and imagined, frustrated both by her own ambitions and by her husband's blind absorption in his work. In the beautiful house these two made each other tolerably miserable—perhaps because they loved each other intensely.

George Sarton had grown up solitary in his father's gloomy house in Ghent, never knowing his mother, who died half a year after his birth on August 30, 1884. His father, Alfred, did not speak of Léonie: he closed up her piano and continued to travel on business as a director and chief engineer of the Belgian State Railways. George was raised by kind but ignorant Flemish servants trained to remove him from the dinner table when he made too much noise. His father paid him little attention; yet George felt he loved him "exceedingly" in his distant way. Alternately ignored and indulged, he was shy, eccentric, arrogant. He was a stocky young man just over five feet seven, with brilliant eyes that could beam or quickly fill with sentimental tears behind rimless spectacles. He had a radiant smile.

Mabel Elwes had stronger ties to Belgium than to England. From early childhood she and her brother, Hugh, had been farmed out to caretakers while her mother, Nellie, accompanied her civil-engineer husband, Richard Gervase Elwes, on bridge-building expeditions abroad. In her teens, Mabel was sent to the Institut de Kerchove in Ghent to learn French, which she eventually spoke without accent. When her father was ruined in a South African mine failure, Mabel returned to the Institut de Kerchove as a lowly *surveillante.* She had no gift for controlling unruly girls, as Céline Dangotte, a pupil, observed. Céline persuaded Mabel to live with her family and initiated her into their interior design business, La Maison Dangotte. In 1903, her father's temporary prosperity drew Mabel back to England, but a year later she returned permanently to Ghent to make her home with the Dangottes.

Mabel loved her adventurous father, and he, at a distance, loved her. She did not love her mother, whose indifference blighted her childhood.

George and Mabel had met in 1906 through a newspaper ad. He was a student at the University of Ghent, a novelist, and the founder of an idealistic group of young men calling themselves Reiner Leven (Purer Living). She was a designer for La Maison Dangotte and a member of the

Wondelgem, May in baby carriage, 1913

Flinken (the Bold Ones), a group of emancipated working women. When Reiner Leven advertised in a Ghent paper for new members, the Flinken unexpectedly answered. They discovered they were all more or less intellectuals, socialists, vegetarians, teetotallers, and women's rightists. Surrounded by women for the first time in his lonely life, George Sarton promptly fell in love with pretty Mélanie Lorrein, but turned for advice in the matter to a pair of close Flinken friends, Céline Dangotte and Mabel Elwes.

Eventually Mabel proved more interesting than Mélanie, and George began to open his heart in letters. "Sarton," Mabel replied in 1907 to one of these confessions, "thank you for your letter, thank you for trusting me enough to choose me when you need to talk to someone at times. . . . Oh, Sarton, Sarton, there is something in you that I like so much—I seem to be always arguing and disagreeing with you, but indeed in spite of that I feel that you are not such a horrible long way off from me as almost every-one is from every-one else."

But there were obstacles to winning Mabel: George's self-absorption, his doubts about marriage, his determination "that in no way will I undertake the support of [a] wife," and Mabel's equal determination to have a career and independence, as well as her fear of sex. "Je vous aime de toute mon âme—mais sans passion," she confessed. The turmoil caused by George's sexual desire coupled with her desire for a career and fear of marriage caused a nervous collapse. She had to give up the miniature portraits for which she was beginning to win commissions and escape to Zurich to learn bookbinding at the Kunstgewerbeschule.

They tortured each other with dozens of soul-searching letters: "Oh, I want you, I want you—more than you believe." He did not believe in her love, he replied. She replied that she knew the absence of her body, which she could not give, tortured him.

Mabel returned to Ghent and La Maison Dangotte. She found her fears confirmed. There was a difference between the way she kissed George and the way he kissed her. She realized that embracing her made him suffer in strange masculine ways. Women, she decided, never could love like men. "I feel that in spite of the sympathy and affection that exists between us, that I am not the fit woman to be your wife." Friends told her she was torturing him unmercifully. She withdrew.

Then one night, she and George unexpectedly caught sight of each other at a concert. Frisson. The next day she came to his study in the ancient Dominican monastery. George was waiting to be asked: his father's death in 1909 had freed him financially; he had begun his doctoral dissertation. On March 21, 1910, they became officially engaged.

Still there were doubts. George brooded on "the sadness and waywardness" of his youth. Mabel assured him she forgave his trespasses. But would he forgive hers? Sending for her birth certificate, she discovered that she had been born out of wedlock; she sobbed all night. Then they had a terrible fight over how, if marriage proved intolerable, they would divorce. She signed herself "Your Wild Bird," hinting at the ferocity of her nature. Yet they were driven inexorably toward marriage. In May 1911 George received his doctorate magna cum laude from the University of Ghent in physics and mathematics, and on June 21 they were married at the town hall. "Though I loved her passionately," said George, "I did not hesitate to tell her that my work was more important than herself."

Wondelgem was to be the home neither had known. A passionate gardener, Mabel immediately hired a boy to turn over earth for planting;

George immediately plunged into the creation of his brainchild, an international journal of the history of science. He worked among his books until teatime, absorbed, indifferent, "a sleepwalker."

She discovered that he was hopeless about the house, incapable of boiling water or nailing down a loose board. He had warned her he had no intention of earning a living; she did not know what would happen when money from the sale of the fabulous wine cellar ran out, because certainly she could not support them with occasional art work. Yet he was tight with money, commanding her to keep track of every penny. When she brought her accounts, however, he waved her off: "I haven't time for that, I have work to do!"

Then Mabel discovered she was pregnant. Doctors had advised the perennially ailing woman against childbearing; and then George, who called her "Mother," wished to be the child in the house. They had tried to prevent her conceiving but, in George's words, were "too impetuous and maladroit." "Mabel is as well as possible," he jotted in his diary as the gray Belgian winter settled over Wondelgem, "but I can not help feeling anxious. The child is expected to arrive in May."

Mabel's words about her marriage and pregnancy are few but significant. There is her deadly fatigue, understandable in the person who was obliged to make the marriage work—for George Sarton remained what he had been: selfish, boyish, enthusiastic, and almost totally absorbed in his work. There is her "hungry" letter to her beautiful Zurich friend Méta Budry, to whom she longed to give "a long 'mothering' sort of kiss." Mabel had intense friendships with women—Céline Dangotte, Madeleine Van Thorenburg, Méta. She preferred women, perhaps, to men. Now there would be a baby, sealing her marriage. Typically, she made "no fuss." Of all her admirable qualities, George most admired the "no fuss."

Late on the afternoon of May 3, Mabel's labor began. She continued setting strawberry plants, moving along on her knees between pains. George sent for Céline and the best doctor in Ghent; he was aghast when the doctor merely glanced at the patient, settled himself in an armchair, and lit a cigar. Nearly as wracked as Mabel, George stayed by her side, "holding her hand, stroking her arm, wiping her forehead and uttering every word of encouragement and endearment" as hour after hour of hard labor dragged by. Periodically the doctor would remove the cigar and call encouragingly, "Poussez, Madame, poussez!" When a girl was finally born, she was put into Céline's arms.

"Petite May est arrivée le soir vers 10 et ¼ heures après avoir fait souffrir sa maman pendant 4 à 5 heures," George noted in his diary with relief and triumph. "Elle pesait en naissant 3045 gr. et était ma foi très gentille: elle avait de longs cheveux noirs et poussait des cris perçants." The birth of a six-and-a-half-pound, black-haired daughter uttering "piercing cries" now seemed a miracle.

They named the child Eléanore Marie, changed "Marie" on the birth announcement to "Mary," then changed "Mary" to "May" and dropped the "Eléanore." George Sarton liked short names. But there was another birth that month more important to George than that of his daughter: "Two children were born to us in 1912," he would always say. This second child, his journal devoted to the history of science, he christened *Isis* after the mother goddess of the Egyptians. *Isis* would be his true daughter—disinterested, rigorous, pure: a beacon illuminating the great scientific discoveries of the past. Of *Isis* he was both creator and priest.

A month after May's birth, Mabel went to rest at Knokke on the sea, taking the maid, Marta, to care for the baby. Céline and her new husband, Raymond Limbosch, accompanied them. Raymond was George's closest friend, a member of the Reiner Leven, a poet, socialist, and philosopher whom George had thought poor until he rang the bell of the Limbosch dressmaking establishment in Ghent and was admitted by a butler. But even with friends, Mabel was nervous and unhappy. From afar she dared to criticize George's aloofness. "You are always in a sort of hurry. I always feel your work dragging at you. *I need* you. I feel suddenly that you *must* give me what I ask—that I ought not to beg for it."

The child was both joy and burden. Mabel agonized when May Baby's "queer long silky black hair" fell out, rejoiced when golden hair came in—though "it still stands straight up all over her little head . . . as if she were wildly surprised at life in general." Little May's incredible energy—"like a tiny white *wind-mill* when one sees at a distance over the edge of her carriage, the little arms beating the air so restlessly and continually"—exhausted her. The baby was always hungry, screamed with rage if she was not fed fast enough, so that Mabel had to sit on one side of the highchair and Marta on the other, spooning the open mouth. She sucked everything in reach, "including her hands—so dreadfully." Mabel returned to Wondelgem, hardly rested, often in tears. "Pledge to spend more time with Mabel," George wrote guiltily in his diary. In a broad straw hat he went out to plant an herb garden next to Mabel's works of horticultural art; yet all his consulting of herbal lore failed to coax a green shoot out of the ground. With profound relief, he returned to his study.

In January 1913, Mabel fled to the Dangottes at Rhode-St.-Genèse. "I do not think I am capable of giving up entirely my work," she wrote her husband. "The desire to work is a real passion—only second to my love

*Mabel Sarton
and May*

for you—(perhaps equal)." She confessed she should not have married—
"voilà la vérité." She stayed with the Dangottes through August, her let-
ters litanies of complaints. She seldom asked after her daughter.

Then Mabel discovered she was pregnant again. Her friends were furi-
ous with George, but what else could be expected from a "maladroit"
couple sometimes sharing a double bed? By April 1913 Mabel was so
unwell that they decided to deliver May to their good friends François
and Véra Bouny-Tordeur, living near Mons. Five days before her first
birthday, George boarded the train with little May.

Céline, not her mother, first cradling her. Handed over to maids as an
infant. Abandoned by her mother and largely ignored by her father. Now
a prolonged exile from both parents at Mons. Sadly, George and Mabel,
both neglected as children, had already established that pattern with their
own child.

Mabel gave birth to a boy, a blue baby. "Let us run to the hospital!"
said Céline, holding the dying infant in her arms. "No!" said George.
That at least was the story eventually told May by her mother and Céline.

Recovering from her second confinement, Mabel thought guiltily of her exhausting little daughter. "May Baby has been away at Mons for nearly 4 weeks," she wrote Méta. "May Baby is *very* good & yet she tires me. She is put to sleep in her new cot & left to go to sleep alone! . . . She no longer wets her napkins!!! (sauf exception!) . . . I am trying *very* hard . . . not to spoil her!!! I sent her away partly for her sake. . . ." By the end of summer she was no better.

Clearly Mabel's illnesses during these first years of marriage were largely psychosomatic. Serene on the surface, sentimental, even cloying, in letters to Méta, she had a fierce temper inherited from an irascible mother: not for nothing had George nicknamed her "Petit Coq." Her father had advised her during childhood tantrums to go pound a nail with a hammer or break sticks. But pounding a nail could not now assuage the need for solitude, creativity, and independence which marriage and motherhood denied her. Her suppressed rage found outlet in violent headaches, an accelerated heartbeat. She was as neurasthenic and sensitive as George was vigorous and sanguine. "Mabel's health was the only persistent cloud of our married life," said George.

There was another cloud forming on the horizon, yet the placid Belgians largely ignored the rapid German buildup of railway terminals and supply depots on the Belgian frontier. George had joined the *garde civique;* finding their training "shockingly amateurish," he'd felt justified quitting the organization in 1912 to concentrate on *Isis.* Belgian neutrality, guaranteed in 1839 by the five Great Powers, seemed inviolable. Belgium was at peace, George working among his notes, Mabel carrying little May to the garden to show her a rose or a marigold. "We were innocents," said George.

Determined to have a career, Mabel was designing furniture and embroidering emerald-green curtains and bright pillows for Céline's business, Arts Décoratifs Céline Dangotte, to be exhibited in June at the Salon de Bruxelles, which for the first time would showcase the new *art décoratif.* Finishing the suite of furniture meant a trip to Austria to consult with carpenters; and Méta Budry came to Wondelgem for a month to care for May.

May attached herself fiercely to beautiful Méta, who played delightful games with her, tossing her into the air on her big bed. Perhaps it was during Méta's stay that May wandered into the strawberry beds and painted herself head to toe with red juice. Or that she was discovered howling in the pantry, balancing on a chair atop a table, the pot of new jam still out of reach. Mabel returned to experience the episode of the bowl of goldfish in the shop window: May in white coat, hat, shoes, and stockings—denied the object of her desire—flinging herself headlong into a mud puddle in revenge. The doctor recommended plunges into cold tubs for frequent tantrums, but May regarded this as something of a game. Then the child had to be sent away again to the Bouny-Tordeurs. Little May wept so bitterly at still another separation from her mother that George wept too. But at the Bounys'—it was already a pattern—May attached herself violently to Véra. She became "very demanding and spoiled there," snatching toys from the Bouny children triumphantly.

On the other hand, the little girl was so quick, so laughing, so alive to all things beautiful, so miraculously responsive to a tender word or caress that she could not help delighting her parents. Though her father, crying "Wa wa! Wa wa!" as he flung her into the air, could terrify her, she adored her mother and was passionately attached to a bright flower, a kitten, a cloud, a butterfly, a tree—like her mother, loving the sun and the earth and everything on it. And the earth was beautiful that June of 1914 in the country at Wondelgem under the large oaks.

Then, on June 28 at Sarajevo, a Serbian nationalist shot the Austrian crown prince, Franz Ferdinand. Austria immediately declared war on Serbia; France rejected Germany's demand that she remain neutral; Germany declared war on Russia and France. There was only one route to Paris. Germany invaded Luxembourg on August 2 and sent Belgium an ultimatum demanding free passage for German troops. Belgium declined and accepted a state of war, but the country was scarcely prepared to withstand the masses of gray German troops that poured into the country like a river of steel. Liège fell on August 7.

"Naturally we've heard nothing from you since communications were so abruptly cut off," Mabel wrote Méta on August 15. "The first days were a nightmare—now life is somewhat back to normal 1) because the Belgians rose so admirably to the defense of their country and their honor, 2) because one gets quickly accustomed to this terrifying state of waiting. George volunteered for the Red Cross—without success. Both of us will work here with an ambulance, I hope. I do not foresee danger here for quite a long time. . . . I wonder if and when you will receive this card."

On August 20 the Germans entered Brussels. So much for Mabel's stunning work for the Salon de Bruxelles. George was issued an old gun, a police whistle, and a lantern and told to guard the railroad crossing. Pacing back and forth in his military greatcoat under the stars, he reflected that he was not sorry he had been devoting less than ten percent of his time to breadwinning. What did it matter—what did anything matter now? The world was in chaos.

"We are well," Mabel wrote Méta on September 19. "May is growing fast and is a great and tender joy in these times. *We are staying here* until the last minute—to protect the house if possible, to help protect the peasants and to help them to *remain calm* if that becomes necessary. . . . We've had five refugees from Malines in the house for three weeks."

Like Belgium itself, the "innocents" had not been prepared. They managed to dig a hole in the garden one night and bury a trunkful of George's precious notes. They deposited their many love letters in the Banque de Flandre in Ghent. For the rest, they gathered up what George could carry and what they could stow in the perambulator with May, including the copy of *Leaves of Grass* Mabel had given George on his twenty-sixth birthday and the published volumes of *Isis.* At the last minute George was able to hire a peasant cart to haul a few valises. They left Wondelgem on Monday, October 12. At the Dutch frontier, they took a train to Terneuzen, then ships to Vlissingen and Harwich: Mabel's country seemed the only possible destination. "At any rate," George remembered afterward with philosophy lacking at the time, "May and *Isis* were leaving with us and we had ourselves." Yet now they were refugees.

CHAPTER 2

Refugees: 1914–1919

"We got here safely all 3 on Thursday," Mabel wrote Méta from her mother's house at Ipswich. ". . . We have had of course to abandon our house & furniture but packed & hid all small things & mattresses & bedding etc. We had to lodge & feed many Germans—food was scarce—we had hardly any more money—fighting was near—only 2 miles off—& all these reasons forced us to leave. May & I stay here for the present. . . ."

England was flooded with Belgian refugees, yet most Belgians remained in their country. Had George not had a British wife who was helping him learn English and whose relatives could take them in, he probably would have waited out the war in Ghent, working on his history of science. Mabel decisively turned George Sarton toward the broader reaches of the English language.

George got a job as a censor in the London War Office, spending his lunch hour at the Reading Room of the British Museum taking scientific notes. Since Nellie Elwes did not want them long, Mabel and May began their erratic pilgrimage across southeastern England from relatives to friends to any stranger who would take them in, Mabel often not knowing from one day to the next where they would sleep.

The uprooted child was by turns brave and brattish. She constantly tested her will against Mabel's, until Mabel deliberately burned her fingertips to prevent her playing with matches, or locked her away in a room. "She is so very rude to Sophie & Mrs. Jackson," Mabel wrote George, "that I am ashamed. . . . I made May beg her pardon but it took

¾ hour!! She had ended by saying that Mrs. J might not even speak & each time Mrs. J attempted to, she screamed & threw herself off her chair. I put her outside & then she kicked the door & pulled at the handle. . . . I have no doubt that the best cure would be for her to have a brother or sister— but oh! my body is *so* tired. I don't think I could nourish a second little life ever again—& May tires me so, that I feel sometimes I should go mad if there were two. I really do think I must be a woman with an insufficiency of the 'mother' in her. . . ."

Staying with Lady Barker at Clare Priory, Suffolk, May fell ill with a severe abscess and raging temperature. "Me a big girl, me not cry. Daddy will be glad," she vowed in rapidly deteriorating French. Daddy had sailed for America, influential Belgian friends having heard of his plight. Arriving in New York on April 7, he was helped by Professor D. E. Smith at Columbia University, then by Leo Baekeland, a university associate and now a wealthy man thanks to his invention of the industrial plastic Bakelite. An appointment as a summer-school lecturer at the University of Illinois materialized, and George, speaking broken English, set off to endure a sweltering midwestern summer.

Mabel wrote George of her daily humiliations, her want of even a little pocket money, her inability to pay anything for May's keep—and relentlessly of her problems with May. "May is certainly a very tiring child to be with *all day long*—she is *noisy* & does love to talk all the time loudly . . . & is so used to always having *someone* to play with her that she is very exacting. I feel every now & then as if I were, as mother told you— an *incapable* woman! . . . I cannot tell you how she tires me!—till I am on the verge of tears & I long for the time she goes to bed as for a release. Yet she is *really* a dear child."

The dear child was sent to Nellie's niece Alice Dorling in Framlingham. Rosy-cheeked, with bobbed hair, May arrived in "a little red coat with white collar and cuffs, beautifully embroidered by [her] mother, and a little bonnet to match." Her cousins were delighted with "Belgian May." As usual, May attached herself "like a limpet" to the family. But she had terrible temper tantrums and could be "violently passionately naughty."

From Framlingham, mother and daughter went to friends at Grantham, where May immediately came down with measles. Then Mabel broke out in red spots and was extremely ill. Dr. Francis Hardy refused payment because they were Belgian; when May recovered, he took "that *topping* little girl" with him in his buggy on his rounds. But he advised Mabel, for her health, to "get rid" of May. Yet how could she get rid of a child who pleaded, "*Love* me, Mummy!" "Poor little daughter," Mabel wrote George. "I do not *want* to be rid of her. She is my greatest consolation & she needs me." If she were only strong enough, she might join George in America; but she was weak.

As an old woman, May Sarton told her biographer a terrible story: how George had left her mother stranded penniless in England, how she begged him for money, how he replied brutally, "Give May away." "My mother should not have told me this, but she did," said May. "I was a teenager. It left deep scars. I have never forgiven him."

Yet: "COME ALONG YOU BOTH BELOVED, COME ALONG AS QUICK AS YOU CAN," wrote George upon receiving a $1,200-a-year appointment as a lecturer at George Washington University in Washington, D.C. Mabel replied that she was terribly ill; perhaps she *must* give May away. "If you prefer to come alone do so," George replied; "but I am afraid we cannot be completely happy without our sweet little May. . . . What I want is to save you both—equally beloved. I don't really know whom I love the most and best: the mother or the baby . . . I love them differently." He covered pages with X's for them both.

Confronted with this letter in 1993, May Sarton exploded. "He was *acting,* of course!" But perhaps, missing Mabel, George was willing to include their daughter. Or perhaps, after years of difficult marriage, Mabel deliberately transferred Dr. Hardy's "Get rid of May" to George, wanting to fuel May's resentment of her father. Or perhaps May *wanted* her father to have said it, to justify her rage against him.

They sailed from Liverpool in September on a blacked-out ship. The deck rolled and the Irish sang hymns all night, but finally they came up on deck into sunshine and saw the Statue of Liberty as they sailed into New York harbor. The Baekelands took them in.

For May, America was first a huge St. Bernard named Teddy, a steep lawn that dropped away into a jungle of poison ivy before pitching down to the Hudson River, a big house with turrets and a polar-bear rug in the drawing room. She quickly felt Dr. Baekeland as "some frightening masculine force—a god who must be placated, a piece of weather." His wife, "Bonbon," a small, round, deliciously warm fairy godmother of a woman, was a different matter, and May attached herself to her.

Apparently Mabel never recorded her feelings about her child's intense attachments to other women—Céline, Méta, Véra, and now Bonbon Baekeland. Many mothers would have been resentful, but Mabel seemed very willing that May share the troubling heat of her young love. George had always been enamored of Mabel's "heart and soul more than of her body"—luckily; for Mabel, who had not been caressed as a child, found it impossible to give her husband and now her daughter the physical love they craved. Besides, George, not May, was the center of Mabel's life; she was "very wrapped up in trying to please" her husband. Father and daughter competed fiercely for Mabel, and George won. May turned hungrily to other mothers.

Despite Bonbon's kindness, the child sensed her fragility in this new golden land: knew that the St. Bernard and polar-bear rug were only on loan from more privileged friends. They left the Baekelands for a "dreary boardinghouse near Morningside Park," because George could not yet afford to have them join him in Washington. Friends of the Baekelands had admired May's simple peasant dresses, fashioned by Mabel of unusual Belgian colors embroidered with birds and flowers in brilliant wools and silks. Mabel now took orders, sewing all day in their dark room to make money to subsist on.

Eventually they joined George in a boardinghouse near the Washington Zoo, where wolves howled at night. They were very poor, and George had to borrow small amounts so they could buy furniture and bedding. But he was determined to write a history of science and publish *Isis;* he was teaching only one course at George Washington University so he could continue research. "During the early American years," he later admitted, "my main anxiety was, How shall I do my work—not how shall I support my family. People will remark that I was very selfish." It was a selfishness that Mabel supported. But guilt for not earning an adequate income for his family sometimes troubled George. "*Great distress,*" he wrote in his diary.

Not yet four, May got a kindergarten scholarship to the Little Potomac School, fell in love the first day with Willem Van Loon, the son of friends of her parents, the Hendrik Van Loons, and proposed marriage to him "sitting hand in hand on a washbasket."

Denied her valuable connection with Arts Décoratifs Céline Dangotte, Mabel found a carpenter who could design chests and cabinets, and began creating a line of simple furniture young couples might be able to afford. Then she met Margaret Gillespie, a businesswoman who was impressed with the marketability of Mabel's embroidered peasant-style coats and dresses. Together they founded the firm Belg-Art, Mabel designing and training other women in European-style embroidery—an artistic and financial connection as important as ADCD.

George secured an appointment at Harvard for the academic year 1916–17, yet the post was the kind of low-paying lectureship he had held

at George Washington University, and Harvard showed no interest in
funding either *Isis* or a history of science. The Sartons left Washington
and found an apartment at 10 Avon Street in Cambridge. There was no
garden for Mabel, who longed to get her hands into earth again. They
were terribly poor. The remains of George's inheritance was frozen in
Belgian banks; Mabel had been torn away from her new association with
Belg-Art, though she planned to submit work from Cambridge. They
looked about for a school for May and found one in Shady Hill, a coop-
erative open-air school founded in 1915 by the Harvard philosopher
William Ernest Hocking and his wife, Agnes, on their front porch, now
occupying unheated buildings at the foot of Shady Hill, the old Norton
estate. May entered in 1917—about the time Mabel discovered she was
pregnant again.

In later years George Sarton explained that May was such a success
that he and Mabel tried to have more children. Unlikely. If doctors had
advised the ailing Mabel against childbearing at thirty-three, what doctor
would recommend it at thirty-eight? Besides, they were refugees, hardly
able to support one child. And Mabel did not *want* another child; she
wanted to work. George himself was totally absorbed in his work. And lit-
tle "windmill" May had the energy of ten tigers. Far more probable that
George and Mabel, though no longer "impetuous," were still "mal-
adroit." Predictably, Mabel's doctor classified the pregnancy as high-risk.

The baby was due in early August 1917. Meanwhile, Mabel made sev-
eral trips to Washington to confer with Margaret Gillespie about Belg-Art,
comforting May with letters:

Little May, little May, you are so dear to us already—shall we some-
day be very dear to *you?*—be your best friends?—you must help us
you know. We will try to love you for yourself and not for us—try
to be really "near" you and not misunderstand when you will
think differently to us because you will be young and we shall be
old. . . . You won't have forgotten me will you when I come back,
little girlie? Now good-bye, daughter of ours—go on being very
quiet and good so Daddy can write and Mother not fret about you
both.

Letters like this put May in a double bind. If Mummy and Daddy
loved her, then why was she so often lonely and alone? It must be her
fault. Her parents told her she was happy; adults didn't lie; obviously she
had only herself to blame. She shouldn't need them so much; she

shouldn't ache so to be hugged and kissed. Then there was Mabel's subtle blackmail: Be a good girl so Mummy won't fret. With all her charm, Mabel liked playing the martyr: "Enjoy yourself, darling. Mummy"—*sigh*—"will be all right." Unsurprisingly, May developed a stunning guilt complex.

In late June May was sent to the Baekelands so that Mabel could rest—another wrenching parting. By now the habit of shifting May to the care of others was relentless. It played havoc with the child's nervous system. She had very early developed a kind of emotional promiscuity, the ability to attach herself immediately to anybody who was kind. She had also acquired a "geographic" instability, a nervous need to be constantly moving from place to place. They were survival techniques.

"Dear Mother," May printed carefully that July, "We have two little jackets to send you. We will make a little pair of shoes for the baby." On August 3, her thirty-ninth birthday, Mabel gave birth to Alfred Hugh, a sickly, underweight boy. George himself had fled to the Harvard Club in New York, unable to face the dangerous birth. Twenty days later, the baby died. Mabel went to stay with friends.

"Mrs. Baekeland will have told you that the little brother was so ill that even the kind doctors and nurses could not save him. I know how disappointed you will be, and so perhaps you can guess how very, very sad Mummy has been and still is, and how much she wants *you* now." Their friends the Booths had found them a house at Annisquam until the fall term, and next week Daddy would fetch her and take her to Annisquam—not to stay with Mummy, though "you can come to see me often and we will be down by the sea together. Don't you think that will be nice? . . . Here is a big, *hard* kiss for each little brown cheek—the sort that leaves a little dent. . . ." Mabel preferred delivering big hard kisses through the mail.

Typically, the Sartons stayed at Annisquam gratis; during these hard years they were very much dependent for luxuries on the goodwill of new friends, who were delighted with the shy, brilliant Belgian scholar, his *spirituel* English wife, and their fervent little daughter. These were Mabel's conquests, for though George's beaming smile could charm, he had little skill or time for cultivating people. They were chiefly women—cultured, artistic, intelligent: Louise Inches, Lucy Stanton, Mary Bouton, though Charles Bouton, a Harvard mathematics professor, was a colleague of George's. The warm, outgoing Mrs. Bouton quickly became "Aunt Mary" to May, who latched on firmly to the family of three girls, Betty, Margaret, and Charlotte, across the street at 9 Avon Street. "Here comes trouble!" the Bouton maid would say, catching sight of May flying for their front door. May, said Charlotte, was "always there."

Shady Hill also did much to satisfy the need for family the child so intensely craved. Shady Hillers quickly realized they were a breed apart from children who attended mere private schools like Buckingham and Browne and Nichols. Shady Hill prided itself upon cooperation, spontaneity, creativity, and civic duty. Innovation was the word—morning exercises, unheated classrooms, folk dancing, poetry under the trees. In winter, Shady Hillers could be recognized by their bulky knee-length sweaters and shiny black rubbers worn over sheepskin boots. For the classroom pupils pulled sleeping bags over their uniforms, painted and wrote in mittens, answered questions with puffs of white breath—and bounced up and down in the bags at the end of class to restore circulation. Hot cocoa came at eleven. Discipline could be nonexistent, or swift and Olympian. Oddly enough, Shady Hillers were proud, even smug, about these privations. They saw themselves as the Chosen.

May quickly established herself as a bright, eager, responsive pupil, though she could be boisterous and demanding. She was by now fluent in English, and her marks were excellent—though her writing could be "a little careless at times." She clung to her teachers, willing them to love her. She wanted terribly to belong.

For the 1917–18 school year, Harvard gave George an office in the new Widener Library in exchange for minimal teaching, but he remained dissatisfied. He was primarily a research scholar with a simple pedagogical approach: "If [the students] did understand me I was very glad, but if they did not, if they showed no interest, well that was their own lookout." He was mastering English with the help of Mabel, who patiently corrected both his speech (he would never lose his accent) and his writing. She was stern, insisting he break one ponderous sentence into two or three, condemning his "French" exaggeration, annihilating a locution like "It is not necessary, of course, to add that . . ." with "Then why say it?" What he needed now for his work was funding: he would earn only $2,750 in 1917. Yet he allowed himself to spend one workday a week at the Boston Museum of Fine Arts studying the Chinese paintings. Mabel might have asked him to spend that day earning money, but she did not.

Then in 1918 something wonderful happened. Through a meeting with its president, George was appointed an associate of the Carnegie Institution in Washington, D.C. He would keep his office in Widener, teach his class, and receive in addition to his Harvard salary a stipend from the Carnegie Institution and support for his work. George called the appointment "our salvation": "Harvard would never have permitted us to live—not to mention publishing my work." His allegiance was now to the Carnegie.

Another great event occurred in November that year: armistice after four years of the bloodiest war in the history of civilization. Mabel wept to see the handwriting of the Dangottes, the Bouny-Tordeurs, Madeleine Van Thorenburg, to know they had survived. The Sartons' thoughts flew to Wondelgem—had *it* survived? And George's papers, buried in the garden? By the spring of 1919, they knew they must return.

On May 20 George appeared before a notary public to testify for the Carnegie Institution his need to return to Europe for six months—to see his next of kin, settle his inheritance and what remained of his country house, confer with scholars, and resume publication of *Isis*. His wife, he argued, must accompany him, since she was far abler than he to cope with family matters.

But they did not intend to stay. On May 19 George had filed in district court in Boston his declaration of intent to become an American citizen. His Carnegie appointment had convinced him he must settle permanently in the United States.

CHAPTER 3

Two Worlds: 1919–1925

"Triste, la guerre," sighed the old peasant. Belgium indeed was sad, its landscape scarred by trenches, shattered trees, ruined barns and houses. They stood at the gate of Wondelgem and saw the plum tree heavy with blue fruit and the garden rioting wild. The house itself still stood, a casement shattered here and there, its roof ripped open by artillery. They pushed open the gate and walked in, May following her parents. She was very quiet; she sensed that this strange homecoming belonged to them alone.

Inside, desecration, filth, ruin. Ironically, occupying Germans had treated Wondelgem well until the end of the war, when undisciplined troops began to sack and loot—though whether the Germans or the Belgians had finally done more damage was impossible to say. Wandering heartsick through the gutted rooms, Mabel suddenly cried, "Look, George!" and retrieved from a heap of rubbish one long-stemmed Venetian glass glazed with dirt. Then a peasant neighbor came to the door with a stack of fine plates; one by one the Germans had traded them for butter and eggs: she had kept them, hoping one day the Sartons might return. George had more reason to be thankful: the Germans had spared much of his library, and the buried trunk of notes had survived.

There were other survivals. In the cellar they found furniture intact, including the big, heavy Flemish bahut and the desk of satiny inlaid woods Mabel had designed for the ill-fated Salon de Bruxelles. But there was nothing to do but sell the house. The sexton of the local parish had grown rich buying up abandoned property; now he offered to buy the

May with Jacques and Claire Limbosch

Sarton place. He would demolish the house and sell the grounds as small lots. Sickened, George had little choice but to sell. Anyway he was eager to begin his work.

They made the mistake of visiting the house after it was sold. The climbing roses were rioting in full bloom, the orchard fragrant with fruit. As they wandered through the empty rooms, they heard a noise "like tearing silk" and saw roses cascading to the ground as workmen tore the trellises from the walls. May would not forget her mother's agonized "Couldn't they wait till we've gone?" That same day the sexton began assaulting the three-hundred-year-old oaks. They fled to the Chekhovian ringing of axes.

George left Ghent to visit the libraries and scholars he had not seen since before the war. Mabel and May stayed with the Limbosches, both at their suburban Brussels home at 52 avenue Lequime and at Les Assels, the Dangotte country house. But soon Mabel was in England, leaving May once again with a family to which she attached herself furiously, playing sister to Claire and Jacques, falling back into French, sipping the beer Auntie Lino insisted was good for children. Uncle Raymond was gentle, moody, intellectual, a little reserved; Céline, vigorous, opinionated, passionate, and earthy—like a loaf of "warm bread," thought May, burrowing into her bosom hungrily. Still, she wrote many letters to her parents, underlining her good behavior: "Dear Mother thank you very much for the card you sent me. I worked very well yesterday. I'm getting much fatter. . . . I'm sleeping very well. I havent cried once, nor dreamed aloud. . . . I'm really a nice big sister. . . . I eat a lot of apples and fruit. . . ." She enclosed an accomplished drawing of houses, trees, and flowers that showed the influence of Mabel's *art décoratif.*

George returned gratified by the support he had found for *Isis* in the European scholarly community. Mabel too had restored vital connections with women friends and a country dearer to her than her native England. And May had discovered another world to which she belonged by birth. She realized now her life had two dimensions: she was both Belgian May and American May, a hybrid of the Old World and the New. She felt as though she'd been given a very nice present.

Halfway across the Atlantic, American May re-emerged rather glumly. They were returning to Washington, where she had not been happy, and she was enrolled not in her beloved Shady Hill but in Gunston Hall Primary and Preparatory on Florida Avenue, where there would not be the immense comfort of Willem Van Loon. They were still engaged to be married and wrote each other faithfully.

As it turned out, Washington did not suit George and Mabel either, despite Mabel's business connection in the capital. They returned to Cambridge with its intellectual bohemianism that was a kind of revolt against Boston's closed social circles, to an apartment at 24 Agassiz Street, and George again took up daytime residence in 183 Widener.

And then it was summer and time to pack again (though not for George); for anyone who was anybody in Cambridge had summer places which they lent to friends, and the Sartons tended to know these people. This time Mabel and May vacationed at Pemaquid Point on the Maine coast. There were "gloomy dark woods, mushrooms, a long walk to get water every day," and Mabel was depressed. May stood barefoot on the rocks and shouted angrily at the sea. Its thrash and suck frightened her. The sea was restless and fierce—like her, but not a friend.

Mabel returned to Cambridge: she could leave her daughter, but not George for long, for he could not feed himself or find a clean shirt without her. "I can swim 55 strokes just plain 80 on my back 3 on my side and I can float on my back," May reported to her parents from the Hockings' in Greensboro, Vermont. "I am learning to dive and I can dog paddle. . . . Please send up my miday and bloumers [sic]." In late July May transferred to the Boutons' summer cabin in Kearsarge, New Hampshire, in the

*May during the
Shady Hill years*

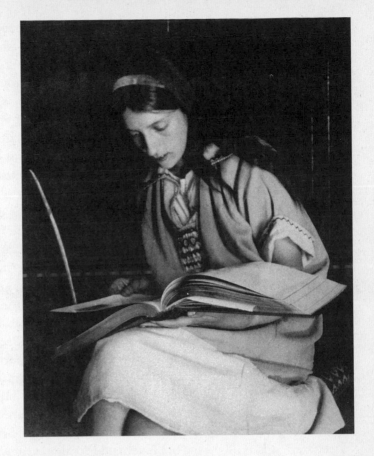

White Mountains. Considered one of the family by now, she was still—
with her fierce energy—the leader, especially in the game of creating lit-
tle villages out of sticks and evergreen boughs and populating them with
twig people, whom she vigorously bossed. She tended to monopolize
Aunt Mary too, but that (the Bouton children understood) was because
she needed attention so badly.

At Shady Hill, too, in the next years, May emerged as a leader. Partic-
ularly she was "a delight" to Agnes Hocking, who did not merely teach
but lived poetry with her pupils. Mrs. Hocking considered May's "a fine
imagination and unusual power of expression"—and in fact, a poem
called "A Pigeon" surviving from this period shows keen observation:

> He eyes you for a moment, with a glance
> That is both curious and afraid;
> Then blinks and chuckles in his throat,
> Opens his beak as if dismayed

And flaps his wings, coo's a mournful note
Blinks again, and settles on his branch.

Dorice Adams Hall, the composition teacher, also found May "most original," her flights of fancy quite astounding. Her work in history, mathematics, and French was usually excellent, and she showed dramatic flair in the plays Shady Hillers loved to produce, starring, for instance, as the doctor in the French class's production of *Le Médécin malgré lui.*

May's closest friend at Shady Hill was Barbara Runkle, dark and pretty, spirited, creative, and dramatic like May. They called each other "Tig" interchangeably, invented a private language, Oyghee, in which they were both "Tioga"—"Tioga, how is theuta weonig?" In letters, they were "This One" and "That One." "This One," Barbara might write, "wonders whether That One might tarry overnight at his house." They were deep co-conspirators, bonded soul mates.

The Bouton girls were still friends, but they went to Buckingham, a private girls' school, so May saw them chiefly on weekends. The Bouton house was particularly magical at Christmas, when Professor Bouton allowed the girls to take over his study for their dolls. They established the dolls' kitchen under his big kneehole desk with a refrigerator and a black cast-iron stove; they baked and cooked for the dolls and had elaborate Christmas teas and games—and May's dolls bossed this delightful world where they played endlessly.

There was also the home of Henry and Rosalind Copley Greene at 38 Irving Street, with four girls—Joy, Francesca, Ernesta, and Katrine, who was in May's class at Shady Hill. The particular attraction at the Greenes' was the mother, Rosalind, very beautiful, very dramatic, very *exaltée.* May adored her. The family had a country home at Rowley, and May would spend weekends there when she wasn't with the Boutons. Neither the Bouton nor the Greene children were ever at the Sartons'.

Looking back at their childhoods, Joy Greene Sweet classified May as "a latchkey kid." George Sarton led a programmed life; Mabel's duty in life was maintaining that program. She woke at four in the morning, often with a splitting migraine; crept down to the kitchen to make herself a cup of tea, which she carried back to bed for "her hour" with books on painting, design, and china; then sent George and May off to school with breakfast. Most of their friends had maids and cleaning women, but the housework was all Mabel's job. They had no car: Mabel would take the trolley into Boston to buy groceries and flowers for her friends at the markets, then lug her purchases from the trolley stop back to Agassiz Street. Tea was a ritual when George returned laden with books late in the afternoon—a sacred time, the only time the two of them were alone together. Then he listened to music in his study while Mabel fixed the evening meal. She washed up afterwards, almost too tired to stand.

May didn't fit conveniently into this schedule, particularly since Belg-Art took Mabel frequently to Washington. "I hope you arrived safely," May wrote her mother during one of her absences. "I washed my hair this morning and have written to Grannie and auntie Lino. I went skating yesterday with Margaret and Charlotte Bouton. . . . My skates fit me perfectly and are very comfortable. Daddy is taking me to *Robin Hood* this afternoon."

George admitted that, like his own father, he was an indifferent parent. Yet he did try to amuse May. When Mabel sailed to England in July 1923 to see Nellie, May could report (without punctuation) that "On Monday Daddy took me to see the Natural History Museum in Boston on Tuesday we went to see the glass flowers in the Havard [*sic*] Museum on Wednesday we went to the covered wagon on Thursday we went to the art museum and on Friday to a vaudeville which was interesting but vulgar." Yet he usually took her to places that amused *him*. Since he was entirely helpless about the house, he could not take care of her. The nightmare was dirty clothes: she didn't know how to wash them; she couldn't talk to George about the problem. She relied upon other people's mothers, who invariably became "Aunt" Mary, "Aunt" Agnes, "Aunt" Louise. Her own parents simply could not supply the love, security, and attention she craved and deserved. And they certainly did not have the means to provide her with the sailing, horseback riding, swimming, and hiking she enjoyed as a guest.

Yet the Sartons did vacation together every summer at Ogunquit, Maine, courtesy of the painter Lucy Stanton, who lent them her studio in the seaside artists' colony. Mabel and May frequently stayed on when research called George back to Cambridge, and May could tell him one June that "Mother is feeling much better and looks very well. I keep wishing you were here so that I could go for long walks with you. . . . When will you be back? I hope before the fourth of July. . . . Mother went in bathing yesterday, she enjoyed it very much. I hope thou art feeling well this merry day. Much love from thy little daughter May."

The letters are always cheerful, bristling with X's for kisses and O's for hugs. She seldom asks for things, only that Mabel might join her for a day or two. She tries hard to sound responsible, serious:

I am keeping an account of the money I spend here and at Ogunquit, here it is.

OGUNQUIT		INTERVALE	
on hand	1.15	on hand	.50
bow and arrows	.60	ice cream cone	.05
present	.05	7 cards	.15
	.65	present	.25
balance	.05		.45
		balance	.05

May put on a brave front. Her parents assured her she was a lucky girl and she tried to believe it, even when the endless shuttlings back and forth didn't work very well. "Miss Coit has written and says she wants me on the 30th of July to the 17th of August," May wrote her father in 1923 from still another friend's summer house. "Please write to me your plans as to how I am going to get there. . . . I would like to see you before I go." On July 30 she was put on a train for Miss Coit's camp at Gloucester, Massachusetts—only: "I arrived safely at the station, nobody was there so I took a taxi walked to the camp, when I got there nobody was there." Miss Coit eventually appeared, but this lonely vagabonding was very hard on an eleven-year-old girl.

George's sabbatical for 1924–25 meant giving up the Agassiz Street apartment and storing the furniture in an attempt to economize. May was plucked from Shady Hill to sail for England with Mabel on September 13. George would join them the following June. May was twelve, not the easiest age to give up one's close friends, teachers, and schoolmates for an entire year.

They arrived in England September 21, and May continued the diary she had begun aboard the ship: "England is perfectly lovely. . . . Little old houses sourrounded [sic] by green rolling hills that look like velvet, with flocks of fat sheep or herds of cows, and often two or three horses. Sometimes we saw a picturesque woman pulling a barge along a canal, or again a manufacturing town, and as we were higher than the street we saw before us a forest of chimneys. I have never seen so many chimneys! At last we came to London and our trunks and valises were taken by a porter in a bright red coat and hat. . . ."

From London they travelled to Ipswich to stay with Nellie Elwes, then ferried to Antwerp to be met by Raymond and Céline Limbosch, who exclaimed over May's resemblance to George. Besides Claire and Jacques, their family now included Nicole ("dark and much like an elf") and Jacqueline ("chubby and fair with blue eyes and two little light pigtails"). Mabel was ill from the crossing: "Tomorrow we have been gone a month & I have only *one* letter from you!" she scribbled to George. "I love you dearly." It was necessary to reassure him, for here she was back in her beloved Belgium with dear Céline and Raymond in their large country house south of Brussels in Rhode-St.-Genèse, her dearest Méta Budry within reach, and a designing job with Arts Décoratifs Céline Dangotte.

May's two accounts of her year in Belgium tell different stories. The first emerges in letters to George and to Mabel, who was often in England during the year—cheerful, guileless accounts of daily activities. The Limbosches have eight ducks, eight pigeons, two hens, two roosters, and a dog, Rouly. With Claire and Jacquot, she takes gymnastics classes three times a week. Uncle Raymond has a marvellous wireless and they hear Big Ben strike all through the house. The children are raking leaves at twenty-five centimes a wheelbarrow and saving up for the circus. They hunt for beetles and chrysalises and tritons in the pond, and are furiously collecting stamps. They will spend a holiday with Raymond and the *gouvernante,* Bobo, at Knokke.

May's letters to George are more formal than hers to Mabel. "I am delighted with your plans for this summer," she tells him, or "My youth's companion is a joy, and I look forward to it and the other magazines you send, eagerly." She punctiliously thanks him for books, stamps, letters, the white roses he sends for her thirteenth birthday. She assures him she has begun to speak French—"My tongue I believe to be untied"—and encloses *dictées* and *rédactions*. She writes him vivid descriptions that flout punctuation: "The policeman [in *A Kiss for Cinderella*] who was played by Jule Delacre the chief player and director of the theatre acted wonderfully. I liked the ball scene the most. The lord mayor was very good he had a rather high thin voice and he said quite a lot of times 'Oui, oui, oui, oui, oui, oui place pour tous et moi aussie [*sic*]' he had a long red cloak and was quite tall and very thin. The censor too was interesting he was all in black with a great red axe and a black half mask."

May's adult reminiscence "A Belgian School," however, paints a much darker picture. That year she attended the Institut Belge de Culture Française in Uccle, a suburb of Brussels. On school mornings, Raymond, Céline, Mabel, May, Claire, and Jacques all piled into Raymond's ancient car. During the fifteen-minute ritual of firing the engine, May agonized over being tardy, a fear not diminished when the three children were dropped a mile from school while the adults drove on to ADCD. Clad in gray cloaks and rubber boots against the constant rain, lugging their books in a strap, they descended the long avenue de Fré toward the Institut, May feeling like a soul bound for hell. Her French grammar was very uncertain; the foreign metric tables confounded her. Worse, subjects were taught by rote—an approach the opposite of the Shady Hill "think for yourselves" philosophy. One memorized the textbook, nothing less.

The lower class was ruled by Mademoiselle Marie Gaspar, a tiny bombshell of a woman with snapping black eyes. A born actress who used her classroom as a stage, she terrorized students by the ferocity of her anger, tears, and smiles. True that after a burst of scorn at some idiocy, "Titi" was known to leave her podium to comfort the student sobbing onto the black-oilcloth-covered table. May, who loved dramatics herself, wept often. Still, the volcanic Titi was a harrowing experience for a girl entering puberty in a foreign land, struggling with the language, and with no real country of her own.

Another experience was equally harrowing. Raymond Limbosch, no longer a politically radical anarchist, continually searched instead for keys to the mysteries of existence. That year he found one in a psychologist named Marcel Letendart, who specialized in *iridologie,* the belief that a patient's mental and physical state could be diagnosed by gazing into his eyes. All the Limbosch children were subjected to Monsieur Letendart, who thought nothing of divulging his verdict in the patient's hearing.

May has rapid perceptions with stable reflexes, he informs her, but a feverish personal judgment, which might, however, improve with maturity. Her brain is average but of a great sensitivity, which will run to irritation and fatigue if overworked. This sensitivity necessitates that she be guided with the greatest gentleness and tact. Her imagination is limited, though feverish. As for her character, she is timid, angry, and stubborn. Given these qualities, she will make a lawyer or a dancer—not a charming or graceful dancer, but a supple, vigorous *danseuse.*

Letendart's diagnosis of the female brain as undeveloped, feverish, and fragile was a standard, chauvinistic nineteenth-century medical view that persisted well into the twentieth century, functioning to keep women subordinate and noncompetitive; but May did not know this. "I was deeply offended and frightened by his diagnosis," she remembered, "and the fright took the form of a waking nightmare. I imagined that I carried around, instead of a brain, a small, very active spider which was eating me up. With this image in my consciousness all the time, it became harder and harder for me to concentrate. Any intellectual effort brought the blood to my head, and for a time I was convinced that I was going mad."

*Marie Closset,
the poet Jean
Dominique, head of
the Institut Belge de
Culture Française*

Diagnosing a child's physical and mental constitution by looking into her eyes is pure charlatanism, yet somehow Monsieur Letendart had drawn a bead on May. She *was* willful and argumentative, highly emotional and irritable, extremely imaginative, perceptive, and sensitive. On another front, he was positively prophetic. "She will be precocious in love," he warned; "it will thus be necessary to avoid her initiation by older companions. She does not have a mother's nature, but the nature of a lover. . . ."

Given the terrors of Mademoiselle Gaspar and Monsieur Letendart, May's letters to her parents, on closer reading, reveal a subtext of unhappiness that she hid even from herself. They are frequently written from bed, where she has retired with stomach complaints or fatigue. She is often lonely among the clannish Limbosch family. Her distress is genuine when Céline suddenly refuses to pay forwarding postage on letters from

George to Mabel, which May customarily opened: she needs to know she's competing successfully against her father for Mabel's love. The celebration on May 3 is a disappointment: "I had a lovely birthday," she writes George, then substitutes "happy" for "lovely," while Mabel adds, "May had I think a happy birthday, but not nearly so much so as at home—I really think she missed you." Even stamp collecting wasn't all fun: "Aunty Lino . . . divided her collection of 1100 stamps between her four children. It was a little hard for me because I didn't get any but I guess it was good for me."

There were two compensations for the hardships suffered that Belgian year, both women. One was Céline Limbosch. "Please thank Aunty Lino for me," May begged Mabel, "for having been such a dear darling sweet little mother for me while you are gone. About 5 times I have had it on the tip of my tongue but I simply couldn't. I am not courageous. You have no idea how I shall miss Aunty Lino in America. I should like to simply hug and kiss her until she became like a jellyfish, but of course I could never do that and even if I could I wouldn't have the courage."

The other woman had been a presence felt rather than experienced. The Institut Belge de Culture Française was occupied by three women: Marie Gaspar, the novelist Blanche Rousseau, and the school's guiding spirit, Marie Closset, better known as the French poet Jean Dominique, whose verses the young George Sarton had carried in his pocket. She was a tiny woman in frail health, with huge, speaking gray eyes and a face made luminous by intense spirituality. She had founded the Institut to teach literature not as an exam subject but as a living, passionate experience. May was only dimly aware that across the hall from Titi's turbulent classroom lay another realm, guided by a creature so intense yet inward, so quiet yet compelling, that the older students entered this sanctuary in awe. But she knew that when "the Master" deigned to comment on a composition sent up by Mademoiselle Gaspar, she had received the highest accolade: "Bien senti!" Someone understood, then, the passionate intensity she had already made her cult. Her sensibility was not dangerous, febrile; it was an instrument through which the world might be "truly felt."

George Sarton arrived on the Continent on June 14, 1925, to begin a summer of travel and research. In July he and May were together in the Pyrenees, May keeping a careful journal in French; Mabel joined them in August. In early September they sailed on the *Suffren* for America. Mabel was returning to a job: she would teach design at Winsor, a private girls' school in Boston, as well as continue her work for Belg-Art. Though she didn't know it, in the reunion with her husband she had again conceived.

May was returning to ninth grade, her last year at Shady Hill. She had begun to think in French, and she was terribly attached to Aunty Lino as well as to Claire and Jacquot. Nevertheless, in mid-Atlantic she once again felt the irresistible tug of the New World, once again felt herself metamorphosing into American May.

CHAPTER 4

"That Lyric Time": 1925–1929

Sometime before May's Belgian year, Shady Hill had decided that the school needed a real principal, an outsider with broader experience and a broader view. They found what they were looking for in Katharine Taylor, past head of the Parker School in Chicago, a woman whose rapport with young people made a huge impact on the "show me" Shady Hillers. Katharine Taylor was in her thirties, tall and slender, with long hands and feet, pale skin, and russet hair—not at all pretty, but original-looking. May instantly worshipped her.

K.T., as May and her friends called her privately, had recruited Anne Longfellow Thorp to head grade seven. Anne was the granddaughter of the poet, tall, gentle, and femininely pretty, with fair hair and a "wide, generous child's mouth." Unlike Katharine Taylor, she was a recognizable Cambridge type, with her love of the outdoors, noble aims, innocence, and lack of frivolity, though not of fun—an outstanding teacher, but even more, an inspirational personality. Of the extraordinary teachers at Shady Hill—and they were essentially the only professional women most of the girls knew—Katharine Taylor and Anne Thorp influenced May most.

But May's last year at Shady Hill was dominated by Taylor, who also taught literature, composition, and poetry. It was K.T. who sympathized when May appeared in her office to demand "more poetry, as a right"; K.T. who inspired May to exalted heights of feeling and achievement. Too exalted, thought Miss Putnam, the science teacher, grimly, jotting on a March 1926 report, "It is a pity to see such splendid ability wasted in effervescence." Ruth Edgett, the mathematics teacher, agreed: "May does

36

Katharine Taylor,
principal of Shady
Hill School, and
May's first Muse

not stand up well when tested. She needs a quieter outlook." But May won only praise from K.T. for her "thrilling depth of appreciation and sureness in catching beauty. May has been pure joy this year," K.T. continued as the school year drew to a close. "Her burning poetic spirit, her hunger for deeper thinking, her keen-edged gayety, her growing warmth of human understanding—how we shall miss it all!" Katharine Taylor was the adolescent poet's first Muse.

In June 1926 May graduated from Shady Hill in a class of twelve. The school had given her more than an education; it had given her a blueprint for life. In the fall she would enter the large Cambridge High and Latin, but first, thanks to Mabel's earnings from the Winsor School and Belg-Art, she would have a summer at camp.

The past January, Mabel had suffered a miscarriage. George had the fetus sent for analysis to the Carnegie Institution in Washington, hoping to discover the reason for the failed pregnancy. Even to unworldly George, the answer could scarcely have been surprising. Mabel was forty-seven. She had never been in good health or wanted children and had given birth to two babies who quickly died. The pathologist called her womb "tired." Mabel recovered from the experience in Washington, staying much of the spring and part of the summer with the Gillespies, designing for Belg-Art. It is hard to believe she felt the miscarriage a tragedy.

She was in Washington when May took the train for Temple, Maine. Day Mountain Camp, on a lake near Farmington in what in 1926 was unspoiled up-country, had been launched by Mary Alice Bradford, an enthusiastic, colorful teacher who wore wire-rimmed glasses and bloomers. Twelve campers slept on cots covered with tarps and mosquito netting; the old renovated barn housed dressing rooms, a living room, a crafts room, and a kitchen. The girls swam, hiked, camped out, climbed thickly wooded Day Mountain, and around the fire roasted marshmallows and sang "We're so dandy, always handy / In our middies spick and spandy" to the tune of "The Caissons Go Rolling Along." May chummed with Barbara Runkle; they were close as almond halves. Everything that summer was "peachy," "marvy," and "scrum."

Activities were fiercely competitive, and May competed fiercely. At the track meet she won the running broad jump and captained the winning relay team. She earned the most points for the canoe race, breast and back strokes, and assorted dives. She won first in the song competition. She was chosen to play Robin Hood in the DMC play. And finally she triumphantly sewed her Red Cross badge on her swimming suit as a Junior Life Saver.

That September May and the few Shady Hillers who hadn't gone to private schools plunged into the cold waters of the High and Latin, hiking silently (talk was forbidden) down corridors to Latin and Chemistry, mixing with large classes they didn't know. For May survival depended on maintaining ties with K.T., Thorpo, and ex–Shady Hillers like Jean Clark, as well as sticking close to "the Snabs"—her close friends Jean Tatlock and the younger Letty Field. Still, she quickly became chief of an elite band who walked across town to school every day. To Jean Clark she was intimidating: "May . . . was the chief source of my abysmal inferiority complex," Clark confided to her diary:

> What had I that could compare with May's rich living? I saw May
> as the leader of this group. She was a keen, ardent, emotional girl:
> she seemed to have more will power and capacity not to dawdle
> . . . than almost anyone else I had ever met. She read voraciously

May (center, on her stomach) at Day Mountain Camp, Barbara Runkle top left

and talked well. Everyone who came in contact with her felt her magnetism. I too, and I hated her for holding me under her sway; I was desperately envious of her will to learn, her absorption in a goal rather than in other people's impressions of her, the fact that in a room full of people all the most interesting ones were inevitably drawn to her.

The four were bound close by their passion for poetry. They all wrote it, dedicating poems to "K.T.," "A.L.T," and each other. They all copied favorite passages of Millay, Dickinson, Sandburg, Housman, and H.D. into leather notebooks bought at the Harvard Coop. They chanted Francis Thompson's "Hound of Heaven" as they tramped along the Charles River or climbed the tower in Mount Auburn Cemetery. Privately Jean Clark and Letty felt that they wrote "deeper" poetry than May, who did not plumb the black depths of her soul to their satisfaction. But all four were intensely serious, passionately idealistic—and not infrequently absurd. They despised the opposite sex—or pretended to. Traitorously, Jean Clark had a secret crush on Harry Dolan, "the wildest boy in school."

Letty's older brother Hermann, fair, slender, rebellious, with Byronic open collars, knew himself among the despised. Though he too attended the Cambridge High and Latin, as an insensitive male he was not allowed to walk with the group to school. Privately he considered his sister's Shady Hill friends "intolerable snobs"; still, he was intrigued—by volatile May with her sharp features and shingled hair; by brilliant Jean Tatlock of the thick black lashes and greeny-blue eyes; by the artistic but rather goody-goody Jean Clark. He did his best to become more "perceptive"; to impress the group, he became editor of the school's *Cambridge Review* and tried to raise its tone by sponsoring a poetry contest. As a reward for these endeavors he might be allowed to sit in when the girls gathered upstairs in Letty's room at the Field home on Berkeley Street to smoke, drink cocoa, ruthlessly dissect each other's poems, and discuss *life*. Still, he felt he was not taken seriously.

"To me rest and poetry are the same thing, they merge into each other for it is poetry which taught me to rest," May wrote in her journal that November 1926. "To me poetry is the thing that lifts the soul to something higher and more beautiful that comes the nearest to truth." Rest may have been an ideal ("*Do* rest, May," one hears parents and teachers pleading), but May seldom achieved it. More accurately, poetry crystallized intense emotions and exalted states of mind. Poetry disciplined a fervent imagination even as it allowed its expression; it was legitimate, sanctioned as the noblest literary form, the natural form to express the feelings of a girl drunk on the beauties of the world.

May (right) with "the Snabs"—Letty Field (left) and Jean Tatlock

Poetry was also the medium of love. May's earlier poems to Katharine Taylor apostrophized her as "the very essence of life . . . worthy / Of your ship of truth!" But exile from the principal of Shady Hill magnified her glamour, and soon May was writing ardently of her love. Wise in the ways of adolescent girls, Miss Taylor counseled restraint and objectivity, answering May's passion with good-humored teasing. May raged against this breaking of her spirit, vowed never again to write K.T., immediately broke the vow. She proclaimed her manifesto of love a month before her fifteenth birthday:

> Loving is more essential to me than Truth . . .
> You may smile, O quiet ones,
> At the profusion of my tropical love,—
> You who love simply, purely,
> Blessed be you!
> But not for me is peace in love—
> I am too wild, too free a heart. . . .

Similarly, she assessed herself in her journal that June of 1927: "I am very proud but not self-satisfied. I am naturally selfish. I have a hot resentful temper which I am slowly learning to control. I am foolishly sensitive and self-conscious (that is partly my age). I think too much. In work I am of average intelligence and can concentrate well. I have no presence of mind whatever. I have an impossible memory. I have a strong will. I am impetuous, very! I love a few people intensely. If I grow in soul and understanding I shall be a poet."

In contrast, May's letters to Mabel in Washington that March and June are curiously naive: reports of helping Anne Thorp after school, attending a production of *H.M.S. Pinafore,* coping with domestic crises that George dismissed with "Let nature take its course!" A maid, Catherine, had been introduced into the new Raymond Street apartment to care for George, while May shunted between the Field, Runkle, Bouton, Greene, Hocking, and Clark homes when she was not looking after herself. "I went to town yesterday," she wrote "Miutsie" (her new pet name for her mother) as the school year ended, "with great success. I couldn't get a bathing-suit at Shepards but I got one in Filene's basement. Unfortunately it is black. It cost $1.95. I got two dozen handkerchiefs, one dozen at five cents each and one at twelve cents. They are men's because I thought for camp the bigger the better. Then I went to Raymond's and got for $1.45 a very nice blue middy suit extra, isn't that wonderful!" The connection between the letter writer and the poet-journalist seems remote. Though George and Mabel

encouraged May's love of books, art, and music, they—like most parents—
were ignorant of their child's private emotional life.

May returned to a better-organized Day Mountain Camp the first of
July. Wooden camp houses on stilts, called "Bungs," replaced the old barn;
May and Barbara Runkle bunked in I, overseen by their favorite coun-
selor, "Humpie." This year there were horses and a Harvard graduate
named Hans as riding master, and May quickly adored cantering and gal-
loping, though she bounced on the trot. Theatricals were enormously
popular: May played the Prince in a Cinderella pantomime, "a fat old
sleepy monarch" in *The Knave of Hearts,* and Oberon in *A Midsummer
Night's Dream,* and the Tiogas made up and performed a playlet called
Much Ado About a Lot. She continued her avid reading: Sir Edmund
Gosse's biography of Ibsen, James Boyd's *Marching On,* T. E. Lawrence's
Revolt in the Desert, and William Allen White's *Woodrow Wilson,* which
struck her as "impartial" and "true in the main."

During a three-day camping trip to Squirrel Island, Charlotte Bouton
was struck by May's seriousness. They were all lying in their wool blan-
kets, looking at the stars, and May talked a great deal about the Sacco-
Vanzetti case, currently polarizing liberals and conservatives across the
country. Chussy didn't know anything about Sacco and Vanzetti; she was
impressed that May seemed to know and care so much. May *was* serious,
writing in her journal July 19, "I have consecrated my life to the search of
truth. . . . I believe in Christ as a great personality who has come the
nearest to truth of any man. . . ."

Back at the Cambridge High and Latin that September, after a long
visit to the Fields' at Woods Hole, May was restive. Her studies did not
engage her; too often her reveries were interrupted by "the sharp voice of
a teacher asking a question / I don't care to know." She gave vent to her
fifteen-year-old ennui in a poem "School-fever":

> There is nothing worth my living for
> And nothing worth my dying for. . . .
> I look at the dried petals of a yellow rose
> And wish I were going mad.

The adored Katharine Taylor continued to be elusive. "If I dare,"
wrote May, "I shall put on a magenta and orange cape / Then gayly storm
your heart." Yet she was beginning to realize that K.T. found her ardor
absurd. Hurt, May withdrew: "I must never tell you / Anything of my
heart again." Yet her reverence for the woman remained: "If you should
ever be unworthy of my highest admiration / I would murder you."

Eva Le Gallienne, who invited May to become a member of her apprentice group

Katharine Taylor as Muse, however, was eclipsed that autumn by a new discovery. It was George who took his daughter to the old Hollis Theatre in Boston to see Eva Le Gallienne's Civic Repertory company in Martínez Sierra's *Cradle Song.* May went actress-mad. Eva Le Gallienne stunned her with the "clear-cut azure" of her eyes, the "fine stillness" of her mouth. May returned for *The Master Builder;* she haunted the Hollis. In December she saw the Boston Repertory actress Katherine Warren in *A Doll's House,* and walked to school the next morning in the first snow dreaming of slamming doors herself. By the new year, 1928, she had made a momentous decision: she would be an actress.

That January she saw Le Gallienne again in *The Good Hope,* this time daring to send a bunch of flowers and a note requesting a brief audience. After the play May waited in the line outside Le Gallienne's dressing room before admission to the sanctuary. Le Gallienne was removing makeup in front of a mirror; she burst out laughing when the crop-haired girl blurted out her wish to play Hedda Gabler, yet asked her to come round again. That month May began to keep a diary, hoping a daily account might cure self-consciousness and teach her restraint, ease, and fluency. The first event she recorded was her delight in Mary Garden's *Jongleur de Notre-Dame*—"She is a great force!" Determined to make theatre contacts, she wrote Garden a letter, and was thrilled by a prompt reply in "a huge, windy writing full of life and love of life."

When Jean Tatlock's crush, Katherine Warren, sent her a six-page letter, May competitively fired off a special delivery to the actress: "Ibsen at present makes me burn to act—Hedda Gabler, Hilda Wangel, Nora, Rebecca West—but especially Hedda Gabler. There is no reason for my telling you that you were exquisite almost hurtingly beautiful as Hedda Gabler but I will tell you it. . . . Why can't I send you a snow-flake, clear and frosty and fine-wrought instead of words and words." May's appeal won them an "almost perfect afternoon" with the actress, who showed them the set, her dressing room, and how to apply stage makeup. Best of all, she told the star-struck girls about a drama school she planned to start in New Hampshire, and even cast them in her first play. Dazzled, May fled from the interview to pour out the adventure to Letty, then dashed back to Jean's for dinner, then, still too excited to go home, "ran over to the Clarks to pour it all out there."

When she did go home, she sat down and frantically typed up a group of poems to send to *The Atlantic, Harper's, Vanity Fair,* and *Poetry* in hopes of earning money for Katherine Warren's school. Encouraged by Miss Sullivan, her English teacher, and Agnes Hocking, who said she would introduce her to Robert Frost the next time he was in Cambridge, she already had been sending poems to *Poetry.* "Monday," "A Friend," and "The Doll's House" had been returned, yet she had been heartened by the editor's note: "Not yet—but these show promise."

But George Sarton had no intention of letting his daughter go on the stage. He was displeased with her latest grades, and May herself wept over them—a D in Latin, "fair" in algebra, and only a "good" in English. "When will they finish educating me?" she lamented. "The aching part of it is that I don't believe it is worthwhile. I feel all the time as if I were wasting time, time so terribly precious." But George insisted, and she applied to Vassar.

When Katharine Taylor went to lecture at Vassar that February, May went along to look over the college. Thrilling to sit across from her not-quite-ex-idol on the train to Poughkeepsie; May found herself pouring out her hatred of the barren grind of school. Miss Taylor nodded sympathetically, but argued that she "must go through with it and do it really well." She herself had dreaded the office work that being a principal involved, but the rewards had been greater than the sacrifice. The confession thrilled May: K.T. had never spontaneously revealed herself before. Still, there was always an emotional distance between them.

May had brought along a sheaf of poems; Miss Taylor kindly asked to read them. When she came to "Renunciation"—"I must never tell you / Anything of my heart again"—she grew thoughtful. "You often feel that way about grownups, don't you? I wonder why." May could not answer, but she agreed with K.T.'s judgment that the poems must leave more to the reader's intuition. Self-indulgence and sentimentality, warned Katharine Taylor, were the negation of poetry, self-discipline its essence.

They stayed in the alumnae house, and that night she walked with Miss Taylor through the snow over a campus lit by the bright windows of studious Vassar girls. When she was about to go to bed, Miss Taylor came in, wearing a blue wrapper, her "browny gold hair down," her changeable eyes like "Vermeer's blues," and kissed May very hard on both cheeks. For an ecstatic moment she had K.T. to herself. Tomorrow there would be the lecture and a meeting with President Henry Noble MacCracken. For K.T.'s sake, she could almost visualize herself at Vassar.

But then Eva Le Gallienne reappeared in Boston in *Hedda Gabler* and annihilated Vassar for May. This time, as an acquaintance of the star, she took Anne Thorp, Jean Tatlock, Letty Field, and the Clarks around to Eva's dressing room. She went back again and again, catching moments with Le Gallienne whenever she could. By June, her infatuation for the great actress was so intense she felt she must renounce her:

> I am going to lose the key
> To the little gilded chest
> Where I have kept your words
> With perfume and spices,
> The tang of exotic adventure.
> I am going to forget
> Your small white face
> And grey eyes. . . .

She did not forget Le Gallienne, of course, or her dream of becoming an actress. Even in the midst of College Boards that spring, she begged George and the absent Mabel to allow her to attend the Gloucester School of the Little Theatre, a semiprofessional summer acting company run by Florence Cunningham. She prevailed, as she tended to do, and packing her old camp clothes, spent the summer as an apprentice to all aspects of the craft in productions of *Ghosts, The Taming of the Shrew, Enter Madame, The Wild Duck,* and *The Circle.*

She was immediately inspired by Cunningham, whom she christened "Ariel" and lauded in verse as "a sea green princess" with "sensitive, passionate goodwill" and intuition like "a flash of crystal appreciation." The theatre enraptured her; yet another force, equally strong, persisted. "Words are my passion," she wrote in a poem, "Creation," that summer. Yet at this point, her passion for words and her passion to act seemed one and the same.

She returned determined to leave school forever after graduation the following June. Le Gallienne had assured her that four years of college were useless to an actress. She was abetted in her rebellion by the boy to whom she had proposed marriage long ago. Willem Van Loon, living in

May photographed by Bachrach for her 1929 graduation from the Cambridge High and Latin

Germany since 1925, now confided that against *his* father's wishes he wanted to be a dancer. Admitting that his massive body did not obviously lend itself to that calling, he still proclaimed himself "the child of Isadora." They were both "Moonchildren," the exuberant Willem told her, and should dance under the moon, forever young, "taken care of by the fairies." May agreed: they were not ordinary mortals and need not obey ordinary rules. She would act.

"Never!" roared George Sarton. Yet one evening not long after, when they were standing in the lobby of Symphony Hall at intermission, he pulled out a box of Murads and, offering her one, murmured the slogan, "Be nonchalant." She accepted her first public cigarette. He then produced a letter from Le Gallienne, which May read with delight: "I felt somehow in her possibilities for theatre work. She seemed so alive with a very definite enthusiasm and idealism, as well as, of course, being highly intelligent and of a pleasing personality." She understood that she had won; that the gesture of the cigarette signalled her father's willingness to let her go on the stage.

Mabel surely had a great deal to do with George's capitulation— Mabel, who had always respected her daughter's freedom, whose own quest for freedom had left her daughter free willy-nilly. George too must have realized not only that May had been much on her own for years, but that he himself had been a headstrong young man. And then, Eva Le Gallienne herself was offering May her patronage.

May Sarton's formal education thus ended in 1929. Mabel had sailed for England, but May hardly cared, for winning the French prize and reading the class poem at the graduation ceremony seemed unreal. She hardly cared, either—or told herself she didn't—that many close friends would be going to Smith and Vassar that fall. How could she care, when the Gloucester Little Theatre rehearsals of *The Master Builder* with May in the starring role of Hilda Wangel began in less than two weeks? And when the great Eva Le Gallienne had summoned her to New York?

CHAPTER 5

Searching: 1929–1930

At seventeen, what were May Sarton's qualifications for the stage? She was slender but not tall—a little over five-three. Her posture was rather poor. Her face was striking with its strong, straight nose, large gray-blue eyes, high cheekbones, and firm chin—classical, like the face of Pallas Athene on a Greek coin. Her front teeth protruded slightly, a fault braces could have corrected; yet the imperfection gave her mouth a curious charm, as though eager words were always bubbling behind her lips. Her boy's cut was growing out; she would pull her straight brown hair back from her face with a round "Alice" comb. Her voice was strong, and with training could become a fine instrument. But it was not really May's physical qualities that had captured Le Gallienne's attention; it was her spirit. Jean Clark called May "magnetic." She was indeed: fired with passion, ardor, and idealism, alive in every atom of her being. She radiated energy and love of life. And she was burningly ambitious.

On June 26 she was installed in a "delectable room" in East Gloucester. She had bought a pair of high laced boots for six dollars at Sears, Roebuck to play the mountain-climbing Hilda Wangel, and quickly began to get inside Hilda's skin at rehearsals in a room looking out onto seagulls floating low over the blue bay. *The Master Builder* opened on July 3; Katharine Taylor was coming the first night, the Clarks and the Dewings on Friday, George on Saturday. "So I shall be well-rooted for," May wrote Miutsie, who was staying with the Limbosches, with a hint of reproach.

As Ibsen's ruthless young idealist, May lit up the stage. "The symbolism of the play was strikingly advanced by having May Sarton play

Hilda," wrote a local critic. "Miss Sarton is herself a symbol of that strange, visionary, captivating 'younger generation knocking at the door,' her eyes those of a mystic, her attitude that of fearless, jubilant youth." Indeed, May felt no barrier between her soul and Hilda Wangel's; she played herself, thinking all the while of the Master Builder, Solness, as Katharine Taylor.

She was next cast as Masha in *The Seagull,* working meanwhile as a general hand to get *Yellow Sands* and *The Last of Mrs. Cheyney* on the boards. Yet beneath the "frightfully thrilling" surface of theatrical life, she was troubled. "If only I cared less for people and more for ideas," she confided to her diary. Katharine Taylor had warned against her obsession with older women, but she *was* obsessed—this summer with Florence Cunningham. She was on a continual high, except when she was plunged into despair, which she hardly understood, "a strange dark mist" that kept her from seeing straight. "Someone is getting a glass of water in the kitchen," she wrote in one of those moments in her room. "I try to will that if it is Ariel she come and kiss me good-night. That is another strange dark part of life. Why can't I just someday tell her that I love her and am lonely for her? Why do I suffer each time our eyes meet and imagine that these wispy meetings are tinged with portents? I'm a fool."

When, a few days later, she dared take her poems to Cunningham, they laughed and talked and kissed each other; still, she was not reassured. "Isn't it silly that a contact like that throws me off balance? Even now as I write I burn. I feel as if this passionate pouring of my spirit into the stream of one person would someday ruin my life. To-night I am filled with forebodings."

She was struggling to understand the lesbian impulse in herself, as well as her creative nature. "I know that I'm not a genius," she wrote in her diary, "though if someone told me I wasn't I would violently contradict them. I know that if I get as far as I want to, it will not be through genius but through intelligence, intensity of purpose, and will." All these she possessed; yet she feared where her violent need to intoxicate herself with a woman would lead.

She found she was expected to report to the Civic Repertory Theatre in mid-August; she had planned to visit Letty Field at Woods Hole in September before braving New York. Home from abroad, Mabel was dispatched to find her daughter lodging in the city, while George was delegated to send to Gloucester the phonetic pronunciations of all the names in *The Seagull*. Letty was on hand to see her quite fine performance as Masha the weekend of August 17. May left Gloucester soon after,

May at the Gloucester Little Theatre, Summer 1930

planning a quiet week at home before New York; but, visiting Katherine Warren backstage at the Cambridge Playgoers' Theatre, she found herself pressed into the ingenue role of Myrine in W. S. Gilbert's *Pygmalion and Galatea.* That left only hours for packing before she took the late sleeper for New York on the 31st.

Mabel had booked her a room at the McLean Club, a boardinghouse for young women at 94 MacDougal Street on the edge of Greenwich Village, near Washington Square. She spent the morning unpacking clothes, arranging books, and hanging photographs of Duse and Le Gallienne, feeling already quite at home. MacDougal Street, "a whole little Italy," fascinated her, as it had Edna St. Vincent Millay, with its speakeasies, a small café called Dante Alighieri, and a tenement with cats on windowsills. After supper she went out to wander the Village, feeling the night "full of portents," longing to knock at tantalizing doors and say, "You look very nice. Let me be your friend." Back in her room she wrote her parents and Ariel before falling into bed with poetry and *The Return of the Native*. Next morning she would report to the theatre.

In 1926 Eva Le Gallienne, twenty-seven and a star, had left Broadway to inaugurate the Civic Repertory in the old Fourteenth Street Theatre on the corner of Sixth Avenue. Envisioning the theatre as "an instrument for giving," not a "mere dollar-making machine," Le Gallienne had pulled together a company to stage, for half the price of a Broadway ticket, plays by Chekhov, Molière, Shakespeare, and Ibsen. And people had come—chiefly for Le Gallienne, of course, but also to see the best repertory group in America.

Le Gallienne had also founded an apprentice program to train young people for the theatre. Tuition was free. Students attended all rehearsals of the Civic Repertory Theatre, or CRT, were recruited for small parts, and took classes in makeup, voice, dancing, and fencing. More important, they staged their own plays for critiquing by Le Gallienne's company. This was the group Le Gallienne had invited May to join.

She arrived at the theatre Monday morning, three hours too early for the rehearsal of *The Cherry Orchard*. Toward noon, about thirty young people began to assemble. May thought they looked "an interesting lot" and was delighted to be chosen by Le Gallienne to play a nun in *Cradle Song*. She quickly discovered that an apprentice's lot was not an idle one: a rehearsal of *The Seagull* lasted all afternoon, and that evening they rehearsed *Cradle Song* till after midnight. Meanwhile, the students had chosen Barrie's *The Admirable Crichton,* which would go into rehearsal next day. May was disappointed: "It's a stupid play."

She managed to carry on the exacting routine she had planned for herself, finishing a section of Rolland's *Jean Christophe,* reading poetry, copying Chinese verse in her journal, studying *Saint Joan,* attending an afternoon rehearsal of *The Seagull,* having supper with friends down from Cambridge, and not falling into bed until 12:30 a.m. after a rehearsal of *The Master Builder.* With such a driving schedule, how strange then for her to write Jean Tatlock of her "stagnant despair":

I am in the valley of the shadow at present. I wander about like a person in a nightmare with no reason for anything. I am utterly uncreative and not even very receptive. I gaze continually at my

soul which is a deep well in which I see nothing. I feel as if I was
going blind, and all the time as I walk about or talk to people I feel
a nail being driven into my head—the aloneness of myself. . . .
There is noone here who even faintly approaches me except one
very innocent girl who has implicit faith in God and the goodness
of man, but who loves me—there is small comfort in that.

May's despair was hardly "stagnant," a condition alien to her mercur-
ial spirit. Quite apart from the shock of transplant from provincial Cam-
bridge to New York, there were other tensions. Very conscious that her
father considered her woefully uneducated, May was putting herself
through a Great Books course, reading poetry, novels, history, and philos-
ophy not only in English and in French but in German. She felt guilty if
she did not spend every hour away from the theatre "improving her
mind." She had always tried to impress George, sending him lists of the
books she was reading as though he were her schoolmaster. Now, instead
of immersing herself in the theatre, she was cramming Descartes and Ger-
man verbs.

There was a more severe conflict with George. May loved spending
money—like Mabel, George would have said: Mabel, who was sending
money to a Russian émigrée princess in Italy as well as to her improvi-
dent brother, Hugh, in Mexico; Mabel, who seldom resisted buying
thoughtful little gifts for friends. May's opposition to George in this was
implacable. She resented his meanness (as she saw it), his stubborn refusal
to admit that Mabel contributed substantially to the family income. But
May was a dependent, living on checks George deposited in an account
at the Amalgamated Bank in Union Square. She bit the bullet, sending
him weekly accounts of expenditures for everything from cigarettes to
sanitary napkins. But she was always overdrawn. She couldn't help buying
a bunch of yellow chrysanthemums, a book of Verlaine, two turtles and
three goldfish, a Victor portable phonograph for $35 because she missed
music terribly, "a wonderful Russian blouse" for $25, tickets to the plays
for friends. Couldn't help begging for a green leather fur-lined coat for
$175—"I'll be willing to go without any luxuries all winter if I may have
it and no Christmas presents. . . . O *please, please.*" Her letters became pre-
dictable: apologies for spending, pleas for more money, vows never to
overdraw again. She claimed she was thrifty, admitting at the same time, "I
do seem destined to have bad luck in money don't I?"

A deeper conflict lay in a choice of vocation. She felt sure she had
a gift for the stage: she considered her dynamic Masha better than Le

Gallienne's, "although in places hers is overwhelmingly great." Acting Saint Joan aloud one day in the library of the CRT, she decided, "I know that I have genius for acting. I know it and I fear." She feared because, traitorously, her deeper allegiance was to poetry. On September 16, she had found a note in the mail from *The Harp* accepting her poem "Friendship"—her first publication in a professional journal. She was waiting to hear from *Poetry*. But a Le Gallienne apprentice had little time for poetic creation. A day like September 21, when she could record "a little poem was born out of nothing, and that was the one scarlet leaf in the day," was rare.

She was so lonely that she was touched by the sight of a boy and girl holding hands, not a spectacle ordinarily to move her. She didn't know anybody at the McLean Club: they ate their meals in little groups she didn't have the courage or desire to join. She wrote constantly to Barbara Runkle, Jean Tatlock, Jean Clark, and Letty, passionate letters, enclosing copies of her poems; they replied in kind, yet they weren't there. Adults often did not satisfy, on paper or in person. "Yesterday I got a letter from Ariel. . . . As usual it is frightfully disappointing—a carefully composed and unrevealing document of thanks." As for K.T., "Why does she write when she has nothing but politeness to say?"

She made friends with a drugstore clerk and argued with him about art and politics over coffee at Child's. One evening Hans, the riding master from Day Mountain Camp, escorted her home on the bus: "Perhaps he is in love with me. I don't know." Egon Brecher, an experienced actor in Le Gallienne's company, had his eye on her. Then there were young women friends who troubled her with their intensity. Margaret Coolidge, a scenery assistant at Gloucester, spent the night, but was "so obviously trying to discover and explore" her that May felt "suffocated." Margaret Brown, also from Gloucester, spent a too-long afternoon that was "at times embarrassing"; she dismissed Margaret's too-ardent letter: "I don't object to slosh but slosh apologized for has no excuse." Obviously, her energy, poetic sensibility, and high spirits made her very attractive to women, even to wise women like Florence Cunningham and Katharine Taylor, who tried to curb her passion.

Not a whisper of these conflicts emerges in her frequent letters to Mabel and George. Teenagers *don't* discuss sexuality with their parents, but May's letters go to extremes to insist that life is heavenly; her reiterated "Isn't that fun?" and "Isn't that marvelous?" beg her parents to find it so too. For her parents, the "frightfully disappointing" letter from Florence Cunningham turns into "a dear little note"; Margaret Brown's "embarrassing" visit becomes "a lovely afternoon"; lessons in dancing, at which she's rotten, become "more fun all the time." German is delightful (it was hell); she adores every book she reads; she is so in love with the French language that she hates English. And of course she's economizing like crazy.

Hypocrisy in one so young—or a desperate need to please, to live up to her parents' high standards, to belong to their world? "You are the most enterprising of any of us, and have much the most will-power," Jean Clark had written, a common view of May among her friends. Obviously she felt terrific pressure to succeed. Beyond this, however, she seemed to have adopted the official stance that not only should daily events be "dear," "sweet," and "charming" but life in the large sense thrilling, heroic, and lived to the hilt. This is a noble view of life, but also damnably unrealistic; hence the incorrigibly cheerful, false note one hears with Mabel and George.

Psychiatrists have said that an only child never believes she is loved. It is difficult to believe that May felt unloved as streams of letters, books, records (for years the Sartons would box up their heavy 78s to send on loan), money, clothes, room furnishings, and clean laundry flowed from Cambridge. Yet it was her own frequent letters that spurred answers; her flood of requests that kept the supply flowing. "My demands must seem endless," she admitted. Indeed. Yet ultimately they were demands for attention. Notice me, she pleaded. Keep me always in mind. In the same spirit, she kept in constant touch with Katharine Taylor, Anne Thorp, Mary Bouton, Bonbon Baekeland, Florence Cunningham, Shady Hill friends. Think about me. Pay attention. I exist.

She made her first appearance on a New York stage in *Cradle Song* on September 17. She read "so abominably" that she was passed over for the student production of *The Lower Depths*. She was chosen to be a wolf in *Peter Pan,* then promoted to an Indian, then won her first speaking part in *The Living Corpse*—a maid with four lines. She joined Actors' Equity. She was taking fencing, which she adored, and voice lessons from Egon Brecher. Then in November the girl playing Natasha in *The Lower Depths* dropped out and she got the part. To celebrate she moved into a fourth-floor room at the McLean Club, with lots of sky and a view of the garden.

She was looking forward to coming home at Christmas on the *Nighthawk,* getting into Boston at 6:38 a.m. on December 24. "So could you send me the money? I'll come back on Christmas day on the 1:00 that gets in at 6:00. I'm so excited!" George sent a check with a rebuke.

"I thought I explained, Daddy, that that money was for my ticket," May answered, stung to complaint at last. "If you did understand and still think I should pay for it I shall be glad to return the check. I've tried to be a good sport about money, but you still seem to think I'm trying to grab more than I need. I am hurt."

For Christmas in Cambridge Miutsie gave her Katherine Mansfield's *Journal*. It made a huge impact. "Once in a while you come upon a person who seems to be grafted onto your soul," she wrote in her diary, which immediately had become Mansfieldian. Poetic: "My mind is thin and cool like the ice round the edges of a little marsh." Elliptic: "I remember that once in a train like this K.T. looked very tired and smiled at me." Evocative: "Willem and I always ate the doughy center of bread first and then buttered the thin crusts—I remember how I hurried to get to the crusts." Rather pretentious—the usual result of innocence imitating sophistication.

But Mansfield also articulated the eternal tension between the demands of life and art. "For the last few weeks I have been having a fight with panic—the panic of people closing over me—I have a horror of that," May wrote Jean Clark. "I felt as if hundreds of starving people were begging my soul and I couldn't give it to them. . . . You see, before this year, it is always I who have asked and other people given—I imagined that to be a giver, the one loved, instead of the lover would be a perfect thing. I wanted madly to give. Now I find, when people ask, I can't give—I become terrified—I am afraid of being shut up too tightly. It is only to the people who have no need of me that I could give all of myself."

She copied this letter to Jean into her diary "because I want to remember, never to forget that panic—E.B., M.B., N.B., and W.v.L."

Some of these demands were sexual. George and Mabel had never mentioned sex; she was a complete innocent. Egon Brecher frightened her. He French-kissed her; sitting in the dark theatre, he grabbed her hand and made her masturbate his hard penis. "I am not worthy of life itself. . . . I allow E.B. to use my body—yes—admit it—simply to give himself strength I suppose. He looks deeply into my eyes, but he must be blind because he sees no revolt." Nine days later she could write, "I respect E.B.—he is so wise and gentle. Yesterday he talked to me about Thomas Mann so beautifully. I love him." But her "inconstancy" tormented her, perhaps accounting for this High Decadent style:

> Being what I am—an incomplete
> And faithless lover; in the end, my love,

I will not follow you, nor is it meet
I wear inconstantly the faith you wove.
Take my vermilion heart, take it and fuse
The crystal shape into vermilion glass.
It is my wish—when I have gone—you use
This scrap of faith, remembering faithlessness.
Fill it with golden milk the slowest bee
Bears on his thigh through the deep, drowsy noon.
Drink whiter wine than that you drank with me,
And sleep more sweetly when you sleep alone;
But if you love again, and end the matter,
Being what I am: Heart, break. Glass, shatter.

In letters May was being pressured for love by the passionate and bril-
liant Jean Tatlock. More than her other friends, Jean had shared May's
heroine worship. While May wrote lyrics to Katharine Taylor, Alla Nazi-
mova, and Le Gallienne, Jean was worshipping at the temples of Kather-
ine Warren and Duse ("I can no longer speak the name of the Duse
without being torn to shreds"). They debated endlessly the merits of their
respective idols, were furiously jealous of them. Then, in June 1929, they
spent a night together.

"I want to know," Jean wrote May urgently, ". . . did something really
happen the last night or did I dream it all? The next morning after any-
thing you are always untouched and oblivious . . . I felt a passion that
night that was pure beauty. . . ."

Nothing had happened that night—at least, the two girls had not
made love. But Jean had fallen in love with May. Separation was torment.
"I love you with my blood at this moment. O, to touch you, to lie down
with you in the sand. Why do I talk about peace? I ache and ache for your
presence. . . . Why & why are you so afraid of the body? My God how
unbearable is this. . . . But I am not Lesbian. Are you?"

It was a question May couldn't yet answer. There was Egon Brecher.
And for all their talk of "passion," it remained only talk. Their burning and
yearning was much the same emotion they felt at a poem of Amy Lowell's,
or the acting of Sacha Guitry and Yvonne Printemps, or a Chopin noc-
turne—which is not to deny its fundamental sexuality. They *lived* to feel
intensely. All May could say at this point is that she was disturbingly attrac-
tive to females, disturbed by male sexuality, and turned off by marriage.

·   ·   ·

*May and George
Sarton, Christmas
1929*

That February 1930, May opened a letter from Harriet Monroe, the
editor of *Poetry:* "Although we are accepting almost nothing because of
congestion, your two poems seem to me too beautiful to decline." She
did not tell her fellow actors about the triumph; it was a secret to carry
like the big peppermint in her pocket when she climbed the red maple
at Shady Hill and the wind whipped her hair into her eyes and she ate
the peppermint very slowly, licking out its middle through a hole in the
chocolate. But she felt her difference from them. Her secret set her
apart.

   She needed this distinction because she didn't seem to be getting any-
where as an actress. A page in *Romeo and Juliet,* a grandmother in the stu-
dent production of Jean-Jacques Bernard's *Martine*—the parts she wanted
went to others. It was some consolation that Le Gallienne told her she was
very like herself and must conquer the same Anglo-Saxon inhibitions.

Still, she was discouraged with the season, though relieved to know she'd be back next year. George Sarton was more confident. "Had good talk with Eva Le Gallienne," he wired Mabel from New York. "She believes May has real vocation; advises us to encourage her." May herself staggered back to Cambridge the first of June under double the load she'd taken with her. She had wildly hoped that George and Miutsie could spend the summer with her at Gloucester. She often hoped for such intimacy; it seldom occurred.

A week before graduating from the Cambridge High and Latin, Letty Field was hospitalized with severe menstrual bleeding. She telephoned, "Please come and see me," but May had a Gloucester rehearsal and did not go. The surgeon, not a gynecologist, botched the ovarian surgery; peritonitis set in. "Je ne dis rien, ayant trop à dire," May wrote in her diary on Tuesday, June 10. "Letty died on Monday." She dealt with her grief and guilt by writing a tribute to "L.F."

> She loved poplars, the sea. At first she loved truth more than beauty then beauty more than truth. . . . Music was her luxury. She knew it with her whole self—intellectually as well as emotionally. All physical things pleased her. . . . Her leather coat, woolen mittens, new moccasins. She possessed her books—just turning the leaves of a new one gave her almost sensual pleasure, and she couldn't bear anyone else to read it first. . . . She loved to exhaust herself physically, but physical pain terrified her. . . . Abstinence and self-discipline were her creed. . . . She wanted to be a doctor but was tormented by that fear of physical pain and the belief that she lacked perseverance. It was difficult to talk with her because she was so humble. . . .

On June 26 she escaped to Gloucester, where she wrote publicity to help pay her tuition, had a minor role in *The Swan* ("I'm really glad you're not coming . . . it is not awfully good"), then went on to bigger things as Asta Almers in *Little Eyolf,* "a gushing lady" in *Enchanted April* ("Don't you think you can both come?"), and the Helen Hayes part in *Dear Brutus.*

Her grief for Letty renewed her need for a woman they had both loved. May deluged Katharine Taylor with letters that summer. On July 28 she took a train to Cambridge to lunch with K.T., "waited and waited and waited—until I was a thousand tigers," and finally saw her for dinner. Anticipation made the meeting anticlimactic: "I wore a violent blue dress—it was awfully hot—I felt sick—her eyes were just the color of her dress, very soft blue like some dark pigeons—but trying to talk over a table is hell."

Back in Gloucester, she tried to analyze her feelings for the older women in her life. Anne Thorp—"I love her largely," she wrote Jean Clark, "but I never have with her that queer excitement of being suspended between two planes of soul that I do with K.T. . . . I don't feel ill, or icy, or burning. . . . With Miss C [Florence Cunningham] I think it's only a terrific tenderness that seizes on me when I'm with her—she is so tiny and slight, between a star and a flower, exquisite—but when I'm away I forget her. K.T. is not like that. K.T. is half my soul." May was emphatically not half Katharine Taylor's soul; yet her gifts and the sheer urgency of her emotional demands had woven her into the older woman's life.

On August 16, Willem Van Loon turned up from Vienna, where he was studying dance against the wishes of his father, who deplored his choice of career. May was secretly horrified to hear he would stay a week: she had lines to learn and was deep into Emily Dickinson. They picnicked on a rock overlooking the sea, May struggling to learn *Dear Brutus,* Willem pirouetting on the rocks, drenched in spray. He told her he was homosexual and that she was the only girl he could talk to. Talk he did—endlessly, lyrically, exhaustingly—to his fellow "Moonchild." Finally the "tempest of words and dancing" whirled away. "I loved him for a week," May told Jean Tatlock, "—another would have killed one of us." Willem returned her sentiments: "I feel you are so strong. I am glad I got away."

By September 7 May moved into a new garden room at the McLean Club, which she changed a few weeks later because it was small and hot. She was writing again after a long drought—something that thrilled her even more than being a member of the new First Studio of the Civic Repertory Theatre. Directed by Robert Ross of the CRT, this select band would stage six matinee productions of works by new playwrights during the season, with critics (they hoped) in attendance. The self-governing group of twelve included Helen Brewer, Arnold Moss, Estelle Scheer, Howard da Silva, and Burgess Meredith.

Her first project was translating Jean-Jacques Bernard's play *L'Âme en peine* for production, while the First Studio opened with *The Jest,* "an old rag worn thin by the Barrymores," with no part for May. She was dissatisfied enough to ask Le Gallienne for a leave of absence; Eva insisted she stay. "It seems hard when I'm not being paid, haven't a single new part, and am not in the first play of the studio," she wrote George and Mabel. ". . . I eat balloons of hope for breakfast, lunch and dinner. As a steady diet they are rather undigestible." Eventually she was given the part of the

Willem Van Loon ("Puck") dancing on the sands

fat nurse in *The Jest;* but when Jo Hutchinson, a major CRT actress, could not open in *Siegfried* because of appendicitis, Eva would not let May audition because she was "too fragile-looking"—a blow since six First Studio members got parts. As an actress she was going nowhere.

Proofs from *Poetry* early in November broke the dismal spell. The magazine was publishing four: "First Love," "Let No Wind Come," "They Also," and "Fruit of Loneliness." Then the volume itself arrived. "My heart *did* leap up when *Poetry* came," she wrote George and Mabel. ". . . Did you see the note at the back . . . 'She is a daughter of the distinguished scientist, George Sarton'?" With the check for $18—her first literary earnings—she flew to Brentano's and bought a book of José Clara's drawings of Isadora Duncan for $17.50.

The four poems, three of them sonnets, proved that at eighteen, May Sarton had a gift for poetry. If they were derivative and traditional in form, so are most first poems. "Fruit of Loneliness" leaned heavily on Keats, Christina Rossetti, and the English decadents:

> Now for a little I have fed on loneliness
> As on some strange fruit from a frost-touched vine—
> Persimmon in its yellow comeliness,
> Or pomegranate-juice color of wine,

The pucker-mouth crab apple, or late plum—
On the fruits of loneliness have I been fed.

"They Also," however, sustains its effective bird imagery skillfully throughout:

The earth is slim between two who have seen
How a white pigeon floats across the wind;
It is not wide for them. The earth between
Bird-minds is thin, and the world's end
Only as far as a white pigeon's wing. . . .

May needed, at this point, strict form to control her fervid imagination and tempestuous feelings. Poetry was a necessity: a spiritual discipline, a tamer of what she called "this luxurious heart." And yet love, inevitably tempestuous, was its inspiration.

CHAPTER 6

Finding: 1931–1932

We came together like two deer
Their horns in velvet still, erect and slight.
Their fur like silk, their large eyes amber-clear,
Startled and dazzled in each other's light. . . .
We came together softly in great wonder
Not dreaming of this lightning-love, this thunder.

Grace Marie Daly also boarded at the McLean Club. She had come from a poor Irish family in Lawrence, Massachusetts, to try her fortune in New York, where she'd acquired little fortune but a patina of sophistication. She was thirty-one, tall, with a good figure, dark eyes, dark hair—very handsome.

"Why did you kiss me that first time?"
"You asked for it. It wasn't so difficult. . . ."
"I shall spend hours and hours trying to find a word for your voice—your *being* and find none."
"Is it so lovely?" Ironically.
"Don't—I don't like that."
"It's part of me. You have to accept it."
"I accept it. I accept it all."

May had longed to be kissed, and Grace had kissed her. A stranger, so different from the familiar Jean Tatlock, whose tortured emotions had been chiefly confined to paper. A mysterious other, into whose empty mold May could pour her imagination. A catalyst (she realized instinctively) to speed her poetic pulse. But most of all, someone for whom the kiss had been easy—someone who would dispel her shyness and shame.

Still, May's falling in love with Grace did not quite solve the problem of her sexual identity. Was she a lesbian, or simply a passionate young woman who hadn't found the right man? The exchange of letters with Jean Tatlock had intensified her self-doubt. "I'm surrounded by homosexuals," she'd written the previous fall, "—how strange that [at] every turning they play with my life. I begin to wonder—Eva Le Gallienne, Willem, Nancy, now Jean. Why?" Eva had made scandalous headlines the previous July when her lover, Jo Hutchinson, divorced her husband; exposed publicly as a lesbian, Le Gallienne suffered contempt and hostility. Her humiliation gave May pause. After all, Grace might be merely one last terrific crush on the road to heterosexual maturity. They hadn't gone to bed together yet. And there had been Egon Brecher.

Though flattered by May's ardor, Grace was also terrified. Here was this daughter of an internationally famous Harvard scholar, member of Le Gallienne's handpicked First Studio, a published poet—and not yet nineteen! May's very room intimidated her: oh-so-artistic blues and oranges, vases of flowers, piles of books, photographs of Duse and Isadora Duncan, Beethoven crashing from the phonograph—the whole thing reeking of a cultured world Grace had never known. Most terrifying of all was May's astonishing fluency washing over her in poems, letters, declarations of love. "People are afraid of words," May challenged. "You are. Why?" Grace didn't know, but she felt inadequate. What to do? She decided that she too had a calling. With any chance at all, she knew she could be—a sculptor.

Nothing could have whetted May's ardor more. She loved an unfulfilled soul to which only she could grant completion, she loved to make things happen, she loved (very humanly) to feel superior and in charge. From the moment Grace admitted her secret calling, May mentally established her in a studio. Grace might not have believed in her destiny; May did.

Meanwhile, she had set her own plans in motion. Despite her triumph in *Camille* that February of 1931, Le Gallienne had announced the closing of the Civic Repertory for a year. Quite apart from the closing, however, May was dissatisfied. First Studio plays were endlessly proposed and withdrawn, and even though Le Gallienne had kissed her hand after *Martine,* saying, "I adore you in this," she was not getting good parts. She had almost decided she wouldn't return, even if Eva asked her: "One gets sucked into someone else's center here—and that's bad."

So, though she'd had to beg nine dollars from her father for Equity dues, she now proposed that George finance a year abroad. She was, as usual, persuasive. The Depression, inaugurated by Black Friday in October 1929, was now in full swing; but in England or Paris, acting jobs might be available. Jean Tatlock and Jean Clark both would be in Paris in June. She could economize part of the time by staying with the Limbosches in Brussels. Willem would look out for her. She could use this time away from the grind of the theatre to write. Secretly, like a primrose opening in her heart, there was the thought that if she got abroad, Grace must join her.

George could hardly say no to Paris, since he and Mabel were quitting Raymond Street and leaving for a year abroad at the American University in Beirut, where George intended to master Arabic and Hebrew. Literally, May had no home. Then there was the family vacation they'd been talking about for years. George decided they all might rendezvous on the Continent in August.

That spring, May refused a small part in *John Gabriel Borkman* as proof of her coming independence from the First Studio. Nazimova, one of her idols, was back for *The Cherry Orchard,* "exquisite and apparently as young as spring," but May's real life was centered on Grace. "It has been a very peaceful golden day," she wrote her parents on her birthday, which she spent with Grace, thanking them for chocolates and stockings. "I think nineteen is going to be a very nice year—I have great forebodings of happiness."

Had her parents known, "peaceful" in May's vocabulary was a red alert, meaning, nine times out of ten, that she was in the throes of passion. May was a stranger to "peaceful," but she came to use the word compulsively. It masked her sexual interest in women; it denied she felt passion at all. "Peaceful" was a sop for George and Mabel, lulling them in the belief that May was leading a calm, orderly life. With Grace, May began the sadly necessary deception that would last her parents' lifetimes.

By mid-month she was home in Cambridge, writing Grace urgently. "You see this isn't a new way of loving for me—it's the old way come to a circle. In spite of ourselves we *are* part of earth turning very slowly towards something—like an orchard of trees. Nothing is complete in itself—I'm myself plus something of you, and whatever you may think, there is a new color in you which is mine. There is a flower in your blood, there is a flower in mine, and the perfume of these two flowers makes a strange, new, poignant scent which is our togetherness."

Grace's noncommittal reply pained her. If only Grace had "put a hand in [her] pocket and brought out, one by one, the broken pencil, the peanut, the blue marble, and the jackknife with two blades—and said, like a little boy, 'Look, this is what I have.' " May was urging a rendezvous in New York before the *Lapland* sailed: "Really unless you do this arranged meeting in a hotel (I can see the towels on a rack, and stiff impersonal furniture, and I wanting desperately to ask for a thimble across a waste of carpet)—unless you do, it will be horrible."

On June 11, May said goodbye to her parents in their emptied apartment and trained to New York, where she greeted Grace in a hotel in new red-and-black pajamas. What she desired did not happen.

The next day headlines announced that Eva Le Gallienne had been critically burned at her country home in Weston when she lit a match to investigate a malfunctioning water heater in the basement and the propane gas exploded. Though she had thrown her hands over her face, she had suffered severe burns on her hands, face, arms, and legs; doctors doubted she would live. May apparently did not see the papers, since she cheerfully waved goodbye to friends at the pier.

She found her shared cabin full of bouquets and baskets of fruit. Almost immediately she wrote Grace. "I'm sitting in the writing-room with a cup of coffee and a cigarette, feeling old. . . . I have a strange sense of fatality about your coming—it will never happen, will it? unless one can count on the faith that moveth mountains which I doubt." In her heart she believed Grace would come, and that it was right, though she wished she could confide in Katharine Taylor. "So far I have always done what I felt and then found reasons afterward," she wrote her mentor. "Usually it wasn't hard." At nineteen May had formulated her creed for life.

She arrived at Plymouth June 22 and crossed to Paris, where she met Willem, passing through from Amsterdam. They wandered from the Gare du Nord to the Palais de Justice, hunting without success for the overalls May imagined herself wearing at the Limbosches', consoling themselves finally with *glaces* at a sidewalk café. Willem proposed that since he would be on tour all winter, May take his studio apartment a few minutes south of the gates of Paris for thirty dollars a month, furnished. May had been leaning toward spending her *Wanderjahr* in Paris; this decided her.

May introduced the idea of Willem's apartment to her parents as a possibility, but had already made up her mind: "Just in case we take the apartment—could you make a bundle . . . with my blue indian blanket, the green pillows and little black ones and the green spread—and any other things you can think of which might be useful (perhaps the grey curtains from mother's room, as the studio has no curtains)." Of course Mabel made up the large parcel and George resigned himself to paying for Willem's apartment.

The two Jeans were already in Paris; they would leave for Pontivy that week. Meeting Jean Tatlock would be difficult; for while Grace had intervened in May's life, May was still central to Jean's. May found her "wonderful and strange . . . so wise, *anciently* wise in some ways, and then suddenly childish." They had two "glorious weeks of swimming naked in *fiery* blue seas"; but by the end, Jean Tatlock's tormented *pudeur* had defeated them both. Jean terrified and humbled May; they were too different to come together.

"I think it was good we didn't find each other," she wrote Jean after they parted,

> because things in both of us were complicated, a too-consciousness of feeling, a tense restless remembering and wanting, and we were each divided and tortured within ourselves. Sometimes I was stretched with wanting your mouth, and I had a feeling of being choked and sealed in some strange way from pouring myself over you. . . . We are so conscious of our bodies, at least I am. That's why G. seemed wonderful—because she knew and took it all for granted so simply. . . . But for us there is only struggle, like the difficult opening of a rose. . . . one day there will be no struggle but we will flow together. O my darling, don't let's lose each other in long apartness.

"I hope to God we will one day simply love one another," Jean answered from America. "Do you think it might happen?"

She went to the Limbosches' ready for work, expecting that once Belgian May was on European soil, words would come. Instead, though she resolved to write five hundred words a day, she could not. The "great slow curves" of the Belgian earth against the sky—more sky, surely, than anywhere else in the world—moved her, but the constant wind and rain, the fast clouds scudding across that huge sky, made her want to throw pen and paper aside. When Grace came, she told herself, everything would happen.

More unsettling than that huge moving sky was the despair of the Belgian people. Apart from the constant rain, darkness hung over the house. On this visit, even philosophical Uncle Raymond was grim. Who could trust the word of a country that had already kicked Belgium in the teeth three times? Clearly Germany was again the rising power in Europe, while France, a dying nation, watched a soaring German birth rate producing a new war machine and did nothing. The Belgians were particularly bitter toward America for allowing Germany to evade every pact for repayment since the Treaty of Versailles. If a pact could be broken, declared Raymond, then there was nothing for Belgium to depend on except the certainty of another German invasion. May listened as an outsider, hearing "a passionate sound of heartbreak at the centre of the world."

On August 6 "the most intellectually ascetic man I know" arrived in Europe, and father and daughter joined Mabel in Geneva. George was basking in scholarly acclaim at the publication of the first volume of his history of science, dedicated to Mabel Elwes Sarton, the mother of "those strange twins, *Isis* and May." (It was like him, thought May, to put *Isis* first.) The three had two wonderful days in Geneva; the second, a rainy day, in a house full of flowers before a blazing fire with Méta Budry. As a small child, May had adored Méta at Wondelgem; now she was entranced with this beautiful woman who seemed her age rather than Mabel's. "She curled up in a purple chair," she wrote Grace, "and laughed in a strange fairy-way, as vermillion poppies would sound if they could laugh! I read poems—altogether one of the rare days—I think one has about forty allotted for a lifetime. . . ."

Half in love, May could not resist writing the enchantress from Zurich: "I have a most awful nostalgia . . . for a fire and a magenta curtain and you curled up in a chair. . . ." Nostalgia and constant rain made Zurich less than exciting, though George walked "tirelessly about like a wet duck" while Mabel visited old friends. From Zurich they went to Vienna. By September 24 the Sartons were off to the American University in Beirut and May was back in Paris, poised on the threshold of what she assured her parents would be a great, productive year.

She discovered that her hotel, the Louvois in the rue Notre-Dame-des-Champs, was "simply a roost for unmarried American hens" demanding endlessly of each other, "Ahvez-vuz aytez o Comayday Frangsayz?" May sat in her little room staring at a list of names of theatre people she intended to call, letters she intended to write, schools where she might study; it all had seemed so probable in New York. Instead she wandered the Paris streets, browsing in the book stalls along the Seine, drinking coffee in sidewalk cafés, reading Baudelaire on a bench under a chestnut tree.

She was not lonely: familiar Americans surfaced everywhere. She ran into Katherine Warren at a book stall; they walked to the Tuileries and sat in the sun while pale leaves drifted to their feet, and May was amazed to feel so little of what she once felt for this lovely woman. Florence Cunningham and Roswell Hawley, a "heavenly middle-aged" actress from Gloucester, also materialized. So did Irene Sharaff, a set designer for the CRT; together they went to a performance of the astonishing Josephine

Baker, very slim, "like flowing metal." Back at the Hôtel Louvois, she spent her mornings writing letters. Occasionally a poem was born:

> We who had been so wounded and so cloven
> Were grafted like two trees into one bark
> And our two colors sharply interwoven,
> The delicate and bright, the tawny dark.
> Out of our mingled blood, petal and flower
> With a sharp fertile perfume of its own
> Love came upon us softly in that hour:
> We did not see that love lay there alone.
> And when we woke out of the dream she made
> Nothing had changed—the earth was just the same.
> And we, so wounded, strangers and afraid,
> Standing apart saying each other's name,
> Looked down and saw love luminous and wild
> Lying between us like a sleeping child.

This cloven other was Grace; and if only Grace came, May could write.

When she sent the sonnet to George and Mabel in Beirut, George thought it so beautiful he offered to underwrite the publication of a book of May's poetry. "I too, find in it a beauty that startles & arrests my heart," wrote Mabel, ". . . partly because before my very (inward) eyes a transformation takes place of the image I have of you, into a different being, but it is partly the joyous & yet awe-inspiring thing that happens when *any* poet reveals something within himself: as if his body became mystically transparent to shew a radiant, beating heart like a flame within him, which dazzles." If sensibility can be inherited, May had her mother's.

By October 22 she was installed in Willem's studio at 42 place Jules-Ferry. There was a grand piano; she decided to keep it at 172 francs a month and take lessons, since she must study something. She quickly got into the habit of going out early to the *marché,* coming home with an egg, a tomato, or a wedge of cheese tucked into a basket of narcissus and yellow daisies. A young Polish friend of Willem's came to practice the piano every morning: she breakfasted and made her bed to Chopin and Liszt. "I have a sense of freedom here—and peace," she wrote her parents.

Dangerous word! Freedom, certainly. When Willem returned, he constantly threw parties for his artistic crowd, mostly homosexual, many of them Duncan dancers, with lots of wine and dancing, which May found she adored. All kinds of friends and friends of friends found her apartment. The artist Olga Brodsky was painting her portrait, as was Irene Sharaff, and she was constantly rushing out with people to cafés and night spots. Francs vanished like smoke; she prayed that Anne Thorp and Bonbon might give her money for Christmas. "I shall need *badly* my Nov. allowance on the first," she warned George, admitting privately to Miutsie, "I myself don't see how I spend, but it seems to be a blindness I can't get over." She had begun to sign letters "Your Mouse," accompanied by a sketch with a long tail.

But she was in Paris for the theatre. She got permission to sit in on rehearsals of the famous acting family the Pitoëffs, and the equally famous Compagnie des Quinze, but found herself watching finished performances of mediocre plays. Besides, she was sick of sitting passively in dark theatres; she wanted to *do* something. In "a fit of fury" she wrote the famous actor-impresario Lugné-Poë. "Where is the theatre?" she demanded. "And why can't I act Hilda Wangel to your Solness?"

A phone call the next morning: "Mademoiselle, vous êtes folle!" rumbled a voice, which subsided into an exasperated "Come and see me if you like!" The next day May took the Métro, finally arriving in a shabby courtyard in the rue Tourgot inhabited by a dirty boy in sabots who told her Monsieur Lugné was not at home. She was playing with the boy, a pail over her head, when a large man with bushy eyebrows, big nose, and white hair under a huge black hat strode in. The pail did not amuse him; abashed, she followed him up a dingy staircase into an office with a big rolltop desk piled with dusty telegrams. The founder of the famous Théâtre de l'Oeuvre told her again she was mad to think of acting in French. Yet quite soon they were laughing and teasing like old friends, and he had discovered that she wrote poetry. He promised to try to find her a small part in a play or perhaps the *cinéma,* and told her to return. She did, but there was nothing. Still, they were charming friends, and she called him "Mon Éléphant."

May, Irene Sharaff, and Mary Chilton, a quiet, studious young woman from the Hôtel Louvois who was taking classes at the Sorbonne, celebrated Thanksgiving at Elsa Lee's American restaurant with turkey and cranberry sauce. A few days later May had dinner with two other Americans in their luxurious borrowed apartment overlooking the Seine and Notre-Dame: Eva Le Gallienne and Jo Hutchinson. Eva had come to Paris to recuperate both from the notoriety of their publicized liaison and from the terrible burns suffered in the explosion. Eva and Jo were in their

dressing gowns, relaxed and amusing, and suddenly they decided that they
must go to the Médrano Circus to see the famous Fratellinis. They had
front-row seats for the thrilling performance, though the plunging horses
terrified Jo. "I want to see you again for a real talk," Eva whispered to
May as they parted.

Their first talk over tea led to nothing. Le Gallienne did not make an
offer when May hinted that she might return to New York to look for a
job in stock. "I see more and more that there is nothing here for me,"
May wrote Miutsie in disappointment, "and if you and Daddy think it
wise I would like to plan to go back in the middle of March. If I were
doing a lot of writing here, I wouldn't mind. But I see too many people."

"Too many people" would be a lifelong hazard for May, who could not
help charming multitudes with her gaiety and enthusiasm, and who herself
needed people like a fix. Yet she didn't want to go back to New York at all;
she was in the throes of a feverish campaign to bring Grace Daly to Paris.

Miutsie was not a part of it, since she wasn't currently earning money; instead May stormed Katharine Taylor and the wealthy Anne Thorp. "You see for me it is Grace," she wrote K.T. that December. ". . . You can't *deny* this very deep, very quiet thing called life—you *can't.*" May next cabled Anne Thorp, asking her to loan Grace Daly $250 for her passage.

Understandably, both Taylor and Thorp were dismayed. They were fond of May (Anne had given her money for Paris) but knew how her emotions galloped away with her. Anne cabled May that she could not possibly loan Grace money without knowing more, and summoned the stranger to the big Longfellow house at 105 Brattle Street.

Ironically, Grace herself had considered Paris out of the question. She hadn't any money and knew that leaving her secretarial job at Brentano's in the midst of the Depression was financial suicide. All autumn, however, the surf of May's enthusiasm battered her. May was miserable without her, could not write a word. Paris would be Grace's salvation: she could study sculpture: the two could work blissfully side by side. By the time Grace walked into Anne Thorp's home, she was as "blind and unrealistic as a child." It was Paris or die. Alarmed, Anne passed her along to Katharine Taylor, who concluded that though Grace was the older, May was leading her by the nose. Obviously Grace had been "caught up in the current of May's enthusiasm and power for action and in an admiration for May's mind which she thrilled to but could not wholly meet." May had established enormous control over Grace by the sheer energy of her demands. Both women declined to lend Grace passage money.

In truth May's longing for Grace had little to do with writing. It was sexual. Paris had liberated her. *À bas* New England puritanism! *À bas* Anglo-Saxon inhibitions! As Marlene Dietrich once remarked, "In Europe it doesn't matter whether you love women or men, it only matters that you're charming." May was drunk on this discovery. How exciting to discover lesbian cabarets where boyish girls in tuxedos tangoed you pelvis-to-pelvis across the polished floor, to have chic women caress you in the streets with their eyes. Even Le Gallienne and Hutchinson were relaxed and free away from the puritanical United States. In Paris May and Grace would consummate their desire. She accelerated her campaign; cables flew across the Atlantic; she became possessed.

One day Eva asked May to bring over some poems because her father, Richard Le Gallienne, the English poet and critic, was in town and had agreed to read them. May quickly typed up ten or twelve and brought them to Eva's apartment; Le Gallienne took them away with him. Then Eva asked her to supper and a play afterwards, and May suddenly felt deliciously like one of the family, lounging in their living room as Jo played the "Moonlight" Sonata and Eva chuckled over the Bernard Shaw–Ellen Terry correspondence. After dinner with champagne, a play seemed too much like work, so they went to La Fourmi to hear the indestructible Dora Stroeva sing in Russian to her guitar; and May went quite mad over her. After this a cabaret, and there in the smoke and din May persuaded Eva, who thought she was too young, to let her direct the Apprentices at the CRT next fall—fifty students and her choice of plays.

"ENGAGED BY EVA THIRTY FIVE A WEEK WHAT ABOUT TYROL," May triumphantly cabled Beirut. George sent a cold reply: extravagant to talk of vacations in the Tyrol, and how did managing a student group advance her literary career? Was she sacrificing poetry to a paycheck?

"I thought you would be rather proud of your only daughter—and pleased," May shot back. She was not abandoning poetry: Richard Le Gallienne had been *very* enthusiastic about the poems; she carried his letter of praise in her pocketbook everywhere. But poetry was not a job:

I don't think if I felt my profession was writing I could write a line. Also the life of the theatre is great stimulation—I only write when I work. Here I write nothing.

As for the stage it would be madness to give it up now—as a matter of fact I would go crazy if I did. Instead of sand it is the *one* rock I cling to—it's the only thing I have which doesn't change— poetry is so much a thing of mood. . . . It is dear of you to offer me such permanent support—but after all . . . I could never never never earn my living writing poetry (noone ever has!) . . . Already next year I shall earn $140 a month. . . . It means a winter coat— concerts—it means not feeling always on the verge of bank- ruptcy. . . . Remember too that you are an exceptionally ascetic person who wants to live simply—also you are a man. As a woman I have to have clothes. . . . [Also] I want to be able to invite a friend to dinner occasionally, and later in a few years to have a cabin somewhere in the country where people can come for week-ends and rest and have fun. A car—I hope when I'm twenty-one. . . .

Though she had gone to the First Unitarian Church as a child with the Runkles, May was an agnostic like her parents. ("May always left the room when God was mentioned!" Polly Thayer Starr, an artist friend from Boston, would observe.) Yet the beautiful Christmas pageants initiated by Katharine Taylor at Shady Hill had touched some deep need in her to formally celebrate love, light, and friendship. Christmas was a special time for May, who loved to give even if she could only afford a card. She had hand-painted and sent more than a hundred this year; in return, greetings and gifts large and small came to place Jules-Ferry. From K.T., a poem— "To darling May—Who light of heart / With keenest dart / Shall every dragon slay." Parma violets and a cable from Anne Thorp, a necklace and money from her parents. Christmas Eve was magical: Mary Chilton hired a car and chauffeur, and she, May, and Irene Sharaff drove to Chartres for the evening service, dining at a charming *auberge* on the way. May woke next morning in the French countryside to the "*coldest wettest* Christmas morn" she'd ever seen, but the day ended warmly at Eva's with dinner and Eva's gift: a tortoiseshell pen with "M.S." engraved on the gold band—"To write poems with," said Eva. Later May came to look upon that gift as prophetic, as though Eva had divined that her future did not lie in the theatre.

But the greatest gift arrived in the new year. She immediately wrote George and Mabel "the extravagantly joyful news": Grace Daly would arrive on the *Lafayette* February 14. "I don't know how she got the money or how long she is staying, but isn't it wonderful!"

Before Grace's arrival, May took Irene Sharaff to the Limbosches'. The visit, she argued, would save money, since they would be guests, and perhaps with Irene there "that dark cloud" that had dampened her last visit would evaporate. She and Irene went for walks in the beech forest, explored Bruges, heard Ravel conduct his own music at a gala attended by the king and queen. The trip did not save her money: Auntie Lino charged them board—"perfectly fair but rather disgruntling." Yet the Brussels visit initiated one of the key friendships of her life.

One morning May set out for the Institut Belge de Culture Française to discover the mystery that had ruled the other classroom: Marie Closset, the poet Jean Dominique. With her housemates Marie Gaspar and the novelist Blanche Rousseau, the mystery was in residence: a tiny, androgynous woman of fifty-eight with thin, boy-cropped hair and enormous gray eyes. May read her own poems, and a quick sympathy sprang up between them. Here was a woman who had loved both men and women, and to whom she could say anything . . . a person whose heart was as transparent as her own . . . a poet "toute intérieure, toute spirituelle," who understood her own poetic soul. She came away knowing that something momentous had happened.

Back in Paris she immediately spent Miutsie's Christmas money from Anne Thorp on freesias, anemones, violets, and lilies of the valley to be delivered to Jean Dominique every week for a month. "Adorable" notes rewarded her: "Return when you can to our house. All three of us await you—three 'old ones' who have faith in your 'luminous and wild genius' and who love you well." She had, she told her parents, "a place there, more I feel now than at Aunty Lino's."

But now there was only Grace and the consummation of their love. May said she didn't know how Grace had gotten money for the trip. Not true. She had finally persuaded Anne Thorp to lend Grace $250, telling Grace she would repay it. She had arranged for sculpting lessons, hired someone to clean the apartment, and stocked it with wine and flowers on

$100 borrowed from Willem because she had spent her $100-a-month allowance cabling Grace and sending Dora Stroeva flowers. On February 13, she left for Le Havre to meet Grace's ship.

Grace hardly recognized May. Her straight brown hair was permed into curls; she wore makeup and fingernail polish, a smart purple suit, and, shockingly, no hat. By eleven the next morning they were back in Paris, May trembling on the brink of her first love affair.

It did not happen. Grace was still handsome—but nervous, defensive, cool. She was appalled to discover that May had the apartment only through March and little money for them to live on. She never took the sculpting lessons, nor was she interested in browsing through book stalls or museums. She wanted to eat in expensive restaurants and go to the Folies-Bergère. She really didn't think they had much in common. She certainly did not want to make love. The chic Parisian May terrified her more than the boyish poet of the McLean Club.

"A dark day," May wrote George and Mabel a week later, "and I have nothing to send you but heart-ache. G. is here—writing letters at the moment. G. is here, but it's all rather a flop." "Flop" put it mildly.

According to May, she felt such guilt for luring Grace to disappointment that she began borrowing money right and left to give her a good time. One of the people she turned to was Edith Forbes Kennedy, a former Shady Hill teacher vacationing in Paris. Edith was divorced, with three sons; intellectual, sophisticated, wise, and sympathetic. Eventually she confided her version of events to Mabel:

> May and Irene were living a good and interesting life in Paris—up to the moment of Grace's arrival. . . . Both girls came here often—and I enjoyed them and scolded them and fed them. And then came Grace. Grace epitomizes the kind of situation that a sensitive imaginative playacting inexperienced girl can get herself into with a hard-boiled commercial New Yorker. May had no equipment whatever with which to meet the kind of dominance that Grace gained over her. How could she have at 19? . . . Her reasons [for liking Grace] were so adolescent, so poetic and pretentious, so far from any reality that I felt like shaking her & weeping over her all at once! It was just the old situation of Grace's making May feel imaginative and so on—and out of her own emotion endowing Grace with heaven knows what glorious potentialities that Grace was actually without. So you can imagine that when the hard rapacious & rather common New Yorker met

again in Europe the dreaming superimaginative & absurdly impractical May—a great mess was bound to come of it all. . . .

I know that May has borrowed considerable money in connection with this affair, but I do think too that she should pay it back herself from her salary—without help—because in my opinion May needs more than anything a hard core of common sense . . . and the sound residue that comes from trial & error and result. She seems to face everything obliquely—not because she is not *au fond* an extremely fine & distinguished character—but because she has allowed her emotions & imagination to mess up her really excellent mind. I've said every word of this to *her*.

"The spring has come with terrific heartache," May wrote her parents. Soon they would have to leave Willem's apartment. With no place to go, May decided that England might be economical, since Margaret Brown had invited them to stay a few days at Northampton; besides, she owed Grace England. She cabled Anne Thorp on March 21, asking for a loan of a hundred dollars to get them there. She saw her salvation now in eventually getting to Florence, where she would live in a cheap pension, work all morning, see absolutely no one, then meet her parents in Rome before sailing home—though she had no money for that, either.

Anne Thorp cabled no to London. On March 26, May appealed to George and Mabel: "Could you make me (for her) a loan of one hundred dollars which I can repay out of my salary next year? . . . This is a mess— I don't know what to say." Quite apart from the London-Northampton trip, May also had to loan Grace money to live on until she sailed April 19. Traveling in Palestine, the Sartons did not reply.

Desperate, May borrowed 300 francs from Edith Kennedy and cashed two-thirds of her April allowance check. In London Grace spent most of it shopping. They returned to Paris, May with 800 francs against debts of 1,276, and took a room in a cheap hotel. They sat in the shabby room listening to incessant rain, too broke to buy cigarettes, hardly speaking. Finally May cabled Anne Thorp: she was stranded in Paris, her parents were in Palestine, she needed, she said, $150 to meet Mabel in Florence.

Anne cabled $250. The day it came May and Grace took a train for Florence, travelling in different cars—but not before May had borrowed $50 from Willem because Grace needed tip money for the voyage home. Irene Sharaff met May the next evening. She had booked her a room next to hers in the Pension Piccioli, Via Tornabuoni. Grace would stay with some

May in Florence,
1932

friends of hers. They parted at the station in Florence. May had financed Grace's trip; Grace would not return a penny. On her return voyage, Grace fell in love with a woman, who asked her to come to California. She did.

Word of May's financial distress had reached George in Jerusalem. "You seem to manage your own affairs so badly that I *feel* guilty for having giving you a freedom which apparently you did not deserve," he rebuked her. On April 15, a chastened young woman sat down to make her confession: "Here I have come, to try and find some peace and draw up an account with myself. The last months have been strange—I don't think I have ever been in such a continual suspended state of pain and anxiety in my life." Besides unpaid Paris bills, she owed Edith Kennedy 300 francs, Willem 700 francs, and Irene 800 francs, though soon it would be more since Irene was lending her enough to live through April. She owed Anne Thorp $500. "If it is in any way possible could you send me fifty dollars before you come," she pleaded. She offered elaborate, impractical schemes for repayment. George sternly refused.

Walking in despair through sunny Florence streets a few days later, she bumped into Roswell Hawley from Gloucester. Over a cup of coffee she spilled out her plight, and Roswell promptly loaned her $500. May flew to the telegraph office: "I have since found a way to get through it alone, and please let me. . . . Discussing is useless. We only get hurt and upset."

"I had thought that Mother & I might indulge ourselves a little—because we are both getting older and have both worked hard; but it is clear that we can hardly do it now," George replied. "As long as the uncertainty & danger which you introduce into our lives is not removed, we shall be obliged to deny ourselves." Miutsie, however, assured May that she believed her promises to work hard and live simply next year:

> It will need will & long-drawn patient 'drive,' it will need the sudden sharp denial to yourself of generous impulses. . . . And though Daddy may doubt *temporarily* & give way to a fit of depression & dismay, he really has a deep-seated belief in your intelligence & power to learn. . . . Of all young people I know, I believe you need a foundation of spiritual serenity to live upon. . . . One thing more, beloved child—one warning from deep in my own life: do not let emotional blindness alternate with rational self-judgment in violent, sharp contrasts *with any illusion that they more or less balance & justify each other.* Be aware of those extremes in yourself. . . . I thank you, dear child and loyal friend for having told us all about it.

Thus May's year abroad ended in debacle. Though she continued to address George on paper as "Dearest Daddums," she never forgave him. "Unloved, trapped, without the guts to send [Grace] back at once . . . I allowed myself to be used and got into debt," May said of the Paris crisis years later. "My parents were in Beirut. My father washed his hands of the debts and never, even later, asked me how I had paid them. . . . My mother had no money and went through hell over it. He was not a father to a 19-year-old daughter in real trouble."

But in this case May's lifelong resentment of George obliterated the truth. In fact, that summer George helped her pay back $400. "It is very generous and like you," May replied. "But I would like it to be a debt to you which I shall little by little pay off . . . thank you from way down in my heart from a place where it is difficult to speak—and bless you." Talk of repayment was idealistic.

The year, however, was not a total loss, because she had made a crucial discovery: "By the time I was nineteen I had accepted that my affective life would be involved with women rather than with men." Irene Sharaff had helped May to this realization. On the rebound from Grace, May had taken Irene as her first lover in Florence. Or had they become lovers in Paris? May's lifelong guilt about Paris, as well as her insistence on Grace's betrayal, suggests that May herself may have been the betrayer. Grace's inexplicable behavior makes sense if she had come to Paris only to discover May with Irene.

In any case, her preference had been clear from earliest childhood: Mabel, not George; Céline, not Raymond; Bonbon, not Leo Baekeland. She might have realized by now too that it was older women who roused the deepest emotions—Katharine Taylor, Le Gallienne, Jean Dominique. In old age, May Sarton would be deeply angered by the suggestion that in her love affairs she searched all her life for her mother; that in choosing "impossible" women, she replayed Mabel's rejection again and again. But young May's life was marked by her hunger for mother substitutes, as well as by her losing battle with George to be first in Mabel's life.

They were very alike, George and May. "It is really *I* who am the Mouse," Mabel would tell them, "& you & Daddy are the lions!" Anne Thorp recognized the similarity. "I never can feel the driving power that is in both of them without feeling in the next breath your presence," she wrote Mabel. "The unfailing understanding and love and support that has fed them and watered them and given them space in which to grow." Yet May needed far more love than her mother could give. What she missed in Mabel, she sought in other women.

May realized that year that her "affective life" would be with women; did George and Mabel? The subject was never discussed. In retrospect, she knew that Miutsie knew, wasn't sure whether her father knew or not. But surely the Grace affair would have alerted the blindest parent? Certainly Edith Kennedy knew the score, though believing May's proclivity could be "corrected." "May I add that I think May should see more of men?" she wrote Mabel. "She has the most absurd complex about them that ever a really beautiful looking girl had. Her point of view is too female." A friend like Hermann Field had known May was lesbian for years. "She was *never* interested in boys. A friend of mine tried to date her. Nothing doing. She didn't put men off, she just didn't respond to them." Whatever Mabel truly felt, she never rebuked her daughter. Perhaps she realized that she herself would have been far happier in an artist's studio with Méta or Céline or Madeleine Van Thorenburg.

Certainly Mabel's sympathy during the Grace Daly crisis won May's violent partisanship for life. "*We* together are different, somehow," she

liked to insist. Mabel widened the breach between father and daughter by
endlessly complaining of George: his refusal to divulge their bank balance,
his self-absorption, his insensitive demands on her limited energy. May
added other crimes: his habit of leaving Mabel at the curb while he
bounded across the street; his pleading an "invalid wife" to avoid socializ-
ing—even though the invalid kept the household and George running
and worked part-time. She branded his insensitivity to her mother's needs
"criminal." Still, she had to admit that her parents not only respected but
loved each other: there was no mistaking that special look between them.
And no question that, skillfully as Mabel played the double game, George
always had and would come first.

A second Paris discovery was equally crucial, though it too had been
apparent for a long time. Love, requited or not, engendered poetry. "If
only I cared less for people and more for ideas," May had lamented. She
never would. It would always be people—women—who fired her imag-
ination. Though the affair ended in misery, Grace had given her poems:
she had a collection ready for publication. Now she needed a publisher—
and a new Muse.

CHAPTER 7

Disaster: 1932–1935

Arriving in New York on June 20, May felt "bewildered and very foreign," but quickly renewed contact with her myriad friends. Private talks about Grace with Anne and K.T. turned into "heart-rending" lectures about the evils of borrowing and the danger of using power like hers over people. Feeling helpless to explain, May took all the blame. Worse, Grace had told Anne that May and Irene were lovers. Both Anne and K.T. recoiled. "One part of them has never grown up and it is just that part of me which has in the last year," she wrote Miutsie, shaken to discover that these two admirable women didn't seem to understand passion. There were no such criticisms to George; chastened, she assured him, "I'm trying to be very sensible, Daddy, I really am."

She returned to Gloucester for the fourth and last time, had a success in *The Rise of Silas Lapham,* and afterwards a round of visits with the Fields, the Greenes, and Edith Kennedy—she still had no home to go to. She also saw Mary Chilton's mother in Boston. Shockingly, the pale, serious, "rare" Mary had died in Paris that summer, the second tragic death of a young friend. Mary had been in love with May, and May had hurt her.

In mid-August she was back at the McLean Club, though her salary wouldn't start until October 8. Le Gallienne was opening out of town in *Liliom,* so that for a time she would be in complete charge of the Apprentice Theatre. She had decided to begin with scenes from plays, then the more ambitious *Brothers Karamazov.* On August 19 she met with a group that included Theodora Pleadwell, Kappo Phelan, Margaret English,

Eleanor Flexner, Alexander Scourby, Norman Lloyd, and Burgess Mere-
dith. "I have no fear," May wrote George and Mabel afterwards, "and feel
full of power." To impress her parents with her new seriousness, she had
also signed up for German at NYU—could they send her $55 for tuition?

By the end of September, May felt she had won the confidence of the
Apprentices. Still, her position as director isolated her. Norman Lloyd felt
other differences between May and the group. She dressed smartly in
well-cut slacks and silk scarves and blouses that didn't come off the rack—
"not Bohemian yet definitely not middle-class." She smoked constantly
and was a fascinating talker. To the young Brooklyn-born actor, she
seemed European, sophisticated, cultured, yet much warmer than the cool
Le Gallienne. Still, she was temperamental and obviously in charge.
Nobody ever clapped May Sarton on the back with "Hi, how are you?"
He quickly realized that her approach to the theatre was intellectual, lit-
erary: she could never do a pratfall; the words "show biz" had no place in
her rarefied vocabulary. Lloyd minded his manners, pretended he'd heard
of Jacques Copeau and T. S. Eliot.

It is impossible to exaggerate the frantically busy life May led this fall
and winter of 1932–1933: rehearsing the Apprentices in *The Brothers*

*May as director of
Le Gallienne's
Apprentice Theatre*

Karamazov and *La Mauvaise Conduite;* meeting with the group to discuss stagecraft; rehearsing Le Gallienne's *Liliom, Cradle Song, Dear Jane,* and *Alice in Wonderland,* in which her parts ranged from walk-ons to Eva's understudy; German class from nine to ten a.m.; constantly searching for and translating plays; studying and reading; weekend excursions with friends. "It seems ages since your mouse has squeaked," she wrote Cambridge the end of October, "—I really don't know at the moment what time of day it is or how long it is since I've had more than a snatch of sleep. . . ." Often she operated on three or four hours of sleep. She had the additional pressure of knowing that Le Gallienne still thought her too young for the job.

After fifteen years of Cambridge apartments, that fall the Sartons rented an attached house at 5 Channing Place, a quiet, attractive cul-de-sac off wealthy Brattle Street, again about a mile from the Harvard Yard so that George could have his daily constitutional. It had three floors plus basement: a pleasant long living room with fireplace on the first, May's and her parents' bedrooms on the second, and George's and May's studies on the third. It was a large house to manage for Mabel, still plagued with migraine, nerves, and heart palpitations, though Mrs. White, the black laundress, came once a week, and there were live-in maids— young, untrained, fresh from Ireland. But Mabel had a garden at last, and immediately plunged into seed and bulb catalogues, dreaming of spring. Meanwhile she sewed and embroidered dresses and blouses for May, having more time because Belg-Art, like so many businesses, had failed with the Depression. Her efforts fell short: "I never have any money, even for stockings," wailed May, who had managed to repay only $20 of her $400 debt to George "—and all my clothes are either dirty or dilapidated, so I have no sense of self-respect when I get up in the morning."

On her return to New York, May had confessed her affair with Irene Sharaff to Jean Clark, now married to Hermann Field. Jean replied:

> I am relieved about Grace, but almost surprised about Irene. . . .
> You seem to be more settled than in Cambridge, that you are
> absolutely going to be permanently Lesbian. . . . I have been think-
> ing about Lesbianism and discussing it with Hermann, and it seems

it might be a much less complete thing than hetero-sexuality. The most obvious thing is of course that you can't have children. . . .

What about the secrecy? Would you, when you settle in your apartment, let it be carelessly known that you were lovers? You say it would be bad for the theatre to know about it—why? do they frown on it in spite of Eva's example? . . . I cannot bear to think that you must have a life of petty deceit before you; it seems you must toward Cambridge people—your family always? don't you feel as if you were acting before your mother?—even if not in New York? And you can never be possessively proud of your lover as married people are of each other. . . . The last thing I wondered about was the complement of character which it seems could not be complete in a Lesbian relationship. You say you and Irene are utterly different; that is fine; still you are both women; both feminine—I used to deny vehemently that there was anything inherently different in men and women, but lately I have seen some rather universal differences. . . . I have not got this matter straight—have you suggestions?

May's answer apparently does not survive. Yet by the time the Apprentice Theatre season was underway, Irene had pretty much been replaced by the actress Theodora Pleadwell. Theo was something of a mystery: twenty-four, well travelled, financially independent, aristocratic, "very quiet but awfully nice." She was unusual-looking—tall, very pretty and dark, with hair that "seemed to stand on end" and a masklike face whose partial immobility had been caused by an illness. She owned—enormous asset—a car. This made possible all kinds of delightful excursions to Cobb's Mill, an inn near Le Gallienne's country place in Weston, sometimes with other Apprentices, like Jock Bauer, Ted Wilkes, and Margaret English, sometimes just the two of them.

Ironically, after her well-published anguish over Grace Daly, May's real sexual consummation with a woman went unsung. This is because neither Irene nor Theo were Muses, those romantic, often unobtainable, women who inspired May to poetic song; they were just friends who happened to appeal to her. By January, May was spending most of her time at Theo's: "She makes breakfast for me—and we are very gay." Peaceful too, she might have added. George chided her for wasting the money he was paying the McLean Club. Yet, on the surface at least, all was affectionate. May called him "My Old Rat," he called her "Excellent Duck," and she was always their "Elf," their "Mouselet," their "Pigeon."

. . .

The Civic Repertory Theatre's *Alice in Wonderland,* with set design by Irene Sharaff, opened to acclaim that December, though Broadway was crying hard times. In January, Eva's burned hand was operated on and May played her White Queen in *Alice* ("a swell performance," said Eva) at the New Amsterdam. Yet by the end of January May could tell George that "the theatre is for the first time in great peril. I have never seen Le Gallienne really discouraged before—to raise the subsidy necessary to continue is practically an impossibility this year. . . . So I fear the possibility of having nothing to do next year. It is a grave prospect."

If the Civic Repertory Theatre was in trouble, the Apprentice Theatre seemed doomed; yet May was determined to keep the group together at all costs. Realizing money was almost impossible to raise—Roosevelt had closed the banks in March, and May was living on small checks from her parents and credit at Child's—May met with the apprentice Eleanor Flexner's father, Abraham Flexner, founder of the Institute for Advanced Study at Princeton, to discuss "angels" who might back a fledgling troupe. The struggle to raise money would, in fact, become May's personal nightmare for the next years—and she enlisted everyone she knew in the fray. The Henry Copley Greenes were an early target: Henry had done lighting for Shady Hill theatricals, Rosalind had wanted to be an actress. And Katrine Greene was enthusiastic, donating a legacy of $500, finding them a dilapidated old house with barn for the summer in fashionable Dublin, New Hampshire, and volunteering to run it.

In recognition of her twenty-first birthday, May signed herself "Your grown-up daughter." It had been a punishing season: the Apprentices had performed seventeen plays as well as acting in CRT productions. And the Civic Repertory was finished that spring, beaten at last by the Depression, which had put some 16 million Americans out of work. Eva offered May a place in her touring company that fall, but May refused to give up her dream of heading an independent group like the Compagnie des Quinze or the Moscow Art Theatre. She was applying for grants. Something *must* turn up.

By mid-July she was in Dublin. Then came wonderful news: Alvin Johnson, the director of the New School for Social Research in New York, invited the group to put on plays for an accredited course. She still didn't see how they could manage financially—perhaps the Apprentices could live at home and commute to New York—but this was good news with which to greet the impoverished actors on their arrival. Meanwhile she was raising money for the group to live on: the Flexners had donated $425; Anne Thorp, $500; Mabel and Francesca Greene, $90—more than $1,000 to last till fall. (Leo Baekeland would refuse a request for $5,000.) The Apprentices still had faith in her. "If anyone can do it May can," said Katrine Greene.

That summer May's friends were pressed into providing chairs, tables, dishes, and food for Lerned House. The twelve young actors pitched in doing dishes and mowing the lawn. In their free time they played baseball and table tennis, listened to classical music on May's phonograph, or strolled into the village to buy ice cream cones. Mostly they worked.

Frictions were inevitable. Theo Pleadwell was a thorn. Obviously she and May were lovers; she was not a good actress, yet May gave her plum parts. There were also arguments about whether they should produce plays that would stretch their abilities or plays that could be used at the New School that fall; and Kappo Phelan, a director, threatened to resign. More serious, rumors were circulating that Lerned House was a nudist colony and, worse, a hotbed of perversion. This struck close to the bone, and May persuaded the influential Greenes to scotch the rumors. "I must confess I am furious," May wrote George and Mabel, "—these wealthy gossiping creatures who can patronize me. . . . I'd rather have an audience of workmen." So effective were the guardian-angel Greenes, however, that May could soon report that the Apprentices had crashed the country club—"swimming, dancing, tennis 'n everything!"

After visiting Dublin, Mabel wrote the Apprentices her appreciation: "Dr. Sarton & I have been immensely heartened & comforted now that we have seen May's 'group'—have glimpsed you as individuals, have been stirred by such of you as we saw act, & have above all 'sensed' that by some miracle May has found an astonishing number of young people who believe in & will *live* her idea. . . . *You* can help her—best of all—*you* can forward the thing she is striving for, this vital thing which has never been attempted in America before & which has never been needed as much, perhaps, as now."

Though Le Gallienne had offered Norman Lloyd fifty dollars a week, Lloyd chose fifteen dollars and major roles in experimental plays with May that fall instead. Morale, in fact, was high. May left Dublin with a black kitten named Pirandello to move in with Theo and her dog, Noë, at 307 East Forty-fourth Street. The Apprentices did not have to stage their first play, *The Secret Life,* until November 6, but May was wild to have Eva critique a rehearsal. Meanwhile, she coaxed support for the Apprentices from anyone with influence: Alexander Woollcott; Arthur Hopkins; Harold Freedman; Anita Block of the Theatre Guild; Edith Isaacs, the editor of *Theatre*

Arts Monthly; John Mason Brown; Hallie Flanagan; Brooks Atkinson; Samuel French. She also booked the Apprentices for one-night stands at the Cambridge YWCA and Vassar's Experimental Theatre.

Le Gallienne did attend a rehearsal and afterward gave them a two-hour critique: "the best time of my acting-life I think," said May. Despite doubts, she also provided an endorsement: "I am most interested in the work of the Apprentice Theatre and in their future development. They have a true and simple approach to their work and their devotion to ideals of what the theatre might be makes one hopeful for their eventual achievement." Buoyed by Eva's approval and $1,000 from Abraham Flexner (May had shrewdly put Eleanor's name on official AT stationery), May and Theo escaped to Cobb's Mill with its waterfall, red sumac, and quiet walks. It would be a frequent retreat.

The Apprentices put on an amazing eleven plays between November 1933 and March 1934 at the New School: *The Secret Life, Still Life, The Children's Tragedy, Naked, Dr. Knock, The Call of Life, The Sowers, Martine, Fear, Gentlemen Wanted,* and *The Armored Train*—all by the foreign playwrights May preferred. K.T., Rosalind Greene, Mary Bouton, and Anne Thorp showed up. Sometimes the bigwigs came—Arthur Hopkins, Archie Selwyn, Brooks Atkinson, S. N. Behrman, Harold Freedman. More often they did not.

May continued to flog the Apprentices to anyone who would listen, alienating some. "What I dislike about you," wrote Edith Isaacs, "is that you seem to me entirely without humility, superficial, full of affectations, and pretenses, mistaking bravado for courage, and jealousy for criticism, and rationalizing all of these faults to your own advantage." Anita Block thought the Apprentices almost professional in *The Secret Life,* but deplored the choice of a "valueless play" and the serious miscasting of Theodora Pleadwell. May herself vaulted between hope and despair. "God knows how we will ever get through next year—and the thought of spending the delicious month of April talking to stupid people about what I am trying to do and asking for money makes me sick just to think of." Still, by the end of the term a few things were clear: Norman Lloyd and Alexander Scourby were Broadway material, Kappo Phelan had talent, and nobody but May Sarton could have pulled off such a season.

Everyone needed a vacation. May drove with Theo and her dog to Pebble Beach, California, arriving at sunset the first of May, drunk on the scent of eucalyptus, cypress, and cedar. They had their own little house in the garden of friends of Theo's, a pool, a beach, the Carmel mountains, and the blue Pacific. May thought she might relax.

Theodora Pleadwell,
a member of the
Apprentices.

Her birthday, which began with breakfast out of doors, telegrams from Mabel and George, and a whole pile of little packages from Theo, was happy, but the Apprentice Theatre would not go away. Lloyd and Scourby gave notice. Internecine war raged: if Kappo had to have anything more to do with Eleanor Flexner, she would leave. On the other hand, the actor Eliot Cabot had volunteered his services as director for later this year, and the still-enthusiastic Greenes had offered their farmhouse and barn in Rowley for summer rehearsals.

May continued to press family and friends. The Apprentices needed fourteen beds for Rowley. "I said you would take charge of furniture," she wrote Mabel.

I don't think we should spend more than $25.00 on household furnishings and I leave that to you. Anne will advance it. I think for the porch two deck-chairs (I think they can be got for about $2.00 apiece). K.T. said Shady Hill would lend us a trestle table and four benches (but verify this, because it was all said very casually). The benches would eliminate the necessity of chairs for the dining-room and the chairs there could go into the bedrooms.

I wish we could have some sort of old *sofa* for the living room. Have you any ideas? I think Mrs. Dewing might be able to help about that sort of thing.

Will you get the linoleum for the tables? Also the dishes, silver, kitchenware, etc. Ask K. Greene if there is any silver or china left from last year. . . . After Shady Hill closes I'm sure Anne would love to drive you up and you could make it a picnic.

Rounding up furniture and its transportation to Rowley while her daughter vacationed in California was hardly a picnic for Mabel. But she and George were escaping to Europe—an extravagance, George admitted, but why should he alone save money and be called a miser in the bargain? "No man can save *against* his family."

Except for Theo, Norma Chambers, and Carl Urbont, the eighteen-member company this year was new. Since Eleanor Flexner was abroad, Kappo Phelan had returned to direct. The eighteenth-century farmhouse proved frightfully dirty and infested with fleas (exterminator, $25). They plunged into Clemence Dane's *Will Shakespeare* (Kappo directing) and *The Master Builder* (directed by May). When Eliot Cabot arrived on August 1, they tackled Bernard Shaw's *You Never Can Tell,* May reluctantly playing Dolly; Cabot, Valentine. The barn rang with the building of scenery, and real costumes from Brooks arrived in a big trunk. Cabot had secured bookings for four performances in nearby Ipswich and Magnolia. May shuttled back and forth between Cambridge and Rowley, beating the bushes for patrons. Mr. Dewing spotted her at the Harvard Coop charging plays to George. "Are you in the red?" he bellowed.

They always were. Dozens of possibilities were offered but collapsed. Still, May called *You Never Can Tell* "a grand success" (actual proceeds $130), and again she scored as Hilda Wangel in *The Master Builder.* A New York angel, Joseph Verner Reed, bailed them out temporarily with $1,000. There was much talk of a southern tour, but more certain was a season at the Wadsworth Atheneum in Hartford's Avery Memorial Hall. May took the train to meet A. Everett "Chick" Austin, the director; over cocktails and dinner Austin talked of selling out the first night to three hundred people who would pay $7 for a subscription, putting $2,100 in

*May as Dolly, Eliot
Cabot as Valentine,
in Shaw's* You
Never Can Tell

the bank. He was impressed that *Theatre Arts* had noticed the Apprentice
Theatre as "the child of Eva Le Gallienne."

It rained twenty-two days in September. The company bought a truck
for $225, cleared out the Rowley house, and returned its contents to their
many lenders. May dashed from Hartford to Cambridge to Boston to
New York, interviewing business managers, scenic designers, publicity
people, and actors who could support themselves for the winter. The
Apprentices brought a private performance of *Uncle Vanya* into New York
for Le Gallienne. She didn't like it.

By November 2 May and Theo were settling into an enormous room
with a fireplace but scant furniture in an old house in Hartford. The first
play was *Multiplied by Two,* adapted by May from a French version of Plau-
tus's farce *The Menaechmi.* May had found a "genius" of a set designer in
Shepard Vogelsang, and an "excellent" new business manager, Theodore
Adams. "Everyone is in a perfect ecstasy of excitement at having a theatre
all our own in such a beautiful city," she wrote happily. They were send-
ing out five thousand circulars and getting stories into local papers, she
was sitting to Bachrach for publicity photos. She drank tea with the
Rotary, the Women's Club, the Professional Women's Club, the College
Club, the Junior League, and the Lions till it ran out her ears. She worked
like fifty horses, then discovered that their opening would coincide with
Arthur Hopkins's new play starring the popular Hope Williams—"It's
really bitter."

Multiplied by Two had three performances and favorable notices. It
earned $700, "not bad at all"—except that with costs totaling $700 the
actors didn't get paid. May redoubled her efforts to find money, almost

*Publicity photo of
May for the
Apprentice Theatre*

impossible before Christmas: a friend of Chick Austin's loaned $200; Le Gallienne and Anne Thorp each contributed $100. Meanwhile the Ballets Russes de Monte Carlo played Hartford. The Apprentices were invited to a fancy party where they almost rubbed elbows with George Gershwin, Archibald MacLeish, Salvador Dali, Léonide Massine, and Alexandra Danilova—thrilling, yet a grim contrast between fame and obscurity.

They gave *One More Spring,* based on Robert Nathan's novel, for a few performances in January. May thought the audience warm, but the *Courant* panned. "It will be a miracle if we get through this next month," she wrote Miutsie. When no one answered her pleas for money, the Apprentices were forced to disband for two weeks. In February they pulled together a brief revival of *The Master Builder,* but few seats were sold. The depressed company split and May was back in New York, looking for cheap places to stay, looking for backers, running hither and yon. Le Gallienne told her she was giving up the heartbreaking theatre. Not May. Incredibly, she persisted, pinning hopes on everything from a ferry-boat theatre (if it docked in Manhattan, they would almost have a Broadway production) to a wealthy dowager in Colorado Springs funding them ten thousand dollars. Mad schemes, hopeless schemes, young schemes. Meanwhile, could her parents advance her ten dollars?

Incredibly too, though she was dead broke and in debt, she decided to go abroad with Theo from mid-May to mid-July. Touched by her superhuman efforts to keep her company afloat, George had substantially raised her allowance the past year; he had also begun putting away a small sum for her each month. Now he gave her money for Europe. And Theo had money. Even Mabel was earning something again: she had started buying china through relatives in England and selling it at a profit in Cambridge, chiefly to friends who felt sorry for dear, charming Mrs. Sarton. But money or not, May went to Europe because she wanted to, and she always did what she wanted. She left Miutsie to handle all her unfinished theatrical business: reading scripts, corresponding with old and potential Apprentices, sending out her articles to *The Stage, Theatre Arts Monthly,* and *The New Yorker.*

They stayed briefly with the Limbosches, then drove south through Avignon, Aix-en-Provence, Pau, Rapallo, Florence, and Saint-Jean-de-Luz. By May 30: "I need about fifty dollars—actually I was mad to come with so little—when I left the boat I had only fifty dollars with which to get half across France and live two weeks in Florence." At Saint-Jean they had a magnificent room on the sea at the Hôtel Maïtagarria, but the resort was almost deserted except for Gertrude Macy, Katharine Cornell's manager, and the actress Margalo Gillmore. A cable announced that Joseph Verner Reed had coughed up more money; *The Stage* rejected her article; Miutsie managed to send fifty dollars of her hard-earned cash. When May finally arrived in New York on July 13, none of the formidable problems of managing an acting company had disappeared.

That fall the Apprentices rehearsed at High Acres Resort ("Chicken Dinners a Speciality"), in High View, New York. For luck, they changed their name to the Associated Actors Theatre. Dr. Richard Cabot, a prominent Cambridge physician, had advanced $5,000. May had acquired Waldemar Kappel as co-director, and, happily, Norman Lloyd had returned to play the leading role in *Dr. Knock.* Theo was also back, and furious at finding no leading parts. If May indeed had "a sweet little room to [herself] at the top of the house," as she wrote her parents, then Theo was also out of May's bedroom. *Gallery Gods* was a second play, with May in the lead; a third was violently debated. There were casting problems: actors arrived, actors left, actors got sick, actors quit. They needed 1917-style costumes

May rehearsing Norman Lloyd (third from left) in Dr. Knock *at Highview, New York, 1934*

for *Dr. Knock*—could Miutsie find two men's fur-lined coats with beaver collars? They needed a theatre to perform in. On the strength of the Cabot name, they booked Boston's Elizabeth Peabody Playhouse for November. On October 11, May wrote Mabel and George:

Dears, we are in a frenzy. . . . Our problems are multifold. There is still the question of the third play—we looked over the costumes of the Plautus and they are in very poor condition—also I'm afraid it wouldn't go terribly well in Boston. . . . I feel more and more that *Gallery Gods* is just a good Broadway play and would like very much to have one strong play of ideas. On the other hand it has to be *so* well acted and Theo will have to play the girl: I'm not sure she can do it. Also the boy's part is terrifically difficult. . . .

It will be necessary to raise two thousand dollars in Boston to cover publicity and so on. . . . As usual everything is costing more than we expected. . . .

The costumes for *Knock* look excellent—incidentally have you anywhere any large costume pins—brooches—or crosses on chains such as a well-to-do farmer's wife would wear. The little bags are excellent. . . . O Daddy it is wonderful to have such a *large* allowance thank you! I have invested in a grey-blue homespun tyrolean suit which you will like!

As their third offering, the Associated Actors finally chose Maxwell Anderson's controversial Sacco-Vanzetti play *Gods of the Lightning.* Joseph Losey had offered to direct; he immediately replaced Theo with Natasha Lewis, and the humiliated Theo left. There were plans to incorporate so they could sell stock. Mabel was asked to spread the word that they were coming to Boston. Gorgeous photos of May appeared in the local papers, accompanied by exalted statements of the young company's creed. They left High Acres on November 4, and May at fever pitch descended upon Channing Place.

George had had enough. "For heaven's sake my dear child," he pleaded, "if you must follow that path [the theatre]—& perhaps you are right though I am convinced you are wrong—leave me & mother alone. We—at any rate—are not made for it. How would you like it if I dragged you into *my* business? . . . All I need is quietness—silence and secrecy— but that I need absolutely. Lovingly, Dad."

Katharine Cornell was playing *Romeo and Juliet* in Boston that November; Le Gallienne was at the Colonial Theatre. The Associated Actors Theatre opened at the Peabody on November 11 with *Gallery Gods.*

Nobody was interested. Nobody came. By November 27 the whole enterprise had collapsed.

May blamed her defeat on the Great Depression; no doubt it was the chief villain, with theatre all over America struggling to survive. Later she could say, "The company failed because I think I was never willing to make a complete sacrifice to it." But there were other reasons. Even the idealistic Le Gallienne knew you had to give audiences their *Peter Pans* and *Camilles.* May chose esoteric, highbrow European plays; then, realizing too late she should go American, mischose for Boston the controversial *Gods of the Lightning.* Some common show-biz sense would have helped.

Though she erred with Theo, she was better at choosing actors— almost everyone who left the Apprentices after the Hartford season got a job. Norman Lloyd became a distinguished stage and film actor; and Alexander Scourby, the best voice-over in America. Could May herself act? Lloyd thought her Hilda Wangel burned up the stage. May's friend, Molly Howe, the Irish playwright known professionally as Mary Manning, disagreed. "Whatever the role, May Sarton was always May Sarton."

May had business managers, but they could not protect a company from her financial idiocy. Then too, she relied too much on friends for support. The sponsors' list for the Associated Actors Theatre read like a who's who, yet financial deals are made not with Boston Brahmins but in New York—or in those years of federally supported theatre, Washington. The Cabot connection only postponed the inevitable.

In the end, though, the whole Apprentice experiment was something of a miracle. "Enthusiasm is an insufficient word for what Miss Sarton inspires," said Eliot Cabot. True: she could fire actors with dreams, coax money from disbelievers, convince people the Apprentices were the theatre's Great Hope. Her energetic idealism worked wonders. It just couldn't work them for long.

George had warned that the theatre was sand. Six years of it had left May exhausted. The burden of success or failure ultimately had been hers; she had been alone. Looking back on the "nightmare," however, one particular personal betrayal hurt her most. After the Boston rout, she proposed to Radcliffe's Ada Comstock that if she raised $5,000, Radcliffe would give the Associated Actors a berth for a year. President Comstock agreed. May told Rosalind Greene and Katharine Taylor her plan. According to May, K.T. and Rosalind went to Comstock and said, "You can't have a company with lesbians at Radcliffe." Ironically—though May and Theo's liaison was obvious—Rosalind and Katharine did not implicate May herself. Comstock withdrew her support. May never forgot that two cherished friends had turned against her.

CHAPTER 8

The Poet: 1935–1937

In later years, May Sarton said that after the Boston disaster she collapsed and was taken to Anne Thorp's country house, ending her connection with the theatre forever. Actually, the sword did not cut clean. After *Gods of the Lightning* failed, she and Theo moved into an apartment on East Thirty-seventh Street in New York, complete with a maid to cook supper ("a great saving"). Since she blamed her business manager for the failure, she tried to coax more money from her archangel Joseph Verner Reed; when he refused, the Associated Actors decided to disband, but only temporarily. There were board meetings, talk of New York repertory, incorporation, summer theatre.

May herself read for the role of the Player Queen in Leslie Howard's *Hamlet,* tried out for *The Women* and *Jane Eyre,* met with Lawrence Langner, Philip Moeller, Richard Aldrich, Herman Shumlin, Katharine Cornell, Le Gallienne. Nobody hired her, but it wasn't until Guthrie McClintic's office informed her in November 1936 that *High Tor* was cast that she gave up, because by then she didn't care.

During these years, it was rumored that Eva Le Gallienne had entrusted the Apprentices to a novice because she and May were lovers. While May certainly pressed for sexual intimacy with the actress of the "cobalt eyes," Eva rejected her, as "Two Sonnets for Eva" makes clear. "O would you open then, or let him hover / This bird who is myself and is your lover?" asks May, an importunate seagull blown against Eva's window. Le Gallienne "let him hover." Obviously, however, Eva's personal support encouraged May in these years of discovering her lesbianism.

"The best one can do is to be decent one's self and realize that lack of understanding always promotes a kind of cruel criticism and censorship," wrote Eva to a May hurt by homophobia. "People hate what they don't understand and try to destroy it. Only try to keep yourself clear and don't allow that destructive force to spoil something that to you is simple, natural, and beautiful." As for May's failure in the theatre, Eva had given her that Paris Christmas not a copy of *Hedda Gabler* but a pen.

Le Gallienne would remain a friend, and the theatre had won May two other lifelong friends: Molly Howe, married to Mark Howe, a Harvard law professor and civil rights activist whom May admired; and Polly Thayer Starr, a gifted Boston artist. Polly drew May in 1935, a startlingly wonderful portrait of the young May Sarton. "She was a phenomenon," said the beguiled Polly. "A dragonfly—flashing, mercurial. A person who raged at life, a person alive to the nth power."

Yet this was a difficult time for May, the theatre fading, her work still unpublished, though Molly Howe sent a collection of May's poems, *Encounter in April,* to Houghton Mifflin in January 1936. She knew she should get a job, yet "everyone says there isn't anything." She knew George was fed up; his anger at her thriftlessness had erupted in a "savage letter" about two Flemish books she'd borrowed for props and not returned. "I am afraid of his power to hurt," she wrote Miutsie (she rarely wrote George these days). "The world seems such a senselessly cruel place that I hope at least I shall never be cruel like that. I'm afraid it is a hopelessly dated point of view but it still seems to me that human *hearts* are the most important thing in the world." Yet even as she waited in Broadway offices, she was planning to sail for Europe in March. If job offers came, "I am telling everyone to write to you," she told Mabel. A strange way to find work. Obviously May didn't *want* a job: she wanted to be a published writer.

She sailed March 24 on the *Manhattan,* sent off royally as usual with telegrams, flowers, fruit, books, and, this time, news that the *Saturday Review* had taken some poems. Again George had funded the trip—not, however, without a stern letter of advice. May replied from the boat, defending her indecision as part of a general malaise: "There is no doubt that many things are unresolved in my mind—the people of my generation are turning almost without exception (among my personal friends) to communism as the next necessary step in the advance of civilization. Much in my education and temperament is revolted by the idea, but there is no doubt—witness innumerable philosophers and thinkers—that we are going through a difficult period with *economic* maladjustment paramount." The ascetic

George Sarton, busy collecting honorary degrees for his selfless devotion to science, was unpersuaded.

She went first to Cornwall to stay with Charles and Dorothea Singer, historians of science and colleagues of George. She was enchanted to see crowds of daffodils in the headlights as they drove into the grounds, enchanted to find the house filled with primroses, daffodils, and camellias. The Singers had an overnight guest, a "thin stork" of a man. Julian Huxley was the grandson of Thomas Henry Huxley and the older brother of Aldous; a well-known intellectual, writer, and scientist; currently director of the five-hundred-acre zoo at Whipsnade. He was in Cornwall looking for a place to grow eucalyptus trees for the koala bears he hoped to install at the zoo. This too seemed enchanting, as did their tour the next day in pouring rain through huge estates lush with palms and camellia trees as big as elms; and Julian told her to call when in London.

Julian Huxley in the 1930s

In London May found a room in York Street. She had a considerable number of Cambridge connections: she constantly went out to tea, dinner, the theatre. She was trying to get published in England. Faber and Faber returned *Encounter in April:* though T. S. Eliot had liked it very much, the firm was committed to modernistic verse like Auden's and Spender's; she should try Jonathan Cape. "It really is quite thrilling that they liked them," she wrote her parents, "—I think I am partly so lacking in faith in the book because of Macmillan, years ago, telling me to 'stick to the theatre.' I have never quite gotten over it." She sent the book to Cape and continued to job-hunt long-distance without luck. "One must be on the spot I'm afraid," she concluded belatedly.

She looked forward to seeing Jean Dominique. May's letters had progressed since their last meeting from "Chère Mademoiselle" to "Cher cher Jean"—indeed they were love letters. "The frightful sensation that we will die without having known each other—known each other profoundly as only love can know—terrifies me," she had written in 1934. "Do you understand? I am not wrong to believe . . . that you love me and understand me better than anyone else, am I?—and that it does not shock you to be addressed with the total frankness of a daughter? Only the question of age has no place here. The soul does not have age. And my soul is not young, nor yours old—they are fresh and eternal." Now Jean Dominique granted her the afternoon of April 27.

She went first to the Limbosches'. Their only son, Jacques, had been killed mountain-climbing in 1935. Raymond had become completely cynical: "La vie n'est qu'un accident." Aunty Lino looked exhausted but said that if she did not drive herself, she would go mad. Everyone talked of Hitler and the inevitability of war. If only, May raged, "they had some *faith*—in either God or man." Pessimism, cynicism, and irony were completely foreign to her temperament; fond as she was of the Limbosches, she felt an abyss between them in all the "deepest and dearest things." One of these was her poetry. Raymond made her analyze the metrics of each line: "I felt absolutely *déchiré*—like a butterfly whose wings have been torn off. . . . We approach [poetry] from the opposite sides of the world."

It was very different in the rooms above the Institut occupied by "the Peacocks," as Jean Dominique, Blanche Rousseau, and Marie Gaspar humorously called themselves. There May was wrapped in a woman's world of sensibility and light. "Et ne me répond si le printemps est mort," Jean-Do had written—Do not tell me if spring is dead. It could have been May's motto. Jean-Do talked to her of her early life, read May her poetry.

Raymond and Céline Limbosch, close friends of Mabel and George Sarton and of May, 1950

Though she was pinched financially, there was a serenity, a nobility in Jean-Do that May worshipped. She was moved to find how many people the poet sustained with her generosity and wisdom. She stayed until six that day and came back the next afternoon and the next, fearing that her intensity would exhaust the fragile woman, yet unable to curb the violence of her feeling. In parting, she gave Jean-Do the silver bird pin K.T. had given her. "I believe that *anything* is possible of life," she wrote Mabel, "when I think that somehow across such a vast distance in time, language & place Jean Dominique and I have met each other." She knew she must return.

Back in London in a new room in Taviton Street off Euston Road, Jean-Do's influence lingered. If May was indeed serious about being a poet, she must *choose* it above any other calling. "[I] am lazy," she wrote Jean-Do, "and I have always thought of poetry as a luxury—I have not been strict enough with myself—I am too facile—and it seems to me that I must now find discipline, an *absolute*. . . . Tomorrow I will be 24 years old—is it the beginning of a profounder life? I want to be fiercely *pure* and whole. . . ."

Yet it was supremely difficult to tear herself away from too many people, to force herself to sit for consecutive hours and write, to be quiet

May taking tea at the avenue de l'Échevinage with two of the "Peacocks," Blanche Rousseau (left) and Marie Gaspar ("Titi")

within herself. Also to commit herself only to poetry: for after Jonathan Cape and Leonard Woolf returned *Encounter* that spring, she turned to sketches and short stories.

Delightfully distracting were the harpsichord notes of Bach next door. The musician turned out to be John Summerson, a tall, dark young man of thirty-one with heavy black brows and "a long English face, a little like an intelligent sensitive sheep." An architect himself, John was working on a book about great English architects. Since May always borrowed his teapot, they fell into the habit of having tea together in the afternoon after stints of writing. He was witty, charming, and cultured—and May fell in love. One night she allowed him to deflower her; the next day she asked him to marry her.

Though she was no Radclyffe Hall, May felt society's relentless pressure to be "normal." In the late nineteenth century, the terms "lesbian" and "sapphist" had come into general and clinical use to describe deviant, "sick" women who preferred their own sex. Society valued women by

their relationship to men; a woman who loved another woman was dou-
bly inferior. Even from intimates, May felt pressure: George's suspicion,
Katharine Taylor's disapproval, Mark Howe's "slight sneer" at a woman
whose chief interest was not men, Molly Howe's insistence that she find
a "fellah." She felt it necessary to believe that Anne Thorp "should have
had a dear pipe-smoking husband and a huge family," to tell Polly Starr
that "an out and out tuxedo girl makes me shiver with horror," to look
upon same-sex relationships as dangerous: "over-*refined,* over-intense,
lacking in an essential *core* of life." Women had always attracted her, but
nothing was yet written in stone. And Summerson was enormously
appealing.

Alas, he told her that he was already engaged. Perhaps May had
guessed something of the kind before she asked him. But it was a blow,
though several years later when she heard that his wife had had triplets,
she felt she'd had a miraculous escape.

As compensation, John Summerson took her to meet Elizabeth
Bowen in her elegant Nash house at 2 Clarence Terrace in Regent's Park.
She found the novelist a sketch by Holbein: red-gold hair; pale blue eyes;
bold, handsome face. Alan Cameron, Bowen's "Colonel Blimpish" hus-
band, hardly fit this "cool underwater drawing room," yet he kindly made
an effort to put her at ease. Difficult to feel at ease listening to the brilliant
flow of conversation among Bowen, Summerson, Isaiah Berlin, and David
Cecil; for the first time, May realized what an uneducated, naive little
American she was, with "really nothing to offer except admiration." Yet
Bowen autographed a copy of *To the North* for her and promised to invite
Virginia and Leonard Woolf for dinner. May left in a glow.

She dined with the Huxleys in their apartment with great windows
overlooking the velvety green of Regent's Park, and was enchanted by Juli-
ette Huxley's heart-shaped face and slight Swiss accent. Julian was about her
father's age; she was enormously flattered that he seemed to find her attrac-
tive. But she delighted everyone; she dined out almost every evening, while
through Richard Cabot, the Singers, and Lugné-Poë, she had introductions
to Conrad Aiken and Basil de Selincourt. And every weekend she was
someone's guest deep in the green English countryside, spooning figs and
cream, listening to the clop of tennis balls on grassy courts.

In June she returned to Brussels to see Jean Dominique, though she
stayed with the Limbosches, who charged her board for a bed and writ-
ing table on the verandah. But she was writing—four stories and about
thirty poems—between visits to the Peacocks in the avenue de l'Éche-
vinage. She was very keen on Miutsie's meeting Jean-Do (Mabel and

George had sailed on the *Queen Mary* for Europe). Aunty Lino was jealous of Jean-Do, teasing May about her *schwärm* for the poet; but "don't be put off by anything," she urged. The self-satisfied clannishness of the Limbosches continued to annoy her: "They destroy *everyone* outside their own circle."

She ended her holiday at Grundlsee, Austria, the view from her balcony overlooking the mountain-ringed lake "fairyland." Yet she knew that her pleasure was very much at George's expense. "Altogether this holiday has been I feel a great luxury but I *have* enjoyed it," she wrote him, "—and have really started to write seriously so that even while looking for work in the theatre I shall have steady work to do. If I have not *seemed* grateful, I *am* . . . and now I feel I must do something great for you and Mummy—at least something solid. I am eager to get to work." She was franker with Mabel: "I am quite terrified at the thought of living alone in New York and looking for work."

She disguised the terror. "Dears, I am wildly happy—all unpacked," she wrote from 239 East Seventeenth Street. "The room is perfect and I *know* I can work here—the park is very charming with thin sweet trees, gold now, and people sitting mournfully on the benches." She had got a Chinese-green couch cover and chartreuse pillows from Macy's; Polly Starr had sent a huge jar of African daisies; she was painting bookcases. Would Miutsic please send towels and her stuffed duck, which she could not live without? "It is *wonderful* to be in a place of my own! Love to you dears from your ecstatic mouse."

The discovery of bedbugs marred the ecstasy. But as usual, though there were no jobs, there were dozens of people to see at all hours of the day: "I must run—it is difficult to capture any particle of peace—the *sweep* of time eludes me." This season May's friends included Molly Howe, Polly Starr, May Potter, Liz Johnson, Eleanor Flexner, Gert Macy, Olivia Thompson, Theo, the artist Neyan Stevens (who was painting May), Kappo Phelan, Margaret English, Ted Adams, Irene Sharaff, Klaus and Erika Mann (as long as May paid for Erika's expensive lunches), and Ashley Montagu. There was also Robert Hale, a friend of Polly's, "a dear sensitive man." He fell in love with May, phoned her constantly, took her to wonderful restaurants, read Virginia Woolf to her when she had the flu. May tried to love him and failed.

And then, with an agent turning down her short stories and theatrical doors slamming in her face, Houghton Mifflin announced it would publish

Encounter in April early in 1937. And from England came two guineas for three poems from *Time and Tide*.

As well as letters from Julian Huxley, disturbingly intense. Though she had just moved into and furnished a place of her own, she made plans to give up the apartment and sail to England. Conrad Aiken had offered to rent his Jeakes House in Rye, a mere hour from London. With Kappo, May Potter, Liz Johnson, and Margaret English, she decided to take it for April and May. She sailed late in March, waved off by Bob Hale and Erika Mann, with flowers, letters, telegrams, and dozens of books, including Julian's *Religion Without Revelation*. "Dears," she scribbled from the *American Trader,* "—it is wonderful to be on the way to work and peace though I hate leaving you." Julian would meet her boat.

She seemed to be running away from the public reception of *Encounter in April*. All her life, May Sarton would face her work with a volatile mixture of conviction and doubt. But she need not have worried. Unlike many first books of poems, *Encounter in April*—dedicated to Jean Dominique, with Polly Thayer's fine pencil portrait of May as frontispiece—was not ignored, though major publications did not review it. Criticisms there were: that the high polish of the sonnets, for example, had sometimes been achieved by "pre-fabricated emotions" as well as by imitation of Edna St. Vincent Millay. But there was also the feeling that here was a fresh new voice, a real poet. "After the cold cerebral deluge that we've been weathering in the name of poetry," said Marion Strobel, a future editor of *Poetry,* "her passionate simplicity is not only exciting in itself but, like the first crocus, *must* be a portent. More poems springing from sincerity and genuine emotion will follow. And when they do, Poetry, the Art, will revive!"

As a poet, May was singularly isolated. She belonged to no literary cliques, groups, or schools. She was not an objectivist, a realist, a surrealist, a populist, an avant-gardist, a southern agrarian, a vortecist, a reactionary, an imagist, or a confessionalist. She was totally isolated from academe and the poets it promoted. She felt nothing of the contemporary poet's "smart despair" and alienation. Nor was she part of the recoil from the exploded ideals of the leftist thirties. She held the "hopelessly dated point of view" that "human *hearts* are the most important thing in the world."

Encounter in April is lyric poetry of evocation, perception, and sensibility. The poems in general are defiantly traditional, with a vocabulary that does not blush at archaisms like "cloven," "bursten." They are lushly sensual ("pour yourself over me like burning honey"), their imagery often startlingly violent: love rockets, blazes, explodes, flashes like lightning, devours like the fiery sun. Difficult to believe that the many images of tearing, piercing, thrusting, clearing, splitting, shattering, wounding do not reflect May's fear of heterosexual sex. Much of the energy comes from juxtaposition: rich/barren; drought/rain; fire/snow; noon/dusk. In fifty-two poems, she uses the words "heart" and "love" (or "lover") ninety-five times. Sarton's subject is not in doubt: "I think really I am a troubadour and my business is celebration of the people I love."

Least successful are poems of place, like "Kew," or Sarton's patent Japanese imitations. Occasionally, one wishes for stricter pruning. But a handful of sonnets have great beauty if not the strictest metrical precision: "We came together like two deer," "If I have poured myself without reserve," "We who had been so wounded and so cloven." Most original is the long free-verse poem, "She Shall Be Called Woman," the story of Eve/Everywoman's creation: the first realization of her body lying against the curve of the earth, her wounding by Adam's desire, her healing, the waking of her soul, her joy in her fertile body. A more *female* poem would be difficult to imagine.

May, therefore, arrived in England a poet. Julian met her boat, delayed in the Thames by fog, and rushed her away to dinner at the zoo northwest of London in the Chilterns, where the Huxleys had an apartment. On the way and during the drive back to London, he told her he wanted to have an affair.

May greeted the announcement with violently mixed emotions. "I wish you were here," she wrote Miutsie, "—I can't help being deeply troubled about Julian and the intensity of his feelings for me." The difficulties seemed staggering: her lesbianism, her attraction to the lovely Juliette, her objection to breaking up a marriage. But then she and Julian had a long talk. He had had many affairs; Juliette understood. They were all intelligent adults; what could be the objection? She capitulated. "I know that both May & I are 'safe,' " Julian wrote Juliette triumphantly the next day, "—& know it very definitely today for, my dearest, I spent the night with her last night at a hotel. It was very beautiful & happy. . . ."

Juliette was devastated: "*Must* I be made miserable so you may be happy? . . . Your selfishness can be so cruel." She must. Julian took May to a gynecologist to be fitted for a diaphragm. Because Juliette received her, May was ignorant of her pain. "I understand everything much better," she assured Mabel, "and that we are really in love (though his marriage is, thank goodness, *indestructible*). . . ." She was thrilled that such a distinguished man loved her; convinced that whatever happened, a relationship with great people like Julian and Juliette could only "bear fruit." She felt that at last she was really *living:* making love with Julian, she felt herself part of a vast primal force—something she had never felt with Irene or Theo. She felt that after all she might be "normal." Going to bed with Julian proved it.

After the trauma of Edward VIII's abdication, London was festive for the coronation of George VI, and May plunged into the social and literary stream. She left a copy of *Encounter in April* with a bunch of primroses at Virginia Woolf's door. John Summerson took her to an architects' party. She read Juliette two chapters of *The Single Hound.* She had tea with Elizabeth Bowen, who liked May so much that she invited her to stay the night whenever she came up from Rye. On April 11 she left for Jeakes House, having invited half of London to visit, knowing that Julian would be there often.

The house surpassed her expectations: a sunken living room leading to a flagstoned garden walled with trees and flowers, a studio and bedroom of her own. By the time Margaret English and Kappo arrived, May had found a char and a girl to come in every day for fifteen shillings a week. Rye itself was "like an operetta set with lovely views out into the cool flat marsh, a windmill and an old castle in the distance." And so May settled down at Jeakes House "to work, to be silent."

Hardly. On April 15 she was dancing and drinking champagne with Julian at a London charity ball. The next days, cocktails with Elizabeth Bowen and *Henry V* at the Old Vic with a young man from Cambridge she'd met on the boat. By April 17, she was back in Rye with Julian ("such a lovely peaceful week-end"); on April 21 in London lunching with her newly acquired agent, Patience Ross, dining with the Huxleys and marvelling that all three of them could be quite happy together; on April 23 back at Rye, having had to borrow five pounds from the Singers for travel expenses.

On May 1 Julian came down to celebrate her birthday. He gave her a blue ring with "*almost* my flower in it in pearls"—the lily of the valley, a motif she had adopted as her signature on letters. Though May got up at six-thirty to make breakfast for Julian, who had to leave early, May 3 turned out to be sunny and warm, with telegrams from Mabel and George, letters from the Peacocks, a camera case from Kappo, a stuffed llama from Juliette, a cake—"altogether a lovely birthday."

Incredibly, the novel was "striding": incredible since she was back in London on May 6 for Gluck's *Alceste* at Covent Garden with Julian and dinner afterwards at Rule's. That night she stayed with Elizabeth Bowen in Clarence Terrace, and Elizabeth stretched out on the couch for one last cigarette while May poured out her hopes and fears. The next day she went out to tea, dinner, a musical, the Café Royal. The Huxleys called for her Saturday morning to take her to Whipsnade, a cold, gray day, but they picnicked at an old bridge spanning a river full of flowers and "chased each other about to keep warm." Julian gave her a tour of the magnificent zoo as soon as they arrived—fortunately, since it poured the rest of the three days, which were such a success, however, that she was "simply walking on air."

Juliette seemed to accept her, even when Julian took her to Paris the next weekend. May tried to explain the ménage à trois to a worried Miutsie: "Really everything is all right and I think I am being a help and not a hindrance—creating life, not destroying or obstructing it. . . . The fact [is] that everything is open and clear between us all three—and that J. and I accept so completely that it is something *outside* our lives, and Juliette also understands that (she is *amazing!*) and loves me." May felt less guilty on learning from Julian that Juliette and Alan Best, the handsome assistant director of the London zoo, were lovers.

She spent the weekend of May 22 in Oxford visiting friends (Julian was there, not coincidentally); danced her feet off at a grand coronation party at the zoo under a marquee in the middle of the floodlit grounds. When Elizabeth Bowen came down to Rye for a few days, May and her friends had already decided to give up Jeakes House the first of June. "Six weeks in this house has been lovely," she wrote George and Mabel, "but now it is time to go." She had hardly spent six days there, thanks to Julian's persistence and her own dragonfly nature.

Which could never be pinned down by Julian alone. Looking back at those intoxicating English days, May was rather horrified by her feverish emotions: "I fell in love every day." She had fallen in love with Elizabeth's chestnut hair, cat eyes, and glamour. She knew that Elizabeth had loved at least one woman. After supper one evening, May led Elizabeth up to her study at the top of the house with its view over the misty moonlit marshes. They smoked and talked and finally, according to May, Elizabeth yielded to her importunity and made love. For May, it was the exalted climax of weeks of frustrated emotion; for Elizabeth, a graceful yielding to a mood that would not be repeated, since she was on her way to Boulogne to meet her lover, Sean O'Faolain.

Living at this frenetic pace and falling in love "every day," May still managed to write. While she was disappointed at the low sales (314 copies)

May and Julian Huxley in 1937

and few reviews of *Encounter in April,* Patience Ross had sent *The Single Hound* to Cresset Press, and its chief reader, S. S. Koteliansky, an intellectual Russian Jew and close friend of D. H. Lawrence and Katherine Mansfield, liked it. Certainly she was being treated like a writer in London, where, after leaving Rye, she spent "the most extraordinary and glamorous five days of my life."

They began with Koteliansky, looking "exactly like a bear with a shock of gray hair standing straight up on a square head" and "a kind sad face," coming to the Huxleys to talk about her book. While there was some difficulty about publishing terms, Kot told her again and again, "You are a writer"—no small compliment from a man of great literary integrity.

The next day the Huxleys gave a huge cocktail party for May, Kappo, and Margaret, with waiters, hundreds of delicious little sandwiches, and masses of people. Elizabeth was there, looking heartbreakingly unobtainable, though she invited May to Bowen's Court in Ireland in September. Mark Gertler, the painter, was there, and Kot, and the Irish poet James

Stephens; and if May was rather dazed by all the people, there was always "a little home circle" to go back to. After the party, Julian took May, Kappo, and Margaret to dinner at the zoo, where they adored stroking the penguins' tummies and making the gibbon sing, a perfect ending to the day.

The next day Juliette gave them a tea with T. S. Eliot, Ruth Pitter, Robert Nichols, and Kot, which began awkwardly, since the men were late, until Julian sent for the bear and lion cubs to entertain them. May was struck by "how New England [Eliot] seemed, that deprecatory very slow quiet way of speaking." When she asked him how his play (*The Family Reunion*) was going, he replied, "If I didn't like it better than anything I have done, I would drop it"—a remark that struck her as profound. Then May, Kappo, Margaret, and the Huxleys went back to London and saw the ballet, and afterwards May went to Elizabeth's in Clarence Terrace, where she slept alone. The next day she was going to Whipsnade for three "peaceful weeks" of work: the Huxleys were loaning her their apartment, though they'd be down weekends.

She did alight for a few days, revising about fifty pages of *The Single Hound,* but then the Huxleys arrived for picnics and drives into the country, and after a week she was back in London to meet Virginia Woolf at Elizabeth Bowen's, a miraculous event. Yet May discovered that her feelings about the great writer were mixed. Woolf extracted confidences with flattering attention, but none of Elizabeth's warmth: she seemed to be "a highly sensitive, immensely curious *voyeur*" who absorbed the lives of others but gave nothing of herself. Still, how thrilling when Virginia invited her to tea.

The Woolfs' apartment over the Hogarth Press in Tavistock Square was "almost rococo," with Vanessa Bell's panels and screens, French books in light papers, lots of flowers, and small, bright objects scattered about. Of course May wondered about Virginia's reaction to the poems she'd left on her doorstep; Virginia said tactfully that "she really hadn't read them yet" because someone had run off with them. But she was "infinitely and charmingly curious" about May's writing, and volunteered that she worked on many scenes of a novel at the same time, depending on her mood. She also said that she thought prose more difficult and, in these experimental days, more interesting than poetry; May guiltily agreed. May stayed till six and only left because Alan Cameron was driving her to Whipsnade. "I can feel a bird of friendship flying about over our heads," she confided to her "dear bear" Kot, "and I think soon he will settle." Had she fallen in love with Virginia? Of course.

May (center) picnicking with Juliette and Julian Huxley

A weekend with the Basil de Selincourts; then Elizabeth came to Whipsnade to read the novel, which Cresset had refused to buy until it was finished. On a cold gray day the Woolfs appeared at the zoo and seemed happy and interested, though to May *everything* seemed to go wrong. Incongruously, the delicate Virginia smoked cigars while they talked amiably enough about America and animals, though the bird of friendship still hovered. The next day May left Whipsnade for London and Elizabeth's house. That evening she and the Huxleys dined with H. G. Wells, a "*most* thrilling night." She liked his bright blue eyes and "queer squeaky voice, his conceit and his undeniable charm," his house in Regent's Park full of flowers and Chinese objets d'art. After the ballet back to Wells's for a drink—"the whole evening had so much *glamour.*" Then an excursion with the Huxleys into the country to see their son Anthony at his school near Marlborough; then dinner with Elizabeth ("peaceful"); then moving all her luggage to the Huxleys' in London, though she'd wanted to be quiet and have a last visit with Kot.

Her last weekend wildly climaxed three frenetic months. Eventually, she tried to account for her behavior to Kot:

I cannot explain the *désarroi* in my heart at having to change plans so often. I was really in a wild state—and instead of crying and crying I went to the other extreme. On Friday night we all went dancing (Alan, Juliette, Julian and I). I flirted with *everyone*—something I never do unless I am temporarily mad—Juliette said that I went around "lighting bonfires" and it is quite true—a sense of flowers falling on my head and that I must reach everyone's *heart*— so I made quite a scene with Juliette and the next day she persuaded me to go [to] Whipsnade. Before I knew what had happened I found myself *caught*—of course I saw nothing of her in the end—did not even have time to read her this poem which I wrote—but Julian and I were together the week-end and I think he was happy. Well, as I had seen Elizabeth not at all I arranged to go there for a drink Sunday night and *after* that you telephoned— it all sounds too complicated for words. And it is. My darling, I really have a *daemon* you know. And I do realize that it is this, this "*génie de l'amour*" as Jean Dominique calls it which is the one thing which might keep me from doing good work.

It is a terrible thing. You know me well enough and understand me to know that none of this is *light*—I do not go into these things lightly, but only from a consuming need to reach the *essence* of people and to give them mine (and often, alas! this is only possible in love)—

By the time Sun night came I was so exhausted and miserable because I felt really like someone who has been shamefully drunk—that I was only half there. My dear, I am sorry and you must forgive me and go on scolding and loving me if you can.

This is possibly the most honest letter May Sarton ever wrote. Her insistent energy *was* demonic. The compulsion was twofold. Profoundly insecure, she needed endless validation of her existence. But she also needed to conquer. She was the initiator, the aggressor—the one who lit bonfires, who gave the first kiss. She could be disarmed; to Juliette: "You spoke and saw my sword-point fall indeed / That was aimed at your heart and but for this / Would have been merciless and made you bleed." But ultimately she must prevail. It was a kind of sickness, as her letter admitted; frighteningly, this *making* people love her was equally the source of poetic inspiration. She had to have it, like a fix—again and again and again. "I don't think I shall ever be destroyed by emotion—it is my business to *build* into it," she said truthfully, but with scant regard for the chaos left in her wake.

The next day she left for Belgium on her way to Grundlsee in Austria, where the Huxleys would join her. Sitting exhausted in a café opposite the Gare du Nord in Brussels, washing down an omelet with red wine, she assessed the astounding three English months that had climaxed in an orgy of *génie de l'amour.* In calmer mood, she felt she had made four solid friends: Elizabeth Bowen, Koteliansky, and the Huxleys. Decidedly she had not swept Virginia Woolf off her feet. As for the Huxleys, "In a curious way I am almost more fond of her than of Julian," she wrote Koteliansky as she sipped her wine. "She is less *great*—but she is more *special,* you know? She comes closer to my world." She had tried to seduce Juliette that last week-end, but Juliette had withdrawn and left her to her husband.

She left that evening for Grundlsee hoping to see again the enchanting hostess of Seeblick, Maria Stiasni, who, Kot now heard, "provides sufficient *glamour* to destroy my peace of mind." Yet she missed Juliette terribly. She smoked the Russian cigarettes Kot had given her and comforted herself with his "Of course it will not be good. Just work and don't worry—it is a first novel." She sketched Maria Stiasni and wrote poems for her, hiked with Franz, a young Czech friend, and waited for Juliette. No publisher had taken *The Single Hound,* but she wasn't worried. Someone would publish it, and Juliette was coming.

Juliette did not come. She had decided, said Julian, arriving in high spirits on July 24, that she couldn't afford it. "I am really heartbroken," May wrote home, "as I had kept thinking how she would love it and how sweet she would look in a dirndl." Instead she had Julian, who enthusiastically joined in the hikes, games, costume parties, boat rides, and poetry reading. But she was not happy. After all, "Julian was not a good lover," she later confessed. "I always felt like a nurse rather than a mistress. He was neurotic, often ill, needed a lot of TLC, which I was good at." Worse, he did not really understand her: he expected that as soon as the right man came along, she would marry.

Pressure mounted. "I think there must be an *inner* revolution in me sooner or later," she wrote Kot. "Since Julian has come I haven't done much work—it is a paradox (that is life) that this heavenly holiday should just come at the moment when I should be absolutely alone with *infinite* time—So I feel caught—and one part of me says to the other 'It is your job to make J. happy, it is only two weeks and it is so sweet.' The other part says 'You have a job to do and that must come first if you are to be a writer.'"

This is every writer's conflict, but intensified in May's case because a man was making the demands. Two egos collided: the male, expecting compliancy from a woman, and the artist's, ruthlessly sacrificing others to its fulfillment. Prodigally squandering her time in England, May now chafed under Julian's domination of her hours. Men did not inspire, they drained her. Though Julian's tenderness for her was as great as ever, she was horribly depressed, mortally tired. Finally she managed "four blessed days alone" and finished *The Single Hound,* though she cried bitterly at the end, sure it wasn't good enough. She took some comfort in James Stephens's reaction to her poem "Dark Answer": "This is written by a fine poet: none better done by any of ours."

She read *The Single Hound* to the Peacocks in the avenue de l'Échevinage, where she had come for ten days, and they were not pleased. The autobiographical story of a failing young writer, Mark, who seeks inspiration from the Belgian poet "Jean Latour," betrayed too much of their lives. They asked her to take six months and rewrite until they were unrecognizable.

This was a blow, as was Miutsie's unexpected call to England to care for her old mother, since surely May must cancel her visit to Bowen's Court and go to Ipswich instead. George had paid for Mabel's boat fare but had given her no money for England. "Dearest Daddy," May pleaded, "I shouldn't tell you this and you must not let her know that I have but I think Mummy is very worried about money. . . . Perhaps you could pretend that you don't know and send her a small sum as an unexpected present." May herself couldn't help: she owed part of her bill at Seeblick. Finally Jean-Do (who called George "le cher pingouin" but understood his parsimony) wired Mabel money she could hardly spare.

On August 26, Julian and Kot met May's train, and as the Huxleys couldn't have her, she took a room opposite Kot's house in Acacia Road, St. John's Wood. She wanted to see Virginia Woolf again; she wanted Miutsie to meet Kot and James Stephens (and, said Kot, "I want to have the pleasure of hearing J.S. telling your mother what a precious darling you are"); she longed to visit Elizabeth Bowen in Ireland.

None of these delights occurred. "I'm so sorry, I shant be in London again till October, when I suppose you'll be gone," wrote Virginia from Monk's House in Sussex. Vanessa Bell's son, Julian, had recently been killed in Spain, but even without that family sorrow, Virginia would have given May short shrift. "Have you," she wrote Elizabeth Bowen that October, ". . . despatched that goose May Sarton, who sent me a gentian picked by Julian Huxley—and so on." Mabel could not leave her ninety-year-old mother to come to London, and by August 29 May had given up Ireland to help move her grandmother to a home in Ipswich.

*The poet James Stephens and S. S. Koteliansky in Kot's kitchen at 5 Acacia Road,
St. John's Wood*

But there were the Huxleys and Kot and James Stephens. Lunch or tea
at Kot's were really poetry sessions, Kot cooking in his bright kitchen
with its tomato plants and rows of plates, while James, inspired by Kot's
special herbal martinis, recited his poetry. He declared that the only two
women poets today were Ruth Pitter and May Sarton, but warned that
May must work much harder to refine each poem—and she agreed. Then
Cresset said they would take *The Single Hound,* though they would
advance her only fifteen pounds—"the bastards."

Before sailing on the *Importer* September 11, May lunched a last time
with Kot. She was assured of the friendship of this difficult, fierce, loyal
"Lion of Judea." The Huxleys were more problematic: Julian loved her;
she was in love with Juliette; Juliette had a lover. Yet miraculously they
were all friends. She would return.

On the voyage home, she gave Julian's lapis-and-pearl ring to a young
woman who momentarily struck her fancy.

CHAPTER 9

The Novelist: 1937–1939

May returned to Channing Place to work in her study at the top of the house, a room she quickly made her own with her furnishings from New York, Mabel's rugs and pillows, jugs of flowers. No more talk of finding a job: she was a poet working on a first novel to be published simultaneously in New York and London, reason enough for George to accept her under his roof. She was still revising *The Single Hound,* trying to defeminize her protagonist, Mark. Kot had advised her to make Mark a girl; May admitted she had failed to create a real young man, but would not change Mark's sex. But the Peacocks were the real problem. They had asked her to change the site from Brussels to Bruges; now May wept in frustration at Jean-Do's insistence that there be *no* suggestion of a sexual relationship between Mark and Jean Latour. May cabled Jean-Do that nothing would be published "without her love and faith in each word" and returned to her typewriter. At the same time she was planning a second volume of poems for next fall and another novel. Yes, she assured Kot, she remembered his warning that she must not *rush* her writing.

Dining out one evening, she saw Katharine Taylor; but Katharine walked by. The incident shook her, because for two years K.T. had withdrawn. She went home and wrote "A Letter to the Living":

Who are you to whom I came when you seemed all wisdom and peace
When I brought you the early poems, early ardor, and the early shame,
And because you were needed your door was open as it always is,
And because it was a child, love did not need a name. . . .

> Autumn is here. Last night I saw you in a restaurant
> (That eagerness of mind beholding you and the heart's praise)
> You did not see me and passed by—a simple accident;
> The leaves are falling. I fear the shortness of the days.

Katharine Taylor had reacted more negatively to the Grace Daly affair than Anne Thorp. If George didn't know his daughter was a lesbian, K.T. did. But K.T. had really not abandoned May: she saw her struggle "between worlds"—the hetero- and homosexual—and stood by, though powerless to help. Yet this was not enough for May, who demanded intimacy.

She could not be out of love long. Returning from abroad, May always ran first to Edith Forbes Kennedy, whose gift of listening made her foreign adventures seem real. One evening "a very strange experience" took place at Edith's shabby little Shepard Street house. In a moment of frankness, Edith admitted that she and Sean O'Casey had been lovers. "Looking right down into her heart," May fell wildly in love. Poems burst forth, all immediately sent to the Muse. May trained all her guns on Edith: bunches of personally delivered flowers, handmade gifts and notes, poems copied into decorated books, urgent telegrams, phone calls, visits, much seizing of hands. Edith affectionately told her not to be an ass. Still the insistent poems came—thirty in sixty days:

> This room is charged now with an atmosphere:
> You must be caught. You cannot break the spell.
> Enchantment of a curious kind is here—
> We are seduced, my love, you know it well
> Though with this heavy head against your breast
> The knocking heart must still deny it rest.

Escaping from her own intensity to New York in November, May heard that Edith Kennedy had fainted and was hospitalized with a concussion and broken cheekbone. "There was nothing I could do," she wrote Kot, "she can see no one, and especially not anyone who might be emotional strain, so I stayed in New York in a kind of nightmare of panic (one can't help thinking people are going to die) and remorse, though on serious thought I do *not* believe I was instrumental in wearing her out. . . ." Rather chastened, May returned to Cambridge to begin a second novel, determined it must be "deeper, truer, less dramatic and lyric this time," offering obeisance to the austere god of form in a poem, "Prayer Before Work." Yet being kept away from Edith tormented her; little comfort to visit Edith's deaf old aunt

Edith Forbes Kennedy, mentor and Muse

and shout poems into her ear, or watch Mabel embroider flowers on a jacket May was giving to Edith. "I haven't heard from Edith for three weeks," she wrote Kot on December 6, "—she has gone to the country to rest. The silence is a *nightmare*."

Her obvious infatuation with Edith finally roused George. "*You should get married,*" he told her brutally. May flung herself at him, wild with rage, weeping, pummeling him with her fists.

She was finally permitted to see her Muse under strictly controlled circumstances. "I think some curious inner revolution has taken place in her," she wrote Kot, "and eventually she will tell me about it. Meanwhile I can only be horribly patient and good." She was neither. In mid-January 1938, Edith finally protested:

Nature being what she is, it is clear to me that romantic love, except in relations to men, can have no place in my being. . . .

I thought that you would eventually sense this, and so not require this abrupt black and whiteness—but your persistence requires an explanation. As I've said before I realize that all passion is passion—but the feminine use of it is not for me & would, I think, very quickly prove either boring or revolting—or both, as far as I'm concerned.★

On these terms any time you wish to come over I'll be delighted —as always—to see you.

Affectionately,

Edith Kennedy

★You know well that I have no hoity-toity moralistic views on all this!

"The inevitable end" had come. That night she visited Shepard Street, a guest among other guests. She was exhausted from her passion, discouraged with her poetry: "Now and then a gulf of fear opens at my feet that I am not a poet at all but living in a private deluded world." As for prose, she had torn up fifty "cheap and shameful" pages of a novel based on the Julian-May-Juliette-Alan quartet. But none of these setbacks mattered— not even Hitler's annexation of Austria on March 11, 1938—because she was sailing back to Julian and Juliette and Kot again on fifty pounds advanced by George against Cresset's payment for *The Single Hound.*

Or thought she was. Deductions shrank the fifty pounds to sixteen. Alarmed by poor advance sales of *The Single Hound,* Houghton Mifflin refused an advance on a second novel. George lectured her at length about extravagance; she would starve to death when he was dead. Channing Place was not comfortable at the best of times, according to Molly Howe, who was afraid of Dr. Sarton when she came to visit. The house had to be absolutely silent for the great scientist; she thought him stiff, withdrawn, an egomaniac. Mabel impressed Molly as a typical English governess: gentle, well-bred, *repressed.* Always eager to break a lance for Mabel, May seethed with resentment against George but could not openly rebel because he supported her. "The apparent completeness of a family," May wrote bitterly of these years, "—and then suddenly the hole at the center." Desperate, May began interviewing heads of schools for part-time teaching jobs. She dashed off pathetic and unsubtle missives to Kot, Julian, and Elizabeth Bowen bemoaning her plight.

Then the miracle. "Only a poet and, perhaps, a young poet could have written this beautiful and distinguished first novel," said *The New York Times. The Single Hound* was a *succès d'estime,* despite Willa Cather's private dissension: "I venture to prophesy that Miss Sarton will never write anything good, because she thinks she is a little tripping fairy—and she is not." George melted, and May sailed on the *Normandie.* She would see him, she told Kot ecstatically, April 10. And, of course, Julian.

Grace Eliot Dudley, owner of Le Petit Bois, and Muse

· · ·

At Anne Thorp's suggestion, May looked up Grace Eliot Dudley, the granddaughter of a former president of Harvard, in cabin class. She discovered an elegant middle-aged woman lying in bed in a room with no portholes, quite willing to be amused by visits from May, who soon was walking Grace's dog and having tea, thrilling to the voice "like a wet flute." May kissed her passionately on the mouth. Grace was unable to resist her charming young ardor. "She is a nice peaceful woman," May wrote Kot, announcing a sudden change in plans: "I must go to Paris—I feel it would be tempting fate to put off seeing Lugné-Poë again." Her real destination was Le Petit Bois, Grace Dudley's house in Vouvray.

"It is the most utter peace, deep in the country, the fruit-trees all in flower, and Grace Dudley one of those rare people who moves in *peace*," she wrote George and Mabel. England now seemed more an obligation than a pleasure; she would rather stay in Vouvray than go to the Huxleys' at Whipsnade. She had her own room, but spent her nights in Grace's.

Grace Dudley was a typical Muse. She was cultivated, well off and well connected (May was an unashamed snob), middle-aged, *spirituelle*. Like Juliette Huxley and Edith Kennedy, she was a "complete" woman, having had a husband (though no children)—"I have never been attracted to the typical 'lesbian,' " said May. More important, she seemed to need love. She had lost her father early, was divorced from William Dudley and at an age when men's eyes passed over her for younger women. For May, these neglected women were plants, needing only her ready fountain of love to burst into bloom. It was also delightful if these women had lovely homes where she could work, for poems were sure to come. And Le Petit Bois in a little woods in the wine-growing Vallée Coquette where the nightingales sang was lovely. It was all she could do to tear herself away to England, though Grace's letters followed: "You are part of the Petit Bois now . . . I rejoice at the thought of you. There are *no* tears on my horizon."

Recovering from a sinus operation when she arrived, Julian evidently did not notice that her emotional center had shifted. When she told him she must return to France to work on her novel, he announced that he would follow. A vacation would do him good.

Kot was still Kot: opinionated, pessimistic, tender. He would try to get *The Single Hound* well reviewed. "For the sake of your mother and father," he explained sternly. "Not for you. Because it has absolutely no importance." He was determined she should publish a big book of poems in England in the fall. She saw Elizabeth Bowen for lunch, but Elizabeth would not review the novel, she said, because they were such good friends. Letters from Jean-Do righted the balance. May had scarcely believed that after her violent opposition to the novel they could resume their old footing, but *The Single Hound* was, the poet declared, *un vrai succès*.

"I have decided to go next week (27th April) to France for a month and spend June instead of May here when Julian will be better and feel more like doing things and when I shall have done a good piece of work," she wrote Cambridge. On April 25, *The Single Hound* was in the London bookstores. Kot professed himself delighted with the first reviews, though May thought them less good than the American. Then Virginia Woolf invited her to tea.

It was not a happy session. Virginia did not want to discuss May's novel; she found May's terrible suspense about her verdict "absurd in the extreme." Finally she admitted she hated the "whimsical" old ladies; thought the second part best; thought it would be interesting, with May's talent, to see if she really had anything to say. Write essays, she advised: essays curb excess feeling, make one think things through. "What a curious woman," May told Elizabeth, "—I kept wanting to say for God's sake be simple—it was like looking down into one of those spiral shells." The great novelist's chief criticism went unspoken: *The Single Hound* was too Virginia Woolf.

With the jury still out on her novel, May left England. Her faithful old "Éléphant," Lugné-Poë, met her train in Paris before she raced to Le Petit Bois. Since she was suffering from a nervous stomach, Grace put her to bed: "She is the most peaceful treasure," May sighed blissfully. Peace was short-lived. Julian arrived, carried her away with him to Tours. "Perhaps I shall get my reward in heaven," May wrote Kot, "—for it is really tearing up my soul to leave here now and all the peace shattered." Her coding of the word "peace" for "sexual satisfaction" had become obsessive.

They sat on camp stools and sketched old farms in pastels, drove to Chenonceaux in pouring rain through shining green woods—and since Julian still loved her and was happy, she felt "useful." But she raged at his sexual demands. Why couldn't he accept her spiritual love, which she gave him honestly, since she was deeply fond of him? The physical act was humiliating, debasing. Yet she still allowed it.

She felt the responsibility of being twenty-six on May 3. "I must work terribly hard and get away from all softness, that everything be very *true*," she vowed. "It is so easy to become literary, to become (that is my horror) a sort of perpetual lace valentine." She expanded on the subject to Elizabeth. "No more emotional excursions. Work. Now that I have a little confidence and think I am not merely charging at a windmill, I see how awfully long it will take before I can write anything good, rooted, secure and finished. . . . I see so clearly now in [*The Single Hound*] its impatient and avid point of view, its superficial pretty sort of wisdom." Reviews from England had sobered her: despite all Kot's efforts, no *really* distinguished critic had championed the new American novelist.

The Single Hound was not "rooted" and "secure," but a novel of shifting moods: of emotion lost before translation into action, of words evaporating before utterance. Impermanence is the theme of this story of a poet who discovers himself through the empathy of an old poet, Jean Latour. Love affairs, like Mark's with Georgia (Elizabeth Bowen), are dreamlike, impermanent. Nothing abides but faith in oneself and one's work. Finally one understands Jean Dominique's importance to May Sarton the writer, who, like her hero Mark Taylor, felt her work irrelevant because she was not politically involved in causes like her more radical friends, was not an alienated intellectual. Be yourself, Jean Latour tells Mark: your gift is making the mind and the heart speak together. That is your personal world. Trust it.

Sarton the poet, the novelist, and the letter writer merge. The same images, the same life-view, permeate all the work. Juliette's "lighting bonfires" becomes a central image of *The Single Hound,* just as Mark's description of the painter Georgia as a swan has its roots in the poem "Memory of Swans." Georgia's "desire at the bottom of her spine like a poison" continued the violent, negative metaphors for heterosexual passion of the early poems. Mark's "My peace, my peace" at Georgia's surrender is May's private metaphor. And Mark's discovery of Jean Latour's "transparency" was already an image May used to describe her own work.

Julian the lover left and May returned to the beloved. "Kot, I really can't believe in this peace and this happiness, it is so good. I feel as if I were being born all new and clear. . . ." Poems to Grace welled up from May's deep joy:

> The wind which swept the earth has mounted the trees
> So we sit in a quiet below the leaf-blown skies,
> Silence touches our eyelids and enfolds our knees,
> Breaks blue as butterfly wings across your eyes.
>
> The wind which crackled the leaves along the path
> Has risen up, has flown to the tops of the trees.
> Here there is silence and a quiet aftermath:
> Passion that shook our eyelids and our knees
>
> Now takes its way to the heart in a quiet flood.
> Silence touches our eyelids and we find sleep good.

On June 6 she reluctantly left Le Petit Bois with plans to return in July, having roughly finished the first part of *The Waterfall.* Back in England, she plunged into the whirl: Whipsnade (Juliette was modelling a head of her); Kot's and Elizabeth's; another weekend with the de Selincourts at Kingham; a driving tour with Julian through Thomas Hardy country ("I am determined to learn to drive"); a weekend at Rye with Conrad Aiken; a dozen other engagements—during which she heard that the Cresset Press would definitely take a book of poems.

Addressed to "Pussy-puss," "Darling Mayling," and "My little love," Grace's letters followed her, though they did not always contain good news. Her former husband, William, who lived nearby in his château, Mon Bazon, with his ex-mistress as housekeeper, had proposed they remarry and keep separate establishments. A woman friend would be at Le Petit Bois in July. "If you slept in my room (which you would any-way—if I know you!) & only unpacked yr toothbrush—we could still crowd into the house. . . ." The next letter was a blow: Grace and William had reunited.

May left for France. "I think I can help," she wrote Kot, "(for certainly there is no happiness for G with her husband) and perhaps I can provide a sort of peaceful companionship and love. . . . I feel curiously aloof and happy." She had actually written a poem that did not contain the word "love." "I have made a resolution to write now only impersonal poems or at least take personal feeling about someone—which will always be the starting-point—one step further. This is I think what James [Stephens] was driving at."

After five bitter days she wrote again. "I have decided that it's best to leave. . . . I think now I shall have to be silent for awhile—no poems and no novel. . . . Grace has gone off with her husband for the evening and I have the whole quiet house and the garden to myself. I am going to sleep." She had witnessed Grace's obvious love for a man who had treated her badly. She could do nothing.

William Dudley's reappearance emphasized the fragility of a lesbian's claim on an essentially heterosexual woman. Freighted with prerogatives, the husband could easily prevail, relegating May to the status of guest. But to pity May would be foolish. She was a survivor, who not only refused to acknowledge setbacks but throve on them. Besides, Grace had fulfilled her function. Bernard Shaw warned Mrs. Patrick Campbell that whatever the outcome of their romance, he would get plays from it. May had just sent *Inner Landscape,* containing sixty-four new poems, to Cresset. As she told Kot, the worst thing was not the emotional but the physical displacement from Le Petit Bois, which interrupted the rhythm of her work. Yet, unquestionably, it had been a rout.

Paris: Lugné-Poë. Uccle: Jean Dominique ("I feel that I am entirely again 'L'enfant de la maison' "). Avenue Lequime: Uncle Raymond less depressed. London: Kot, James, the Huxleys. On August 10 she sailed aboard the *American Importer* a month earlier than planned, exhausted by the ongoing battle with Julian over sex. In retrospect, Juliette seemed the most precious of these wonderful people. In mid-Atlantic she could think of her with "no chance that Alan will suddenly come in—or Julian—or one of the boys—to stop the thread and shut up the heart in its usual box. . . . You must never let me slip out of your life, Juliette." She enclosed a poem. And so a voyage begun to return to Julian, but diverted to Grace Dudley, ended with May sending Sappho's "Ode to Aphrodite" to a woman still unconquered.

She joined her parents at Rockport, Massachusetts, at a hotel full of old ladies reading *The Single Hound.* May worked on short stories, stopping every now and then to watch George caress the vacationing Sarton cats in a voice he never used with people. But Rockport only postponed the inevitable: she *must* make money. If no school hired her, she would try to entice this year's debutantes to enroll in a private poetry course.

As always, her European adventures now seemed eerily insubstantial. Did Kot's silence mean he was sick to death of her? Elizabeth seldom wrote. Julian wrote that he would not accept a platonic relationship. She replied, pleading for friendship. Juliette did not write. Impending war weighed on everyone's mind: the Sartons woke each morning with a sense of doom. Mabel felt the oppression more than May. "I wish you were near," she wrote Kot, whom she had met in London and instantly loved. "I could talk with you with such deep pleasure as I rarely have with anyone—talk and listen & be silent together."

May got a job teaching writing to five "intelligent, nice talent-less creatures" at the Stuart School. Two elderly women paid her for private poetry lessons. She accepted fifty dollars from Concord Academy to direct a play so that she could pay off debts, then spent $300 on a blue Dodge convertible to get her there. May economics.

Her attitude toward her own work volleyed between satisfaction and despair. She had finished a second novel, *The Waterfall,* but, feeling it lacked the stern purity she was aiming for, shelved it. She was reading Rilke. She was waiting for the publication of *Inner Landscape* in England: "I feel very far away and as if I should be there to guard them from evil, teach them how to curtsey. . . . It is a real pain, the idea of their going out into the world, to be wagged on people's tongues. . . . I cannot understand why anyone ever wants to publish anything, it is so awful." She felt she would never write a personal poem again; instead she turned to war's brutality:

> There are too many deaths to be assimilated.
> The mind refracts them like a shallow mirror.

None crashes through: we are not implicated.
We have learned facility with horror.

She felt that since returning from Europe she had "crashed through a new floor" in herself, gotten one level deeper.

A "darling" letter from Juliette came with the new year, 1939. But Julian continued to torment her. Will "he ever see that *love* is the important thing and that if we love each other it is blessed and enough without a messy physical side which will only destroy *my* love?" she wrote Kot. "He cannot, *will* not see it. And he is wrong." Though she was saving money for England again in June, "I dread so terribly a repetition of the hell that Julian can create." He was having an affair with another woman—a relief, but terrible for Juliette, who didn't know. And terrible for Julian, this constantly seeking "intoxication and pleasure" instead of love and understanding.

Inner Landscape appeared in March. May bought fifty copies to send to friends, feeling quite ashamed now of the double dedication to Edith Forbes Kennedy in America and the Huxleys in England, the result of "an excess of love, a longing to give the same thing to too many people." American reviews were few, though the poet John Holmes called *Inner Landscape* "among the few really excellent books of the season," and *The New York Times* praised the subduing of emotion by form—like a butterfly imprisoned in ice—but wished she had not so strictly curbed her Pegasus. "You are wonderful to have managed two reviews," she told Kot, "—here absolutely *nothing* has been done, not a single advertisement, very few copies given away except the ones I bought. . . . Ah well, it doesn't matter. I am rather indifferent by now!"

She certainly was not indifferent to Basil de Selincourt's three-column review in the *Observer*. "If her verses deserve notice, it is because the intense experience which underlies and unifies them has engendered an uncompromising determination to forge and refine the tool for its expression, a tool which needed to be, and indeed already is, deep-searching to the point of ruthlessness, and very delicate." Here was someone who understood, though de Selincourt was hardly in the van of poetic fashion. James Stephens called her one of the most notable poetic talents writing at the time. Other reviewers talked about strength and wisdom, delicacy and precision, sensitivity and originality.

But there were dissenters. "I believe [the poems] are unsuccessful," wrote one British reviewer; "she aims at a precise vision, but does not achieve it because she does not use words precisely." The *Spectator* agreed: "Miss Sarton's language is trite ('smitten with fire at the heart's cockle') and she is content with vague approximations to the meaning she wishes to convey." For instance, the couplet "If it were snow it would fall soft as wool / Wrapping the senses with a silken spool": "wool" and "silk" were very different entities; moreover, if one took "spool" as a cylindrical object, the image was patently absurd. In America, Dudley Fitts in the *Saturday Review* concurred: "It is not only that the writing is flat, the diction usual: what really vitiates the book is a curious disregard of the implications of metaphor, a failure to perceive that figures may work at more than one level and that a surface effect is worse than useless if contradictory forces are contriving absurdity beneath the surface. . . . *Inner Landscape* is a disappointing performance."

These highly conflicting reactions can partly be explained by May Sarton's flagrantly unfashionable lyricism, by her adherence to traditional patterns, and by her eschewal of "smart despair." Yet they also can be explained by her volubility. Poetry poured out; in "an excess of love" she gave the same thing to too many poems, as she did to people. She should have taken accusations of trite and imprecise language with dead seriousness; for, even more than rhythm, language is the soul of poetry. A cliché like "I was smitten with fire at the heart's cockle" indeed undermines the otherwise fine poem "Afternoon on Washington Street." The lines "You who ask peace, peace is not in your nature / You cannot hope to rest," belong to a hymn. And in a poem like "After Silence," one longs for one striking, concrete image to focus abstractions like "mind," "forms," "praises," "spirit," "silence," "solitariness," "love," "will."

Yet *Inner Landscape* was in many ways an advance over *Encounter in April*. James Stephens had advised May to "forget your love, your little war, your ache; / Forget that haunting so mysterious face / And write for an abstracted beauty's sake." May insisted correctly that poetry inspired by one haunting face could be universal, but she had taken Stephens's advice to "seek for sterner stuff" seriously. Poems like "Prayer Before Work" and "Architectural Image" invoke the spirit of form—"the central nerve, the living spine"—which must discipline passion into a soaring spire. The passionate but derivative young poet of *Encounter in April* was learning subtlety and refinement.

The cold spring dragged on, Mabel as usual worrying about money. She tried buying and reselling paintings, tried selling her embroidery designs, with no success. That May old Mrs. Elwes died, severing Mabel's last filial tie to England; the two hundred pounds Mabel and her brother, Hugh, might have divided, Nellie Elwes willed to her caretakers. May herself was subdued, "almost drowning" from "the demands of all these unimportant people with whom I have deliberately surrounded myself against loneliness." *Inner Landscape* had sold only forty-one copies in England, and Cresset billed her seven pounds. She ached for England and Belgium, still feeling much more European than American. She had no work and no love—"a kind of illness." No money to get to Europe, either: "However something will turn up."

Comic relief was provided by George, who was learning to drive. Though short-sighted and hopelessly absentminded, he managed to pass his driver's test. The first time he took the Dodge out alone, he ran into another car and fled the scene, writing an eloquent letter to the chief of police proclaiming his innocence. He sallied forth again; hit a second car. When its driver said menacingly, "Follow me," George did not, but only, as he explained even more eloquently, because his car would not start due to his nervous failure to insert the key in the ignition. Mabel prayed he would desist, but George was cheerfully convinced he was the only good driver in Cambridge.

Something did turn up—three hundred dollars from George, as usual— and on June 14 May sailed on the *Normandie*. No coincidence, Grace Dudley was also on board, and May went up to her cabin daily for "nice peaceful times together reading poetry and talking"—which in May idiom probably meant that they were again lovers. She had no idea in what frame of mind she would find the mercurial Julian, but she vowed that from now on there would be no sex.

She had a room at Rosslyn Hill, overlooking Hampstead Heath. And though there were little dinners at the zoo, and Julian showed her Eton and rowed her on the Thames past fields of daisies, she refused to go to bed with him. Still, the relationship had its complications. One morning as May was waiting for Julian to collect her for a Cambridge weekend, Juliette phoned to say that Mark Gertler, Kot's last friend from the old Lawrence–Mansfield–Lady Ottoline days, had committed suicide. Would May go to Kot immediately? Realizing that Juliette knew nothing about the weekend, May stammered agreement before Julian whisked her away in the car. Halfway to Cambridge, she insisted he drop her; she would train back to London to see Kot, return to Cambridge to meet him for tea. But when she phoned, Kot savagely dismissed her concern as hysterical. She had no choice but continue to her clandestine weekend, feeling she had betrayed both Kot and Juliette. She depended enormously on Juliette's goodwill; Juliette's acceptance permitted her this circle of wonderful English friends.

Tea with Elizabeth Bowen in her beautiful room full of roses, dispelling May's fear that Elizabeth was through with her. Tea with the Imagist poet Hilda Doolittle in her dimly lit flat in Lowndes Square. (Though H.D. had been an idol of her youth and had written her warmly about *The Single Hound,* May was "not frightfully taken with her really.") Tea with Virginia Woolf, who agreed that there was something essential lacking in the poetry of the currently fashionable Auden and Spender. Lunch with Julian at Vita Sackville-West's Sissinghurst, Vita feminine above the waist in an orange silk blouse and dangling earrings, masculine from the waist down in riding pants and boots. They drank a bottle of hock each and talked of poets until four. (According to Polly Thayer Starr, May had an affair with Benedict Nicolson, Vita and Harold's son; one hardly sees how she had time.) Driving home, she and Julian agreed that the aristocracy were absolutely different from ordinary mortals, taking their luxuries for granted as a right of blood—though Vita couldn't have been nicer.

Word from home that the beautiful, otherworldly Ernesta Greene had shot herself. "I just can't *bear* it for Rosalind," May wrote Miutsie. Ernesta's and Gertler's tragedies starkly revealed the fear underlying the social gaiety that summer of 1939. "It is so dark everywhere—people live under such a strain. But love is the answer I'm sure," May concluded. "It *abides.*" Kot disagreed. On the evening she left for Belgium, he told her she should not have come. No American could understand the agony of England, whose wounds from the Great War had scarcely healed. She had come like a tourist on holiday. She had been brutally tactless.

Who am I? wondered May, falling easily into French with the Limbosches and the Peacocks. Belgian May seemed a different being from English May, American May different from both. Her American friends thought her European; her European friends, a spoiled American. She felt spoiled as she noted margarine on the Limbosch table, no meat except an occasional slice of ham, Aunty Lino and Raymond doing the chores instead of a cleaning woman. Yet living on the edge of the abyss had stiffened their spines.

She sailed for home August 23. Kot had recanted his harsh words, but a "sad, kind and *final* letter from Julian," who could not accept a platonic relationship, made the distance between her and England seem wider than the ocean. Ironically, she had never honored him as she did now; it was impossible to think of life entirely without him. But especially without Juliette. "Please do not let me go altogether out of your life," she begged, "even though I seem now so terribly far away and incapable of understanding because I am not there. . . . I do love you and wish I had some great beauty to lay in your hands. . . ."

On September 1 Germany invaded Poland; two days later England and France declared war. The Europe that May loved was closed to her indefinitely.

CHAPTER 10

My America: 1940–1944

George was so depressed and weary that the Sartons drove to Florida to restore him, returning to Cambridge early in January 1940. May had discovered that a third novel, *Fire in a Mirror*, still was not right: she was skating on the surface instead of crashing through to realities, experiencing such "fears and doubts" that writing seemed "an illness rather than a profession."

Julian came to the States to see Aldous in California and drum up support for War Aims, a group dedicated to helping Britain through the crisis. Though he had sworn they could not be friends, he and May spent four days together and the miracle happened. "I really felt he was happy as I was and that somehow all this hell we have been through *hasn't* been just destructive," she wrote Juliette. ". . . I feel a *well* of gratitude and deep joy to you and to him, and as if a great peril in which one's soul was in the balance has somehow been passed."

Grace Dudley had returned to Boston. Her reunion with her husband had not lasted, but that didn't make Grace available, since she was "absolutely enclosed in her love for him, like a nun or a saint." Grace made her feel "peaceful"—a new usage, meaning "resigned to not having an affair." But she was lonely. Though still a friend, Edith Kennedy was off bounds, and could heartlessly report, after an evening with the Sartons, that her sons had found Mabel "marvellous" and George "such a charming guy." This reminded May of a visit from Jean Tatlock, currently studying for a Ph.D. in psychology at Berkeley. Tall, slim, and stunning, Jean had walked straight into the arms of Mabel and George, with whom she'd lived the year between high school and college. She was very left fringe; had even got her lover, J. Robert Oppenheimer, interested in radical causes. She wasn't much impressed with May's two books of poems or the novel. May was stunned. After all that passion, all those protestations of love!

May's own life seemed scattered, purposeless. She was teaching classes in creative writing at the Stuart School, had agreed to direct more plays for Concord Academy. Still paying for her Grace Daly infatuation, she sent another one hundred dollars to Roswell Hawley. Professionally, she felt stagnant. She complained of her neglect as a poet to Louis Untermeyer; while at a beer party at Jean Stafford's, Richard Eberhart, "a fat boy who teaches at St. Marks and another of these 'Do you know so and so' climbers," made her sick with envy because he had written one wonderful poem, "The Groundhog." But then contact with living poets terrified and depressed her. "I haven't *touched* for a month any part of myself which is poetry or silence," she recorded the end of February.

In March she fell in love with "V.L.," probably a teacher at Concord Academy; but V.L. was cool when May read her the poems she'd inspired. "An interesting idea," mused May after a disappointing session, "—that one has no *right* to lay the burden of articulate intense love on someone unless they want it." To Kot she wrote, "I have been going through a sort of salutary personal crisis—salutary because to be in love is to be alive . . . a crisis because it is founded as usual upon *impossibility*—a woman—and can have no end." By the end of March she dismissed V.L. as "like rayon."

Gloom was thick in the Sarton household: Mabel white and exhausted, George grim because *Isis* had been suspended again. "It is really quite difficult to live here," she confessed to Kot. She began sending out prospectuses to colleges all over the United States, offering herself as a lecturer on poetry. By mid-May she had fifteen invitations from "queer out of the way colleges" in Tennessee, Texas, and New Mexico. If ships had been crossing the Atlantic, she would have taken one. But Europe was closed to her. Open, America.

She sent the finished novel to Houghton Mifflin (who at last had published a good book, May thought: *The Heart Is a Lonely Hunter* by someone named Carson McCullers). Her novel seemed "dead and unreal"; the thought of the critics sickened her, but that, she realized, was because she lacked an "inner *core* of conviction." When Houghton Mifflin told her to put more sex in the novel, she blew up and took it to Knopf; Blanche Knopf turned it down "with Spanish compliments." Back at Houghton Mifflin, Ferris Greenslet said it needed "heightening" but thought it worth the struggle.

At the end of June, all three Sartons left for the Straitsmouth Inn at Rockport, though George would commute to Harvard daily. The minute they arrived, Mabel started making a garden; George energetically spaded in manure, realizing that in petunias and snapdragons Mabel sublimated her furies. He wore a white hat like an inverted bowl against the sun and smoked cigars in a long holder to discourage mosquitoes. Evenings they sat on the porch wrapped in rugs, lulled into amity by the surf. But May's friends followed her to Rockport. "Yesterday I woke up and burst into tears just at the idea that there would be no solitude in the day." For May the conflict between compulsively giving herself to people and needing solitude was insoluble. She saw it as the perennial conflict between life and art, without realizing that she needed eighty percent more "life" than most artists.

Shortly after hearing that Lugné-Poë, her dear old Éléphant, had died in Paris that July, May fell in love. The woman was Margaret Foote Hawley, a professional portrait painter, the sister of Roswell. Margaret was sixty-three, with short, wispy hair, great charm and energy. They became lovers, and poems came to May again, among them the fine tribute to Lugné-Poë, "What the Old Man Said." When Margaret left Rockport mid-August, May's letters pursued. "Darling . . . I am in a state of grace and that is thanks to you. . . . There is nothing about this that is not right including the fact that I am so much younger. . . . Let me know where you are. Poems like to have a destination for their flight." She now existed in a "strangely exalted state," steeped herself in Yeats, poured out poems, telegraphed, dreamed of Margaret coming to Cambridge ("Mummy would adore to have you. She feels almost the same way about you as I do"). She was alive again, empowered, drinking deep of the "secret life-giving river."

Margaret was older, wiser. "We must be free," she told her ardent lover. May reassured her. She knew her insistence had destroyed her relationship with Edith Kennedy; this would be different. Margaret must write only if she felt like it, and feel no responsibility. "I suppose the reason I am absolutely not afraid of giving myself away is that way down deep I have an implacable core that can't be given away or possessed," she wrote her, "and that makes me invulnerable." She would begin her lecture trip in Washington October 2 and wanted to see Margaret in New York on the way: "We might have dinner and a long peaceful evening." The stay in Margaret's studio apartment proved so peaceful that May sang all the way to Washington, contemplating the love poems she would write for her Muse.

George had bought his daughter a Mercury convertible for the lecture trip, which would take her through the South to the West Coast and back through the Midwest. Although May intended to earn money (George had cut her to fifty dollars a month), she had already proposed a travel book of poetry and prose to Greenslet, who liked the idea. Charleston, New Orleans, the southern plantations, the deserts, the Rockies, and San Francisco would unlock the spiritual secret of America to a foreign poet. She also wanted to promote poetry—including her own. Her lecture, "Poetry as a Dynamic Force," argued that poetry was the spiritual force of the nation; poets, the nation's conscience. She intended to wake up young people to the necessity of examining and evaluating their lives through poetry. She intended to wake people up to May Sarton.

The trip would have killed a person of less vitality. A few colleges let her off easily with one lecture and a cocktail party; most demanded lectures, poetry classes, roundtables, and private conferences with students, as well as faculty luncheons, teas, dinners, cocktail parties, and evening poetry readings. In a morning she might drive one hundred miles to reach the next campus; at night, after fulfilling her obligations, she hauled out her typewriter to write poems, travel impressions, and dozens of letters, then fell into bed with the increasingly ugly war news. And because she needed American material, she worked sightseeing into her days, driving to Monticello and in West Virginia exploring a mining town. She talked to farmers, people in drugstores, hitchhikers, hotel keepers.

Only occasionally did she crack. At Guilford College in North Carolina she was given a cheerless cell, seated at dinner without a drink with people who had never heard of her, and, when she pulled out her Luckies, told that "Guilford girls don't smoke." She burst into tears. Questions like "As a Belgian, what do you think of Hitler?" and "Why didn't Belgium fight?" also provoked tears and fury.

Not surprisingly, she found many of the students apathetic, their poetry weak and unimaginative. On the other hand, she discovered that she was a knockout speaker. Her strong, classic beauty magnetized people. She galvanized audiences with her energy and conviction, her physical élan. Her powerful contralto voice irresistibly conveyed both authority and deep feeling. She read poetry magnificently, her own best of all—not in the "American idiom" pioneered by William Carlos Williams, but with an elastic vitality that freed traditional form. She radiated, she inspired. Female English teachers fell in love at first sight. Colleges felt her a Presence. "I have been dead for two years and now I am alive and useful again," she wrote Kot joyously from Black Mountain College in

Dynamic May lecturing on "Poetry as a Dynamic Force" in the early 1940s

North Carolina. "I am being used to the top of my energies and bent, till I am utterly exhausted and it is wonderful. . . . People come at all hours and sit on my bed. . . . I am seeing so much that my eyes burn all the time and my mind bursts like a rocket. . . . I feel so busy inside it's wonderful."

She found time to miss Margaret Hawley. "I have saved $50.00. Will you come to Asheville. . . . I'll sit for you if you want to do experiments but will have to work myself two or three hours a day—and we could go for drives—*and* laugh—and make love—and sleep." Poetry had earned the fifty dollars: "It must be spent for love," she coaxed, enclosing train schedules.

"Terribly sorry but I can't break off work now," Margaret wired. May was bitterly disappointed; considered flying to New York, only "I'm afraid of what my father would say"; pleaded again that Margaret come south. She refused. "I never really believed that you would come," May replied, "knew in my heart that you *couldn't*, but had fun imagining and planning it anyway." But the idea of a person who would not desert work for love chilled her. She wondered whether there really could be room for her, or anyone, in Margaret Hawley's life.

She left for Charleston with the news that FDR had been re-elected and Coventry and London savagely bombed. Savannah; Chattanooga; Memphis; Mobile; Natchez; New Orleans; Denton, Texas; Colorado Springs; Denver. An audience of six hundred, an audience of six. Attacks of colitis. Migraine. But on December 9, high in the mountains, she came to the wide open bowl where the adobe village of Santa Fe lay in a purple and blood-red moon landscape patched with white snow. Nothing had prepared her for this vastness, this impersonality, this exhilaration.

She had come to Santa Fe on the strength of a letter from the poet Haniel Long praising *The Single Hound* and a subsequent invitation to break her lecture trip in Santa Fe over Christmas. The minute she walked into Alice and Haniel's adobe home with its heavy, dark furniture, books, jars of flowers, and huge open fire smelling of piñon, she felt spiritually at home. She talked and talked and drank cups and cups of tea and felt as though she had known the tall, lean poet and his "absurdly like a dove" wife forever.

She stayed with the Longs' friend Lura Conkey in her house on Canyon Road. On December 13, she drove to Albuquerque to lecture at the University of New Mexico. In the audience was a Frenchwoman of forty with a "camellia-white face, clear brown eyes, a high pure forehead and tender mouth." When she introduced herself afterwards, May heard an accent like Juliette's, doing the same delicious things to words. Marie Armengaud had come to Santa Fe hoping to cure her tuberculosis. She taught French in Albuquerque, had a house in the hills behind Santa Fe. May fell in love.

"My only booking in Cal. has fallen through," May wrote Mabel and George, "and if I can get the schools around here to give me one or two lectures I may just settle through January. I long to stay." She left Lura Conkey's house to lodge for eighteen dollars a week with Agnes Sims, a tall, boyish artist with an endearing sense of humor whom she'd met through the Longs. Weekends she shifted to Marie Armengaud's house— "It reminds me of 'spending the night' with Tig [Barbara Runkle] or Miggy [Margaret Bouton] when I was in school," she wrote home with the sad, necessary deception.

Edith Kennedy had accused May of sexual and emotional promiscuity; Juliette Huxley had called her *"un coeur multiple."* May temperamentally could not love one person long. Lacking a sense of self-worth, she needed the constant stimulation of falling in love, often with qualities in the beloved that proved illusory. Love also focussed her and made the

*Portrait of Marie
Armengaud in
Santa Fe*

poems come. That's why she never wanted to be the passive beloved. Like
Don Juan, she needed to conquer. She would be in love with Marie until
Marie too no longer inspired her.

"My heart beats fast because of the altitude and because I am happy,"
she wrote Margaret, eventually spelling it out plainly: "I am very much
absorbed in the discovery and love of Marie Armengaud. . . . You are a
very remarkable woman because I can write you this. The important
friendships are always more or less passionate with me as you know." May
was a more faithful friend than lover; though the romance was essentially
over, she continued to write Margaret affectionately for the next ten
years.

Christmas, as usual, generated a frenzy of activity. She mailed greetings
and packages to dozens of people—or, lacking an address, sent the pack-
ages to Miutsie to mail, rather a chore since Miutsie was sending the novel

to publishers as well as shipping to May the mittens, scarves, socks, gloves, nail scissors, and books she requested. Social invitations poured in: she was immensely popular with the artistic crowd. On Christmas Eve she drank hot buttered rum with friends, then drove through snow to San Felipe for the Indian dances in the Catholic church. Christmas telegrams and presents to open (though no word from Jean-Do or Julian)—Millay's poems from Miutsie, Swiss handkerchiefs from Bonbon, a red cigarette case from Margaret Hawley; then Christmas dinner with Alice and Haniel Long. She now intended staying in Santa Fe through February.

The new year, 1941, brought a severe letter about finances from George, who had been worried about his Carnegie Institute appointment ever since the new director told him, "Of course, Sarton, to me your work is irrelevant." "Dearest Daddy," May replied guiltily, "I was very glad to have all your news of the financial situation as I have been thinking for some time that I should begin putting in to the family budget instead of taking out. . . . I realize that you have been the most generous of Daddys in supporting me so long and making possible by so doing my work in peace. But I have it definitely in mind to become independent within the next five years." George could not have been enchanted by the five-year plan or the announcement that she must return to Santa Fe in summer to "see the landscape in a new light." And she was broke, as usual—perhaps money worries brought on three wretched weeks of colitis, even though Margaret Hawley sent a check. Yet by the end of January she had a batch of new lecture engagements for the spring. And she *was* writing poems— too many; she couldn't stop.

She finally left Santa Fe on March 16. In Springfield, Illinois, she opened the *Atlantic Monthly* to two of her poems, "Charleston Plantations" and "In Texas." In St. Charles she burst into tears when told that Virginia Woolf had committed suicide. "It matters a great deal that she is dead just now," she wrote Kot from Chicago. "She was one of the few people delicately and persistently establishing relationships, making a *wholeness* however much was destroyed. . . . For three days . . . I have sat in this hotel room above this loud boisterous and cruel city, thinking of her. It is like a hole that nothing will fill. And O Kot, I had so hoped I would someday do something she would like. . . ." Virginia had definitively eluded her. In Detroit she heard that Marie Armengaud was back in a sanatorium. And then she was back in the loved and hated house that was both sanctuary and prison.

Rather embarrassingly, Rosalind Greene gave a dance on May's twenty-ninth birthday for her and Francesca, a not-so-subtle hint that it was time she got paired off, while at home George's "You should get married" still hung in the air. And the money problem was everlasting. She, who signed herself "Your little pigeon," "Your little Easter bunny," was indeed still dependent.

They went again to Rockport. "This has been a hellish two weeks," she wrote Kot July 13, sick with "self-hatred and self-despair. . . . My book of American poems in which I believe, has just been turned down by [Houghton Mifflin] with the acid comment that it would only interest my friends, in other words it is 'amateur.' " She had felt her America poems less poetically pure than the early ones, yet a step forward because at last she'd got out of the prison of self; ironically, Greenslet felt they had little value except as private experience. But she hadn't only failed with the poems; she had failed with Marie, whom "unfortunately" she had seduced and abandoned. "I say unfortunately because it is simply a nightmare," she told Edith Kennedy. "And I am incapable of love. In order to love well one cannot be in such a state of confusion and despair. It is a wholly selfish state. I have failed her imaginatively in a thousand ways. . . ."

Though they couldn't cure her "forever of impatience and ambition," reading Flaubert's letters proved comforting, because Flaubert too wrestled with the precarious balance between life and art. "I am at peace," she could tell Kot as summer drew to a close. She had twenty-six American poems she considered worthy; the rest would come. But she would not send the finished manuscript to Houghton Mifflin. "I cannot explain it but I feel they are through with me and I am through with them."

She returned that fall to the Stuart School. Without a college degree, full-time teaching was almost impossible; yet full-time teaching would be hell. And she loathed the thought of a "commercial" job. The problem seemed typically insoluble.

With the bombing of the fleet at Pearl Harbor on December 7, the United States finally entered the war. May had been almost too embarrassed at America's neutrality to write English and Belgian friends; now overnight she felt the whole country exchange guilt for the zest of unified struggle. December also brought Julian to the States again. He showed up at Channing Place for a Christmas Eve party May threw for "all the waifs, refugees and old friends who might not have anywhere to go." On Christmas Day May drove him into Vermont, where they stayed at a village inn. "I really had a lovely time with Julian," she wrote Juliette. "He has so much gusto and is so *dear* and appreciative of whatever there is to see or do." Julian still wanted sex; yet, as May told his wife, he really "didn't seem to mind my un-satisfactory-ness too much."

. . .

In the new year, the family closed about her like a fist. She brooded upon the "queer pain" of a child's relation to its parents. "I really think I shall *die* every time I leave home and yet at the same time I am relieved," she wrote Juliette. "When I am here as now there is something hermetically sealed about my life. I am in a way untouchable. I am quite absorbed in my parents and that is of course the charm of our life. We have wonderful conversations at table and I fight with my father and we gleam at each other across the table and each have our work. But still there is a constant awareness of the umbilical cord. I couldn't for instance *possibly* have an affair while living at home. It would be spiritually impossible." It was perhaps no accident that during these months she conceived an idea for a book about modern martyrs.

Trying to feel useful, she volunteered for motor transport service and enrolled in a first-aid course, contemplated factory work, sent out feelers for another lecture tour. She could not rid herself of the shame of not earning her living; she had made only $250 in 1941. If she could write one good poem, her soul might be saved; but she could not. Fatigue, irritability, inertia, depression increasingly tormented her. Then one day at lunch George announced that their 1942 income tax would be three thousand dollars. They would have to give up Channing Place and May must support herself. "For me it is good," she wrote Juliette. "I shall simply *have* to find a job."

In New York she looked for part-time teaching. She stayed with Gertrude Macy, Katharine Cornell's stage manager, whom she had known since the theatre days, and Gert tried to seduce her and failed. Back in Cambridge, however, May flooded Gert with poems and letters, while telling her "your physical attractions aren't overpowering." Yet May was willing to rendezvous. Gert was coming to Boston with Kit's production of *Candida*—"Could you spend the night at my hotel?" May agreed. Gert found May ill, nervous, and unhappy. What Gert hoped for did not, apparently, happen. "We layed a lot of foundation—more is needed," she wrote May back in New York. "I do love you and in a nice way."

But May didn't want to be loved by Gert. She was sick in mind and body. Finally a doctor diagnosed simple colitis, prescribed a sensible diet, and sent her to the hospital for tests. There she was told she was on the verge of a nervous collapse and ordered to rest. She did not. "Near to tears all the time," she recorded on June 17. "Smoking too much." Two days in the hospital followed. Then the ever-loyal Anne Thorp offered her country house for the ordered six weeks' recuperation.

"I have been worrying very much about your illness," George wrote her there, "and the more so because it awoke reminiscences of my own youth." Lonely and disillusioned, he had cured himself with work, for which he expected no reward but self-satisfaction. "I do not know to what extent you have found your own path. As soon as you find it, are sure of it, and expect nothing more but to follow it quietly, unobtrusively, you will be all right again."

"The difficulty in a nutshell," May replied, "is that I know *very well* what I am and want to do: I am a poet BUT it is not possible to earn a living by being one." At least her collapse temporarily relieved her guilt about not working. In fact, she guessed that her sickness had been a revolt against the idea of finding a job. "It is clear that if I teach full-time I shall not have strength for anything," she told Koteliansky. "I don't *want to,* Kot. The idea revolts me, like being put in prison. . . . Anyway I cannot solve it now for a few months—that is a relief!" Instead she read Henry James, helped Anne's German-refugee couple shell peas and make jam, tried to rest and cut down on cigarettes.

On September 18, the peerless Edith Kennedy died from complications of an enlarged heart. She was only fifty. "She was the touchstone for all ideas, the perfect sounding-board, and not to me alone but to innumerable others," May wrote Juliette. ". . . She can die but we cannot do without her. There is the enormous human egotism. I felt it once before, when Virginia Woolf died, a sort of *rage.* Virginia Woolf, Edith, Lugné-Poë, Jean Dominique, Kot, you. These, in the absence of God, were my gods and three are dead, one lost in the hell of silence."

That November she set out on a lecture tour that included Buffalo, five small Ohio colleges, Bethany College in West Virginia, and Briarcliff Junior College in New York. No car this time: she had sold the Mercury to buy war bonds. In Bethany, she stayed with Florence Hoaglund, the head of the English department, "a great large *sun* of a woman" whom she had liked on her previous visit. One benefit of lecture tours was the opportunity they provided for love affairs. Realizing that there was "something dangerous" in her terrible compulsion to conquer, she nonetheless seduced Florence; and Florence, who had given up hope of personal fulfillment, fell deeply in love. As May reported to Miutsie, "It is very peaceful here."

A severe attack of colitis coincided with this seduction, caused by guilt, the renewed necessity of finding a job, and her dread of home. In fact she did not return immediately to Cambridge, but went to Katrine Greene's apartment in New York. There, after talks with Kit Cornell, Eva Le Gallienne, Gert Macy, and the poet Muriel Rukeyser, whom she had met through friends, she decided to return to New York immediately after Christmas to look for a job. But there were other reasons for wanting to be in New York. Florence Hoaglund was flying up to stay at the Murray Hill Hotel with her. And she was decidedly attracted to Muriel.

Florence fed the still-queasy May breakfast in bed, read to her, patiently waited to be loved. She left New York on January 3. A few days later, May and Muriel were lovers.

May considered Muriel Rukeyser the most promising contemporary woman poet. "A great dynamic girl" with a large round face like Kuan-yin, the Chinese goddess of mercy, she wore odd, often dirty, clothes and no girdle. She seemed to live at a pitch of conflict which had to be resolved in action. She stimulated May tremendously: "It has been a long long time since anyone has entered my life with such seeds in their hands." Muriel's most potent "seeds" were powerful feelings expressed in powerful language. Not since Jean Tatlock had a woman lyricized May's "white wonderful flaming face" or, in her poetry, "that delicate wiry line on which you have always built." Or turned a too-brief lovemaking into literature: "That was a brief and flaring and bitter time. Snatches of time, and sweetness flowing across the moment, across the flesh. . . . At the glimpses of your wish I sprang to myself, and the room flared into your face and your throat and your body. . . . You burned on my life, not like fire that leaves a burn, but like some pain of burning that leaves fire. Darling . . . find me when you are ready."

To Juliette she tried to justify being fed by two spoons. Florence was far away. "I can see her I suppose for three or four weeks a year at most. And O Juliette what a hunger there is in me for continuity and permanence, for peace and returning at night, for what marriage should mean." Yet she felt terrible lying to Florence. Her betrayal would cut Florence "at the root."

Emboldened by distance and Mabel's despair at leaving Channing Place, May tackled George that January.

> We do not need to decide about an apartment—Mother knows more about the cost of living than you—and I am not at all sure

The poet Muriel Rukeyser, "a great dynamic girl"

that an apartment is the solution. The Browns pay $75.00 for 3 *miserable* rooms. We would need four at least. We would have to have someone come in to get the dinner (that is Mother's *lowest* ebb of the day and I know she couldn't do it). I am in favor of looking for a small *house* in an *unfashionable* part of Cambridge . . . and of having a maid. . . . Dear Daddy, I know you will do what is best—and this is not meant as criticism but only to beg you to leave some of the responsibility to Mother. She will find a way (when she knows exactly what she can have to spend). *She always has.*

At the same time she defended her dependency: she would not take just *any* job.

She interviewed for teaching jobs; refused them. In February *The New Yorker* sent a check for thirty dollars for a poem, "Navigator." Muriel was currently working in the poster division of the Office of War Information (and being investigated by the FBI for left-wing activities); she was trying to pull strings for May. May herself was often sick—flu, sore throat, colitis, tonsillitis, trench mouth, heavy colds—though she was seeing people constantly: Willem Van Loon (in the Army), Theo Pleadwell, Margaret English, Gert Macy, Le Gallienne, Katrine Greene, Polly Starr, Margaret Hawley, and her new friend William (Bill) Theo Brown, a painter, gay, in the Army. Finally in March she landed a job with the East and West Association, an organization headed by Pearl Buck whose purpose was to promote relations between the United States and China. Then OWI wanted her as a scriptwriter for its film unit. This appealed to her more than East and West—besides, she was terribly jealous of the renowned Buck. She began a script for OWI on the Tennessee Valley Authority project, and in April flew to Tennessee for work on the TVA film. "Everyone is amazed that I got the job—it is a plum." She assured her parents that OWI was a good place to meet men.

As a salaried employee, she celebrated her thirty-first birthday more happily than in recent years. Muriel arranged a treasure hunt for small packages, with cryptic quotations from May's poems attached to each. George gave her a book of war poems; Miutsie, money for a coat and gloves, which she wore to see Ethel Barrymore in *The Corn Is Green*. Her work on the TVA film was going well: "I like more and more the associate producer, Philip Dunne. . . . He is inspiring and easy to work with . . . a good man." She was assigned another movie script, *Chicago*. Yet how frustrating still to be begging George for money: OWI paychecks were irregular. And she was constantly on the move, shifting from the Murray Hill to the Hotel Albert to the Brevoort (when she wasn't at Muriel's apartment on East Tenth), all of which cost money.

In August May and Muriel vacationed at Newcastle, New Hampshire, a boat-building and lobstering town three bridges away from Portsmouth in the bay. They had the top floor of Mr. Amazeen's lobster house, and Mr. Amazeen, who lived across the street, boiled pots of beans and unlimited lobsters for them. Mr. Amazeen was salty, wise, slow of speech; despised Maine dwellers, ignored daylight saving time. May and Muriel took long walks, rowed about the islands in the river, lay on their stomachs in the sun reading E. M. Forster.

Back in New York in September, May took a studio apartment near Muriel. "The two things I really need are the studio couch and the black Chinese cabinet from my study, and the little low black table beside the couch. . . . The thing I will need eventually is an armchair and a standing lamp. I am sending a separate list of all the items to be sent and I'll let you know exactly when. . . ." George lifted his eyes and prayed for the one hundred thousandth time that his daughter might manage her own affairs,

though it was Mabel who would do all the packing and shipping. Miut-
sie responded with a typically martyred letter contrived to make May feel
both guilty and resentful of George:

> Do forgive me for not writing—it has been "one of those
> weeks." . . . I can't even remember each day's tasks & they are not
> worth recounting but must fall into the past & be "sunk without a
> trace." The great thing is that we have heat when we want it—I
> know how to work the furnace & thermostat . . . so that if any-
> thing went wrong (which it never has) I could shut *everything* off
> in perfect safety. As dear Daddums is absolutely no good in an
> emergency I feel glad to know this. Several days I got absolutely no
> rest at all—I have only once sat down at my desk all week till now!
> & in bed at night & in early morn. I have not been able even to
> read intelligently. But I am over the top of this hell & today I
> refused to ask anyone to dinner, & on the contrary asked Daddy to
> take me to the Square, which he did very cheerfully. . . . This
> morning I got up late because I felt sleepy—& had to hurry
> because of the organ concert at 9:30 which has become [Daddy's]
> compulsion. It is a pity for I do long for one lazy morning but
> please be sure not to mention it, or it will cause a far worse situa-
> tion. . . . I don't like to feel I must *always* have breakfast ready in
> time for it—Daddy is so kind: if I tell him, he will say, "Well—just
> don't get the breakfast," not realizing that I can't really rest, when
> I hear his urgent feet on the stairs nor can I deprive him of his
> breakfast. . . . No, it is just a thing I must adapt myself to. . . .

Practically, May was applying for a Guggenheim Fellowship and buy-
ing bonds when she could. Inspired by the pianist Myra Hess's free
wartime concerts, she had persuaded a number of famous poets to read at
the New York Public Library. One hundred people were turned away at
the first event on October 19, when Marianne Moore, in a huge black
hat, delivered a witty, profound, eccentric lecture. William Rose Benét,
big and virile, with a good voice, disappointed May: his superficial invok-
ing of God was "a shame for both poetry and for God." At following
events William Carlos Williams was "nervous, a bit showy-off, dynamic
and rapid and rather like fireworks"; W. H. Auden seemed negative;
Horace Gregory, strangely beautiful, young, and suffering. Drinks with
Gregory afterwards was good for Muriel, who had been badly hurt by an
attack in the *Partisan Review* inspired by Delmore Schwartz. Thank God,
thought May, she'd never been socked in the guts like that.

Yet that was the trouble. Muriel was a somebody, had poets and editors interested in her, while May, though charming everyone from Lillian Hellman to Marianne Moore to Bennett Cerf, was not taken seriously by the literary establishment. Insecure and jealous, May, however, overestimated Rukeyser's security as a poet. She belonged to no literary clique, no poetic school, had no powerful critics on her side—Louise Bogan, for instance, refused to review her in *The New Yorker*. What Muriel had was faith in her poetic vision.

May could not compete with or satisfy Muriel as a lover. For May, sexual satisfaction was secondary to emotional exaltation. One orgasm per evening satisfied her. Muriel liked a lot of sex with a variety of people. More than once, May sat in the hall while Muriel entertained a lover behind the locked door. But she stuck, because she needed Muriel's warm strength, while Muriel stuck because "I love you, I'll always love you, May, whatever."

Inevitably, May grew disenchanted with OWI, where everyone wanted a finger in her scriptic pie; by January 1944, she'd had enough. "I am going to use every means to be able to do my own work," she told Juliette. "And then whenever necessary economically take a job for awhile. But I am simply *determined* not to get caught up into a standard of living that has to be 'kept up' at the expense of the spirit." She wanted to get back to poems and a new novel about the Limbosches.

That January Mrs. Field, Letty's mother, called with the shocking news that Jean Tatlock had drugged and drowned herself. Jean's father, a professor of medieval literature at Berkeley, had found her with her head in the bathtub. Mrs. Field was sure Jean's trouble had begun with Letty's death, but May knew better. Jean's affair with Robert Oppenheimer could not erase her lesbian guilt. She had left a note: "I wanted to live and to give and I got paralysed somehow. I tried like Hell to understand and couldn't. At least I could take away the burden of a paralysed soul from a fighting world." Of the three "Snabs"—Letty, Jean, and May—only May was left. To May the awful thing about Jean's death was its humiliating posture—kneeling.

Life in New York was breaking up. Muriel sent her new book of poems to her publisher and left for California on holiday. "Now it only remains for me to do something!" May wrote Mabel and George, whose monumental work on the history of fourteenth-century science was finally in galleys. George offered a remarkable solution to his daughter's insolvency: "It occurred to me that when Muriel comes back from California & you

Mabel and George in the garden of 5 Channing Place

are tired with New York, the best solution would be for *all* of us—Muriel included—to live here. Cambridge is an ideal place for a writer—for it is sufficiently quiet, isolated & provincial—& yet all the resources of a great city are within easy reach." George's cordiality was matched by OWI's farewells: "Phil [Dunne] praised my work very much and was altogether very warm and kind." Then she heard she'd gotten a Guggenheim; then that George had decided to buy 5 Channing Place. They would own their first house since Wondelgem.

A long period of frustration was coming to an end. Back in Cambridge, she threw herself into the Limbosch novel, *The Bridge of Years*. She was reading Turgenev with delight: "so human and warm and pure, without being sugary. This is what I would hope to do in my new book." Cambridge seemed "very beautiful and precious" to her now; and after all, there were "no better, deeper nor more loveable people in the world" than her father and mother. She didn't miss New York: she really hated the literary crowd. She was working on a long war poem. She had a new agent, Diarmuid Russell. And conspiring with her contentment, the war in Europe seemed to be drawing to a close with the invasion of Normandy on June 6 and the liberation of Paris in August.

Vacationing at Folly Cove near Gloucester, May and Muriel knew what the knot of flowers at the foot of a statue of Joan of Arc meant. May wept, thinking not only of France but of Belgium and the friends who had been silent so long. Kot had not written for more than a year. And Julian, fired as director of the zoo but working feverishly at a dozen war projects, had had a nervous breakdown. She still felt English and Belgian friends the real ones, as did Mabel, who one day sobbed, "I want to go home." But perhaps reunion was near.

May had a new book of poems, *The Lion and the Rose,* going the round of publishers. Diarmuid was very pleased with part two of *The Bridge of Years.* And just when she was reduced to borrowing money from Muriel and Margaret Hawley again, the Cabot Fund awarded her $1,000 for poetry. By the end of the year she was on the final third of the novel. She had two poems in *Best Poems of 1943,* and *Poetry* had taken "Sestina: For Friends in England," "Homage to Flanders," and "To the Living."

Only her emotional life seemed balked. Though she and Muriel were still lovers, and occasionally Margaret Hawley, and Ella Winter, the widow of Lincoln Steffens, who let her "be free in bed," and though the undivided affections of Marie Armengaud and of Florence Hoaglund were hers for the taking, she was profoundly dissatisfied. "I wish that I could marry now," she wrote Juliette. "It is time and for the first time in my life I think I am ready *inside.*"

CHAPTER 11

Judy: 1945–1947

Finished in January 1945, *The Bridge of Years* sets the story of the Limbosch family against a political background, 1919–1940, charged with socialist, nationalist, liberal, communist, and fascist tensions. After struggling with two unpublishable novels, May wrote *The Bridge of Years* with relative ease; it was a subject she had known intimately since childhood. Its completion coincided with the first letters from the Limbosches and Jean Dominique since the war: a propitious sign.

Contact re-established, May immediately began sending packages of tinned meat, soap, coffee, and tea to the Limbosches and Jean-Do, dunning her friends for contributions. The Limbosches accepted the largesse coolly. "It is extraordinary how very much more anxious you seem to be in America," Céline had written Mabel in 1940. "Is it innocence on our part?" Now Céline sent thanks for chocolate, ham, and nutmeg, but discouraged further parcels. Kot too growled over the packages of jam and tea May plied him with; indeed, he seemed to have shut her out of his life. Some Europeans were too proud to accept American charity gracefully.

Stifled at home, May left on March 4 for Santa Fe on Guggenheim money—Santa Fe, the holy land of poems. Not only Marie Armengaud but the exhilaration of that austere country had inspired her. In Chicago, she was reminded powerfully of Virginia Woolf. Four years earlier when she'd heard of Woolf's suicide, "the city died." Now, as lines came, she found Woolf again:

Wherever I looked was love,
Wherever I went I had presents in my hands.
Wherever I went, I recognized you. . . .
I send you love forward into the past.

In Santa Fe she had a sunny, whitewashed room with mountain views in Mrs. Ricketson's boardinghouse at 940 Acequia Madre. Other occupants included a police dog and "a very nice English teacher on sabbatical from Simmons College," who was friendly but did "not impinge and make demands." May immediately sought out Haniel and Alice Long, Lura Conkey, and Agnes Sims, as well as Dorothy Stewart, with whom she drank Cinzano and watched the sun set over snowy mountains.

Marie Armengaud was more difficult. May knew very well she had hurt this sensitive woman and caused her periods of severe depression. Not to see Marie, however, would be to admit her guilt. May counted on her charm to heal the wound. "I have seen Marie Armengaud twice and am greatly relieved to find that everything is really all right and we can now be good friends. . . ." Not quite. May believed everyone had her resilience. Everything was not all right; they did not become good friends.

Farrar and Rinehart did not find the characters of *The Bridge of Years* sufficiently sympathetic, a verdict May justifiably dismissed. The novel went on to Knopf; but meanwhile Santa Fe had worked its spell. The "poems are coming," she wrote home, "only I am afraid really of doing too much too fast out of sheer excitement and I must try to be quiet— and go slow." By the end of March she was "in real *full tide,*" not only in the midst of a long poem, "My Sisters, O My Sisters," but writing a play about the French Resistance. Every morning she woke "simply on fire," and every morning she read the previous day's work to the nice, appreciative English teacher.

Judith Matlack was forty-seven, a Quaker of old New England stock. Her beautiful, flirtatious sisters, Barbara and Constance, had always eclipsed the quiet, serious, intelligent Judith. She was single, not from choice but from shyness coupled with irony and detachment. Her Quakerism showed itself in restraint: one glass of sherry before dinner, serviceable clothes, silence rather than outspoken anger. She was a slender, handsome woman with dark brown eyes. Under the reserve lay humor and good sense. Her students adored her.

Soon May and Judy were cooking delicious little dinners and having long talks by the fire. Meanwhile, Muriel Rukeyser had come to understand the impossibility of loving May. For a year May had avoided sex

Judith Matlack and May in Santa Fe, 1945

with her by pleading, "I must be free to marry"; had even named a mutual friend, Alfred Marshak, a geneticist and political radical, as a prospective husband. But, as Muriel discovered, it was always another woman. "Last summer was made more of a Hell than it needed to be by those daily letters from Marie and your never really being honest with me about her," Muriel wrote her now. ". . . You have always had someone *in reserve* if things didn't go well with whomever you were with at the moment, just as you once told me that you make two or three dates for dinner and then break the two which at the last minute you decide are less what you want. . . . It is really not much good to insist that you love someone and at the same time be insisting to someone else that you love them in the same way." Hardest for Muriel was May's refusal to level with her. "You have always been in a white rage of contempt that I should even ask the question of what was happening. You accuse me of writing painful letters but you never answer them except to point out how miserable you are. That is avoiding the issue."

"We are going through a strange time because I suddenly decided that I must have this time to myself and I fear I have hurt [Muriel's] feelings," May told William Theo Brown. Her fear was justified. At the end of April Muriel was considering a blond New Zealand engineer; in July she became the wife of the painter Glyn Collins. A few weeks later the marriage was annulled on the grounds that Mr. Collins was psychotic. "I feel sad about her," May confessed to Bill, "because I really can't help her—I think I only make her sad for the past and there is no going back."

If May felt some guilt at abandoning her lovers, she felt no guilt at falling in love. "It always seems like an angel coming in, you know. It always seems so beautiful and right that I never think, 'Oh, I mustn't do this, it's wrong.' It always seems to me absolutely the most beautiful thing that ever happened."

This new angel had one great advantage: she lived in Cambridge. May's affairs had often collapsed because of distance. Still the emotionally dependent child, she could not leave her parents. But now the perfect solution offered: living with Judy Matlack, she would be out from under the repressive roof but still next door. May considered that her love made an old-maid schoolteacher burst into flower. But Judy would spring May from Channing Place.

The blow of Franklin Delano Roosevelt's death that April was softened by V-E Day on May 8. As for May, her birthday had never been so lavishly celebrated: a trip to the Indian dances, dozens of presents and telegrams, a party with punch and two cakes, and May presenting everyone with a poem tied with a yellow ribbon. Everyone was delighted to celebrate the nativity of this vivid, enchanting person whose vitality energized everyone around her. Especially Judy, who sent George and Mabel "my own love & thanks to you for your lovely lady-daughter."

By June, May had sent off the finished *Underground River* to Eva Le Gallienne and "My Sisters" to *Poetry*. Doubleday wanted to see the novel; and May dared hope that the long waiting game might be over. But she now felt rather dissatisfied with the impetuous poems. "I see all the faults so clearly," she wrote Bill Brown, "a sort of romantic over-emphasis for one, and I do wish I could get away from such personal poems. . . . I can imagine such a wonderful poem about a rock or a tree but when I come to write, the old romantic fallacy pops up, and there I am talking about myself and my own sensations as usual! I have been reading Millay again and feeling this weakness in her very strongly. I just pray that I may grow out of it."

Written out, she was sick of mountains, desert, scrub, high altitude. New England reasserted its charm; she imagined tea in the lush garden at Channing Place, though Cloudy, the prolific favorite Sarton cat, had died. Judy was leaving. Lecture engagements were coming in for the fall. It was time to go home.

. . .

Back in Cambridge, she found that Doubleday was advancing $1,000 for *The Bridge of Years,* more than countering Le Gallienne's rejection of her play. Armed with this success, as well as acceptance of poems by *Poetry,* the *Atlantic Monthly,* the *Kenyon Review,* and the *Yale Review,* she told her parents that she intended to move into Judith Matlack's apartment. It was, she recognized, a huge step. All those apartments and rooms in New York had been like playing house. This was the real thing. She was making a home with another person. This was the "marriage" she had longed for.

On October 1 she moved into Judy's big, shabby apartment at 139 Oxford, one of Cambridge's busier streets. There was a fireplace in the dining room, and a study, and—in aid of her writing—a mate who taught all day at Simmons College. May was not domestic, but it was wonderfully pleasant to greet Judy with a glass of sherry at the end of the day, the table laid with wineglasses and flowers, a steak casserole bubbling in the oven. To read aloud to each other in front of the fire. To invite George and Mabel to Sunday lunch. To plan the future.

Yet there was a problem. Though Judy had submitted to sex in Santa Fe, she warned May, "I could never feel for a woman what I would feel with a man physically." Often she pleaded, "We love each other too much to be passionate tonight." Now she was clearly so unhappy as a lover that May was forced to give up pressuring her for sex. "I do occasionally wish for a little more warmth than she can provide," May told Bill Brown. Yet Judy's sexual reticence was easier for May to cope with than Muriel's earthy, honest passion.

Now that May had a home, it did not follow that she would stay in it. A week after moving in with Judy she left for a lecture trip to colleges in Wisconsin, Illinois, Iowa, and Missouri. She returned in early November to find Judy more precious than ever. "I feel like a man who finds haven after years and years of tossing about on foreign shores," she told Juliette. "I just pray that being given so much I will at last be able to prove that I am a builder and a person fit for an enduring relationship."

She had sent the new book of poems, *The Lion and the Rose,* on its perilous rounds of publishing houses. She was fiddling with a fifth novel, begun in Santa Fe; yet feeling at a creative low, she had turned to short stories. She booked another series of lectures in March and April; accepted a post as poet in residence at Southern Illinois University at Carbondale—

"It means quite a lot of money." Money, yes; but the lecturing and teaching stints meant far more. They charged her batteries. They satisfied her need to talk, to dominate, to influence. They gave her recognition as a poet, which the critics thus far denied. And they belied the terrible Monsieur Letendart. Ever since he'd analyzed her eyes in Belgium, she'd believed herself stupid. College teaching proved him wrong.

When Diarmuid Russell astounded her by selling a poetic story, "The Old Fashioned Snow," to *Collier's* for $600, she began to churn out more stories. In contrast, *The Bridge of Years* had sold only two thousand advance copies (not surprising when it was promoted as "the story of a good woman"). She sent a copy to the Limbosches, hoping that "this mixture of memory and imagination" would not offend, copies to dozens of friends, and waited for the reviews.

The press that noticed *The Bridge of Years* praised Miss Sarton's "genuinely distinctive novel." "Its style is limpid, unpretentious, beautifully expressive," said the *New York Herald Tribune,* "and its content is beyond all things warmly and humanly emotional. . . . Entering the magical circle of the Duchesnes is a rare privilege indeed." A pity so few entered it, for *The Bridge of Years* is a fine novel in its portrayal of the dynamics of family relationships. It is May's tribute to the surrogate families she had "clung to like a limpet" from childhood. It is also a successful attempt novelistically to do what she had been trying to accomplish in poetry: to look at the world apart from her own immediate sensations. As such it was not so much an advance over *The Single Hound* as a broadening of her powers. And something else: in *The Bridge of Years* she had deliberately eschewed the consciously lyric, poetic style of *The Single Hound* for the deeper use of poetry as place, time, theme, and character—poetry not laid on, but embedded in the novel's texture.

The novel has flaws, the most serious the last-minute introduction of "a tiny ball of camel-colored fluffiness, fast asleep." This sentimental symbol of "hope" or "rebirth" insults a family that has toughed out the Wehrmacht; the Duchesnes don't need a puppy to face Hitler. And since she has developed into a complex, stoical character, it is also wrong that Mademoiselle Louvois exits the novel in hysterics at the approach of the Germans. But these are minor crimes in a fine novel. The trouble was, American readers weren't interested in Belgians. May didn't understand that to sell in America she would have to go American.

In May her agent sold another short story to *Liberty* for $350—nearly half the airfare to England, for which she was wildly nostalgic. She had worked herself into a state of frustration, simultaneously writing a novel, poems, short stories, and lectures for Carbondale; giving speeches locally; seeing too many people; making plans to go abroad. In early June she and Judy prepared to sublet the apartment, since Judy would be attending a Quaker congress, then going to Sky Island for the summer. May was leaving for Carbondale June 6, but before that the Huxleys came for lunch and a tea in their honor at Channing Place.

She had not seen Juliette since 1939 and was disappointed by the "abrupt, teasing meeting." New York, where Julian had come to explain to the United Nations the mission of UNESCO, of which he had been elected director general, seemed to have changed them. Juliette was decked out in the latest fashion, almost extinguishing what May liked to call her "petite flamme bleue." Julian struck her as jazzed up, annihilating intimacy with his "nervousness and speed." "I do love him so much," she eventually wrote Juliette, "and was happy to see him—but sad too. . . . He rushes around like a humming bird tasting this and that, but does any of it get digested? Is it *real?*" A fair description of her own state that spring. She was bitterly disappointed not to see Juliette alone.

At Carbondale she had a room in the women's dormitory. With temperatures in the nineties and hydrangeas and roses lush everywhere, she felt "buried in the heart of America." Twenty-three students, including a Baptist minister and the head of a public school, in her Background to Modern Poetry class; mostly farm kids in Teaching Poetry. When students threatened to drop because of low marks, she announced that she did not intend lowering her standards. In her spare time she read Kierkegaard, wrote dozens of letters, short stories (which Diarmuid returned), and a series of poems called "Poet in Residence":

Here in the center of America
Steeped deep in the tiger-lily June . . .
Here in the center of America where it is always noon,
On the secure sidewalks of the typical town,
I go alone and a stranger, a haunted walker,
Full of self-questioning and wonder,
Waiting for the speech, for the word
To break the tension like a clap of thunder,
"How can the books be broken to yield the dynamic answer,
And we embody thought in living as does the dance, the dancer?"

At the end of her stint, people congratulated her on her tough stance with students. "You have made a depression, Miss Sarton," said one professor, "and that is better than an impression." Then she was back at Channing Place for the rest of the summer, facing the strain of being both "oneself and one's family's child." She was rearranging her book of poems *The Lion and the Rose,* pulling out some, adding "Poet in Residence." She felt it quite good at last. She had given up plans for Europe: impossible to get a visa for England. Instead, between July 10 and September 1, she and her parents entertained forty-five people at Channing Place for tea, lunch, or dinner, or overnight.

In September, after a "heavenly" week in Vineyard Haven with Judy, she returned to find Mabel hospitalized with a throat infection, so that instead of settling back into Oxford Street she spent her days dashing between the hospital and Channing Place, where she gave George his tea and supper. She bitterly resented having to wait on him when she felt like writing. When Mabel recovered, May was obliged to drive her in a borrowed car to the doctor four times a week, as well as keep Channing Place running, since Mabel was still extremely weak. She vented her anger in a long, hot letter to Doubleday, blaming them for the financial failure of *The Bridge of Years.*

She managed to see Judy evenings and some weekends. The serene household she had imagined was rather a joke. In a year she had spent perhaps five months at Oxford Street. Now as they planted scilla bulbs for spring, she reflected that she would probably be in Europe when they came up. Judy would "have them for consolation."

That fall she worked on the new Santa Fe novel, "a drama between a person and a landscape." By the end of November, however, she felt she might scrap it, a feeling her agent confirmed when he returned it with the comment "Nothing happens"—though he had sold another short story for $850. Finally, in February 1947, Doubleday confirmed the worst: the novel needed complete overhauling. Since she had a March lecture trip and passage to England in April, she shelved it.

Before sailing, she had another financial battle with George, though he had just given her "a large crowd of guineas" for England. The cost of living, she argued, had risen thirty percent since he decreed Mabel's $150-a-month housekeeping allowance.

At nearly seventy she deserves for this the distinguished service medal, and I know you think so too! . . . How can we help her? Well, in the first place I certainly plan to spend at least two weeks this summer at Channing Place taking all household cares from her back. I had hoped before I left to be able to leave with her a sum of money so that she could afford a few clothes and things she sorely needs—but luck has been against me these months. . . . What I suggest is that you think of raising mother's allowance a little— even twenty-five a month would make an *enormous* difference in her peace of mind. . . . Then I wish you could see your way to giving her perhaps an Easter present for some clothes. She will never ask for these things for herself as she knows only too well the awful strain you are under and does not want to add one atom to it.

How to reconcile George Sarton's constant generosity to May—trips to Europe, cars, monthly allowance—with his tight-fisted treatment of Mabel? May believed that Mabel had lost the money battle at Wondelgem when George refused to look at her accounts, not *wanting* to know how much it cost to run the house. At that point she literally should have thrown the book at him. But May was a fighter, a tiger. George feared the ferocity that her "Dearest Daddums" hardly masked. He could lug home heavy art books from the Widener for Mabel but refuse her twelve dollars for a new corset. "He was a little crazy about money," said May. And the mother-daughter conspiracy to "bankrupt" him crazed him more.

May sailed April 9 on the *Queen Elizabeth* with the good news that Rinehart would publish *The Lion and the Rose.* The voyage itself was less than pleasant: fog cut visibility to zero, and May had one of her fearful colds. May rushed to Kot through a London that seemed miraculously unchanged until one unexpectedly came upon a crater or a park stripped of its traditional iron railings. But she would not only see friends. She was the family ambassador, renewing Elwes and Sarton ties severed by the war.

She found Kot thinner and older, but as feisty as ever. Cantankerous about the packages she'd been sending, swearing to smoke more than ever despite the higher cigarette tax, fiercely proud that St. John's Wood had been heavily bombed during the war, furious with both Tories and Labor. James Stephens was there for tea, looking like "a small wizened tramp" in a coat out at the elbows, madly railing against the world—all very much the same. But Kot was not the same; nor did she understand his ethos: "I do not need tokens of friendship," he replied after she sent him a book as a thank-you gift. "Having taken you to my heart and mind, from the moment we first met, you may be sure that you remain there, in peace and safety, whatever you do, for ever and ever. . . . Keep well, May, and do not mind if I do not write to you."

She stayed with a friend named Jane Stockwood in the apartment in Southampton Row she shared with a painter, Anne Duveen. She paid visits to her Suffolk relatives, Evelyn Mann and her sister, May Pipe, who remembered little Belgian May in the red embroidered coat; lunched with the Singers; celebrated her thirty-fifth birthday at Kingham with the de Selincourts (George and Mabel celebrated it at home with Judy and Anne Thorp); with Ruth Pitter stayed at Penns in the Rocks, Withyham, the home of the poet Dorothy Wellesley, the duchess of Wellington, now, alcoholic, "a ruin of what once was great beauty and power." Though England was heartbreakingly green and tranquil that spring, talk was of taxes and rationing. Dorothy Wellesley was pathetically grateful for May's present of a bit of bacon.

Armed with a horrid chest cold, but also with the news that Diarmuid Russell had sold two short stories for $500 and that Rinehart would advance $200 for the poems, May left for Belgium May 9. Aunty Lino met her boat, carrying a bouquet of May's flowers, lilies of the valley. At 18 avenue Lequime May immediately toured the garden with Raymond, Nicole, and Jacqueline. The supper of cold fish, potatoes, fresh mayonnaise, and salad was excellent, but here too everything was rationed. And the old animosities remained. The Limbosches were savagely anti-Russian, lenient toward the Germans, which sickened the savagely anti-German May, as did Raymond's cynical distrust of all the democracies.

She found Marie Gaspar and Blanche Rousseau much aged, Jean-Do the same, though she was now seventy-four. But the poet was nearly blind. "The darkness crowds her," May wrote Kot. "She cannot read, she who lived on books, with books—it is a kind of starvation. It is this last winter that has nearly killed everyone. The bitter cold, as in England. And she cannot finish a study of Katherine Mansfield which was to be her last work. . . ." Jean-Do's annual income of eighteen thousand francs was now worth a third that sum; she still taught to make ends meet. They did not talk of that, but of May's books and battles, and of her contentment with Judy.

After emotional meetings with Madeleine Van Thorenburg, George's brother, Jean Sarton, and his sister, Vera Sarton, May left for Paris to see the Huxleys. The first day was UNESCO hell: the phone rang five times while May tried to read Juliette a poem, creating in the poet severe indigestion. Then they all went into the country for three wonderful days, putting up at an inn, picnicking in the forest of Fontainebleau. No sign of the war except blasted bridges and hundreds of young people crowding the highways, on holiday at last. Julian darted here and there, intensely interested in everything from birds to bikers. Back in Paris she was swept by Juliette into the UNESCO social whirl. But they also stole time alone. And what had hovered for ten years happened: the angel descended and May fell violently in love. "Juliette," she wrote Kot, "has become something very wonderful."

How maddeningly inconvenient that Grace Dudley was collecting her to drive to Le Petit Bois! Fortunately Julian was going abroad on UNESCO business the following week, which meant she *must* get back to Paris. Poems were spilling in ecstasy. She left with Grace for Tours on June 3; by June 7 she was back in Paris, unaware that Kot had tried to commit suicide that day and was in Holloway Sanatorium. "I am having a lovely peaceful time with Juliette," she wrote George and Mabel. " 'While the cat is away, the mice will play.' Dear Julian, the cat, arrived safely in New York and now is off on his huge trip to South America."

Love transformed Paris. With Juliette, May wafted blissfully through an evening at the theatre, a drive in the Bois, an afternoon with the sculptor Constantin Brancusi, an exhibition of Flemish painters. Juliette had always been adorable, with her beautiful heart-shaped face and forget-me-not eyes; now she was ravishing.

May tended to fall in love with two kinds of women: the glamorous (Katharine Taylor, Anne Thorp, Eva Le Gallienne, Edith Forbes Kennedy, Grace Dudley, Méta Budry) and, in her words, the needy (Florence Hoaglund, Judy Matlack). Juliette was both, a glamorous woman whose sexuality (May felt) had not been tapped. Juliette herself had admitted Julian's inadequacies: "You should be with a man, May. What a pity Julian is such a bad lover!" Now May's ardor ignited *la petite flamme bleue;* Juliette responded emotionally if not physically.

Hell to say goodbye; to see, like Romeo, Juliette gazing down from her balcony. Back in Belgium, she spilled everything to Jean-Do: the miracle of Juliette, her despair at the prospect of *eight* days without mail during the coming boat trip to Holland with the Limbosches. Jean-Do twinkled. Long ago she had concluded that May, like herself, was born to fall in love. They agreed that if *they* were renting the boat they would "simply tie it in a canal near a post-office and write poems and drink wine like Chinese philosophers."

"I remember everything," May wrote her love:

how the light flowed on the pavement outside Socrates, how the Arc de Triomphe looked, the little chairs under the chestnut on

Juliette Huxley

the Ave. Foch, the David leaves, your piercing loveliness as we drove toward the Orangerie and I looked at you, the palms of your hands. . . . I am so full of poems, of marvelous *inépuisable* joy!:

> The glittering leaves are still
> That shook down light and shadow
> Until the static pavement flowed
> Under our feet like broken water. . . .

It was torture not to hear immediately from Juliette, for perhaps her ardor, awakened so daringly, had cooled. "I do so wonder, o, I do so wonder, and I want to write you so many things but I do not dare until I have some olive branch in the beak of a dove from you—or a thorn—or whatever it is to be. Suspense is the only killing thing. Everything else can be *used. . . ."* Juliette wrote, extending the branch, but warning that she was a married woman. But the branch was enough, and May exploded with importunities: "And on your part I understand how deep your marriage goes. . . . But also I have no guilt about Julian because for a long time now it seems he has not been able to nourish you, but only to take from you. If I could give anything whatever to you, I would be giving it *also* to him. I think I shall try to come to Paris. Would you dread it very much?"

As the Bouton maid used to say, "Here comes trouble!" Trouble because May would not give up until she possessed Juliette physically. She had to prevail. "You can say *no,* you know," she assured Juliette, but May would not accept no. And Juliette did say no in many ways, but May did not take the hint: "I bet you forget to give me your address in Neuchatel, but if you have a grain of natural feeling, cruel one, you will have a letter for me here by the 30th full of the balm of meeting—or at least *some* balm!" She was, she told the cruel one, "desperately sad."

When Juliette did write, May wept in gratitude, admitted she had been "frightfully quick," swore she had "truly renounced all violent hopes" of another meeting this summer. But on the boat with Céline and the girls, she could not renounce everything. "I have invented a game of imagining that perhaps I shall see you but I *believe* it won't be—so don't let it add a featherweight to all the little and big worries you juggle, *darling,* my dear wonder."

Sailing on Dutch canals with a loutish captain bawling Flemish turned out to be a nightmare. She hated Holland. Every day they rose at six and spent the whole day furling and unfurling sails; when the wind died, they had to row. At night they tied up, May tortured in the airless bow clunking against the dock. "The boat was really Hell," she wrote Mabel and George, "and I fear I didn't behave very well: it was so awfully uncomfortable, small and never any peace for always one must pump or fix a sail or lift an anchor or get a meal—the only 'convience' a pail and no privacy. I was so dirty and depressed . . . I cried several times. Aunty Lino and the girls were awfully kind . . . but the fact is that they are ten times as strong and enduring as I. . . . I had the worst migraine I've ever had for the first three days. There was no hiding that." To Kot she was franker: "I am much too old and cross to live in uncomfortable circumstances, let alone *without mail* for a week!"

On $115 cabled by Anne Thorp, May left for England to stay with Jane Stockwood and Dorothy Wellesley. Though Julian, to her chagrin, was back in Paris, she now planned "to fly over just to kiss you both and see you once more." In London she heard from his good friend Marjorie

Wells that Kot was sedated and could not see her. She feared for him, for surely his terrible depression had been caused not only by dear friends dying around him but by his own ruthless cutting himself off from life.

She paced the London streets in a "rage of absence." Juliette had written that she "could not receive another person's gifts"; she was unworthy. "Darling," May replied,

> how *can* you lie to yourself any longer? . . . It is not the transference of guilt which is killing you, but the fact that you have not got through to love, you have not really accepted. And how can a person made for love, not resent not having love? *Of course* you resent it. . . . That's what I sensed. That's what drove me to all of this. . . . If you now deny this love, this riches which has come out of poverty, then you will make us both poor. O darling, don't do it. Accept me with all I am, if you can, for I am no saint, God knows. I am all torn up with egotisms and desires and selfishness and wanting you *for myself.* . . . There has never been anything quite like it for me. I feel all the time on the brink—Only let me come on the 17th. Do not say no. I know it is asking a great deal, but I do ask it, because I must.

Juliette relented. "I shall not really live again until I see you and thank God you say to come," May replied joyously. "I think I can be happy with you both—as long as you and I have some time together and that we shall have during the day. I dread the nights without you." But "no pressure. I won't make any. I promise you that." Instantly breaking that vow, she booked until July 21, overstaying the Huxleys' invitation but "the only flight *back* I could get." The irony of the reversal did not escape her. She had originally entered the Huxley house as Julian's lover, begging Juliette's acceptance. Now she came as Juliette's lover, praying for Julian's clemency.

She found the Huxleys in a luxurious new fifth-floor apartment in the avenue Foch with airy views of treetops and the Arc de Triomphe. Juliette was extremely nervous; Julian, badly hurt in an auto accident in Buenos Aires and just out of a cast, in pain with inner bleeding. May could not be entirely sorry. "I think perhaps it is a good diversion that I am here as he needs jacking up with little visits and I can release Juliette now and then," she wrote her parents.

But though they sat on the red sofa and Juliette laid her head on May's shoulder, they did not go to bed together. Still unconsummated and deeply in love, she wept at leaving Juliette; yet back in London she wrote her paeans of gratitude: "I wear you in the lining of my heart and on my breast. You are with me. You go where I go. You can't help it, darling. It's done! Glory be to God!"

Juliette's feelings were rather different. She was ashamed of loving a woman, guilty at not having given herself, and still ambivalent toward May as Julian's former lover. She was also exhausted: "You have seen me in Hell with my misery," she wrote May, "—with *your* misery which I am bound to add to mine, and you have beaten your heart against my prison. Oh darling—all the time I want peace—I only want peace and gentle love. I cannot reach those stars you live amongst, and I am desperately tired of the great effort to live."

May tried to comfort her:

But do not be sad that you did not love me. . . . There was no physical magic this time, even for me—you know that. Partly because of my curse. Partly I know because something did crack in the flood of my feeling for you after the first night and morning. I had come so very open and frightened and loving—then it seemed all cut off, so absolutely cut off. . . . But it would have been awful if I could not have touched you at all or come close to you and the physical expression is fearfully important to me. I don't mean that it isn't. Only that the angel didn't come down. . . . But all the time love was there, so beautiful. There is so much love in you towards me. You mustn't say there isn't. I feel it all the time. And that is all that matters in this world. . . . *Does* Julian guess or mind? I wonder.

And what about Judy? For one thing, May felt that Judy's refusal to have sex tacitly freed her to find it elsewhere. For another, Judy must understand that May required a Muse to be a poet—and that she was no Muse. And then May believed that her love for Juliette did not lessen her love for Judy. She could bathe them all—Judy, Juliette, even Julian—in her ever-flowing fountain.

Meanwhile, May reassured Judy, back in Cambridge cleaning May's closet, shellacking floors, sending May's clothes to the cleaners, visiting the Sartons, forwarding May's mail, and paying her bills. "I miss you terribly," Judy replied; "all the little amenities have just dropped out of sight for me, and I feel sort of impoverished and barren in many ways." Judy was missing, in Mabel's words, the "endless bonds," the "endless *sharing*" that May wove like a spell around those she loved: little notes on a pillow, the cozy glass of sherry before dinner, the latest book inscribed "To darling Judy with love," May's intimate confessions, the joy of making plans. "I do not know how I ever found such a person," May wrote Judy now, "nor how I deserve such understanding and love. But I love you very much and that is where my root is all the time."

Still, rather tough on Judy.

CHAPTER 12

Cast Out: 1947–1948

She sailed back across "that great monster who divides my heart and separates me from all I love." When Judy met her in New York, she announced she was booking passage to England for the following April. In Cambridge she found Mabel shockingly old and worn; George, beaming and immersed in compiling English, Chinese, and Greek indices to his huge history of early science. She spent the day after her return crying; that evening she told Judy about Juliette. May had feared that Judy might plunge into one of her depressions, but the next morning she seemed the same. "Of course I have now got rid of my burden and laid it upon her," May wrote Juliette. ". . . I have a deep inside feeling that all is well and will be. This is entirely because she is, where people she loves are concerned, of an almost infinite generosity and imagination. I do not deserve so much."

Now she did not regret Juliette's lack of passion; the miracle had been that Juliette—Julian *in situ*—had been as loving as she had. "Love really does open the world. . . . Passion is so exclusive and violent. It closes out the world. So all things considered I have come to believe that for us the absence of passion is a saving grace—perhaps *the* saving grace. Especially as in a state of such delicate equilibrium it may happen at any time." She wanted Julian to see the poems: they would force Juliette to acknowledge their love.

She agonized over the final selection for *The Lion and the Rose.* Punctuating was hell, reminding her of those red "May, your PUNCTUATION!" reprimands on school themes. (Personally, she believed that "if a poem

164

needs punctuation it is a failure.") Should she include the poems to Juliette with those to other lovers? She decided she must. She was also overhauling again the Judy-inspired Santa Fe novel and churning out short stories (they had brought her $2,000 in 1946) since she was stone-broke until her November lectures.

"I have to keep reminding myself, tortured by ambition as I am, that all that really matters is the intensity of the life lived," she wrote Juliette. She told herself this because the novel was not going well, because the stories were superficial, and because she now found some of the poems in *The Lion and the Rose* labored, didactic, and stale. So, since she was "very angry with everything" except the new poems, she comforted herself with notions about the intensity of life.

Thus she found ample time for friends, though less for George and Mabel. Time to write to Kot, home from the sanatorium, roaring subduedly. Time to congratulate the unmarried Muriel on the birth of a boy ("*Perhaps* she will remember to change his diapers"), though she was jealous of this biological creation which she had determined never to experience. Time to talk to Will Hawthorne, back in the States with Barbara and their two children. In England, Barbara had confessed that though Will was a genius and a saint, she did not love him. Now Will told May sad stories of a wife so disturbed she could not get a meal, choose a pair of curtains, or boil water for a cup of tea. And of course time to dine with the Huxleys in New York on their way to Mexico, Julian looking better than he had in Paris, Juliette a dream in a blue feathered hat.

After that pulse-quickening event, she set out on a lecture tour to Missouri and Iowa, returning on November 18 to the "fabulous news" that Diarmuid had sold "The Paris Hat" for $1,000 and "Today a Woman" for $750. She immediately banked $1,000 for Europe and rushed to the shops to buy pâté de foie gras for Dorothy Wellesley and bacon for Kot. But the year ended, as many did, in a crescendo of frustration. "My life seems to be a matter of swimming madly like a pursued mouse, trying not to drown," she wrote Bill Brown that December, ". . . and now, damn it, Christmas on top of everything fills me with bitterness and horror—and yet I buy much too much myself. . . . I am working at the novel, but really it needs a long hibernation and uninterrupted period of confinement, six months labor pains! And instead I let myself get in for a radio speech on Civil Liberties (using poems) and all sorts of bothers." Recipients of this woe felt guilty for taking even more of her time; but May wrote compulsively to friends, though *real* letters (she felt) only to Juliette, Jean Dominique, and sometimes Kot.

. . .

The Sartons were going abroad and leasing 5 Channing Place, which meant readying the house for their February departure. May cleaned for three days and brought Mabel meals in bed—"What hell!" She looked forward to their trip as relief from Miutsie's constant woes. His doctor had told George he must give up working through lunch and come home for a hot noon meal—a horrid blow to Mabel, who counted on those hours for visiting friends, flower markets, or museums. Sometimes she simply was unable to do the housework and prepare three meals a day—as, for example, the day she was prostrated with a temperature of 102: finding no dinner, George stormed to his study and wrote a German colleague, "It is really disgraceful that I, with what I have on my back, have to do all the housework"; then showed the scientist's commiserating reply to Mabel. He refused to pay for a housekeeper. But now, with his tremendous work finished, they were sailing to Europe. May did not forgive him. "Men are terrible creatures," she wrote Juliette. "Their selfishness is beyond telling. . . . Women are always too good for men as far as I am concerned."

In the midst of Channing Place bustle, *The Lion and the Rose* arrived. Exciting, yet she had steeled herself for little advertising, minimal reaction. Once a book was out, she felt, it was curiously finished, for meanwhile its author had grown new skin. When she got back to Oxford Street, she found a note from Judy: "It seems to me that *all* the emotional poems are especially lovely, and no matter who inspired them, I cannot feel anything but pride and joy in them." But then Judy, as May was realizing, suffered like a saint—silently, not inflicting pain upon its creator.

Her first public response came from William Rose Benét, who had read *The Lion and the Rose* in proof. He admired her intensity, which to him was "the sinew of the real poet." He thought "My Sisters, O My Sisters" one of the most remarkable poems by a woman ever written; he admired "Not Always the Quiet Word," "Who Wakes," and "The Clavichord." A pity this praise came from the poet who had alienated May at poetry readings with his appeals to God. "Of course Benét is old-fashioned, God bless him!" May wrote, Benét-like, to Bill Brown, ". . . but at least I have one friend—among the savage beasts—and that is a great boon."

The beasts, however, were not unduly savage. The *Saturday Review* called *The Lion and the Rose* "an achievement of the first quality" and May "an artist of remarkable powers." Other critics distinguished between the clarity and "troubling beauty" of the New Mexico and love poems and the didacticism of "Place of Learning," "Celebration," and "Monticello," in which Sarton's material failed to undergo "alchemical translation." *Poetry* titled its review frankly "The Rose and the Oration," contrasting the ease of

> In Texas the lid blew off the sky a long time ago
> So there's nothing to keep the wind from blowing
> And it blows all the time. Everywhere is far to go
> So there's no hurry at all, and no reason for going.

with the exhortatory deflation of the last stanza of "Monticello":

> The time must come when, from the people's heart,
> Government grows to meet the stature of a man,
> And freedom finds its form, that great unruly art,
> And the state is a house designed by Jefferson.

Since this criticism is valid, the question is, How does a lyric poet become as well a didactic poet, drumming the virtues of freedom, charity, peace, and tolerance into her reader's ear? May would later confess to the sin of self-righteousness. Because she was still an outsider in America, she shored her ego with passionate convictions, feeling it her mission to preach to the purblind citizens of a remarkable country. Then, too, she had vowed to temper personal poetry with the poetry of ideas. Combine with this the belief that action can remedy ill and a taste for abstractions, and lo, the preacher. In December 1943, she had begun to send long, annual, didactic poems to friends and acquaintances, proclaiming herself, as it were, Poet Laureate of Years Past and Future. She admitted these were epistles rather than poems; yet the urge to exhort was irresistible:

> You teachers, mothers, poets, politicians,
> Builders of bridges—bridge these new divisions.
> Match the fierce discipline of body and of will
> With discipline of mind and the heart's miracle;
> That with the fire of love, the fire of charity
> We may this year set ourselves truly free.

No accident that she wrote her poems to be read aloud: preaching is an oral art. But her beliefs about the purpose of poetry are also significant. "One boy came up after the chapel speech," she wrote Bill Brown after a

lecture tour, "and told me that my 'Work of Happiness' had helped his
mother out of a serious neurasthenia and actually cured her—a slight
exaggeration no doubt—but it was good to hear. I cannot believe that the
publishers matter a hoot when I hear things like that." Gratifying, yes; but
a broken ruler by which to measure a work of art. Art is not a Band-Aid
or an aspirin or an hour with a psychiatrist. A poem may inadvertently
comfort or sustain, but healing is not the business of a poem. Its motive is
its own internal truth of form and meaning—its beauty.

May confused art with healing because writing poems kept her sane.
She was tormented by guilt, not because she loved women but because
she spread her dragonfly affections thin—"an excess of love, giving the
same thing to too many people." She might rationalize her need to
repeatedly conquer by love, but was not quite blind to the pain caused by
her promiscuity. She knew she had hurt Judy, knew she would hurt her
again and again. She objected to being loved, not only because she liked
to play the active role, but because she felt profoundly unworthy, know-
ing she would betray. The poems, the writing, were her justification for
living. In her best work, they turned her sickness into art.

Now May had only a lecture tour of Virginia and North Carolina col-
leges before flying to Juliette. At Mary Washington College in Freder-
icksburg, she read from *The Lion and the Rose* to an audience of twelve
hundred and "really heard the poems ring out," yet she most enjoyed
Durham's North Carolina College: "The Negroes here talk freely and
very wisely about the race problem and I feel much more at home with
them than in the narrow-minded white 'Christian' colleges where I've
been on this trip," she wrote Mabel and George. Her America, she con-
cluded, was materialistic and bigoted. At the end she had to say goodbye
to black friends outside the train station since they were not allowed in
the white waiting room.

Back in Cambridge, she almost regretted leaving April 7. "I do not
dare to think too much about seeing you," she had told Juliette. ". . . Do
you realize that we have had only about eight days together in all our lives
in love? . . . Thank God you do not know me as I really am, driven,
always in a hurry, much too keyed-up and tense. I have felt this same devil
in Julian and I know that I have got to tame it before I can do really good
work. . . ." Suddenly Judy seemed very precious. "In some ways I wish I
were not going," she wrote Bill Brown, "and yet I know how the poems
will start again and how I shall feel alive and full of joy again—and it is
irresistible!"

She sailed on the *Queen Mary* with a new dark blue silk coat and a nest egg of forty-seven pounds in a London bank from short-story sales. Hearing that Rebecca West was on board, she sent up a copy of *The Lion and the Rose* and was rewarded by the writer's descending twice from first class for drinks and talk about the poems. From the ship she tried to lull Juliette's fears. "Now, my love, please do not torture yourself about anything concerned with me. I am happy and peaceful and think of you with rushes of excitement, but no *pang*. I am really rather tired and very gentle, you know, and getting old, so please 'take it easy' as we say in America. All will be well—all will be *very* well!" Any decoder of May Sarton would hoist the hurricane flags.

She stayed again with Jane Stockwood in Southampton Row, went to the de Selincourts in Kingham (Basil offering to fund publication of the *The Lion and the Rose* in England), lunched with Elizabeth Bowen and with Rebecca West in the country. She saw Kot, who had been charmed by George and Mabel as well as by *The Lion and the Rose*. "Your daughter," he told them, "is the best poet in America!" After shock treatments and rest, he seemed his prewar self, "a wise old God, a kind of standard of purity and true values"—yet if Kot *were* God, one would certainly want to be one of the elect in his rigorous kingdom.

Every nerve strained toward Juliette, who had granted her four days. May arrived in Paris the evening of April 28 in an agony of desire frustrated by cramps, indigestion, and a sinus attack that made the first twenty-four hours hell. Then came "three unbelievably passionate days." At last Juliette acknowledged the physical wasteland of her marriage and succumbed to May. A "*wonderful* peaceful time with Juliette," Miutsie was informed.

She left for Belgium the morning of her birthday—shaken, exhausted, happy. "I understand now how much I needed passion," she wrote Bill Brown, with whom she could frankly discuss sex, "and how rare it is." But passion was also intoxicating, like wine. She didn't want to be drunk; she wanted to be alert so that poems would come. "Now the storm of flowers is over," she wrote her lover from Belgium, "and all is green and at peace and fulfilled and silent." Now again she could think and write and, at a distance, find herself rather revolted by her behavior in Paris, by a nature "which exploits itself to such a point."

May had usurped Céline from her mother the past eleven years; now Mabel reunited with her friend. And Céline, who had never thought George good enough for Mabel, this time liked him very well, though she was appalled when Mabel confided she had to beg money for trolleys and postcards because George hadn't given her a cent since they'd left. Once again May was forced to "discover" that Miutsie had no money and shame George into opening his wallet. He might have reminded her he was sending Mabel's eternally indigent brother twelve hundred dollars a year, but probably did not. Her heart closed tighter against him.

Every other day she visited Jean-Do in "a state of perpetual lover's anguish" over her affliction; yet the poet herself was "full of bitter wisdom and laughter and *douceur*." Her *fidèles,* six students who had come every week for twenty years, were still faithful, as were other friends; still, May wept all the way back to the avenue Lequime. Of course she told Jean-Do about Juliette, though she felt she had been circumspect with Kot, to whom she had written only: "Apparently Juliette told you that I was ill all the time, a slight exaggeration, to conceal perhaps her joy and mine (but that is a secret)." She longed for Paris again: would Juliette have her? "Let me know. But I hope, I hope—though I shall never *expect* anything, you know."

Arriving in Paris on wings, she was appalled to find Julian ill in the apartment, "which makes this a good deal less peaceful than I had hoped." She smouldered as the Huxley life took over: phones ringing, UNESCO business, plans for a trip to the Balkans. Julian announced he might go to London for the weekend; she lit candles. Meanwhile on May 26 she went to George's lecture at the Collège de France with Julian and Juliette. George was often an overwrought speaker, jabbing home points with forefinger and flashing spectacles; this time he charmed his audience. She felt it good that after the long, lonely struggle he was being praised and fêted. Also good was walking with Juliette in the Bois de Boulogne or drinking wine at sidewalk cafés—and when Julian did go to London, a "peaceful weekend" with her love. Yet this time Paris exhausted more than fulfilled; she was not entirely unhappy to leave with Grace Dudley for Le Petit Bois on June 3. "I am getting over my extravagance of Paris," she wrote Kot from the country, "—too many cigarettes, too many poems, too much life. . . . It is time perhaps to be silent."

May was shocked to find Grace old and depleted; it became apparent she was very ill. X-rays revealed an obstruction in the stomach; her doctor confided to May that it was certainly cancer. Grace entered the American Hospital in Paris June 20, May postponing plans to meet her parents in Switzerland. As a close friend, she couldn't abandon Grace—and Juliette was in Paris. It was indeed cancer, though Grace was not informed. May stayed with Juliette, paid daily visits to Grace, who had given her one hundred dollars to subsist on until the June 30 operation. Grace's whole

stomach was removed; still, the surgeon pronounced the operation a suc-
cess, and May bought her ticket to Montreux.

Her last days in Paris were good farce. Julian returned, promptly got
May into bed, told all. Juliette was furious. Every night May crawled to
Juliette's door, pleading, "Julian just wanted a place to lie down!"—an
explanation Juliette spurned. Retaliating, she evicted her lover from a
family dinner with Aldous and Maria Huxley, so that a very tired May was
obliged to sit out the evening in a café. Meanwhile, May was visiting her
former lover in the hospital daily. Between crises poems leapt out.

On July 6 she joined George and Mabel at the Hôtel Bristol in Mon-
treux, immediately lapsing into a coma of family boredom. She hated the
lake, the hotel, the Victorian flowerbeds, the rain, quoting Gide in her
diary: "The admiration of mountains is a Protestant invention." Mornings
she pretended to write while agonizing over her conduct with Juliette—
fearing silence meant Juliette's hatred, knowing too well why it might.

Méta Budry's arrival diverted her—Méta handsome at sixty, with bril-
liant golden eyes and snowy-white hair. She had been the mistress of a
wealthy man who had promised her five hundred thousand francs; when
he died, the bank told her there was nothing. She married Marc Turian, a
vigneron, not for love. May found Méta as fascinating as ever, but really she
was marking time until she left for Paris and her "swan and love and star."
The Huxleys would have company on the weekend. "I am very tempted
to stay till Sunday because of the lack of beds, a paradox which you will
understand," she wrote Juliette, at the same time assuring her "it will not
be a long nor a difficult visit."

Not long, but very difficult. Juliette was always reserved at first meet-
ing; distressed now by the violence of May's feelings, she did not thaw. She
was horrified by May's total lack of restraint, her insistence that she
respond passionately, all the time. When Juliette recoiled, May suffered
loud and long. She left for the Limbosches after "three days of sheer Hell
with a little peace thrown in at the end, thank God," realizing she had
alienated Juliette, though unaware of the extent of the damage. "It is dan-
gerous to love so much," she wrote Bill. "I got to the point where I just
ached all over if I even looked at her and that is foolish." To Juliette she
admitted that the qualities Juliette "hated" about her permeated every-
thing, even her writing style—"the too-muchness," the exaggeration.
Still, she pleaded for Paris in August. Juliette replied that they must not see
each other again that summer.

May left for London August 9 to stay with Kot, hoping her gift of but-
ter, salami, gin, and tea would not anger him. (It did.) Although she had

Mabel Sarton and Méta Budry Turian, influential in both mother's and daughter's lives

promised to say nothing about her relationship with Juliette, she told him everything. And though Juliette wanted silence, she wrote.

Just because our natures and our needs are so very different, we must *include* each other or everything breaks apart. I know that in order to make this happen I must learn to love you less terribly. . . . Only now you mustn't leave me quite outside. . . . You see, darling, I have come to you so often full of that most vulnerable joy of meeting and love, only to be slapped down and shut out. . . . My suffering seemed to become the great sin. To the point you could write to me over and over "be *happy.*" I wonder if the explanation of this is not that you have so decided that I am "over-intense" and excessive that you confuse this real failing with the reality of my feeling. That even the tears were not *real,* and therefore the love not *real.* . . . O my darling, think of me, please try to remember some of the good. . . . I have lost all faith in myself.

She continued her litany of complaint in letters of August 15, 17, 18, 19, 20, and 25, though she received only restrained replies. Meanwhile, she felt Kot close against her. He had been, she was sure, in love with her himself. Now something had ended, though she pleaded:

Let us forget this between us and remember only the truth which is that there is a great deal of unused love floating around in this world which attaches itself here and there, sometimes well, sometimes badly—but from all of it one learns each time to be a little wiser, a little more detached, to love a little more as angels do. . . . As I tried to tell you (but you did not want to hear) I became well at Basil's and now I *am growing* every day and I think this has been a great summer and now it is time to be silent and to learn from it all there is to be learned. . . . I am so terribly sorry that I had to be in Hell just the days I came to you—will you forgive me someday?

Kot did not answer. She turned to his friend Lady Beatrice Glenavy, who had invited her to Ireland. Rockbrook House proved to be a large, stone Georgian establishment at the foot of the Wicklow Hills above Dublin overlooking the bay. Though Lord Glenavy was in residence, May fell rather in love with red-haired Beatrice, flirted with her, confessed her passion. Beatrice bluntly told her to stop tossing the word "love" around like a bean bag. Wasn't she supposed to be madly in love with Juliette, not to mention some maiden schoolteacher in the States? What kind of adventuress was she!

Meanwhile, nagged by guilt, May confessed to Juliette she'd told Kot they were lovers. "I think it made him terribly angry. Nothing was gone into. I just burst into tears and went away and came back and we never spoke of it again. . . . I feel I am in his mind *beyond the pale.*" The absolutist Kot had cast off Katherine Mansfield, Dorothy Brett, and John Middleton Murry for lesser crimes. Yet May did not realize what had happened. She appealed to Beatrice to intervene. The practical Beatrice scolded her but promised to write to Kot in her behalf. After May left, Beatrice felt rather sorry: "I felt I had said such horrible things to you— you looked such a beaten little girl in your school girl's dressing gown—

& I was awful to you, but I had to set it straight. . . . Perhaps it all boils down to this—you mustn't confide about erotic love to old outsiders, they only feel it is ridiculous & disgusting!"

May would not take the advice, or admit her follies. "Anyway I am now on good terms with myself," she wrote Bill from the *Britannic* as she sailed for home, "and very ready to go on living and as I look back on the summer it seems almost incredibly rich and wonderful."

At the Limbosches', Mabel had discovered a lump in her breast. Typically, she did not tell George, not wanting to spoil his sabbatical. Back in Cambridge, she went into the hospital to have the cancer removed. Knowing how fond Kot was of her mother, May wrote him about the operation. She extorted a brief word in reply.

She still didn't fully realize how she had alienated him, and how her passionate, belligerent letters to Lady Glenavy were turning off that new friend. "I think you are good to look at, with nice clothes, amusing, very intelligent, charming, companionable, with a very interesting talent," Beatrice replied. But "May—could you write a letter without any 'darling' in it or any 'love' in it—'restraint is the greatest emotion'—ask yourself do you make these words cheap? . . . Let's be friends."

May fought back. What was wrong with emotion—and wasn't Beatrice flagrantly emotional herself? She continued to send "darling"s along with packages of tea and soap, defending her right to be passionate, insisting that her advances to Beatrice had been only a poet's appreciation of beauty and kindness.

Beatrice was growing weary of May's insistent narcissism. No one had impressed her more favorably on first meeting, but then "I saw that you & your work had to be admired without question: you have a quite attractive generous way of handing yourself & your work out like presents, but it must be all accepted at your own valuation."

In November, Lady Glenavy visited Kot. Juliette was there. May was the hot topic. "The crying, the crying!" exclaimed Juliette, shuddering at the memory of Paris. "Did she cry with you too?" "Yes," said Beatrice, not remembering whether May actually had or not, but thinking it likely. Kot said angrily that he considered May's note about Mabel's operation "intolerable" since it forced a reply, told Beatrice to tell her that once he was finished with a person, he was finished forever. In short, May was thoroughly trashed. Eventually Juliette wrote May: her tears at Lady Glenavy's were the final proof of insincerity.

"Betrayal!" raged May. She had *not* cried. There was a conspiracy against her. Beatrice was jealous of her friendship with Kot, would do anything to turn Kot and Juliette against her. She turned to Bill:

> Juliette got together with Kot and Beatrice . . . and they did a perfect job of destroying me for her. Beatrice had enough truth to tell to damn me, I guess, but she also lied cruelly, such as telling Juliette I had *cried* (which I know I never did) and now J. has written me a very cold letter saying she is through with my "devious ways," asking me to burn all her letters which I did yesterday, and saying that Kot and B. are through with me but for old lang syne she will still write, and ending with the contemptuous phrase that she is glad the poems are *selling*. The worst is that J. said "so all those tears you cried for me were just as easy to cry for someone else within a few weeks." Bill, it is so terribly hard to explain all this, but what I wanted from Beatrice was comfort, was to be taken in and sheltered—I believe this is a weakness, but every one has his own way of dealing with the shocks of life. I believe my way is better than taking to drink, for instance. It is a loving way and does not at least lead to bitterness. But Beatrice is really a treacherous person. I'm convinced of that now. . . . Judy is really so wonderful in all this. She said last night that it was clear that none of them understood me at all nor my kind of love in which sex has little part, and she is so right. I do not really deserve such kindness, but it is a blessing, I must say. . . .
> It is a fearful shock to be thought a monster by three people one trusted, two of whom one has known for more than ten years.

May would always claim that because Beatrice Glenavy betrayed her innocent flirtation, Juliette and Kot cast her out of their lives. In 1993, however, May put into her authorized biographer's hands a folder of letters from Juliette Huxley written after Julian's death in 1975, when May pressed her for a reconciliation. "You see, what happened between us in Paris left its mark on me," Juliette replied, "—and the last thing I want is to harp back on the final disaster of our relationship. That it was a disaster is not in doubt—for when you threatened to 'tell all to Julian' I really felt betrayed in so absolutely unexpected a way. It is a great pity that the memory of this remains so clear in my mind—as I have always felt so much admiration for your courage and your great gifts."

Thus, Juliette's break with May had little to do with May's overwrought passion in Paris, her telling Kot about their affair, or her flirting

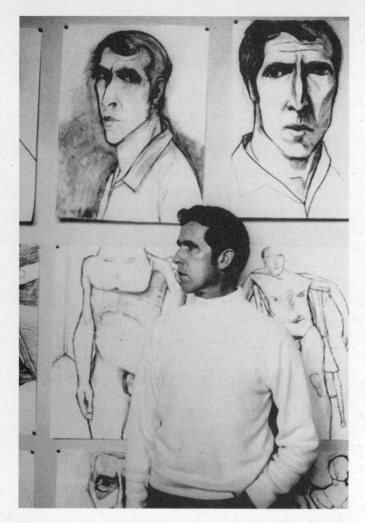

*The painter
William Theo
Brown, May's
"brother" and
correspondent*

with Lady Glenavy. Juliette repudiated May because she had threatened blackmail. It was a crime that her guilty love could not survive.

How could May not only blackmail her lover but expose their liaison to Kot and, protesting love for Juliette, try to seduce Beatrice Glenavy? Not to mention hurt Judy—but that May discounted. One can only conclude that she was strangely blind to the consequences of her actions. Everything she did was inevitable, right, angel-sent. She was almost totally self-absorbed— perhaps not surprising in a person who had been both extravagantly neglected and coddled as a child. Fuming at his daughter's recklessness, George never disciplined Tiger May, avoiding responsibility by burying himself in scholarship. Mabel, a failure as a *surveillante* in Belgium, had no weapons against May's furious tears except appeals to sweet reason and her own sufferings. May never learned a code of honor or responsibility.

She was right when she confessed that the qualities Juliette distrusted in her permeated even her style. Reading her letters, one is struck by the absence of cause-and-effect words like "because," "thus," "therefore," "since," "nevertheless," "as a result," "consequently." May's favorite connector is "and": "I wish you and Julian were here in a little adobe house and I could cook for you and read you poems and read Thurber aloud with you, and then we would laugh until we cried and we would embrace each other, and we would be happy together." A writer who perceives experience as simply linear—"I became well at Basil's and now I *am growing* every day and I think this has been a great summer and now it is time to be silent and to learn from it all there is to be learned"—ignores the intricate connections between actions. May's simplistic "and"s deny cause and effect, as she denied that her behavior turned Kot and Juliette against her.

Juliette and Kot were more important to May than she was to them. She had lost two valuable supporters.

CHAPTER 13

Loss: 1949–1950

May was sure that Mabel's breast cancer had erupted from suppressed fury at George. Certainly Mabel could not forget the humiliations of the European sabbatical. She withdrew from George, sometimes not speaking to him for days. Then she would climb the stairs to his study, put her arms around him, and murmur, "You know, I really love you." George would look up, spectacles glinting. "What's all this about?" He hadn't noticed. May called Mabel every day. "Is it any better, Mother?" "No," Mabel would whisper. "I can't. . . . It's some sort of block." In one last try at financial independence, she had tried writing short stories for publication: she had a real, if unhoned, gift for writing. "Ordeal by Water" described George making for shore at Ogunquit against an undertow, leaving her—if she could not save herself—to drown. Life with him had been a series of such indifferences; now she raged inwardly against them. Yet he had always loved her, in his way. During the operation and the X-ray treatments that followed, he could not speak of her without tears in his eyes.

May was driven to writing more short stories for cash. She had decided against lecturing in 1949, though it meant living on George and Judy. In the aftermath of the disastrous summer, she was feeling thoroughly dissatisfied with everything she had written. Juliette, Beatrice, and Kot had been right in a way: she was still too emotional, too self-absorbed; still took her work too seriously—though she knew she was compensating for what she considered her "total lack of success."

For though she won praise from individual critics, she was still ignored as a poet by the literary establishment. This was because, she believed, she had emerged as a poet just after the heyday of Elinor Wylie and Edna St. Vincent Millay into a climate hostile to lyricism. *The* female poet of the 1920s, Wylie was now branded escapist for her inability to deal with cruelty, degradation, and tragedy. Millay had been extravagantly admired; reviewing the *Collected Lyrics* in 1943, however, a critic in *Poetry* was able to cull only twelve poems that still seemed worthy. Academe, which promoted intellectually and structurally ambiguous poetry for professorial explication, further buried Wylie and Millay. May felt the hostility of male critics acutely. "I think men do not want women poets to talk about their feelings. It's the *feminine* poet men don't like." To her that explained the acceptance of Marianne Moore, Elizabeth Bishop, and Louise Bogan. They played men's games, curtailing emotion.

In January 1949, she began another novel with herself as the young male protagonist. Its title, *Shadow of a Man,* stood metaphorically for coming into manhood, though "shadow," as May knew, also meant lesbian—an appropriate code for a novel dealing with May's passion for Juliette Huxley. The novel's central theme reflected May's creed that love, no matter how stormy or impermanent, begets more love: Francis Chabrier's brief affair with Solange teaches him to love the patient Ann. Rival cultures are also a theme: Francis is torn between his American and French roots. And finally the novel is the story of a son's struggle to come to terms with his dead mother, Persis, a woman who gave him freedom but not love—interesting in the light of May's frequent assertion that the greatest proof of Mabel's love was the total freedom she allowed her.

May could fictionalize herself readily as a male because society equated the qualities she saw in herself—energy, will, aggression, anger, and, above all, creativity—with maleness, a judgment most women still accepted. And she had played the male role with the resisting, feminine Juliette naturally, just as she unselfconsciously referred to herself in letters as "he" or "a man." Besides, not loving men, she would have had enormous psychological difficulty creating a male love object.

As for portraying same-sex love, in 1949 neither publishers nor May could risk it. More significantly, May still didn't think of herself as "lesbian." She not only could say that she wanted marriage but could decide that her gay friend Bill Brown was ripe for marriage to some nice girl. "There is just no doubt that a 'normal' relationship is better from every point of view if one is capable of it," she wrote him that February. May, therefore, did not so much lack the courage to write about lesbianism as not intellectually credit it herself.

Shadow of a Man admits the havoc she created in Juliette's life. But Francis's clean break with Solange was pure fiction, for in reality May would not let go. Juliette had attempted to pacify May's fury at the "Glenavy betrayal" by offering friendship. But as May continued to demand love, Juliette recoiled. "There is now such a thick cloud between us that I find it almost impossible to write to you. . . . I cannot give you what you demand of me, I have no love alas. . . ." May threatened to confront her in London that spring. "I do not wish to see you in the spring," replied Juliette, "and . . . if I do, it will be the last time. . . . Your last letters have killed any feeling I had left." May responded with tins of sweets, eggs, and meat. "Please don't send any more," Juliette rebuked, "we really have no need." May could not seem to understand that coercion and bribery were less than endearing. "I feel just as I did," she wrote Bill sadly, "and she has changed."

Since Mabel seemed well that spring, May charged George to hire a cleaning woman and booked passage on the *Queen Elizabeth,* docking at Southampton May 3. With little prospect of a reunion with Juliette, she had invited Judy to join her in Belgium in early July. Though she saw the Singers, Ruth Pitter, and the writer-traveller Freya Stark, and celebrated her thirty-seventh birthday with presents and a "colossal check" from George, not only the London weather was cold. Humiliating to have to learn about the Huxleys from a mutual friend; to be told by Kot's friend Marjorie Wells she might call him. She expected a receiver slammed in her ear; instead he inquired quite kindly after Mabel. She hung up in a burst of grateful tears; still, he could not see her now. Baffled, she bought a ticket for Belgium. She had assessed herself bitterly in her diary that week in London, when the only solace had been the discovery of a book Kot had long recommended, Thomas Traherne's *Centuries of Meditation:*

Now she is 37, nearly forty
Without wisdom, without learning,
Fatally spontaneous,
Having suffered too much for the wrong reasons.
[Been] lavish where restraint would have paid
As little afraid of wasting love as money,
Thriftless, impatient, driving herself too fast.
Whatever depth there may be, forced upon her by her own failures

The price (grant she has paid it gladly) sometimes very high
Given too much of herself to too many people,
She will open her heart to an acquaintance on a bus,
Dreading to telephone, quickly lonely if it doesn't ring,
Aching for solitude, but eager to meet new people,
She is childish without being gay
And suffers a good deal without growing wise—
At 37 looks forward to being old and kind,
Tolerant of the young . . .

Brussels was cold, windy, and wet, Uncle Raymond depressed, Aunty Lino aged, though still the comfortable loaf of bread. As soon as May unpacked, she went to Jean-Do. Blanche Rousseau, Jean-Do's housemate for twenty-five years, had died. Now they sat in her room, in which nothing would be changed until the deaths of the other two Peacocks, and talked of old times and of how they had all laughed with George and Mabel last summer. Though Jean-Do missed reading and doing errands with Blanche, she was not desolate. "All this love around them has helped tremendously," May wrote home. ". . . A soft shining radiance goes out from the house and penetrates farther than any of them know. I am sure of that."

May continued *Shadow of a Man,* translating each chapter and reading it to the two Peacocks. On May 20, she walked to the end of the avenue Lequime to meet Eugénie Dubois, a friend of Jean-Do's, who had admired *The Single Hound.* Madame Dubois turned out to be a pretty, shy, dark-haired woman with a large German shepherd named Roy on a leash. They walked four kilometers across fields to her house in the village of Linkebeek while May learned that she taught French, had two grown children and a husband, Jean, whose hobby was astronomy. She found Madame Dubois charming.

But May's thoughts were on a car for Judy's forthcoming visit. She was told she could buy one secondhand for a mere 5,000 francs—$120. A mechanic friend of the Limbosches would see she wasn't sold a lemon. And she could resell the car at the end of the summer, saving money otherwise spent on train fares or rentals. The idea quickly possessed her.

"Dearest Tata, a little boon I crave," wrote May, announcing the purchase of a Renault "in very good condition" for 15,000 francs. She'd had to snatch it immediately, for its owner, Monsieur Muraille, hinted at another buyer. It was ten years old, but with new tires and a new battery—and she had christened it La Vieille Caroline. "I shall have the car until Judy and I leave the continent in Aug. and then I shall resell it surely for not less than

10,000 francs. . . . That means that I shall have had a car at my disposal for two months for $100, no trains or porters and our trips to Tours and Brittany included." She needed $200 until the resale in September. . . .

George complied. But Old Caroline refused to start in Monsieur Muraille's garage. After two hours tinkering, he found that the contact had been left on, draining the battery. Much embarrassment, much swearing he would produce a running car. "I'm sure he is an honest man and will give me the car in good condition," May reassured her parents. Meanwhile, insurance cost another 1,850 francs.

At last May possessed Caroline and set out for Jean-Do's along roads mined with potholes; the motor died. "One must expect a few such things," she wrote home cheerfully. A garage fixed the motor for two dollars. Then Bill Brown came for the weekend and they toured far and wide in his new Peugeot with only one flat tire—a pleasure that only emphasized Old Caroline's disabilities. For when she next took her out, Caroline threw a rod. Repair, the mechanic informed her, might cost 6,000 francs. Outraged, Aunty Lino stormed Monsieur Muraille. She won from him the cancellation of the last 1,500 francs, but also the admission that the Renault was fifteen years old. "The fact is that I fear I have been done," May wrote Cambridge sadly.

The garage issued grim bulletins. Piston rods needed replacing, the motor was shot, and even if she invested 6,000 francs in repairs, another part would blow in a week. May now owned a car that wouldn't run and no one would buy. The Limbosches gathered round, clucking sympathetically. Then a knowledgeable car man turned up, took one look at Caroline, and announced that the carcass was a repainted Green Taxi that had run all during the war, making it closer to thirty years old.

May admitted defeat, but nothing ultimately could faze her. She arranged to rent a new Renault for 9,000 francs at 100 kilometers a day, 2.50 francs for each additional kilometer. Judy would surely kick in, but of course it was George who absorbed the loss from the Renault and paid for the rental. "So, dearest Daddums you have saved your little mouse," May wrote happily. "Will you have this money ($200) *cabled in dollars.* . . . It is something learned anyway!" The terrible head cold and violent colitic cramps that followed this debacle were probably Old Caroline's legacy.

Though they had been rather jealous of Bill Brown, the Limbosches were highly pleased with Judy, whom Aunty Lino thought distinguished and so much more adept at French than Bill, who could only say "Tiens!" May had a great deal of fun showing Judy Belgium with the Limbosches, for whom she and Judy paid all expenses, meanwhile trying to find time for Jean-Do. She dreaded their parting, more painful each year.

On July 14 they left for Paris, noting the difference between tidy Belgium and dirty France in every village street. Judy stayed with friends, May at the Hôtel Saint-Simon. She dined with Paul Child, Edith Kennedy's onetime lover, and his wife, Julia, "a big, simple kind Californian girl"; took Judy to the circus, the theatre, and boating on the Seine; saw people for lunches and dinners. If comparison of this summer to last year's with Juliette pained her, she did not admit it. "Judy is happy as a lark and so am I. . . . I do not deserve it but I am enjoying it as if I did!"

From Paris to Le Petit Bois, picnicking on the way on the banks of the Loire. They found Grace Dudley a skeleton of ninety-six pounds, existing on beer, which she sipped all day, too weak to see anyone very long. They stayed with Grace's neighbors the Lestanvilles, supped on lamb chops grilled over a wood fire and Vouvray, were told that 1949 would be one of the great wine years.

From Le Petit Bois down the Loire to Nantes, through a primitive part of Brittany with cottages buried under haystacks, to the sea, and then to Pontivy and Mabel's old friend Elsie Masson, both May and Judy "in a perpetual state of joy and admiration" when not appalled by war damage, much of it inflicted by American Flying Fortresses. Then back to Belgium and the ferry to England, where they stayed in London as paying guests with Jane Stockwood. May would sail August 13, Judy stay on with friends into September.

Despite dinner with Ruth Pitter and "a heavenly afternoon" with the Huxleys' son Anthony, his wife, and their three girls, London was grim. Kot, she was told, was too depressed by the recent burglary of his house to see her. "The evil spell" seemed broken when the Huxleys invited her and Judy to tea; but the tea was a nightmare—other guests, Julian depressed and silent, Juliette's lovely chin in the air. She and May did not exchange a word. And though May wrote them both warm letters from the boat, they did not reply.

She returned to Channing Place (Judy had sublet their apartment), disgusted with Europe for the first time. Martyred Mabel complained she had had no help all summer, so May pitched in as dishwasher and scullery maid. Sleepless at night, she battled Juliette, rehearsing her wrongs. "I really had never imagined that pain could be so acute over so long a period of time," she wrote Bill. "And I grind my teeth at the waste, the waste of real love—if they only knew and could see. But I will not give up yet," vowed the eternal orphan. ". . . All I want now is to feel included again. . . ."

News that Rinehart liked *Shadow of a Man* hardly cheered her. "I am not really a novelist as everyone knows. . . . I know in my heart that at best it is just another novel (and there are so many!) when it should have been good. The thing is that a novel exposes one's every lack—in maturity, style, understanding etc. and requires such a *large* imagination, whereas poetry only needs perhaps a certain depth and intensity in one area. . . . It is devilishly difficult." Yet she had not kept *Shadow* back to nurse into excellence.

On October 24 she left for the Midwest to earn $700 lecturing on "Why Read Poetry?" in Carbondale, Cape Girardeau, and Lindenwood, and at Beloit and Cornell Colleges. In Carbondale she was immediately stricken with colitis, a product of the terrible nervousness she always felt before speeches. It cheered her that people there had read *The Bridge of Years;* these trips, then, were worthwhile as publicity. Writers, it seemed, were either notorious successes, like Truman Capote and Tennessee Williams, or unknowns. Frustratingly, she still fit the latter category.

As a reward for nerves, small audiences, and student apathy, she spent two weeks at Agnes Sims's guest cottage in Santa Fe, arriving on November 14 with a monumental cold. "I really have a pain all the time that you have never been here," she wrote Mabel and George, "and so really cannot imagine it. . . ." This time, however, Santa Fe did not work the poetic miracle—and, back in Cambridge, the inevitable distractions of Channing Place, friends, and Christmas shattered her concentration. She had made only two thousand dollars in 1949, was—as usual—in debt, and forced to beg George for money. "I am absolutely cut off again from poetry here in a bog of depression and short stories and looking for a teaching job and doing accounts," she wrote Bill in the new year, "and were it not for dear Judy and the cat I should be feeling very low indeed. . . . Christmas is really a disastrous time for me—so wasteful of time and energy and so depressing for some reason. . . . The root of all my sadness is that I feel time passing and realize that the best of my energy is not going into what my real gift is, and so my life seems a sort of betrayal."

Yet she was polishing a Santa Fe poem, "On a Winter Night," in which the speaker, "feeling old, strange / At the year's change" finds in the ashes of a fire not annihilation but rebirth:

May with Elizabeth Bowen in Cambridge in the 1950s

> For then I saw
> That fires, not I,
> Burn down and die;
> That flare of gold
> Turns old, grows cold.
> Not I. I grow.

The poem was important not only as affirmation but for the discovery that she could use experiences that happened long ago—that is, photograph an experience in a burst of poetic energy, but develop and print it later. Yet she simply could not feel intensely now about anything. No one excited her, inspired her—not even "wonderful, kind, appreciative, warm and real" Elizabeth Bowen, staying with them two nights at Oxford Street on a lecture tour. "Sometimes I feel like a prisoner," she moaned, reflecting the mood of another poem, "The Tiger." There would be no Europe this summer. Could she, without passionate love, generate her own creative excitement?

Shadow of a Man was published in May 1950, to less than popular acclaim. A certain *New York Times* critic used to categorize novels as good-good, bad-good, good-bad, and bad-bad. *Shadow* falls into the bad-good category, a novel of style and a certain subtlety that doesn't come off. Its hero catapults from happiness to confusion to blankness to misery to savagery to humility to radiance—to little purpose; for the story of this young man's passage through the Venusberg of an older woman's love never grips. For all his violence, savagery, and rudeness—perhaps because of them—Francis does not cast the shadow of a man. Rather, the novel reflects May's own violence, muffled by a didactic ending: "But now at last I can have my own shadow, the shadow of a man. It means all kinds of things, Ann. It means responsible love; it means what I can do in teaching and as a father and as a human being, and it means maybe what I can be as an American, an everyday kind of person really . . . for that's what we believe in, isn't it? In the unlimited power of being human." May on her soapbox again. By October *Shadow* had sold only 3,400 copies—"a dismal failure."

That late spring, Mabel was decidedly unwell. In July she was hospitalized; doctors diagnosed lung cancer. On August 19 May brought her terminally ill mother home; three weeks later Mabel, the woman "with gardens springing up under her feet," visited her garden for the last time. In mid-September May and Judy moved to a house at 9 Maynard Place, but she was often at Channing Place, where Mabel's lung was drained every three days of a quart of deep red fluid. "I must say I find it hard to imagine the end and that queer emptiness," May wrote Bill, "but the only thing is to take each day as it comes. And she has had a good deep life full of riches she has made herself. What more can life be than that?"

Glib words concealed the intense conflict Mabel's dying roused in her. She forced herself to go to Channing Place; but the sight of the fierce spirit struggling in a dying body alienated her. Perhaps because Mabel had deserted her so often in childhood, she could not now give her lonely mother the companionship she craved. She brought armfuls of flowers, tidied the bed, bought the champagne and oysters which were all Mabel could eat ("What is this?" complained George, coming upon May coaxing Mabel to swallow an oyster. "A *party?*")—but she fled the house, unable to bear either her mother's suffering or her father's aloofness. For years George had stuffed his pockets with peanuts for the squirrels in the Harvard Yard; now he tried to show a similar solicitude for Mabel, but his remoteness was ingrained. "I cannot reach him to take his hand in mine," said Mabel, "—instinctively he withdraws it, even resents such an attempt as presumptuous: *only another man of science* can understand or comfort him."

George brought his wife illustrated books on West African bronzes, but Mabel preferred bulb and seed catalogues, though she knew she would never plant again. On November 18 at seven p.m. May said good-bye to her mother and returned to Maynard Place. Shortly after nine, the night nurse called to say that Mabel had died quietly in her sleep.

"She was beautiful and herself to the end though literally wasted away," May wrote Bill, "and after it is over I know how I shall feel her radiant presence by my side. Now it is just the emptiness, the telephone calls, the flowers to acknowledge and so many people to tell." A simple memorial service was held November 21. A few days later, "Aunt Mary" Bouton told May it was her duty to move into Channing Place and take care of her father. May wept all night. The next day she wrote George, lecturing in New York:

Perhaps she imagines, as some people may, that I could ever be a substitute for mother in your life or that a daughter can in any way replace a wife. What I can be and must be is myself to the fullest limit. . . . I think you do understand that Judy and I have now formed a real partnership which will, God willing, last out our lives and though this is not a marriage, it is an abiding relationship. . . . If we should come and live with you, it would be a different thing—we should be living your life and not our own. . . . Mother knew it. Anne Thorp knows it.

In the last fearful months I have felt so close to you, dearest Daddy, as I never did before, loving you too in a new way because of your infinite patience and loving kindness with mother and with me. Surely the crown of all those forty years was the last months when I felt you and mother newly wedded through pain.

So now we can go on hand in hand, living our separate lives but truly parallel and sharing so much. I shall never be worthy of my two parents, but at least I do know that and am humble before it.

George immediately hired a housekeeper, Julia Martin, to care for him. Reading friends' testimonials to Mabel's grace, sympathy, generosity, and tact, he was struck by remorse. He attempted to assuage his conscience by beginning a biography, *The Adventures of a Scholar's Wife.* He proceeded in a scholarly way, researching Mabel's family, writing letters to Belgian and English friends, using material from his own diaries. His discoveries did nothing to relieve his guilt. They reminded him that every one of Mabel's colleagues at the Koninklijke Academie voor Schone Kunsten, where she studied from 1905 to 1908, had become professional artists. They reminded him that she had resisted marrying him for years because she wanted a career. They reminded him that he had deprived her for much of their married life of a car, money, companionship, and, above all, a garden.

Guilt burdens this work of intended homage. "I failed her in many ways . . . I cannot forgive myself . . . I was very inferior to her." In the end, however, George probably learned little from his well-intentioned effort. He found he was unable to describe Mabel because he had never really looked at her. He found himself indulging in elaborate footnotes—more notes finally than text, many about himself. His immense relief when, having dispatched Mabel's family, he could turn to himself was comic: "The reader must now put up with me for a few moments for I am about to describe Mabel's marriage, and a marriage concerns very specially and equally two persons. In order to appreciate it one must know the bridegroom as well as the bride." Had he been able to read the biography objectively, he would have discovered that it was, finally, a testimony to his monumental self-absorption. Perhaps this is why he abandoned it.

May's guilt for "abandoning" Mabel would last a lifetime. And the brutal finality of death haunted her:

> I saw my mother die and now I know
> The spirit cannot be defended. It must go
> Naked even of love in the very end. . . .
>
> Let us be gentle to each other this brief time
> For we shall die in exile far from home,
> Where even the flowers can no longer save:
> Only the living can be healed by love.

She set about creating from a humanly flawed woman Saint Mabel Sarton, a martyr tortured by the ogre-husband their daughter hated. No one, least of all herself, could utter a word against this deity: "Everything is perfect about my mother." Her dying, May argued, was in one sense a relief, because nothing worse could happen to her in her lifetime.

CHAPTER 14

New Novels, New Poems, New Lovers: 1951–1955

In 1950–1952, May taught two composition courses twice a week at Harvard as a Briggs-Copeland appointee. The large house at 9 Maynard Place was partly subsidized by student renters. Without Judy, May would indeed have been forced to live with George, for she earned a bare subsistence.

Life with Judy was good, safe; yet May was often dissatisfied. Denied passion, she could be jealous of Judy's colleagues, the "Silver Fish," who met once a month at each other's houses for dinner; once she hurled a frying pan at a Fish's head. "You can give friendship to Edie, to Dorothy—to anyone except to me," she accused. ". . . I can it seems, be good for everyone, except you, be loved by everyone except you, communicate with everyone except you. It is strange, so strange that I sometimes wonder if this is a bad dream and I will wake up."

But Judy knew May's power over her, knew that May would seize love, sympathy, and sex wherever she found it. She also understood May too well for May's comfort, realizing that her frequent migraines, violent colds, and attacks of colitis were products of tension and guilt, knowing the extent to which May compulsively demanded attention: "You write too many letters to too many people *all the time*."

The Christmas of Mabel's death May sent lipsticks, stockings, and chocolate to Juliette, vainly hoping that door might reopen. The death of James Stephens occasioned a subdued letter of condolence to Kot: "I send you my love and many thoughts and much gratefulness for the good days when several times I drank tea at your table with James. Do you remember

189

the wonderful drink you made in the square cut glass bottle? How fine it was to be a little drunk on it and poetry, together." Though Kot remembered, his door too remained closed.

Frustrated in writing and in love, May sailed for England May 24, going directly to the de Selincourts', where every day there were delicious excursions to Oxford and the Cotswolds, though she was suffering one of her terrible colds. London from June 5 to 20, the city echoing Kot, James, Julian, and Juliette. Then the avenue Lequime. She had hoped to recapture her mother there, but when Céline spoke of Mabel, May felt she had never known her. When she hurried to the avenue de l'Échevinage and into the darkened study, she saw for the first time that Jean-Do was sick and old. The frail poet had hoped to be the first Peacock to die; but now that Marie Gaspar too was dead, she felt a sense of liberation. Yet, quite blind, she was as dependent upon the ministrations of strangers as an infant. She did not seem to mind. By stripping down to essentials, she was instinctively preparing for death.

May saw Eugénie Dubois again, and what she had (surely) planned happened: Eugénie fell deeply in love. Again, this was the kind of disillusioned middle-aged woman to whom May appealed extraordinarily, not least because she believed she was giving May poetry. As she expanded in that green summer under May's ardent lovemaking, she confessed her woes—the husband who told her, "I shall never be faithful but you must never give me up," who cried impatiently "Vite! Vite!" when she failed to reach a quick climax. And May too fell in love. "Eugénie under the trees, the barley waving its long tassels together in the wind. She, like a blue sky opening over a prisoner's head, saying, 'But you *must* love, for the sake of poetry!' " The prisoner was freed, morally and creatively.

When May met Judy in Paris, Eugénie's letters followed, often written in English so that her husband could not surprise her unpleasantly. "All that has happened seems extraordinary to me. The whole of the world has suddenly turned into paradise. . . . I love your being the ardent initiator— a river of fire." Eugénie was already dreaming of next summer, wondering whether she could keep the secret of their love entirely to herself. Yet May must not hurt Judy.

From Paris May went alone to Méta and Marc Turian in Satigny, Switzerland. Their home, La Roselle, was set on a rolling plateau with vineyards rising against the purple Jura Mountains. The house was divided into Marc's quarters downstairs, where all the cooking was done for the

*Eugénie Dubois
with her son Eric*

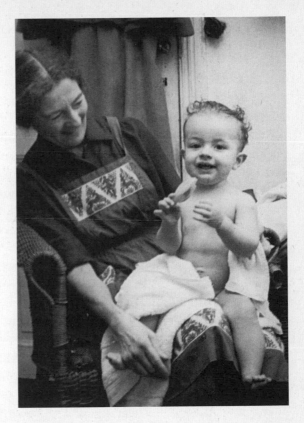

laborers, and Méta's flower-filled domain above, which Marc never visited without pulling felt slippers over his *vigneron*'s boots. Perhaps May expected to find Mabel here too; instead she found Méta. What was it like, psychologically, to have a sudden, furious affair with her mother's "old flame"? An exorcising of Mabel? An attempt to find her in the arms of her dearest friend? A way for the desperately insecure daughter to feel included? Or simply another adventure for all-conquering May?

She told Eugénie—Eugénie, who was visiting Céline and Jean-Do just to hear them utter May's name. Eugénie took it nobly. "I like to think of Méta, like you une allumeuse, une enfant terrible, une Bacchante. And I wonder what beautiful fire you are able to light together." She wondered whether her own fire with May had been a dream.

May sailed from Cherbourg August 8, writing Eugénie from the boat that she must tell her husband about their affair. Eugénie answered in distress: May had promised not to interfere with her happy little family. Yet she could not be angry with her lover long. "I was starving and you brought me such peace as I had never experienced. . . . And then you are so understanding, so gentle, with such sensitive imagination that I too feel I must tell the truth. . . ."

Europe had worked its old magic—nourished roots, tapped the creative sap. Arriving in New York, she immediately booked passage for the following June, then went for two weeks to Breadloaf, Vermont, for a writers' conference, where everybody drank too much and she taught the short story. She was already seventy pages into a new novel inspired by Elizabeth's Irish manor house, Bowen's Court, which she had finally visited after the Glenavy disaster in 1948. By November, despite advanced writing classes at Harvard, she was driving to finish *A Shower of Summer Days.*

Sometimes the thought of her two loves terrified her, for each was ardent—and there was still Judy. Eugénie's letters were hymns of joy to the pure love she had found with May. She continued to visit both Jean-Do and Céline regularly to talk about her lover, but became decidedly disillusioned with Céline, who "*cannot* leave off being a narrow moralist who does not understand any form of neurosis. . . . She is a force of nature and I like her, but I do not agree with her, not in one thing. . . ." She wished May would make their Linkebeek home her headquarters next summer. May wrote Aunty Lino, begging off; received a volley of protest; compromised. Meanwhile, Méta waited to clasp May in her arms again. And Judy was planning their summer jaunt with Jane Stockwood and Anne Duveen through the Dordogne. It promised to be a full summer.

She sent her novel to Rinehart, who replied in January 1952 that it needed expanding. She finished it at Channing Place, where she'd taken refuge until Judy found them another place to live; in April Rinehart accepted the manuscript. It was at Channing Place that she celebrated her fortieth birthday. Her hair, permed and swept back, was streaked prematurely white, a striking contrast to her perfect skin, straight nose, and high cheekbones. She was slenderer and handsomer than she'd been at thirty. She wore clear red lipstick, sleek suits with exotic scarves, and draped slacks. She had a trick of throwing her head back, infectious laughter spilling out. And she still had the energy of forty tigers.

She sailed in early June, her new Austin aboard. "There you are—on the boat and free at last!" Eugénie wrote ecstatically. "Free" was not the word: the summer was the kind of frantic hell only May Sarton could survive. As she and Judy were settling down in Brittany before the drive with Anne and Jane through France, she heard that Jean-Do was dying.

"Damned sentimental friends *made* me drive back 500 miles to Brussels for 24 hours to be in at the kill. However she pulled through that time, only I think I spent my last reserve of feeling and strength there. . . . By the time we started out I had really begun to hate the car and wanted only to sit by a roadside and chew a piece of grass forever. Instead we hurtled down through Chartres . . . Poitiers, Perigueux . . . Brantome. . . . Then we pulled up stakes to go South as the English friends longed so for heat (!) and the Mediterranean." As driver and planner—and longer for Eugénie—May was tense, irritable. Finally she left her companions at Dieppe, sped to Belgium, "and there I found again my love and really the deepest of such experiences I have ever had." Poems came, among them the sensuous "Prothalamion":

> How pure the hearts of lovers as they walk
> Through the rich quiet fields
> Where the stiff wheat grows heavy on the stalk,
> And over barley and its paler golds
> The air is bright . . .

The affair was serious enough for May to talk about leaving Judy, whom Eugénie had come to resent. Judy actually dared criticize May for snubbing the Limbosches, actually reproved her for her tantrums. Judy was harshly judgmental because, said Eugénie, in her heart she disapproved of May's life. Whereas she, Eugénie, longed to protect "the vulnerable, thin-skinned emotional side" of May.

Meanwhile Jean Dominique was indeed dying. May spent hours in the dark room holding the tiny hand until she lapsed into a coma. Four days later she was dead. "It is queer but I still cannot feel much about Jean-Do except relief for her that the long struggle is over," May wrote Bill. ". . . Yet I know later there will be an immense hole—and already I find myself wondering 'Whom will I *tell?*' "

Then May heard that Méta was partially paralyzed on one side from a nervous shock. She was waiting for May's return like the second coming, hoping that the miracle of May's passion would cure her. May arrived at La Roselle and was immediately stricken with colitis. She knew its cause: "I simply this time cannot divide myself." Her feelings for Eugénie were too intense for her to switch to Méta. Finally she told Méta she could not possibly make love. "I hope that in spite of her awful grief, slowly the tenderness I do feel for her very deeply, will make up for the loss of passion," May wrote Bill. "But it has been a fearful strain, I must confess."

She stayed at La Roselle until August 28, then drove back to Brussels for a tearing goodbye to Eugénie. She talked of leaving Judy; but this would be difficult when Judy was back in Cambridge finding them and Tom Jones, their cat, a place to live. May sailed for home September 7, feeling "cut off again from all inner life."

Finding no suitable apartment, Judy had bought a small house at 14 Wright Street, a short, narrow block tucked off Massachusetts Avenue. The converted harness shop was barracks-like from the outside but had two big study-bedrooms, a formal and an informal living room, and a garage for the Austin. May plunged into classes, quickly feeling "like a neurotic rat caught in a trap. I give an occasional desperate squeak and then get back on the treadmill, my little feet running as fast as they can till I drop exhausted." The only way to get through the year was "to regard teaching not as a job but as a *gift,* to give all I can freely, without reservation—otherwise it is a nightmare of frustration." But it was impossible for her, a writer, to give everything. Nor was she temperamentally a teacher: "The values which interest me passionately have to do with feeling. . . ."

A Shower of Summer Days was published October 23. Critics and readers applauded this lovely evocation of an Irish country house and its effect on a rebellious young American who comes to spend the summer. Violet Gordon, the chatelaine of Dene's Court, is not Elizabeth Bowen, though Charles Gordon is very much Elizabeth's kind, long-suffering husband, Alan Cameron. But it is Dene's Court, buried in countryside so lush that its high rooms take on a subaqueous glimmer, that is the main character—a symbol, again, of the cultural grace and permanence May associated with Europe. This was a fine novel, her best because, through a tightly controlled lyric style, she achieved the *atmosphere* essential to all good novels. Yet May was miserable because *A Shower of Summer Days* narrowly missed being a Book-of-the-Month Club selection.

Determined not to do another "feminine sensitive" book, she had been making notes for a novel based upon the 1950 suicide of the Harvard English professor Francis Otto Matthiessen, which had shocked academe. Matthiessen was an idealistic radical who believed (wrongly, it turned out, in those years) that communism and socialism could work compatibly in Eastern Europe. *Faithful Are the Wounds* thus asks the question, "Can a man be right and wrong at the same time?" Yes, answered May: idealism in any cause is preferable to indifference. The novel pitted Edward Cavan (Matthiessen) against a cautious Harvard establishment ruled largely by personal ambition. Yet she eschewed black-and-white characterization, easy answers. "I get terrified when I think of the next book," she confessed to Bill. ". . . a big theme instead of a little one. . . . It will be laid in Cambridge and most of the characters will be men which scares me, but a lot of things scare me about it." Not least, the local setting: *Faithful Are the Wounds* would be May's first really American novel.

In fact in the new year, 1953, things were "looking up in a wonderful way." *Shower* had finally awakened publishers to her talents, giving Diarmuid Russell enough clout to sell Rinehart the new book of poems, *The Land of Silence,* and win May a $1,500 advance on *Faithful Are the Wounds.* In New York she collected a $200 prize from the Poetry Society of America for the poem "Journey Toward Poetry," then heard she'd won a $3,000 creative writing fellowship from Bryn Mawr, which meant release from the dreaded teaching for more than a year. She was being taken seriously as a writer at last.

Ironic that this rush of good luck should come after the deaths of Mabel and Jean Dominique. They had liberated her: "Now I become myself. It's taken / Time, many years and places." She was no longer "the child of the house"—either of Channing Place or of the avenue de l'Échevinage; for Mabel's death had freed her to some extent too of George, whose egoism she had suffered chiefly through Mabel. Though they argued heatedly when she and Judy dined at Channing Place (Judy covering her ears with her hands), she still wrote him faithfully on her travels. But George was experiencing his own freedom. "Do not expect anymore news from me," he wrote jauntily on the eve of a European trip, "as I shall be terribly busy, meeting all kinds of people, & thinking my own thoughts."

Even poetic fashion, she could feel in 1953, might be swinging her way. May always called herself a lyric poet misborn into the austere and pessimistic world of Eliot and Auden. She distrusted intellectuality in poetry. Elinor Wylie's, for example, was "like a metal image instead of a plant," while Auden's, like that of most male poets, was weakened by "this terrible division in him of emotion and mind." In 1940 she had asked Louise Bogan what could be done about the current distrust, even hatred, of lyric poetry. "Nothing, I suppose," Bogan answered. ". . . The only thing to do is: do what one can, and not sell out."

May felt it high time that a Dionysian poet like Dylan Thomas was restoring sensuousness to verse. Bogan, lecturing to a shamefully small audience of thirty (mostly May's students) at Radcliffe, seemed to agree, deliberately reading her austere but voluptuous "After the Persian." May had long admired Bogan's poetry, though thinking her "rather mean to women poets in general." After May championed her poetry that Radcliffe evening, Bogan invited her to see her in New York.

Involved in the new novel, May gave up Europe that summer. With two hundred pages of *Faithful Are the Wounds* written, she went to Breadloaf to teach The Novel from August 16 through 26. Two years before at Harvard, she had been "fearfully attracted" to one of her students but had desisted ("great self restraint I may say!"). When the student turned up at Breadloaf, May felt that virtue had been rewarded. Soon Beth (not her real name) was telling May she'd only begun to feel true passion in May's class. Soon after that confession, she was sharing May's bed; almost as soon she was talking about leaving her husband if May would leave Judy.

All this May reported to Eugénie, adding tactlessly that it was wonderful to be in love for a change with someone her own age. "Does she know how many times you have been just as wildly in love?" sighed Eugénie, increasingly disillusioned with May's myriad lovers, her constant need to be on the move, her endless correspondence. "Even when here, you not only allow letters to pile up (from people to whom you ought not to have given your address!) but feel compelled to rush to one or the other uninteresting person, who then gets more and more demanding."

She did not tell Judy about Beth, who lived in Washington, making weekends challengingly inconvenient. Then in November Beth confronted May: she had been serious about leaving her husband; obviously May was playing with her. This was the hazard with younger women. The Métas, Eugénies, and Grace Dudleys were grateful for spare crumbs; younger lovers wanted commitment. May could not give it. She had the grace to be rather appalled at the "strange and terrifying" emotions she had roused in a woman for whom, after all, she cared little.

Professionally 1953 ended less happily than it had begun. Notoriously hard on herself, she now felt that except for "The Swans," "The Leaves of the Tree," and "The Second Spring," the published *Land of Silence* was "full of faults, impurities and over-statements." At a dinner of fellow poets at Richard Wilbur's, she decided that Theodore Roethke and Wilbur were "the two most interesting younger poets now. . . . I get a kind of ache of humility when I think of them—and really my only hope is a long life and so a chance to improve." (Roethke was awarded a Pulitzer that year.) But she always felt traumatically inferior to contemporary male poets.

A group of them—Wilbur, John Holmes, Richard Eberhart, John Ciardi—met regularly at each other's houses during these years to drink whiskey and read their poetry. May was the only woman in the group. She was writing political poems like "Take Anguish for Your Companion"—

not her forte, and Ciardi in particular savaged them. "May," Richard Wilbur later recalled, "perhaps because she was then more accomplished as a fiction writer, and wished to improve her secondary talent as a poet, played fairer than the rest of us; she took criticism seriously, and often appeared at our meetings with poems which had been reworked and bettered." He refrained from saying that she often ended an evening in tears.

Since he knew May considered herself primarily a poet, Wilbur's remark is deliberately dismissive. Her negative experience contrasts vividly with Anne Sexton's in the Boston area that same decade—Sexton, who won a scholarship to work with W. D. Snodgrass, attended Robert Lowell's seminar at Boston University, delivered the Morris Gray Poetry Lecture at Harvard, and eventually became a professor of creative writing at Boston University. Sexton was accepted; May suffered. When Ciardi left the area in 1955, he could write John Holmes, "I think the one thing I really miss in this shift to NJ is those poetry meetings." Oppressed by male authority and endemic insecurity, May could not say the same.

Ciardi officially blasted May's poetry in a review of *The Land of Silence* for *The Nation,* condemning it as "high-pitched," a quality to which he was "absolutely, fiercely, implacably, violently [and high-pitchedly] opposed." May was devastated. "What he does is to count the number of times certain abstract words such as 'intense' appear," she wrote Bill Brown; "the mean thing is that he quotes 'I tremble with desire' out of context so anyone reading the review would think it is a typically 'poetess' kind of poem and would have no idea it referred to a tiger. This I think dishonest." The terrible fears that seized her after each book of poems appeared turned her "into salt or lead." But then she had always had, since she could remember, "this queer sensation of walking on very thin ice above despair."

Fortunately, the difficult novel was going well, and she had signed a contract with *The New Yorker* for a series of personal reminiscences about Wondelgem and the Belgian school year. "The New Yorker stuff I am doing is easy because I am making no attempt to come to grips with *any* conflict," she told Louise Bogan, "(it would not be for them if I did, and it is not for me at this time)." In January 1954 she could tell Kot, who had written at last to thank her for *Land of Silence,* that she was "happy and full of work."

On January 22 May visited Louise in her apartment at 169th Street with its view of the Hudson River. There in "that robin's egg room where every object means something and is beautiful," she fell in love with the fifty-six-year-old poet with Irish green eyes. "Please accept the fact that you are beautiful," May wrote Bogan, who protested May's fervor, "and everyone must love you."

May would write Bogan seventy-nine times in 1954, telephone her regularly. Bogan responded sympathetically, but with reserve. She rejected a love affair, less because she couldn't love a woman than because, after cataclysmic relationships—particularly with her fury of a mother—she was wary. "So far as desire is concerned, I must wait," she wrote May. All her energies were going now into her work. Yet, "Be happy, dear May, and remember that I proffer you all that I can proffer any human being. Which isn't, I suppose, v. much; but all of it is fresh and real and non-*patterned*." Incautiously she sent May daffodils and iris. "Darling, darling, darling," exclaimed May, ". . . you must not be afraid of me. I do realize that you must be a little afraid (anyone would be after such a deluge of let-ters and calls), but I am very gentle at heart. . . ."

They were very different at heart. Louise had hard-won coolness and irony. She valued her job as the *New Yorker* poetry critic not only as income but because she found analysis congenial. May thought Bogan the critic crippled Bogan the poet: "The critical power stops the creative flow instead of merely disciplining and shaping it." She constantly urged Louise to open her heart to feeling (and to May). Louise as constantly urged May to slow down: "You *do* drive yourself so; you must give your-self periods of *careless* rest and relaxation between pressures."

May was delighted to have this close relationship with a poet who was respected by the critical establishment, but Bogan could be cruel, under-mining May's confidence by casual recitations of poets she planned to review for *The New Yorker,* award ceremonies she attended, inscribed books she received from dear Marianne and Randall. "The great and unexpected news is," May read with dismay, "that yesterday morning I received a letter from Alan Pryce-Jones, the gentleman who is evidently now editor of *The Times Literary Supplement,* asking me to do an article (2000–3000 words) for a special American literature number he plans, on the contemporary situation in American poetry!—Isn't that fantastic?" But how could May be pleased when she knew Bogan would not include her in the article?

Bogan could be severe with May's poetry, considering "My Sisters, O My Sisters" an "indignant essay" rather than poetry. Bogan's demur reinforced May's own doubts:

There are times when I believe that for years I have misunderstood the nature of poetry and hence have been battling to achieve

Louise Bogan, whom May loved as a poet, feared as a critic

something which does not exist. I do think—and I believe you do—that everything is material for poems, everything felt deeply, everything that springs from experience, from the most inconsequential to the most consequential. But there is a huge leap from the material to the poem and I think the great flaw in all my past work has been the belief that unadulterated "life," not sufficiently *transposed* and *depersonalized,* that the formulating of everything that was happening to me was the material of poetry. I think now that I always stood on the threshold and never really got into the sanctuary and this is very frightening. . . . I have wished for a wider range than is usual in the poetry of women, have wished to include everything in fact. . . .

"Of course, everything is material for poems—even the 'passive suffering' (sometimes) that Yeats deplored," Louise replied; "but argument should be dramatized, as Yeats learned to dramatize, rather than projected straight. . . . It is impossible really to argue, in lyric poetry, because too many abstractions tend to creep in—and abstract ideas must get a coating of sensuous feeling before they become true poetic material. . . . Certainly 'unadulterated life' *must* be transposed, although it need not be 'depersonalized.' Otherwise you get 'self-expression' only; and that is only half of art. . . ."

George meticulously recorded in his diary days of work missed because of illness, in late years chiefly chest and abdominal pains. In February 1954, after painful attacks accompanied by fever, he was taken to the hospital, where his gallbladder was drained; and May was forced to give up Italy with Eugénie to move back to Channing Place. On May 17, George had gallbladder surgery. Progressing from miserable-saintly to cranky-recovering, he recuperated in a nursing home and later, more pleasantly, at Newport with May, sea, sun, sherry, and cold lobster.

Between visits to the hospital and the nursing home, May struggled with the "inhuman, monstrous" *Faithful Are the Wounds.* Diarmuid told her frankly that her subject was impossible. A friend warned that Matthiessen's relatives might sue for libel. May battled with the novel all spring, driving to revise and finish. Bogan urged a cooling-off period: "I keep thinking that it would be better if you put some time between you and the MS. . . . You are more of a happy-first-draft person than I am; nothing pleases me more than fussing and re-working things, once they have been *cast onto the paper.*" But on June 15 May took the manuscript to a typist. Now she was free for Eugénie in August. For the first time, she would fly.

Belgium was "wintry," and Raymond, the cynical philosopher, had died, increasingly embittered in late years by Céline's domination. May loved Céline as usual, but "at bottom she believes in nothing," she wrote George, "—neither in man, nor in art, nor in God": the heritage of Raymond's long disillusionment. Céline also shut up like a clam when anybody mentioned May's writing, "because she is jealous for Raymond. I must say I miss him *very* much."

A few days later May and Eugénie left on a long-planned trip to Florence via Paris, Chartres, Dijon, and Grenoble, shedding sweaters as they drove south through hayfields and vineyards. On September 3 they arrived in Florence and took an apartment on the Via Sallustio Bandini for ten days, during which May worked mornings while Eugénie explored. Florence itself reverberated with motorcycles and radios, which they escaped by driving into the country for picnic suppers. Méta telegraphed that she expected May September 18, so they left "pagan" Italy via Ravenna for Lausanne, where Eugénie would catch a train.

They parted in a café. After May left, Eugénie sat "completely immobile and submerged" for hours. The trip had not been ideal—May's bursts of temper and restless need for other people distressed her—but Eugénie was more deeply in love than ever. "I love you infinitely," she wrote in French. "The intimate three weeks of the trip elevated all that I previously felt to a new and higher plane." But May did not want to be loved. Wisely and sadly, Eugénie read the signs. "Do not agonize over your New England conscience," she added, "even if you meet immediately someone else who moves you." May would spend part of October at Linkebeek; Eugénie told herself it was enough.

At La Roselle May polished poems begun in Florence, but chiefly took notes for a *New Yorker* piece about Marc Turian, the *vigneron*. The courtyard was filled with barrels awaiting the wine harvest; yet the golden days needed after the rainy summer did not come, for suddenly it was autumn, with frosty nights, and May came down with the flu and one of her prodigious colds. Still, she left October 3 for Paris, where she saw friends and a possible translator for *A Shower of Summer Days,* then pressed on to Linkebeek and Eugénie, who assured her again and again, "I do love you so." It would be difficult expressing this love with her husband, Jean, in residence, but May was used to such intricacies.

In Brussels she collected 36,300 francs willed to her by Jean-Do and spent part of it on a luxurious red Afghan rug so that she would have one fine thing to remember her by. She also bought a dozen copies of Jean Dominique's *Selected Poems,* just out. On All Saints' Day, November 1, she and Eugénie walked miles across the golden countryside to the cemetery where Jean-Do was buried to lay chrysanthemums on her grave, but they arrived late and the gates were locked.

After a week with Céline, she flew to London. From Satigny she had written Kot: "I really have nothing to say except that I think often of November when I shall be in London and hope to drink gallons of tea with you." But Kot could not see her. She called the Huxleys ("How courageous!" said Eugénie). Julian was in America, Juliette busy. So she searched for a despatch case for George's seventieth birthday before visiting the de Selincourts', where Basil, helpful as usual, went over her poems. She also saw Roger Fry's sister Isabel in her unheated sixteenth-century farmhouse; Ruth Pitter in Bucks; Leonard Woolf at Rodmell; and countless other friends and acquaintances. In Cambridge she found Barbara Runkle Hawthorne, her beloved Tig, drinking heavily. She still could not boil water for Will's tea, but Will was a saint and loved her.

May flew home November 28. The next evening she and Judy dined with George at Channing Place. During her trip she had written the man she claimed she hated thirty-three communications—a letter or postcard every 3.3 days. Love could hardly do more.

In January 1955, she heard that Kot was dead, a series of heart attacks following deep depression. The now permanent loss of this remarkable friend occasioned a flood of memories. "So many thoughts," she wrote in her diary. ". . . So glad Leonard Woolf went to see him before the end. It will have meant a great deal. On Kot himself, peace at last—but how to imagine him *not* there, sitting in his kitchen with the stove at his back, lighting cigarettes with long bits of paper. . . . The deal table smooth—the plates on shelves, fruit in a bowl . . ." He had called her "Maylume"—luminous May. He had told her, "I am so fond of you that I should like to protect you against the ills of life." He had warned, "I want you to be aware of what you call your 'steel,' and what I call your wisdom. . . . I mean, that whatever mad or chaotic things you do never forget that there is your ultimate wisdom that must keep you safe and whole." He had loved Mabel: "Your mother is wonderful. There is no one like your mother. When we meet I'll entertain you to a long discourse on the superiority of English women to all other European women." And he had said, "I am not good at 'making' friends; true friends happen like great and rare events." He had been such an event in her life.

Memories of Kot prompted "three beautiful dreams of reconciliation with Juliette one after another! But the reconciliation was possible because I had (apparently) decided to take her *lightly,* and could say 'You were cruel' very lightly without reproach." Thoughts of Eugénie were more troubling: "Where is the wound? why only think of her with a kind of painful resistance?" Because Eugénie loved her, and she could draw no sustenance from being loved. As a result she began to quarrel. May angry could be terrifying, even by mail. "I am a little afraid," Eugénie replied. Why could she accept May's beliefs, but not May hers? "Now I am going to await an answer to this, *trembling. Please* do forgive." Eugénie retreated, writing less often. Still, she dreamed of the summer to come.

By March the excellent *Faithful Are the Wounds* was garnering well-deserved praise—her best review ever from *The New York Times.* But she soon discovered that certain elements at Harvard were not pleased. Harry

Levin, a distinguished professor of comparative literature and the solitary Jew in the English department, was convinced he was the model for Cavan's antagonist, Ivan Goldberg, particularly since May had given Goldberg Levin's foreign wife and ill child. May's personal assurance that she'd based Goldberg on another Harvard professor she'd seen exactly once didn't satisfy him—rightly; for May certainly knew that her fictional Goldberg would be linked to Levin. What she didn't know was that Levin would be hurt, or that her portrait would stir up the anti-Semitism lurking behind Harvard's civilized exterior.

"It may interest you to know," Levin answered, "that I have been asked, in Japan and Hawaii as well as in California, how I liked being a character in your novel." But Levin's objections to *Faithful Are the Wounds* went deeper. "I have never believed that you deliberately intended to lampoon me, and have minimized that view when others have taken it. But, having lived on close terms with Matty's tragedy, I am bound to feel the immense discrepancy between what happened and what you describe; and I find it hard to condone the insensitivity that has sought to exploit the association."

May believed that Levin forthwith launched a vendetta that scotched her rehiring as a Briggs-Copeland instructor and prevented her nomination to the prestigious Academy of Arts and Letters. But though Levin was wounded by Goldberg, this kind of revenge-taking, according to Walter Jackson Bate, chair of the Harvard English department at the time, was simply not in his character.

In the 1970s, May would again be attacked for not daring to make Edward Cavan a homosexual like F. O. Matthiessen—a criticism as reasonable as insisting that fiction be fact. May was not writing a biography of Matthiessen, but a novel about that universal figure the scapegoat, in this case the radical who atones with his life for the sins of his circumspect liberal friends. She wanted focus and thematic clarity, not literal truth: "I did not feel . . . that I could load my book both with a defence of the liberal and a defence of the homosexual, unconscious or conscious."

Jeanne Taylor, an artist living in Cambridge who knew friends of May's, read *Faithful* and invited her for a drink at 225 Brattle Street. There May met Jeanne's lover, Cora DuBois, the Zumarian Professor of Anthropology at Harvard and the author of a seminal work, *The People of Alor.* Cora was a big woman with a sense of humor who smoked cigars, favored tailored suits, and called herself "the Herr Professor." "And I'd never met anyone quite like her," said May. "That is, a pure intellectual. . . . I fell passionately in love with her, more than I've ever been physically in love with anyone."

Cora fell just as hard for May. "Oh, I know, there are 'problems,' " Cora would write her, "and it will take time, and there will be scratchy patches, and we shall neither of us get all we want, but this *has* happened. In your language—the miracle, and the mystery. In my language, the god-damned lucky break."

That year, 1955, May did what she often did: lectured far and wide, vacationed in Santa Fe, had poems published in *The Atlantic, The New Yorker,* and the *Saturday Review,* taught at Breadloaf, spent a Guggenheim grant for $1,200. The most important thing she did, however, was consult a psychiatrist. She had realized at last the frightening schism in her nature. There was the writer who could tame feeling and experience into poetic form, the wise woman who understood the human heart, the radiant woman who warmed people's lives, the woman of steel who was a survivor. The other May was a chaotic child who wept and raged and banged her empty dish on the table. This infantile May blamed others for her troubles, rationalized, evaded. She demanded exorbitant attention. Unstable emotionally, she could be destructive. Fearfully insecure, she could not be trusted with the security of others.

This problematic person had functioned forty-three years—leaving chaos in her wake, true, but also producing creatively. But the physical passion Cora DuBois aroused terrified May because it undermined her need to control. "I curse it, knowing well that the same thirst / Will turn me back to bless what I have cursed," she had written as a young woman. "How to turn this illness into wellness?" she agonized now. "For the awful thing about passion is that it *destroys* all other values. Nothing else exists—the awful senseless agitation, chaos . . ."

Encouraged by Dr. Pederson-Krag, May logged her feelings.

I loved my mother passionately. . . . In some ways my father and I were rivals and have remained so. It is perhaps significant that my relation with him has become very much easier and better since mother's death. But we are still rivals in some ways. For instance I feel a great deal of inner pressure about my work because my father is able to work so steadily and to produce so much. . . . He is very proud of me, however, as I learn from other people. I have taken the place of my mother as his mother now, and that, I think, is why we have come to an understanding. . . . I believe I have come to forgive him at last about mother.

This may be because I have a lot of guilt about my mother's last months. . . . I spent the summer nursing her and doing the cooking and housework at their house, and then as I was about to begin teaching at Harvard, got an Irish woman to take over. . . . This is a great weight on my mind. I still have fits of awful weeping about it. The loneliness of my mother's last weeks was awful. I see that now.

One more word. . . . In the most profound sense I honor both my parents and feel immensely lucky to have had them. They set each in his own way, high and valid standards for me—my father taught me to respect and demand of myself hard work. My mother taught me all the shades of sensibility toward others. It is a very rich inheritance and I am aware of that fact—it may be one reason why I feel a compulsion to "give," as if I had to give some of it back to life.

But she'd sought help because of another compulsion:

I do believe that creative people have one very great flaw, and this is worse in maturity than when they are young unless it can be controlled, namely to depend upon the excitement of the "love affair" as motor power. . . . For myself at present, it seems to work, to make occasional "excursions" outside, and to have long peaceful workful months with Judy in between. But in the last two years, two things happened which came to a kind of conjunction at Breadloaf and made me feel that I must rethink all this, not because it is not good for me, but because I may be doing harm to others. I have one great and unfair advantage which is that because I am a writer, everything is grist to my mill, and hence perhaps I have in some respects a hard heart.

What frightened her was the increasingly destructive pattern of these "excursions." In her defense, she cited the arguments of two Catholic apologists, Gustave Thiben and Louis Lavelle: that it is only by new affections that we prove our old; that communion with others is the only way to self-communion. Still, "is my whole conception of the love affair a rationalization to permit myself an outlet for certain drives which are in essence destructive?"

May was big on rationalization. At heart she didn't want to conquer a drive she considered fruitful, or confront her destructive self, as her poem "The Furies" makes clear:

Never look straight at one,
For then your self is gone.
The empty eyes give back
Your own most bitter lack,
And what they have to tell
Is your most secret Hell.

"So you really think, my dearest, that a few talks with a psycho-analyst (not even clever!!) will free you from your temperament all fire and earth?" Eugénie was skeptical, but then she believed in astrology. She was also terrified of losing May. "Your gift is love. Why not let it be?" But May could not let it be: she was driven to psychoanalysis to seek absolution for her terrible need to seduce and abandon. And permission. Not that she actually abandoned her lovers. She remained a friend as long as they understood their star had fallen out of her sky.

But now it was all Cora. After initial frustration and misunderstanding, they had a week of bliss. Unfortunately for Jeanne Taylor, the bliss had to occur under her and Cora's roof, since 14 Wright Street was too small for May and Cora to make love privately. Not that Judy didn't know. "Poor Judy," Eugénie wrote bravely, "I think of her with pangs of pain. . . . She must hate to prevent you from going over to Cora as well as fear that you should go."

This year Judy spent Christmas with her family. Neither the season of goodwill nor her Quaker tolerance could make palatable the spectacle of May's passion for Cora.

CHAPTER 15

"No Longer Child":
1956–1958

Lecturing in Texas in March 1956, May sent George a note and a flower: "Daddy dear, Just a little word to say that I am thinking of you especially on this first day of spring (when this reaches you I trust) and of your engagement—your marriage, as I see the many poor ones around seems such a wonderful thing, and how lucky I am to have had such parents. Your loving little Mouse." Early the morning of March 22, George called a taxi to take him to Logan Airport, where he was boarding a plane to Montreal to lecture. Halfway to Logan he felt ill and had the cab return to Channing Place. Julia Martin helped him to a chair, where he died of a heart attack. "My prayer is, when my time comes," George had often said, "God, *make it snappy!*" His prayer had been granted. The last entry in his diary had been, "Lovely day."

Telephoned by Julia, May felt such shock that for some time she was unable to call an airline or pack her bags. Eventually she pulled herself together and got a plane that hopped about the country a great deal before setting her in Boston, where Judy met her. Cora wanted to be at the airport to take May in her arms, but decided that was Judy's privilege.

May found that George had left things in order. He had chosen the music for his funeral—two Brahms choral preludes, the slow movement of Beethoven's "Archduke" Trio, Bach. He chose for a text I Corinthians 13 ("Though I speak with the tongues of men and of angels, and have not charity . . .") because it had been read at Mabel's funeral, though it "was not appropriate for him," said May. A blizzard paralyzed Boston the day of the funeral; mourners coming from New York, Chicago, Washington,

Philadelphia, and Canada were turned back; the Harvard Chapel, which May had expected to be packed, was half-empty. George probably would not have been dismayed. The man whose motto had been "I need neither hope to undertake, nor success to persevere," knew that his work was his memorial.

A few friends came back to Channing Place after the funeral. Later, May and Judy were sitting alone in the drawing room reading condolatory messages when the doorbell rang and John Malcolm Brinnin and Henry Schuman, George's sometime publisher, came in. Neither had been to the funeral, and Brinnin hadn't even known George, but May offered them sherry. Immediately they plunged into literary gossip. May began to smoulder. Finally she jumped to her feet. "*We were talking about my father,*" she said in a white fury. The men precipitously left.

Mabel and George had requested that their ashes be mingled. With Judy, Anne Thorp, and Mary Bouton, May made the pilgrimage to Mount Auburn Cemetery, where, high on the hill reserved by Harvard for foreign professors who did not own a burial site, an old gravedigger opened the two boxes and tipped their contents into the small pit. It was a mild, windy day, and a "thin smoke" of ash blew along the grass. The flat, oblong stone was engraved simply with the Sartons' names and dates.

George had modest bank accounts in Brussels, London, and Cambridge; his largest investment was a trust fund of over $60,000 for May with the National Shawmut Bank, yielding an annual income of about $3,600. A pity she was so inexperienced, for his library, which included a 1482 edition of Euclid's *Elements* and many early Arabic scientific texts, might have brought her more than the $5,000 she realized had she not allowed an unscrupulous dealer to steal the gems. Similarly, she might have gotten $75,000 for Channing Place, her chief legacy; but fearing taxes, she had a real estate agent list it for $35,000. Clearing out Channing Place in April, she felt drowning in *things*. She stored the big Flemish bahut and the inlaid desk Mabel had designed for the Brussels exhibit in the basement, along with the eighteenth-century portrait of a Sarton ancestor, Mabel's embroideries and hand-painted mirrors, her own portrait by Polly Thayer Starr, which had hung in George's study, and the silver laurel branch presented to George by the city of Ghent.

She had dedicated *The Land of Silence* to "E.M.S. In Memoriam." Now she celebrated George:

> I never saw my father old;
> I never saw my father cold.

His stride, staccato vital,
His talk struck from pure metal
Simple as gold, and all his learning
Only to light a passion's burning.
So, beaming like a lesser god,
He bounced upon the earth he trod,
And people marvelled on the street
At this stout man's impetuous feet. . . .

And when he died, he died so swift
His death was like a final gift.
He went out when the tide was full,
Still undiminished, bountiful;
The scholar and the gentle soul,
The passion and the life were whole.
And now death's wake is only praise,
As when a neighbor writes and says:
"I did not know your father, but
His light was there. I miss the light."

But to May her parents never died. She saw herself as a vessel contain-
ing their divine sparks. Like George, she was selfish, vital, and persistent.
Like Mabel, she was empathizing and giving. These warring impulses
never let her rest. Privately she could admit that Mabel was "the arch-
neurotic"; no matter what she told the psychiatrist, she had not forgiven
George. But these two dominated her private pantheon. She felt herself
unworthy of them. Guilt pursued her: she had hated her father, knew she
had failed him in not giving him a grandchild; she had never been able to
alleviate Mabel's terrible anxiety about money. They haunted her. How to
"lay down their deaths"? She could not let them go.

Louise Bogan very much admired May's translations of French poets. She
showed her rendering of Valéry's "Palme" to Jackson Matthews, who was
editing the complete Valéry for the Bollingen Foundation. Matthews was
impressed, and May and Louise began collaborating, financed by $1,000 a
year from the foundation. As it turned out, Bogan's French was limited:
May translated, Bogan polished.

The collaboration proved as useful as pleasurable. May felt increasingly
guilty about making love with Cora with Jeanne Taylor in the next room.

Valéry gave them a chance to escape to New York weekends, May work-ing days with Louise and spending nights with Cora. Though Cora cooed over her "Pussy," "Bunny," "Mouse," "Lamb," and "Snooks," May was discovering she had a temper as fiery as her own. She could also be cruel. "As far as I can see, May," she announced, "you have never written any-thing that has any value." Eventually May would come to believe that Cora was the kind of lesbian who hated women as much as any misogy-nistic male. Now love blinded her. They quarreled, May wept and raged, and they had passionate reconciliations.

Almost immediately after the publication of *Faithful Are the Wounds,* May had begun another novel. Yet she thought of herself as a poet rather than a novelist; to be a great poet was her ambition. "I told [a writer friend] if I had to choose between novels and poetry I would choose poetry without batting an eyelash," she told Louise Bogan, "without a *sec-ond's* hesitation and would choose it whether any one ever read the poems or not." Why, then, did May keep on writing novels, especially since George's death left her with enough money, supplemented by lec-tures, to live frugally? Why didn't she make the total commitment to poetry that Jean Dominique had urged years before?

The answer might be simply that she *could* write novels. But she also believed that she didn't have to choose. She had enough energy for nov-els, short stories, *New Yorker* pieces, articles, translations, and poems. And she did not take seriously enough Kot's and Juliette's and Bogan's advice to go slow: to prune, polish, refine, to let months or even years elapse between returning to a piece with a rinsed eye. May was always in a rush. And then she didn't know the meaning of writer's block: words came. Had she ever made a list of great poets who were also successful novelists, however, she would have found it short.

Though May's diary shows she wrestled with it, *The Birth of a Grand-father* had a relatively simple plot. Sprig Wyeth, a sensitive but repressed New Englander, cannot show affection for his family. Then he learns that his close friend Bill Waterford is dying of lung cancer. Paradoxically, Bill's dying releases Sprig's buried emotions. Finally, the birth of a grandson coincides with his own spiritual rebirth as a man mature enough to sus-tain a loving relationship with his family.

By now a Sarton novel has certain predictable features. The characters are drawn from her social experience, which ranges from schoolteachers who talk beautifully and drink dry martinis to wealthy easterners who also talk beautifully and drink dry martinis—and Châteauneuf-du-Pape. Every character is essentially *good:* sensitive, intelligent, responsible, civic-minded, loving or potentially loving. A world peopled by Sarton characters would be a far, far better place—though it might talk itself to death. Characters are based largely on people in Sarton's life. Sprig, for instance, is Richard Paine, Grace Dudley's brother-in-law, a wealthy Bostonian who played angel to May's theatre group. And places: the Wyeths' island home is Greenings Island, where in summer the wealthy Anne Thorp ruled. Plot in a Sarton novel is less important than the portrayal of rapidly shifting dynamics of human intercourse. Like shadow chasing sun, Sarton characters smile, weep, scowl, laugh, sigh, and wince in one beat. What grounds this chaos of sensibilities? The certainty that these people are working toward secular redemption. Community is all, human nature the divine mystery. *The Birth of a Grandfather,* like *The Bridge of Years,* reflects not only Sarton's craving for family but her belief that spiritual salvation lies in sustaining close human ties.

And did serious poets write charming little stories about their cats? *The Fur Person,* published in January 1957, is the tale of Tom Jones, a stray-about-town adopted by Gentle Voice (Judy) and Brusque Voice (May). While the two women initiate him into civilized catdom, Tom Jones teaches them lessons about feline priorities. *The Fur Person* would prove the most successful book May had thus far written: obviously, said critics, the author herself was part cat. May's old friend Hermann Field groaned. He had been imprisoned during the war in a Warsaw cellar, where he'd written a political novel called *Angry Harvest. Faithful Are the Wounds* had impressed him: finally May was stretching herself intellectually. And then *The Fur Person!* He felt it a terrible waste. Yet writers like T. S. Eliot and Jean Stafford allowed themselves innocent fun with cats.

My honey bunny, I want to write you a little paean of praise and love for it seems to me that you are the most wonderful person— and as I watched you walk down the street away from me this morning my heart smote me that I do not tell you this oftener. The hardest thing about all this is the allowing life to do it, the waiting and being suspended. But it is still true as ever that it is beyond my imagination to think of breaking up our life together, this dear house, and all we have invested in it of love and suffering too. On the other hand I do realize that a prolonged life, so divided, with everyone feeling that a half life is going on, is not possible as a long-term thing. At least so it seems now. But, darling, please do know that I have never loved you so much in a very special sense of the

word, love and *honor,* and great tenderness. Whenever I go away I
feel the tug of home.

Thus did May announce the eventual breakup of the Wright Street
house. Judy was suffering terribly, Jeanne Taylor was suffering, May was
suffering, presumably even Cora was suffering, as two people strove to
divide themselves among four. May was not prepared to leave quite yet,
but the "drowning and uprootedness" she complained of to Eugénie sig-
nalled that she already imagined life without Judy, "the earth under my
feet." What she wanted was a place of her own for Cora.

In December 1956, after a semester of Radcliffe seminars and week-
end translating sessions in New York, May ended in the hospital with
severe tonsillitis. There she made plans for Europe the next spring; a wiser
Eugénie knew nothing would be the same. She continued to placate Judy.
"My darling lamb," May wrote the eve of a flight to Hawaii with Cora,
"It is an awful wrench to leave our dear little house, our poor pussie and
you—but I feel we have come to some new and deep understanding—and
I leave more serene in my love for you and yours for me than ever
before. . . . Love and love, my dearest one." Certainly it would have been
easier for Judy had May broken with her cleanly. But May still needed her.

While May vacationed with Cora in Hawaii from March 11 to April
20, 1957, Tom Jones died. "There is no point dwelling on the emptiness
of this house, nor piling up adjectives," wrote Judy. ". . . I refuse to be
maudlin, even in my thoughts." Several weeks later Judy began seeing a
psychiatrist once a week, a radical step for someone so reserved. Her
severest problem was dependence on May, for it was true, as May claimed,
that she had brought love and light into the quiet life of a New England
spinster. But another problem was that in learning independence she
would hurt May, who counted on Judy's unquestioning devotion. And
that would be hard, for, as Judy told her, "I most deeply love you."

Judy did not know how often Cora baffled May's quest for intimacy.
Listening to Cora lecture at the University of Hawaii, May was conscious
of the professor's great power, which she participated in only as a specta-
tor in the front row. Each came "rich with spoils" from an inner life
which ultimately neither could share; thus the intensity of their passion
was "in direct proportion to the distance it must traverse." They were
"the poet and the hero"; yet comparing her gift with Cora's, May felt that
"power in reserve is everything." Cora made her feel inferior, which
made her fierce and defensive, which made Cora bully her the more.

There was another problem with Cora. May was used to playing
Doña Juana, but Cora insisted on making love to May, never allowing her

to initiate or control sex. Intensely frustrated, she felt that Cora was denying, even killing, her sexual vitality. After all, Cora was *her* Muse. She should allow May to woo her.

That year anger with Cora spoiled Europe. In London she found a letter from the Herr Professor deploring her constant need for facile reassurance. The letter was "so sneering and awful," she wrote Kay Martin, an older student from one of the seminars already elevated to "O darling" status, ". . . that I became quite ill with rage. I felt every hair on my head standing on end and it was just like a disease, which is still not cured." To Judy she confessed, "I keep thinking of those awful black rages mother suffered about Daddy, the waste of it—and C. is so like Daddy!"

On June 8 she crossed to Belgium to the Limbosches', where she planned to get back to writing if she could only fight her way through dozens of letters, dozens of people. "An awful lot of life comes at me here, because I am deliberately seeing friends of my parents to get all I can about their youth," she told Kay. It might be different at Eugénie's; at least "I always imagine this, and then there are always everywhere so *many* people." And Cora. The conflict "follows me here—it is one of the very rare times in my life when I feel a sort of awful gray dusty glass of *self* between me and the beauty of the place." She was reading Jung and Zen; she wanted to come back "hard and clear"—but how?

On June 20, though she did *not* get along with Jean, she went to the Duboises', settling into her little room under the eaves looking out over apple trees and fields of flax to huge beech trees on the horizon. And she might have worked if she had not been "locked into rage by Cora." She could not exorcise the demon, though she knew Cora couldn't change. Lack of communication now maddened her: to her anguished letters, Cora simply replied, "I'll be glad to discuss it in August." Sometimes it seemed the only answer was trying to find again the tender love she and Judy once shared. Yet she knew that was irretrievable, and that her own insecurity created much of the conflict with Cora.

Eugénie had conquered her grief over May by sheer will, aided by May's cool instruction to stop thinking so much about her. Now May hardly saw her because of demands of husband, school, grandson, and house, but on July 4 they left for Le Petit Bois for what she hoped would be seven days of quiet productivity. Instead she and Eugénie quarreled.

Eugénie had never told her children that she was Jewish. May argued that hiding the fact was dishonest and cowardly; Eugénie contended that she had done it for their safety during the war. May challenged her to break silence now. Voices grew hot. Then Eugénie cried, "Everybody knows your father was a Jew!" White with fury, May demanded an explanation. George's mother's family, the Van Halmés, Eugénie informed her, were certainly Jewish. Then May remembered: people mistaking her father for a Jew; she herself wanting to snatch a paper yarmulke off his head when they visited a synagogue for fear of permanent metamorphosis; her father storming out of the room when she said, "I think everybody is a little anti-Semitic." Back in Belgium, research into her great-great uncle von Sieleghem's abstruse will seemed to disprove a Jewish heritage—though now she did not dislike the idea. But the quarrel with Eugénie broke something permanently. It had nothing to do with Semitism but with the fact that May no longer cared much about Eugénie. "I have always admired faithfulness so much," May wrote Kay Martin, "and been incapable of it!"

May flew back to Boston July 31, to be met by Cora and Jeanne, since Cora did not drive. Judy had agreed to vacate Wright Street until August 9 so May could be alone there with Cora. They talked until May felt first again in Cora's life. Then unexpectedly Cora and Jeanne went out and bought a house on Coolidge Hill that they would occupy after Cora finished a year's teaching at Stanford. This demolished May until Cora told her that a small apartment might be made for her in the former servants' quarters so that she "would always have a haven." Yet the house only confirmed the unbearable fact that with Cora she was *not* first.

This fact mixed with liquor precipitated violent quarrels. Liquor in fact had become an unacknowledged problem. As the many drinking episodes in *The Birth of a Grandfather* betrayed, May was very fond of cocktails and wine, but had limited tolerance for alcohol. Cora also drank too much. When she did, she needled May. A pleasant evening could turn into mayhem after two double Scotches and a bottle of Beaujolais. May did not try to control her drinking. Drunk, she could avoid responsibility for her behavior. And she enjoyed the moments of power, the mounting crescendos of fury that ended in floods of cathartic tears. She had already chosen the phoenix as her symbol, the magic bird reborn from fire—in her case, from rage. After the terrible outbursts, weak but purged, the lovers would stumble to bed and reconcile with sex. But the toll these binges exacted should have sobered her. Judy had always been ready to pick up the pieces. Few others, no matter how much in love, could tolerate them for long.

"You are so buoyant that oscillation from hate to love, from rage to tenderness are possible," Cora wrote her. "Slow tortoise that I am, I only slowly accumulate the impact of events. I live in a shell; you in the air. I acquire through slow accretion layer after layer of conditional carapace. You, like a dragon fly, cleanse yourself from minute to minute on wings in the air. . . . Every quarrel, every scene, every rage leaves an indelible streak on my shell. I am embarrassed by the loss of human dignity, and distressed by the sordid impropriety. Please understand, darling, this is not said in a sense of recrimination. . . . To save our love, which I cherish, it may be necessary to reduce the intimacy."

The Birth of a Grandfather appeared at the end of August. Granville Hicks wrote the most intelligent review. The publishing business, said Hicks, always ballyhooed a few novels, neglected the rest. Unfortunately the ballyhooed novels were usually bad—"crude, corny, and sensational" like Grace Metalious's *Peyton Place,* "a slick contrivance" like Gerald Green's *The Last Angry Man,* or "excruciatingly bad" like Ayn Rand's *Atlas Shrugged. The Birth of a Grandfather* was one of the undeservedly neglected. It had faults, true. The reader does not quite believe in Sprig Wyeth's inner change—a failure of Sarton's nerve since, not daring to get inside a man, she explores him only through the eyes of other characters. Yet this was a fine novel, distinguished by the same kind of subtle insight as *Faithful Are the Wounds.* A pity so few would read it.

But everyone read *The New York Times,* where Elizabeth Janeway paid the novel negative attention. And May herself felt that people were rather disappointed. Eugénie criticized her for throwing the game to the men by endowing them with women's sensitivity. Another friend regretted that the awaited grandchild was automatically expected to be a boy. Still others objected to the very quiet plot. "My own private feeling," May wrote Kay Martin, "is that it is not a major work, but a triumph for me to have pulled out somehow from a devastating year. . . . And I can look forward slowly to the next one." But the contrast between *Grandfather*'s quiet reception and the hosannahs greeting James Gould Cozzens's *By Love Possessed* depressed her. True, Cozzens had written a major novel, but she deplored the immaturity of vision that made lust the motivating power of life.

That September the Bollingen Foundation dropped the Valéry project, and May and Louise Bogan were out of a job. May had translated twenty-seven Valéry poems "with infinite labor"; still, her personal struggle to work out "this sense of despair always so close to the surface" so preoccupied her that she hardly regretted the translations. "I am trying to write poems as a sort of therapy," she wrote Kay. ". . . And the results are not poetry. But I am sure this is my way of coming through and growing. . . . One of the things I have got to find out about is why love for me has always been a *wound*."

The jacket blurb for *In Time Like Air,* the new book of poems—"No subject is too large or too humble to be included in her abounding love of nature, mankind and God"—depressed her terribly, but so now, typically, did its contents: "I am in a bad low which makes me believe that I am utterly mediocre and might as well settle for lecturing to elderly ladies and children on poetry."

It is true that a flaw that marked May Sarton's poetry from the beginning still plagued it. "After Four Years," a poem about Sarton's inability to accept her mother's death, begins:

> How to lay down her death,
> Bring her back living
> Into the open heart, the overgrieving,
> Bury once and for all the starving breath
> And lay down her death?

How to reconcile this stanza with a later line—"Mother and marvellous friend"? Suddenly not poetry but banality—"Oh, she's a *marvellous* friend." How can Sarton be so careless, so *lazy* as to let that or the equally hackneyed "Melt itself through me like a healing balm" stand? Surely "healing balm" had been banned from poetry since Ella Wheeler Wilcox; but Sarton hasn't caught on to that yet. One hears Bogan cautioning, "Go slow, prune, revise." But Sarton is like a pianist who after missing five conspicuous notes in a Beethoven sonata says, "Yes, but I played the other ten thousand perfectly grand."

Yet *In Time Like Air* has many strengths. The *Times* called it "the best kind of virtuosity"; it was, "to a poet at least, a book to carry in the pocket and re-read with delight." *Poetry* could be severe, criticizing lapses into "the ease of the professional who has learned to multiply indefinitely examples of her very true competence even when she does not work hard but only rhymes and meters the life out of her objects." Generally, however, *Poetry* praised, comparing the "civilized and intricate" vision of the poems—much to May's chagrin—to Auden's.

Ten of the poems are for Cora. Poems for Eugénie Dubois—"Leaves Before the Wind," "Prothalamion," "Kinds of Wind," "The Seas of Wheat," "The Action of the Beautiful"—reflect the gentle bounty of her nature; Cora's poems coruscate with pain. Rarely is the calm of "I touch your face / The open palm / Marries your bone" sustained. Rather, there is "never-ending battle," impermanence, despair, and the death of desire. But Sarton's deepest conflict in *In Time Like Air* is within herself. The poet battles reason, the Furies, nothingness, falling, the phoenix, death, the dragon—symbols of destruction or the unconscious. In every case she asserts her will—pitting passion against reason, rejecting the Furies, creating out of dreams plenitude, wresting life from the phoenix, cherishing the dragon. Yet these are not simple battles of opposites, but compromises that embody the paradoxes of life. It is only when the phoenix dies that she lives, only when the self dissolves that it crystallizes, only when the poet accepts despair that she is "both grounded and in flight." If this synthesis of opposites was "out of synch" with current thought, as one critic said, it was also (paradoxically) Sarton's strength. Both *In Time Like Air* and *Faithful Are the Wounds* were nominated for a National Book Award.

From November 1957 to March 1958, May taught two adult seminars in the short story at Radcliffe while considering a book based on the *New Yorker* pieces as well as leaving Rinehart, who had let *Birth of a Grandfather* drop into a black hole. She was seeing little of Cora, yet squandering much emotional energy on her—one reason she seemed off track creatively. The problem with Cora was always the same: Cora did not give her enough attention. She could sacrifice an evening with other people for Cora; Cora could not spare her ten minutes. Brief sexual encounters were not enough; May wanted deeper communion.

She had continued to search for a house and finally found it in the tiny village of Nelson, New Hampshire—a charming old farmhouse with a barn on thirty-six acres. Mythologizing her life in later years, May Sarton would say that her move to Nelson was a deliberate retreat. The establishment had ignored her; she would renounce it and let the world come to her if it chose. With her biographer, however, she was frank: "I did it for Cora." And Nelson was hardly the wilderness she pictured. It was close to Dublin, where the Apprentices had summered, and roughly eighty-five miles from Cambridge.

With the papers for the house with her lawyer, May left April 7 to lecture at Agnes Scott College in Decatur, Georgia. Among the English teachers welcoming her was Ellen Douglass Leyburn, a scholar of eighteenth-century literature, a superb teacher, and a distinguished personality whom

Cora DuBois,
Harvard professor
of anthropology
and Muse

one colleague described as "a beautiful green tree." At a concert May sat next to Ellen; feeling her profile, "delicate as a leaf," carve itself into her nerves, she felt desire. During her visit she managed a half-hour visit to Ellen's office, that was all. By the time she left on April 19, Ellen Douglass Leyburn was deeply in love with her.

"All the beauty is in you," Ellen wrote her two days later; "but what pure joy it is to be allowed to be part of the miracle of realizing it." It was both pain and joy to hear May spoken of in the wake of her dazzling appearance at the college, yet to hug to herself the secret knowledge of their love. All day she went around exclaiming under her breath, "My dear! My dear!" In the month of May alone, Ellen wrote twenty-four letters. But she was troubled about Cora and Judy, though since Cora was not a spiritual person, she argued, it was all right for her to give that to May. But she wanted to give more. She dreamed of holding May in her arms and loving her "that way." May now had Cora, Ellen, and Judy in love with her, as well as Kay Martin and half a dozen others, though she was in love only with Cora.

On June 7, the Nelson house, bought with $17,000 from the sale of Channing Place, was hers, though she would not move in until autumn. She had decided to break up Wright Street as gently as possible, leaving many books, paintings, and some furniture behind. Judy was not to consider that May was "leaving" her. There would be weeks together on Greenings Island, holidays to share, Judy would often come to Nelson, she would visit Cambridge. . . .

May had hoped to be worthy of the kind of love and stability Judy gave her; she had appreciated the security:

> In the evening we came back
> Into our yellow room,
> For a moment taken aback
> To find the light left on,
> Falling on silent flowers,
> Table, book, empty chair. . . .
>
> The deepest world we share
> And do not talk about
> But have to have, was there,
> And by that light found out.

But Judy could not satisfy such an emotionally ravenous person. As long as May conducted her affairs in Europe, the relationship could survive. But Cora was in Cambridge and the situation intolerable. So dependent she believed she would die without May, Judy had finally worked through to release. "This letter comes from the deepest heart-searching of all my fifty-eight years," she had written May. "If *you are to have a home of your own,* you must make one as soon as possible, not *after* next year, or the year after. . . . I have done my honest best to meet the situation, to make *myself* into the kind of person we could both live with under these circumstances, but I have not succeeded. . . . You must be *free* to live your own life, and so must I." Losing May would have compensations. For years, Judy had felt trapped—unable to call her home her own, unable to entertain friends because of May's unpredictable, jealous rages, forced to witness May's passion for Cora.

Some people considered Judy a curiously subdued companion for dazzling May. Eleanor Blair, formerly head of the English department at

*Ellen Douglass Leyburn, professor
of English at Agnes Scott College*

*Judith Matlack (Judy), the only woman
with whom May ever had a home*

Dana Hall and a good friend since 1939, disagreed. "Judy was a darling!
She was a rare and beautiful spirit—quiet, but vital and alive. Her students
at Simmons adored her. But how could she compete with May? Judy was
a pleasant glow, May a glare. You had to *look* for Judy. But then in May's
world, it was always May plus supporting cast."

Currently, Eleanor Blair and May were not in communication. This
was because one night at a dinner party at "The Hive," Eleanor's home
in Wellesley, May had run down Judy. Judy, May said, was terrifically neu-
rotic. She was also terribly limited. She was not her equal and, frankly, May
could not go on with her much longer. Cecile de Banke, Eleanor's long-
time companion, was so outraged by this betrayal that she insisted Eleanor
never see May again. Eleanor was very fond of May, but fonder of Cecile.
She dropped May.

CHAPTER 16

Nelson: 1958–1960

I moved into my house one day
In a downpour of leaves and rain,
"I took possession," as they say,
With solitude for my domain. . . .

I moved into my life one day
In a downpour of leaves in flood,
I took possession, as they say,
And knew I was alone for good.

Moving into her Nelson house October 1, May probably felt "alone for good." But she would seldom be alone in the physical sense, since she was incapable of spending more than a few consecutive days in her own company. Yet in a deeper sense she was indeed alone. Whether she realized it or not, her self-absorption, radical mood swings, and violent temper made her impossible to live with. Like the little girl with the curl, she was either very, very good—or horrid.

Yet that had not been her reason for buying the house. "Here at Nelson I shall see you for the first time in a place which I cannot be 'asked to leave' or 'allowed to stay'—in which I am not helplessly in the power of an atmosphere created by others. Here *I* create the atmosphere. You can come or go as you choose but you *cannot* make me leave." Thus May gave Cora notice that she had established her own turf. Cora might visit, but May was boss. Since Cora had left for Stanford, however, the test was not yet.

In 1958 Nelson was a charming village of about four hundred souls tucked in rolling New Hampshire hills near Silver Lake and Mount Monadnock. May's house, in the center of the village, faced a tiny green. Nelson had a town hall, a handsome, spired Congregational church, a brick schoolhouse, and a minuscule library. No stores, no gas station—people did business in Keene. Bessie Lyman and Myra Hardy, the minister's daughters, lived next to the church. Across the road from May in a big yellow house lived the Cobleighs. Kitty-corner from May, next to the town hall, lived the Quigleys in dilapidated poverty. Mildred Quigley worked as the town clerk, Quig painted pictures, made frames, gave art lessons, repaired violins, and played at local square dances. Win and Dorothy French lived just out of town on Center Pond Road. Win drove the school bus and delivered mail. Way down that road the Warner family eked out a living farming with huge Belgian horses. Doris Warner cleaned houses in the village; her daughter, Gracie, cared for a menagerie of animals from rare ducks to miniature ponies. Summer people, like Helen Millbank, didn't really count as Nelson natives. Natives were independent, hard-working, proud, generally poor, taciturn, and salt-of-the-earth. They lived pretty much as they chose, which meant that if the fish were biting, Mrs. Cobleigh or Miss Lyman didn't get her grass cut that day. Enter May Sarton.

She brought with her as heavy psychic baggage her current turmoil about Cora and Ellen, whom she had visited in Decatur in July and met in New York in September. Cora had demanded an answer to the "ultimate question." Yes, said May defiantly, they had made love. Ellen was "part of that whole fountain which has been stifled for so long"—her ardent, dominating self which Cora had tried to destroy as she was trying to destroy her creativity. Being able to give Ellen bliss had restored May to herself.

She also told Ellen about Cora, in infinite, painful detail—and Ellen, who had thought after the first night of passion that she was May's only lover, now heard that Cora possessed the part of May that felt "married," like a woman to a man. She now realized that the poems May had sent her had been written for Cora; Cora was the Muse. Her anguish was intense, not only because she felt physical ardor for May but because she felt cheated of spiritual intimacy. She thought of May in exalted religious terms—and the knowledge that May was not her personal savior devastated her. She began to take sleeping pills; sometimes she thought she was going mad with the pain of it. She prayed for both their souls at church on Sunday. May would eventually realize what she made this honorable, intelligent woman suffer: "I did a terrible thing to Ellen Douglass Leyburn, one of the things I am most burdened with guilt about." Now she thought only of her own suffering. "Darling, I cannot go on any longer," she wrote Cora October 7:

I am too tired. I am too starved for lack of being able to use my ten-
derness, my real love, starved for the poetry that is in me to be used,
to nourish someone somewhere who does not feel they have to
"resist." It is too harsh and bleak a world where you make me
live. . . . I must be able to look into human eyes again without
being accused of "voyeurism"; to be able to send poems to people
who can read them with their hearts, who are not afraid. If you have
to resist me to be yourself, then it is too sad, too bad. . . . I am really
dying. I am frightened. I have to try to live. It is not lack of love. It
is just that I have lost my hope. I can't write to you any more. I must
be silent. You must try to understand. It is not lack of love.

Meanwhile there was the moving in, involving over the next months
dozens of trips from Cambridge and dozens of friends. As everyone had
predicted, May was spending fearful sums on repairs: new clapboards,
pump, electric box. The house was not large, but it was nicely symmetri-
cal. The fanned front door opened onto an abrupt staircase. To the left was
the "cozy room"; to the right, May's study. Behind the cozy room was the
big kitchen with a dining area; behind May's study, her bedroom and
bathroom. There were two fireplaces in unfinished guest rooms upstairs, a
fireplace in every room down. May installed bird feeders outside her study
and kitchen windows; two big sacks of birdseed at the foot of the stairs
became a fixture, as did the rifle next to the back door for scaring off
woodchucks and coons. She started planning gardens.

Almost family, Céline came by freighter to help baptize the new
house. On October 11 Judy and Louise Bogan joined the party—more
people under her roof at once than May would ever have (or want) again.
They were dropped off by friends of Louise's who, uninvited, came in for
so many martinis that May finally offered them lunch at two p.m.—an
outrage to a person who invited guests at a specific hour for a clearly
specified time. Louise downed martinis like water, unsociably passed out
after her third. At least Céline was amused. After naps and tea, they set out
to "beat the bounds" of May's property. Judy and Louise soon dropped
behind, but May and Céline plowed through brambles, thick brush, and
woods till they triumphantly reached the brook bounding the southern
edge. Faint cries told them that Louise and Judy were less happy with the
outing. The next morning, Louise announced reproachfully, "I *seem* to be
all right."

After Louise left, Céline observed that she had not been kind. No, said
May, Louise *was* kind, but not warm; still, she was "a dear true friend." Yet

*May in the
"cozy room" of her
Nelson home*

their relationship, after the Valéry project fell through, was problematic. Louise could be hilariously cruel about May to others. And May never forgot that after promising to review *The Land of Silence* in *The New Yorker,* Louise merely gave it a few lines at the end of a long Edith Sitwell review.

Before coming to Nelson, May had sent Rinehart a collection of revised *New Yorker* pieces titled *I Knew a Phoenix.* The memoirs, written in a clear, fluid style that May liked to call "transparent," are notable as the beginning of the myth May Sarton was starting to create of her life. Most writers mythologize themselves, consciously or unconsciously: Charlotte Brontë dramatizing bleak Haworth in letters to her publisher; Bernard Shaw creating the colossal GBS; Lillian Hellman styling herself the incorruptible, hard-mouthed heroine. Sarton's central myth in *I Knew a Phoenix* is that a young person nurtured by extraordinary people cannot help being extraordinary herself. George and Mabel, Jean Dominique, Katharine Taylor, Le Gallienne, Lugné-Poë, Koteliansky, Woolf, Bowen, and the Huxleys

The Nelson house that May immortalized in Plant Dreaming Deep, *photographed by Lotte Jacobi*

take on secular divinity. They are delightful, gifted, noble, and flawless except for the few charming weaknesses May chooses to disclose. And they are all bewitched by May.

May's myths are, of course, grounded in reality. But as Bogan told her, "You leave the hell out." Indeed. The passionate crush on Katharine Taylor, the Grace Daly disaster in Paris, Jean Dominique's bisexual sophistication, Céline's intellectual pretensions, the affairs with Julian and Juliette, Woolf's coolness, the rending quarrel with Kot and Juliette do not exist. "Oh," exclaimed May, "all that book does *not* say!" There were good reasons: Taylor, Daly, Céline, and the Huxleys were still alive; besides, most affairs and quarrels postdated the *Phoenix* years. And *The New Yorker* hadn't wanted the "hell" even if she'd been tempted to include it. Yet the patina glossing these memoirs has less to do with practicality than with May herself. Paradoxically, this violently conflicted woman avoided serious conflict in her writing. Writing purged the agony. The product was serenely transcendent—the rebirth from ashes of the phoenix, the eternal bird that was her symbol.

That first fall in Nelson May worked on another novel. She had always been impressed by great teachers she had known: Agnes Hocking, Lillian Putnam and Anne Thorp from Shady Hill, Kay Martin, Ellen Douglass Leyburn, Cora DuBois, Nadia Boulanger. She would create a plot around different types of teachers: the teacher's teacher, the teacher who molds, the teacher who leaves her students free, the brilliant classroom performer who privately is a driven neurotic (May herself), the new teacher. And students, one of them an intelligent and susceptible girl, "an only child who has lost her mother and feels great guilt about all she did not do— tense, scared, a tendency to be *exaltée*"—May again. These characters were evolving into *The Small Room.*

This year of new independence ended, as many did, with May sick— ten days before Christmas in the hospital with a throat infection caused less by a virus than by "inward depletion." Her hospital room was crowded with stacks of her Christmas poem waiting to be sent ("Reflections by a Fire," eighty copies for Cambridge alone), roses, chrysanthemums, cyclamen, gift books, Christmas cards, and a chocolate Santa wrapped in red tinfoil. Scoffing at her illness, Cora sent a card, no flowers. May read *Dr. Zhivago,* brooded on her impossible love.

She celebrated Christmas at Wright Street, the rituals intact, though Judy seemed depressed. May dreaded the arrival of Ellen on the twenty-ninth. She had told her not to come, then relented; they would drive to Nelson for three days. The weight of Ellen's love exhausted her. No matter how often Ellen told her, "Do not grieve over being the cause of suffering to me for what you cannot give me," she could not erase the vision of Ellen down on her knees in Decatur praying for the strength to conquer passion.

But May had weapons against suffering in others. "The next morning after anything you are always untouched and oblivious," the unhappy Jean Tatlock had told her. Now when Ellen emerged of a morning in her blue wrapper, May was already outside, filling bird feeders, shovelling snow, confabbing with Perley Cole, a tall, silent Nelsoner commandeered for odd jobs. In the face of this oblivious energy, Ellen was helpless. May made breakfast, pounded her typewriter all morning, made an excellent lunch preceded by sherry, napped in the afternoon, walked Ellen up to the cemetery on the hill talking nonstop, introduced her to the Quigleys, Bessie Lyman, and Myra Hardy. Then she lit the Christmas tree and it was time for drinks in front of the fire before sitting down to the excellent veal stew for supper. After supper May read to Ellen from *The Small Room,* then talked of the agony of Cora late and long. When Ellen finally retired to May's bedroom, May was not in it, having graciously yielded it to her guest, who tossed all night, inhaling May's English lavender on the pillow, dreaming tragic dreams.

Incapable of deception, Ellen had believed in May's love. She left a wiser woman. For a time she pretended that their new platonic relationship improved on the old; that they could now meet without "this awful expense of spirit." But May had given her the coup de grâce, and she knew it. Her great dignity prevailed: her letters cooled, slowed; she resigned herself to the role of understanding friend. Particularly she buttressed May's fragile creative ego, battered by Cora—*The Bridge of Years, A Shower of Summer Days,* and *Faithful Are the Wounds,* she insisted rightly, were fine works. She thought often of the beauty and the sadness of the Nelson days.

May's relationship with Cora had become a chronic illness. Futile to chart its violent ups and downs. Recriminations, justifications, accusations from both sides flooded the mails. This was the "claggy" quality of lesbian relationships that Elizabeth Bowen deplored—so hyperintense that one longed for a cold splash from the bucket of reason to shock the parties into sense. But May said it herself in *The Small Room:* "Women wear each other out with their everlasting touching of the nerve."

On March 10 May flew to California to see Cora, where they resumed the vicious hate-love cycle. Cora called May's novels "undistinguished." She said May obviously had gone in over her head with the Nelson house, panicking and making everyone else suffer. She called May a spoiled brat and a paranoic.

Back in Nelson, May retaliated. Cora had poisoned all the wells—the house, her poetry, and now the novels—because she was jealous. But she defied her: "I shall get well here alone. From the first day I knew that it had to be that or nothing. I made the house out of despair. There is no angel here except the angel of solitude. I dread your presence here and all that it will bring of hostility, destructiveness, and poison." Yet in the next breath she could write, "I do love you and I always will. I have not the slightest doubt of that." And Cora herself replied, "I love you a very great deal."

That spring May decided that she needed a psychiatrist again to help her understand Cora's "terrible cruelty" as well as her own inability after four years to accept Cora's relationship with Jeanne Taylor. There were other questions she might have asked. Why, in the same letter accusing Cora of poisoning wells, had she begged for a loan of $1,000—though she had more than $70,000 in the bank? Obviously May lent, gave, and borrowed money to bind people to her. But did she understand this, and why she still needed that kind of security? Again, she called Cora both father and mother; yet Cora was punitive. Why did she still crave punishment from Mabel and George? And were May's terrible furies, hysteria, and constant need for self-justification tied to this vision of herself as victim? What created the anger? Was it enough to say, as she sometimes did, that her anger was "the other face of *hope*"?

In her first interview on May 5, she told Dr. Kitty DeForest that she had lost her sense of self and that Cora's lack of response was driving her mad. "What is your *need* for response?" asked the psychiatrist. May's reply is unrecorded, but Dr. DeForest's final words, "What I can't understand is what *you* are doing in such a situation," suggests that May still portrayed herself as the innocent victim. Dr. DeForest should have understood what May was doing in such a situation because May was always in them.

But the sessions could not last long, because May was taking Judy to Europe. After she collected (along with Cora) an honorary degree from Russell Sage University, as well as excellent reviews for *Phoenix,* they sailed on June 28 on the *Empress of England.* She left the Nelson house in charge of Kay Martin, who would forward mail, feed Pezou, the cat, chopped kidney and haddock, and coax into bloom the large perennial bed May had had dug and planted. This European trip would be different for several reasons: for the first time May was going as a tourist, with plenty of money and no plans to rendezvous with a lover.

Though she saw an old love. "I have found again in friendship my dear Eugénie," she wrote Kay happily, "she who was so hurt when I fell in love with Cora that I thought we would never be friends." But second and third meetings were less satisfactory. She felt "invisible walls." Eugénie now seemed under Jean's thumb, sure he was right about everything. And then she didn't really seem to understand the artistic temperament—May's. Decidedly, it was not the same. And Cora, about whom May was dying to talk, could not be mentioned.

May went on to La Roselle to celebrate Méta's seventieth birthday, then to Paris. There she heard that Méta had been operated on for cancer and was not expected to live. Every morning she called Geneva expecting the worst. When a telegram finally reached her in Vouvray, she felt "only relief. Much later I shall have slowly to get used to her not being there—now I am only happy that she is no longer suspended between life and death and that I no longer feel like a plane circling and circling and unable to land."

London without Bowen, Kot, and the Huxleys. Belgium without Jean-Do and Raymond. Le Petit Bois without Grace Dudley. And now Switzerland without Méta. Yet May's eager questioning of Kay betrayed how tenaciously she lived in the present. Had any of the herbs grown? Were the two clematis still alive? Had any California poppies flowered? How destructive were the woodchucks? How did Old Home Day go? Had the Warners come to mow the big field, or had there been too much rain?

During the trip she had achieved a new understanding about herself and Cora. "I see that far more than I had understood this whole crisis in my life has to do with identity—I mean my relation to myself rather than with my relation to others. Cora, in other words, is less central than she appeared to be at first." Yet the thought of their reunion unnerved her— "the dread of arriving exhausted after the long flight and once more having to come with my heart open and singing although at any moment I may be punished and beaten, by Jeanne, or by you, and knowing that when you are there together I am absolutely alone and will not be defended or helped, but must be punished for both your sakes. I think I shall go to a hotel, from there straight to Nelson and that perhaps you might come up by bus. Would not this give us a small better chance of peace?"

And for ten days Cora did come to Nelson. For the most part they managed to be civil. Pezou slept with them in May's bed; the weather was cool but sunny; and while May napped in the afternoon, Cora went out and performed herculean tasks of weeding, pruning, organizing the vegetable garden, and hauling stones. But then Cora started saying bossy things like "If I were you I'd have corn against the barn," until May's teeth chattered with rage; worse, she barged into May's study to read her what she'd just written, though May knew Cora would never tolerate such interruption from her. One Sunday noon after the Quigs, as May called Albert and Mildred Quigley, had been over for martinis, they almost had a terrible fight until they said, "Let's eat our lunch separately and cool off." As for sex, "She did make love to me," May told Kay, "but we were both so exhausted the next day (this is very strange) that I was almost relieved it didn't happen often—and I felt she was making a supreme effort."

It was autumn in more than one sense. Something irrevocable had happened with the terrible fight over Jeanne Taylor the previous August, and they both knew it. "She will never love me as she did then, in those

Albert and Mildred Quigley and family, at Nelson

first years. We are mending a broken cup and it will still be useful but it
never will be the same again." May drove Cora back to Cambridge, came
home, and wrote "Der Abschied" (The Farewell), reaching through
poetry a philosophical detachment she rarely achieved in life:

> Here is the room where you lay down full length
> That whole first day, to read, and hardly stirred,
> As if arrival had taken all your strength;
> Here is the table where you bent to write
> The morning through, and silence spoke its word;
> And here beside the fire we talked, as night
> Came slowly from the wood across the meadow
> To frame half of our brilliant world in shadow.
>
> The rich fulfillment came; we held it all;
> Four years of struggle brought us to this season,
> Then in one week our summer turned to fall;
> The air chilled and we sensed the chill in us,

The passionate journey ending in sweet reason.
The autumn light was there, frost on the grass.
And did you come at last, come home, to tell
How all fulfillment tastes of a farewell? . . .

What stays that can outlast these deprivations?
Now, peopled by the dead, and ourselves dying,
The house and I resume old conversations:
What stays? Perhaps some autumn tenderness,
A different strength that forbids youthful sighing.
Though frost has broken summer like a glass,
Know, as we hear the thudding apples fall,
That ripeness and the suffering change is all.

At the end of September May went to Boston to have her perennially troublesome tonsils removed at the Eye and Ear Hospital. She would recuperate with Cora at the new house on Coolidge Hill; she resolved to be very good. Vain resolve. Going back to Cora and Jeanne was like "going back to the old vomit." Cora seemed slavishly dependent upon Jeanne, who could do no wrong. And she virtually ignored May, daring to have a boy come to garden and lunch one day when Jeanne was gone, so that nothing could happen between them. In a long, grievance-ridden letter, May told Cora "This is goodbye," and moved to Anne Thorp's.

It was not goodbye. A few days later she drove Cora to Nelson, then back to Cambridge. After a lecture in Philadelphia, she stayed again at Coolidge Hill. "I saw Cora for the last time last night and we had a literal knock-down drag-out fight," she told Kay Martin. "She hit me very hard in the face and I hit back and we ended by knocking over and breaking to pieces the only really beautiful object in their living room, a small end table that Jeanne had lovingly rubbed down years ago." Actually, they did not knock over the table; May hurled it at Cora, and though she missed, the table shattered. "Now you leave," said Cora contemptuously. May drove home, wrote Sonnet 13, and eventually to Cora:

There is no doubt that I have lived with rage and misery too near the surface for too long. . . . Your pattern toward me for a very long time has been alternate punishment and withdrawal and mine toward you tenderness, passion, and *hysteria*. The spiral we are caught in is that when you withdraw, I batter at the walls and when I batter at the walls, you either punish or withdraw or both. The withdrawal is legitimate and necessary; the punishment is not. You will never tame me by punishing me; people of this temperament always fight.

. . . We both needed and need to get away from each other. But this does not mean there is no love and I think you are unnecessarily hard about this. It is not quite human to put someone in outer darkness so suddenly after such a close relationship.

. . . Let me lay it on the line. The door is open and always will be. . . . If and when you can say, "I love you, I need you," I shall be here. Until then I am not here for you and I must beg you to respect suffering because it is real. . . .

I'll send the letters shortly. Please destroy mine or do what you will with them. I do not want them. I would be very glad if you would return my novels to me. You surely cannot wish to have works which have taught you nothing and which have no distinction cluttering up your library, and it troubles me that they should be so exposed.

Let's be as happy and fruitful as we can, darling. I am managing pretty well and you must not worry about me. Ever your May.

So still it was not over.

May returned to Nelson. It is instructive to examine the kind of "solitude" she was experiencing there. She had returned from Europe in early September, taken Cora to Nelson with her for ten days, driven Cora back to Cambridge, then returned to Nelson. Shortly after, Rosalind Greene visited, and May drove her back to Cambridge. Then the operation, then back to Nelson with Cora, then with Cora back to Cambridge, then back to Nelson because Aunt Mary Bouton was coming up for lunch, then farewell drinks with the Quigs before leaving for Cambridge again. Then Philadelphia. Then the fight with Cora in Cambridge. Back to Nelson. November 6 to New York, where she had lunch with Louise Bogan and dinner with Katrine Greene. Then west on a lecture tour that took her as far as Seattle. Back east, Thanksgiving with Judy in Cambridge, then Nelson for five days with Judy. Back to Cambridge for dental work. Back to Nelson for eleven days to be alone and address six hundred Christmas cards ("The Annealing"). Back to Wright Street, the Silver Fish to dinner December 16. Dinner the twentieth with Cora, who did not say a loving word. Christmas Eve at Wright Street, many people in. Down to Plymouth to see a friend the

night of the thirtieth. And in January 1960, lectures all month before mov-
ing back to Cambridge to start creative writing classes at Wellesley. Pre-
sumably the "angel of solitude" that guarded May's Nelson door wore a
smile.

Yet to a person who lived so intensely, three days at Nelson may well
have seemed three weeks or three years, especially since Nelson was a
place that focused experience. She had already begun to mythologize the
village and its inhabitants. The impoverished Warner clan, living in ram-
shackle buildings back in the woods with a manure pile higher than the
house, were heroic peasants of the land; the daughter, Gracie, never sent to
school, a modern Saint Francis. The Frenches were salt-of-the-earth New
Englanders; the taciturn Perley Cole, the Abe Lincoln of Nelson. Some
people saw Mildred Quigley as an ordinary woman forced by her hus-
band's indigence to neglect her own house and children working for
other folks; May saw her as a thwarted intellectual. Quig himself was not
a good painter and, the village said, bone lazy; May saw him as the Gen-
uine Craftsman, spurning materialism to follow his own truth. With his
shock of white hair, long sensitive hands, and shy but kindly eyes, he was
a father figure like Julian, Kot, and Lugné-Poë, a man who, unlike George,
could show her affection.

The people she idealized were not social equals. She became their
patron, hiring them to work for her indoors and out. She lent money to
the Quigs; eventually she would replace their outhouse with a real bath-
room. She gave Gracie Warner money to care for her animals and buy
winter boots. True, she had Mildred and Quig in for drinks in front of the
fire; but she did not go to their house for drinks. She was the lady of the
manor, dispensing largesse, taking a keen interest in the children of her
employees, carrying soup to them when they were sick. She did this with
charm and enthusiasm, and the Nelsonites were disarmed.

But she was essentially alone. She had seldom been able to establish
successful relations with her peers. As the director of the Apprentices, she
had been apart from the group. As a writer, she shunned other writers,
had no coterie. As a lecturer, she was a solo act. When she taught, she was
alone in the classroom. Now, despite her presence at village meetings and
musical events and her contributions to the Congregational church
(which she did not attend), she was not really a villager. Yet that did not
matter, because she was making Nelson her own.

CHAPTER 17

Wellesley: 1960–1968

Teaching at Wellesley meant moving back to Wright Street and com-
muting to the college twice a week. Of the largely male English
department only the Chaucerian scholar Helen Storm Corsa seemed to
welcome her, and May, as a poet on a semester appointment, did not feel
part of the close-knit community. Her first set of papers made her laugh
and cry over literary endeavors like "The ashtrays were filled with the
corpses of dead cigarettes, their brief glows of life extinguished in the
remains of their relatives." Still, her students were "so young and eager
and sweet, I shall grow to love them and presumably should be able to
teach them *something*." Three mornings a week she worked on *The Small
Room* at Wright Street. And she continued to lecture at colleges in the
area.

Louise Bogan had asked Kay Martin to call her if May ever talked sui-
cide. May *was* talking suicide; and Bogan recommended Dr. Volta Hall, an
analyst "sensitive to the creative problem." Apart from Cora, May was
trying to deal with the terrible sense of inferiority she had always felt as a
writer. Talk at a dinner party about fashionable writers made her "dwin-
dle and pine away." Recently she had judged the National Book Award
in poetry, the pain of reading good-bad poetry exceeded only by that of
reading good-good. Now she feared her work linked to Cora. "I can con-
fess to you," she told Kay, "that I feel in some indefinable way as if my star
rose with Cora and now is setting—my star of work, of everything—as if
it had been some great Hope, now lost. . . . What I miss is the challenge
and excitement we were together for one another."

During spring vacation she escaped to Nelson, where she finished *The Small Room* "feeling like a small machine going much too fast and hard." "I know it is nothing of what I dreamed," she wrote Kay. "I just made myself do it and now it is done. Also I need the money. But I have this terrible fear that I am mediocre and never will be anything else. A middle aged cart horse who once imagined he was a race horse." One consolation was Nelson. Increasingly she saw that she had created something beautiful and good there that nothing could take away:

> The cat sleeps on my desk in the pale sun;
> Long bands of light lie warm across the floor.
> I have come back into my world of no one,
> This house where the long silences restore
> The essence and to time its real dimension;
> All I have lost or squandered I examine
> Free of the wars and the long searing tension;
> And I am nourished here after the famine.

Yet the serene summer she anticipated was anything but. Louise came, "like a gentle giant baby" calmly expecting to be waited on, and for twenty-four hours May ran about madly, finally putting her on the train with relief. Louise's self-protectiveness alienated her, even though she knew it was a necessary technique after still another breakdown. Then Cora. The Herr Professor was far less trouble than Louise, working away at scholarly articles at the trestle table with a gin and tonic at her elbow, digging flowerbeds and setting tomato plants. But the emotional storms she still inspired shook the farmhouse.

Then came Ellen Douglass Leyburn, but the dreaded visit was calm. Finally May was able to see Ellen as she really was—"like very fine steel, or a strong but delicate flower"—not a martyr to love. Kay Martin followed, and since she was also in love with May (and May not at all with her) there were tensions. Meanwhile, there was obligatory socializing with Nelson people like Helen Millbank and the Tolmans, and hordes of miscellaneous day-tripping friends. Twenty-four actual hours of solitude was broken by the arrival of an attractive Wellesley professor. "Nell [not her real name] is here," May told Kay Martin, "and all very peaceful and calming." Which meant that they were lovers. After a PEN conference in Rio de Janeiro, which might have been fun except that she knew she was a last choice and her hotel was second-rate, Nell again for ten days. Then she fetched Judy from Cambridge for a blessedly unemotional week. Then to Cambridge and back to Nelson to brace for another stream of visitors. Cora. Barbara and Will Hawthorne, for whom she cooked a rabbit in cream.

If May needed people, people needed May. Her spark made them burn almost as brightly as she. She immediately got down to cases, talking of sex, money, and trauma so uninhibitedly that conservative New England heads spun. She told people about herself—all about herself. And she radiated hope—a belief in beauty and happiness and in life itself that was irresistible. Yet people often discovered they meant little to May. Kay Martin poured out her soul in hundreds of letters. Ultimately May dismissed her as "no one important."

Nelson, meanwhile, exercised its spell. She had seventy-five small trees taken out below the garden, opening vistas of large maples and stone wall. She sat up late at night scanning catalogues for plants unattractive to woodchucks. She had a lightning rod installed on the barn and planted three tree peonies. A new cat, Scrabble, had kittens, which all had to be taken to Keene for spaying. Perley Cole came and scythed down the long grass to the barn, a poem in motion. It did not rain for Old Home Day, when residents and friends ate box lunches on the green, bought chances on a quilt, and listened to speeches and band music. Then it was autumn, and she was picking flowers against the frost, massing great bowls of zinnias and phlox as the sun slanted lower in the west and the morning grass was drenched with dew, and there were hundreds of narcissus and daffodil bulbs to plant in the stony field in anticipation of a Wordsworthian spring.

She had sent *The Small Room* to Rinehart in late August, still smarting from the commercial failure of *Birth of a Grandfather*. Stanley Rinehart replied that though *The Small Room* was her best, he must retract the promised $5,000 advance. She turned to Houghton Mifflin, her first publisher; but Houghton Mifflin too decided the beautifully written novel would not sell. Diarmuid sent it on to Viking, as all the doubts Cora had planted came back to haunt her.

At the end of October she closed Nelson for the winter, relieved to get away from so much physical labor and back to Judy, who was at her dearest. Cora too was dear, for Jeanne Taylor had a new lover, and for the first time that impregnable relationship seemed threatened. It was decidedly pleasant to listen to Cora agonize over Jeanne, as well as worry about the rigors of her coming sabbatical in India. The Herr Professor was human after all.

As, she was discovering, George Sarton had been. With Dr. Hall she explored the impact of his absence. She missed his buoyant certainty, his innocent belief that hard work would right the world. Reading his essays

Basil de Selincourt, May's British literary mentor, at Nelson

at the Widener was like hearing his voice again, arguing that time is more precious than money or that the brilliant student is rarely the genius. He said the obvious, but "with such conviction and so sweetly" that it seemed new. That December she attended the first George Sarton Memorial Lecture in New York, "quite thrilling though I did not quite get used to being a 'symbolic' person instead of myself." Cora was linked to this new acceptance of George, though whether her father now seemed more human because she'd come to terms with Cora, or Cora because May had come to uneasy terms with George, she did not know.

In January 1961, Eric Swenson, a colleague at Breadloaf, accepted *The Small Room* for Norton, as well as the next book of poems. The $250 she had spent on publicity photos by the gifted photographer Lotte Jacobi now seemed less frivolous. This good news was tempered by word that Quig, ill all fall, had been hospitalized. Immediately she left for Nelson and for several days drove Mildred back and forth to Keene. Her last gift to Quig was a pocket edition of Delacroix's *Journal,* which he did not let out of his hands while she was there. When she went again January 23, he was clearly dying. He slipped away at eleven-thirty that night, seventy years old. "I feel as if I had lost my father again," she wrote Kay Martin, "for Quig gave me all the tenderness and sweet love and faith my father could never *utter*—it is very hard to imagine life here without him."

The next morning May made Irish stew for Mildred and dashed down a poem for Quig, forty-six lines, ending

> Lover of ceremony, and all courteous graces,
> He was one of the last fiddlers, jigs and reels,
> And "Call your partners." We'll dance in the old hall
> A last dance for Quig, the fiddler, whose tunes kept
> Our feet light, our eyes open, our hearts true.
> I tell you his joys are with us. We are not alone.
> (But, God it's an empty village that we have to fill!)

She got the *Keene Sentinel* to publish the poem, wanting to do this unappreciated man public honor. Quig had entered her pantheon. Meanwhile, she persuaded friends to buy his paintings—Kay Martin, Anne Thorp, and Dorothy Wallace, a wealthy, recently widowed student in her creative writing class at Wellesley. She shuddered whenever she remembered that Quig was still above ground in his satin-tufted coffin; the frozen New Hampshire ground could not receive him until spring.

Back in Cambridge at the end of January, May, Judy, and Helen Corsa and her friend Molly Slavin celebrated Helen's new professorship, May's Norton contract, Judy's raise from Simmons, and (belatedly) the election of John F. Kennedy with dinner and Marlene Dietrich's show. May went "ga-ga" over Dietrich's beautifully polished performance—"first in a glittering evening dress, then . . . in top hat and tails, singing with such finesse (no voice of course) and every gesture so discreet and telling . . . literally ageless and timeless, the Lorelei, the Siren of Odysseus." It was one of the last relaxed times before Wellesley began February 6. That day May had to hire a man to dig her car out of the towering Cambridge drifts; cried when he said, "There's nowhere to put the snow"; gave him whiskey and sixteen dollars when he at last succeeded.

Besides the difficulty of commuting that snowy winter, May had other grievances with Wellesley. Like George at Harvard, she was defensive about her position. By mid-April she was frustrated enough to complain to the head of the English department:

> My big question about myself and my place at Wellesley is whether you are really using me to my full capacity? Whether also it is out of bounds to wish to have the chance to follow through on students of mine from 200 who might wish to go on with me? . . . My light may be a small one, but it is a true light and I have a feeling that at present it is being rather carefully hidden under various bushels called 200, 301, 304. I have both a new novel and a Collected Poems coming out. There is no one in your department who can approach my standing in the world "outside." . . . I feel humiliated to have to make such a point. But I am disturbed, I must confess. I would like to be used for what I am worth. . . . It is significant as a minor point, that I have never been asked to read poems at Wellesley except at a sorority. You do apparently want to hide your candles. . . . But I am too old and battered a candle now to really give a damn. Either you want me to stay or you don't. Let me make it crystal clear: I am not a charity patient or a walking wounded. . . . And if you cannot use me, others can.

May did not endear herself to the department by avoiding meetings, refusing faculty invitations, and luring some of the best students to her classes. And "outsiders" always inspire academic jealousy. But she won another appointment for the fall 1961 semester. Cora was bemused. Why was May maneuvering like a campus politician? "T'aint in character."

It wasn't in character, and May couldn't keep it up long. Attempting to woo a professor on the hiring committee, she invited Patrick Quinn to Cambridge for drinks. She warned him that martinis made her aggressive, but they drank several rounds. Then they went out to a French restaurant, where they ordered wine. "Which check shall I put the wine on?" asked the waitress at the end of the meal. Quinn said nothing. Furious, May paid for both dinners, then blew up. "I've never in my life had to deal with a cold, repressive atmosphere like Wellesley's! It would be inconceivable anywhere else for a man to behave as rudely as you!" Heads cranked.

Abashed, Quinn murmured, "Next time you will let me do the honors." But there would be no next time.

By November *The Small Room* had sold 13,110 copies, and May bought herself a new Peugeot. Decidedly she was happy with Norton, and with her editor, Eric Swenson, who wrote her charming, enthusiastic letters. And with the reviews, which generally were excellent.

Everyone called it her Wellesley novel, but since she'd begun it two years before, Appleton College could be any prestigious eastern girls' school. She had based the plot on a friend's experience with a brilliant student caught plagiarizing Steinbeck's *The Red Pony.* Less obviously, Sarton's Jane Seaman plagiarizes Simone Weil; still, the theft is discovered and Jane threatened with expulsion. The real theme of *The Small Room,* however, is the problematic relationship between professor and student. Does one teach students to think only, or also to feel—and at what peril? Outside the classroom, how much personal involvement is healthy, for the professor and the student? And one character, at least, voices the idea that Sarton began with: "Great teachers are great people. You can't get away from that."

Within the novel's deliberately narrow scope, the cast of characters is rich and immediately recognizable to anyone familiar with academe. Carryl Cope, the brilliant medieval historian who had she been a man would certainly have occupied a Harvard chair. Hallie Summerson, the great teacher and human being. Jennifer Finch, at home a slave to her invalid mother, at college meetings the respected diplomat. Jack Beveridge, the idealistic English professor. President Blake Tillotson, steering a precarious course between the shoals of student, faculty, administrative, and alumni interests. Henry Atwood, a new professor painfully eager to fit in. Lucy Winter.

In some ways, Lucy Winter is May herself—a new English teacher, unwilling at first to meet her students on any but a professional level, learning painfully that love and compassion have a place in the curriculum. But Lucy Winter belongs to Appleton in ways May never would belong to Wellesley. She has a Ph.D. She is immediately accepted by the campus powers. She is poised and welcome at social events ("I almost never come home from any social occasion without feeling that I have behaved like an outlander, a woman from Mars, or a plain rude child," said May.) Lucy becomes a power herself, teaching her jaded colleagues that a school must educate the total human being, not just the mind. And again May's protagonist is heterosexual.

When the *Wellesley News* gave *The Small Room* a "mean review," May stormed the office of the president, Margaret Clapp, and found that austere woman ensconced at a long trestle table in a Gothic room with bare floor and one straight hard chair for supplicants. May took it and poured out her woes: the uncertainty of her position at Wellesley, the unwarranted snideness of the review, the impossible situation at the *News,* which, she believed, had no communication with the administration. The last was a slap at the president, who, May accused, lacked a *human* approach to the students. President Clapp listened, said coldly, "I think they are doing a very good job." May persisted. "Miss Sarton," said President Clapp, "I have a very heavy schedule."

The success of *The Small Room* did not make her feel secure. "I just quiver before the poems' coming out," she wrote Kay of the awaited *Cloud, Stone, Sun, Vine,* a collection of seventy-six titles, including twenty sonnets to Cora, "—I know so well what a let-down *that* is going to be." She sent the book to Louise Bogan, who replied:

> My objection to the sonnet-sequence is in part a general objection: I don't think that such sequences can be written, nowadays, with any hope of effectiveness. . . . *Women* should not write them, any more! The linked formality makes chance of discursiveness too great; and the sonnet, *as such,* is *never* discursive. . . .
>
> I think, too, that it should be clear that your sonnets are written to a woman. . . . These are the two main objections. One other small one: I feel that the sequence should end in a kind of unresolved positive *anger,* not in questioning acceptance. "To hell with you."—But that's my Irish *vulgarity,* no doubt!
>
> Otherwise, I think that the book *marches;* proceeds, opens out. You know how much I have always admired "Humpty Dumpty." From here on you begin to come down to facts—and state terms. And the *actual* begins to break in. "Somersault" is excellent: a true image for a spiritual complication. ("The Phoenix" and "The Furies" are also v. good indeed.) The poems on the deaths of your mother and father are also v. moving—and true—and difficult to do. I must admit to almost total dislike of the poems in "To the Living" section. *With* the exception of "What the Old Man Said," which is *lovely.* "These Pure Arches," *also.* You have transcended the awkwardness which *must* reside in the "humanitarian" poem, here.—You know how much I like the European evocations. And the Nelson poems.

On the whole, you have a *metaphysical* bent; you desire the universal behind the apparent; you have a passion for the *transcendent.* That is why I am perturbed when you seem in the sonnets to put so much spiritual capital in the *temporal:* in a *person.*—I feel that you will not need to do this again; that this is a transitional phase; that your *big, unrelenting, drastic* poems (*life or death*) are to come.

Now, take all this as the advice of one so *much older,* whose every second thought must be of death!

High praise from the stringent critic—though May disagreed that women should not write sonnets. Marianne Moore also praised, and Eric Swenson himself was endlessly encouraging. So that a book signing over Thanksgiving in Keene at which only one friend appeared in a deluge was not as traumatic as it might have been; and May not unhappily dashed about all December getting shots and examinations and her troublesome teeth fixed in preparation for the world tour she had been planning for 1962, with Cora in India as its focal point. Then there was the mad rush of semester end and Christmas: correcting papers; getting off hundreds of Christmas poems; buying presents, liquor, food; carting it all, in addition to Judy and the cats, to Nelson. At Nelson, the tree trimming, then the Warners, the Frenches, and the remaining Quigleys in for separate celebrations. The Warners loved ice cream with ginger ale, the way Mabel served it; and "Aunt Sally" Warner always made a Christmas-tree cake frosted in a poisonous shade of green that had to be consumed as May distributed presents like the local squire. Then last-minute wrappings and preparations for Christmas dinner and hanging stockings on the mantel. And then on Christmas Eve, May opened *The New York Times Book Review* to a notice of *Cloud, Stone, Sun, Vine* by the Pulitzer Prize–winning poet Karl Shapiro.

It is pointless to be cruel about bad poetry, but sometimes there is no escape. Whatever May Sarton's other accomplishments as a writer, she is a bad poet. The present collection covers a twenty-year period of writing and none of it is distinguished in any way. Her poetry is lady-poetry at its worst—this at a time when poetry is very much the art of women. Her poems are personal in the sense that the reader is invited to participate in the higher life, as tourists visit the house of the Duke of Bedford. But the tour turns out to be a walk through the chamber of clichés; her high literary attitudes (Rilke and Yeats) are only hastily mastered techniques, duly applied for the occasion—I am sorry to say this. I apologize.

May wept for three days, Christmas in shambles, her fears of mediocrity seemingly confirmed. Useless for Ashley Montagu to fume that Shapiro was too "eccentric" to be trusted with reviewing, or Helen Storm Corsa and Basil de Selincourt to write dissenting letters to the *Times*—they were friends. Useless, too, the favorable reviews that followed. "The hardest thing to bear is that I shall not be defended," she wrote Bogan. She was right: no one from the literary establishment—Moore, Roethke, Eberhart, Wilbur, William Carlos Williams, Bishop—came forward. Not even Bogan.

Hardest to bear was the fact that Shapiro's devastating critique contained some truth. Except for "What the Old Man Said" and "These Pure Arches," the poems in the "To the Living" section were May at her worst—on her soapbox, righteously haranguing. And she could be sentimental. "I had her take out two mentions of 'kittens,' from one poem," Bogan once wrote her friend Ruth Limmer. " 'Cats,' yes, 'kittens,' no." But Shapiro had arrogantly condemned the whole for a part. What finally hurt most was his condescending "I apologize."

John Wilson Croker's harsh review of *Endymion* in *The Quarterly Review* did not kill Keats, nor did Karl Shapiro's review of *Cloud, Stone, Sun, Vine* kill May Sarton. But she never forgot it. She added it to the lengthening list of "betrayals": Grace Daly spurning her in Paris, Rosalind Greene and K.T. warning Radcliffe about lesbians, Theo continuing in theatre without her, Kot and Juliette shutting her out, Ciardi omitting her name from his account of the Cambridge poetry sessions. "There is something in you which does not allow the wounds to heal," Kay Martin told her. They could not heal, for May's accusations of betrayal reflected her own betrayals; and her unacknowledged guilt for these endlessly tormented her.

After a lecture trip that took her again to Agnes Scott College and Ellen Douglass Leyburn, May left for Japan March 4, 1962. Because George and Mabel had been "a little in love with Japan," she was prepared to embrace it. As a guide, she hired a pretty college student named Kyoko, happily almost as ignorant as May about her country, so that she didn't tax May with information. May wanted impressions and got them, memorably at the old seaside house of her father's colleague Shio Sakanishi at Oiso, where she bungled like any tourist:

> Rushing into the house
> To get bird-glasses,
> I forgot to take off my shoes—

Profanation
Of the clean, sweet-smelling
Grass mats.

Later,
Having worn socks
Into the garden,
I brought bits of dry grass
Onto the velvety blue rug
In the Western-style room.

Twice-shamed!

From Japan she went on to Hong Kong, Bangkok, and finally to Bhubaneswar and Cora. She stayed in the state guest house, from 10 a.m. to four p.m. literally, since it was too hot to go out. A thinner Cora seemed very much in command and deeply interested in her teaching and research, despite the frustrations of Indian disorganization. "She seems like a large maternal figure on the landscape, surrounded by her students, Indians, and one sad American who wants to lean and whom she pushes away like a mother cat who is weaning a kitten," May wrote Kay Martin. ". . . We are very relaxed, and loving, not a sign of tension or strain so far." May had been sending Cora cigarettes, cigars, caviar, Camembert, and pâté de foie gras; now she brought Scotch, which Cora was willing to drink ("thank god!") in private. As for India, May did not feel at home with the people as she had with the Japanese: "There seems very little light in an inward sense and one has the feeling of either decadence or half-baked efforts at the huge creation of the new India."

With Cora she visited Kashmir and the Taj Mahal, then flew to Athens, where she celebrated her fiftieth birthday by climbing the Acropolis in the white morning light. Then Patmos, Lindos, and Delphi, the high point of the trip. From Florence to La Roselle; then to Paris to see the poet Camille Mayran, with whom she had begun a literary correspondence. On July 6 she arrived in London. The next day she had tea at the Huxleys' for the first time in fourteen years. Julian, now seventy-five, seemed well and inclined to hold forth on the "aristocracy of genes." Juliette, still adorable, brought them their tea and left the room. Julian shrugged. Yes, it was a shame. After May he'd had a violent love affair that had almost broken his health and marriage. May left, having nothing from Juliette to take away; though her trip had proved a poetic lode to mine.

. . .

She had not forgotten Shapiro, or Bogan's lack of support. On August 30 Judy and May were having drinks in Nelson on the screen porch Judy had given May when Louise rang from Boston, asking May to meet her bus the next day at Keene and drive her to Peterborough. "I have just been to Keene all day and I don't want to a bit," said May; but of course they met Louise's bus, drove her to Pete, and lunched there. Louise didn't even offer to buy them a drink. On September 4, May sat down to address this difficult friend, quoting Sir Thomas Wyatt's "*Noli me tangere;* for Caesar's I am, / And wild for to hold, though I seem tame":

> I shall not bore you with a long lament about my position in the *world* of poetry: it is certainly a peculiar one. But I have no doubts about my position in relation to *myself* as an instrument for poetry (for better or worse, and whether I ever "succeed" or not). I find, for instance, that the Shapiro review coming as it did after such a long sustained struggle (20 years of it) did break some spirit in me. No doubt in the long run I shall see that this was right—that I had to withdraw whatever little antennae had been out towards the world of poetry, that I had to "give up" once and for all the hope that I might be *heard.* . . . I have come to see that I cannot afford to expose myself at all in places and among people where the *world* of poetry operates. This is a neurosis, if you will. Neuroses are always defenses, I suspect. I have to defend myself somehow against rage and despair (those two sides of the same coin).
>
> Now the troubling thing is that you are my dear poet, but you are also—alas—a critic. I find that this makes for ambivalence in my feelings toward you, and even hostility. When the Shapiro thing came out, I wrote you, "The hardest thing to bear is that I shall not be defended." I meant defended by my peers. And I was right.
>
> You told me once that Babette Deutsch (whose work you do not really respect, or so you have said) badgered you into getting her into the Academy. I have never in my life approached anyone of influence to work on my behalf, and I never will. This is pride, false pride perhaps. But if this pride implies choices . . . then I have to choose not to see people of influence because it is just too upsetting. . . . What to do? I felt that the only thing was to be honest with you and tell you that I have to suspect you as a critic, or cease to believe in my own work.

I am a wounded bear, my dear, and I just must go on somehow and not be prevented from what I can do. When I see you, the wounds begin to bleed and I want to roar with misery. . . .

But to the poet, most loving greetings. . . .

Louise replied in "Of course we'll always be friends" fashion, but for May the pain went deep. She was seeing Volta Hall regularly in analysis, trying to deal with rage against the world of poetry which excluded her. Hall approved of the letter to Bogan: rage was more constructive than depression. In seeming proof, May had actually written that month "two major and longish poems" (perhaps "A Child's Japan" and "Japanese Prints") and was contemplating during the coming months a children's book based on a charming tale about a donkey told her by her Greek guide. And then on November 1, the day before her next appointment, she heard that Volta Hall was dead of a heart attack.

Panicked, she asked Louise to recommend another psychiatrist; but three days with rain and quiet and Haydn on the phonograph persuaded her that Nelson itself might be the therapist. Yet she mourned her Virgil: "Who listens so, does more than listen well. / He goes down with his patient into Hell."

Nelson did not get much chance to heal May in 1963, for she was rather seldom there, though after poetry readings in January at Bryn Mawr, Radcliffe, and New York University (arranged by Bogan), she finished *Joanna and Ulysses,* the Greek donkey tale, in three weeks at Nelson. The news during those weeks of Robert Frost's death hit her "amidships." She ranked him high as a poet and influence, along with George Herbert, William Blake, and Yeats; the fact that academic circles had turned against him endeared him further. In April and May she lectured on "The Writing of a Poem" from Washington, D.C., to California. At Scripps College she heard that the *Ladies' Home Journal* had bought *Joanna and Ulysses* for $10,000—delightful, yet "quite preposterous to get so much for a minor work of 100 pages."

The previous February she had read Betty Friedan's *The Feminine Mystique,* a polemic that was playing a large part in the new feminist movement stirring the country. It was no accident that by autumn she was planning a novel about "all the wild parts of me I subdue" and about "being a woman poet—the search for the muse." The idea tantalized and frightened her. Though they celebrated her sixtieth birthday on

Margaret Clapp, president of Wellesley College when May taught there in the 1960s

October 26 happily together, with presents and a cake, Cora was no longer a Muse. And May needed a Muse.

Margaret Clapp was fifty-three, petite and pretty, with a dry sense of humor; a Pulitzer Prize winner for her biography of John Bigelow; a forceful administrator. Like a schoolgirl with a crush, May fell desperately in love. Margaret was not available; but long ago May had discovered that the pursuer has more fun than the pursued. Possessed, she began an all-out campaign to win her. Apparently she did not consider what the scandal of a lesbian love affair would do to the career of the president of Wellesley.

That fall semester of 1963, May began begging Margaret Clapp to spare a moment for "an idle lunch." Through her secretary Margaret refused. When she finally yielded, she took May to lunch in a crowded, noisy faculty dining room. Unsatisfactory, but May was rocked by an inner explosion. Poems came—*Letters to a Silence,* May would call them. Of course she sent them to Margaret. Margaret did not reply.

May took a year's leave from Wellesley in 1964 to work on the new novel. Frustrated, more in love than ever, she wrote the Muse from Nelson:

I think, on the whole, your silence is kind. But it forces me to rely on hunches to an extent that is sometimes nerve-wracking. I have had the odd hunch that some door which had been left slightly ajar has in the last four days closed. There is no heartbreak here, I am too grateful for the unexpected flood of poetry. . . . But, I did sometime ago, ask whether you could spare an hour either on February 29th or on Sunday March 1st. . . . I do not want to see you again in a public place. Is it too much to ask that I come to the house? . . . Let me make things as easy as I can for you, since utterance . . . seems next to impossible for you. I enclose a card with some questions on it which can be answered *yes* or *no.* I am arranging for flowers to be sent for your desk about once a week. This is a gift to the college (like those rugs) as well as to you, so I hope it may be acceptable.

Yours to command

Margaret Clapp refused May that hour and announced she would distribute the flowers among other offices. May continued to phone her office (she did not have her private number). "Margaret," she said once, reaching her in the evening, "there's a full moon, you'd better go look at it." Margaret laughed. She could be friendly, and May was, after all, very appealing; but finally her secretary said, "Miss Sarton, I think you'd better stop calling." But Miss Sarton did not. "As usual the person is impossible," she wrote Rosalind Greene, an unlikely confidante, "—so impossible in this instance that I received *no* answer to 20 or more poems, so 'important' that she cannot be reached by telephone . . . so that the brief encounter will of course not sustain the stream of poetry very much longer. Or will it?"

Maddened by lack of response, May drove down from Nelson to attend a Wellesley chapel, knowing the president would be there. Afterwards, she accosted her: "Margaret, I've sent all these poems and you've never answered." "I haven't had time to read them," said Margaret, getting into her car. May jumped into her own car and tailed her, so furious that she almost rammed her. She wanted to, but some good goddess prevented this utter folly.

May wrapped up a precious signed eighteenth-century netsuke figure of a cock and went to Margaret's house. No one was at home, so she opened the door and put it on a hall table. The gift was not acknowledged. She continued to call the president's office after the spring semester ended, coaxing her to name a lunch hour. Miss Clapp wanted no fixed lunch engagements for the summer, said her secretary, and would be much out of town. Somehow, at some point, May managed to confront the president in her office. There she read to her a poem about the sacrificial bull who, for his passion, dies in the ring. At least, pleads the narrator, throw him a rose before the kill:

> If we must do him in, poor passion,
> The mythical beast, too rough and bold,
> Then give him the moment of truth in royal fashion:
> Show me your warmth, Ma'am. You and I grow old. . . .

"It destroyed our relationship," said May, "—which didn't exist, except in my mind."

Since 1960, May had taught at Wellesley on one-time appointments she'd been fighting to convert into a three-year contract. In November 1964 she received a letter informing her that she would not be reappointed for 1965. In the storm of emotion unleashed by this rebuff, she knew that Margaret Clapp had fired her. In the following weeks, however, she changed her mind, for the president assured her she had nothing to do with the committee's decision, and May wanted to believe her. Clapp offered plausible explanations. Wellesley was in the throes of curriculum change. No writer had ever been permanently employed by the college, since the program was designed to expose students to a variety of philosophies and techniques. May herself had been uncertain of her commitment to Wellesley—witness this year's leave.

May had other explanations. "It was because the English Department was jealous of me. You see, I was taking students away from them because I was very popular. And published. I put a copy of *Cloud, Stone, Sun, Vine* on the table in the faculty lounge and *no one* mentioned it, except Fred Perry, also a poet, and he said, 'It has a nice cover.' The English Department was mostly men and they didn't like me. I didn't woo the Department and I should have."

During 1964, May had finished her very personal "coming out" novel, about a lesbian poet's search for the Muse. In time, May would claim that *Mrs. Stevens Hears the Mermaids Singing* cost her her job at Wellesley. But though this fits May's perennial vision of herself as victim, it does not fit the facts. First, *Mrs. Stevens* was not published until September 1965, more than ten months after Wellesley decided not to reappoint her. Second, Wellesley under an enlightened feminist president could hardly be called homophobic.

Why, then, did Wellesley terminate May Sarton? Undoubtedly there was jealousy in the department. Karl Shapiro's review may also have played an insidious part. But Wellesley could cite irrefutable arguments for getting rid of her. May did not have an advanced degree. And Sylvia Berkman, the writing teacher she had replaced, was returning.

Yet surely May's own behavior ended her employment. Her love affair with a Wellesley professor. The fact that too many of her students developed passionate crushes on her. Her constant complaints that Wellesley treated her like a dog. The restaurant blowup with Patrick Quinn. And finally, her relentless pursuit of the president. As the Boutons' maid said, "Here comes trouble!" Academe couldn't take it.

May received Margaret Clapp's letter of termination November 14. Tears, bitterness, helpless rage. Shortly afterward she left for Yaddo, Saratoga Springs, for six weeks of writing. She had replied immediately and briefly to Clapp; now she wrote at greater length:

> I have thought a lot about the college, about myself in relation to it, about the writing of poetry as an academic discipline. The parallels between me and my father—the way he was treated by Harvard, the way in which he had to fight *against* the committees for *his* discipline—have been much in my mind. He too for many years, years in which he was honored outside Harvard by the international academies, was treated like a lackey and felt it bitterly. The difference between us is that he never loved Harvard. I had come to love Wellesley. . . .
>
> But I have come to see that, after all, I was only *allowed* to teach poetry by an accident, by Helen [Corsa]'s wit in seeing a blank opposite a number in the catalogue. . . . What I represent is not a part of the scheme of values within which the college operates. So, for me personally, it is a huge relief to have been forcibly cut off from loyalties which could not be reciprocated, and therefore could not, in the long run, *operate*.
>
> I was grossly overpaid. Treated a little worse than I presume you treat your charwomen, not respected, as they are, my salary was huge. Whatever I cannot change at Wellesley, I can change with this small segment of the past. As soon as I can confer with my lawyer in New York, my will [will] be altered so that every cent Wellesley paid me will come back to the college after my death. There will be no strings attached to that $16,000. . . . I simply wish it to be known that, although Wellesley College could not honor the teaching of poetry, poetry honored Wellesley, not for what it is, but for what it may become, an academy open to the spirit.

Recognizing that May's offer came from hurt pride, Margaret Clapp answered quietly a month later, thanking her for her letter, some lovely roses, a poem. May owed Wellesley nothing; she was the creditor. Eventually May recovered her balance and gave up the idea. She began to believe that Wellesley's rejection was the best thing that could have happened to her.

Still, she did not give up on Margaret Clapp. For Christmas, 1965, she sent her a huge star crystal engraved, "An inward music is just within reach." In January 1966, she wrote. "Everything is in order in my mind, except one thing: when am I ever going to see you? Although you wish to be inhuman, I cannot afford to be. . . . Three years ago I said that if I could see you for an idle lunch once a year, that would be enough. . . . If you could bring yourself to tell me that I can see you in June or July and that you did receive a Xmas present—well, my dear soul, that would resurrect the dead."

Margaret did not answer; May continued to write. Then Eleanor Blair called to say that Margaret Clapp had resigned from Wellesley to head a girls' college in Mandurai, South India. May felt a shock of joy. She has done it for me, she thought—she has resigned to become my lover! Ex-president Clapp, however, gave no indication of falling into May's arms. May stepped up her writing and telephoning campaign that summer, claiming she only wanted to end a chapter in her life "filled with mystery and anguish from its beginning." This could only happen if Margaret consented to see her: "For a little while, from July 1st to August 1st, perhaps, you will be a human being. I think it is mandatory that that human being write a few words to this human being. Let us lay aside poet and president. If I could see you for one hour, it would be an immense help." If you'll see me, you'll be rid of me. But Margaret Clapp understood that if she gave May an inch she'd demand a mile.

Home again after her appointment as cultural attaché to India for the United States Information Agency, Margaret discovered that May hadn't yet quit, even though her only business now was to press for the return of the spurned crystal, apparently lost in the packing up of the president's office. Correspondence back and forth. Finally, in January 1968, Clapp's secretary located the gift and returned it to Nelson. Margaret herself sent a brief letter of apology, spelling Sarton's name "Mae."

In April May picked arbutus at Nelson and drove to Tyringham, Massachusetts, where Margaret had a house. Poems started coming as she drove; she had to stop the car to get them down. Years later she told her biographer that she knocked at Margaret's back door and, receiving no answer, walked into the house. It was still, but a grocery list on the table made her sure Margaret was there. Eventually she left, certain she was being watched from an upper window. In another version, she said there had been a "tremendous scene," and that was the end.

"It was like being possessed," said May. "In a way, because she was completely unavailable, she was the best Muse." But the Clapp possession had made May unemployable in eastern girls' colleges. Fortunately, she was on the verge of a success that would make teaching unnecessary for the rest of her life.

CHAPTER 18

Mrs. Stevens Dreams Deep: 1965–1968

Mrs. Stevens Hears the Mermaids Singing was a watershed in May Sarton's career, as well as the most difficult novel she would write. Although *The Birth of a Grandfather* explored Jung's theory that in middle age people turn sympathetically to their own sex and *The Small Room* introduced same-sex lovers, May had never before made her protagonist a homosexual. Of course she hedges: Hilary Stevens is a "Mrs.," after all. But never before had May openly revealed her lesbianism. Never before, too, had she so frankly revealed her troubling nature: someone who feels too much, yet is too detached to be quite human; someone who asks, "When did I learn—shall I ever?—that conquest is not the point!"

Like *Faithful Are the Wounds, Mrs. Stevens* poses a question: What is it to be an artist—and a woman? May had already considered the problem of the woman artist in "My Sisters, O My Sisters":

And now we who are writing women and strange monsters
Still search our hearts to find the difficult answers,

Still hope that we may learn to lay our hands
More gently and more subtly on the burning sands.

To be through what we make more simply human,
To come to the deep place where poet becomes woman,

Where nothing has to be renounced or given over
In the pure light that shines out from the lover,

In the warm light that brings forth fruit and flower
And that great sanity, that sun, the feminine power.

During an afternoon with two interviewers, Hilary searches her heart for difficult answers. She is, she admits, androgynous—a concept of human nature that would be re-explored by feminists in coming decades. In Jungian terms, she is psychologically bisexual, powered not only by *anima,* the feminine principle, but *animus,* her unconscious masculine self. This claim—that in every woman there is man, and in every man, woman—would become one of the more enlightening ways of thinking about human nature in the feminist-powered last decades of the twentieth century.

Yet the conclusions Hilary Stevens draws from androgyny can be disturbing. As rigidly as Freud, Sarton identifies "feminine" with nurturing and emotion, "masculine" with mind and creativity. "After all, admit it," says Hilary, "a woman is meant to create children not works of art—that's what she has been engineered to do, so to speak. A man with a talent does what is expected of him, makes his way, constructs, is an engineer, a composer, a builder of bridges. It's the natural order of things that he construct objects outside himself and his family. The woman who does so is aberrant. . . . Oh, we are all monsters, if it comes to that, we women who have chosen to be something more and something less than women!" In short, being a woman and a writer is "a contradiction in terms."

While Hilary Stevens might outrage those who believe that women artists are not deviants, her claim that women must find their own language and subjects in the dominant world of men's literature was a radical concept in 1965. Mrs. Stevens's idea of "woman's work" also goes far to explain the puzzle of May Sarton's own oeuvre: how such an aggressive, volatile, and violent person could produce novels and poems that ultimately transcend conflict. Like Hilary Stevens, May believed that her creative demon was masculine, her sensibility feminine—George's masculine power driving her to write, Mabel's feminine sensitivity allowing her to sublimate conflict in "a celebration of life itself."

Mrs. Stevens Hears the Mermaids Singing was also written in self-defense. "People want to become you," Dr. Pederson-Krag had told her; "when they find they can't, they want to kill you." May saw the Cora and Wellesley disasters as attempts to kill her as an artist. "Under all the superficial praise of the 'creative,' " says Mrs. Stevens, "is the desire to kill. It is the old war between the mystic and the nonmystic, a war to the death. . . . I was the enemy, the anarchic, earth-shaking power." Yet May Sarton does not claim genius for Hilary Stevens. "A small, accurate talent, exploited to the limit," says Hilary, "let us be quite clear about *that!*"

May Sarton: poet,
novelist, essayist,
photographed by
Lotte Jacobi at
Nelson

May agonized more over this "horrendous gut-destroying novel" than anything else she wrote. It was one thing to masquerade as a male lover in *Shadow of a Man,* quite another to openly admit her passion for Edith Forbes Kennedy (Willa MacPherson) and Cora DuBois (Dorothea). She did not dare put Margaret Clapp in the novel; instead, Margaret is the Muse to whom it is addressed. Though the Muse fertilizes the seed that generates poetry, the Muse herself has no responsibility toward the poet. "Oh, the Muse never answers, that's sure," Hilary tells the interviewers. ". . . The Muse opens up the dialogue with oneself and goes her way."

Visiting Nelson, Ellen Douglass Leyburn read *Mrs. Stevens* and told May she was not sure she would be asked back to Agnes Scott College. Judy was terribly anxious about its publication. Puffing a cigarette, Cora said, "I suppose this new novel will create a scandal?" Eleanor Blair was more optimistic. But May had decided that none of her friends, busily trying to find themselves in the characters, would ever consider *Mrs. Stevens*

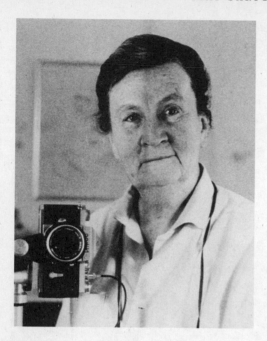

Eleanor Blair—friend,
copy editor, house sitter,
photographer

a work of art. Norton, however, loved the novel and promised publication in August 1965.

With the death of Cecile de Banke, Eleanor Blair had re-entered May's life. She would become the most useful of May's supporting cast, functioning as editor, proofreader, and typist, as well as house sitter and confidante. Eleanor also took good photographs of Nelson, the cats, and May at work, contributing tangibly to the myth May's life would become. She was a cheerful, gregarious person whom May never considered an equal; therefore they got along well.

The Wellesley slap still hurt. "I wake up in tears every day and feel unable to cope," May wrote Kay Martin. "But it is high time this long period of self-pity and joylessness came to an end and I am very cross with myself." Despite the demands of Nelson, abscessed teeth that needed pulling, lecturing, stacks of letters to answer, and visits from Cora, Eleanor, and Judy, May managed to get the new book of poems, *A Private Mythology,* off to Norton in July 1965. Then she and Judy left for Greenings Island, leaving Eleanor with gargantuan tasks of weeding, watering, cat care, and forwarding all mail. "It is really wonderful here," she wrote Kay, in the process of being replaced by Eleanor, ". . . swims in the warm sea pool, walks on the soft moss and pine needles and across the great mowed field . . . that sense of being sheltered and safe. . . . Our room has a little porch where we sit and have a drink and watch the yachts sail by. I really believe that Anne Thorp is the most beneficent person I have ever known. . . ."

That fall she went to teach at Lindenwood College in St. Charles, a town of elms and old houses above the Missouri River, where she loved her spacious apartment at 604 Clark Street and was at last treated by a college like a VIP. Agnes Sibley, a teacher in the English department, had got her the job; unfortunately, Agnes was "a sort of saint, but *unconsciously* very demanding"—and she burrowed into May like a tick, making all kinds of demands that May once had half-encouraged.

Meanwhile May had not left worries behind. She was sending checks to Mildred Quigley and her daughter, Tami. After a double mastectomy several years before, Ellen Douglass Leyburn lay dying of abdominal cancer in an Atlanta hospital. May firmly believed her mother's cancer was caused by anger and frustration; hard to think of that now, with Ellen. In New York, Katrine Greene was also fighting cancer. Basil de Selincourt, her old champion, who had visited Nelson and was profoundly shocked to find her writing poetry to Haydn and Mozart, hung to life by a thread. Then there was Judy, retired from Simmons College and depressed about her sudden poverty. May sent her $350, heard nothing, rang Judy and wept at her ingratitude, which included lack of sympathy about May's *Mrs. Stevens* anxieties. All her close friends seemed to be scared off; worse, "that rat, Virginia Kirkus," had given the book "a deadly *sneer.*" She took comfort in the fact that Norton liked her proposal of a series of novels about New Hampshire.

Mrs. Stevens Hears the Mermaids Singing got a lot of attention—most of it adverse. While *The New York Times Book Review* praised its deceptively simple plot, subtle mood, and intense feeling, most reviewers could not handle a novel about an aging lesbian who asserts her validity as an artist and a human being. If not as widely read as the *Saturday Review* and *New York Herald Tribune* critics, John Gardiner in the *Southern Review* attacked in vicious ad hominem style, dismissing Hilary Stevens as "a posturing, self-pitying phony" who "talks to herself in the stagy manner of an elderly lesbian (which she is). Miss Sarton, for understandable reasons, can't see through her. . . . And there are others, a brilliant cast of fops, mostly gay. Mrs. Stevens teaches people that 'we have to dare to be ourselves.' One wonders if such people *ought* to be themselves."

"What hurts is that nowhere was it given for review to any critic who counts," May wrote Eleanor, house-sitting and correcting the proofs of *A*

*Anne Thorp, former
Shady Hill teacher
and matriarch of
Greenings Island*

Private Mythology. Small comfort a *Cleveland Plain Dealer* critic called it
"not only the best novel I have ever read about a poet and the creative
experience, it is one of the best novels I have ever read about anything";
the *Plain Dealer* didn't count. All October was "sheer Hell because of the
d——— reviews." And there were less public, but hurtful, reactions as
well. Some teachers at Lindenwood deliberately shunned her. The head of
Shipley School cancelled a $500 lecture. The *Christian Science Monitor*
decided it didn't want her to launch its series on poets. Suspiciously, both
Radcliffe and the Guggenheim Foundation rejected her applications for
fellowships. There was one tenuous compensation. May had sent *Mrs.
Stevens* to Margaret Clapp. "I sense that the quality of the silence between
us has changed," May wrote Eleanor of her eternally aloof Muse.

By December 1 *Mrs. Stevens* had sold only 6,500 copies. Frustrated,
May offered Norton $1,000 if they would match the sum. The result was
a full-page ad in *The New York Times Book Review* with a fine photo of
May by Lotte Jacobi and a quote by Julian Huxley. But *Mrs. Stevens Hears*

the Mermaids Singing was a novel before its time. In coming years, as the gathering momentum of the feminist, gay, and civil rights movements raised America's consciousness and women's studies departments sprang up on campuses across the nation, *Mrs. Stevens* brought its author a fame she had sought all her life.

The first copies of *A Private Mythology* were in her hands February 7; she sent one to Margaret Clapp inscribed, "For Margaret, a final gift to your college with love from the recipient of almost intolerable silences." Meanwhile, she had added another string to her bow: writing short pieces on village life for magazines like *Country Beautiful* and *Woman's Day.* She was also planning a new book of poems, *As Does New Hampshire,* illustrated with photos by Eleanor Blair, whom she was also recruiting for house-sitting for May and June while she and Judy were in Europe. And returning to the light mood of *The Fur Person* and *Joanna and Ulysses,* she had also found time to write a little fable called *Miss Pickthorn and Mr. Hare,* which Eric Swenson loved.

Miss Pickthorn was May herself; Mr. Hare, an itinerant named Edgar Poland, who lived in a derelict chicken house in the woods next to the Cobleighs across the road from May. Edgar Poland drank, scrounged from the dump, and let his dog run; and May had been furious enough at the sight of his insolently smoking chimney to protest this unsanitary squatter at a weekly meeting of the selectmen. Eventually there was an uneasy truce; May even hired the outcast for odd jobs. Then one bitter winter night Edgar lapsed into a drunken stupor and let his stove go out. The next day, still drunk, he told May he thought his feet might be frozen. She drove him to the Keene hospital, where both feet were amputated to the ankles. She visited him regularly. He wanted to come back to the chicken house, but the village denied his request, and he was not heard of again.

Written before the amputated feet, *Miss Pickthorn and Mr. Hare* is the story of an eccentric Latin teacher's unconscious identification with the Thoreau-like Trumbull Hare. When he disappears, his absence becomes even more vivid than his presence had been. Finally, Miss Pickthorn understands. "Trumbull Hare was a poet, a myth-maker, don't you see? . . . There he was, living inside poetry all the time, right across the way." It is a truth that we persecute what we fear in ourselves; as Miss Pickthorn says, quoting Horace, "Change but the name and it is of yourself that the tale is told." May was not too eccentric to know that her status in Nelson was becoming almost as problematic as Edgar Poland's.

Katrine Greene died on March 11. "Meanwhile Ellen Douglass lives on, a tortured animal," May wrote Kay Martin, "who begs to be released. They drained out 40 pounds of liquid day before yesterday. I wait for the phone to ring and pray as fervently as I ever have for her quick release. . . . I have never felt more keenly the Hell of life." She began packing for Europe. Before leaving, she was given a book party at the Hotel Pierre by the New York PEN Club for *A Private Mythology,* her first—and heard that Ellen had died. Then she fled the reviews, as she had so often, comforting herself that Eleanor, Judy, and Helen Corsa all raved about the poems.

She and Judy began their tour of France on the Côte d'Azur, then drove through the Dordogne, lovely except they both had flu. By May 3 they were at the avenue Lequime, where an avalanche of birthday mail greeted May. She was horrified to find Céline old and plagued with high blood pressure. The whole atmosphere felt strange: Céline would not talk about Mabel and said indifferent things like "Well, your face is still all right." Besides, May knew too many people, and talked and visited too much, pushing herself past the limit. Then too, there was a lawsuit in Athens against *Joanna and Ulysses,* accusing May of "stealing the soul" of Joanna Carayanni, May's guide in Greece and the source of the story. Judy braced for bad weather.

Judy had found a friend in Eleanor Blair, back in Nelson coping with mice, weeding, watering, pampered cats, and now, in May's absence, the Joanna business. "Every time May's deluge of mail arrives, I'm reminded of your faithful post of duty and remember how fortunate we are to have you supervising our general 'cattery' and taking so much responsibility on all sides," Judy wrote from Céline's. ". . . May carries so much anyway (sometimes, I feel, quite unnecessarily), that I am always bothered by a little sense of guilt, and to know you are more or less always in the picture while we are away is a very great relief. . . . The general atmosphere here has been, on occasion, somewhat touch-and-go. These good kind friends . . . were apparently not prepared for the temperamental outbursts which I hoped we could avoid, but I soon saw that they were inevitable. . . . Of course, my own shortcomings and increasing lack of memory and absent-mindedness are no help whatever." Judy had left her purse in a wood near Chartres, only discovering the loss an hour down the road. "I have to be very much on the qui vive because of J's absent-mindedness and really have to take responsibility about everything so it is not a rest," May complained to Eleanor.

She was back in Nelson by mid-June to discover the miracles Eleanor had wrought: mouse baffles, gleaming silver, the kitchen table sanded and stained and furniture rubbed to a deep gloss, the chaotic filing cabinets organized, bushes pruned, plants planted—"I know that you loved doing it which makes me feel better!" But Eleanor had the temerity to stay on two days, and May blew up, outraged that she imposed at a difficult time. Actually she was jealous of Eleanor's decided popularity with Nelson.

Though there was praise for *A Private Mythology,* some reviews would not handle the poetry tenderly enough. William Pritchard's notice in the *Hudson Review* typified the kind of scorn May could arouse in male critics: "Miss Sarton has taken a journey round the world and come back alive to tell us about it. In *A Private Mythology* she stands forth proudly as an o-so-sensitive globe-trotting madam on whom not the least nuance of experience has been lost." Pritchard found the poems, as he did the novels, "lordly, reverent, and condescending by turns or all at once." Yet Sarton was "impartial in her patronizing." "A Recognition" celebrates the virtues of Perley Cole:

> I wouldn't know how rare they come these days,
> But I know Perley's rare. I know enough
> To stop fooling around with words, and praise
> This man who swings a scythe in subtle ways,
> And brings green order, carved out of the rough.

Of course, complained Pritchard, "she does not stop fooling around with words and by the end of the poem Perley has been formed into Brancusi, in the course of which one more beautiful self-congratulatory object has been wrought."

Though the review would cut May deeply, now she was angry that *The New York Times* had ignored the book. Francis Brown, the editor, professed astonishment and remedied the oversight. Though the *Times* found, with justice, the Japanese poems too porcelain-like and the Greek too full of white columns and blue sea, it praised the "savage brilliance" of the India poems and found the same "wrathful commitment" in two important elegies, one for Méta Budry Turian, the other for Volta Hall.

It was naive of May to believe that a trip around the world could automatically evoke great poetry. Nelson is the best inspiration in *A Private Mythology;* poems like "The House in Winter," "An Observation," "Learning about Water," "An Artesian Well," "A Late Mowing," and "A

Village Tale," the most powerful. As one reviewer observed, May Sarton was not a confessional but a teleological poet, her best work expanding from the concrete image at its core into universality. The short, haiku-style free-verse form of the Japanese poems could not be as effective, therefore, as the longer contemplative poems, where thought could gather resonance as it expanded.

In July, the rebuked Eleanor Blair returned again to caretake while May and Judy went to Greenings Island, a respite that somewhat slowed May's pulse, for she had been taking belladonna for nerves and stomach pain. One night May read the guests *Miss Pickthorn and Mr. Hare*, interpreting ripples of laughter as approval. And she was working on another book, a series of reflections about Nelson, trying to decide whether to call it *A House for All Seasons, The Silences of Nelson*, or *Thirty-six Acres of Solitude*. Eventually she decided on *Plant Dreaming Deep*, using "plant" as a verb from her poem "Heureux Qui, Comme Ulysse," which describes the hero returning "seasoned and stretched to plant his dreaming deep." Returning to Nelson, she found all in order and the house stocked with the best Scotch, gin, and vermouth. Eleanor fondly waved as she drove off, but May was already on her knees rooting in the annual border and did not look up.

In late September, May brought Eugénie Dubois, now seventy, to Nelson. Eugénie's face had been operated on for cancer, leaving a disfiguring patch on her cheek; and May had decided during their last meeting in Belgium to cheer up her demoralized friend. While Eleanor stayed at Nelson still again and cleaned under the sink, May drove Eugénie through the glowing fall colors of Vermont and Maine, though Nelson itself, as Perley Cole said, was "beyond beautiful." But then Eugénie's son, Eric, wrote to say that Jean Dubois had had a stroke, cutting short her visit.

With relief, May went back to *Plant Dreaming Deep*, consulting Eleanor, an editor for Ginn, closely: "Just read over these chapters fast, tell me anything you feel essential, and send them back. . . . I have a few questions to ask you, the first reader." Was the prologue too long or irrelevant? Too much detail about her relative John Elwes? Too much detail about the Nelson house? Eleanor could be a stiff critic, faulting May for "small name-droppings," suggesting cuts, advising her to stop thanking people so liberally. May was grateful for Eleanor's sharp editorial eye. "The real problem is that I have too much to say, too many lives have touched mine over the years and here, all interwoven. . . . I think the quality of the book will depend in part on my being honest about the fact that I have gone through bad depressions here—otherwise it is all just too good to be true. . . ." Yet how to be honest? Perley Cole, for instance, had black rages against her; as she was writing him into *Plant Dreaming Deep,* he announced he was through working for her and made cruel insinuations about her private life. There was so much about that life she couldn't say.

Miss Pickthorn and Mr. Hare was published on November 28. Norton sent out a letter with an order form to May's friends and acquaintances, touting the book as ideal for Christmas giving; but though May's friends were myriad, the charming fable fell into limbo, *The New Yorker*'s favorable review misclassifying it as juvenile. May shot off a furious letter to Eric Swenson, charging that Norton hadn't even made bookstores aware of *Pickthorn*'s existence. Swenson was an equable editor, but May's "totally untrue" accusations stung him.

In January and February 1967 she was driving to finish *Plant Dreaming Deep,* inviting Eleanor to Nelson, where they worked together at the big trestle table, or sending her chapters regularly for revisions. "Darling, I can only make a silent prayer about your understanding re my blow-off," she apologized after one stormy disagreement, "—I have a sort of inbred violence against detail (so unlike my father in this)—it creates awful frustration in me for some reason. I felt it again when your *dear* envelope came as I was deep into the final chapter—but then when I set to work and *saw* what you had done, all resistance vanished and I felt such a flow of gratefulness that some small atom of it must have reached you and made your ears burn."

Often she was *not* grateful: "I did not sleep last night, had bad migraine, because I felt after reading this chapter that in this one you have become in some way over-dominating. . . . And this rouses fears about the whole book—it is certainly much smoother than I could have made it alone—but is it like a piece of sculpture, over-handled, having lost just the rough edge that is the sculptor's *own mark?*" She dug in further against her "kind but extremely enervating friend." She would not delete all the "magics," "myths," and "silences": "the whole book is about magical, mythical, silent Nelson!"

Curiously, as she was finishing the Nelson book, she had thoughts of leaving. That February she'd visited Beverly Hallam, the painter, at her studio on Shore Road in Ogunquit, "a glorious revelation of what the ocean there can be in winter." Molly Howe thought the Nelson house dreary. And Eleanor Blair urged leaving, until May came to believe that she was indeed being both stifled and overworked in Nelson and perhaps *should* give it up—in about ten years. But then a humiliating experience

May going over the manuscript of Kinds of Love, *1969*

in Washington, where, as a recipient of a National Foundation for the Arts grant, she felt "snubbed and humiliated" by Carolyn Kizer on the platform in favor of the poet Duncan Grant, made quiet Nelson and the masses of daffodils seem again like paradise.

Spring and summer, as usual, flowered with visitors. Polly Thayer Starr, visiting Nelson overnight for the first time. Molly Howe, whose husband, Mark, had recently died (May's "The Rock in the Snowball" commemorated the civil rights activist). Lotte Jacobi, to photograph. Joy Sweet, the surviving daughter of Henry and Rosalind Copley Greene. Judy. "I am really worried about her inability to *focus* on anything," May wrote Eleanor. ". . . I have never loved her more—such a dear companion—but her presence here does not relieve me of any responsibility and that is, frankly, what would be good right now. . . . She *three times* put out tray cloths instead of place mats when setting the table—each time I carefully and patiently explained the difference and showed her where each group is laid in the drawer—but this kind of thing is humiliating for her and hard on me."

Beverly Hallam. May's inferiority complex kept her away from writers, but she liked artists. With Beverly she could talk frankly about the

A relaxed May at Nelson

problems of the creative life. "I can only say . . . that what I have had to kill, the big DRAGON, has been ambition of the wrong kind. In the end one's work is between oneself and God, not between oneself and the critics, the fashion, or the dealers. Yet there is this terrible need to *crash through* somehow—I used to feel as if I were buried alive and trying to lift myself out over a gravestone." She felt close to Beverly because they were both "good animals i.e. direct natural people."

Eleanor Blair, with whom she frequently lost her temper—as, however, she could with anyone, apologizing to Beverly for "the awful things I say and do, my tears, rages and general behavior lately of a child just teething." May's temper, in fact, rocked Nelson. On summer evenings, after a few Scotches, her furious telephone calls to friends who had wronged her flew through open windows across the green. She had monumental battles with villagers over stray dogs. She could be violent at town meetings. Joan Cobleigh Gerbis with her husband, Harold, and their boys visited her mother and had run-ins with May, who hated noise. That only provoked the Gerbis children more—"Let's go make May mad!" Joan didn't try to stop them: May notoriously snubbed Mrs. Cobleigh when she came across the road to talk when May was gardening. Perley Cole, no temperamental slouch himself, gave May's rages a wide berth. Now she apologized to Eleanor: "I know only too well that I am a difficult and exasperating person. I can only say that I suffer real anguish and guilt because of my behavior. But I think I know that if I really calmed down, I would have ceased to write, ceased to be a poet etc. This is not an apologia but a statement of fact. The real conflict is and always has been between responsibility in a human sense and responsibility towards work. It will never be solved."

Yet the Ladies Aid gladly sold copies of *As Does New Hampshire,* a slim book of regional poems printed in Peterborough to celebrate New Hampshire's bicentennial. And Eleanor gladly returned to house-sit and battle fleas so that May and Judy could spend two weeks again on Greenings Island. People forgave May.

Katharine Taylor did not come. Unlike Anne Thorp, she had cooled toward May over the years; and though May sent her everything she wrote ("What a sensitive, strong, tender, beautiful thing you have done," Katharine had replied to *I Knew a Phoenix*), May resented the distance K.T. maintained like a clipped lawn between them. "Don't ever feel you must explain about not asking me to Nelson!" Katharine now answered May's apologies. "The idea never occurred to me—never occurs. . . ."

This time Kay Martin came to care for the Nelson house, gardens, grounds, neighbors, and cats when May went abroad that September. "I have known from the beginning that the true presence of the house can be felt only when one is alone here," May had written in *Plant Dreaming Deep,* "so I like to lend it to a friend when I myself am absent." Not the whole reason, though Kay found inspiration in May's habitat.

The trip was a frank assignation. During her last visit to Belgium she had met Baroness Hannie Van Till, a Hollander, painter, friend of Queen Christiana, survivor of seven years in a Japanese prison camp in Indonesia, and admirer of May's work. The baroness was a large, fierce, insatiable "fire engine" of a woman. She made it clear to May that the invitation to Bussum meant sex. After years of hopeless passion for Margaret Clapp, what the baroness offered seemed refreshingly simple.

"Of course I knew when I decided to come what she wanted," May wrote Bill Brown,

> but I was not at all sure of what I might feel—or *not* feel (so scary). She is not at all my type to put it crudely, but she is, in her *grand* great way, irresistible—and after all the ambivalent people I have been involved with over the past ten years or so, it is almost unbe-

lievable to me to be with someone so absolutely *straight* and whole. It is doing me a world of good, though I must confess that her pace is staggering and I sometimes fall by the wayside . . . but notes for poems hover in the air again after such a long dry time when I was trying to *force* things, and I must say that on a less personal level I find the immense, always changing skies over the flat lands deeply exciting and moving.

("Don't believe all!!!!" Hannie scribbled on the envelope, horrified that May was telling Bill about their affair.)

As with Muriel Rukeyser, May found herself overwhelmed by an appetite larger than hers. "She was a lioness who wanted to eat me alive! After spending the night with me, she would climb into her husband's bed so that he would suspect nothing. I had no choice but to give in to her." It was, she told Eleanor Blair, like being "caught up in the eye of a hurricane."

Back in Nelson October 12, she felt still the suck of the Dutch undertow—"any major love affair when one is 56 is bound to be at the same time a great *charge* (electric charge for work I mean) and a huge complication," she told Bill. "H. is terrified that Hans will know—I had to promise *not* to publish and feel terribly depressed and *stifled*. . . . But I think maybe I can get the feeling down impersonally (Dutch Interior). It was all very sudden, brief and overwhelming—we are *so* different. She is non-verbal (that's bad when one is so far away) and expresses herself by exclamation point and underlining. I feel queer and cut off. . . ." With Eleanor, she was direct: "I now look at the Dutch episode as a big mistake on my part. . . . I am back in those areas of anguish which I hoped to have left forever."

May was willing to "gather the grapes from any vine, / And make rich wine, and make rich wine." Yet Hannie did not inspire major poems. Instead, May found herself committed to the proposed local fiction series. "I am in a laocoon struggle with the first of the N.H. novels which I now begin to fear were a great mistake," she wrote Bill. "I wonder if this is not all forced stuff and not within my talent. It is rather joyless, five pages a day, come Hell or high water—and exhaustion at the end of that daily stint. Then I wake up in a sweat of anxiety 50 times a night . . . but slowly the characters begin to live and maybe I can pull something viable out of the reluctant subconscious, at least enough to satisfy my conscience about that d——— grant!" Her working title was *The Cold Winter*.

. . .

In January 1968 she sent out first copies of a work well within her talent. "That lovely, *lovely* book!" exclaimed Katharine Taylor. *Plant Dreaming Deep* was indeed a lovely book, an artful evocation of the discovery of Nelson woven into the deeper texture of the discovery of self, a revelation of how the poetic spirit finds truth and beauty in the everyday. Brooks Atkinson in *The New York Times* and Granville Hicks in the *Saturday Review* loved it; and Norton's president, George Brockway, was moved to congratulate her on a stunning press. More important, readers loved the book, reread it, talked about it, passed it along to friends. By mid-November 1968, *Plant Dreaming Deep* had sold 11,145 copies and was still moving nicely. Not a runaway success, but a success.

Plant Dreaming Deep brought May Sarton a new kind of attention; it brought her fans. "I have seldom heard a book speak so directly to me" . . . "I have placed it next to *Walden* on my shelf " . . . "I lived every moment with you" . . . "You have taken me to the depths of life" . . . "Oh, yes, Sister!" Most of these fans were women discovering a wonderful woman: courageous, independent, in harmony with nature, warm, loving, frank about her shortcomings. May Sarton was what they wished to be. These fans were sure they knew the author like a friend. They could easily imagine themselves sipping a martini in front of her fire as they admired the flowers, the cats, the portrait of The Ancestor, Mabel Sarton's wonderfully wrought desk. May's gift for immediate intimacy was as seductive in prose as in life.

May's lip justifiably curled over these assumptions. She had given herself away, like most autobiographers, in only the most circumspect way, far less than in *Mrs. Stevens Hears the Mermaids Singing.* Or sometimes not at all. The dedication to Judy, "who believed in the adventure from the start," is sheer audacity considering the fact that May bought the Nelson house for Cora. There are inadvertent revelations, of course. The prologue imagining her forebears Duvet de la Tour and John Elwes feeling quite at home in New Hampshire says a great deal about May the cultural orphan, an outsider even as she immortalized the village. The invoking of a "guardian angel" who oversees the finding and creating of the house is May-the-eternal-child's longing for a protective, loving parent, as are her tales of the good ghosts that haunt it and the magical appearances of neighbors whenever she needs help. And, of course, her making a myth of Nelson is fundamentally a need to bolster a painfully insecure ego by creating a self larger than life.

Gardens and gardening are central to this myth. What lifts *Plant Dreaming Deep* out of the realm of ordinary memoir is Sarton's genius for using nature as a metaphor for human life. Thus the stringent and cathartic task of weeding is like writing a poem. Planting a bulb in October enacts the eternal ritual of life in death. Cutting down an old maple wrenches the soul like the death of a friend. An ice storm reflects Sarton's own rage. Drilling a well to tap water eighty feet deep is like finding an inner resource when one's spirit has hit rock bottom.

Sarton's metaphors are so powerful that we almost cease to question. "Is there a joy except gardening that asks so much, and gives so much?" she asks. So mythically is Sarton's gardening associated with birth, life, death, and rebirth that both garden and gardener are sanctified. In her powers of creation, Sarton is God.

This is not to criticize. *Plant Dreaming Deep* is imaginative, not factual, truth—May's life as she idealized it: aesthetically and spiritually rich; shored by faithful friends; charged with just enough conflict between Life and Art to make it clear she's not one of the masses. The raw truth might have made a best-seller, but *Plant Dreaming Deep* was more important than that. Brooks Atkinson called it a "small, but tender and often poignant" book. Small it is not. *Plant Dreaming Deep* is an impressive exercise in the creation of a female cultural heroine, and as such, a book of genuine import.

CHAPTER 19

"Time of Burning": 1968–1970

Plant Dreaming Deep brought May floods of letters, exacerbating the perennial torment: how much for people, how much for art? This violent ambivalence would last a lifetime, accelerating as she won new readers. She could not live without mail, yet could hardly live with it. Mail time became the focus of her day, shattering her concentration an hour before Win French stuffed her mailbox full of letters. She began to use sherry to push herself "into a final hour of letter-writing between noon and one." From time to time she hired a secretary, but nothing could rid her of the burden, just as nothing could stem her voracity for it. Eleanor Blair chided. "I appreciate all you said," May shot back, "but you must remember that it is far harder to cut people off than you realize. . . . From the outside it sounds *easy*, just don't answer, just close the door. It is *not* easy and that is that."

Fan mail was corrupting in another sense. It reinforced May's vision of herself as a healer rather than an artist. Years before, she had been pleased that a poem helped a woman with depression. Grateful letters poured in now: a son had committed suicide, a husband had beaten a wife, an old mother was failing—and *Plant Dreaming Deep* had helped the reader weather the crisis. May took these letters to heart, dismissing one from a California woman who asked her, apropos *Mrs. Stevens,* whether she ever revised. Suppose the characters in that novel *did* rub their foreheads ten times in ten pages as if no other gesture were inventable (where was May's editor?). If *Mrs. Stevens* helped someone deal with trauma, that's what mattered.

Ironically, this sybil, this Wise Woman of Nelson—as readers saw her—could offer guidance when her own life was in chaos, as well as when she had no direct experience of the problems of her readers, who were wives, husbands, divorcées, siblings, parents. She who frantically struggled to center her own life could center the lives of others. Ironic indeed, because May had not much *real* sympathy. As she confessed to Eugénie Dubois, "Personne ne m'intéresse, excepté moi-même." But her immediacy, her zest were irresistible. Eugénie understood the paradox: "As to those who enter your life through your books, and believe you are serene, well . . . You give such a sense of intimacy and such a special quality of life, freed from anxiety, from loneliness, from despair, that one wants to drink at the same spring. You have the gift of . . . feeding the hunger that real life has not fed."

Plant Dreaming Deep also brought May money, both from sales and from the magazine *Family Circle,* which now offered her $1,000 a month to "just babble on about life in the country, me, cats, trees, whatever I feel like." "What luck," said Harold Gerbis when May told him about the contract. "*Luck,*" roared May, "had nothing to do with it!" With the money she bought an emerald-green chair for the cozy room, commissioned a monotype from Beverly Hallam, paid $380 to have Gracie Warner's teeth fixed, and eventually bought the carless Quigleys a blue secondhand Plymouth for $650. "I am now getting so rich that I am feeling very poor," she wrote Beverly. "That is a sure sign of being rich-rich, I fear." But producing columns for *Family Circle* wasn't easy, especially since many topics proved to be assigned. "I had to get drunk to be that submissive."

New prosperity that spring of 1968 coincided with a diet, for May at fifty-six was no longer svelte. To conquer a portly waistline, she tried drinking only tea, bouillon, and fruit juice for one week a month. Dieting would become a pattern: periodically, with immense discipline, she would shed twenty pounds, only slowly to regain it with noon sherry, evening Scotch and wine, and her own superb cooking. But she set out for an April lecture tour ("Thank God two of the colleges are Catholic where at least I do not have to apologize for soul") five pounds slimmer.

Incredibly, May was only now giving up Margaret Clapp. "I called her late this morning," she wrote Eleanor, "and have finally elicited a rebuff which makes further communication impossible but also freed me to write her one last letter of explanation which I have, so far, refrained from doing. It is a *relief.* Five years of hopeless hope is too much and has

May with Esmeralda, Nelson, June 1968

undermined my real self, a self which should be joyful but has not been."
Museless—"will I ever be a *poet* again?" May mourned—she hit upon the
idea of borrowing inspiration that summer in the person of the Warners'
arthritic donkey. Perley Cole fenced off her field and readied the barn, and
the Warners hauled the recalcitrant Esmeralda to May's place. Everybody
thought she was crazy.

"She lay down for a while today in the soft grass and looked very con-
tent, and she waits eagerly now for my comings and goings as I have either
a lump of sugar or a carrot in my pocket!" May reported to Eleanor. "It
is quite easy to clean up after her in the barn (really just grass rolled up in
neat oval balls!). . . ." On June 24 May was ecstatic when Esmeralda gave
her first bray. But revived by cortisone treatments for the arthritis, Esme-
ralda proved as difficult as her mistress, escaping from the field, devouring
ten pounds of oats, tearing about the village with a string of panting locals
at her heels. And then manure shovelling quickly lost its enchantment.

And Esmeralda could not substitute for the finally lost Margaret
Clapp. "I am too old," May wrote Beverly Hallam. "I have asked so little,

and on it depends *poems* . . . why? Why? Why? I cried so much last week that I have swollen glands around the eyes and look like HELL. I have turned frustration into poems for five long years. But now it is the end and I do not know where to turn." But then Esmeralda came through after all, in the guise of "an angel" who commanded her "to write a small *Pickthorn*-like book, humorous and wise (we hope) about Andy Lightfoot, a poet who loses his Muse and finds a donkey."

If only she could get to it, because summer as usual was hell, with pilgrims in search of *Plant Dreaming Deep* added to hordes of friends. Two of these pilgrims stayed for three hours, exhausting her with their problems; another turned out to be a horrid woman who owned an artificial-flower shop. May got violent and was told, "You are a fat, embittered old maid!" There just wasn't time for writing and gardening—"my ideal life here, which I so rarely seem to live!" Finally in August Eleanor Blair came to be indoctrinated into donkey care while May fled with Judy to Greenings Island.

Yet between struggles with the Nelson novel, "an ornery nut" that wouldn't crack, *The Poet and the Donkey* got written, and May did achieve the desired tender, humorous tone and, with the help of Eleanor's rigorous editing, a "more distinguished" style. Chiefly, however, *The Poet and the Donkey* is a charming defense of May's quite indefensible behavior with Margaret Clapp. Andy Lightfoot finally decides that Miss Hornbeam, the college administrator who is the object of his passion, is not "entirely human in the way a poet must be." "I suppose that is why Plato would not have allowed poets into his Republic," muses Andy. "They are, inevitably, disturbed and disturbing people, vulnerable, anarchic, never quite grown up, feeling their way by hunches, in touch at times with mysterious powers, always engaged in knocking walls down, opening locked doors, and making nuisances of themselves." Poetry demanded that the poet "give himself away," keep himself "absolutely transparent" and therefore terribly vulnerable. How could an administrator, governed by formality and reason, comprehend the poetic soul?

Esmeralda had served her purpose; and to Andy, as it had to May, came the revelation that he did not have to keep the donkey forever. "For he had done what he meant to do—made her well, able to run away and to have her joys, to be the complete, balky, whimsical animal she was meant to be. And she, meanwhile, had helped him recover his sense of himself: runner after the impossible on desperate—oh, yes, sometimes desperate!—feet." Bud Warner carted Esmeralda back to the dark stall from which May had liberated her. For when the Muse has fulfilled her mission, the Muse may move on.

Baroness Hannie Van Till and May

That October the hungry Baroness Van Till descended upon Nelson. May kept her busy planting bulbs—not possible, of course, at night. "As long as it is not a terrible burden to you I should accept Hannie's fountain of passion without too much questioning," wrote Eugénie, still reluctantly May's confidante. "Up to now, it has always been *your* role to overwhelm other people with your passionate feelings. . . . It struck me before how little caught you were by [the] passionate feelings of people towards you."

But a real Muse was on the horizon.

Monica (not her real name) was a college educator. She loved May's poetry and *Plant Dreaming Deep* and, like so many readers, felt her life changed by the sympathetic author. May liked Monica's intelligent letters, and in the spring of 1969 accepted an invitation to read poetry at her college. "I decided I was going to fall in love with her," said May. "I just thought, this is going to happen. I mean, I didn't decide in the sense of *will*. . . . But I was on a trajectory. It was very strange."

Monica was younger than May, with dark hair and a pretty face set off by brilliant sapphire eyes fringed with black lashes. She had energy and charm and a strong will (which boded ill), and that spring they were lovers. May cancelled a trip to see Céline, exiled to an apartment in Brussels. To Rosalind Greene, May poured out her joy:

> It is a miracle at 57 to meet the right, true person, but I have *no doubt*. The well fills up. At first I simply collapsed into days of weeping . . . too absurd . . . like a starving person who cannot eat when bread is there, because of so much deprivation. For *twelve long years* since I came here, I have fought depression, fought suicide day by day. . . . I can say this now because all that is *over*. Cora, I think, nearly killed me. . . . Then I followed a will o' the wisp for five years, a person who made poetry flow out like blood, but *never* answered anything—*never!* So I measure fully what a change of style happiness is . . . happiness, sharing, a mutuality at last. . . . 57 and a newborn babe!

Hannie Van Till had insisted May tell her immediately if she took a new lover. Hannie's rage made May quite ill, though the baroness's fury, she reasoned, might cauterize her wound. On June 24, Monica came to Nelson for a week, and because poems like "Inner Space" and even the Nelson novel were flowing again, May gave a whole week to holiday. They took out a canoe at Pebble Beach in a stiff wind and almost capsized, went on long hikes, grilled steaks, laughed hilariously at nothing. And Monica, "intoxicated" by this "stimulating, sensitive, intelligent, and perceptive" playmate, thanked God for the gift of May. As May assured Beverly, "There will be no conflict, only understanding."

"Now that poetry is humming again, mayn't there be some that are *not* love poems?" Eleanor Blair wrote dryly. Secretary, editor, critic, typist, house-garden-and-pet-sitter, Eleanor had hoped that she could become to May what Cecile de Banke had been to her. She had weathered May's passion for Margaret Clapp as well as Hannie's passion for May. Monica, sadly, finally put her in her place. "I have been useful," she told May bitterly. "God knows you have!," May replied the next day:

> I think . . . I hope . . . that we have been useful to each other, for after Cecile died, you needed a creative person in your life. . . . I provided a central person when you needed that most. And Nelson, a new *place*.

But I believe you knew from the start, after C's death, that you could never be that for me. And almost at once there were angry times when I felt caught in a relationship in which I could not function as my total self, a relationship which gave me so much that I was always in the position of being an ingrate. . . .

It is not good for me to see very much of someone who is the cause of so much guilt and stress. It is not good for you to see much of someone who harries and upsets you for no rational reason. . . .

Where we stand now is truly united toward the work of a writer in whom you have faith (and sometimes even I have faith in her!). There is *no one* to take your place there. . . . It has not happened fast . . . I rebelled like a donkey on the first books . . . but slowly and by sheer understanding, by thinking and feeling so deeply with the poet, you have come to stand *inside* the work itself, the heart of the work, as no one else ever has or ever will. How to measure what this means? Is there not great *love* on both sides in it, love and earned trust on both sides? I have many friends. I have had many lovers. I have never had *anyone* who does what you do for me in my work. There, it seems to me, we each serve something greater than either of us. . . . I love you more than ever now this is said.

So Eleanor had to be satisfied as the acolyte of May's work. That fall it was chiefly the novel, an "inward journey to a village" which she wanted, variously, to call *Willard, Right On!* or *Old Devotions.* It had given her great trouble from the beginning, partly because she felt she had used so much of the Nelson experience in *Plant Dreaming Deep.* Poems were coming too—"The Invocation to Kali," "After the Tiger," "Night Watch"—and she wanted to do a book "about solitude and this place . . . more naked and deeper than *Plant,* on a different level, more about *inside* me." Meanwhile, Norton had reprinted *I Knew a Phoenix,* and *The Poet and the Donkey* had appeared September 27. Though May disliked the illustrations, *The New Yorker* called the fable "sophisticated and elegantly sentimental." And in November, on the strength of a hundred pages, Norton offered a $10,000 advance for the Nelson novel, making her keenly regret having signed with a New York agency for a 1970 income-padding lecture tour.

"Love is glorious but it sure is hard to fit in." This was as true for Monica as for May. Arriving at Monica's primed with crises and frustrations, May often discovered that Monica's week had been even more arduous and that in consequence she was exhausted and remote. This baffled May, who took the centrality of her concerns for granted; but May was in love and Monica as yet could do no wrong. "Never has anyone I loved really cared about my work," she told Beverly, ". . . and she does. What a difference that alone makes. But I also care about hers . . . I am an educator at heart!" And Monica too was in love, and what would later strike her as "mid-life madness" still intoxicatingly new.

Judy came to Nelson for ten days during the Christmas holidays—Judy, whose memory loss was now diagnosed as Alzheimer's. Kind friends suggested a nursing home; then new pills seemed to help for a time. May's dilemma was acute. On the one hand, Judy was sweeter and more pliable than before; on the other, she was no help at all to May, who expected visitors to relieve her of work. More deeply frustrating, Judy was drifting away: May's love affairs, crises, and tantrums no longer engrossed her. Trying to explain this outrage to old friends, May was told, "You must be serene." Instead, she "hit the ceiling, cried hysterically half the night." No use reminding May that she had left Judy. May felt abandoned and betrayed.

Now a terrific snowstorm prevented her from driving Judy home—and Monica was expected in hours. She finally paid a villager fifty dollars to return Judy and her cats to Cambridge. "My best Christmas present was [Monica] for a week," May told Beverly. "I felt amputated when she left."

Though May complained to Bill Brown of Eleanor's "turtle-like progress at typing the Mss, a real agony as she will not take pay and will not be hurried," May spent long weekends at "The Hive" in Wellesley in January and February 1970, hammering out revisions. Eric Swenson strongly urged not rushing the novel, yet warned May that neither she nor Miss Blair should relax their efforts for a 1970 winter publication. May had more time to work on the manuscript because *Family Circle,* to her combined relief and fury ("I cannot be put into an ashcan in public"), cancelled their contract. And she was writing poems.

In February she heard that Louise Bogan was dead, "alone in her N.Y. apt.," she wrote Bill, "as so many other solitaries must do . . . in deep depression (not suicide I gather, though) . . . it hits me hard. Mostly because she was such a great poet and had managed to write so few poems for the last 20 years, all the honors came when she had ceased to write. . . . Muriel called me yesterday . . . and said she had seen Louise (who for 30 years never reviewed M.) who told Muriel (drunk I presume), 'I have not had a bath for three weeks' . . . she was clearly again on the verge of breakdown." Despite bouts of severe depression, Louise Bogan had never contemplated suicide. Her death on February 4 was perhaps from a heart attack brought on by mixing diabetes medicine with cigarettes, tranquillizers, and alcohol; certainly from indifference to life. "Yet what remains," May concluded, "is the best lyric poetry of our age . . . how strange it all is."

She immediately wrote an elegy for Louise, as she had on the deaths of virtually everyone important to her except Mabel, whose loss could not be encompassed in one poem. It is a bad elegy ("Louise, Louise, why did you have to go / In this hard time of wind and shrouding snow"), perhaps because while Sarton the poet valued Bogan the poet, May could not forgive Louise her withering ironies and critical neglect in *The New Yorker.* One can imagine Bogan's lip curling at lines like "Where are they now, the aqueous green eyes, / Her violent heart, her innocent surprise?" Yet May was sincere when she praised Bogan's "singular light" and "clarifying pain."

For spring vacation, May and Monica flew to Bermuda, where Monica learned more about life with May. She stuck to a fixed routine: work and letters in the morning, rather a lot of sherry before lunch, a nap, then playtime. This suited Monica, who wanted to sightsee while May was occupied. But May wanted Monica within reach. Even while she napped, she insisted Monica stray no further than the balcony. Then there was the terrible *suddenness* of the rages. "Listen to this poem," May might say. "I want your reaction." Trustingly, Monica gave it. May turned on her in fury. "*I don't need my poetry discussed!*" On her part, May was discovering that Monica was rather conventionally middle-class, with none of her own cultural sophistication. May also disliked Bermuda, wet and too cold for ocean swims, infested by college kids on motorbikes and philistines buying cashmere sweaters. "But after all Bermuda was for love," she wrote Bill, "and we did have a most loving peaceful time . . . wonderful to be so at peace."

Just back from Bermuda, she flew to Belgium on April 9 for three weeks, finding Céline at eighty-seven in a large apartment in the avenue Maréchale Joffre, "a rich bourgeois section of Brussels . . . not a tree in sight." In this uncongenial setting, May judged more harshly. "Céline has always been an egotist and dominator (she lost her three children by trying

to over-control) and now is worse," May wrote Beverly. "I felt like a pris-
oner. She is in love (there is no other word) with a French woman who
works for her and cooks. . . . Said woman is an *angel,* I must say. But I had
to listen day and night to her praises and felt it unnecessary to have made
the supreme effort and spent $1000 to show my faithful love." One night
May threw up from sheer jealous rage. "I hated Belgium. The umbilical
cord is cut right off."

She returned for her fifty-eighth birthday, "a tearful magnificent cele-
bration of friends" with four bottles of champagne, daffodils and narcis-
sus. Monica drove up the day before; they vowed never again to endure
such a long separation—a vow broken when May learned that an old
friend from abroad would be visiting Monica that summer, leaving them
only July 24 to August 9 together.

May's reaction to this news was violent and prolonged. Terrible
scenes, nights of weeping, rages, blowups at hapless friends and strangers,
after which she would flee to her car and weep wildly over the steering
wheel. The slightest comment she took as personal insult, any check (she
was not allowed to visit the very ill Lotte Jacobi) as total rejection. By the
end of June, however, she had begun to realize that after "a lyrical year of
passionate love," the problems with Monica were familiar. Stolen, spo-
radic weekends. Living Monica's life on those weekends instead of her
own. Disguised affection: Monica was so nervous that she wouldn't meet
friends who knew about their relationship. Monica's demanding job. "I
came to see that my loneliness (acute and awful) was really a loneliness for
myself," she wrote Bill Brown, "and what I had to do was get back to my
blessed solitude. My motto, the opposite of dear Forster's, has become
'only disconnect.' "

But she realized too that her misery had other foundations. "The
point is, Bev, that my rage and woe come from great and prolonged suf-
fering that the critics have never never given the poems a break. I see the
mediocre winning and I suppose to keep going I have to get mad . . . bet-
ter than committing suicide. It is the fight to *survive* somehow against the
current. I am a salmon leaping up the waterfalls."

Work maintained sanity—work and the garden and the cats and the com-
panionship of Punch, the green parrot who had replaced Esmeralda as a
Muse of sorts (his "stuttered staccato scream" was compatible). Eric
Swenson was enthusiastic about *Kinds of Love* (Norton's title) and had
sold the novel to *Reader's Digest*—$15,000 for May. And with the help of

Eleanor Blair, she was pulling together a new collection of poems, called, from Matthew 17:20, *A Grain of Mustard Seed*. Eleanor's help went beyond typing. The last line of "Once More at Chartres," for example: May wanted, "For here the suffering child must become the mother," but couldn't get it to scan. "Any ideas?" The line emerged as "The suffering child here must become the mother."

A Grain of Mustard Seed reflected Eleanor's influence in another way. Although the volume was dedicated to Monica ("M.H.H."), it contained no overt love poetry. Of course, love inspired many of the poems; but Margaret Clapp, Baroness Van Till, and Monica were all off-limits, and May transposed discreetly. Hannie's overwhelming passion becomes "the wild skies overhead" in "Dutch Interior" and "A Vision of Holland." Margaret Clapp is, anonymously, "The Muse as Medusa" and, in "Easter Morning," the "Presence" that might visit the poet if she has the patience to " 'wait, / When all is so in peril, and so delicate!' " Even Eleanor would not have known that "The Invocation to Kali" was inspired by Monica had May not written, "It came flowing out of a real agony of mind and as the result of a night of weeping when I believed that I would have to give [Monica] up for *her sake*." On July 6 she sent off the manuscript, and Eric replied that *A Grain of Mustard Seed* was wonderful. "The quality and productivity of your mind never cease to awe me."

Inevitably, *A Grain of Mustard Seed* reflected the turmoil of the sixties: the assassinations of John Kennedy, Robert Kennedy, and Martin Luther King, the escalation of American involvement in Vietnam, nationwide protests, peace marches, desegregation marches, student sit-ins, police brutality. In the spring of 1970, as May was completing the volume, the Nixon administration bombed Cambodia; at Kent State University, National Guard troops shot four student protesters dead. May's political temper was Mabel's: fiercely black-and-white. She was pro-liberal, anti-war, anti-segregation, anti-Republican. Martin Luther King was a hero. Her activism might go little further than local campaigning for Eugene McCarthy and George McGovern or reading poems in a Boston ghetto, but her concern was real, as was her championship of the underdog. If this seemingly contradicted her social snobbery and narcissism—well, May was nothing if not a paradox.

"The Ballad of the Sixties" testifies to America's "season in Hell" when "only the mad are sane . . . And only the lost are well." "The Rock in the Snowball" is May's tribute to a fighter for human rights, Mark Howe. She sings "The Ballad of Ruby" for a black child facing southern racism. "Easter, 1968" mourns Martin Luther King; "We'll to the Woods

No More, the Laurels Are Cut Down," the four students murdered at Kent State.

Most of the poems in *A Grain of Mustard Seed* are personal, yet even the protest poems are strongly tied to May's own temperament. The sixties were, to her, primarily "the time of burning," the hour of the tiger. In that sense, they reflected her own lifelong personal rage and desperation. Which were, this late summer of 1970, escalating.

The two weeks at Nelson with Monica were far from serene. May's outbursts were growing more and more frequent. So insecure that two visitors could throw her into a panic because they might talk to each other instead of her alone, she could hardly bring herself to accept the presence of the old friend in Monica's life—though she herself had Judy. And Judy's senility was increasingly infuriating, since she could no longer give May the attention she craved. Yet Monica was the chief difficulty, if only because May still loved her. "I do feel sure this time that the relationship is valid," she wrote Bill Brown, "and worth a struggle."

> How much rage in your suffering?
> How much suffering in my rage?
> Who can tell?
>
> How much danger in your safety?
> How much safety in my danger?
> Who measure?
>
> How much truth in my conflict?
> How much conflict in your truth?
> Who unravel?
>
> I don't know, my dear, I don't know.
> Where do we go now, what do we do?
> I don't know, my love, I don't know.

In mid-September May turned to the Yellow Pages and chose a psychiatrist named Marynia Farnham. Dr. Farnham had retired from a New York practice in 1968 to work in Brattleboro, close to her one-hundred-acre farm in Winchester, New Hampshire. In 1947 she had co-authored a notorious best-seller, *Modern Woman: The Lost Sex,* which argued that in deserting traditional homemaking and nurturing roles, women had only injured themselves and society. More recently she had specialized in child and adolescent psychology, founding the Society for Adolescent Psychiatry and, in Brattleboro, working with the Children's Special Services Center. When May walked into Dr. Farnham's office at 8 Park Place, she found a thin, gray-haired woman of seventy—witty, dynamic, sophisticated, and cultured. Immediately she felt enormous rapport.

"I am back with a psychiatrist," she wrote Bill:

. . . For the last four months I have wasted too much psychic juice in rage or its obverse, suicidal depression, and it is time I went back to the cradle (where I had tantrums of course) and try to find out what the matter is. Anyway this old woman whom I saw last week for the first time, seems just right . . . tough, wise, and with a sense of dry humour. . . . I am doing this to try to salvage my relationship with [Monica] who is not a person who can "talk things out" so too much resentment gets buried and then explodes in anger . . . so I am always in the wrong as I was with Cora. The neurotic *repetition* is clear and that is what has scared me literally nearly to death.

That fall and winter May believed that Marynia Farnham had literally thrown her a lifeline. The weekly sessions became "a dialogue where doctor and patient / Battle together / In a quiet empty space / On neutral ground." To May, they seemed like salvation. Yet the quickly developing relationship with Marynia Farnham would be one of the more disastrous of May's life.

CHAPTER 20

Chaos: 1970–1972

Norton backed *Kinds of Love*—22,500 copies in print, a full-page ad in *The New York Times Book Review,* her photograph on the jacket to cultivate public recognition of "a good face." *Kinds of Love,* Eric Swenson told her, "might well be the breakthrough." This hope coincided with a wonderful New York weekend with Monica—entirely attributable, May felt, to Marynia Farnham's miraculous help. Then May read Richard Rhodes's review in the *Times* of November 29:

> *Kinds of Love* is one of those books a reviewer has trouble deciding how to take. The work of an accomplished and prolific poet and novelist, it is yet flawed in style and flabby in content. . . . It reads like a book intended for a private printing, in the sense that Miss Sarton assumes by her style that we already know, somehow, the people and events she portrays, and that assumption—not, presumably, deliberate—makes shallow what might have been profound. . . . Miss Sarton leaves us on the outside, as if she, and we too, are summer people. Perhaps the flaw is that she tells us of feelings rather than showing us.

"I am drunk as usual these days, I fear . . . recovering from a really *annihilating* review in last Sunday's *Times* (*the* most important place) by a man no one has ever heard of," May wrote Bill. ". . . What hurts is not this stupid man who will soon be forgotten, but that Francis Brown, the editor, did not feel I had a sufficient rep to find someone adequate to the task. . . ." Other reviews praised, *The New Yorker* calling *Kinds of Love* "a complete success"; readers found the novel "smoting," "powerful," "beautiful." But they were not the *Times*. Betrayed again.

In *Kinds of Love* she had undertaken the formidable task of character-izing a New Hampshire village, centering the action in the decision of the wealthy Chapmans to winter in Willard and Willard's preparations for its bicentennial. More than forty characters (seven of them dead) evoke Willard from Revolutionary times through and beyond the present, while the novel's themes range from class conflict to debate about environmen-talism and pacifism: an even more ambitious undertaking than *The Bridge of Years* and *Faithful Are the Wounds*.

"Perhaps the flaw is that she tells us of feelings rather than showing us." Certainly the characters in *Kinds of Love* talk about feelings; that is the trademark of a Sarton novel. They also write about them: reflecting May's new penchant for journal keeping, many events are told through Christina Chapman's journal, reflections upon action rather than action itself. *Kinds of Love* was, said the *Boston Globe,* "an intensely feminine novel." Translation: a novel about feelings, relationships, "the heartbeat" of Willard—enough, perhaps, to put off a male critic.

Yet the *Times* had a point when it complained that *Kinds of Love* "does not bring the reader in to share the depth of these characters' experi-ences." While the tough and bitter Ellen Comstock (Mildred Quigley) lives on the page, the Lovelands (Warners) are passed off easily as salt-of-the-earth farmers, with no mention of their shocking poverty and igno-rance. The novel never comes to terms with Old Pete (Edgar Poland again, of *Miss Pickthorn and Mr. Hare*), just as Nelson refused to. Jane Tut-tle, local botanist and mentor to the young, is portrayed as "a saint," ignoring such a character's inevitable conflicts with spinsterhood, loneli-ness, and sexual frustration. The Chapmans' children, in-laws, and grand-children are idealizations of the family May never had. *Kinds of Love* thus inevitably reflected May's own isolation in Nelson. Always an outsider, not least because of her self-preoccupation, she wrote the novel sympa-thetically, but often from outside.

Yet thousands of enthusiastic and deeply moved readers ignored the *Times*. In the new year the novel hovered just below the best-seller list, with sales climbing toward 19,000 by spring; but, as she told Bill, "that awful review took all my joy away." Monica, no longer so understanding, decried her bitterness, but May told her, "If I got the Nobel prize tomor-row it would not make up the for humiliations of the last thirty five years. . . ." She was working: "The journal of solitude creeps along but the danger that it is a scorpion eating its tail remains . . . a self-devouring thing at best, and I really don't know what value it has or might have."

Although May still insisted that she loved Monica "wholly," the stolen romantic weekends often ended in disaster. Once May exploded because Monica wouldn't introduce her to some cousins; "madness," said Monica. Another time as they were standing by the kitchen sink at Nelson, Monica inverted the gift bottle of whiskey she had brought, remarking, "My father said you should always turn whiskey upside down before pouring it." May erupted. *"You think you're the only one with a father!"* The torrent of abuse so shattered Monica that she fled across the road to hide in the Cobleighs' garage. Eventually she crept back—"My greatest mistake was not getting into my car and driving away." Although they had a delightful time vacationing on Captiva in the Gulf late in March, and though May wept behind dark glasses at their parting, the relationship was in serious trouble.

At first May felt only intense gratitude for the skill of Marynia Farnham, "that great genius of a psycho-therapist." Eventually, if she could not reach Marynia by phone, she panicked. Then, in February, sitting in the doctor's office on Park Place, she had just written on the notepad Marynia provided, "I am afraid of my dependence on you," when Marynia announced that she was moving to Mexico. Shock and disbelief.

Marynia's decision could well have been inspired by May's asking her to spend the dreaded solitary winter months at Nelson. She was, as her patient divined, fond of May, but also wary of the pressure of May's intense need—a need that became imperative at the prospect of losing her analyst. Marynia herself was vulnerable: drinking heavily, at the end of her career, quarreling with her daughter. Unwisely, she allowed May to invade her private life.

"Yesterday I saw her house for the first time," May wrote Bill:

It looks like a witch's house, a very low, red farm—very old. . . . Instead you walk into a huge *elegant* drawing room, absolutely stuffed with works of art . . . all very gay, sophisticated. She herself also, rather like the beast turned into beauty, looked very handsome and young, sitting in a big chair with three exquisite tiny Italian greyhounds draped about on an arm, above her head and behind her back . . . like some lady in a tapestry. The whole thing was such a shock to me that I felt absolutely *mad* with nostalgia for all she has and is and represents in my starved state . . . for Nelson is impoverished and there is no one with that rich taste. I came home and simply howled like an animal.

By the end of March, May was shaking with excitement before their sessions just imagining Marynia's ironic smile, clipped voice, and masterful parrying of May's turbulent emotions. She had progressed from patient to lover, in her mind at least. The only thing that disturbed her was Marynia's contempt for women; she always spoke of men "with amused homage," while "no woman ever built a bridge." The dogmatism of Farnham's book *Modern Woman: The Lost Sex* distressed her; its emphasis on sex made her "quite ill. Other things are, I am sure as important if not more so, like love, tenderness, compassion, some attempt to meet each other, men and women, black and white halfway . . . to make bridges not tear the bridges down." Naively, she believed that Marynia's scorn for women did not affect the value of the therapy.

Because May always talked about one passion to another, Monica unwillingly began to hear a great deal about Marynia Farnham. But that was May, thought Monica: she seemed to have "no sense of privacy—or honor." When Monica objected to being tortured by May's obvious infatuation with the psychiatrist, May advised her to go into therapy with Dr. Farnham herself. Monica recoiled. She considered Marynia Farnham dangerous.

That spring of 1971 a number of factors influenced May to give up Nelson. Monica told May that after all she could not live with her upon retirement, destroying the dream of permanent companionship. Then the impact of Marynia's sophistication had been enormous: May now felt that Nelson was the North Pole of culture. Besides, Marynia was moving to Mexico; May now envisioned wintering there each year. More important than either Monica or Marynia, however, was the fact that as a writer she had exhausted Nelson. *Miss Pickthorn and Mr. Hare, The Poet and the Donkey, As Does New Hampshire, Plant Dreaming Deep, A Grain of Mustard Seed, Kinds of Love,* and now the new journal had all been Nelson-inspired. What more was there to say?

But the clinching factor was an offer of another place to live. In April, Beverly Hallam and Mary-Leigh Smart, a wealthy patron of the arts, drove over from Ogunquit to pick up Beverly's monotype for a retrospective exhibit of the artist's work. When May reminded them she'd always wanted to live near the ocean, they produced photographs of forty-six ocean acres in York, Maine, that Mary-Leigh had recently purchased.

*Marynia Farnham,
psychotherapist and
Muse, photographed
by Lotte Jacobi*

Mary-Leigh and Beverly intended to build a large duplex for themselves next to the water; meanwhile there was this older house on the property. Would May be interested? May studied the photographs. "It's far too large!"

She went to look at Wild Knoll in April, then again with Judy on May 3, her fifty-ninth birthday. From exclusive York Village one took the back road to Kittery, branched off, then branched off again onto a private road that ended at the sea. Wild Knoll had woods behind, a terrace and gardens in front, a big field running down to the sea. She was slightly disappointed that, with two neighboring houses in view, the spot was not as isolated as she had imagined. Inside, her heart sank. The living room was huge, the fireplaces undistinguished. She could envision writing only in a small panelled third-floor room with an ocean view. The big screened porches daunted her; perhaps they could be enclosed or shut off. Because May could not possibly afford to buy the place, Mary-Leigh suggested that she become a permanent renter for $225 a month, plus expenses for grounds care. There was no hurry about the move. Their duplex would not be completed until 1973.

Despite doubts, May came home and dreamed of sea. At York, she imagined, she would not be lonely. There would be communion with

Beverly, an artist who understood her, and the benefit of Mary-Leigh's undoubted social connections. And the rent was so reasonable that she could pay it from the seven-percent interest on the $35,000 she would surely get for Nelson.

That spring May was paid a visit by Carolyn Heilbrun, a professor of English at Columbia University, a feminist scholar, and, under the name Amanda Cross, the author of an elegant series of academic detective novels. Heilbrun's admiration had been roused by *Mrs. Stevens Hears the Mermaids Singing,* and by *Plant Dreaming Deep* ("I honor you for writing it"). She wanted to learn more about the writer.

Heilbrun stayed at a motel but had dinner with May; washing up afterward, she put some ivory-handled knives in water. May's outburst astonished her. But the professor also disturbed May by telling her that writing about a woman's solitude was her best theme; May wept bitterly over the prison-sentence of that verdict. Yet Heilbrun was the first professor from a major university to extend a hand. At her suggestion, May began looking about for a library to buy her papers, and found an interested purchaser in Lola Szladits, curator of the New York Public Library's Berg Collection. A longer-term consequence of Heilbrun's visit would be the phasing out of Eleanor Blair as literary advisor. May had a real scholar interested in her now.

Still, she sent Eleanor the new manuscript of poems that July. Norton would publish *A Durable Fire* the following year on her birthday. She had deliberately held back love poems from *A Grain of Mustard Seed,* wanting to publish them triumphantly at sixty. There were two major groups in the new book, the "Autumn Sonnets" for Monica and "Letters to a Psychiatrist" for Marynia Farnham, as well as eighteen other poems inspired by Monica. She was still working on a major poem, "Gestalt at Sixty." Would Eleanor read carefully? "If any of these seem very weak, suggest cutting. I do want, however, the sense of love that goes through pain as well as joy. . . ."

With Monica, joy and pain alternated with breathtaking rapidity. May spent the week of July 14 at Monica's summer home. Bliss, storms of tears, reconciliations, quarrels. But after she left, May told Beverly that Monica "now appears to understand just how hard she has been on me . . . and to appreciate what we have together. . . . I feel like a man who has been putting his weight to pull a big rope and suddenly the rope goes slack and he is flat on his back laughing." Then Marynia Farnham's casual announcement that she was not moving to Mexico after all flipped May flat on her back again. Suddenly life teemed with possibilities.

Monica came to Nelson for a week on August 3, and May took her to see Wild Knoll. Monica was delighted to meet Beverly Hallam and Mary-Leigh at lunch, bowled over by York and the house. York was also working its enchantment on May, that "immense radiant meadow and ocean which I go to sleep visualizing. . . . I begin to love the house too." And, as Monica pointed out, York was only five miles farther than Nelson for their weekend commuting. They also talked seriously about the new poems that week, and Monica (fortunately) made May excise tritisms like "our dream come true" and make further cuts, though May had revised a poem like "All Day I Was with Trees" dozens of times. It was a loving, fruitful week.

On September 3, Eleanor Blair came to cat-sit while May spent Labor Day weekend with Monica at her place on the ocean. They were getting along happily until they went to an Italian restaurant for dinner. Suddenly May exploded. Afterwards, Monica could not remember the cause. She only knew that she was utterly fed up with May's scenes. She stood up. "I'm leaving," she said. They drove to Monica's house in bitter silence. May stormed upstairs. Minutes later they confronted each other, May at the top of the stairs with her suitcase, Monica at the bottom. "I'm leaving this house," said May. "Good," said Monica, "because I won't stay here with you in it."

Monica burned May's letters and returned the many gifts of jewelry. The fire had not been durable after all. Yet May had ended the relationship deliberately. "I finally said to her, 'I don't like you'—which was the worst thing I've ever said to *anybody*. And that was the end. I mean, I wanted it to be. I meant it to be." Because May believed that Marynia Farnham was now available.

Though they exchanged a few visits and letters for a time, May did not remain a friend. She did not forgive Monica for not tolerating "the destructiveness implied in growth." Worse, Monica had a will of her own: "We fought an awful lot. We were both very dominating women, that was the real trouble." As for Monica, she decided that May was two people: the writer, sensitive, intuitive, wise; and the chaotic child, irrational, angry, demanding. She could not reconcile "the angel and the fury." Yet she was devastated by the sudden ending and still in love. It took her a long time to cure herself of May.

"The investment on both sides was very great, of course," May wrote Eleanor Blair. Yet May came out ahead. Only Cora DuBois inspired more published poetry than Monica. They are rich poems—"Dear Solid Earth," "The Return of Aphrodite," "The Tree Peony," "The Snow Light"—lacking the coruscating pain of the Cora poems, reflecting the deep joy of the first year and a half of the relationship:

> We hold it in our keeping, even apart,
> Twin trees whose pollen has been swiftly crossed,
> And all this sumptuous flowering of the heart
> Will grow rich fruit, nor anything be lost.

Of course there is conflict: Sarton acknowledges her "grieving fury," her "infant anguish." And there is elegiac regret for the transience of love. Yet ultimately May had few regrets. As she admitted in "Autumn Sonnet 8," "My life has asked not love but poetry."

May complicated her life not only by falling in love with Marynia Farnham while in love with Monica, but by permitting fans to fall in love with her. After all, she didn't have to reply warmly or permit their visits. Lee Blair, an artist, wrote one fan letter, then another. Soon May had woven her into her life. Anne Woodson, a young, attractive aspiring poet and painter, the divorced mother of three, had also entered her life through *Plant Dreaming Deep*. At first, Anne "made rather a pest of herself," writing every day. Eventually she simmered down, accepted May's friendship, became a welcome guest, then "a deep friend." May felt she was the only friend who knew her faults yet wholly accepted her.

A third young woman had become a problem. "I am very tired of people falling in love with me, or rather projecting their needs onto me," May wrote Bill Brown that September. ". . . More and more I become aware of the dangers of over-giving. On my side I do it because I feel guilty that I cannot 'love' the person, on their side because (unconsciously) they hope to bind me to them by *giving* too much." Kathy (not her real name), like so many of May's fans, wanted to be a writer. She was theatrical and flamboyant, "pathetic," thought May, "a failed person . . . a disease I have to cope with." Most disturbing, Kathy in her demands was "a grotesque cartoon" of May herself.

Returning with Judy to Nelson after the aborted Labor Day weekend with Monica, May found Kathy camped in the house, drunk. May promptly packed her off to a motel. Hurt and enraged, Kathy telephoned, talking anguish and suicide. Judy fielded the hour-long phone call. They discovered that Kathy had filled the refrigerator with casseroles they didn't want—trying to "bind" me, thought May with disgust. She recommended that Kathy go into therapy with Marynia Farnham. If she thought she was getting rid of her—or helping her—she was wrong.

That fall May began to pressure Marynia for love. Staying overnight at the farm, May went into the psychiatrist's room, lay down next to her on her big bed, took her in her arms. "For me, it was not sexual *at all*," May wrote Bill, ". . . but apparently it upset her terribly and she later used the word 'obscene' which boomeranged so that for 24 hours I was in real despair, lost the sense of myself and felt like some horrible monster. But I guess *she* feels it obscene to feel what she does for me . . . and it is bad for her, so I am making a real effort to allay the pressure and to be quiet."

May was never quiet. Her insistence tortured the psychiatrist, for whom a personal relationship with a client was taboo, and who was not lesbian. Yet she found herself deeply moved by the ardent younger woman. That December she yielded,

> and we spent the night in her great bed with *two* dogs . . . laughing till tears rolled down our cheeks, because Marynia kept quoting over and over a TV ad which goes "Try it—you'll *love* it!" It is part of her charm that she would finally break the barrier between us with humour and I love her for that. No passion . . . that's not what I need from her . . . but a lovely night of tender love. . . . Next day I called Marynia and said "I feel so peaceful" (the truth) and she said "I feel peaceful too." . . . But I do see clearly now that she has been in real agony . . . and just pray that it may be over for her now she sees that she *can* give what I ask, and not be pressed beyond what she can give.

But this was not a fortuitous time for May to be asking anything of Marynia Farnham. Drinking heavily, becoming daily more paranoid, the doctor was slipping rapidly into senile dementia. She had almost stopped eating, was gaunt as a stick, had lost most of her patients, could not pay her office rent. Worst, she viewed her daughter bringing in a geriatric specialist as hostile. That expert said that Dr. Farnham must give up her practice altogether and enter a hospital for observation and treatment; but how could they get her into the hospital, agonized May, when Marynia flew into towering rages at the least interference?

Though May was not the least interested, Kathy reported her continuing sessions with Marynia in detail. The neurotic young woman had in turn fallen in love with Marynia, so that now May was the enemy; and Kathy did her best to turn the ailing and paranoic Marynia against her. Given Marynia's guilt at loving a woman, this was not difficult. Marynia resumed her struggle against May's insistence that she sleep with her. "If I did," said Marynia, "you would have me in thrall." "Forget me," said Marynia. May's response was "a cry of anguish":

> Woman, who are you? What are you doing
> To me and to yourself: "Forget you"?
> Who lays despair on one who truly loves
> Lays the stigmata on him, makes him a bleeder.

> "Forget me," you say. You say, "Don't be sad."

> Christ, break this heart, this Christmas.
> Relieve us of despair, Help us to live!

"My Hell, a kind of limbo, I suppose, is to be in love with a mad person," May wrote Bill.

A kind of chaos. Marynia still refused to enter a hospital, yet in 1972 she closed up her house, leaving furniture in payment for office rent. On February 28, May drove Marynia with her three greyhounds to New York, a trip that in microcosm embodied the nightmare this relationship had become. May called Marynia's daughter, Linda, asking her to recommend a kennel for the dogs. Linda told May accusingly that her mother's maid blamed May for driving Marynia to drink; May hung up in a rage. Because Marynia had not brought the dogs' inoculation records, no kennel would take them; finally, after a two-hour wait in a veterinarian's office, they were accommodated. When they got to the Cosmopolitan Club, May discovered that Marynia had brought only bedroom slippers and no good clothes, so they had to have dinner sent up. It was then she finally realized Marynia was senile, yet she had to leave her alone in New York. With profound relief May heard the next day that Marynia had collected the dogs and taken the train to Sarasota to visit her rich sister.

Though she didn't need the money, May left for Georgia March 14 to teach at Agnes Scott College, in pain with shingles down her left arm due to tension over Marynia. The first days in her apartment overlooking a woods she wept and slept, tortured by the plight of the woman she loved. Extremely restless, a primary symptom of her malady, Marynia had not stayed put in Florida, but was wandering about the country with the greyhounds. There were constant, despairing letters ("I must leave here; it is death") with no return address. May managed to trace her through "hundreds of long distance calls" (phone bills, $250 a month).

Then in early April she heard that Judy was in the hospital with a ruptured appendix, and extremely disoriented. Perhaps now was the time to decide about putting her in a home, for in Nelson at Christmas she had haphazardly served scrambled eggs on top of corn muffins and in Cambridge unwittingly left her phone off the hook for five days. It was hell having both an old love and a new barely *compos mentis;* but May was determined not to desert either of them.

She had thirty-five earnest students who produced poetry beneath contempt. As she had at Wellesley, she did battle for the place of the humanities in the curriculum. But "I do not really fit into the academic world at all," she concluded once again, having been hooted down by two male professors deep into structural ambiguity for praising a poem as "sincere." To comfort herself she bought a new Audi, "a dream of a car."

When not teaching or reading papers, May typed the final draft of *Journal of a Solitude.* The person whose advice she now heeded was Carolyn Heilbrun, though she still placated Eleanor Blair, who was adverse to making the highly personal work public: "There is no doubt in my mind that I want to publish this journal, as coming from a new freedom and ability to talk of intimate matters from a philosophical point of view. It is written from the place where I am now, the place also expressed in Gestalt at Sixty." Yet this freedom was limited. Monica not only insisted that she appear as "X," with no gender or incriminating detail, but that she personally vet all relevant passages. Then there was Marynia. The journal ended in September 1971, before she and May shared a bed and before the onset of obvious senility. Why include her at all? "There are still many people who believe that going to a psychiatrist is an admission of failure or an act of cowardice," May argued. ". . . I am a fruitful person with a viable life and I believe it would be helpful for people to know that I have had help and did not fear to ask for it."

There was another motive for publishing *Journal of a Solitude. Plant Dreaming Deep* "has given an entirely false idea of my life and what it costs. It looks too easy and delightful . . . so the book has gotten across to a lot of 'squares' (many people write me long descriptions of their houses and I am bored to death reading them), but the people I want to touch are those highly aware and agonized souls who could be given courage when they see my struggle. . . ."

"I am glad to be sixty and my own woman," said May, celebrating her birthday on May 3 with a catered champagne party for the more congenial younger faculty. That day too, she signed two typed copies of *Bridge Over Troubled Waters*—forty-eight poems written to Marynia Farnham between September 1971 and March 1972, twenty of which would eventually appear in poetry reviews, May's own journals, and a later book of poetry. Many poems celebrated the mystery of the woman who had given much, yet not all:

> When you are most alone and I not there,
> My passionate guise, my fiery air,
> Think of me kindly and the six-dog nights.
>
> Remember the huge map of tenderness
> Laid on your bed, and all that did bless,
> The strange withholdings and the strange delights. . . .

The semester over, May stopped in Weston on her way home to see Eva Le Gallienne. Le Gallienne had strongly disapproved of *Mrs. Stevens Hears the Mermaids Singing.* Now May poured out the story of Marynia, and again Le Gallienne recoiled. That night she came to May's bedside in her nightgown and begged her to leave off therapy. It was cowardly; one should face one's problems alone. Le Gallienne's lack of sympathy further widened a breach that Monica had noted the past summer when May refused to go backstage at Stratford, where Le Gallienne was acting. May had always said they were too alike to be lovers. But the difference between the reserved actress and the confessional writer was profound.

May returned to find that Marynia had rented a house in New Hampshire, though she refused to unpack. Kathy was in frequent attendance, May's bitter enemy. Marynia's maid-housekeeper (reportedly) hated May more than Kathy did. Between them, they persuaded the paranoid woman that May was dangerous, even insane. As a result, Marynia took sheafs of May's importunate letters and the manuscript of *Bridge Over Troubled Waters* to her lawyer, asking for protection against her former patient—and informed May that she had done so. May also believed she had discovered a plot by Kathy to whip her into a rage, then have *her* committed.

"I simply cannot talk about the punishment I am getting here," May wrote Eleanor,

> but at least now I think I have been convinced that I must abandon all hope of ever seeing Marynia again (and of course I don't want to see [Kathy] again or I might kill her). She got Marynia to a lawyer to accuse me of threatening phone calls, and of threatening to kill Marynia. I saw this lawyer today and at least I know he now sees that these were wicked lies. But every time I get myself centered again more trouble breaks out. No one will ever know how I have been tortured for three weeks. I have to keep very still and just wait till the pain eases off. But in order to do that I become hard and very very lonely, for I will never look to another human being for help or trust one again. Animals are my only comfort. I have become a leper.

May demanded that Marynia return the *Bridge Over Troubled Waters* manuscript. When it was not forthcoming, she sued through her own lawyer for its return. She also announced that if pressed, she would sue for character assassination. Marynia's lawyer returned the poems.

Threats to kill, lawyers, harrowing phone calls, turgid letters, plots and counterplots—all very sordid. It didn't help that Marynia and Kathy drank heavily, and that May after two double Scotches was hardly rational. And of course May was not in the least convinced that she must "abandon all hope of ever seeing Marynia again."

A Durable Fire appeared that June. Some reviews praised its "delicate strength" and "understated lyricism." The *Times,* however, ignored this tenth book of poetry, and several reviewers were harsh. Writing in *Parnassus,* Rose Ellen Brown declared *A Durable Fire* "the failure of a style: the voice of the poet who neither confesses the actual occasions for his feeling, nor makes us, by any metaphoric substitution, feel it or see it with him, but names an emotion and, more often than not, leaves us standing there with it, our hands utterly empty." Other critics agreed. "May Sarton in this volume seldom confronts the emotional issues she writes about with candor, openness, or a sufficient sense of honesty. The underlying skill is so evident, however, that we await her next volume with optimism."

This judgment inexplicably ignores fine poems like "A Burial," "Autumn Again," "The Fear of Angels," some of the "Autumn Sonnets," and the plangently moving "Gestalt at Sixty." Yet charges of lack of candor

are valid in the "Letters to a Psychiatrist" because May never honestly ana-
lyzed her relationship with Marynia Farnham. Most of her pieties about the
balm of therapy are bunk. Marynia couldn't help May understand her com-
pulsions, because May didn't want to. What she wanted was unconditional
attention from a fascinating new Muse onto whom she fastened "like a
limpet." She also wanted poetry. The paeans to Marynia "the psychic sur-
geon" are really paeans to Marynia the Muse. A person who cannot face the
truth about her own behavior cannot write honestly about it.

And yet how dependent that behavior was on May's conception of
herself as Poet. "Poets," said Andy Lightfoot, "are, inevitably, disturbed
and disturbing people, vulnerable, anarchic, never quite grown up, feeling
their way by hunches, in touch at times with mysterious powers, always
engaged in knocking walls down, opening locked doors, and making nui-
sances of themselves." All her bad behavior, May told herself, could be
forgiven because she was a Poet. But what if, as some reviews of *A Durable
Fire* suggested, she wasn't a poet at all? The abyss this thought opened
beneath her was too dizzying to contemplate.

All summer she fought with Eleanor Blair about the publication of
Journal of a Solitude. Carolyn Heilbrun had enthusiastically approved the
completed manuscript, Marynia omitted. Anne Woodson felt strongly
that it would win May new readers. Even Monica had admitted it might
be her best work. When Eleanor continued to resist, May opened fire:

> From the start you have showed neither generosity toward Carole
> Heilbrun nor understanding of the very great importance it has for
> *the work* that a critic of stature, a critic who will gain in *weight* with
> time . . . a critic who has many PHD students working with her
> all the time (and hence who can get my work looked at by young
> professors who will write about it and later teach it) means to me.
> I have waited all my writing life for *one* such critic to appear. . . .
> It is as if you had an unconscious block *against* anyone entering my
> writer's life in this role at this time. But I have needed it it so badly
> and for so long! Can you grudge it to me now? You have helped
> me immeasurably, but you are a professional in your own right, and
> you must know that there is a difference between an editor and
> copy-editor and a *critic*. Carole can be what you never could be[:]
> a way through into the public I have never reached, and into my
> being taken seriously by the literary establishment. . . .

Effectively, this was the end of Eleanor Blair. Oh, yes, May still wrote
affectionately once or twice a year, drove to "the Hive" on Eleanor's

birthdays with flowers and a chocolate cake, invited her occasionally to York, dropped in at Christmas. But Eleanor had been replaced.

That late July, May and Judy went again to Anne Thorp's on Greenings Island. Judy was managing at home in Cambridge with close supervision; she had completely forgotten the recent five weeks in the hospital. She was pleasant, uncomplaining—but, May felt despairingly, it was like talking to someone behind glass.

"Animals are my only comfort." On her return to Nelson May went to Win and Dot French's to collect her new sheltie puppy, Tamas. She was decidedly a cat person, currently feeding and trying to tame six wild cats on her property, half-succeeding with a spotted orange-and-black female called Bramble. "The Pussies" had been a strong bond with Judy; Judy still brought "the Old Cats" with her when she visited Nelson. Readers of *The Fur Person* felt that the author was part cat herself. Now, her first dog. May had no idea how to discipline or train an animal; but fortunately Tamas from his box was a born gentleman. "Tamas was very *good* to May," said Mary-Leigh Smart.

Besides the comfort of Tamas, May was delighted when an old friend bought a property twenty miles from Nelson. May valued the artist William Theo Brown for many reasons, including his cultural sophistication and appreciation of her work; but chiefly he had been someone who understood her myriad conquests. Now Bill and the painter Paul Wonne had undertaken the remodeling of an ancient farmhouse and invited May to view the results.

It was a gala occasion: wonderful food and drink, good talk about art, music, and Bill's friend Igor Stravinsky. Then Bill put on a record of Kirsten Flagstad singing Wagner's Wesendonck Lieder. May associated the five songs with Cora. An "earthquake of woe" shook her; she lifted her head and "howled with grief." "How could you play that, Bill! Don't you know I can't take music of that sort!" Floods of violent tears as she distractedly paced the floor. Bill went cold with rage, but Paul took her in his arms; she confessed she feared she was going mad. Bill still held himself aloof. "I'll go home to Tamas," said May accusingly. "*He* licks my tears." Since Bill and Paul had moved to New England largely on May's recommendation, this was a less than auspicious beginning, and next morning May was ashamed—to a point. "It was an outrage and I myself felt it as such. Yet I was not at fault . . . the voice of Flagstad had opened the source of pain to a point beyond my control. I was in woe because I have not written any poems for six months.

That whole part of me, dependent on Marynia as the muse, has been murdered."

Her behavior inspired her to analyze "the tiger of rage" coiled inside her, ready to spring at the slightest frustration. "The Imaginary Psychiatrist," an unpublished twenty-page document written that fall, reviews the recent disasters. A lunch at Kay Martin's house during which, though she made "quite an effort to do well in a threesome," she couldn't handle the presence of Kay's friend Marilyn; then, next day, utter fury when Kay explained she had been afraid to be alone with May. Dinner at Mary-Leigh's house, when her casual remark that the English were stuffy sent May into "a whirlwind of rage." I don't attack your midwestern origins," screamed May, "why should you attack mine?" When neighbors called the police, Mary-Leigh explained that the television was turned on loud. Next morning Mary-Leigh told May that her lawyer advised her not to rent to May. "Betrayal, betrayal!" cried May. Beverly took the weeping May into her arms. "Now you've spoiled everything," she said. But Mary-Leigh relented. After all, May was a superb gardener.

Alcohol unleashed these tigers, even with Judy. May often drove to Cambridge to spend a day or two with her mentally failing friend. Often Judy had no food or drink in the house, which May took as personal rejection. This time May telephoned the night before, reminding Judy to have breakfast things in the house, but when she got to Cambridge after dark she found only three slices of bread.

"But this time I thought you would have things in," said May, summoning patience.

"Well, you know me by now," said Judy cheerfully. "It's a geriatric problem."

May laid in supplies. They had dinner, May two double Scotches. "My rage against her is always the same spiral. I shout and scream, 'You lead a totally selfish life! You say you love me but you don't even have food in the house! I have to do everything!' " Then May would sob that she was lonely and had no family, and who but family could be counted on?

She was the more devastated because she had read Judy's will. Long ago they had agreed to leave each other the major part of their savings; May willed Judy the income from her trust for life, about five thousand dollars a year. Now she discovered that Judy had left her only a fifth, putting nephews and nieces on an equal basis. She didn't need the money, but realizing she was not first in Judy's life caused convulsions of anguish as acute as the discovery that Judy did not prepare for her visits.

Why, asks the Imaginary Psychiatrist, do you continue to be outraged by a senility that you accepted rationally long ago?

May struggles to define the source of her rage. "Maybe it is the infant who expects love and being cared for as a right, as 'the way things are,' and is outraged when he does not have his expectations fulfilled?" Of course, the bursts of fury create terrible guilt, which in turn fuels anger— May resents the victims of her outbursts for making her feel conscience-stricken. Then there is her unlovely sense of self-righteousness, "a much worse and more corrupting fault than anger," which is surely caused by her sense of failure as a person. It too must derive from "some primary insecurity that goes back deep into infancy." Ultimately, however, she excuses both her self-righteousness and her rage as productive. Psychiatrists call this rationalization. May called it "the necessary self-forgiveness of sins." Fortunately, May had an outlet, if not a cure, for her affliction. Her writing stabilized her. Literally, writing was transcendence. Through it, she was able to live a productive life. Yet it was a life lived on the edge, constantly threatening to disintegrate. Nothing could cure the trauma that lay at the core of May's nature: lack of self-identity.

That August, May had managed to see Marynia for dinner with another former patient. "It all went off well, except that my after-reaction has been complete devastation and collapse . . . the whole awful harrowing of these last months . . . and because there can never be any clarity . . . any *real* understanding." Saying goodbye to Marynia, May pleaded, "Please don't be angry with me any more." "I have never been angry with you," said Marynia. But whether Marynia meant it or had just forgotten the accusations and lawyers, May couldn't tell.

Torment over the lost psychiatrist continued. Kathy seemed to have moved in permanently, reputedly was buying Marynia liquor by the half-gallons. The dinner gave Kathy the idea that May was once more back in the fold. She telephoned May and said that she was coming to Nelson with a group of young blacks to kill her. ("People want to become you and when they find they cannot, they want to kill you.") May took this hysterical nonsense hysterically. One evening she burst into the Gerbis home across the road, where Joan and her children were sitting around the table after dinner, and began pouring out the story of her doomed love for Marynia Farnham. No particular friend of May's, Joan was astonished, then very angry. What right had May to inflict her lurid love affairs on three impressionable teenagers! The writer, decided Joan, had definitely worn out her welcome in Nelson: "One by one she alienated people by her lady of the manor snubs, her temper. Frankly, I thought she behaved like a spoiled brat."

"Nelson has been totally desecrated now," May told Beverly Hallam, "it is like a place in Belgium where the Gestapo worked, I see the walls as covered with blood. God didn't hear those screams any more than He hears mine. These are the places where human beings are tortured who cannot defend themselves and degraded out of all human dignity. But I know I have got to stay here until I have written this nightmare off, finished my novel, and can start a new life in the clear."

Work was, as usual, the only sanity. That fall she sent *Journal of a Solitude* to Norton and pushed on with *As We Are Now,* the searing tale of an old woman confined to the cold comfort of a nursing home. Anger could be productive.

She dreamed of the spring, when she would move to Wild Knoll. Maine would cauterize deep wounds. "I feel that coming there," she wrote Beverly, "is going to bring a whole new creative phase for me."

CHAPTER 21

Guru: 1973–1975

By the time May moved into Wild Knoll in late April 1973, she had made it her own. She had the north porch blocked off and the south enclosed to create a dining-sitting room, bird feeders outside the window. She had the kitchen painted mustard yellow, the floor slabbed in dark gray. She turned the formal dining room into a "cozy room" with a sunny plant window behind the sofa. The large living room looked comfortable with a thick, shaggy yellow rug, bright blue tweed sofa, recessed book-shelves, and the big Belgian bahut against the wall. A carpenter built bookcases for the second floor, and she bought a good desk—her first—for her study on the third. Next to the desk in a revolving bookcase she placed "the great influences": Jung's *Psychological Reflections,* Traherne's *Centuries of Meditations,* Thoreau's *Walden,* Florida Scott Maxwell's *Measure of My Days,* Dinesen's *Out of Africa,* Freya Stark's *Journey's End,* Louis Lavelle, Martin Buber, Simone Weil. Outdoors, Raymond Philbrook, Mary-Leigh's gardener, was tilling a picking garden that sloped toward the graveled road.

Tamas told her politely that Wild Knoll suited him; wild Bramble scourged mice in the meadow. On May 3, Beverly and Mary-Leigh came with champagne and "a noble feast" and pronounced themselves pleased. The Quigleys drove over for lunch. "Even the sky seems bigger here," said Mildred. "How strange and far away Nelson now seems," May wrote Bill Brown, who had moved to San Francisco with Paul, disillusioned with the New England wilderness. "I never had a moment of nostalgia, a closed chapter."

Thin and white, Judy had been taken to Walden House in Concord, a "terrible nursing home," thought May, who cried every time she left her, though Judy herself was quiet and dignified, only asking gently, "Why can't I go home?" May would assuage the terrible guilt she felt about Judy by having her often at Wild Knoll, though a two-week visit was difficult, for Judy could not occupy herself and tended to wander off, so that May had to stop typing to search the neighborhood. This infuriated her, and there were quarrels, which Judy mercifully forgot.

The sad soap opera starring Marynia Farnham, May, and Kathy was still prime-time. May had lunched with Marynia, "a poor pathetic waif," in April, when Marynia spoke of Kathy "with contempt and loathing," assuring May she had never done anything wrong. Marynia's lawyer agreed that Kathy must go, but failed to see a legal way to evict her. Yet two days after the lunch Marynia called and said, "I bid you goodbye." Obviously Kathy was in sway. Then came news of a tape, purportedly a discussion among Marynia, Kathy, and another psychiatrist of May's "falsifications," and a testimony by Marynia that May had swung a chair at her and threatened to kill her. May immediately called Marynia, who denied all knowledge of such a tape; but then Marynia had lied before. May concluded that Kathy had made the tape without Marynia's knowledge to use against her in court. Off the record May's lawyer branded the tape slander. So went the dismal dance.

That spring *Journal of a Solitude* appeared in bookstores. It was, as May intended, more intimate and honest than *Plant Dreaming Deep*—no musings about ancestors, but an immediate plunge into confession:

> I feel too much, sense too much, am exhausted by the reverberations after even the simplest conversation. But the deep collision is and has been with my unregenerate, tormenting, and tormented self. . . . Now I hope to break through into the rough rocky depths, to the matrix itself. There is violence there and anger never resolved. I live alone . . . for the reason that I am an impossible creature, set apart by a temperament I have never learned to use as it could be used, thrown off by a word, a glance, a rainy day, or one drink too many. . . . I go up to Heaven and down to Hell in an hour, and keep alive only by imposing upon myself inexorable routines.

Bravely said at last.

Journal of a Solitude offers other themes, among them May's theory of poetry. Still haunted by Bogan's "You keep the Hell out," May answers her critic: "I have thought much about this. I have felt that the work of art (I am thinking especially of poetry), a kind of dialogue between me and God, must present resolution rather than conflict. The conflict is there, all right, but it is worked through by means of writing the poem. Angry prayers and screaming prayers are unfit for God's ears. So there is a Hell in my life but I have kept it out of the work." In other words, May purifies her writing in atonement for her sins. This alone excludes her from the "confessional school" of Roethke, Sexton, Berryman, Lowell, and Plath, for she transcends in poetry as well as prose.

Yet May did not believe in a personal God, or in personal salvation, or even, perhaps, in God's existence, since "Give me to be in Your presence, God, even though I know it only as absence" was for her the only possible prayer. The notion that poetry is resolution also conflicts with her definition of poetic power as "tension in equilibrium" in her fine 1962 essay "The School of Babylon," where poets learn "to walk into the furnaces / And whistle as we burn"—their anguish never resolved, only perilously balanced. Perhaps "God" in this context refers to Sarton's half-held belief in a power that granted her poems when she was in a state of grace. Then indeed she might fear to alienate this power with rage and tears.

May feared that "the insoluble problem" of reconciling her needs for people and for solitude had become "the leitmotif of this journal"—a fear well founded: the problem is the leitmotif of her life. *Journal of a Solitude* pleads for communication even as Sarton complains of intrusions. A true solitary would not publish photographs of her house so that fans could zero in with binoculars or camp on her doorstep (a not infrequent occurrence), or declare that a room without flowers throws her into deep misery, so that fans rush her flowers, for which she must thank them. A true solitary would not complain publicly about solitude, inspiring hundreds of people to relieve it. But then May was a solitary only because of her impossible temperament.

Which was actively alienating the village of York. The Garden Club invited her to a program and tour of gardens; May made fun of the local ladies, slamming in her own face many York doors. At first Beverly, Mary-Leigh, and May exchanged dinners once a week; May was, said Mary-Leigh, "a fabulous cook." But May couldn't handle the two good friends together, so eventually the dinners were discontinued. And though she told Beverly, "Never feel I can't be interrupted," both Beverly and Mary-Leigh soon learned not to interrupt.

Still, Mary-Leigh tried to involve May with local people. She got the Cadwaladers, wealthy newcomers, to ask May sailing. Unfortunately, dinner was delayed aboard the yacht till nine, while May tossed down Scotches. Her outburst, said Mary-Leigh, rocked the boat. When Dean and Sylvia Frieze, close neighbors, invited her for dinner, May asked for a double Scotch, then another, then drank a lot of wine with the food. Suddenly she jumped to her feet, hysterically accused Mary-Leigh of never inviting her to her house, burst into tears. "It was a terrible scene," said Mary-Leigh, "—horrible. I was totally embarrassed. Her behavior went all over York. No one wanted to invite her." At the end of 1973, May could tell Bill that Raymond Philbrook "is my one true friend here."

Yet May's public reputation was booming. Fan mail poured in, while friends and fans crowded York that summer of wall-to-wall visitors and lobster salad. In August she went to New York to tape three television shows, one of them a Barbara Walters special on "Women Alone." (Sandwiched between a divorcée and a widow, May felt the unmarried woman hadn't much of a chance.) The Modern Language Association announced a Sarton panel at its December 1973 meeting in Chicago. Wherever she read poetry or appeared to sign books, she could feel the enormous elation of the crowds. And after stormy phone calls, tears, and threats to find another publisher, Norton was backing the new novel, *As We Are Now.*

As We Are Now was published September 23 to a chorus of praise. Brooks Atkinson called it "masterly"; Madeleine L'Engle, "important, brilliant"; the *Times,* "brave and beautiful." For once May could not complain about her press. Fueled by her rage at Perley Cole's lonely, institutional death in 1970 and by her frustration with both Judy's and Marynia's disintegration, *As We Are Now* is an old woman's testimony from "a concentration camp for the old, a place where people dump their parents or relatives as though it were an ashcan." Finally, May had included the Hell. Caroline Spencer's torments are May's imagined own: loneliness, neglect, lack of love. And for once, a Sarton heroine does not sublimate or rise above her anguish: she burns the damned nursing home to the ground. Action at last, and a fine novel.

Coincidentally, on October 2, Marynia Farnham went into Eden Park, no concentration camp but an upscale nursing home in Brattleboro. May drove the three hours to Brattleboro, only to be told that Marynia was happily painting and playing bingo and could see no one. She left books and flowers, confident that she would be allowed to see Marynia as soon as the medication took, glad that phone calls from Kathy were forbidden. Under the illusion that she was still on professional duty, Marynia eventually stationed herself behind the reception desk. The staff liked her and tolerated the game. Doubtful whether she thought of May—or Kathy—at all.

May had already begun a new novel, called *Crucial Conversations,* about the "peeling of the onion, a man who is forced to face how many times he denied his authentic being, lied to *himself.*" But when it began to feel "like lifting a corpse every morning and trying to make it breathe," she realized it would not be a great book. She had begun it because she could not stop writing. Even though *A Durable Fire* and *As We Are Now* had recently appeared and Norton planned the *Collected Poems* and a reissue of *Mrs. Stevens* on May's birthday in 1974 (how many writers have books published as birthday presents?), May could not pause to let the well fill up.

Her endemic insecurity still flared in encounters with other writers. The success of *As We Are Now* was quite spoiled because another nursing-home book, by Ellen Douglas, was nominated for the National Book Award. Doris Grumbach was all right, since she had praised *As We Are Now* in *The New Republic.* But though Muriel Rukeyser wrote a fine advance report of the same novel, May recoiled when Muriel's biographer, Louise Kertesz, telephoned for an interview, all her old envy of Muriel's "connections" resurfacing. Then Louise Bogan's published letters gave her "a bad blow." The editor, Ruth Limmer, "has decimated my wonderful letters from her," May wrote Bill, ". . . and (worse) kept in a single sentence very near the end of her life, in a letter written *to* the editor: 'I wish May Sarton would stop writing sentimental poems.' It hit me hard as a last word from the dead . . . but I guess the fact is Louise always treated me rather badly."

The suicide of Anne Sexton that December would not move her. "She had painted herself into that corner and the only possible next thing as far as 'fame' was concerned had to be suicide. How sick can such art be? But as I write this it sounds too cruel. Perhaps it is more that when the poem never transcends the personal problem, the problem ends by devouring even the poet." Yet what comfort trashing Sexton when, opening the 1973 *Norton Anthology of Modern Poetry,* she discovered Elizabeth Bishop, Josephine Miles, Gwendolyn Brooks, Margaret Avison, Denise Levertov, Adrienne Rich, Anne Sexton—and no May Sarton.

That December, at "the professors of English thing," as May called the Modern Language Association meeting, a woman at the Sarton panel stood up and said, "Anyone interested in Sarton's work should read the Louise Bogan letters." "May is not altogether pleased by the editing of

that woman, Ruth Limmer," Carolyn Heilbrun replied. "I am Ruth Lim-
mer," said the woman to audible gasps, and launched an attack on May's
too emotional correspondence. The young Theodore Roethke had writ-
ten emotional letters to Bogan—but Roethke had grown up. Heilbrun
objected: "Yes, maybe May is emotional, but Roethke and Bogan ended
up in mad houses." "That is a profound and wonderful remark," said
Limmer. Yet the feeling remained that true poets—Hart Crane, Sylvia
Plath, Roethke, Randall Jarrell, John Berryman, Anne Sexton—may have
ended in madness and suicide, yet did not write too-emotional letters. If
only May had committed suicide at thirty-three . . .

Yet who would guess her insecurity when she strode onto a lecture
platform in an elegant black pantsuit to be greeted by storms of applause,
then rapt silence as the poems rang out, or into a crowded reception room
full of eager young people with whom she joked and laughed, talking
around the cigarette in her mouth as she autographed dozens of books? In
January 1974 at Providence, a young poet attempted to warm up the
audience by a long introduction; but, said May, "the audience were
already persuaded!" She was like good champagne, dazzling audiences
with her strong, buoyant personality, that aristocratic, resonant voice.
Some of this audience was lesbian, seeing in the author of *Mrs. Stevens* a
champion; most were not. As for lesbians, "The fact is that I don't hold
any brief for such a life and feel it usually ends in tragedy of one kind or
another," May told Bill, blithely ignoring the fact that her life was
emphatically lesbian. She had always tried for a universal breadth of sub-
ject in her poems. As for her love poems, they too were intended to
express feelings common to anyone in love.

As her audiences grew, so did the fervor of her fans. "I feel eaten alive
as though by human ants," wailed May. A stream of presents kept the
York post office busy. These guru-fan relationships had a definite pattern:
intense communion at the first meeting, during which the fan felt visited
by the Goddess; scores of intimate, soul-baring letters from the fan over
the next years; a terminal explosion from May, sick of the intrusion she
had invited. Many fans fell passionately in love with her. And she became
many a hopeful writer's Muse.

Some visitors were different. Morgan Mead, twenty-four, starting to
teach, hoping to write, confused about being gay, had written May a fan
letter about *Kinds of Love;* to his astonishment she invited him to tea.
Recalled Morgan:

Went. Had strong bourbon. Sat in a blue wing chair looking
towards the ocean in the library while May sat opposite drawing

May at her third-floor study desk at Wild Knoll

me out in a manner both genuine and extremely flattering considering that she was the author and I was the fan. Stunned at the ease with which she talked about sex and money—the two topics I had grown up considering forbidden. She told me she had made 50 grand on *Kinds of Love*—the most she'd ever earned at that point. And, in the course of a discussion of *Mrs. Stevens*—which I had not read—she casually mentioned her own lesbianism. I remember leaving there in a state of great excitement because the conversation had been so intense and so illuminating and honest. . . .

May was just as impressed with Morgan Mead, who was "beautiful to look upon, tall, very blond with Dutch cut hair and very blue eyes, and arrived with a huge bunch of garden roses from his grandmother, and a marvelous *Belgian* cake made by a Dutch aunt." Morgan's grandfather was an aviation pioneer, his father a surgeon. "They are a great clan and live at Squam Lake all summer. I feel we shall remain friends."

That visitor-infested summer she managed to revise the new novel, "the last I shall ever write I trust under the influence of Carol [Heilbrun], for I feel it could have been a stronger and richer book had I used the

May enchanting her audience at a poetry reading

omniscient view. I felt in a strait jacket the whole time. It's a dry hateful yet (perhaps) powerful statement and not, I think, a work of art."

She had intensely disliked Heilbrun's introduction to the reissued *Mrs. Stevens.* Praising May's open and ceaseless struggle against her personal demons, "Sarton," wrote Heilbrun, "has not avoided the dangers inherent in such an openness and such a dialogue: the appearance of self-indulgence, self-pity. These dangers might as well be mentioned in their harshest form, together with her other sin: a certain laxity of style, a tendency to seize the first metaphor to hand, rather than search out the one, perfect phrase." This was just criticism, but May couldn't take it. Heilbrun came to dinner; well into the wine May charged: "Everybody thinks you're a lesbian because your hair is short!" When Heilbrun didn't react, May launched a violent attack on Jewish Harlem slum landlords. Heilbrun rose. "I'm leaving," she said.

But though May might weep for days over Heilbrun's stringencies, she would not, could not, reform. She was already planning a collection of prose portraits called *A World of Light.* And Harper's had accepted a second children's book, *A Walk Through the Woods,* even as a *Times* reviewer was finding *Punch's Secret,* a tribute to her late, beloved pet parrot, darkly complex. Though May scoffed, she as a lesbian—caged by society's homophobia, forced to have secret friends in the dark—definitely had something in common with Punch. And she would finish *Crucial Conversations,* her fifteenth novel, on schedule if it killed her.

That September 18 she flew to Europe, going first to her cousins the Alain Sartons, then to Eugénie. From Linkebeek she visited Céline in Brussels—Céline, now ninety-one, stone deaf, attended by day and night nurses, "suddenly grown tiny and frail," yet undaunted by dependency and writing bad sentimental verse. May had deliberately planned nine days in Belgium so that she could see Eugénie "quietly and well"; she found her friend at eighty doing all the housekeeping and cooking and, carless, walking two miles a day to buy food. By "bitter mischance" Eugénie had an English guest, so that it was six days before May saw her alone. May got sick, "simply crowded out by ghosts (Jean Dominique) and the terrible old. It rained the whole time."

She went to London, still pursued by ghosts and the very old, the latter a Miss Spencer in a nursing home who had written, "I *am* Caroline Spencer!" so that May felt obliged to travel to Aldershot to see this admirer of *As We Are Now* and declare the two of them friends. On her last day she had tea with the Huxleys. "Francis [the Huxleys' younger son] was there, looking more like Aldous than ever. . . . Julian sat in the corner of a sofa wrapped in shawls like an ancient frail mouse, very interested in his tea." Looking "exhausted and bitter," Juliette deigned to remain in the room, venting her disgust at the way writers about Bloomsbury denigrated her former employer Lady Ottoline Morrell. "The whole visit left a dry ashy taste in my mouth," May wrote Bill. "There was no warmth toward me at all, nor interest in what I am up to. . . . And I felt the British superiority and insularity forcibly."

Yet Europe still worked a spell. Back in York, she could listen to music again, something that anguish over Marynia had made impossible. And she launched a new journal on November 13. "I feel . . . that we are on a very fast and terrible decline," she told Bill, "the whole civilization . . . and I want to *record* at least what one person went through." More to the point, *Plant Dreaming Deep* and *Journal of a Solitude* had been very successful. And May *had* to keep producing.

Christmas had gotten out of control. Although she had not produced a Christmas poem since "Blizzard" in 1966, May allowed countless other demands on her time. She decorated a little tree for Marynia and took it to Brattleboro. She drove to Nelson with dozens of gifts. She baked cookies. She bought and wrapped gifts for old friends, from Anne Thorp to Eleanor Blair, as well as for people who worked for her. She mailed hundreds of cards, decorated a tree. Then she collected Judy for the holidays— Judy, who still sounded plausible when saying of an adored brother-in-law, "Tell me a little about him. What is his background?" but who was lost in a world of her own. May kept up their old routine of having people in separately for brief, strictly controlled periods: Beverly and Mary-Leigh; Anne Woodson and the sculptor Barbara Barton; the Garretts from York Harbor, among her few local friends; Raymond Philbrook, the gardener. Last-minute shopping. Then the grand opening of presents on Christmas Eve, Christmas breakfast in bed with Judy and the opening of their stockings, and finally the excellent Christmas dinner she prepared herself.

"The fact is that Christmas has become a deadly life-consuming horror," she wrote Bill, "and why one goes on doing it and falling in with so much is beyond me. It took 6 weeks out of my life this year!" Her fans had been particularly active this Yuletide, but May was not grateful. "I became quite enraged at opening so many stupid ugly presents I didn't want and had to thank people for. I mean, how *can* people send one cheap imitation Disney china rabbit made in Japan?"

In the new year, 1975, the book of portraits absorbed her. "It has been an earthquake to go back into that dazzling time in the thirties when I knew Bowen and everyone else. I dream a lot and feel quite harrowed. . . . I mean simply that this 'work' is so full of buried anxieties I feel I am crossing a mine field every day." Parent-haunted, she would include portraits of George and Mabel in *A World of Light,* along with Céline Limbosch, Edith Kennedy, Grace Dudley, Alice and Haniel Long, Marc Turian, Albert Quigley, S. S. Koteliansky, Elizabeth Bowen, Louise Bogan, and Jean Dominique.

What were the minefields May had to cross as she wrote these "portraits and celebrations"? One explosive, certainly, was sex: the fact that she had seduced, or tried to seduce, Edith Kennedy, Grace Dudley, Méta Turian, Elizabeth Bowen, and Louise Bogan. Obviously, this must be treated very lightly, or ignored. Another mine lurked in her real, rather than celebratory, feelings about these people. She still bitterly resented her father; this could not be said. She now realized that Mabel's abandoning her so often as a child had left her pathologically insecure; this too could not be said. She knew that Céline's arrogant domineering had alienated Raymond and her children. And her feelings for Louise Bogan were ambivalent in the extreme.

But the deadliest mine lay buried in the reality of these people's feelings about her. Edith Kennedy had ordered her to cease and desist. Marc Turian was not blind to May's and Méta's passionate attraction. Quig felt affection; but to him, a proud man, she was also the lady of the manor, employing his wife as cleaning woman, giving his family money—doubtful that he felt as spiritually akin to May as she felt to him. Kot had shut his door on her. Louise Bogan sniped at her ruthlessly. And Elizabeth Bowen, too, back in the mid-fifties, had suddenly shut her out of her life. May decided to tell that story obliquely.

> I did see Bowen's Court again, under strange circumstances—a disastrous visit which I recount here in order, perhaps, to exorcise it. . . . The mood and the atmosphere changed with the arrival unexpectedly . . . of Miss Lovelace, a charming and beautiful young Californian who arrived with all the flurry and excitement of the adorer who has found her way to the promised land. If I had been a little at a loose end before, I was now in double jeopardy and had become what Elizabeth once called herself—"an agitated observer" of a scene in which I clearly was expected to take no part, but which I recognized with a pang as the mirror image of my own first stays at Bowen's Court when I was the welcomed young adorer myself. . . . It was as acute a case of psychological discomfort as I have ever experienced.

For reasons she would never know, continues May, "I had become a second-class citizen in Elizabeth's province. When I had not heard from her for several years I cabled a New Year message, and when that was never answered, I had to realize that our friendship had come to an end." But May knew very well why Bowen ended their friendship. A frequent visitor at 14 Wright Street while lecturing in the States, Bowen had become very fond of the wry, understated Judith Matlack. Then came Cora DuBois. To justify leaving Judy for Cora, May ran down Judy to Bowen. And Bowen, as May finally admitted to her biographer, never forgave that treachery.

News of three deaths accompanied this voyage into the past. Céline died January 30. On February 15, May was watching the evening news when Julian Huxley's face appeared on the screen; all night she tossed with turbulent memories of Julian and Juliette, who now was free. Then on March 3, Rosalind Greene died. In a burst of frankness, May recorded her feelings in the new journal, *The House by the Sea*. Rosalind might have been a great actress. Her own failures she revenged upon her daughters by setting impossibly high goals. "Every one of the girls was brilliant. Katrine might have been a really good painter. But all were short-circuited by their mother's standards, too high, even ruthless toward beginning efforts. Rosalind was in many ways a terrifying mother. What kind of mother is it who expects a dinner party to be given in her honor when on a brief visit to her daughter? And expects to be the prima donna?" Her surviving daughter, Joy Greene Sweet, agreed: "Yes, the grandchildren got the glow; we were burned." Yet May had felt closer to Rosalind, as she had to another dominating mother, Céline, than to any of her daughters.

A year of loss, of hectic activity. She lectured and read poetry at the University of New Hampshire ("pale smug profs emerged from under their stones"), New England College, Clark University, Ohio Wesleyan, Bates College, Cornell, Dartmouth, the University of Minnesota—most of the time suffering a low-grade virus infection, finally losing her voice.

Meanwhile, Norton brought out *Crucial Conversations* on her sixty-third birthday. "I DON'T like it," May had told Bill. That did not mitigate her fury at Norton's apparent refusal to advertise. "Not one single ad," she wrote Eric Swenson May 12. "O.K. I'll put $2,000 or more into small ads in the Daily Times. I am shocked: why give a big advance if you intend no backing?" Eric was a patient man, but really, he told her, she shouldn't jump down his throat before she knew Norton's plans. The book had sold 10,532 copies in seven days. Ads were waiting for reviews. Yet he forgave her anger. "Hell, if you didn't care enough to cry—or to blow a gasket—you wouldn't be the creator you are."

May resented Carolyn Heilbrun's criticizing her "undue admiration for marriage" in novels like *The Bridge of Years, Birth of a Grandfather,* and *Kinds of Love*—not fair, she felt, from a woman with a husband and children, nor accurate, since her novels celebrated not so much marriage as the family she never had. Thus May planned *Crucial Conversations* as a middle-aged *Doll's House,* with Poppy Whitelaw walking out of twenty-seven years of marriage to reclaim her stifled soul. The novel's crucial conversations debate the wisdom and morality of her act.

In fact the novel takes place almost entirely at the level of debate—Sarton intellectually answering the question: "What happens when a middle-aged woman walks out of a marriage?" The *New York Times* critic disliked this detachment: "The trouble is . . . no real person was ever as uncompromising and articulate and morally self-conscious as Miss Sarton's characters. Nobody ever acted the way they do except in daydreams of marital squabbles and plays by Eugène Scribe. No one was ever so free of the weight of history or the demons of irrationality. . . ." Sarton had tried to link the Whitelaws' story to history by having Vietnam and Watergate wake Poppy to the falsity of her marriage—"though this will seem preposterous." It does, because the linking is perfunctory.

There is another perfunctoriness. "It's such a dirty world we live in," Sarton could tell Bill Brown. "I stand on the edge of some *panic* about mankind in general—man is so *cruel,*" she wrote to another. Yet Sarton loves the term "human": "a complete human being," "a whole human being," "an authentic human being." In her novels she seems unable to admit that "human" encompasses not only the virtues but the brutality of the most vicious species on earth; that an "authentic human being" has fully as much potential for evil as for good. It is as though her right hand refuses to acknowledge the sinister.

This remains true even though Sarton often applies a specialized meaning to "whole human being." As she wrote Morgan Mead: "The whole imposed criteria are crumbling and people are learning that to be human one has to accept the male in one if one is female and vice versa, and *not be afraid of it.* What a world we could make if men really could be gentle and loving! And women trust themselves and be aggressive without paying the price of being called names." To be whole in this sense, then, is to be androgynous, to cherish one's animus and anima. It is also, crucially for Sarton, to be a lesbian and still be considered by the heterosexual world not a cripple but "an authentic human being."

To list her visitors these years would be like compiling a telephone directory. Among them was Katharine Taylor. Despite the coolness between them, May had continued to send K.T. all her books, and though K.T. favored *The Bridge of Years,* "*Kinds of Love,*" she had written, "will I'm sure prove to be your *best.*" Now Dorothy Wallace drove the eighty-six-year-old Katharine to York for a post-birthday celebration for May, who met "a frighteningly thin skeleton, walking gingerly with a cane, but the spirit flaming alive, all her wits as keen as ever, and her wonderful genius for being absolutely *with* whomever she is with, of all and any age, untouched by time." May served lobster, Dorothy poured Pouilly-Fuissé, and they had a grand reunion in front of the fire, though they were forced to speak of another Shady Hill teacher who had not kept her wits—Anne Thorp, fast slipping into senile dementia. May spent a bad week on Greenings Island that summer, terrible heat, both Anne and Judy confused. Still, May would not give up.

More precious than visitors that summer was a letter from Juliette
Huxley. May had read a tribute at a memorial service for Julian in New
York in June; now she struggled to answer Juliette's question: "But who—
who—who really was he?" She dreamed of the Huxleys often; it was part
of the journey into the past she was taking with *A World of Light*. And she
dared hope for a reunion with Juliette.

That November she sent the finished book of portraits to Norton,
minus Rosalind Greene's, excised on Carolyn Heilbrun's advice; Norton
enthusiastically offered a $12,500 advance. But looking back, she decided
that 1975 had not been a good year: too many deaths, too many visitors,
too much fan mail, too little time for concentration. And she *had,* she felt,
to write a book a year to meet expenses and be able to give money away:
$5,000 to Anne Woodson, for example, so that she and Barbara Barton
could buy a twenty-five-acre farm near the White Mountains. But the
worst of it was that she had not written any poetry since the unpublished
poems to Marynia. Poetry had always depended on the Muse; but she was
going on sixty-four: what chance of falling in love again at her age? If she
were to write poetry, she would have to find inspiration without the help
of love.

There was another problem, less articulated. "I do not think it is the
business of a poet to become a guru," she had written in *Journal of a Soli-
tude.* A poet's job was to remain simple, receptive, and vulnerable to all
experience. Yet with the highly intrusive following her recent books had
earned her, how perilous to remain in that open state. When she did, her
energy went into seeing fans who insisted she receive them or into advis-
ing readers who considered her the "Dear Abby" of literature. To these
readers, May Sarton was a symbol of "the whole human being," some-
thing they must touch, like a bishop's ring. But the inordinate amount of
time and energy she lavished on these readers should have been expended
upon her real work, not counseling the troubled. May knew the agony of
giving herself to fans because the critics wouldn't have her, knowing
those fans would eat her alive.

CHAPTER 22

Poetry Again: 1976–1978

"I am making deep plans," May had written Bill in August 1975. She would finish *A World of Light* that Christmas, then take six months off and "hope that, given time and space, I might find my way back to poems *without a muse*. It is the last great hurdle and I just pray I can open that door again somehow." In the bitterly cold January of 1976, May did make tentative tries at poems, gazing from her desk at the frozen field and dark sea. But six free months were an illusion.

"A hippie girl turned up one whole day, having hitch-hiked from Ohio with a knapsack full of my books, knowing the poems by heart, dressed in over-alls and heavy work boots and a tam o'shanter," she wrote Bill:

> . . . When I asked her why she liked my poems, she said, "They're so trippie," meaning having the same effect as LSD. . . . I tried to suggest that commitment to an art, a person, a life work is really far more dangerous and exciting and difficult than what looks like adventure in her sort of life. I left her standing on Route 1 in the dusk, a frail figure, waiting for a ride to Boston.
>
> . . . I realized after she left how little the young *really* interest me. I miss old friends and people my own age who face some of my problems. All the people I see regularly or communicate with regularly are my inferiors (this sounds snobbish but you know it is not . . . they are kind dear people who floated into my life by their choice not mine).

These encounters left her lonelier. "After another day entirely alone in the bleak cold, some sort of breakthrough that has been coming since Christmas happened. I think it had to. I wept torrents of tears. . . . I am simply too isolated and starved. And it is not the easiest thing to solve . . . there are people I could call, who would gladly come and have dinner if I invited them. But that becomes a great effort, breaks into my meditations, destroys all real work for the day, so it is not a solution. What I need is a 'family.' . . ."

Wondering where the poems had gone, she left in March for a literary festival at Notre Dame University, where the young in whom she was not really interested gave her a standing ovation after she read from *As We Are Now* and the poems. Their enthusiasm made it, for once, a pleasure to listen to other poets: Louis Simpson ("a little dry and self-conscious"), Stanley Kunitz ("exactly like a koala bear"), and Galway Kinnell ("authentic genius I felt"). There were parties every night, and she returned to York high on happiness, but soon learned "that this champagne fizz has nothing whatever to do with creation. . . ."

There were compensations. Reading poems at the University of Oklahoma, Clark University, and Vassar in April, she discovered again that *Mrs. Stevens, Plant Dreaming Deep, Journal of a Solitude,* and *As We Are Now* had made her a celebrity as a fighter for women, one of the sisterhood. But not necessarily of the lesbian wing. Finding most "lesbian" poetry and novels "simply terrible," May was "terribly loath" to actively identify herself with homosexual women. At the same time, she realized that "coming out" in *Mrs. Stevens* had contributed to her work winning recognition, even made her a heroine. A conflict, to say the least.

In May, the University of New Hampshire and Bates and Colby Colleges in Maine granted her honorary degrees, and she celebrated "a singularly happy" sixty-fourth birthday, waking to dozens of gifts and phone calls from admirers who had become friends: Lee Blair, Beulah Jenkins, Laurie Armstrong, Irene Morgan. Judy's niece Patricia Warren brought Judy for lunch. Avalanches of flowers poured in all afternoon. But the chief celebration took place two days later with Anne Woodson and Barbara Barton, who brought the phoenix statue May had commissioned. It was her chosen symbol: the ardent spirit rising again and again from the ashes of defeat. She installed it beside a yew in the formal garden, where "it does just what I wanted, gives the sense of an uprush of *flight.*" It was appropriate for a year in which she felt she was, at last, coming into her own.

Countless summer visitors. She ended *The House by the Sea* on August 17 and sent a copy to Carolyn Heilbrun. Heilbrun was blunt: "This is the

May receiving an honorary degree (one of eighteen) from the University of New Hampshire, May 23, 1976

material for a work, not the work itself, and no amount of editing and cutting will change that. The journal is fundamentally too self-indulgent, too formless, too repetitive, and promises more than it delivers." But Eric Swenson liked it, and she eagerly accepted his word—"Only I wonder whether maybe Carol is right, that's the trouble. She is not a country person . . . maybe that is partly why she didn't like it, but I feel sometimes it is thin and shallow compared to the other journal. I am haunted by the memory that the Japanese when happy and at peace produced no great art, only painted fans!" Her doubts multiplied that fall: "I'm already quaking at the idea of how I shall be skinned next year when the journal comes out . . . but I have to have money to live on to write a new novel, and at least I'm glad Norton will publish."

By encouraging one or two Sarton books a year, Norton was making money but inevitably promoting mediocrity. Few writers can produce consistent quality at that pace. May knew this at heart, yet was so eager for attention, so starved for acclaim, that she *had* to publish, even while dreading the results. Her excuse that she had to write to support herself is true—but only because she gave so much money away. She attributed her prodigality to horror of George's meanness; it was a way of rebelling against him still. She had even adopted a Greek family financially, as Mabel had her Russians. Yet giving was also an attention-getting device, a subtle blackmail: You must love me, I have given you so much. Giving away thousands a year also ensured that she would be forced to write: writing was, she admitted, the only sanity. Then, too, giving allayed the deep guilt of the narcissist who could admit, "Personne ne m'interesse excepté moi-même."

Publicity appearances for *A World of Light* and readings at Mills College, at the Unitarian Thomas Starr King School, and in Milwaukee and Chicago soothed fears. May disliked Erica Jong's novels for their sexuality (and hated Henry Miller's and Norman Mailer's) and thought her poetry bad, but Erica had obliged with a blurb—"May Sarton is a national treasure"—and May was pleased to meet her in New York, "a warm sweet vulgar girl with a diamond heart set into the base of one eyeglass!" And *A World of Light* (dedicated to Carolyn Heilbrun) was garnering praise for the vivid portraits of people who had touched her life: a book reminiscent of Lillian Hellman's *Pentimento,* but with its own generous, graceful style. May had disguised the minefields well.

Only *The New York Times* "as usual was mean." After praising May's "keen talent for friendship" and "considerable intuitive skill," Pearl Kay Bell got down to business. Neither Elizabeth Bowen nor Louise Bogan came into focus, because of Miss Sarton's overfondness for "sentimental and ardently vague generalities." Moreover, much of the material had been published before. "It thus seems rather disingenuous for her to claim in the Preface that she has brought a wealth of hard-earned new judgment and feeling to the present book. . . . Not enough, it would seem, to prevent Miss Sarton from resorting to the pouring of old wine. . . . *A World of Light* makes it clear that, at least for the time being, four volumes of autobiographical reminiscences and self-exploring memoir have been more than enough."

Hard words when the author knew that still another self-exploring memoir waited in the wings. Ms. Bell was correct that some of the essays had appeared in print before. Yet the reviewer's essentially trivial sniping might have been avoided had May not written that disingenuous preface. But of course she wrote it precisely because she *was* recycling some material.

May had her own interpretation of the review. "The critic turns out to be a sister of Alfred Kazin, so we are back with the Jewish mafia which runs the literary world," she wrote Bill Brown. ". . . The woman had *asked* for the book, and she has done this before . . . asking for a book she means to destroy. [Doris] Grumbach has written to complain to the editor." The question Why did Pearl Kay Bell wish to destroy May Sarton? remained unanswered.

In December May returned to New York for a reception at the Public Library celebrating new additions to the Berg Collection, including six cases of Sartoniana. Muriel Rukeyser came to the event, though not for May personally. She'd had a stroke, and May thought her former lover looked awful, with makeup smeared on eyes and mouth: "It was *sad.*" The white wine and pretzels also seemed a sad sign of New York's financial woes, but at least, May told Bill, "I did not get drunk."

The Berg had paid her $20,000 for the cache; but by January 1977, though the trust was intact, she had only $400 in a savings account depleted by $12,000 in taxes and the fact that "people have got used to large money presents." On January 3, spurred by finances, she started a sixteenth novel, about a woman dying, like Mabel, of lung cancer. "I had forgotten how literally impossible it seems at first, so many people to invent. . . . I really have no confidence whatever, as usual. I realize how careless my style is for one thing. Lack of primary intensity I fear is the key to that, for when I look back at some earlier novels, which is quite fatal, I wonder how I wrote so well!"

They say that when a writer goes back to earlier works for inspiration, she's finished. May had written five fine novels—*The Bridge of Years, A Shower of Summer Days, Faithful Are the Wounds, Mrs. Stevens Hears the Mermaids Singing,* and *As We Are Now.* (Many readers would add *Kinds of Love,* some *The Single Hound* and *The Small Room.*) By now she was writing novels on automatic pilot—and she knew it. No wonder that by February she was struggling in "a quicksand of despair."

That January she had paid a last visit to the dying Anne Thorp in her apartment over the barn behind the Longfellow house on Brattle Street. Though Anne had fought wildly against leaving Greenings Island the previous summer, sensing she would never return, she was not suffering now, just sleeping much of the time, letting life go. For May, her death meant more than losing a childhood idol or ritual days on Greenings Island: Anne Thorp was the last person who had known both Mabel and George intimately. On March 5, May spoke a tribute to this wealthy, benevolent, essence–of–New England woman at a memorial service at the First Parish Church, Cambridge. "A big piece of my life dies with her."

But a phoenix is always reborn. From Tennessee that March came an invitation to read poetry from a wealthy widow who had come to May's work after her husband's death. The invitation was not the first: May and Dinah (not her real name) had actually met, since the latter sum-

mered in New England. May had held back—not liking the mutual
friend who had introduced them, intimidated by the heiress's wealth,
reluctant to make a fool of herself again at the ripe age of sixty-five.
Now she accepted the invitation; and there, amidst dogwood, daffodils,
and anemones, she "fell into a trance of passionate love for a strange and
beautiful woman."

Dinah's wealth was definitely an attraction. So was her childhood,
which, she admitted, had been emotionally deprived. The star treatment
Dinah gave her was also definitely flattering. And they shared similar tastes
in art and music. But what really stunned May was the transformation of
a curly-haired afternoon tomboy in shorts into the queen slowly descend-
ing the staircase in a stunning gown—the embodiment of unconscious
erotic androgyny. May kissed her passionately. Dinah was astonished. But
she did not throw her guest out of the house.

Exultant, May immediately wrote Bill. "She has a great head like mar-
ble, the most *contained* face I ever saw . . . noble like a piece of sculp-
ture . . . very bright glancing dark eyes"—a departure: blue eyes had
always enchanted May—". . . a haunting deep voice." But she did not ask
Bill to congratulate her on falling in love; she asked him to rejoice "that
poetry has come again." Lines already hummed in her head. Now she
regretted her forthcoming trip to Europe in July, just when Dinah would
be in New England. But Dinah would come to Maine for her birthday,
and meanwhile there were phone calls and "absurdly reserved letters." "I
was preparing to die," she told Bill not a little melodramatically, "and now
I must prepare to live."

Before Dinah's visit May went again to New York for interviews and
readings. Lola Szladits worried about an audience until "four acolytes
brought four vases of lilac to the altar." "Acolytes" and "altar" describe very
well the religious fervor that May ignited in her audiences; and as usual
now, she received a long standing ovation before everyone adjourned for
cider and birthday cake.

A reading at Barnard's Lehman Auditorium the evening of April 28
was similarly packed, elation high. Deborah Pease, a former student at
Wellesley, now a poet herself and the publisher of the *Paris Review*, was in
the audience. "What a performer!" thought Pease admiringly. After the
reading, May fielded questions with éclat. A young woman sitting next to
Pease, obviously very depressed, timidly raised her hand. "What do you do
about torment?" she asked in a barely audible voice. "Just die!" said May
on a great gust of laughter. Deborah shivered. The laugh was chilling, as
was Sarton's "sailing on to the next topic with no concept of what she
had done."

Next day a signing at a gay bookstore in Greenwich Village was a fes-
tival of love. "I do have some reservations about being affiched as gay or
lesbian," she told Bill, "but they are our people, and I am coming to rather
like being with them." A radio interview excited "hundreds of calls"
from people eager to find her books because in these corrupt times May
Sarton came across "as so uncorrupted."

Back in York, festivities celebrated both May's and Anne Woodson's
birthdays and Dinah's arrival in May's life—champagne, lobsters, and a
fabulous catered dessert because Dinah loved sweets. Yet May was the star,
Dinah unobtrusively refilling glasses, removing plates. She stayed four
nights and five days and, miraculously, seemed to be as much in love as
May, "so the nights progressed like some great piece of music, creating
reverberations in all my secret caves."

In June May went south to Dinah and the Spoleto Festival in
Charleston, South Carolina, an orgy of music, though only Schubert's
Quintet in C Major touched her, that and Handel's Water Music, which
she and Dinah heard lying on the grass. "Then the bliss of going to bed
together at last after the long day of not touching. . . . I simply am speech-
less before the quality and depth of this relationship, Bill. It was quite a test
in Charleston because of the pace, but there was never a moment of ten-
sion in all those days, just perfect understanding and communion on every
level . . . lots of laughter, too." The only irritation, back in Tennessee for
three days, was the blasted dogs, who occupied all the good chairs in the
house. Dinah called the dogs "daughter." "Who," asked May caustically,
"is the father?"

The novel, she wrote Eleanor Blair late June, "has been such an albatross for
so long." It was typical of her frenetic pace that she should consider six
months and nineteen days long; she was determined to get it into Norton's
hands before she left for Europe July 25. "It is about a woman dying of can-
cer. . . . I have been dying for three hours every morning, no joke. Title: *A
Reckoning.* Whether it is any good or not remains to be seen but I am philo-
sophical as it is quite clear to me now that I wrote it because I was dying
from lack of poetry and a muse. If it is a dud I am still determined to take a
year off in '78 and not do another book until I have had a fallow time."

Doris Grumbach, now a friend, came to house-sit; May flew off to
Europe after making passes that Doris rejected. She stayed with Eugénie
until August 2, walking in the rain across the wheat and barley fields, talk-
ing endlessly about Dinah and her recent triumphs, ignoring Eugénie's
attempts to talk about her own exploration of Indian philosophy. ("Nous

*May with Tamas,
looking seaward
from the terrace of
Wild Knoll*

sommes sur des chemins différents," Eugénie would write her sadly: "We
are on different paths.") She walked also with Jacqueline Limbosch under
the tall beeches in the Forêt de Soignes, where they had played as chil-
dren. But the purpose of the trip was Juliette. "One day you must tell me
what you really think of Julian," Juliette had written. ". . . During his life
I have tried to keep the Image. . . . I am now trying to forget what was
left of Julian in the last years of his life . . . and recover the good." She had
refused to let May stay at 33 Pond Street, but agreed to a meeting of not
more than two hours.

May found a still-lovely woman looking more like sixty than eighty-
one. Julian's photographs were everywhere, forcibly reminding May that
Juliette had immolated herself for his sake. They talked of his curious intel-
lectual charm, the fact that he had never really grown up, his destructive
demon. Worst of all, he had "survived himself so cruelly." Juliette was

May with close friends Barbara Barton (left) and Anne Woodson

writing her memoirs. She would not mention Julian's many love affairs and was happy that he had omitted them from his. She did not hate these women; she had forgiven May. But she was still wary, bitter. The love affair between them could not be mentioned.

"Two hours after thirty years in the doghouse was too little," May wrote Bill. "I felt sad that she still had to make recriminations. Perhaps she was telling me that the wall is still there and always will be. She said she felt I was 'dangerous' and 'exploited' people. I think I am indiscreet, but not in a malicious way, only very open. . . . It never occurred to me that I could have made recriminations too. But then I really loved J and still do. . . . Next morning I woke up in floods of tears so that ever since I have been trying to come to terms with feelings of guilt."

Except for a production at the National Theatre of Harley Granville Barker's *The Madras House,* which she saw with her "charming, bright-eyed, discriminating, and self-made" young cousin Alan Eastaugh, she hated a London jammed with tourists, was delighted to get away to the Isle of Sark, where she dreamed of Dinah and never having to travel alone again. Dinah was writing almost every day, "but never a word of love of course!" Eric Swenson was more outgoing, cabling of *A Reckoning,* "More than splendid, perhaps your best"—but she didn't believe it, and was still upset about Juliette. She ended the trip in Dublin with Molly

Howe, flew home August 23, and in September was at Dinah's summer place deep in the woods.

Though there were only the beloved dogs as competition, Dinah still did not give May enough attention. She was a good cook, a fastidious housekeeper; seven hours of the day seemed to be spent preparing or cleaning up after meals. When May wanted to share a convivial bottle of champagne before dinner, Dinah was in the kitchen making a chocolate soufflé. When May protested, Dinah answered, "But I made the soufflé for *you*." When May wanted to sit next to Dinah, the dogs were already in residence. "I think this whole relationship is a kind of culture shock for me and it remains to be seen whether we can really make a go. . . . Although Dinah has great respect for the poet she does not appear to understand the kind of *person* who does the creating. And to resent that I am not a German cook at heart. . . . I know I am quite impossible . . . but that doesn't help either." On the other hand, they were very much in love. Again life was filled with companionship and *plans*.

One day May drove Dinah in her new Dodge Aspen to Nelson. If her Europe was haunted by the dead, her Nelson seemed to have vanished. New owners had painted her white house a drab olive green and neglected the garden. Mildred Quigley, sick with a thyroid problem, weighed eighty-four pounds. The Frenches had sold the sheep that used to delight her. And the Warners—how had she ever been able to ignore the terrible poverty of their lives? She drove Dinah up to the cemetery to show her the plot she had bought next to Albert Quigley's on the hillside. She would be cremated and buried there, with Barbara Barton's phoenix for a headstone. She didn't want her ashes scattered; she wanted a place, so that people would come.

The House by the Sea, with photographs by Beverly Hallam, was published that fall of 1977. "I feel it is rather bad but how can one tell?" May asked Bill. One way was to admit that "primary intensity" during its writing had often been lacking, making it easier to quote a fan letter or an article from the Op-Ed page than clothe an issue in one's own words. Another was not to blame faulty punctuation on the typist: "Two thirds of the exclamation points should have been removed. And all those ' . . .'. Punctuation has always been my weak point. (It was also V. Woolf's and Leonard did that among so many other things he did for her)." But the punctuation was ultimately May's responsibility. Or Norton's—but Norton seemed curiously reluctant to edit May's manuscripts. Of course

Sarton's loyal band of admirers bought everything she wrote, no matter what the quality. No wonder she dreaded reviews.

Which were generally favorable: "moving testament," "delightful discovery," "inspiring." A Chicago critic, however, admitted he could be impatient "with her chatter about dogs, cats and flowers" and bored "with her views on public policies, which sound like an echo of liberal conventional wisdom." And Doris Grumbach had reservations:

> Sarton is a curious literary phenomenon. She has written thirty-one books. . . . Yet she has been received into no academies and recognized with no prizes or grants as far as I know. True, seminars in her work are held regularly at Modern Language Assoc. meetings, but her true recognition comes from her extraordinarily loyal band of followers who watch for her every published word. Her loyal publisher, recognizing this phenomenon, brings out a new book of hers every year. She seems to speak to the young as well as to those of her own generation. . . . Sarton's new journal will please her admirers and, as it has ever been with her books, gain her new ones. I have a few reservations that concern her lapses into sentimentality, her occasionally trite or effusive prose, her over-reliance on the word "lovely," her fondness for the exclamation point. Her writing sometimes turns to gush, but more often it is evocative and successful. Her strengths are all on the side of her warm, humane person, her sensitivity to the world, to persons and to animals.

Sadly, this kind of review could have been avoided. Had May heeded Carolyn Heilbrun's objections or submitted the manuscript to Grumbach's cool eye, then *acted* on their suggestions; had she insisted that Norton groom the manuscript; above all, had she waited two or three years before launching a new journal—then surely she would have produced another fine work like *Plant Dreaming Deep* or *Journal of a Solitude*. But that loyal band of followers corrupted both author and publisher. *The House by the Sea* inspired so many fan letters that May felt like "a well that is silted up."

Her close friend Anne Woodson blamed the move from Nelson for the falling off of *The House by the Sea*. May had left a distinguished house which she herself owned and created to rent a too-large, undistinguished house in an alien, highly affluent seaside resort community. Though May remained an outsider in Nelson, she had established genuine relationships with people like the Quigleys, the Frenches, the Warners, and Perley Cole. Life was often hard in Nelson; that alone had put steel in her spine and her writing. But Nelson was also a distinctive place. Its quality gave May quality. "She betrayed herself by leaving," said Anne. "Nelson was deep in her soul. She left something vital of herself behind in that village when she came to York."

In October May left to give talks at the University of Wisconsin–Madison and the Midwest Modern Language Association meeting in Chicago. Madison had been a radical campus in the sixties; now May found herself "in the midst of the Lesbian Nation." An informal talk at the feminist bookstore A Room of One's Own ended with a discussion of erotic poetry, which May disliked, especially lesbian erotic poetry. It took some courage, surrounded by militants, to voice that decidedly unpopular view, but she did: "I feel poetry is an essence and a good love poem should apply to any kind of love." The reading the next night to about two hundred went well; but May finally concluded that to women's liberationists, any poet who said what they wanted to hear was a good poet—though much feminist poetry (to her mind) was "sloppy, self-indulgent, and narcissistic or, even worse, simply propagandistic."

In Chicago she shared the platform with the radical black lesbian poet Audre Lorde, a huge presence in a turban and loudly patterned dashiki. Most of the women at the MLA wore pants; May felt self-consciously ladylike in a black dress. She did not like Lorde's poetry, or the way she attacked the audience for not being on the streets of Soweto. She herself was introduced as a writer who was a total failure until the women's liberation movement came along—"a little hard."

The next day a discussion of women's poetry bemused and amused her. "I write with my womb," said one woman. Another said, "I write with my whole self, often in the crouching position of giving birth. I write naked and often look at myself full length in a mirror." To May's astonishment nobody laughed. Finally she blew up. Art was written with the mind and soul, not the body. Art should be judged as art, not as propaganda. Afterwards people came up to say that they agreed but hadn't dared speak out against the militants. "For the first time in public appearances I felt suddenly absolutely *passée*," she told Bill, "and came home rather depressed." Yet her appearances in both Madison and Chicago had created euphoria among her admirers.

. . .

May finished revising *A Reckoning* in early January 1978. But Dinah and the poetry she was inspiring dominated her life. They had "a marvellous cementing week" in January: two days in Boston at the Ritz, then four days of long walks in the snow in York. In February they met in Washington, staying at the Hay-Adams Hotel, visiting the Phillips Collection and the zoo, whose primal roars had terrified May as a child. The stoic Dinah confided she had been in pain recently with her knee, almost as thrilling as when she'd admitted, "It's good to let go." Yet she baffled May, this "secret, passionate, often somber, stubborn, unique, devastatingly fascinating [Dinah] *behind the screen*"—something Doris Grumbach recognized when at a dinner party May paid Dinah exaggeratedly deferential attention. But the four days were rich and full, and she assured Bill Brown that they had "reached a place now of solid love." Frustrating, then, that Dinah's letters continued to be as impersonal as ever.

For their first "anniversary," March 29, May went to Dinah's home for a week, having warned her in advance that she didn't want to socialize, even though she'd enjoyed buying a fancy evening dress—the first she'd ever owned—for Dinah's occasions. It was a sore point between them: Dinah wanted to give elegant luncheons and dinners for her famous friend; May disliked sharing her with others. Besides, May was inept socially, unable to make small talk or cope with a situation in which all attention was not focused on herself. Dinah had agreed, and an exultant May got off the plane "full of love," bearing presents "to commemorate an extraordinary year." When she found Dinah unprepared to admit the anniversary, she reacted with rage and tears. Deeply reserved, accustomed to impeccable social manners, Dinah loathed emotional demonstrations. "I apologize," she said coldly.

Back in York, May struggled to analyze the disaster.

What I have come slowly to understand is that your unconscious flooded the whole thing . . . you *could not* recognize an anniversary that did not have to do with you and [your husband]. . . . I do understand. I do not blame you. But that doesn't mean that I am not in pain. . . . I will never be in [Tennessee] on that day again, and the word anniversary will never be used by me. . . . All that is asked of you now is to understand why I can no longer be open as I was, and loving in the way I was. I'm sure there are good times ahead, and I am going to try not to feel so much. Then there won't be rage or tears. . . . I think you can take it, if I succeed, as a proof of love.

May could not change; Dinah could not change. The more May raged and demanded, the deeper Dinah's chill. As a result of the anniversary fiasco they did not see each other until the Spoleto Festival in June; then, however, "somehow we felt at home with each other in a new way." Perhaps, May decided, she was getting used to Dinah's reserve.

In late June, May left for the University of California at Berkeley to give five two-hour seminars. Preparing for them had taxed her; she was "rather scared about the whole Berkeley thing," for which she was being paid a mere $400.

During the California week May had tea with Joy Greene Sweet's daughter, Gay Scott. At one point, Gay left her two-year-old son, Gulliver, with May while she made tea in the kitchen. When she returned ten minutes later, May was crouched on the sofa in hysterics—*the child had attacked her!* How could Gay have abandoned her to a two-year-old? Gay was too astounded to do anything but apologize. Her mother later analyzed the bizarre incident. "I have no doubt that May was genuinely terrified. She saw the child as an alien force—that is, *someone not responding to her needs.* Gulliver was absorbed in his toys, not in May. She was not getting the total attention she demanded. Two universes collided, Gulliver's and May's. It also may be significant that the child was male. At any rate, May never forgave Gay and never stopped telling the story. It remained a thorn between us. And the absurdity of a grownup claiming she'd been attacked by a two-year-old never struck her."

Though May occasionally gave them a picnic, or tolerated them with their parents, she did not particularly like children. Neither did she really like dogs. This was part of the difficulty when she went in late July to stay *en famille* with Dinah, her daughter, her granddaughter Victoria (not her real name), and the dogs for two weeks. There is only May's account of the disastrous visit, though Dinah's daughter said much later that May was "very difficult," and Victoria admitted, "I was afraid of her."

According to May, Dinah met her with hostility. "We had a bad scene through a screen door (so symbolic)—when Dinah told me she did not want to be 'absorbed into my lesbian world, did not like my friends and would choose her background against mine anytime.' " May had brought wine, potted basil, and—dreading Victoria—dominoes, books, crayons, and a drawing book. Dinah ignored the first and rebuked her for "trying to buy [Victoria's] affection." For May that was the beginning of two long weeks of humiliation. Some of her grievances were legitimate, for Dinah expected people to live by her code and could be oppressively "rich." Chiefly, however, May suffered because she wasn't the center of attention: "There was never praise" . . . "Never can *they* be in the wrong" . . . "I was never once at table asked a question that would have made any conversation possible" . . . "[Victoria] is *at all times* the center." After two weeks of "relentlessly cruel" treatment, May stormed back to York. Victoria's refusal to say goodbye was the crowning humiliation.

> I'm learning all the time [she wrote Dinah]. Next time if there is one I'll bring hand-knitted pot holders, home-made bread and butter pickles, and perhaps a hand stitched apron and thus not appear to be above my station. I might even be able to bring that new "in game" which is called Feeling Superior to May Sarton. It's easy to play and you really can't lose, because she is so vulnerable. The only problem is finding enough players, but since two people in the social register are already avid players, surely others will follow. . . .
>
> I brought basil I had potted for you. I gave you one hour of my precious poem-time to cut up kidneys for the dogs. . . . I made beds, helped with the dishes, tried in every way I knew how to be a good guest. But I couldn't win because for two solid weeks your mood towards me never changed. You never really got over the anger with which you met me and which, alas, I had elicited—and so you had to punish me and you did over and over again.

Writing to Bill, May was more analytical. "What it all adds up to is that somewhere way off is THE WRITER whom she respects, but nearby is THE PERSON, May whom she finds impossible and at times actually hates. What she cannot see is that they are the *same* person." Dinah also, May judged, was "in a homosexual panic," terrified at being with May in a close family situation. May could feel sorry for her: "I sometimes think of [Dinah] as a strangely wounded prehistoric animal who has been given into my care. She sometimes looks like a small dazed wounded little bull who does not really understand what is happening or where the hurt comes from. I come back to her again and again because I know what a deprived person she is. . . ."

Still seething, she attacked the typewriter. In the 115-page novella *We Aren't Getting Anywhere,* Susie visits wealthy Cousin Anna, her daughter Liesel, and Liesel's two children on their Maine island. Susie discovers she is always to be in the wrong: she brings too much luggage, spills the soup, forgets to scrub the bottom of a double boiler, fumbles the boat rope, drops dishes—while Cousin Anna and Liesel exchange meaningful glances.

Learning fast, the children treat her like a servant. Susie is driven to tears, wild outbursts, and more mistakes. "I don't dare be myself" . . . "They take it for granted that their way of doing things is the right way" . . . "Why had it been made to seem such a dreadful faux pas?" . . . "I have no identity any more" . . . "If anyone had ever praised me" . . . "They're so mean." Mean, mean—one of Sarton's favorite words, a childish word, typifying her view that the whole establishment is against her. Significantly, Susie is a very immature eighteen. In other words, May realized that a story about a grownup reacting this way would be ludicrous.

We Aren't Getting Anywhere reveals Sarton's infantilism (Susie calls herself "an embryo") as well as her pathological sense of isolation and lack of identity. It also reveals a confused sexuality. Susie dislikes feminine women because she is not "womanly" herself. "If I could become a woman, a real woman," she says wistfully. Crying, supplicating, and adoring, she does play feminine with masculine Cousin Anna; yet Cousin Anna is not a friend. Men are friends: Liesel's husband; the islander Patrick O'Halloran; a male dinner guest; even the child Peter. "Why is it that little boys are so much more lovable than little girls?" asks Susie, or, "Men are nicer than women I decided long ago." Yet male sexuality terrifies her. Sarton's novels contain almost no sex; it is startling when Liesel's husband kisses Susie hard on the mouth. Susie is devastated—a young woman who feels unfeminine, thus preferring masculine women and neutered men.

From the humiliations of those two weeks also came a poem like "Control":

> Hold the tiger fast in check
> Put the leash around his neck.
> Make it known a growl will tighten
> The collar. Browbeat. Frighten. . . .
>
> You may have complete control.
> There will be no roar or growl.
> But can you look into those eyes
> Where the smothered fire lies?

Dinah did not appreciate, or often understand, the poetry she inspired. In "The Lady of the Lake," for example, May admits that Dinah's marriage stands between them:

Somewhere at the bottom of the lake she is
Entangled among weeds, her deep self drowned.
I cannot be with her there. I know she is bound
To a dead man. Her wide open eyes are his.

But May is able to transcend that barrier, something Dinah could not admit: "I come / With him, with her, into a strange communion, / And all is well where the drowned lovers sleep." At Dinah's she had wrestled for days with the poem "At the Black Rock":

Anger's the beast in me.
In you it is pride.
When they meet they lock
There is no pity.

When she read it to Dinah, Dinah said, cutting picnic sandwiches, "It's so sad." "Sad"! How could she call the spilling of one's lifeblood "sad"?

They continued to see each other. In August May threw a clambake on the rocks for forty people in Dinah's honor. Dinah returned to Wild Knoll in September and again in October. For Thanksgiving May flew south, determined to probe the still-aching wounds of the blighted anniversary and summer visit. Dinah met her head-on. She had never wanted sex, had only complied for May's sake. They were too old; it was disgusting. She preferred to forget that aspect of the past year.

Devastating—for despite their quarrels, Dinah had been capable of passion. May suddenly felt old, disgraced; the poems Dinah inspired now seemed lies. "This morning I couldn't bear to sit opposite her at breakfast after a sleepless night, and fled to my room with my coffee," she wrote Bill. "I helped plant bulbs, had no lunch because I couldn't face sitting at the table, and have been here in my room trying to sleep. . . . It is now five and I must soon get into evening dress—a grotesque red-eyed elephant, for we are going to a dinner party in my honor." May returned to York knowing that even the affection Dinah showered upon the dogs could not be hers.

What frightened her was the pattern. Cora, Monica, now Dinah: intense love for about a year, then such intense hostility she felt they wanted to kill her. She might have recognized another pattern. Grace Dudley, Juliette Huxley, Eugénie, Judy, Monica, Marynia Farnham, and Dinah considered themselves heterosexual women. Once May's dazzle wore off, they recoiled. Guilt fueled their anger—and fear of their own sexuality. May became the villain who had led them astray. She must be punished.

"It may be that by imprisoning every spontaneous feeling I have towards you," May wrote Dinah that December, "by entering your prison—but it must be done through a kind of abnegation that will take very hard work on my part—it may be that if I can really bury all that is precious about me as far as most people see me, bury the poet, bury the loving person who so needs tenderness, bury every spontaneous gesture, that the *surface* will satisfy your need for absolute control and the death of the spirit so that all may appear to be orderly. I cannot promise this."

Dinah could not promise to put up with May's demands. Still, they were not through with each other yet.

CHAPTER 23

Intimations of Mortality: 1978–1982

Dinah's sexual withdrawal doubly devastated May because it coincided with a "scurrilous review" of *A Reckoning* in *The New York Times,* where Lore Dickstein claimed that Sarton's real theme was not dying but lesbianism. Why disguise *A Reckoning* as a woman's final battle with cancer, asked Dickstein, when the crux of the novel was Laura Spelman's "I think this whole journey towards death has been in a way joining myself up with women, with all women"? Why play coy?

Actually, Sarton does not play coy: the lesbian theme announces itself plainly on page 14; moreover, it is perfectly plausible that a woman facing death finally confess her affective priorities. More damning to Dickstein than Sarton's reticence, however, was her failure to deal with either cancer or homosexuality effectively because of a style "which tends toward the ready cliché and occasionally teeters on the edge of sentimentality."

Writing to Dinah after she'd read the *Times,* May forgot that she could call her own novel "*very bad.*" "I had put too much hope, once more, for the 32nd time, into what a good piece of work might do to relieve me of constant pressure to over-produce. I have now come to terms with the hard fact that I am second-rate, not quite 'the real thing.' This time I almost made it. But in my work as with you I have given the best that is in me and I have failed." She was particularly incensed that Dickstein had branded "My Sisters, O My Sisters" lesbian. She did not write *lesbian* poems; she wrote universal poems about love and life.

The novel raised another question: Was May Sarton an artist, or a healer? Is *A Reckoning* fine fiction, or a self-help text for cancer victims?

Neither, actually. True, countless readers found inspiration in Laura's battle to die with dignity. But that isn't the real problem with *A Reckoning*. At the core of this novel's weakness is "lack of primary intensity." The ratio of good, solid, fictional creation to easy clichés of women's-liberation philosophy is skewed: as in *Crucial Conversations,* Sarton's fictional world is thin. After all, Charlotte Brontë laid down eleven dense chapters before she allowed her heroine to cry "I longed for a power of vision . . . desired more of practical experience . . . more of intercourse with my kind"; and Ibsen, a whole play before Nora walked out of the doll's house. But for Sarton, received feminist doctrine is ready to hand, easy to substitute for both character development and action, so that a few words are enough to convert intrepid old Aunt Minna:

> LAURA: I think that however original and powerful a woman may have been—and as you surely are—we have allowed ourselves to be caught in all sorts of stereotypes. What is a woman meant to be, anyway? We don't think of men as "meant to be" primarily married and fathers, do we?
>
> AUNT MINNA: You know, I never thought of it quite like that before.

Similarly, with one glance into her doctor's eyes Laura can say, "Thanks, Jim. I never knew what it meant before that we are all members of each other." She might be thanking him for a lift to the supermarket.

Disarmingly, Laura's insights were—for many educated, awakened, middle-class women and men in 1978—profoundly true. The novel chokes with truths—but with so little invention that Laura's daughter wanders about the room picking up various objects and setting them down on page 162 just as Laura's very different sister picks up objects and sets them down twelve pages later. Most novelists would at least describe the objects.

What Sarton does do uncannily well is convey the physical and mental processes of dying. Readers feel in their own lungs and heart Laura's gradual weakening, growing discomfort, loss of appetite, tears of frustration, terror of the hospital, and, through it all, conflicting resolve to live vividly yet let life go. Though the novels are hardly comparable in quality, readers of *A Reckoning have* lung cancer, just as readers of *The Magic Mountain* have TB.

A Reckoning is also intriguing biographically. Again Sarton places her protagonist at the center of the large family she never had. Central to the novel is her struggle to come to terms with a real woman, the beautiful, thwarted, destructive Rosalind Greene (Laura's mother, Sybille). Just as May could not solve her relationship to that difficult personality, Laura cannot finally "reckon" Sybille's powerful influence. Another woman is even more important: Ella—May's friend Barbara Runkle Hawthorne. Laura decides that this passionate friend means more to her than family or her dead husband, just as May would consider Barbara her soul mate to the end: "Time and other people don't really matter."

May wrote this novel of dying, she told Eleanor Blair, because she herself was dying for lack of poetry and a Muse. There is much of May in Laura: her self-absorption, her desire to let someone else take over the intrusive business of life, her constant tears, her love of animals, her feeling most comfortable with people who "don't displace much atmosphere." Pure May is a moment like, "Tears slid out from under her lids. It's hard, she told herself, it's just plain hard that I am not to have my one last day before it is all taken from me," or the scene in the hospital elevator when Laura becomes incensed when interns converse over her head. But difficult behavior in a well woman is understandable in a sick one: Laura Spelman, dying Mabel's death, is a sympathetic character.

Christmas that year was "simply excruciating." May had flu, a rainstorm knocked out lights and heat, and Judy was too far gone to notice the tree. Since May complained bitterly of her coldness, Dinah's gift was an electric blanket; she had a sense of humor. The fact that she was sharing a festive Christmas with her daughter and grandchild in snowy New England galled. She came to Wild Knoll in January 1979 with the two dogs—one, incontinent, transported on a mattress. All the pain got raked up again, Dinah repeating that she had long been revolted by sex. This time May flew at her, fists flying. An explanation followed Dinah to Tennessee:

> For me, sex is not primarily an aesthetic experience. . . . I think I "fall in love" always with a face, and with the secret person behind it, that secret person whom I want so desperately to reach and to make mine . . . and at the same time to give my secret self to that person, "to take them in" if you will, and to be "taken in." For you the aesthetic is far more important than it is to me. The mysterious thing, however, is that when there is desire a secret place in a person opens, very much as a flower opens . . . and this is quite beyond the will. . . . Although you deny it now, there *was* desire in you or you would have been closed. Sorry, but that is a physical *fact*.

For me the sexual act, especially with a woman, is primarily a spiritual thing . . . a giving and taking of something enormously secret and private, hence precious. The moment of climax becomes then a kind of ecstasy for a few seconds. One is melted and fired at the same time. All tensions are released and one is made *new.*

You have chosen to shut out all that and to think only of things that revolt you because you refuse to remember what you *felt.* Sex when contemplated cold is always ludicrous if not actually revolting.

"Things are very good with [Dinah] (maybe because we are apart!)," May was able to tell Bill in February. "I sometimes think my violent attack on her the night she was here cleared the air. . . . She *believed* it." Both were looking forward to two weeks in England and on the island of Sark in May.

Though Juliette wrote, "One book a year is TOO much," May had begun another journal in December, a novella in January, and was revising love poems for a new volume, *Halfway to Silence.* The journal had become a habit: comparatively easy to write, a way of restoring "a sense of meaning and continuity" to her life—and marketable. May could thank the women's movement for the booming market in memoirs. Women's studies courses taught the diary and journal as a feminine genre reflecting women's traditionally inward, private lives and fragmented time available for creation. Professional writers like Sarton and Anaïs Nin, of course, wrote "privately" to publish, quite a different thing from Dorothy Wordsworth's journal keeping, Virginia Woolf's working diary, or Sylvia Plath's journals—though no twentieth-century writer could be unconscious of publication. As May said, her recent journals were "hostages to fortune": cautious, complimentary works written with an eye on libel suits. Actually, she considered journals "a low form of creation."

In *Anger,* the novella, May recast her battles with Dinah as battles between Anna Lindstrom, a temperamental singer, and her husband, Ned Fraser, a conservative banker. A bad attack of diverticulitis in February as she was working on the book clearly announced that writing about anger did not necessarily dissolve it. It did not help that she knew she was forcing this book; in fact, she eventually laid it aside.

That late winter and spring she hit the road again, suffering her "usual reaction of self-loathing and self-doubt after all the applause and all the people wanting to devour me and get *inside*." In Washington, a meeting with Doris Grumbach, whose novel *Chamber Music* had been a success, intensified anguish. "How can I help making comparisons? For the moment I have lost faith in my capacity to write. . . . But I have to believe that I can make a come back eventually. It is too frightening to imagine even for a second that I am finished as a creator."

Before leaving with Dinah for England May 8, she discovered she had a breast tumor. Like Mabel, who hadn't wanted to spoil George's holiday, she kept the news from her friend. And they did have pleasant days on a barge on the Thames and on Sark, Dinah "as tender and loving as is possible for her tightly-censored feeling self." She returned to news of Marynia Farnham's merciful death, days of filming for a movie two admirers were making, and the prospect of losing a breast. "Remembering my mother I am convinced that cancer is psycho-somatic," she wrote Bill. "I knew last summer that no one could have to suppress so much justifiable rage and not break down either mentally or physically in some way."

Martha Wheelock's and Marita Simpson's movie crew arrived on June 1 to film May gardening, walking through the woods with Tamas and Bramble, collecting her mail at the York post office, talking about being a poet, and reading poetry. Martha was writing her dissertation on Sarton's work; Marita was a young filmmaker. "Martha and Marita have managed . . . to create an atmosphere so appreciative that I have not felt self-conscious, but able to transcend physical weight and old age, and to feel transparent and alive. I am grateful." Despite one huge blowup during the four days, May did transcend. The camera lingers lovingly on details of house and furnishings, on her strong, unlined, handsome face, then pans to shore and waves as the rich voice delivers poems like "Of Molluscs," "June Wind," and "Gestalt at Sixty." By the time the half-hour *World of Light* ends with May's response to "What do you want to be remembered for, as a writer and as a person?"—"I guess for being fully human—if I am"—viewers are enchanted by this strong, immediate, open personality. Of course the film idealizes: neighboring houses are invisible, May's daily amble looks like a genuine hike, and she seems to own, not rent, Wild Knoll. Yet the serene power May emanates is remarkable considering that she was currently depressed about her work, in despair over Dinah, and facing a mastectomy. Much of what she said in the film—particularly about Americans being afraid of feeling—was aimed at Dinah, "the insoluble enigma of which I sometimes believe I am dying."

. . .

Her doctor allowed her one last poetry reading at Camden on June 15 before removing her left breast two days later at York Hospital. "I'll go into the operation remembering your handclasp," May whispered to Dinah. "I'll spare you the banalities; they are beneath you," Dinah replied. "I felt," May told Bill, "like an abandoned child." Back at Wild Knoll, "very weak and lonely," she telephoned Dinah in a rage, then tried in writing to account for Dinah's "curious behavior" where she was concerned:

> Of course I may well be wrong . . . you may actually be a person from whom ordinary human compassion, sensibility, was simply left out at birth. I cannot believe this. What I have come to believe is that at some point at the end of our first year you became afraid of your own feelings toward me. . . . One door after another was closed against me and because you were afraid you began to punish me as the carrier of what plagued you. . . . No, you are not inadequate, darling, but you are slowly succeeding in "wasting" me and our love, what is left of it—out of fear. Fear of *yourself.* That grand being, I loved once.

May would eventually invent for herself the myth that Dinah rejected her sexually *because* of the mutilating mastectomy. "If you're the lover of somebody and they've had a mastectomy," she told her biographer, "you *have* to make love to them." But Dinah had ended that part of the relationship the previous November.

Neither of them was ready to give up, however. In October they miraculously discussed their differences calmly in York. May spent Thanksgiving in Tennessee, with only one huge blowup the last day; then travelled to Switzerland that Christmas as Dinah's guest ("great fun, a real holiday"). Obviously Dinah still valued May as a companion. And though May wanted love, she wanted "the heightened consciousness" she still experienced with Dinah more.

She rejected love that winter from a forty-five-year-old woman named Karen Saum, who, with three sons, had fled an abusive husband. May's writing, as it had for thousands of readers, turned Karen's life around. She approached May about making a video; friendship rapidly developed. That November she'd moved into May's house, where she cooked, ran errands, walked Tamas, and wrote poetry. "I feel she is my daughter," May wrote Bill. ". . . Luckily she does not attract me sexually! But I like her a lot." May was seldom attracted to younger women.

But Karen was in love with May. It shows in Karen's video *She Knew a Phoenix;* she is too love-struck to be an effective interviewer as May talks about her rocky career as a lyric poet in a nonlyric age. Only the ironic and the outrageous are admissible, says Sarton—witness Anne Sexton's popularity; "feeling" is a dirty word. As if in defiance, May actually begins to weep reading the lines "Then the boy at my side / Whom I hardly know / Said, 'The petals leave' / (As he turned to go)." Backed by Mozart and Haydn, *She Knew a Phoenix* is a loving look at Sarton by a sensitive woman deeply in love.

World of Light had premiered to an invited audience in New York that October and quickly found its way into university classrooms. May loved it; everybody did. "I certainly give my soul away in that half hour—but it is beautiful and moving and (except when gardening when I am a stout elephant) I look 'fabulous' as a friend on *Vogue* wrote me. . . . I am so grateful to Martha and Marita for making something of such substance as well as beauty." Certainly the film solidified the public's belief in Sarton as the solitary mystic, the sagacious poet. The Healer. The Wise Woman with her hands in the earth and her soul on the wind.

She felt foolish sending Eric Swenson a book of love poems, but Norton accepted *Halfway to Silence* with alacrity. *Anger* was still shelved, but on November 30, 1979, she had concluded her journal, *Recovering.* The title referred to three recent "mutilations": Dickstein's "drop of poison" in the *Times,* the failed love affair with Dinah, and the mastectomy. "I feel devalued and abandoned at the center of my being," wrote May. "I sometimes feel that everyone else manages to grow up and harden in the right way to survive, whereas I have remained a terribly vulnerable infant. When poetry is alive in me I can handle it, use it, feel worthy of being part of the universe. When I can't, as now, when the source is all silted up by pain, I think I should have been done away with at birth." Deprivation, especially of love, had made her a monster. Yet *Recovering* ends in hope: "I have been badly hurt again but I see this morning that it does not really matter because I perceive the truth. Rage is the deprived infant in me but there is also a compassionate mother in me and she will come back with her healing powers in time."

Norton advanced $18,000. Carolyn Heilbrun eventually read proof and sent "a hard letter saying it is very badly written. But she advised me not to publish *House by the Sea* so I can't get too upset. Norton thinks it is magnificent and the best of the journals. I think the first half is much less good than the second half . . . well, I can't change anything now, so why worry?"

In February 1980 she began *The Magnificent Spinster,* a novel about Anne Thorp—a challenge since Anne "never talk[ed] about her inner life and I don't know much about it." As she was working, *A Reckoning* got three fine reviews in London before the *Times Literary Supplement* branded it "Sophomoronic Sapphism": a "shock like having shit thrown in one's face," but, she decided, the reviewer's homophobia was not *her* problem.

Still very much in love, Karen Saum left March 1 to find a job. Passionate love letters followed, which May filed. That month she went to Captiva to stay with a "darling new friend" and fan, Marion Cannon; visiting Dinah on her way back, she decided again that Dinah was incapable of love. Not May: "And after two years / Without touch / The seed is still there."

Norton published *Halfway to Silence* for her sixty-eighth birthday. Undedicated, the work is nevertheless for Dinah, who had given May, halfway to muting death, poetry again. "It's a beautiful little book and is prominently displayed," said Dinah, a remark that a year ago would have blown May sky high. By June it had sold 5,000 copies and Norton was printing 6,000 more—impressive for a book of thirty-six poems, hardly reviewed.

If, as May claimed, the "holiness" of a poem depends on the quality of the experience that precedes its writing, then her love for Dinah had been quality. Some of the best poems are deceptively simple: "After All These Years," "Two Songs," "The Myths Return," "Three Things"; but the more ambitious "Lady of the Lake," "Of Molluscs," "Pruning the Orchard," and "Old Lovers at the Ballet" are equally fine. May thought "At the Black Rock" the best; yet its second stanza offers problems of prosody strange in a poet who so prided herself on form that she could "never *believe* a poem in free verse is a true poem." "Mal du Départ" is also problematic:

> After you have gone
> I walk up and down
> The strange chilling tomb
> This lively house has suddenly become.
>
> Even your white tulips
> Turn brown at the lips,

Their freshness gone,
And ashes on the hearth. I am alone.

Absence infects the air
And it is everywhere.
How can I shake off woe,
On what bed lay me down without you?

What healing sacrament
What ritual invent
And quietly perform
To bring back life and make it warm?

Another day a letter
Might tell you I am better,
The invalid has taken
Some food, is less forlorn and shaken.

But for today it's true
That I can hardly draw
A solitary breath
That does not hurt me like a little death.

The concluding lines of stanzas one, two, and six are iambic pentameter. The last line of stanza three, however, if iambic, is missing its last beat; it can be read as trochaic pentameter—awkwardly. The concluding lines of stanzas four and five are iambic tetrameter; the last line of five, beginning with a spondee, is iambic trimeter with an extra beat. Impossible to believe that Sarton could not invent six iambic pentameter lines—or a consistent and felicitous rhyme scheme. Why the irregularities from a writer who expressed her poetic ideal in "Monticello": "all given rein, / But taut within the classic form and ruled by it"?

The question of form has vexed poets and critics since Modernists tossed most of its outward conventions to the winds. Obviously, form is not a rigorous structure imposed upon a poem from without—a kind of mold into which the poet pours words. Form is inherent, the poem itself creating its structure. Perhaps all one can say is that a good poem establishes a persuasive musical pattern. Too many of Sarton's poems do not. One understands Basil de Selincourt's horror at discovering that she listened to Mozart and Haydn while she wrote poetry, instead of heeding an inner music of her own.

. . . .

She had planned to go to the Spoleto Festival again with Dinah, but when Dinah replied to a list of grievances, "just more of the same," May cancelled. "I did truly love you," she wrote in July. That month a tumor her doctor removed in his office proved malignant. May blamed the recurrence of breast cancer on her private suffering.

As she did her attacks of colitis. Apart from monumental colds and sinus problems, which never slowed her for a minute, May had been healthy—except for an intestinal tract that since early childhood had tied itself in knots during emotional stress. Often love affairs brought on attacks of colitis, or public appearances, or too many visitors—or guilt over her rage at all three. In 1969 she had landed in the Keene hospital with a severe attack of diverticulitis, during which Monica had rushed to her side. Obviously May's anxieties went to her gut. But the breast cancer she hauntedly connected with Mabel and suppressed rage—though May hardly suppressed rage.

Removal of the tumor did not stop her from giving five lectures and a poetry seminar in July, nor did nauseating radiation treatments prevent her from reading poems to one hundred Methodist ministers and their wives in August. As a young girl, May had gone to the Cambridge First Unitarian Church because the Runkles did and because she adored its famous minister, Samuel McChord Crothers. She had never forgotten a sermon with the text "Go into the inner chamber of your soul and . . . shut the door." Appropriately, May had long been the unofficial poet of Unitarians, ministers using her poems in birth, marriage, and death rites. Now her reception by the Methodists was "tremendously moving for this old non-believer," she wrote Bill. "I saw the poems work in beautiful ways." Asked whether she believed in a personal God, she said no. Nor did she call herself a Christian, not only because she didn't believe in Christ's divinity but "because I believe that to do so would require giving up all material things and literally going among the most destitute." But she felt spiritually akin to this "loving fellowship of people who are liberal, full of self-doubt, very endearing."

On leaving the conference, she went to Dinah "in a state of grace, I suppose, and when I saw her face, so innocent, innocent like a dear cow, unconscious of what she does to destroy, I just melted and we had a peaceful time and a tender night and I suppose we are back where we were except that I have become less dependent."

But they could never be back where they were. Still wretched over the relationship, May embarked on four therapy sessions with the research psychologist Laurence LeShan, who, through reading her journals, believed he could help her. May's chief problem was self-esteem: Dinah's scorn corroded her self-confidence, undermined her identity. Of course May did exactly the same to Dinah, making her feel inadequate because she could not demonstrate feeling.

Heilbrun had not liked *Recovering;* Anne Woodson said, "I fear it will get very harsh reviews"; even May admitted it "could have benefited from some editing . . . which I never get from Eric, lovable as he is." But reviews proved favorable, many readers thought it her best journal, and May's fans just wanted her to keep confiding in them. Certainly May had been more honest in *Recovering* than in *Plant Dreaming Deep* or *The House by the Sea.* There are passages of deep pain and soul-searching.

After Thanksgiving with Dinah, which, unremarkably, ended in a row, she limped back to York. She was not feeling well: X-rays discovered radiation pneumonia, a delayed effect from the August treatments, which made breathing hard and sapped her energy. She also was discouraged about her weight, all of it stomach. "I am in a strange state," she wrote Bill that December, "not Dinah, I am used to that . . . but simply that I feel I have come to the end as though I were dying. I am so weary of the endless responding, and feel so empty." She had begun to call herself Mother Pelican, feeding her followers with blood from her own breast. They were, she felt, eating her alive.

Fortunately, Karen Saum returned to stay for long weekends. Dinah had accused May of wanting only sycophants around, "but Karen and I really communicate, as I never can with [Dinah]," she told Bill. "Loving kindness is precious. I only wish I could fall in love with her as she is so in love with me . . . but one can't do that on will, alas."

Karen, though in love with May, was not blinded. She did not believe they communicated. May talked and Karen listened: "She treated me like a groupie, not a peer." May also had a positive genius for complaint, "a unique ability—chronic and destructive—to fasten on to the discomfort in a situation." One might come in radiant from having spotted three deer and May would say bleakly, "Yes, they're starving." Yet while she devastated others, she herself seemed to derive energy from complaint, anger, and destructive relationships. And the self-pity, the tears were never far under the surface. Still, Karen found great rewards in knowing May. "She allowed passion and adoration; she allowed life to flourish in all its complexity. She permitted me to be myself. And she was extraordinarily perceptive. She made the world come alive."

. . . .

It was no use collecting Judy for Christmas that year. She had been moved to Suburban Manor in Concord because her nephew Timothy Warren and May had not been satisfied with the other home. But there "was no question of happiness or unhappiness now." She didn't recognize May and tried to eat the flowers she brought, so May substituted chocolate peppermints, which Judy devoured. Hard to tell what, if anything, was left of consciousness. Before the blinds had been lowered on her mind, however, Judy had pointed out to a visitor the handsome photograph of May on her dresser and smiled. "Wasn't I lucky to have had her!"

Instead, May invited a new friend, Janice Oberacker, to stay four days over Christmas. Janice was an assistant professor of nursing at Fitchburg State College in Massachusetts who had used May's books to teach aging, dying, and death. Janice had not particularly wanted to meet May, but May wanted to meet Janice: "Be at my house at 10:45." May was waiting with Tamas and Bramble. Her face was unlined, Janice noted, her posture stoutly erect. They walked fast, May talking nonstop, occasionally shouting, "Tamas, come back here!" When they'd made the circle, "Come have sherry," she invited; "now, tell me about yourself." Soon May looked at her watch. She was due in Kennebunkport; she ushered Janice out the door. A few days later she rang Janice wanting a quarter of a cord of wood (Janice cut her own). "What time?" "Eleven." Janice delivered on the dot.

May and Karen had been "Ceres" and "Persephone"; Janice was "Rat" to May's "Old Mole." Rather soon Janice was dining with May once a week. She preferred Wild Knoll to restaurants like Dockside or the Whistling Oyster because May behaved badly in restaurants. If she was not served immediately, she would create a scene: "I'm an important person and I'm not getting the service I want!" If a fan recognized her, she was rude; if no one recognized her, incensed. A performer always, thought Janice.

Janice believed she got on better with May than most people did, a common illusion among May's friends. Janice often avoided scenes by changing the subject: May's mind ran divertibly fast. She lived, thought Janice, almost exclusively in the moment, contriving that moment like a stage manager, making things happen. After two Scotches, she was rather more spontaneous. She laughed often but had, thought Janice, no sense of humor. People were towers off which she beamed imperative tales of loves, failures, frustrations, triumphs. "Once I started counting the lovers I've had," she said, laughing richly over a bottle of Châteauneuf-du-Pape, "but I had to give up—there were too many."

To Janice, the remarkable thing about May was the voltage—so much crackling electricity that she charged you. You felt euphoric, on a spiritual high, suddenly confident you could live life on your own terms. May celebrated Christmas, however, on her terms. A big tree in the library. Crackling fires. The lighting of a huge outdoor candle. People over in twos for half-hour visits—champagne, sherry, or hot chocolate, depending. Local friends like Elizabeth Knies and George Garrett were deliberately encouraged to read poems; then May the professional knocked them flat reading hers. On Christmas Eve promptly at four Raymond Philbrook, the gardener, came with his sister. He had composed a poem for the occasion; he read with flourishes. A formal exchange of gifts— gloves, scarves. The lady of the manor having her servants in, thought Janice. After they left, a special supper. Then May read one or two of her poems, cried a little. Christmas breakfast with stockings in bed. Then Mary-Leigh and Beverly at eleven for gifts and champagne. "It was Christmas," said Janice, "but not *my* Christmas."

> Dearest [Dinah]:
> I am struggling to come to terms with something that became clear while I was there. 1) you have never been in love with me. That is the plain truth. So all your efforts were, of course, in vain, and it is an excruciating humiliation for me to think that you did on will what can only be done on feeling, for such a long time. 2) You do not like me very much as a human being. You feel *contempt*. That is poison. You are outraged by my temperament. You think the only reason I am loved is "that I listen to their woes." You are very critical and constantly flick me with mean little statements. . . . 3) You are un-interested in my work. . . . You told me you don't really like the poems. So *Plant Dreaming Deep* is left as your one real enthusiasm. . . .
>
> I have invested so much in this love that I simply cannot let it go now, though reason tells me that I ought to for your sake as well as mine. . . . I need to be with you. You do not need to be with me. . . .
>
> Promiscuity means *indiscriminate* sexual experience. I have been discriminating always. To use that word to me is so ungentlemanly that I can scarcely believe you did, even now. If that is what you think it reflects rather badly on you that you had anything to do with me . . . and I often wonder why you did. That is the real mystery.

It was not May's ultimate, nor even her penultimate, cry; but the cries were getting fainter. That January 1981, *The Magnificent Spinster* at an impasse, she returned to her novella of "hot versus cold anger and all the pain and frustration each can cause." A collapsed lung, so painful that Karen had to lift her out of bed and get her to the doctor, hardly broke her stride, made lighter by the loss of fifteen pounds achieved partly by giving up liquor, which she was surprised she didn't miss. Getting Anna's and Ned's battles down on paper in *Anger* purged the emotional pain, as writing *Recovering* had done. Many of their quarrels were hers and Dinah's: Ned wanting to cool a red-and-orange bouquet with white flowers; Anna loving the flamboyant red and orange. And the major blowup that ends with Anna and Ned barking at each other like dogs.

On February 22, May found a letter from Karen Saum on her bed saying she had left because she no longer could stand the pain of loving her. Karen had been stunned to learn that May was sailing in June on the *Queen Elizabeth II* with Janice Oberacker and spending four days at Easter with Doris Grumbach in Washington. Karen had come into May's life after Dinah; she accepted that bond. But she felt May's casual transference of intimacy to Janice devastating. "I was unbearably jealous," she confessed. "I had to leave." May was sorry to lose this "most delicate and supportive person" just when she felt she was developing "a little family of loving friends" around her. She reassured herself that she had "never led Karen on in any way."

Before sailing, May faced the "ugly and useless" fact that she owed $26,000 in back taxes in addition to 1981 installments on an income of $38,000. Fortunately, royalties earned on books copyrighted before she was sixty-five were nontaxable; next year, when she was seventy, she would receive $660 a month social security. Meanwhile, she borrowed tax money from Dinah, whom she visited on the way home from another holiday on Captiva with Marion Cannon. They sat on the floor to have drinks because the dogs on the sofas could not be disturbed. "[Dinah] is totally *given* to her new dog, . . . who is beautiful but, as usual, totally untrained and so always in the way. I suppose it is a gain that I now fully recognize that it is she not I who is the neurotic. . . . But I do love her face and her physical being." Dinah was becoming very deaf, widening the distance between them. It was a handicap with which May, the great communicator, could hardly cope.

For her sixty-ninth birthday May invited old friends one by one for lobsters and quiet talk. She had asked for a "useless" lover's present from Dinah, who usually sent toasters, blankets, and sheets. Dinah obliged with a small enamel box, but May had wanted a golden bee lapel pin, so once again she felt denied. It was Janice who came up with a pin, more appropriately a gold tiger. On May 8, May picked up another gift: an honorary doctorate from the University of Maine at Orono. The gifted poet Constance Hunting ran the Puckerbrush Press there and had published the previous December a collection of May's addresses and essays, titled *Writings on Writing*. They had a happy reunion. May had christened the delicate, blond Constance "Ariel," for once unthreatened by another poet.

For May in tourist class, the *QE II* was a flop, the once luxurious liner now a second-rate cruise ship, though Janice proved attentive and affectionate. As for Janice, she appreciated May's romantic little gestures: bringing her Scotch in the bathtub, leaving a flower on her pillow. They parted at Southampton, and May went on to Brittany to stay with her cousin Solange Sarton, a look-alike who talked even more impetuously than May. They got along so well that May admitted her lesbianism, and Solange understood perfectly. Chiefly May rejoiced in being able to speak her own violent, voluble French again. In Belgium she stayed with Jacqueline Limbosch ("a little harsh in the Limbosch way") and had long talks with Eugénie. May's latest books meant little to Eugénie, absorbed in Eastern philosophy: May's use of the word "detachment" bore no resemblance to her understanding of the term. She did not say this to May, because she was afraid of her anger; instead she listened. It rained every day.

Nevertheless, "Europe did the trick for me as it always does," May wrote Bill back at York on July 1. Immediately inundated with visitors, she still attacked *Anger* vigorously. She would go back to *The Magnificent Spinster*, which had died on her, after finishing the novella, and begin another journal next year on her seventieth birthday. But this kind of confident purpose could be shattered in a moment.

"What threw me into a night of bitter tears was dinner with Doris Grumbach the other night," she wrote Bill in August. (May's terrible outburst had left Doris aghast.)

She has the same effect on me that Muriel used to. . . . Doris simply has everything . . . 6 [*sic*] marvellous grown up daughters, one adorable grandson of ten with whom she is writing a children's book. En plus her last rather bad novel about Marilyn Monroe has been translated into 5 languages and for a huge sum to paperback. She is writing the biog of Willa Cather and 6 publishers are out to get it, and a novel about a woman poet. But the worst for me is that she has made it up with her love, Sybille . . . it made me feel like an abandoned orphan. No children, no family, and even if [Dinah] and I could make-up there is not enough there, no real exchange. Besides both Karen and Janice, my two young admirers, have each now found a lover. You can see that all this threw me into a real tailspin.

She returned to work on *Anger,* wondering whether suggested sex— the only kind she would include—would work. Then too, she didn't really know where the novel was going, which made it hard to proportion. But she had already withdrawn $5,000 from the trust; if she couldn't finish *Anger* by Christmas she'd be dead broke. On October 28 she took the manuscript to New York and waited for Eric Swenson's verdict with her intestines "in a tight knot." "Of course we'll publish," said Eric, astonished at her anxiety. But now there were the reviews to dread. Feeling desperately in need of a stiff critic, May sent the manuscript to Carolyn Heilbrun.

Unexpected bliss with Dinah in late August had not lasted. A quarrel over the "huge anarchic dogs" had ended an October visit to York: "the last straw was on the last morning when I came in to help make her bed (downstairs in the library so she could sleep with . . . the new dog) and she said 'I'll do it later' because she did not want to disturb [her]!" But of course May was angry not about making the bed, but because Dinah had slept downstairs with the dogs.

Nevertheless she spent Thanksgiving with Dinah, and Dinah came to York for Christmas for festivities that went on and on. As usual May was terribly spoiled: heaps of spring flowers delivered by Foster's Flower Shop on Christmas Eve, "too many presents" from people she didn't know. Predictably, Christmas too ended in a quarrel. According to May, the very deaf Dinah misheard something she said, flew into a rage, and refused to eat the dinner May prepared, detonating May. "It is quite absurd how angry we get!" May told Bill. One can only suppose that by now they both enjoyed the fireworks. Certainly May did. As both Monica and Karen observed, "She was addicted to rage."

May gave herself a Christmas present in 1981: she did not publish a book, a needed respite for herself, if not her readers. And Heilbrun came through with a "marvelous letter" of both "challenge and affirmation," calling *Anger* an important book which needed some rethinking. Squeamish about sex in novels, May had her mature couple conducting a long courtship without going to bed together. "Impossible in 1982!" Heilbrun also considered the ending too optimistic: May transcending again, even when experience told her that a conflict like hers and Dinah's could not be resolved. May agreed, though as for physical details of sex, "I simply cannot do it."

Unfortunately, she rushed revisions of *Anger,* and Norton rushed publication. "The salesmen made such a fuss when they heard *Anger* would not come out til '83," May told Bill, "that Eric pushed it forward and it will come out in the fall. Now I see all its faults of course, but I am relieved not to have to wait . . . now I can give it to my friends for Xmas."

That late winter she cancelled a trip to England and France with Dinah. "I found I chiefly dreaded [Dinah's] hostility and meanness too much," she wrote Bill. "Why stick your neck in a noose? I feel I have come to the end now . . . the end really of caring." The Christmas quarrel still rankled. "You had to make me angry and put me in the wrong," she wrote Dinah. "You *wanted* to ruin Christmas and you certainly succeeded. It is hard to forgive that and I have not forgiven it, and probably never will. It was in fact the last straw."

It was not quite the last straw. But May had snapped nine hundred of the one thousand threads of desire, love, envy, respect, antagonism, and masochism that had bound her to Dinah. In a sense, finishing *Anger* enabled her to let go. On her way home from Captiva in March, she stopped again in Tennessee. This time they did not share a bed even platonically. May had her breakfast on a tray in her room to avoid the always difficult breakfast hour, when Dinah didn't like to talk. Dinah gave May two luncheons, and May was quite fond of her friends. "At least I left this time feeling full of human dignity and in the clear," May told Bill. "No 'scenes,' no tears, no tenderness, no love. I suppose I feel rather relieved to have given up trying. The ball is now in her court. I am again the writer she admires and can show off."

Dinah had wanted more than showing off the writer. "I once thought of our living together," she said. "Of having a home together permanently." May's rages and tears—the "terrible scenes" Dinah came to dread—had ended that dream.

CHAPTER 24

Last Muse: 1982–1984

May's birthdays had become command performances. For her seventieth, Dinah decided to give her a magnificent dinner at the Whistling Oyster in Ogunquit. Janice was in charge of arrangements. Heide Lapirow, a lunch friend, volunteered as wine hostess. Dinah phoned every day; May phoned everyone. Dinah wanted centerpieces from Foster's; May wanted daffodils and jonquils from her own garden (May won). The guest list would include a nucleus whom May had come to think of as her "extended family": Anne Woodson, Barbara Barton, Janice Oberacker, Lee Blair, Edythe Haddaway, and Nancy Hartley—all of whom had come to May through her books.

By late April Foster's and UPS vans were plying the roads to Wild Knoll while the phone already jangled with birthday wishes. On the day itself, "Such a peaceful, windless morning here for my seventieth birthday," May recorded on the first page of the new journal. It was to be a text of triumph and hope, reflecting the spirit of her Hartford College address: "This is the best time of my life. I love being old. Because I am more myself than I have ever been. There is less conflict. I am happier, more balanced, and more powerful."

The celebration went on and on, with the dinner climaxing May's "incredible 70th." By then Janice was a nervous wreck. She knew very well May's trick of conquering by dividing her friends. But since she would be the center of attention, perhaps things would go smoothly, especially with Dinah in charge. Fourteen sat at four tables making a square, Dinah next to May. Everyone stood for the champagne toast to May except Dinah; perhaps she hadn't heard? As dinner progressed, the guests rose one by one to talk about what their first encounter with May had meant to them. Edythe Haddaway, a self-described "garden-variety friend," told how May's books had consoled her after she lost her husband; Anne Woodson remembered how a simple gift of a dozen fresh eggs had established their friendship. But May was most touched by the testimony of the sculptor Lee Blair. The heavy woman did not stand; she said shyly that she had found *Plant Dreaming Deep* in the hospital after a car crash that broke nearly every bone in her body. "May taught me all I know about love." "Most moving," May told Bill—whose gift was an elegant mist-green cashmere scarf—"because we were never lovers (I'm afraid no lover of mine would ever say that as a matter of fact!)."

Lee Blair believed the seventieth birthday party marked a turning point for May. For the first time, her friends met each other; yet May saw that she could handle them all at once. From that point on, there were gatherings.

On Janice Oberacker's fiftieth birthday, May was also the star, presenting Janice with a dachshund puppy, "Fonzi." The minute she walked into the living room, conversation ceased and all eyes focused on May. She held audiences with one guest at a time while the others waited and listened. Utterly quelled, Janice's friends slipped inconspicuously into the kitchen, where "they got tight in despair." It was, said Janice, one of the most uncomfortable evenings she ever spent.

May's birthdays also could be uncomfortable. In the years following the groundbreaking seventieth, it became customary for the six to celebrate the event with May. Each had an assigned task: Janice provided lobster rolls and took photographs, Edythe made the cake, Nancy brought the chocolate sauce. The trick was to keep focussed at all times on May. Only Nancy Hartley and Janice managed to keep cool. May terrorized Edythe Haddaway the most. "Be careful," warned Edythe, "or May will hand you your head!"

Yet the extended family remained devoted. Some had been in love with May; some were frightened of her; all tried to please. Only Janice and Nancy Hartley lived in York; the rest were in summoning distance. Edythe and Janice felt it a privilege to caretake Wild Knoll during May's many absences. Nancy pulled weeds, ran errands. Edythe gave endless presents, but then all May's friends liked to give her things. In turn May could be extremely generous: she had been paying Anne Woodson's health insurance for years; she and Dinah had given Anne and Barbara a small tractor for Deer Run Farm; she brought Janice hot soup and flowers when she was ill, and wrote her birthday poems.

The extended family kept in constant touch. May, a benevolent, exacting, dangerous spider, dominated the center of the web, alert to the slightest quiver along a filament. Yet it was a lonely position. No one really confided in May; they were too afraid of her. Instead they talked privately *about* her; she couldn't know *everything* that went on—could she? Couldn't know that her friends became each other's friends: Lee and Janice, Edythe and Nancy. These innocent subterfuges (what if May walked into the Spice of Life and found Edythe lunching with Janice!) made life adventurous, while May's tears, tantrums, and enormous needs enthralled them. There was always some imperative, some rescue. And then what fun to open the newest journal and find their names, and when May got things wrong, to exchange indignations.

Invoking exemplars of vigorous old age—Jean Dominique, Lugné-Poë, Basil de Selincourt, Eva Le Gallienne, Camille Mayran, Eleanor Blair—May had intended the new journal to reflect the perils and pleasures of arriving at seventy. Instead it became a record of invasion. "People pour in, old friends, friends of the work . . . manuscripts pour in. . . . I am now the universal grandmother, I suppose, but the suit does not fit me!" Particularly tiresome were the endless "young women and men, who don't even empty an ash tray, and expect me to be able to get endless meals, wash up, and still be the May Sarton they know through the books."

More than tiresome were women who regarded her as *their* Muse. One came for twenty-four hours bearing three journals, poems, and a novel. "This is my present to you," she said, filling May's arms. "No, it is *my* present to you to read them," corrected May. It was incredible how inconsiderate May's fans could be—how pushy and opportunistic. Of course, May could have stopped them dead with a resounding "NO!"

She escaped the swarm of visitors to give the Ware Lecture for the Unitarian-Universalist Assembly at Bowdoin College: "2000 people in a vast gymnasium, a sea of faces, but attractive ones luckily, stretched into infinity from where I stood trembling." She was pleased to be introduced as "our poet," thrilled to hear the poems ring out. She received the by now usual standing ovation, as well as the Women's Federation "Ministry to Women" award for "your courage, your honesty, and the healing power of your books." Not bad, she told Bill, "for an old lesbian." It was passing strange to be honored by religions but not by critics. "But I am happy anyway . . . and don't worry about that any longer": a clear statement that May Sarton had forfeited artistry for the "healing power," but an equally clear statement that as a lesbian—an outsider—she was hungry for approval in any form.

May's "extended family": (left to right) Edythe Haddaway, Lee Blair, Anne Woodson, May, Barbara Barton, Nancy Hartley, Janice Oberacker

In childhood her happiest moments had been making little books of poems and prose to give to friends. Nothing had changed. That September she wrapped and mailed fifty copies of *Anger* because "after all the only pleasure I get out of publishing a book is giving it to my friends." Then, "a sitting duck waiting to be shot," she braced for reviews.

Why, asked Sheila Ballantyne in the *Times,* instead of writing a novel about the stereotypical repressed male and emotional female, hadn't Sarton written a novel about women lovers? True, Sarton strongly resisted being labeled a lesbian writer, but she had also wondered in *Recovering* whether "I am after all evading a real responsibility, to write, as so many people ask me, a novel about women in love." For Ballantyne, *Anger* was "an evasion," which perhaps accounted for its facility.

May did not entirely dislike the *Times* review, because "at least I was treated with respect for a change." She could not deny that *Anger* was facile, however, because she'd admitted it herself again and again: "It is a poor work because I have failed often to concentrate on detail, to bring a

scene alive in concrete terms." Though May claimed her least favorite
novel, *Crucial Conversations,* was the only one "written to a thesis," her last
novels had been stripped down to just that—debates. With *Anger* May had
again rushed creation, not fully developing a fictional world.

Whatever its merits, she doubted whether Dinah would ever read
Anger; it didn't matter now. She managed a calm weekend with her that
September because she no longer expected anything. Dinah as usual
cooked interminably, but now she seemed to May only a rather pathetic
deaf grandmother. Was Dinah's deafness protection? "I can't stand the
noise of your anger," Kay Martin once told May: "it hurts my ears." Cer-
tainly Dinah's deafness was an insuperable barrier. May no longer could
wield her most powerful weapon, her vocal cords. Conflict was quite out
of the question. Her adversary had eluded her.

But a phoenix will rise. Elspeth (not her real name), a psychologist from
British Columbia, had written Norton for permission to quote a passage
from *Recovering.* To her surprise, May phoned her. The call led to letters in
which Elspeth, a mother and grandmother, confessed a recent failed love
affair with a woman. May had a tour that would take her to Seattle late
October and November; she now added British Columbia to her itiner-
ary. She was commanding $1,500 to $4,000 per appearance; the trip
would be lucrative as well as (she hoped) inspirational; and in fact she did
six poetry readings which turned out to be great love-ins, with fans bear-
ing flowers and books to sign. But she was dismayed when Elspeth met
her at the Victoria airport with a much younger woman.

She was also dismayed by a dinner Elspeth specially arranged for her
with George's former assistant at Harvard, Dr. Sidney Jackman. Jackman
had also known Mabel, but it was George he admired as one of the great
academic pioneers of the century. Jackman's enthusiasm for her father,
combined with her polite but uneffusive reception that day by the Uni-
versity of Victoria, roused all May's demons of insecurity. "She spoiled the
dinner," said Elspeth.

The last night of the Victoria visit, she took Elspeth out to dinner
"and fell madly in love. . . . Probably you are the only living person who
will not laugh at me . . . at 70, no less," she wrote Bill. "She came back to
the hotel and we had a long and rather loving talk. (She said it was like a
blaze of light)." That night—though Elspeth had firmly resisted May's
attempts at hand-holding—Janice Oberacker's phone rang. "I'm in love
again!" sang May triumphantly. "And there she is now 2000 miles away,"

she continued, back in York, "and in love with someone else. But perhaps the guardian angel knew what she was doing. I hate messes, and the poems are such a present . . . how can I complain?"

> Yes, I am home again, but home has changed.
> And I within this cultivated space
> That I have made my own, feel at a loss,
> Disoriented. All the safe doors
> Have come unlocked and too much light
> Has flooded every room. Where can I go?
> Not toward you three thousand miles away
> Lost in your own rich life, given me
> For an hour.

To May at seventy, the loved one had virtually been reduced to a shot of speed to the poetic vein. Elspeth functioned to focus May's energies just as well two thousand miles away and in love with someone else as she would have next door and in love with May. Elspeth herself had decidedly mixed feelings. She admired much of May's work, was flattered by her interest, and so much moved by their talk in the hotel that she had wept next day saying goodbye. But she was not in love and was uncomfortable with the pressure May immediately began applying. At the end of November she telephoned to say, "I think we should never meet."

May felt "the blood withering inside her." "Never" was a hopeless word. She argued that her parents had died in their seventies: "I want to know you before I die." She pleaded for a weekend meeting in Seattle in January. She wept, threatened. Elspeth recoiled, even when May retracted suggestions of a double bed. But the poems were not lost. "My muse is I think withdrawing," May wrote Bill, ". . . so understandable. . . . Whatever happens now meeting her lifted me out of the sterile summer and into poetry again so I can only be grateful."

For Christmas she sent friends *A Winter Garland,* regretting that the fifteen poems were "not up to the production, muse-less as they were." Edythe helped her decorate a dream of a tree. Then, on December 22 at eight a.m., Timothy Warren called to say that Judy had slipped away in her sleep that night.

Though May had prayed for Judy to die, she "simply collapsed into woe for days and could not stop crying." She felt riving guilt, but reminded herself that Judy had said again and again, "You will never know what you did for me." And it was true: May had seen her blossom those first years "like a plant in the desert that gets rain." There was to be no service, only Judy's ashes buried eventually in the family plot at Matunuck, Rhode Island, where the Matlacks summered. Poems would have to be the memorial:

Judy is dead. Judy is gone forever.

I cannot fathom that darkness, nor know
Whether the true spirit is alive again.
But what I do know is the peace of it,
And in the darkened room before dawn, I lie
Awake and let the good tears flow at last. . . .

Lee Blair came for Christmas to comfort May. Anne and Barbara cancelled Christmas Eve dinner because of flu, but sent one red rose to place under the tree in memory of Judy. Lee had carved a copy of an eighteenth-century crèche for May, which pleased her, and friends came in at intervals for champagne. Starved for quiet work time, still mourning, May looked forward to the discipline of January.

In January, May went on her annual diet to lose twenty pounds. She also went back to *The Magnificent Spinster,* a more formidable challenge. By February, bogged down with facts and records, including Anne Thorp's letters, she realized she'd stumbled into the realm of biography. "I am very bad at this kind of work," she told Bill. "I want to *create.* In the end I may have to cast aside what I have done and make it all happen on the island in her old age."

Though she couldn't write biography herself, she admired Judith Thurman's recent life of Isak Dinesen that February because she felt Thurman had dealt fairly with a very difficult woman. May, a more difficult personality than Dinesen, dreaded the thought of someone writing her life: "I know my biographer will be my enemy," she had told Bill. Now, Thurman's book gave her hope. "I have been so depressed at the way I may be massacred by a biographer that this one is encouraging . . . in fact I wish she would do mine. I wrote her a fan letter in the wild hope that she might." When Thurman did not accept, May authorized Carolyn Heilbrun to record on tape her "life and lovers (!) to be sure a biographer gets the facts right." The thought of those lovers—as well as of all the one-night stands—gave her sleepless nights: "It really frightens me to think how many people there have been."

She put aside the vexing *Magnificent Spinster* to attend Mildred Quigley's funeral on February 20. "It was a long nostalgic draught of Nelson for me . . . for now my Nelson has nearly gone. Except for the Warners and Frenches, Mildred was *it*. I expect the house will be pulled down, as it should be, as it has become an eyesore on the green." (The Quigley house was pulled down, and a fir tree planted on the site.) The funeral at Keene was awful: "The Impossible Dream" for music and a minister who talked about himself and called them "folks." But May was happy to be "part again of the only community I ever belonged to."

The poems written for "the autumn muse" had stopped when Elspeth withdrew; then May received word that Elspeth would detour from a Washington conference to York for a few days in June. Before her visit, May again set out to read poetry, in Charlotte, Boston, California, and St. Paul. Audiences no longer waited until the end to cheer, but rose in veneration when she walked onto the platform. Still, any comparison with other writers could throw her. She asked a Marin College official why the school hadn't hired a larger hall for her sold-out reading. "Too expensive," he said, "but we're hiring a big hall for Doris Lessing"—reducing May to tears.

Jean Clark Lieberman attended the reading and afterward took May to her hillside home in Mill Valley. May hadn't seen Jean often since her divorce from Hermann Field, but Shady Hill and the Cambridge High and Latin were powerful ties. Jean had copied into a black leather notebook the poems that she, Letty Field, Jean Tatlock, and May had written in their teens when they all lived life at the ultimate pitch. Reading over the poems to Anne Thorp, May resolved again to finish the novel for the woman "who had provided an intimation of what passionate love would become."

She came home to huge gardening chores, two hundred presents and letters for her seventy-first birthday, and the completing of *At Seventy*. "In spite of the pressures of what is ahead," she concluded, "—to clear my desk, sow the annuals, plant perennials, get back to the novel—I feel happy and at peace. My life at the moment is a little like a game of solitaire that is coming out. Things fall into place. The long hard work is bearing fruit, and . . . I am coming into a period of inner calm."

When Elspeth came to Wild Knoll, May was appalled to find that the Muse still wanted no intimacies. Elspeth was warily polite, saying things like "What a nice lunch, thanks so much" in crisp British tones. She refused to accompany May, Tamas, and Bramble on walks, but sunned on the terrace a good deal. She also got May to drive her to a shoe outlet in Kittery—"She *used* me," May said forever after, "to buy *boots!*" Since Elspeth wanted to be entertained, May invited Janice Oberacker for dinner: "With Janice she was coarsely self satisfied and overbearing." A restaurant lunch the next day ended in a flaring anger. "You are incapable of a good relationship with anyone!" cried Elspeth. After "48 icy hours" May drove her back to Logan. She was devastated. Why had Elspeth come? "Maybe she was terrified of *herself* rather than me," she wrote Bill. "I certainly did not pressure her in any way."

According to Elspeth, May was greedy and demanding, forcing physical caresses on her and trying to get her into bed. Elspeth found May's aggression disturbingly macho. The writer was *not* a feminist, she decided; her values were patriarchal: she must always be the dominating power. When she tried to tell May how extremely uncomfortable she felt, May exploded. Elspeth felt aggressively *used*. But the verbal pressure was greater: "You are my Muse; I've found you; you have a responsibility to respond—for me and for posterity." "The Muse is not external," said Elspeth, "she is within yourself." Enraged at the time, May would come to this view herself.

May neither forgave nor forgot Elspeth's "cruelty." "No doubt your real face is back now," she wrote her. "I never saw it." Hope that the visit might spawn a poem or two nevertheless was fulfilled:

> The muse is here, she who dazzled the air
> For months at a distance now gives her presence
> To this house, lies on the terrace wrapped
> In her own thoughts, an icy visage, silent.
> No harsh or tender word could now unblind her.
> She has chosen not to see and even not to be,
> Medusa who has frozen herself into a trance. . . .

Elspeth inspired the same image as the supremely unassailable Margaret Clapp: "I saw you once, Medusa; we were alone. / I looked you straight in the cold eye, cold." Elspeth's coldness was more hurtful, however, for May was older now, mutilated by breast surgery, certain that she could never find physical love again.

She sent the journal off to Norton June 8, feeling "it may be a little better than I feared." Summer pressures mounted: "Tim, I'm afraid I can't go with you to bury J's ashes. This month is simply overscheduled to the point of misery." At Columbus, Ohio, at the National Women's Studies Conference on June 27, the audience of one thousand rose as she walked onto the stage—"after the disaster of the muse it certainly did me good." Yet the failure with Elspeth had left her not only demoralized but "dull and lonely, and suddenly old . . . by that I mean I suppose part of a race set apart, the race of the old, as one might feel as a Black or a Jew. . . . I envy all my friends who have a partner and can say 'we' which I never can say." The appearance in the *Paris Review* that October of ten poems "for my horrible muse" cheered her only temporarily, while Elspeth's response—"I am sad I could not give you what you needed"—made her "black with rage."

Haunted by her father's sudden death, she gave up smoking and in November checked in for a physical. Her cardiogram was satisfactory, but the doctor ordered her to lose forty pounds. "Of course I'll feel better if thinner," she moaned, "but Bill, I gave up smoking after 50 years on that powerful drug two months ago and now to have to watch every bite I take is hard. I felt so deprived I cried all the way home."

Losing a mere six pounds in two weeks, she wept in the doctor's office, outraged at having stinted herself for so little result. "You must learn to grow old gracefully, May," said Dr. Lawrence Petrovich. "He should have said, 'You have to grow up first,' " teased another doctor. May managed to laugh in acknowledgment. The deprivation of food reminded her forcibly of the emotional deprivation of childhood, that land of need in which she was eternally arrested.

By the end of January 1984, she had lost fourteen pounds but was smoking again as she retackled *The Magnificent Spinster,* at Carolyn Heilbrun's suggestion changing the narrator from male to female, though she feared it was late to make such a radical change. She felt "buried alive and screaming" at the task of rewriting over two hundred pages. Her desk was a "scene of torture." Worst, the novel seemed "just plain *boring* . . . what could be worse?" It was hell, she decided, writing about a *good* woman.

Yet Anne Thorp had been no saint. May could have had some fun had she acknowledged Anne's inordinate pride in bossing Greenings Island; the conflict of her humanitarian interests and her great wealth; the disparity between her charitable largesse and (according to a niece) her penny-pinching with relatives. Or the sexual repression which May had met head on after the Grace Daly disaster. May had chosen to celebrate Anne Thorp rather than create a believable character.

In eleven years at Wild Knoll, May's hectic life had fallen into a restlessly stable pattern. A lecture tour in March or April to escape the cold Maine

spring. A stream of visitors throughout the summer; short trips. Often a lec-
ture tour in the fall. Thanksgiving with Dinah. The month of December
sacrificed on the altar of Christmas. Regional poetry readings, trips to
accept awards. January, February, and March her real working months. Her
birthday, simmering in April, boiling over in May. Work on journals or
poetry scattered across the year. The omnipresent mail, which just as often
brought "irritating requests and horrible letters from bores" as it did appre-
ciation, yet had become her reason for living. Beverly and Mary-Leigh were
used to the sight of May's Ford Escort charging down the drive. "She *had*
to get to the post office," said Mary-Leigh. "She'd go out in ten below zero,
a blizzard. Nothing would stop her from getting the mail."

This spring of 1984, "a really triumphal" lecture tour took her to San
Francisco and Bill Brown. Nervous before readings, May nevertheless
agreed to lunch with Bill and his writer friend Alice Adams, whom she
wished to meet. Bill and May arrived at the restaurant at 12:20, ten min-
utes early. To her displeasure, he did not immediately order wine. At 12:30
she insisted he call Alice; Alice had left. By the time she walked in at
12:40, May was boiling. Then Bill asked her to put out her cigarette
because Alice hated smoking. May turned on him and launched a torrent
of abuse that left him white and trembling. "I think we should leave," he
said. Alice agreed. "No," said May, "we're here and I'm hungry." For
Bill's sake, Alice was charming to May; but Bill hardly said a word.

Back in York she wrote Bill as usual, explaining that her anger sprang
from Jung's animus and was necessary for creation. Bill did not answer.
She went to New York in May to receive an honorary doctorate from
Union College; left for France June 14; returned to heat and visitors.
"Dearest Bill," she wrote August 27, "it's so very long since I've heard
from you . . . I begin to be anxious." When she got no response, she sent
him a cryptic postcard quoting Edna St. Vincent Millay's "To a Friend
Estranged from Me":

> Farewell—but fare not
> well enough to dream.
>
> You have done wisely to
> invite the night before the
> darkness came.

May's anger had thoroughly shaken Bill: "It was sinister." Now he
interpreted May's message as a suicide threat—with his silence as its cause.

May on a winter stroll with Bramble, Tamas out of view

This ploy, as he saw it, to shift blame from her behavior to his incensed him. And so after thirty-three years her confidant and "true brother" withdrew. Bill called it a rupture, not a quarrel. But it was complete.

The feminist and gay movements had brought May fame. Now she had won another large audience, the elderly. That August *At Seventy* made the *New York Times* best-seller list; by early September it had sold 24,176 copies. "Honest," "revealing," "rich in warmth, perceptiveness, reassurance," "compassionate, wise, comforting"—so went the accolades. To attack "national treasure" May Sarton had become as taboo as burning the flag. Only the *Los Angeles Times* reviewer wondered what had happened to the "passionate poet and elliptical novelist we thought we knew."

Fans didn't wonder. They lined up by the hundreds outside bookstores where she was signing, as much to see and speak with the Wise Woman as to get her autograph. Or they simply appeared. One day she answered a knock at the door. A strange man stood there holding out a thumbed and underlined copy of *At Seventy*. "May I please have your autograph?" he asked. "This book is my bible." What, she asked, had particularly moved him? "That wonderful passage," he answered promptly, " 'I think of myself not as much a survivor as a person still on her way.' "

Not all fans were so lucky. One day Sylvia Frieze met a neighbor on the road, red-faced and weeping. A fervent reader of May's journals, she had ventured to Wild Knoll to express her admiration; furious at the interruption, May had kicked her out. "I never want to see her again," wept the woman.

That November May was on her way to Belgium to observe the celebration of George Sarton's centennial: 1884–1984. May herself was unknown in Belgium, but George Sarton occupied a place in that country's cultural history. Michel Thiery, a University of Ghent professor interested in Sarton's work, was her official host. He had long been friends with the Sartons. George he considered "*so* egotistic yet impersonal, a man attached neither to places nor individuals but to scholarship," while the enigmatic Mabel was "always in the background, brittle, tall and misty, with startling blue eyes." Thiery had last seen George in December 1953 at Channing Place with May for dinner—a memorably huge ham with pineapple. There had been a lot of good talk, but Thiery had felt that George still missed Mabel. Now he conducted May through an exhibition titled "George Sarton's European Roots," and May read "My Father's Death" and "A Celebration for George Sarton" to the assembly of scholars. Since she loathed and feared science, she cannot have had a scintillating time, though Thiery's dedication was charming. She claimed she did not feel ambivalent about the honor to her father: she respected his work, strictly dividing it from the private man.

That November, too, Norton published *Letters from Maine,* her twelfth book of poems, with the ten to Elspeth as centerpiece. They were in a free, nonrhyming, discursive style new to her—a successful style. As usual, the book was hardly reviewed, though Ursula K. Le Guin eventually compared *Letters from Maine* with new volumes of poetry by Mary Jo Salter, Eve Triem, Denise Levertov, and Carolyn Kizer. *Letters from Maine* "is mostly easy going," wrote Le Guin. "The lines flow with facility and the grace of long usage, the rhymes are undemanding, one may be soothed by the conventionality . . . but look out. Sudden authority rings like sword-steel, and the clear old voice [speaks] with awful honesty."

It is instructive to compare May's Holocaust poem, "Survivors," with Levertov's "Thinking About El Salvador." "What they dreamed," writes Sarton,

> Lying on filthy mattresses
> Was to bear witness,
> To tell, to make known,
> To sanctify horror
> By bringing it into the open world
> To be cleansed and purified
> By human tears. . . .

This may be "facility and the grace of long usage"; it is also characteristically abstract as well as elevated in tone. Levertov also writes about atrocity:

> Because every day they chop heads
>   off
> I'm silent.
> In each person's head they chopped
>   off
> was a tongue,
> for each tongue they silence
> a word in my mouth
> unsays itself.

Levertov is directly involved in the horror, Sarton distanced: no matter how genuine her sympathy, Jews are "they." But, as Le Guin said, "look out," citing Sarton's poem "Letters to Myself" as an example of "power that is earned by a lifetime of using power mindfully."

That December she sent her eighteenth novel to Norton. Though she still considered *Mrs. Stevens* the most difficult she'd ever written, her struggles with *The Magnificent Spinster* had been Laocoönian. That Christmas, too, she sent to friends the poem "Absence," a lament for the great white pine outside her windows felled by a winter hurricane:

Must we lose what we love
To know how much we loved it?

It is always there now,
That absence, that awful absence.

The words were written for the lost Muse who might never come again. They were written, too, for the loss of her "true brother," the irreplaceable friend with whom she had shared her struggle with the demands of life and art for so long.

CHAPTER 25

Guardian Angel:
1985–1990

Often into the lives of the old and famous comes a young stranger. He is usually a sincere admirer or adulator. He has read all the works, knows all the paintings, has seen every movie, play, or ballet. The famous one can't help being flattered. The stranger persists. He invites himself to tea, hangs on the famous one's every word. Soon he is running errands, driving the famous one to appointments, reminding her to take her medicine. Finally, sometimes against her better judgment, the famous one takes the stranger permanently into her life. The stranger's power over the famous one grows: he fields phone calls, answers letters, vets acquaintances. Met by a wall, old friends drop away, leaving the famous one even more under the stranger's control. Eventually the now indispensable stranger acquires rights to publish manuscripts or sell paintings or film rights. Perhaps he oversees the changing of the famous one's will in his favor or becomes her executor. In exchange for this power, he is willing to take whatever abuse the famous one chooses to deal out. In retaliation he may publish a memoir. With variations, this theme has been the finale of many a celebrity's life.

In March 1979 Susan Sherman, a thirty-nine-year-old English teacher at Riverdale Country School in the Bronx, had written May a gushing letter requesting the privilege of meeting her. May received many such letters; she answered, thought no more about it; the meeting did not take place. In June 1983, however, Susan brought an elegant picnic lunch to York. May met a small, pretty, intense Jewish woman with lots of graying hair piled atop her head. Then in May 1984, Susan attended a reading in

New York, her arms laden with books for May to sign. The letter she wrote after that event was so exalted in its appreciation of the miracle of May Sarton that May telephoned her thanks. In February 1985, when May was facing the ordeal of having all but two teeth pulled, she called Susan. The warmth of that conversation starkly contrasted with a stiff letter from Dinah a few days later, defending her attachment to dogs. Then one Sunday May told Susan she'd not gotten her *New York Times.* In a dramatic gesture, Susan bought a *Times,* drove all the way to Maine, handed May the paper, and drove back to New York. Little wonder she gained a secure foothold in May's life.

Susan was a genuine friend of the work. She read everything May wrote, listened to poetry tapes in her car, taught May's work, drove miles around New England to hear her in person. She became her most devoted appreciator, on the publication of *The Magnificent Spinster* in September 1985 writing May a four-page single-spaced letter extolling the novel's depth, characterization, and ethos. Much needed appreciation, for real critics were harsh.

May had called *The Magnificent Spinster* boring—and it is. The Anne Thorp character, a curiously dated spinster who chuckles and calls people "dearie," fails utterly. Of course it took a certain courage—if not obtuseness—to glorify a Boston Brahmin in the 1980s: hard to believe that Sarton's contemporaries were not Louisa May Alcott and Laura Ingalls Wilder instead of "such edgy writers" as Jane Bowles, Carson McCullers, and Djuna Barnes. But Jane Reid chiefly fails because Sarton refused to take the plunge and invent her.

Though a brutal male world of war and politics does exist, seldom has a novel dealt more with "the world of women." Sarton's female characters don't need men, rarely think of them. A novel, then, that champions lesbianism? Not necessarily. One reviewer called *The Magnificent Spinster* "a quintessential fantasy of American breeding" in which members of the DAR would not feel out of place, and Sarton the "fairy godmother to the disenfranchised" who, with a wave of her pen, "transports the lesbian community into a WASP Kingdom of Heaven."

Too easy, in other words. Feminist sociologists have long observed that the slightest forms of marginality in poor, Jewish, Hispanic, or black women tend to be viewed as distasteful, threatening, or even pathological, whereas the same deviance in a WASP is treated as amiable eccentricity. The old-family Vassar, Unitarian, New England lesbians in a Sarton novel

May's close friend Maggie (Mrs. William) Vaughan, at her Hallowell, Maine, farm

above all, her love for May; but it was a small printing, recognized chiefly by friends. On her rainy seventy-fourth birthday "only Janice" came to share champagne and overwhelming gifts of plants and flowers, which this year May was too ill to appreciate. On May 8, Dr. Gilroy, in a re-enactment of *The Reckoning,* drained a pint of fluid from a lung so she could breathe more easily; yet two days later, after sensations of suffocation and a liver exam, May was admitted to York Hospital. Edythe dashed to York to care for Tamas and Pierrot.

May had always enjoyed hospitals. They were an envelope against intrusions, and she loved being coddled by attentive nurses. (Once she fell intensely, if briefly, in love with a particularly soothing nurse.) This time, however, she was not happy. "Why do I trust Dr. Petrovich? . . . I do not feel I am being treated as a whole person or that he has the slightest idea what it is for me not to be able to work." Her misery persisted at home when electric shocks did not get her fibrillating heart back to normal. On August 3 she was admitted to Massachusetts General's exclusive Phillips House through Janice's influence, Maggie Vaughan nearby in a motel, but her heart could not take a pacemaker. Through it all, tears, tailspins of depression, incessant demands. Doctors were all against her, didn't care how she suffered.

Yet by August 12 she was home and "myself again." Soon she was lunching everywhere and planning a fall lecture tour as antidote to "that rapid descent into real old age." By September 2 she was well enough to drive to Harwich to visit Irene Morgan.

"I have never understood," said Irene, "why May is my friend. What does she see in me? I had a modestly successful career before I retired and bought my little house—not even on the water!—but I'm just an ordinary person. But every year May drives down to spend a week or a few days with me. Of course, we live by her schedule: her work time, mealtime, naptime, bedtime. I do the cooking—the food she likes. I stock the house with her brands of liquor. She talks, I listen. She thinks we're friends, but I believe friendship involves give and take. She doesn't know me: I don't confide in her. But she's a marvellously lively person, and fun. And she sends me all her books. I don't know what I've done to deserve her attention."

Many of May's friends asked the same question, just as Eugénie had wondered why May squandered so much time on people of marginal importance. Lee Blair finally decided that May wanted control. "May weaves a magic web. If she likes you, she *seems* to devote her whole attention to you. It's a heady experience. But what she really wants is to become *all* to that person. The friend does not become all to May, but May wants to become all to the friend."

That fall when May returned from poetry readings at Dartmouth, Concord, Indianapolis, and Bloomington, Tamas wouldn't eat. The vet discovered a bone deep in his esophagus. The morning of November 6 May was waiting for Edythe to drive her to Logan for a New Mexico lecture when the vet called to say Tamas had died. May was not particularly sorry: "I think it is best for Tamas—he had seemed terribly lame these last weeks, did not want to walk, and we all knew the time was coming when he would not enjoy what had been a wonderful dog life any more." Tamas's disabilities had magnified her own. "I thought of us as two very old people—but now that I am well again I am not any longer the very old woman with a very old dog I was all spring and summer. In one way therefore his absence is a release from sorrow and anxiety." Unlike Bramble, faithful Tamas did not rate an elegy.

But she never really felt released. On December 3 she returned to the inevitable distractions of Christmas. A few days later, Barbara Barton's statue of Persephone shattered when it was blown off the garden wall—a disaster that affected May far more profoundly than news of Hannie Van Till's death. More intimations of mortality when she visited Cora DuBois, now eighty-five, in Cambridge. Cora had undergone major intestinal cancer surgery two years before, could not read for more than an hour—though May faithfully sent her everything she wrote. May found her bitter and despondent about her dependence on Jeanne Taylor. Tragically, "in some deep way" Cora had "repudiated her own life." In contrast, ninety-two-year-old Eleanor Blair, though blind, was cheerful when May visited her at "The Hive." If only she had someone to read to her regularly, sighed May.

Many of the tree ornaments had survived last year's blaze, and Edythe again helped trim the tree. Lee Blair came for the traditional Christmas Eve dinner of scalloped oysters, but May was not happy: "I kept feeling I was being buried under paper, wrapping, *things,* food. Two big dinners to cook on the *day* for Janice, Edythe, Lee and me and then yesterday for Lee, Janice, Anne and Barbara. . . . I realize the energy expended reduces even my spiritual hunger to near zero." It didn't help to realize that she was terribly spoiled yet unhappy precisely because she *was* spoiled and had to thank people endlessly. Storms of tears. "I feel unable to deal with my life," she wrote three days after Christmas, "with the too-muchness of it."

Particularly annoying were the endless books she was asked to blurb. One upset her deeply: Mary DeShazer's *Inspiring Women,* dealing with the Muse's influence upon Bogan, H.D., Adrienne Rich, Audre Lorde, and Sarton herself. The chapter on her friendship with Bogan galled her like "a drop of poison." She was sick to death of everyone, goaded by Ruth Limmer, quoting Bogan's "Cats, yes, 'kittens,' no." For one thing, May had *not* excised the "kittens." For another, she found Bogan's lordly tone unbearable. "I was *not,* as everyone now seems to believe, her acolyte. She was never a muse for me. Because at the root of our friendship there was no real generosity on her part. Always the tone was patronizing, or condescending."

The old doubts tormented her. "I am having to face at long last the unhealed wound of Bogan's attitude toward my work," she wrote the last day of 1986:

> She did not, could not, perhaps, respect it as it deserves. But does it deserve to be? . . . Bogan was an extremely good critic but could not bring herself to praise me in print—as a poet. So either

she was right and I have given my life to a crazy delusion, or she was wrong. And if she was wrong and perhaps knew she was being "mean-spirited"—one of her favorite words—then jealousy is the only explanation. Both of these possible explanations cause extreme psychic disturbance in me. At night I pace around inside my head like a caged animal who can find no rest.

It would help if the correspondence between us could at last be published. . . . But Ruth Limmer's hostility and sneering attitude toward that relationship has, so far, stood in the way. At least it is now understood in academic circles that she has chosen to do so.

Lately I have felt covered with wounds like a tattoo—everywhere I look in the past there is pain.

May had never gotten over Juliette's rejection of her, or given up hope of a reunion. They had resumed writing after Julian's death, though Juliette was reserved. The discovery of May's letters to Julian had distressed her; when May replied they should go to the Berg, Juliette finally read them and experienced "a sort of posthumous shock," though the letters were "curiously impersonal in a way." She had burned many of May's letters to her after Paris; she now asked May to return hers. May's reply that the early ones had gone to the Berg jolted her again, though May promised to burn the rest. Finally Juliette returned May's letters to Julian, begging her to let the whole painful matter rest.

Still, they had in common Julian, "our strange ghost." And May, determined to see her, continued to ply Juliette with chocolates and cases of wine. By 1986 Juliette was writing regularly, sympathetic but rather amused by May's endless complaints. *Why* did May have to travel so often, promote herself, wear herself out with people? "And why do you have to have a cardiograph to tell you to stop rushing into crowds, lecturing to crowds, listening to crowds. . . . Surely you don't *need* to work? Yes, I know. You work because it *is* life itself." She could be ironic: "How I feel for you, those interminable days of waiting waiting," she had written when May was anticipating hospitalization at Massachusetts General, "—and even cooked lobsters and champagne no uplift." May bore the digs. The really awful thing about the stroke had been that it forced May to cancel a "glittering plan" to visit Juliette in June.

Yet there was bitterness. Juliette had not mentioned May in her recent memoir, *The Leaves of the Tree,* blotting her the way Ciardi had blotted her from the Cambridge poetry meetings. When Juliette explained that she had accidentally omitted pages about May which her publisher would not add, May realized she still resented her—how better to punish an offender than excise her from your life? Still, Juliette was writing. Forty years of silence was over.

Seemingly recovered, May found no excuse to prolong *After the Stroke.* Like the others, this journal volleyed between complaint and gratitude. Its main theme, however, is guilty regret: "One reason I do not want to go back into the past, as when, after the stroke, I found myself in a maelstrom of memories, is because I am shocked that I could have loved so many people. Always when I realize this I remember Edith Kennedy saying once—not pejoratively—'You are facile emotionally.' That may be true for all I know, but it does not feel true." Bill Brown had told May that no one else he knew was so parent-haunted. But not only her parents haunted May. So much of the past was torment.

Norton kept *After the Stroke* nearly three months for copy editing, but May disliked the results: "Such a *stupid* person did it." Published early in 1988, *After the Stroke,* however, was generally treated as a classic by a classic. Readers and critics praised the indomitable Sarton's honesty and fortitude. Few noted her "angry and self-pitying resentment of friends and acquaintances who occasionally depart from whole-hearted admiration of her talents, or who fail in their utter attentiveness to her." More typical was Nancy Mairs in *The New York Times:* "Thank you, May Sarton, for the complicated joys and companionship. I've enjoyed this sojourn as much as earlier ones. I hope I'll be asked to return for another before long." At last May was getting a little respect from the *Times.*

The *Kentucky Poetry Review* devoted its spring 1988 volume to her. That spring, too, she began *The Education of Harriet Hatfield,* the story of a sixty-year-old woman who expands her horizons by opening a feminist bookstore ("She borrowed my Somerville house and neighborhood," said Morgan Mead, "though there's little resemblance"). A relapse in late May forced her to abandon the novel—"a wildly accelerated heartbeat, no pain, but one is simply out of breath and totally exhausted all the time." In late August, after the most miserably hot and humid summer in memory, she was back at her desk.

That fall Norton published a thirteenth volume of poetry, *The Silence Now.* Nineteen of the poems had been written earlier: "Letters to an Administrator" for Margaret Clapp and the "Over Troubled Waters" sonnets to Marynia Farnham. The new poems express Sarton's longing for silence, continuity, and respite from the silting clutter of life, as well as her acceptance of the Muse within herself. Predictably the political poem "AIDS" is the weakest; though genuinely concerned, Sarton is seldom inspired by social issues. A delight from the past: "The Muse as Donkey," Esmeralda as antidote to five frustrated years of adoring Margaret Clapp. "Salt Lick," a humorous warning to consuming fans:

> On some cold winter day
> I shall be licked away
> Through no deer's fault,
> There will be no more salt.

And two poems to Mabel, the mother whose death never died:

> Inside my mother's death
> I lay and could not breathe,
> Under the hollow cheekbone,
> Under the masked face,
> As if locked under stone
> In that terrible place. . . .

As usual with May's poetry, *The Silence Now* gathered few reviews. *Publishers Weekly* noted that the "clear-as-crystal diction of recent works" contrasted sharply with the conventional falcon, lute, and tower tropes of the earlier poems. "Luminous new verse . . . beautifully simple language, shorn of all artifice," applauded the reviewer, echoing praise for the "easy simple beauty of the recent poems" and Sarton's "stunning lyric style." Is it carping, then, to object in "New Year Resolve" to a simile like "To clutter my mind / Like dirty snow"? "Clutter" is a jumble of things; calling snow clutter is rather like envisioning hair or coffee as "they." Or to ask that a poem with an *a-b-c-d-c-d* rhyme scheme not break the pattern in the last stanza? Perhaps it is carping, in an age when meaning is totally personal and an ordinary sentence broken into irregular lines goes by the name poetry. Or does Sarton's irrevocably cluttered life irrevocably lead to carelessness: "I fear I am on the verge of breakdown and when I brought two friends up here yesterday who feasted the New Year with me they were appalled . . . for what they saw is miserable, out-of-control chaos . . ."?

January brought a little "clear time, clear water." But one problem refused to go away. In 1987 May had bought herself a miniature wire-haired dachshund named Grizzle, who, it soon became clear, was not innately docile like Tamas. Having neither the patience nor the energy to train a dog, May found herself locked in a battle of wills. Grizzle barked. Grizzle soiled carpets. Grizzle scratched at doors. Grizzle dug into the foundation under the plant window. Grizzle terrorized Pierrot. And the more May pleaded, wept, and threatened, the more Grizzle misbehaved. Actually, Grizzle was begging the head of her pack to lay down firm rules. But May was too old to learn new tricks.

One cold night Janice Oberacker received a frantic call: Grizzle was stuck under the house. Janice took in the situation, sawed off a piece of siding, and retrieved a shivering dog. But Janice did not believe Grizzle had "got stuck." She believed that May, furious with the dog for digging, had screamed, "All right, if you want to dig, dig!" and shoved, then panicked when she saw Grizzle trapped. Janice was glad to adopt Grizzle, as much for the dog's sake as for May's. And May was profoundly relieved: "I had her for two years and loved her, but she was too much for me, and the wild and almost continual barking got on my nerves. Tamas was a saint among dogs and I was spoiled, I guess."

The Education of Harriet Hatfield, her nineteenth and last novel, was in May's hands for her seventy-seventh birthday. "God knows whether it is any good," she wrote a friend; but publicly she was more confident: "I've wanted to do this book for a long time. . . . I have an obligation to tell the truth about myself." Unlike May, Harriet is not torn between the obligations of friendship and art, nor does her private life—thirty years' fidelity to one woman—remotely resemble the author's. In other ways they are close: genteel, snobbish, yet good-hearted older women who, conscious of privilege, wish to reach out to a broader community. Like many of Sarton's novels, this one has a mission. By making Harriet appealing and "exemplary," May hoped to persuade homophobes that lesbians are human beings much like themselves. Elementary education? Not when an estimated seventy-five percent of Americans fear or hate homosexuals.

Some critics found *Harriet Hatfield* not radical enough, the persecutions Harriet suffers too mild. Graffiti scrawled on her shop windows washes off with soap and water; stolen wood is immediately replaced; only a beloved dog is killed. Moreover, the women who come to the bookstore aren't really social misfits—witness the token black who speaks flawless English and is married to a black businessman. And the unfashionable meliorist tone baffled not a few. Novelists had for so long concerned themselves with "irremedial woes" that the *Times* critic had trouble accepting a novel "in which courage, honesty, and a spirit of community are presented as likely to solve just about everything."

A critic who chided Sarton's "repetitive language and surprisingly poor craft" did not entirely blame Sarton: "W. W. Norton, with whom Sarton has published for decades, owed this author better editorial support." Marcie Hershman, one of May's few writer friends, agreed: Norton did not serve May well. Surrounded all her life by Thorps, Taylors, Dudleys, and Huxleys, May naively gave every character in *Harriet Hatfield* a pristine WASP name. "Her editor should have caught this," said Hershman. Of course one searches in vain in *any* Sarton novel for Italians, Germans, Poles, Greeks, Hispanics, even a Scandinavian.

The Education of Harriet Hatfield succeeds, however, where *The Magnificent Spinster* failed, because Harriet is real. She smokes, likes Scotch, buys expensive shoes. Very humanly, she doesn't care to take on the personal problems of everyone who finds her or his way to her bookstore, nor does she necessarily like all her customers. She has courage and integrity and she suffers. (Having her beloved dog killed in front of her eyes is no small punishment.) And meliorist or not, many of her beliefs are sound: love is what matters, whether hetero- or homosexual. Like Sarton, Harriet wants to connect the hetero- and homosexual worlds. As one critic recognized, connecting is a lonely job. "Sarton has called herself 'a solitary.' Indeed she is because the sad, lonely fact about being a bridge is that one does not, in actuality, belong anywhere." Harriet Hatfield shares that solitude; it humanizes her.

Like Sarton, Harriet dislikes the term "lesbian" because " 'lesbian' seems primarily sexual." Her attitude not only reflects Sarton's certain knowledge of the foundation of homophobia but her own distaste for sex as well. Susan Sherman would call May "asexual"—a strange term to apply to a Doña Juana like May. But Sarton *is* curiously nonsexual. Not only is there no sex in her novels, there is very little sensuality. Her characters are intensely oral: they smoke, drink, eat, and talk—like Sarton herself. No passion, no orgasms. Obviously, sex for the philandering May was a way to possess a person, rather than sensual pleasure.

That October she flew to London to see Juliette, Edythe Haddaway her companion, and had "several hours each day of communion" with the "adorable person," now ninety-two. The topic of their love affair could not be introduced; still, according to May, Juliette was miraculously affectionate, even urging that her letters should eventually be published.

May and Susan Sherman, the "Guardian Angel"

Juliette's son Francis Huxley had a different story. "Don't leave me alone with her," Juliette begged. "She frightens me!" Francis stood guard at the tea table the first and subsequent days, until May phoned and peremptorily demanded to be alone with Juliette. It was obvious to Francis that Juliette endured rather than enjoyed the meetings, despite May's splendid gifts of food hampers and a video machine.

Back in the States, it became increasingly clear that May was not well. The strong, audience-thrilling voice had begun to crack. Her heart was weak and the side effects of heart medicine debilitating. When she tried to begin a journal that new year of 1990, she found she had great difficulty getting her thoughts down on paper: words escaped her or she mixed them up. CAT scans revealed no brain damage; doctors told her not to worry, "only your heart is very, very tired and has also lost strength in the past year." The punishing intestinal cramps continued; when the prescribed medicine blurred her mind, she relied only on Kaopectate and Tylenol. She spent days just waiting for the pain to pass. Her weight loss was frightening. On her seventy-eighth birthday, she managed to begin a journal: "It's hard to believe I am still around. . . . I am to settle, or so it seems, for a semilife, or the life of a semi-invalid."

As always, friends and employees rallied. Maggie Vaughan brought suppers of shrimp, mussels in cream sauce, and homemade strawberry sorbet.

Nancy Hartley kept May's enormous files in order and helped in the gar-
den, which Diane York managed on a professional basis. Dean Frieze did
household repairs. Karen Kozlowski, a young friend living in York Beach,
ran errands and tackled chaos indoors. Andrea Rioux catered dinner three
times a week (lamb stew was May's favorite), did dishes and the wash.
Since May was too weak to type, Deborah Pease sent a tape recorder and
cassettes so she could experiment talking the journal. Eleanor Perkins, who
cleaned for May (and resented her condescension in the journals), put in
extra hours. Mary-Leigh had trees pruned so that she could keep an eye on
May's house and garage.

But chiefly it was Susan: Susan who sent extravagant sprays of white
orchids, who stood in for May when she received a thirteenth honorary
degree, who drove up weekends from the Bronx, who made little collec-
tions of May's writings about Judy or Mabel or cats and presented them
on anniversaries; Susan who almost tamed Pierrot, who trained her white
poodle, Cybèle, not to bark, and went about the house on tiptoe, who
concocted wonderful meals. May was not in love with Susan, but Susan
was intoxicated with May.

Meanwhile, she had been working with the large cache of May's
papers. May didn't want a biography before her death, but she gave Susan
permission to edit her letters in many volumes, creating a biography with-
out interpretation, "which is what I fear." With thousands of letters avail-
able—a fourteen-inch stack to her parents alone—Susan would be
occupied for years to come. Working on the letters meant that Susan
knew more about May than May herself did, that she was intimate in a
way no other friend could be.

So it was Susan who, one autumn weekend at Wild Knoll, saw that
May was very sick. She had lost fifty pounds. She had cancer of the lining
of the lung. A doctor had recently drained six hundred cubic centimeters
of liquid from her chest. Her color was terrible. "I think I am dying,"
May had told Dr. Petrovich, who answered, "You probably are." Susan
took a bold step. Taking a leave from the Riverdale Country School, she
moved into Wild Knoll in November. "I don't want her to come," May
told Maggie Vaughan, but for once someone else's will was stronger than
her own. Besides, the prospect of someone completely at her beck and call
was irresistible.

May's doctors had given her three years; May's friends, a year at most.
Except Susan. Susan vowed to make May well.

CHAPTER 26

Dying, and Beyond
1991–1995

And May seemed to get better. Thanks to Susan, every day on the good ship *Susan-May* seemed a step toward recovery. Each day Susan helped her walk a little farther across the room. She catered to her treacherous digestion, concocting endless varieties of digestible soups and purees. She filled the house with flowers, answered the telephone, watered plants, ran errands. She persuaded May to buy a VCR so they could watch movies together. She was completely and abandonedly at May's service. "The time Susan and I spent together through Thanksgiving and Christmas and into late January knitted us into the most subtle, loving friendship I have ever experienced," said May.

While some friends distrusted Susan's motives, none thought May appreciated Susan's services. Lee Blair had watched May change from an independent woman to an exploiter. "May shamelessly uses people like Edythe Haddaway, Nancy Hartley, and Susan Sherman. I suppose it's inevitable now that she's old; but still, she *uses*." Mary-Leigh agreed: the more Susan gave, the more May expected. And May was not grateful. "Susan," she could tell her biographer in 1992, "is not one of my favorite people."

The relationship seemed sadomasochistic: May exacting and punitive, Susan submissive. But May, who needed to be in control, was afraid of Susan's power and constantly fought to "take charge of her own life again." At the same time she had become dependent on Susan. Susan made the York house a home. And Susan had vowed to stay with her the rest of her life.

Inevitably May's old extended family felt squeezed out. Lee Blair had taken a great deal of cruelty from May about her weight: "I don't have enough chairs to give you two," May once taunted her. But Lee stuck until May told her not to come for her seventy-eighth birthday because Susan was there. After Lee moved to New Mexico, they talked occasionally on the phone; May would blow up, then call back and apologize. But their friendship had changed irrevocably. "You can glue a broken teacup back together," said Lee. "But it's never the same teacup."

Anne Woodson, May's closest friend, felt a barrier between them. Though still May's secretary, Nancy Hartley had to admit Susan was chief caretaker now. Edythe Haddaway found her usefulness diminished, though because she and Susan became friends (secretly, of course), she at least had the satisfaction of hearing Susan complain about May. And Susan had a hell of a lot to complain about: May betrayed her private concerns, verbally attacked and belittled her. Rejected by her parents, May compulsively punished those who dared love her.

Janice Oberacker felt totally excluded. "Susan changed May. May was not there for her extended family after Susan; it was as though she shifted into a new era. I had to realize that our friendship was over. Curiously, I don't think May had any concept that she hurt me. People didn't mean much to her. It was as though she was emotionally castrated."

Maggie Vaughan stuck. She continued to drive to York, bringing eggs from her hens, wine jellies, and chicken broth as well as companionship and love. And May telephoned her every day. But Maggie never overlapped with Susan. If Maggie came for an hour when Susan was in residence, Susan disappeared on errands. They were enemies.

"I'll enjoy resuming my solitude after these months of precious companionship and care," said May, though Susan's return to teaching in January 1991 brought on a particularly excruciating attack of diverticulitis. But she was not the old May Sarton. Her 175 pounds had shrunk to 94. Unlined even in her seventies, her haggard face now curiously resembled that of the sharp-featured young May. Her voice was a croak. She could climb two flights of stairs to her study, little more. Dr. Petrovich had pronounced himself pleased with her heart; Dr. Gilroy was satisfied that medicine seemed to be drying up the lining of the lung. Still, when she had her lung drained for the fourth time on January 28—"*hideously painful*"—she wept and felt sure she was dying. Irritable bowel syndrome tortured her relentlessly.

May at her desk, with Pierrot

Theoretically May welcomed solitude after Susan's departure; in reality she needed more people more of the time. Besides Eleanor Perkins, Diane York, and the indispensable Nancy Hartley, she had a great number of helpers, paid and unpaid, coming in and out to wait on her—Joan Pavuk, Andrea Rioux, Nadine Wheeler, Karen Kozlowski. But she did not appreciate unscheduled assistance. One day a fan interrupted her nap. "I'm Helena," said the stranger. "This is not a visit. I just brought you a few things." May went to pieces. "Well, she was there half an hour, and in that time she disposed of a *ton* of food. She *invaded* the refrigerator and *planted* I don't know what—several meals there and innumerable other things, among them cheesecake, which I don't like, and she left twenty pounds of birdseed in the hall. I only give the birds hearts of sunflower seed, because the shells of regular wild bird seed make such a mess under the bird feeder." The intrusion left her feeling "a *prey* to anybody who builds up this kind of obsession, for that's what it is. . . . My whole intestinal tract was tied into a knot. I've been in pain ever since."

Feeling "abandoned by the doctors," she had sought the help of a holistic doctor, Ferida Khanjani, who recommended rice and vegetables to combat diverticulitis. May saw Khanjani twice a week, benefiting more from the attention than from the diet, which she constantly broke. By the end of April she was venturing out of the house, something she would not have dared in March. And she'd managed to keep the journal going.

Since her life had become circumscribed, the new journal clicked the old beads: arriving in the States as a refugee, sent to camp by George without a change of clothes, leading the Apprentices, discovering her sexual bias in Paris, making her only home with Judy, reading Ciardi's cruelty in *The Nation*. Again she chanted the talismanic names: Woolf, Koteliansky, de Selincourt, Bowen, Lugné-Poë, Huxley. (To Cora DuBois's death in April 1991 she was indifferent, though two months later Eva Le Gallienne's touched her.)

Yet despite illness and old age, she reacted strongly to the present. Her political views might be liberal clichés, as one critic claimed, but she responded feelingly to Nelson Mandela's American visit, starving children in the Sudan, global pollution, domestic violence, Iraq's invasion of Kuwait. She was also extremely generous with blurbs for current authors—too generous in some cases. And the VCR had been an inspiration. May always hated going to movies alone; now she could watch *Moonstruck, The Whales of August,* and *Victor/Victoria* with Susan—and critique them in the journal. Still, May's topic is always May. *Endgame,* begun and ended on May 3, the solar day in her universe, is studded with references to her own work. And the year had brought professional rewards, among them French and Japanese translations. The Japanese, her publisher Misuzu told her, were particularly fond of *Journal of a Solitude.*

Was she finally, then, a success?

I'm read by people from ten years old to ninety. . . . At this very moment somebody is discovering me in a public library. . . . One proof of success is if, at nearly eighty, the author is still being discovered, as I am. Another sign is whether the books stay in print. My first novel is now just out in paperback—*The Single Hound. . . .* I don't think there are many writers—serious writers—who make as much money as I do . . . the royalties have amounted to more than fifty thousand dollars a year. . . . If somebody asked me now if you consider yourself a success I would say: Yes, I do, although I'm not a best-seller, never have been, and never will be.

And yet . . . She was not in the major anthologies; inclusion—admittedly a political game—signalled a poet's stature. No major American critic had ever been on her side. She had never won a major literary prize.

She had been snubbed or ignored by the (problematic) literary establishment. These were the haunting failures.

When *Endgame* was published for her eightieth birthday, she could not complain of her press. And fan mail, as usual, poured in. But the literary quality of this dictated journal—as May knew—was poor. Lame structures: "I'm waiting now for Maggie Vaughan, who is coming at eleven for a little talk and to see me." Illogical connections: "Of course, it's been an exhausting afternoon, because they brought the new refrigerator and Mary-Leigh came with the men, and she could not have been kinder." Incoherence: "[Amanda Cross] seems to me to have neatly escaped a very hard thing that she suggested in the book itself was going to be done, was going to happen."

Norton had undertaken to publish *Endgame* by their golden goose. They knew she was barely able to whisper into a tape recorder. *They owed her editing*—now more than ever. Did May's temper discourage Norton from editing her manuscripts? Though Eric Swenson rode out the inevitable "squalls" with equanimity, others at the publishing house found her very difficult. In this sense, she may have been her own undoing. And then Norton reckoned that May's fans were loyal no matter what.

Most, but not all. Not a few university professors who taught Sarton saw *Endgame* as a black mark against her reputation. Many readers shook their heads. "Even devoted fans must tire of such preoccupation with bowels," mused a friend, a remark echoed by another jaded reader: "May Sarton—lobsters and loneliness, diverticulitis and champagne." Sarton, some felt, had joined the Writers of Whine—authors who make financial hay out of their bouts with cancer, multiple sclerosis, alcoholism, manic-depression, or memories of childhood abuse.

In "When Bad Things Happen to Good Writers," Nancy Mairs defended May in the *Times,* arguing that any woman writer who dares air problems invites hostility merely by violating the tradition of female public silence. But Mairs ignores something fundamental. Bad things have *always* happened to good writers. Good writers have turned those bad things into "Ode on Melancholy," *Villette, David Copperfield, The Voyage Out, Of Human Bondage,* "The Lost Son," *The Glass Menagerie, The Country Girls.* The crucial point is whether bad things are transmuted into art. There is no argument when Mairs writes, "As Ms. Sarton's health has failed, infirmity has emerged, gradually and naturally, as a major theme in her work, and in this process she communicates a harsh lesson: aging is the one disaster that, if we escape all other, will claim us in the end." The point is, Is *Endgame* literature? It is not.

The point is also that Sarton could not stop writing. *Endgame* was not the end of the game after all. On May 5, 1991, she began a seventh journal, *Encore.* "It is the second day of my eightieth year. . . . I want to go on for a while longer discovering what is really happening to me by keeping a journal."

That same month, I wrote May Sarton a letter. For my fifth biography, I thought it would be interesting to work with a living writer, much of whose work I admired. Would Sarton consider me as a biographer?

"Dear Margot Peters," May replied on a postcard in purple ink in a minuscule hand, "You are not the first and won't be the last to ask this question. I hope the biog will only be written after my death. There are several books of letters, a new journal still to come out. I'd rather be buried *after* the death." Still, she gave me her phone number. "Give me a ring . . . *not* after 8 p.m. I've been very ill and writing is next to impossible. . . ."

The following September Sarton stood at the gate of Wild Knoll. "I am too old," she said immediately. Expecting the robust Sarton of the film *World of Light,* I was shocked to find a gaunt old woman who hardly reached my shoulder and spoke in a cracked whisper. The smart pants suit, bright silk scarf, and red lipstick only emphasized the cruel diminishment. May invited me in, offered iced tea with ginger ale, "the way my mother always served it," and waved me into a seat facing the bright sea.

"What," she asked, "do you think of Anaïs Nin?"

"A narcissist," I said. "I distrust the diaries."

Sarton vehemently agreed. "I have been reading a life of Piaf," she said, passing English biscuits. "Now there is truly a *monstre sacré.*"

"Yes," I agreed. "And surely they are the most fascinating subjects."

Still, May had reservations. She had little strength for the inevitable interviews. She dreaded raking up the painful past. And I was, after all, an unknown quantity. Yet there were decided compensations. She might be able to control interpretation, "which is what I fear." And a biographer sealed the success she hoped she'd at last achieved. But most of all, a biographer would satisfy her deep craving for undivided attention. After consulting with Carolyn Heilbrun, her literary executor, May took the plunge, agreeing to my stipulation that the biography appear only after her death. She fully intended, however, to read it before that date.

What she dreaded happened. There were questions. "All I ask of life now I can't have, a little time to live in peace and look at flowers and be in touch with old friends and with myself NOW," she cried. "Instead I am being asked every day to resurrect the past and it is making me very ill. So ill that my only hope now is to be allowed to die." It wasn't only me: other biographers pressed her for reminiscences of Le Gallienne, Muriel Rukeyser, H.D. May did provide me with a list of people to interview, however. "Does she have any idea of what a Pandora's box she's opening, giving you these names?!" exclaimed Joy Greene Sweet—a question I often pondered.

Then after reading hundreds of letters from May to her parents, I spoke of George and Mabel as "they." Explosion.

> I want to get something straight right away. Never in relation to me lump my parents together as "they." My relation with my father is still an open wound. . . . The spiritual discipline, the slow agonizing coming to terms with the violence of my feelings, the hatred and livid anger I still sometimes feel have been extremely costly, but I grew little by little to accept my father—*NEVER* as a human being though. Your letter brought it all back. You have to realize how dangerous all this is when you smugly say "biographers have to ask questions." Yes, when they have command of the material and the facts. You don't after a few months work.

She signed herself, "Your ornery May."

"Dear ornery May," I replied injudiciously, ". . . Boswell spent 285 days with Dr. Johnson over a period of 25 years, frequently making a damned nuisance of himself. You will not have to put up with me for 25 years or 285 days, but I'm bound to be a damned nuisance some of the time. Still, I hope we will have patience with each other and believe in the thing we're doing."

It was not the right tack. "When someone tells you they risk nervous breakdown and you say they are ornery, it is such a merciless comment that of course it makes me shut up like a clam," May fired back. "One more such statements [sic] and you will have lost me as a source. I am a free woman. I am not your slave." Her fear seemed to be realized: she was losing control. Her life was in someone else's hands.

But she had more than a biographer to think about. Far from well, she had nevertheless determined to fly to London. Juliette's letters had grown infrequent after 1986. May accused her of coldness, not realizing that Juliette in her nineties was losing her memory. When May telephoned, however, Juliette was warm. She could not lose this absolving friend. Now she asked Maggie Vaughan to accompany her for ten days in March. She packed an arsenal of pills and medications and Maggie wheeled her onto the plane.

The trip would have killed a less determined person than May. After hours of delay on the ground, the plane had to turn back over the Atlantic with hydraulic problems, and the passengers were put up at the Hilton. This setback, however, was nothing to the shock of discovering Juliette's old lover, Alan Best, in the garden when she arrived at 31 Pond Street. May had counted on finding the adored one alone, as Juliette knew. For two frustrating hours, Alan holding her hand, Juliette distributed her attention between her two swains. But what a novella it would make, thought May, appreciating the ironies: three old lovers meeting in a London garden. If she only had the strength to write it!

The celebration of May's eightieth birthday had long been in the works. Susan had conceived the idea of collecting tributes from friends, colleagues, and admirers; Deborah Pease paid for the publication of *Forward Into the Past*. (When May told Deborah the previous year she was worried about medical expenses, Deborah had immediately sent her $10,000.) Susan was excited but apprehensive. Would May be furious that she had secretly invaded her life?

May was enchanted with the leatherbound volume. Norman Lloyd, Burgess Meredith, and her former lover Irene Sharaff had contributed. Gwendolyn Brooks, Madeleine L'Engle, Doris Grumbach, Susan Kenny, Marge Piercy, Constance Hunting, Deborah Pease, Anne Tyler, and Richard Wilbur said graceful things. Her editor, her agent, her literary executor, and her biographer were represented. And many more—including Bill Brown. His tribute to her as a spiritual gardener broke a silence of more than seven years.

Inevitably, she was most delighted by an accolade that reminded her of the magical London years. "You an old woman?" wrote Sir John Summerson:

> I can't see you so
> For me you are a nymph in search of love
> Striding down Gower Street on your way to meet
> Your satyr-lover in his Bloomsbury grove.
> Striding and loving still? I guess you are. . . .

The momentous eightieth birthday was also marked by the publication of *Endgame* and *Coming Into Eighty*, a collection of twelve new poems, many of them in a succinct line new to Sarton's style. "Renascence" celebrates the return of poetry:

> For two years
> The great cat,
> Imagination,
> Slept on.
>
> Then suddenly
> The other day
> What had lain dormant
> Woke to a shower,
> A proliferation of images. . . .

Yet the mood of *Coming Into Eighty* is by no means unclouded. Though the volume is dedicated "to Susan Sherman, the guardian angel," no amount of love and attention could comfort orphan May. The volume ends with "Melancholy"—Sarton "no one's mother, no one's child . . . never able to say 'we.' "

The great eightieth culminated with a three-day symposium of scholarly papers and lectures sponsored by Westbrook College in Portland, Maine, with Carolyn Heilbrun and the feminist scholar Sandra Gilbert as keynote speakers. May would attend only the morning of the last day, her poetry reading the highlight of the conference. Worried about her vocal cords, she consulted a specialist and performed exercises.

The morning of June 13 May arrived early, leaning on Susan. As she made her way from the parking lot across the grass to the auditorium, admirers surged about her, hailing her, snapping photographs. "I can't believe it," cried more than one ecstatic fan, "May Sarton in person!" Understandably, May wanted to get the feel of the stage and the microphone; yet by arriving early she forced herself to exercise the problematic voice in greeting dozens of people. The usual energy drain, the usual compensations.

Bent and frail in a navy pants suit and bright scarf, her stiff, curly white hair a halo, she took the podium while Susan shot photographs wildly and the capacity audience stood applauding in homage. May had not read poems for an audience for two years. Though no longer golden, her voice did not betray her. In fact she read fifteen minutes longer than she had intended, ending with a paean to the "burning sprite" of poetic voice which miraculously "gives tongue, gives tongue!" At the finish the audience rose again with a great, sustained roar of applause.

May had ordered a limousine and asked me to make a luncheon reservation at a favorite restaurant, Roma; but Roma was closed on Saturday, and I had chosen a seafood place on the waterfront. "Will you tell her?" I asked Susan. "*You* tell her," said Susan; "you don't have to live with her all summer."

At the restaurant, Sarton chose a window seat. "Let's have a drink!" She ordered a whiskey sour. When I asked for a gin gimlet, she nodded approvingly: "Elizabeth Bowen used to drink gimlets." Over the lobster salad, May interrupted Carolyn Heilbrun, who had been chatting with Sandra Gilbert: "General conversation only, please!" "But May," said Heilbrun guilelessly, "surely it's all right. We were talking about *you*." At one point, I turned to ask Susan a question. Her eyes locked on May, Susan shook her head mutely. Despite May's obviously beneficent mood I felt tension, as though we were each performing solo for an extremely exacting director.

"The best thing about the Westbrook conference . . . was all these dear friends of the work having a chance to meet each other," May wrote Dinah that summer. "I gave a champagne party here the next day for 25 and it was lovely to see how much they had to say to each other."

And now it would seem as though May had at last come into her own. Norton would publish the *Collected Poems* in 1993 as well as a collection of writings, *May Sarton: Among the Usual Days.* Two collections of critical essays were due in 1992 and 1993: *That Great Sanity* and *A House of Gathering.* Constance Hunting's Puckerbrush Press planned *A Celebration for May Sarton,* papers from the Westbrook conference. Attention, attention was being paid.

In the midst of current triumphs, however, the past exerted a stronger pull. That September Barbara Runkle Hawthorne died. At the service at the First Unitarian Church in Cambridge, May read the poem she had composed in memoriam. For many years they had seldom met, yet

> Without writing letters
> We kept in touch.
> I knew I would call
> If you were dying
> "Is that one dying?
> This one will come."

> We would talk Oyghee
> One last time.
> But no one told me.
> And now there is no ending,
> But wherever I am, you are.

That same month May flew again to London to see Juliette, finding her vague and needing constant care. She seemed to have forgotten Julian, even May; then the sun would break through and she'd pat her cheek, saying nice things like "You're so kind" and "I love you." When Francis Huxley worried that there was not enough money to keep his mother at Pond Street much longer, May wrote a check for $10,000; told of May's munificence, Juliette did not respond. In solo encounters with Francis these years, May spoke triumphantly of getting Juliette to open to her, "as though," thought Francis, "this justified her life." Appreciating her generosity, Francis could not ignore something obsessive in May's pursuit of Juliette. Nor had Juliette been able to ignore it.

She was making more money than ever—$100,000 in a good year, and still giving a great deal of it away. $1,000 annually for Anne Woodson's insurance as well as $400 at Christmas and birthdays. More than $6,000 to the Warners over the years. $600 a year to Susan Atherton, "an eccentric poet." $8,000 for a new truck to Jamey Hawkins, a down-on-her-luck epileptic working with retarded people; hundreds of dollars besides ("I never counted"). $2,000 to Eleanor Perkins. To Catherine Claytor: $750 "because she has no job." Fifty pounds each at Christmas and birthdays to her English cousins Alan, Janet, Isobel, and May. Two or three hundred every year to her British actress friend, Pat Keen. $1,000 to an artist friend, Betty Voelker. And generous birthday checks to countless friends. "It's such a happy thing for me to be able to do this."

Friends voluntarily became minions. May met Margaret Whalen and Barbara Martin when Margaret asked her to autograph Barbara's Sarton books. Though Barbara was the fan, she was wary, even afraid, of May, who quickly discovered, however, that Margaret was infinitely patient and generous. Soon Margaret was delivering May's *Times* on snowy Sundays. In December, May phoned Margaret with the flu.

"I don't know what I can eat."

"Why don't you try some chicken soup?"

"That would be nice, honey, but you see, I don't have any."

Margaret made and delivered chicken soup.

Soon Margaret and Barbara were inviting May to dinner regularly. May would telephone her menu choices: steamed clams, fresh salmon, lobster. Usually she brought the wine. She and Margaret drank Scotch sours: "Martinis are evil for me." Unflappable, Margaret was quite aware May used her, but didn't mind. She found May lively, great fun, and inspiring.

May's menus seldom conformed to Dr. Khanjani's prescribed diet, resulting in a contentious doctor-patient relationship. One day that winter, according to May, she went to Khanjani with the flu in bitter cold only to be told, "I won't treat you today." May burst into tears and recriminations, then suddenly lay down on the floor and curled up in a fetal position. "I was thinking of wolves, when two males fight and the weaker one bows in surrender so he won't be killed. She is a domineering tyrant. You know the Iranian temper." If Khanjani refused to treat May that day, it was probably because she had again broken her holistic diet. But May was through with Khanjani since the diverticulitis seemed cured.

In March 1993 May returned to London—to see Juliette, of course, but also to read poems in connection with the Women's Press publication of *Halfway to Silence*. Again Maggie Vaughan wheeled her onto the plane. On the flight May lost control of her speech for about twenty minutes. Maggie guessed that she had suffered a TIA—transient ischemic attack— not a stroke, which May dreaded. But May was not comforted: What if she had a TIA while reading poetry?

She read successfully to an audience of two hundred, but had to cancel theatre and concert dates with her cousin Alan Eastaugh because of an attack of indigestion at a restaurant so severe that she doubted she could make it to her hotel alive. Then when she was with Juliette the last day, she again lost verbal control, though she managed to make Francis understand what was happening. Above practical cares, Juliette smiled beneficently.

May insisted on going through five promised interviews with her biographer on her return, though she knew she should see a doctor and have a CAT scan. "*Why?*" I asked Eleanor Perkins when I saw that May was exhausted. "She so desperately needs the attention," said Perkins. "She can't get enough, ever. Some days when things go wrong, she cries, 'Nobody cares about me. I want my mother!' She has such terribly low self-esteem. It's sick, really." Yet I admired the grit.

A CAT scan revealed that May had had another stroke, probably at Christmas, when she'd felt weak and disoriented. This did not stop her reading poetry as "an American Icon" to an audience of three hundred at Harvard on April 18 for a New England Poetry Club benefit, but in May she was back in York Hospital, dizzy, unable to keep food down—perhaps a reaction to tranquillizers that she was taking because she lived in terror of another stroke.

When Margaret Whalen visited her, May looked small and frail in the white hospital bed and complained that the toast was soggy. "Hospital toast is *always* soggy," Margaret comforted. Two weeks later they were dining on Scotch sours and steamed clams; two weeks after that May was back in the hospital with pneumonia. For seven years her life had been a battle of will against illness. Illness had gotten the whip hand.

Though she was too tired to write the novella about old lovers in a garden, she had managed to finish *Encore* and had enough fight to be furious with a "mean" notice in *The Women's Review of Books* comparing it unfavorably with Doris Grumbach's memoir *Extra Innings. Encore,* wrote the reviewer, made her realize how small May Sarton's world had grown, how empty at its center: "In the end I was left with a poignant sense of having witnessed a ceremony arranged by Sarton as a commemorative tribute to Sarton, from which the real May Sarton . . . is inexplicably absent."

Comparative reviews aren't fun for the loser; but May's extreme reaction to a minor critic's strictures underlined a vulnerability that eighty-one years had done nothing to diminish. Responding to her dismay, Doris Grumbach and Deborah Pease wrote protesting letters to the *Review,* as did May herself. But nothing diminished the blow, not even hundreds of letters from appreciative readers telling her how much they adored the latest journal.

Norton's publication of the *Collected Poems* bitterly disappointed May that year, beginning with Richard Eberhart's refusal to blurb the book. With this summarizing publication of her poetry, she had hoped at last for critical recognition, even for awards honoring a lifetime's achievement. But though she won *Poetry's* Levinson Prize, it was not, could never be, enough. "I want to die now," she said two days before Christmas—no longer a nightmare, simply because she lacked the strength. "There's no use going on. *Three books out this year—and nothing!*"

Friends were used to May's "I'm sick, I'm dying, I wish I were dead." Few believed her; she had risen from defeat again and again. But though

May did not want to die, she did want life on her own terms—wellness. Dissatisfied with "It's only old age," she continued to search for the magic cure, adding oncologists, gynecologists, and neurologists to cardiologists and pulmonologists. She started taking Prozac for depression, even went into analysis attempting to deal with her terror of illness, old age, and death. In objective moments, she appreciated the irony: the Grand Old Wise Woman—unable in her own life to deal with old age and failing health.

At last she found a doctor who levelled with her. She had gone to Dr. Patricia Locuratolo for a numb left arm, which Locuratolo diagnosed as burned nerve ends from radiation treatments nine years before. But Locuratolo went further, making her feel with her hands what strokes had done to her brain—"Fortunately, you had a lot more brains than most people to begin with!" Faced with frankness, May asked the big question: "Must I accept the fact that I will never be well again?"

"Yes," said Dr. Locuratolo.

She finally heard what she had denied and no other doctor dared tell her. Not that she buckled immediately. She was dictating still another journal, *At Eighty-two*. She was struggling with an introduction and connecting narrative to her letters to Juliette, for which Norton had advanced $15,000. She went out for lobster lunches with friends. But failing neurological functions made it difficult for her to organize herself mentally. She began to lose her wallet, forget lunch dates, drive erratically. "She's *dangerous*," said Maggie Vaughan after a visit. And she really couldn't write anymore, giving up Norton's suggestion of a book about her cat, Pierrot. After the thousands of letters she had pounded on her typewriter, fans now received printed cards of acknowledgment. A May Sarton who could no longer write was not too long for the world.

The Saturday before Easter, 1994, a Foster's delivery man found May on the floor. When he helped her up, she insisted on putting the flowers in water, then climbed the stairs to her bedroom to call Maggie before she lay down. Furious because her lifeline wouldn't stop beeping, she yanked the wires out of the wall. That alerted York Hospital, who alerted Beverly Hallam. Beverly and Mary-Leigh found May frothing, her false teeth half out of her mouth. She refused an ambulance: "Maggie is coming." When they finally got her to the hospital, May was told she'd had a TIA; in fact it was another stroke. She hugged the floppy rabbit Maggie brought her and pressed the nurses' call button often.

On April 5 she went home, weak and on the blood thinner Coumadin to prevent another stroke. Though her left eye drooped, her mouth was back in place: again she had survived. Quite soon she was dining with friends and wrestling with the Juliette letters. The current journal was easier; her new secretary, Judy Harrison, had already typed several hundred pages from her dictation. But she felt terribly weak and alone and insisted she was dying. "I'm May Sarton," she told everyone, "and I'm taking care of a very sick old woman." She could not equate the two. Karen Kozlowski, who took her grocery shopping and to the outlets at Kittery, thought she would not last the year.

Once she'd feared she was losing her life to her biographer, though she'd come to look forward to the interviews. Now she felt she'd lost Susan Sherman, ironically through Susan's Sarton work. Her time absorbed by the *Collected Letters,* Susan came to York far less frequently. When she did come, it was hard for May to wake her early, ask her to help with the journal or go for mail when Susan claimed she'd been up till three a.m. slaving on the manuscript. Nowadays she felt oddly exhausted, rather than refreshed, by Susan's visits. Their quarrels shook the house.

She clung to thoughts of Juliette, since Sir John Summerson's death in 1992 the surviving god of her pantheon; she planned another trip to London in November. The day she phoned Juliette to say she was coming, Juliette had a stroke. Though it seemed she might recover, she slipped into a coma and died the last week of September. Lady Huxley was ninety-six.

"Juliette came absolutely toward me at the end," May insisted. Then permission to include five of Juliette's letters in the Norton volume forced her to re-evaluate. Juliette's strictures leapt out of the page; once more she fought them.

"One book a year is too many." ("There's nothing I've ever published I regretted! And there were five years between the poems. I never published a book of poems every year.")

"Why do you have to have a cardiograph to tell you to stop rushing into crowds, lecturing to crowds, listening to crowds?" ("What you don't understand is the *pleasure* I get from the readings! Something transcendent happens when I come on stage. I feel the poems work, I see how they move people!")

"How I feel for you, an invalid—even cooked lobsters and champagne no uplift." ("I have been hungry all my life!")

But May always seized the negative: no one was harder on May than she was on herself. She might have cherished Juliette's reaction to a 1991 phone call: "Ô *ô oh ô & just then phone rings & the miracle happens of your voice* at the end of magic lines. Your voice, & your *promises of coming.* Ô I *can't believe* it but it must be true." Or a typical ending to a later letter:

"This is to say goodbye for now—with a great armful of concerned wishes, & all the warmth of faithful love—for you know I always love you." Or the fact that Juliette had kept her love letters. Unable to forgive herself, May did not believe in forgiveness.

She went to London anyway on November 3 with Maggie; and Maggie, who had never complained about sharing her with Juliette, was very happy. "We have an aura, people like to see us together," May had always told her; and it was true: doors flew open, cabs and waiters appeared, people vied to push May's wheelchair. They stayed at a favorite hotel, Durrant's, fed ducks in St. James's Park, enjoyed the hotel's beef and lamb, shopped, and read cozily in bed. May herself called it "the best time ever in London."

They returned November 13. Six days later May was hospitalized with a blood clot in her left arm, then released after three days with an increased dosage of Coumadin. Her reply to hints of a nursing home was firm: "I want to die at Wild Knoll." Ill, she still celebrated Christmas with Susan, a tree, and scalloped oysters—better at least than Thanksgiving, when the caterer had infuriatingly forgotten the cranberry sauce. She was momentarily cheered by news that *Coming Into Eighty* was in a second edition and that she'd receive her eighteenth honorary doctorate next spring. She'd begun to devour detective fiction, the only kind of reading she still enjoyed.

I saw her that spring 1995 when she'd returned from still another trip to London. She'd abandoned Scotch sours for straight Scotch. Her voice was stronger, eyes brighter, though she'd had a lift installed to carry her to her bedroom on the second floor and study on the third. She sailed into the interview with gusto:

"Juliette *was* ambivalent up until the end, I see that now. She didn't forgive me for saying I'd tell Julian—though Julian wouldn't have minded. Julian didn't believe in fidelity in marriage, he believed his affairs enriched him. That was terribly hard on Juliette. Maria Huxley, you know, tamed women for Aldous. The young tigress, you know, she broke them in. Sybille what's-her-name [Bedford] who wrote about Aldous was both Aldous's and Maria's lover. . . .

"Kot was the most *whole* man I ever knew. But I couldn't stand James Stephens—such a show-off, drinking gin and reciting his poems endlessly. Kot loved Beatrice Glenavy before he met me. All Beatrice wanted was to separate me and Kot, because Kot did love me. But it was hard to be a guest of Kot's. It was wonderful pushing his gate open, finding him smoking and having tea or gin with buffalo grass in the neat kitchen, but he was fanatic about order. Once I unpacked and some powder from my puff

May Sarton, 1994

fell on his spotless kitchen table. A sacrilege! Kot told Beatrice I was dis-
orderly. . . .

"Muriel was extremely sure she was a genius. We had quarrels in pub-
lic over this. She was *so* unfaithful to me—with Reeves McCullers for
one. Carson adored Muriel. And then there was this woman from the
Midwest, this rich woman who promised Muriel money. Whenever she
came to New York I had to move out of the apartment. That was hard.
But Muriel taught me to play; she taught me it was all right to read mag-
azines in the daytime. . . .

"I've been extremely ill for three years—well, perhaps two. Now I
have like a period, but with no blood. I have to wear a pad. When I went
to the gynecologist about it, I was as near suicide I've ever been. . . .

"If I couldn't drive I would be totally desperate. The car gives me physical power. I can't use my left hand very well; I can hardly walk to the garage. I can't write—I dictate to Judy and Susan. I've become so dependent—and I don't mind. Sometimes a poem comes, but it's gone before I can get it down. I've tried writing one to you. So frustrating. Nobody liked being written poems to; it seemed like a demand, I suppose. . . .

"I've always hated Doubleday because they turned down *The Lion and the Rose*. They gave me an expensive luncheon, then said, 'We can't publish.' I cried all through lunch. When we parted on the street I said, 'I'll never see any of you again!'—and I never did. . . .

"This time in London I had a dream of dying. I was alone, even though people who cared were there. I was terribly frightened. People who come back from dying say there's a tunnel and then one sees light. I didn't see any light. I was so terrified I woke myself up. . . .

"It's hard, I can't write. I've already cut the latest journal and now Norton wants it cut more. It's bad, but I need the money. Carol[yn] helped with this last journal. She suggested taking out all the food references! I said, 'People love to read about food!' In a minute I'm going to have lunch. I have dark chocolate with ginger ale and a cream cheese sandwich with marmalade."

Three months later, on Saturday, July 8, May found it hard to breathe and impossible to talk. The next morning she was worse, so she was taken to York Hospital and installed in the extended-care wing in a large room next to the nurses' station. She was put on oxygen, a sodium chloride drip, and a catheter. Since she was too weak to press a buzzer, someone had to be with her at all times. Susan settled in; a private nurse was also in attendance nights. Though Susan refused to notify Maggie Vaughan of May's illness, she told Margaret Whalen, "This time for sure it doesn't look good."

Friends came to the hospital: Anne Woodson and Barbara Barton, Edythe Haddaway, and Margaret, who on July 12 spelled Susan for a few hours. Margaret hardly recognized the May she'd known: head slumped between her shoulders, face twisted, throat rattling with fluid. "Isn't this unfortunate?" she whispered. "All those books. I can't communicate and I hate it." When Susan returned she began theatrically kissing May's hands. Finding the scene distasteful, Margaret left.

Beverly Hallam came. The once precious mail lay scattered unopened on the blankets. Without glasses, May's eyes were big and clear; she looked, thought Beverly, like her portrait by Polly Thayer. "This is so hard," whispered May.

Though she could eat almost nothing, she was still interested in ordering food and, as always, impatient with bad service. "The food comes just anytime," she complained, "I never know when. The trouble is, they have no routine here!"

On July 12 she started receiving small doses of morphine. Maggie Vaughan came later that day and found Susan in May's room. "I've come all this way to see her," said Maggie. "May I see her alone?" "Surely you can tolerate me in the room?" said Susan. "No, I can't," said Maggie. Susan left. May had always enjoyed the rivalry. Now she smiled, her face relaxed from morphine, and was tender with Maggie, though she could barely speak.

The breast cancer had metastasized, but with her entire system failing, it hardly mattered whether breast cancer, lung cancer, strokes, or congestive heart failure was killing May Sarton. Her living will, which stipulated that she not be kept alive by extreme measures, was honored. On July 13, she was taken off all medication, though remaining on oxygen, the drip, and increased morphine. She failed steadily until she died at 5:15 p.m. on Sunday, July 16, 1995.

May had appointed Timothy Warren, Judy's nephew, as her personal representative. Her will bequeathed $5,000, her automobile, jewelry, clothing, and personal effects to Anne Woodson; $5,000 to Carolyn Heilbrun; modest sums to her cousins; and $5,000 to Susan Sherman, though before her death she had also bought Susan a new car. To Carolyn, her literary executrix, she further gave "all of my interest in all my published and unpublished works" as well as "one-half of the proceeds of any royalties and other income from such works as may be received from time to time." But the bulk of her estate went to the establishing of a Sarton Fund, through which the Academy of Arts and Sciences would grant Sarton Fellowships to poets and historians of science. Significantly, though May had exalted Mabel's artistry while deploring George's self-absorbed scholarship, she did not honor her mother by funding a fellowship in creative design.

May had requested cremation and burial in the Nelson cemetery, with Barbara Barton's phoenix as her headstone. On the morning of October 6, a furious nor'easter lashed the York coast, as though May herself were refusing to go quietly to earth. The day before, Win French had painstakingly tidied the cemetery for May, but overnight the wind and rain destroyed his work. At the cold, rainy burial he stood in the dirt road in a yellow slicker, directing cars to parking places. Twelve people attended the ceremony, at which the Reverend Susan Kershaw, minister of the Nelson Congregational Church, and the Reverend Richard Henry, a friend of May's, presided. Supported by Edythe, Susan made a late entrance. "This marriage will never end," she had told Margaret Whalen in the hospital. Now she kissed the plastic bag containing May's ashes before consigning it to earth. Of the small group, Maggie Vaughan, Anne Woodson, Janice Oberacker, and Beverly Hallam seemed the most affected.

Though fifteen hundred notices of the memorial service the following day had been mailed, the tents set up with loudspeakers on the green proved superfluous, and even the Nelson Congregational Church was not filled to capacity. The rain, many thought, kept people away. May seemed strangely absent in the cold church perfumed by white lilies and roses, though Richard Henry's admirable address attempted to evoke the incandescent spirit whose courage and energy had inspired thousands. Throughout the hour-long memorial, Susan wept conspicuously in a front pew.

On the whole, May would have been pleased with her obituaries, though incensed that Stephen Spender, by virtue of his dying on the same day, got more attention in *The New York Times*. The *Times* saluted her as "a commanding stoical figure and a heroine to feminists," quoting a 1982 review by Sheila Ballantyne: "It is clear that Ms. Sarton's best work, whatever its form, will endure well beyond the influence of particular reviews or current tastes. For in it she is an example: a seeker after truth with a kind of awesome energy for renewal, an ardent explorer of life's important questions." Obituaries in Britain, where May had gained an increasingly wide following, concurred, though the London *Times* slated the poetry for "lacking nuance, ambiguity or the technical mastery that might counterbalance the conventionality of her material." Still, Sarton "was an always interesting—and fervently sincere—writer."

Will May Sarton's work endure? During her lifetime, Sarton literally made her own reputation—selling the poems and novels through countless personal appearances, assiduously cultivating the fans her journals won her. Now her work must exist on the cold page, without the animating force of her extraordinary personality. Will it speak to future generations?

The sheer volume of Sarton's work—fifteen books of poetry, nineteen novels, thirteen memoirs and journals—is in her favor. Her subject matter, the mysteries of the human mind and heart, will not go out of style. Time, careless of fashion, may well treat the best of her lyric poetry favorably. The raging conflicts revealed in the journals are human conflicts and universal: durable fires. If her feminism goes out of style, it will come in again. Her meliorist views are unfashionable only currently.

May Sarton will never be considered a great writer. But she is that equally rare phenomenon, an appealing writer whose work has the power to change readers' lives.

Notes

Sources frequently cited in the Notes are identified by the following abbreviations:

ADF	*A Durable Fire*
ADNH	*As Does New Hampshire*
AGOMS	*A Grain of Mustard Seed*
APM	*A Private Mythology*
AS	*At Seventy*
ATS	*After the Stroke*
AWOL	*A World of Light*
Berg	Henry W. and Albert A. Berg Collection, New York Public Library
CSSV	*Cloud, Stone, Sun, Vine*
E	*Endgame*
EIA	*Encounter in April*
EMS	Eleanor Mabel Sarton
GS	George Sarton
GS/EMS	George Sarton's notes for a biography of Mabel Sarton
HTS	*Halfway to Silence*
IKAP	*I Knew a Phoenix*
IL	*Inner Landscape*
ITLA	*In Time Like Air*
JOAS	*Journal of a Solitude*
LFM	*Letters from Maine*
MP	Margot Peters
MS	May Sarton
NYPL	New York Public Library
R	*Recovering*
THBTS	*The House by the Sea*
TLOS	*The Land of Silence*
TLOTT	*The Leaves of the Tree*
TMS	*The Magnificent Spinster*
TSN	*The Silence Now*

Prologue

Though drawing on several sources, the Prologue is chiefly based on notes taken by Andrea Musher at the Room of One's Own Bookstore in Madison, Wisconsin, on October 25, 1977. I am grateful to Professor Musher for allowing me to quote from her record.

Chapter 1   Wondelgem: 1911–1914

Information about the family, youth, and education of George Sarton (GS) and Eleanor Mabel Sarton (EMS) comes from his notes for the biography of EMS as well as from family, emigration, and citizenship papers; his answers to a Carnegie Institute questionnaire (April 1922); letters from GS and EMS to each other (Berg Collection, New York Public Library), MS's 3-page, unpublished account, "My Mother and Father" (York); MS's notes for *I Knew a Phoenix;* and this biographer's many interviews with May Sarton, who based portraits of her father and mother in *A World of Light* and her chapters about her parents—"In My Father's House," "A Wild Green Place" (written chiefly by EMS herself), and "The Fervent Years"—in *I Knew a Phoenix* on the abovementioned sources.

George Sarton's paternal grandparents were Séverin Bonaventure Sarton, inspector in the Belgian Treasury, and Anne Thérèse de Schodt. His father, Alfred Sarton (1845–1909), born in Poperingen, had four brothers—Arthur, Adolphe, Ernest, Jules—and two sisters—Hélène and Elisa, who became Mère Marie d'Agréda, eventually mother superior of the Convent of Marie Réparatrice in Seville. George's maternal grandparents, the Van Halmés, died young, leaving his Ostend-born mother, Léonie Euphrasie Marie (1860–1885), to be raised by an uncle, Hyppolyte Van Sieleghem. In unpublished notes (York) made for her chapter "The Fervent Years" in *I Knew a Phoenix,* May Sarton speculates from the following letter from Hyppolyte on the occasion of the birth of Berthe Van Halmé, a cousin of George Sarton's and the daughter of Léonie's brother Pedro, that the Van Sieleghems were converted Jews: "Vous aurez besoin de beaucoup de courage pour élever cette fillette destinée par la volonté des parents à la lutte sterile en matière religieuse. Puisse-t-elle ne pas faire naufrage par suite de la méchanceté humaine" (You will need much courage to raise this child destined by her parents' own wish to a sterile struggle in religious matters. May she not be shipwrecked in consequence by human evil). Records of the Vlaamse Vereniging Voor Familiekunde in Ostend indicate, however, that the Van Halmés were Roman Catholic. George knew little about his forebears: "My family can not be traced back beyond beginning of XVII," he wrote in notes for a biography of EMS, "—at least I did not try. I am far more interested in the genealogy of ideas than in the genealogy of my own family." Under the feminine pseudonym Dominique de Bray, George Sarton published two novels, *Une vie de poète* and *La Chaîne d'or.*

Eleanor Mabel Elwes, born to Richard Gervase and Elinor Cole Elwes at Thornton Heath, Croydon, Surrey, on August 3, 1878, could trace her family back to

Sir Gervase Elwes (or Helwys), lieutenant of the Tower of London (1561–1615). This distinguished family, with Nottinghamshire, Lincolnshire, Scottish, and eventually Mexican branches, included Members of Parliament, baronets and knights, high-ranking navy and army officers, high sheriffs, university dons, notable churchmen, barristers, artists, and civil and mining engineers. A publication about the family, "Elsham and Its Squires," notices that "Mabel Elwes . . . married a Dr. George Sarton in America who was a writer and poet of distinction"—though EMS married GS in Ghent, not in America, and GS was not a poet. Mabel's brother, Hugh Geoffrey Elwes, established the Mexican connection when he became a mining engineer in Mexico and married Carmen Martínez. GS cancelled a note in his biography of EMS speculating that the Elweses may have objected to Mabel's marriage to "a social nobody"—and indeed it is unlikely that the Elweses would object to the penniless and fatherless Mabel at twenty-eight marrying into a solid, bourgeois Belgian family; rather, it was the Sartons who were not enthusiastic. Mabel herself, says MS in *World of Light,* never had anything to do with the Elweses; it was only after EMS's death that May discovered her mother came from a distinguished family.

May's early health records are preserved at York: she walked at fourteen months, had ten teeth at fifteen months, and so forth. EMS subjected May to the diagnosis and treatment of Dr. Miele of the Institut des Régimes, Brussels. Constipation was the chief problem; Dr. Miele prescribed special menus, syrups, vitamins, yogurt, potions, and herbs. Yet generally MS was "enfant en bon état."

Sources of quotations are as follows:

p. 8: "Sarton, thank you": EMS, March 18, 1907.

9: "that in no way": GS's journal, quoted in *IKAP,* 60.

"Je vous aime": EMS to GS, April 30, 1908.

"Oh, I want": EMS to GS, September 9, 1908.

"I feel that": EMS to GS, January 17, 1909.

"the sadness": GS/EMS.

"Though I loved": GS/EMS.

10: "I haven't time": MS to MP, October 12, 1992.

"too impetuous": GS/EMS.

"Mabel is": GS/EMS.

"a long 'mothering' ": EMS to Méta Budry, July 19, 1911. I have translated the French portions of EMS to Budry.

"no fuss": GS/EMS.

"holding her hand": GS/EMS.

"Petite May est": GS/EMS. In those notes he states that Mabel's first child was to be called either David or Marie. The birth announcement with EMS's letters to Méta Budry states: "Mr. et Mme. George Sarton ont le plaisir de vous annoncer la naissance de la petite Marie. Wondelgem, le 3 mai 1912," with "Marie" altered in pen to "Mary." GS states his preference for short names in "Why *Isis?*" in *Isis: An International Review* 44, part 3, no. 137 (September 1953): 232–42.

11: "Two children were born": GS/EMS.

"You are always": EMS to GS, June 22, 1912.

11: "queer long silky" . . . "like a tiny": EMS to Méta Budry, June 18, 1912.

"including her hands": EMS to GS, June 25, 1912.

"Pledge to spend": GS/EMS.

"I do not": EMS to GS, January 8, 1913.

12: "Let us run": MS to MP, October 12, 1992.

13: "May Baby has": EMS to Méta Budry, June 3, 1913.

"Mabel's health was": GS/EMS.

"shockingly amateurish": GS/EMS.

"We were innocents": GS/EMS, describing also their attitude toward life in general, including his own disregard of the necessity of earning a living.

14: "very demanding": MS, "The Imaginary Psychiatrist," an unpublished journal of 20 pages, written some time in 1972 in Nelson. In this journal MS tells also of the mud-puddle episode and of screaming unless she was fed by two people at once: "This tale has haunted me for years."

"Naturally we've heard": EMS to Méta Budry, August 15, 1914.

15: "We are well": EMS to Méta Budry, September 19, 1914.

"At any rate": GS/EMS.

Chapter 2   Refugees: 1914–1919

The Baekelands were not friends of the Sartons in Belgium, but connections through the University of Ghent. Leo Hendrik Baekeland (1863–1944) had been a chemistry student of Professor Swarts, whose sister, Céline (Bonbon), he had married. Baekeland had immigrated to America in 1889, when GS was only five. But GS attended Swarts's classes at the University of Ghent and worked in his laboratory, so it may be inferred that Swarts was instrumental in bringing GS and Baekeland together. Baekeland had become a millionaire through his inventions of Velox, a photographic printing paper he sold to Eastman in 1899, and Bakelite. He may well have paid for GS's passage to America in 1915.

The Shady Hill Cooperative Open-Air School in Cambridge still exists, though it has moved to a different location and is no longer "open-air." Its students were chiefly children of Harvard professors. Florence Luther Cobb was its principal when May entered; the management of the school was in the hands of a board of overseers elected by the parents as stockholders; academic policies were determined by an advisory council made up of educators such as Professor George Herbert Palmer, Professor William T. Sedgwick, and Thomas Whitney Surette. The school had an excellent reputation for progressive education, much strengthened by the participation of the parents. The philosopher and Harvard professor William Ernest Hocking, author of the neo-Hegelian *The Meaning of God* (1912), for example, not only oversaw disciplinary procedures but helped stage theatrical events, and Mabel Sarton taught classes in applied design.

Sources of quotations are as follows:

16: "We got here": EMS to Méta Budry, 22 Lower Brook Street, Ipswich, October 25, 1914.

16: "She is so": EMS to GS, December 1, 1914.

17: "Me a big girl": EMS to GS, December 10, 1914: "Moi une grande fille, moi n'a pas pluré. Daddy sera content."

"May is certainly": EMS to GS, April 12, 1914.

"a little red coat" . . . "Belgian May": Letter from MS's cousin May (Mrs. Richard) Pipe, Dakons, Washbrook, Ipswich, Suffolk, November 11, 1991, to MS, recalling May's arrival at the Dorlings' in Framlingham in 1915. I am also indebted to Richard Pipe's description of May as "rosy-cheeked and bobbed-haired" in a letter to MP of January 22, 1992, and to Janet Mann, the daughter of MS's cousin Evelyn Dorling Mann, who described family relationships in a letter to MP of March 26, 1992.

"like a limpet": MS used this phrase often in describing her fierce attachments.

"violently passionately naughty": EMS to GS, May 21, 1915.

"that *topping* little girl": EMS to GS, May 10, 1915.

18: "Poor little daughter": EMS to GS, May 14 [1915].

"Give May away": MS to MP, quoting EMS, October 12, 1992.

"COME ALONG": GS to EMS, Washington, D.C., April 11, 1915.

"If you prefer": GS to EMS, May 25, 1915.

"What I want": GS to EMS, June 10, 1915.

"some frightening masculine": *IKAP,* 87, 88–89.

"heart and soul": GS/EMS.

19: "very wrapped up": Charlotte Bouton Barnaby to MP, April 22, 1992.

"dreary boardinghouse": *IKAP,* 92.

"During the early": GS/EMS.

"*Great distress*": GS/EMS.

"sitting hand in hand": *IKAP,* 94.

20: "Little May": EMS [n.d.] in *Letters to May,* 1.

21: "Dear Mother": MS to EMS, Yonkers, New York, July 17, 1917. Letters from MS to her parents in the Berg Collection begin November 16, 1913 (written in French to EMS for MS by GS), and end with her last letter to GS, October 16, 1954. They comprise a stack fourteen inches tall. The letters include about a dozen very early notes to her parents, either printed in crayon or written for her by others.

"Mrs. Baekeland": EMS, 10 Avon Street, Cambridge, September 3, 1917, in *Letters to May,* 2.

"Here comes trouble!" . . . "always there": Charlotte Bouton Barnaby to MP, April 22, 1992.

22: "a little careless": MS's report card from January, February, and March 1919, a period in which she was absent eight times and tardy seventeen. Since subsequent reports also mention carelessness, I am assuming that the trait was evident in her first years at the school.

"If [the students]": GS/EMS, quoting his attitude as a teaching assistant at the University of Ghent. While GS was of course a responsible professor, he was obviously far more interested in research than in pedagogy.

"It is not necessary": GS/EMS.

23: "our salvation" . . . "Harvard would": GS/EMS.

Chapter 3   Two Worlds: 1919–1925

24: "Triste, la guerre": The peasant woman called "Triste La Guerre" by the British soldiers in Robert Graves's *Goodbye to All That.*

"Look, George!": *IKAP,* 81.

25: "like tearing silk" . . . "Couldn't they wait": *IKAP,* 82, 83.

26: "warm bread": MS to Kathryn Martin, Belgium, August 1, 1959: "Yes, Céline *is* warm bread and I am spoiled here and loved, and can be the child again we all need to be *sometimes.*" Kathryn Martin, a writer, was house-sitting MS's Nelson home while MS was abroad, and working on a journal. ("She was trying to be me," said MS to MP in a telephone conversation of December 12, 1992.)

"Dear Mother": MS to EMS in England, n.d. but August or October 1919. In early August May visited her grandmother Mrs. Elwes in Ipswich, as a photo of them shows (York).

"gloomy dark woods": *THBTS,* 155.

"I can swim 55": MS to GS and EMS, Greensboro, Vermont, July 5, 1921.

27: "a delight" . . . "a fine imagination": Shady Hill Final Report 1920–1921.

"He eyes you": MS's journal, 1924–1929. MS wrote, "I have included in this book everything that I wrote during those years, no matter how bad it is." Many of the poems are crossed out. "The Pigeon" (1924) is the earliest.

28: "a latchkey kid": Joy Greene Sweet in an interview with MP, May 4, 1992. I am indebted to Mrs. Sweet for her highly insightful comments on MS and the Shady Hill years.

29: "I hope you": MS to EMS, January 28, 1922.

"On Monday Daddy": MS to EMS, July 7, 1923.

"Mother is feeling": MS to GS, June 16, 1922.

"I am keeping": MS to EMS, Intervale, New Hampshire, June 22, 1924.

30: "Miss Coit has" . . . "I arrived": MS to GS, July 25 and 31, 1923.

"England is perfectly": MS quoting from her journal to GS, October 22, 1924.

31: "dark and much" . . . "chubby and fair": MS to GS, October 12, 1924. It should be noted that many of the dates on MS's letters have been added later; with a few exceptions, however, they seem to be accurate. As for MS's resemblance to GS: "They all thought I was so like you! Almost everyone of your old friends sees a resemblance immediately, Uncle Michel, the Willems, and Aunty Lino and Uncle Remond" (January 2, 1925).

"Tomorrow we have": EMS to GS, a note added to MS's letter of October 12, 1924.

"I am delighted" . . . "My youth's companion": MS to GS, "soon after March 21, 1925." There are touchingly numerous references to the happiness her *Youth's Companion* gives her.

"The policeman": MS to GS, February 10, 1925.

32: "I was deeply": *IKAP,* 127–28.

33: "She will be precocious": Translated by MP from Dr. Marcel Letendart's written analysis. MS has written on the first page, "Charlatan!"

34: "I had a lovely" . . . "May had I think": MS and EMS to GS, May 1 and 4, 1925.

34: "Aunty Lino . . . divided": MS to GS, February 17, 1925.

"Please thank Aunty": MS to EMS, written on Arts Décoratifs Céline Dangotte stationery, n.d., but toward the end of their stay in Brussels, 1925.

"Bien senti!": *IKAP,* 130. It is important to note MS's own caution that "Titi" (published originally in slightly different form in *The New Yorker*), or "The Belgian School," was written retrospectively and that her real impressions of Marie Closset were formed later. She mentions Marie Closset only once in her letters to her parents that year: "One of the mistresses at my school is called Mme. Closset, I think you know some of her poems" (to GS, November 22, 1924). There were also times when she lost her terror of Mlle Gaspar: "My school teacher 'Mlle Gasparre' is a dear she is much like a teacher that ought to be in my school I which [sic] I could transport her there!" (to GS, February 17, 1925). As MS herself points out, Mlle Gaspar's rote teaching was far from the inspirational instruction that Mlle Closset envisioned when founding the school; on the other hand, Closset recognized that Gaspar's chief job was priming students to pass the all-important state examinations.

Chapter 4   "That Lyric Time": 1925–1929

36: "That Lyric Time": "I am the sole survivor of that lyric time," MS's unpublished reminiscence, probably written shortly after Jean Tatlock's death.

"wide, generous": Interview with Joy Greene Sweet, May 4, 1992. I am indebted to Mrs. Sweet for her vivid descriptions of both Katharine Taylor and Anne Longfellow Thorp.

"more poetry": *IKAP,* 118.

"It is a pity" . . . "May does not": Shady Hill School Report, Grade IX, March 12, 1926.

37: "thrilling depth": Shady Hill School Report, Grade IX, May 28, 1926.

"May . . . was the chief source" . . . "the wildest boy": Jean Clark Lieberman's unpublished diary, n.d. MS and Jean Clark had their ups and downs as friends. According to Jean, she and her close friends at Shady Hill tended to be goody-goodies and were heartily disliked by the rest of the class, including May. In a journal entry of December 20, 1927, May describes Jean as "exact," "penetrating," "not possessed with an extravagant heart." On January 15, 1928, when they were juniors at the Cambridge High and Latin, May records that Jean thinks of her as a scabbard with no sword, and replies: "I could change this impression / By letting you feel the point, / And that I am too kind or rather / Too cowardly to do." And in a letter of November 2, 1929, Jean reminds May that May hadn't liked her that summer. There could also be disagreements with Letty Field over "reason" and "passion," MS writing in a poem to "L.F." on January 1, 1928: "Go on with your spiritual dissection, / I prefer to live!"

40: "intolerable snobs": Hermann Field to MP, April 23, 1992.

"To me rest": Journal, November 23, 1926. "I have changed very much since I wrote this," MS added later.

41: "the very essence": Journal, "Katharine Taylor," December 1926.

41: "Loving is more": Journal, April 1927. In a similar mood, she wrote a poem on June 11, 1927, beginning: "Let us love greatly if we love at all."

"I am very proud": Journal, "Ego," June 1, 1927.

"Let nature take": MS to EMS, Friday [June 1928]: "The gas heater is perfectly fixed now, thank goodness. You can't imagine how funny Daddy was. His theory was the we ought to let nature take its course; I verily believe he would have let the house be flooded!"

"I went to town": MS to EMS, Tuesday [June] 1927. There are numerous letters to EMS these months, reporting final tests and the reading she is doing (Shaw's and Tolstoy's plays).

42: "a fat old": MS to EMS and GS, August 2, 1927.

"impartial": MS to GS and EMS [1927]. One highlight of the post–Day Mountain Camp visit to the Fields at Woods Hole was the discovery with Letty of a secondhand-book shop in New Bedford where she bought "a Keats, very nice plain edition, a beautiful leather-backed and cornered edition of *Pilgrim's Progress,* a little *Cid* and a sweet little complete Burns"—all for $1.50.

"I have consecrated": Journal, July 19, 1927—one of the few entries made at Day Mountain Camp.

"the sharp voice": Journal, "School" (written in school), September 30, 1927.

"There is nothing": Journal, "School-fever," December 9, 1927.

"If I dare": Journal, "K.T.," November 2, 1927.

"I must never": Journal, November 26, 1927.

"If you should": Journal, "A Bitter Berry," April 30, 1928.

43: "clear–cut azure" . . . "fine stillness": Journal, "Eva Le Gallienne," September 26, 1927. In the margin of a subsequent poem to Le Gallienne, "Hedda Gabler" (May 22, 1928), MS later wrote, "Influenced by Jean Tatlock. This is not worthy of me." In late January or February MS attended an "excellent lecture" by Le Gallienne: "She is a marvelous person, much greater than K[atherine] W[arren] as I have always known. She actually said she recognized me at the lecture, and as we left said to me, 'I'll see you again.' "

44: "She is a great": Diary, February 7, 1928. The diary, as distinct from MS's poetry journal, records daily events—large (Mary Garden) and small (washing her hair).

"a huge, windy writing": Diary, Tuesday, February 9 [1928]. "Mary Garden, you have my heart!" MS added.

"Ibsen at present": Diary, Sunday, February 12, 1928, copy of MS's letter to Katherine Warren.

"almost perfect" . . . "ran over to": Diary, Tuesday, February 14, 1928.

"Not yet—but": Quoted in Diary, Monday, February 13, 1928.

"When will they finish": Diary, Tuesday, February 7, 1928.

"must go through": Diary, Thursday, February 16, 1928.

45: "You often feel": Diary, Thursday, February 16, 1928.

"browny gold" . . . "Vermeer's blues": Diary, February 16, 1928.

"I am going": Journal, "Flowers After the Ball," June 3, 1928. MS later wrote "good."

46: "a sea green" . . . "crystal appreciation": Journal, August 5, 1928.

"Words are my passion": Journal, "Creation," August 20, 1928, influenced by MS's reading Isadora Duncan's life.

47: "Moonchildren" . . . "taken care of": Willem Van Loon to MS, November 4, 1928.

"Never!" . . . "Be nonchalant": *IKAP,* 149.

"I felt somehow": Eva Le Gallienne to GS, December 11, 1928.

Chapter 5   Searching: 1929–1930

48: "delectable room": MS to GS, June 26, 1929. May was the first to arrive at Gloucester and the only student back from the previous year.

"So I shall": MS to EMS, July 1 [1929]. Mary and Abbie Dewing were Shady Hill students, though neither belonged to MS's intimate circle. In *IKAP* MS describes Elizabeth (Ibby) Tracy as the only non–Shady Hiller at the Cambridge High and Latin to be accepted by her group.

"The symbolism": Unsigned review dated July 14, 1929, from Cape Ann Shore. *The Master Builder* was performed July 3–6. On June 10, 1928, MS had entered the poem "After Reading *The Master Builder*" in her journal: "Hilda myself, Solness K.T."

49: "frightfully thrilling": Hilda Wangel's exclamation in *The Master Builder* and used by MS, along with "perfectly glorious" and "absolutely heavenly," to excess during this exclamatory period. "Daddy will object to all these exclamation points," she wrote May 2, 1930, "but I'm so happy I can't help it." As for MS overusing "dear" and "sweet," her reaction to Housman's "Loveliest of Trees"—"Isn't it sweet"—is a prime example; however, she was only eighteen.

"a strange dark" . . . "Someone is getting": Diary, Thursday, July 25, 1929.

"Isn't it silly": Diary, Monday, July 29, [1929].

"I know that I'm": Diary, Thursday, August 1, 1929.

50: "a whole little": Diary, Sunday, September 1, 1929. The McLean Club was then run by Mrs. Julia Baldwin. Room and board (two meals weekdays, three Sundays and holidays) was $13.35 a week.

51: "an instrument for": From a 1932–33 Civic Repertory Theatre brochure, but Le Gallienne's words on many occasions—for example, in her autobiography *With a Quiet Heart* (1953). Since its foundation in 1926, the CRT had given 1,024 performances of thirty-one plays, most successfully *The Cradle Song* (1926), *The Good Hope* and *Hedda Gabler* (1927), and *The Cherry Orchard* and *Peter Pan*. During MS's 1929–1931 attendance at Le Gallienne's school, the great successes were *Peter Pan, Romeo and Juliet, Alison's House* (for which Susan Glaspell won a Pulitzer), and *The Lady of the Camellias.*

"an interesting lot": MS to GS and EMS, Tuesday [September 3, 1929].

"It's a stupid": MS to EMS, Thursday [September 5, 1929].

"stagnant despair": Diary, Saturday, September 14, 1929. MS frequently copied portions of letters to friends in her diary. The "one very innocent girl" is Helen Brewer, a fellow Le Gallienne student from Kentucky.

52: "improving her mind": May's reading during this period was prodigious. Besides all the plays produced by the CRT and the student group, books she devoured included *Adrienne Mesurat, Jean Christophe, The Return of the Native, Crime and Punishment,* Verlaine's poetry, German poetry, Descartes, *Cry of Time, Types of Philosophy, Swann's Way, Overtones, Orphan Angel, Fathers and Sons, Letters to Women, A Modern Comedy, The Whirlwind, The Ambassadors,* Katherine Mansfield's *Letters* and *Journal,* a Duse biography, *Eight European Plays,* Moore's *Héloïse and Abélard, La Prisonnière, The Unlit Lamp, De Profundis, A Room with a View, Wolf Solent, Death in Venice, The Magic Mountain,* Emily Dickinson's poetry, *The Life and Mind of Emily Dickinson, Kristin Lavransdatter, Orlando, To the Lighthouse, Mrs. Dalloway.*

"I'll be willing": MS to GS and EMS, n.d. but a few days before October 27, 1929, when she replies to their refusal, "I'm really very glad about the coat because after I had it I would probably feel it was too extravagant. I only hope someone gets it who will love it." MS was photographed with GS at Christmas 1929 in "the wonderful Russian blouse," the jacket photo of *IKAP.*

"I do seem": MS to GS and EMS, March 3, 1930, adding, "Today I feel physically sick with weariness and despair."

53: "although in places": Diary, Wednesday [September 18, 1929].

"I know that I": Diary, Saturday [September 21, 1929]. On July 4, 1931, on rereading this passage, which ends, "I tremble even as I write this. If it were not so?," MS wrote "God!"

"a little poem": Diary, September 21, 1929. Since she wrote Katharine Taylor "a long stupid letter" that day, the poem might have been the unpublished "Gift (To K.T.)."

"Yesterday I got" . . . "Why does she": Diary, Saturday, September 21, 1929, and January 30, 1930.

"Perhaps he is": Diary, Saturday, September 14, 1929.

"so obviously" . . . "suffocated": Diary, Wednesday, September 18, 1929.

"at times embarrassing": Diary, Wednesday, September 25, 1929.

"I don't object": Diary, Thursday, September 26, 1929. The letter embarrassed MS chiefly because "it is so like many I have written and regretted."

54: "You are the most": Jean Clark to MS, November 2, 1929. Jean Clark often frankly expressed her alienation from MS, Letty Field, and Jean Tatlock because she felt she could never live up to their high standards.

"My demands": MS to GS and EMS, October 26, 1930.

"so abominably": MS to GS and EMS, October 5, 1929. MS does admit failures to get parts, a bit of realism amid the "frightfully thrilling"'s.

"So could you" . . . "I thought I": MS to GS and EMS, December 12 and 13, 1929. It is impossible to overemphasize how much MS's letters these years concerned money. Her most desperate appeals, such as the time she lost $20, were addressed to EMS; she also sent separate "accounts" to GS and EMS, EMS paying for more "frivolous" things like stockings, eau de cologne, etc. Even supposed economies backfired: invited to dinner by Bonbon Baekeland, she ended up spending nine dollars on white gloves and taxis.

55: "Once in a while": Diary, January 7, 1930, from a letter to Jean Clark: "I have been swimming in a purple and blue and emerald sea of Katherine Mansfield." MS had immediately bought Mansfield's letters on returning after Christmas to New York.

"My mind" . . . "I remember" . . . "Willem and I": Diary, December 25 [1929], December 30 [1929], February 26, 1930.

"For the last few": Diary, January 7, 1930, letter to Jean Clark.

"because I want": Diary, January 7, 1930.

"I am not worthy" . . . "I respect EB": Diary, January 20 and 29, 1930.

"Being what I am": Copied in a letter to GS and EMS, March 23, 1930. "I think it's one of my best."

56: "I can no longer" . . . "I want to know": Jean Tatlock to MS, often undated, but from circa December 1929 through spring 1930. Tatlock had read Radclyffe Hall's *The Well of Loneliness,* wrestled with the question of whether she was homosexual but concluded she couldn't be because of her "unmasculinity." MS warned MP about misinterpreting the correspondence: "You would think we were having the most passionate sexual affair, but the letters are rather an example of the feverish intensity of my friendships in those days." MS's letters to Tatlock apparently do not survive.

57: "Although we are": Quoted by MS to GS and EMS, February 17, 1930. "The main thing is that I've really broken through," added MS.

58: "Had good talk": GS to EMS, May 8, 1930.

"Je ne dis": Diary, June 10, 1930: "I say nothing, having too much to say."

"She loved poplars": Unpublished typed copy, "L.F.," erroneously dated April 1930. "Switzerland was the place of her roots": Letty's father, Herbert Haviland Field, a humanist and Quaker pacifist, headed a scientific institute in Zurich.

"I'm really glad" . . . "a gushing lady" . . . "Don't you think": MS to GS and EMS, Thursday, July 10, 1930.

"waited and waited" . . . "I love her largely": Diary, July 30, 1930, quoting a letter to Jean Clark.

59: "tempest of words" . . . "I loved him": Diary, September [1930], quoting a letter to Jean Tatlock.

"I feel you": Willem Van Loon to MS, Sunday [August 24, 1930], written on the train to New York the day or the day after he left Gloucester.

"an old rag": MS to GS and EMS, October 5, 1930.

"It seems hard": MS to GS and EMS, October 1, 1930.

60: "too fragile-looking": MS to GS and EMS, October 8, 1930. The part, Mrs. Patchkoffer, went to First Studio member Edith Lane. "I am certainly having to learn patience," wrote MS.

"My heart *did*": MS to GS and EMS, November 30, 1930. By mid-October, Harriet Monroe had accepted four poems instead of two. May had copied out "Fruit of Loneliness" for her parents on April 13, 1930: "I hope you haven't imagined from my poems that I'm in love! Because I'm not, heaven knows." The poems appeared in *Poetry* 37 (October 1930–March 1931); 144–46.

61: "this luxurious heart": from "Fruit of Loneliness."

Chapter 6   Finding: 1931–1932

62: "We came together": first of the published series of sonnets to Grace Daly in *Encounter in April* (1937). The sonnets were written over a period of more than a year; for example, MS reported to GS and EMS on June 13, 1931, that the *Saturday Review* had refused "Leopard," eventually published as Sonnet 4 in *EIA*.

"Why did you": Diary, May 1, 1931.

63: "I'm surrounded": Diary, September 10, 1930.

"People are afraid": Diary, copy of letter to Grace Daly, June 1, 1931.

"I adore you": MS to GS and EMS, December 11, 1930. As an example of May's frustrations, she had worked very hard to translate *L'Âme en peine* into English (as *Marceline*) and had rehearsed it painstakingly with the First Studio for one or two performances to which the critics did not come. Though Le Gallienne assured her she had done in one year what she thought would take her five, May was obviously dissatisfied with her progress.

"One gets sucked": Diary, copy of a letter to Jean Tatlock, April 30, 1931. Jean Tatlock (to MS, February 1930) did not think Le Gallienne's influence all good: "Please don't be like Eva. Don't be. Go away if you are."

64: "exquisite and apparently": MS to GS and EMS, April 24, 1931.

"It has been": MS to GS and EMS, May 3, 1931.

"You see this isn't": Diary, quoting letter to Grace Daly, June 1, 1931. Like many writers, MS tried out images and metaphors several times, writing to Katharine Taylor in November [1930?], for example, "By the way, it's all right—really all right—everything that has and will happen. I feel sure. In spite of ourselves we *are* part of earth turning very slowly and surely towards something—like an orchard of trees."

"put a hand" . . . "Really unless": Diary, copy of letter to Grace Daly, June 6, 1931.

65: "I'm sitting in": Diary, copy of letter to Grace Daly, June 13, 1931. May was fortunate to have only one roommate in her four-bed cabin. Among her bon-voyage tokens: three letters from her parents, handkerchiefs from EMS, red roses from the Dewings, a Marconigram from Renée Orsell, a bunch of African daisies from Robby [?]. She found her table companions "about the worst possible and service interminable."

"So far I": Diary, copy of letter to Katharine Taylor, on board the *Lapland* [June 1931].

"Just in case": MS to GS and EMS, June 25, 1931.

66: "wonderful and strange" . . . "glorious weeks": Diary, copy of letter to Katharine Taylor, July 29, 1931.

"I think it was": Diary, copy of letter to Jean Tatlock, July 26, 1931.

"I hope to God": Jean Tatlock to MS in Zurich, September 9, 1931.

"great slow curves": Diary, copy of letter to Katharine Taylor, July 29, 1931.

67: "a passionate sound": Diary, copy of letter to Katharine Taylor, July 29, 1931. During this period, 1931–1932, according to diary entries, MS confided in and discussed serious issues with K.T. more than with anyone else.

67: "the most intellectually": Diary, copy of letter to Grace Daly, August 6, 1931. May began the letter, "I'm sitting on something resembling a hawser—Antwerp—London—to meet Dad."

"She curled up": Diary, copy of letter to Grace Daly, Zurich, September 17, 1931.

"I have a most" . . . "tirelessly about": MS to Méta Budry, Zurich, September 11, 1931.

"simply a roost": Diary, copy of letter to Grace Daly, October 5 [1931].

"heavenly middle-aged": MS to GS and EMS, October 6, 1931. Roswell Hawley had acted Mrs. Fisher in *Enchanted April* at Gloucester with May.

68: "like flowing metal": MS to GS and EMS, September 28, 1931.

"We who had been": sonnet published in *Encounter in April,* copied in letter to GS and EMS, September 1931. GS wrote in the margin, "That, I find, is a very beautiful poem" and was impressed enough to offer to underwrite a book of MS's poems.

"I too, find": EMS to MS, Beirut, October 14, 1931, in *Letters to May,* 6.

"I have a sense": MS to GS and EMS, October 22, 1931.

69: "I shall need": MS to GS and EMS, October 22, 1931. May understood very well the implications of "Your Mouse," writing EMS [n.d. but 1932 or 1933], "Just a word . . . to thank you for your cheese for your mouse. . . ." Similarly, signatures like "Your Elf" and "Your Pigeon," used until her parents' deaths, emphasized an entirely imaginary, but useful, small helplessness.

"I myself don't": MS to EMS, December 3, 1931.

"a fit of fury" . . . "Where is the theatre?" . . . "Mademoiselle": MS to GS and EMS, November 6, 1931; MS to the Greenes, November 7, 1931; *IKAP,* 166–70. The accounts vary slightly; for example, MS tells her parents that she had proposed to Lugné-Poë that she form a group of young actors to do *The Master Builder,* not that she asked him to play Solness to her Hilda Wangel.

70: "I want to see": MS to GS and EMS, [November 28, 1931].

"I see more": MS to EMS, December 3, 1931. GS was in Egypt at the time.

71: "You see for me": Diary, copy of letter to Katharine Taylor, December 19, 1931.

72: "blind and unrealistic" . . . "caught up": Anne Thorp to EMS [1932]. Anne did not see Grace as exploitative, but saw both Grace and MS as carried away by unrealistic expectations (engendered, however, by MS).

"ENGAGED BY EVA": MS to GS and EMS, December 14, 1931.

73: "I thought you": MS to GS and EMS, December 19, 1931.

"May always left": Polly Thayer Starr to MP, April 23, 1995.

"To darling May": A ten-line poem from Katharine Taylor, Christmas 1931 (York). One of May's handpainted Christmas cards for 1931 depicts a joyous dancing angel holding a scroll of music; the other, "From Pooh and May," a design of a piano, a bar of music, a pen and paper, a potted tulip, and her teddy bear, Pooh.

"*coldest, wettest*": MS to GS and EMS, New Year's Eve [1931].

74: "the extravagantly joyful" . . . "I don't know": MS to GS and EMS, January 28, 1932.

"that dark cloud" . . . "perfectly fair": MS to GS and EMS, January 28, 1932.

"Return when you" . . . "a place there": MS to GS and EMS, February 9, 1932, Jean Dominique quoted in French.

75: "A dark day": MS to GS and EMS, February 22, 1932.

"May and Irene": Edith Forbes Kennedy to EMS, Paris, April 23, 1932. The former wife of Robert Woods Kennedy, Edith had three sons, Robert (MS's age), Fitzroy, and Edmund. She knew EMS slightly from their Shady Hill connection. It is important to note that EFK knew Grace only through MS's disillusioned account of her.

76: "The spring has come": MS to GS and EMS, March 20, 1932.

"Could you make": MS to GS and EMS, March 26, 1932. MS explains that since Grace expected her to have more money and an apartment through April, "I have felt it practically incumbent upon me to make this up to her."

77: "You seem to manage": GS to MS, April 6, 1932.

"Here I have" . . . "If it is": MS to GS and EMS, Florence, April 15, 1932.

78: "I have since": MS to GS and EMS, April 20, 1932. MS sometimes says the loan is $400, sometimes $500. The latter is borne out in MS to EMS, July 3, 1932, and in subsequent letters. MS also claimed that she repaid the money; when I expressed skepticism, however, she said, with a laugh, "Well, I *tried*."

"I had thought": GS to MS, April 26, 1932.

"It will need": EMS to MS, Beirut, April 26, 1932, *Letters to May,* 8–9.

"Unloved, trapped": MS's unpublished notes [n.d.] for the theatre chapter, "Impossible Campaigns," in *IKAP;* she does not go into the Grace Daly situation.

"It is very generous": MS to GS, August 14, 1932.

"By the time": copy of MS's unpublished letter to Dr. Pederson-Krag, a female psychiatrist, September 12, 1955, an important statement of MS's psychosexual nature. The suggestion that she searched for her mother in her love affairs with older women was mine, and angrily rejected.

79: "It is really *I*": EMS to MS, January 22, 1941.

"I never can feel": Anne Thorp to EMS [1932].

"May I add": Edith Forbes Kennedy to EMS, April 23, 1932.

"She was *never*": Hermann Field in an interview with MP, April 23, 1992.

"*We* together are": MS to EMS, July 10, 1932.

80: "invalid wife" . . . "criminal": MS to MP in a telephone conversation of October 5, 1991. MS exploded over my calling her mother's letters "sad": EMS was *not* sad, she was *fierce,* said MS, and deeply resented GS's "criminal" selfishness.

Chapter 7   Disaster: 1932–1935

81: "bewildered": MS to EMS, Commodore Hotel [n.d. but probably June 21, 1932]. I have made no attempt in this chapter to catalogue MS's dozens of addresses, since they would only bewilder a reader.

81: "heart-rending" . . . "One part of": MS to EMS, June [29, 1932]. MS was not the only person to call Anne Thorp repressed. Hermann Field, recalling her walking arm in arm with Manley Hudson, a Harvard professor, speculated that her inhibitions might have doomed the romance.

"I'm trying": MS to GS, Gloucester, July 10, 1932.

82: "I have no fear": MS to GS and EMS, August 21, 1932.

"not Bohemian": Telephone interview with Norman Lloyd, December 4, 1991. Lloyd has written of his years with the Apprentices in "Remembrance of Theatre Past," *Gambit: Magazine of KCET Public Television, Los Angeles* (October 1975): 16–18; and *Early Stages,* a memoir. MS confessed to the isolation Lloyd recognized: "In some ways I am terribly lonely—by the very nature of things, you see, I can't mingle entirely with the group" (to GS and EMS, September 24, 1932).

83: "It seems ages": MS to GS and EMS, "Sunday morn" [October 30, 1932]. Between August 19, 1932, and May 18, 1933, the Apprentices produced scenes from *The Tempest, Paolo and Francesca, The Way of the World, A Month in the Country, Maya,* and *Private Lives* (directed by MS); *La Mauvaise Conduite* (translated and directed by MS); *The Shepherds* (d. MS); *The Brothers Karamazov* (d. MS); *Spring's Awakening; Three Acts; A Bill of Divorcement; S.S. Tenacity; The Guardsman; Will Shakespeare; Scenes from Romeo and Juliet; Miss Julie* (d. MS); *The Constant Nymph* (d. MS); *Rope;* and *Six Characters in Search of an Author.*

"I never have": MS to EMS [n.d. but late fall 1932].

"I am relieved": Jean Clark Field to MS [n.d.].

84: "very quiet": MS to GS and EMS, Tuesday [fall 1932].

"seemed to stand": Norman Lloyd to MP, March 19, 1992.

"She makes breakfast": MS to EMS, "Monday Eve" [n.d. but early January 1933]. Theo lived in the Beaux Arts Apartments at 307 East Forty-fourth Street at this time.

85: "a swell performance": MS to GS, quoting Le Gallienne, January 10, 1933.

"the theatre is": MS to GS, January 29, 1933. Ironically, the 1932–33 season was the Civic Repertory's best financially; it also had recently been granted tax exemption by the state of New York.

86: "If anyone can": Katrine Greene to EMS, Dublin, July 19, 1933.

"I must confess": MS to GS and EMS, Tuesday [July 1933].

"swimming, dancing, tennis": MS to GS and EMS, "Monday morn" [July or August 1933].

"Dr. Sarton & I": EMS to "Dear Group, dear Apprentices" [n.d. but probably August 1933]. The Apprentices produced three plays: *Tom Thumb, The Secret Life* (H. R. Lenormand's *La Vie secrète,* translated by MS), and *The Children's Tragedy.*

87: "the best time": MS to GS and EMS, September 15, 1933. Le Gallienne's rather temperate endorsement of the Apprentice Theatre appeared in all their brochures.

"What I dislike": Edith Isaacs to MS, March 15, 1934, in answer to MS's rather strenuous letter of March 14: "Is there no criterion of judgment, no recognition in America except for 'success'? I refuse to believe it!"

"valueless play": Anita Block to MS, December 16, 1933. The fact that May had translated *The Secret Life* was a potent reason for producing it; her favoritism to Theo was a perennial problem.

87: "God knows": MS to EMS, February 27, 1934.

88: "I said you would": MS to EMS, May 31, 1934. "I marvel more and more at all Mummy accomplished," MS wrote with reason to GS and EMS, July 4, 1934.

89: "No man can save": GS to MS, May 14, 1934. GS tried to give MS sound advice: "I would not believe in a company led by you—*even* if you had won your spurs. For any theatrical enterprise is 50% business, and the leadership of it must be 50% business. I do not think you have any business ability, in that sense. . . . I do not even believe that you are of the stuff of which leaders are made, for that implies such a large amount of conceit and egoism that one can easily disregard the interests & feelings of one's associates" (May 24, 1934).

90: "Everyone is in": MS to GS and EMS, November 4, 1934. MS and Theo were living at the Hartford Bridge Club, 29 Highland Street, West Hartford.

"It's really bitter": MS to GS and EMS, November 20, 1934. *Multiplied by Two* was MS's translation of Jean Variot's *La Mauvaise Conduite,* based on Plautus's *Menaechmi.* Theo had the female lead of Eroti.

"not bad at all": MS to GS and EMS, December 7, 1934.

91: "It will be a miracle": MS to EMS, January 5, 1935.

92: "I need about fifty": MS to EMS, May 30, 1935. Since the Grace affair, MS addressed most of her pleas for money to EMS. Ironically, when she visited EMS's Russian "charity cases" in Florence, they immediately begged her for 300 lire, which terrified her—"Of course we seem well-off to them."

"a sweet little room": MS to GS and EMS, September 12, 1935.

93: "Dears, we are": MS to GS and EMS, October 11, 1935.

94: "For heaven's sake": GS to MS, November 20, 1935. GS had never believed in MS's company; had begged her to either go back to school (he would finance her) or work at writing "slowly and humbly."

"The company failed": MS's diary, copy of a letter to Edith Forbes Kennedy, June 1941.

"Whatever the role": Molly Howe (Mrs. Faneuil Adams) to MP in a February 15, 1993, interview.

95: "Enthusiasm is": Eliot Cabot, "You Never Can Tell," article in an unidentified newspaper, August 31, 1934 (Berg).

"You can't have": MS to MP, March 12, 1992, the only source of this story. Ironically, it was Rosalind Greene who had drawn Ada Comstock's attention to the Apprentice Theatre in 1933. After seeing a performance, Comstock had expressed hope that the group would be able to make their home in Cambridge.

Chapter 8   The Poet: 1935–1937

96: "a great saving": MS to GS and EMS, December 5, 1935, in a letter requesting five sheets and pillowcases, kitchen towels, bath mat, bath and face towels, and blankets.

"cobalt eyes" . . . "O would you": "Two Sonnets for Eva" (unpublished), post-dated 1934.

97: "The best one can do": Le Gallienne to MS, Minneapolis, January 29, 1934.

"She was a phenomenon": Polly Thayer Starr to MP, telephone interview, August 5, 1992.

"everyone says": MS to EMS, January 1, 1936.

"savage letter" . . . "I am afraid": MS to EMS, January 4, 1936. In an undated letter, MS had defended herself to GS, who had recently given her $300: "I *do* know how lucky I am to be given this undeserved security. . . . I also know very well my own tendency to extravagance."

"I am telling": MS to GS and EMS, Sat. afternoon [March 21?, 1936].

"There is no doubt": MS to GS, March 31, 1936, aboard the *Manhattan*.

98: "thin stork": MS to GS and EMS, Kilmarth, Par, Cornwall, April 2, 1936. Sir Julian Sorell Huxley (1887–1975), a biologist and ecologist, was married to the Swiss-born Juliette Baillot, who for a time had been a governess in Lady Ottoline Morrell's house, Garsington.

99: "It really is quite": MS to GS and EMS, April 21, 1936.

"One must be": MS to GS and EMS, April 26, 1936.

"The frightful sensation": MS to Jean Dominique, August 24, 1934. I have translated the correspondence between MS and Jean Dominique, which is in French.

"La vie n'est": MS to GS and EMS, April 26, 1936.

"they had some": MS to GS and EMS, 16 avenue Lequime, Brussels, April 26, 1936.

"deepest and dearest" . . . "I felt absolutely": MS to EMS, 23 Taviton Street, London, May 3, 1936.

100: "I believe that *anything*": MS to EMS, May 3, 1936.

"[I] am lazy": MS to Jean Dominique, 23 Taviton Street, May 2, 3, 1936.

101: "a long English face": MS to GS and EMS, 23 Taviton Street, May 8, 1936.

102: "slight sneer": Molly Howe (Mrs. Faneuil) Adams to MP, interview, February 15, 1993. May, said Mrs. Adams, got along with men well; she had no hidden agenda. May said, however, about a later lover that "men feel comfortable with her as they never do with me" (MS to Polly Thayer Starr, Santa Fe [n.d.]).

"should have had": MS to Polly Thayer Starr, July 28, 1942.

"an out and out": MS to Polly Thayer Starr, May 22, 1938.

"over-*refined*": MS to Juliette Huxley, Jeakes House [April 20, 1937]. May added that "when I left U.S. last spring I was determined to get away from it"—lesbian relations. Today there is still no one definition of "lesbian," though Juanita H. Williams in *Psychology of Women* (New York: W.W. Norton, 1987) offers the following definitions: "(1) a woman whose primary bonds, emotional, social, and probably erotic, though not necessarily, are with other women; (2) a woman who identifies herself as lesbian, though she may not do this publicly for reasons related to children, job, friends, and so on; (3) a woman who may (or may not) be part of a lesbian subculture, or community, or simply a group of lesbian-identified women" (392). At this point in her life, MS fit only the first category.

"cool underwater" . . . "really nothing to offer": "Elizabeth Bowen," *AWOL*, 193. MS's poem "Portrait by Holbein, for E.B." in *EIA* was inspired by this visit.

103: "don't be put off": MS to GS and EMS, Pignon Rouge, June 16 [1936].

"They destroy *everyone*": MS to GS and EMS, Pignon Rouge, June 25 [1936].

"Altogether this holiday": MS to GS, Seeblick, Grundlsee, Austria, July 10 [1935]. Haus Seeblick was founded by Frau Doktor Schwarzwald as a meeting place for intellectuals; the Jewish Schwarzwalds did not survive the Nazis. MS was extremely fond of the Schwarzwalds, and of Maria Stiasni, one of the hosts at Seeblick.

"I am quite terrified": MS to EMS, Seeblick, July 10 [1936]. MS left Grundlsee July 18 to meet Jean Dominique, on vacation, in Luxembourg. She then returned to Brussels to the Limbosches', met her parents in England, and sailed on the *Corinthia* with them August 7.

"Dears, I am" . . . "It is *wonderful*" . . . "I must run": MS to GS and EMS, "Sat. morning" [August or September 1936].

"a dear sensitive man": MS to MP, August 4, 1992. Robert Hale was later curator of American painting at the Metropolitan Museum of Art.

104: "Dears—it is": MS to GS and EMS, aboard the *American Trader* [n.d. but just embarked, so late March 1937]. She sailed with Liz Johnson, recently graduated from Bennington: "I never liked her very much."

"pre-fabricated emotions": *Poetry* 50 (July 1937): 229.

"After the cold": Marion Strobel to Ferris Greenslet of Houghton Mifflin, quoted by MS in a letter to GS and EMS, April 18, 1937.

"smart despair": Diary, MS to Katharine Taylor, January [1931].

105: "I wish you": MS to EMS, Garland Hotel, London, April 8, 1937.

"I know that both": Julian to Juliette Huxley, April 15, 1937.

"*Must* I be": Juliette to Julian Huxley [April 15, 16? 1937].

"I understand" . . . "bear fruit": MS to EMS, Garland Hotel, London, April 8, 1937.

106: "like an operetta set": MS to GS and EMS, Jeakes House, Rye, April 14 [1937]. Though seldom mentioned in the narrative, Liz Johnson, May Potter, and a German girl May met on the boat shared Jeakes House with May off and on during the seven weeks.

"to work": MS to Juliette Huxley, April 12, 1937. MS's first extant letter to Juliette is dated October 27, 1936.

"such a lovely": MS to GS and EMS, Jeakes House, Rye, April 18 [1937].

"*almost* my flower": MS to GS and EMS [May 3, 1937].

107: "chased each other": MS to GS and EMS, Coronation Day, Rye, May 12 [1937].

"simply walking": MS to EMS, Sunday [May 16?, 1937].

"Really everything": MS to EMS [n.d. but May 1937].

"Six weeks": MS to GS and EMS, Jeakes House, Rye, May 20, 1937.

"I fell in love": "Elizabeth Bowen," *AWOL*, 194.

108: "the most extraordinary" . . . "exactly like a bear" . . . "You are a writer" . . . "a little home circle" . . . "how New England" . . . "If I didn't": MS to GS and EMS, 2 Clarence Terrace, London, June 6, 1937. Samuil Solomonovich Koteliansky edited, co-edited, and translated thirty-five works from Russian, among them Chekhov's notebooks, Countess Sophie Tolstoy's autobiography, Dostoyevsky's *Stavrogin's Confession* (with Virginia Woolf), and *The Dream of a Queer Fellow* (with Katherine Mansfield).

109: "a highly sensitive": "Elizabeth Bowen," *AWOL,* 195.

"almost rococo" . . . "she really hadn't" . . . "infinitely and charmingly": MS to GS and EMS, Whipsnade, June 22 [1937].

"I can feel": MS to S. S. Koteliansky, "Wed. Tea time" [June 23, 1937].

110: "*most* thrilling night" . . . "the whole evening": MS to GS and EMS, 2 Clarence Terrace, London, July 8, 1937.

"queer squeaky voice": MS to GS and EMS, Whipsnade, June 22, 1937. MS had met Wells previously with Juliette Huxley.

111: "I cannot explain": MS to S. S. Koteliansky, Seeblick, Grundlsee, Austria, July 16, 1937.

"You spoke": "Martial Music," unpublished poem for Juliette written July 9, 1937.

"I don't think": MS to Juliette Huxley, Jeakes House [April 20, 1937].

112: "In a curious way": MS to S. S. Koteliansky, Brussels, July 11, 1937.

"provides sufficient *glamour*": MS to S. S. Koteliansky, Seeblick, Grundlsee, July 16, 1937. "Mountain Landscape" in *EIA* was written for Maria Stiasni.

"Of course it will": MS to GS and EMS, quoting Koteliansky, Seeblick, Grundlsee, July 25, 1937.

"I am really": MS to GS and EMS, Seeblick, Grundlsee, July 25, 1937. Juliette had planned to come with their sons, Anthony and Francis, for a family holiday. Expense was probably not a factor: perhaps May had alarmed her sufficiently that last weekend in London.

"Julian was not": MS to MP, August 4, 1992.

"I think there must": MS to S. S. Koteliansky, Seeblick, Grundlsee, August 2, 1937.

113: "four blessed days": MS to S. S. Koteliansky, Seeblick, Grundlsee [postmarked August 7, 1937]. MS finished *The Single Hound* on August 12.

"This is written": James Stephens's note written below the poem "Dark Answer," a copy of which she had sent to Kot, probably August 7.

"Dearest Daddy": MS to GS, Seeblick, Grundlsee, August 12, 1937. EMS sailed for England on August 7 because Mrs. Starnes, her mother's housekeeper, was dying of cancer and EMS had to make other arrangements for the care of Mrs. Elwes, ninety years old. Constantly short of money, Mabel had to borrow from Katharine Taylor as well as Jean Dominique to pay a nurse's wages, etc.

"I want to have": MS to EMS, quoting Koteliansky, Belgium, "Dimanche" [August 22, 1937].

"I'm so sorry" . . . "Have you": Virginia Woolf to MS, Monk's House, Rodmell, August 29 [1937] and to Elizabeth Bowen, October 9 [1937], *The Letters of Virginia Woolf,* Vol. 6, pp. 165, 181. MS's lesbianism would not have bothered the bisexual Virginia Woolf; it was probably MS's rather trying combination of heroine worship, persistence, and naïveté that turned off the sophisticated, unforthcoming writer.

114: "the bastards": MS to EMS, Friday [September 10, 1937], a refreshing bit of plain talk.

"Lion of Judea": D. H. Lawrence's name for S. S. Koteliansky.

Chapter 9   The Novelist: 1937–1939

115: "without her love": MS to S. S. Koteliansky, September 25, 1937. Ferris Greenslet of Houghton Mifflin had recently called *The Single Hound* "better than he expected," but suggested making part 2 into part 1 to emphasize the protagonist, Mark Taylor. "I am inclined to disagree with Greenslet," MS wrote Kot wisely October 17, 1937, ". . . and he will agree with me I know in the end." By the end of October, MS had rewritten part 1 three times because of Jean Dominique's objections, one of which was that MS had made Marie Gaspar a clownish figure.

"Who are you": unpublished poem "for Katharine Taylor," dated September 25 [1937].

116: "between worlds": Katharine Taylor to MS, January 17, 1937. K.T. admitted to MS that she had been "hopelessly inarticulate" the past year.

"a very strange" . . . "Looking right down": MS to S. S. Koteliansky, October 17, 1937. MS tries to explain this incident in a letter to Elizabeth Bowen (September 25, 1937): MS suddenly asked Edith Forbes Kennedy, "Why didn't you marry Sean O'Casey?" "No one has ever asked me that before," said Edith. "I think my pride and his inexperience." In the emotional silence that followed, MS believed she had glimpsed Edith's heart for the first time; she fell in love.

"This room is charged": dated October 23, 1937, one of three unpublished sonnets to Edith Forbes Kennedy.

"There was nothing" . . . "deeper, truer": MS to S. S. Koteliansky, November 21, 1937. The resolve inspired the poem "Prayer Before Work," published in *IL*.

117: "I haven't heard": MS to S. S. Koteliansky, December 6, 1937.

"*You should get*": MS to MP in an interview of April 8, 1993.

"I think some": MS to S. S. Koteliansky, December 19, 1937.

"Nature being what": Edith Forbes Kennedy to MS, Cambridge, Wednesday [n.d. but probably January 12, 1938].

118: "The inevitable end": MS to S. S. Koteliansky, January 17, 1938.

"Now and then": MS to S. S. Koteliansky, January 23, 1938.

"The apparent completeness": MS to Polly Thayer Starr, June 20, 1936.

"Only a poet": Jane Spence Southran, *New York Times,* March 20, 1938. Harrison Smith, an old friend of MS, was so angered by Houghton Mifflin's lack of advertising of *Inner Landscape* that he gave HM $200 for advertising, challenging them to match it.

"I venture to prophesy": Willa Cather to Ferris Greenslet, March 22, 1938.

119: "like a wet flute": MS to S. S. Koteliansky [April 28, 1938]. MS's quarters on the *Normandie* were upgraded during the voyage to a "sumptuous" tourist cabin; perhaps Grace Dudley was the benefactor.

"She is a nice": MS to S. S. Koteliansky, *Normandie* [April 3?, 1938].

119: "It is the most": MS to GS and EMS, Le Petit Bois, April 9, 1938.

120: "I have never been": MS to Dr. Pederson-Krag, n.d., unpublished letter of self-analysis. MS's belief in a "typical lesbian" seems uninformed today.

"You are part": Grace Eliot Dudley to MS [n.d. but April 1938]. Grace begs for a letter but no more gifts: MS had sent her an Easter basket and books from Paris.

"For the sake": MS to GS and EMS, 35 Rosslyn Hill, London NW3, April 15 [1938].

"I have decided": MS to GS and EMS, April 19 [1938].

"absurd in the extreme": Virginia Woolf to MS, May 19 [1938], *The Letters of Virginia Woolf,* Vol. 6, p. 228.

121: "What a curious woman": MS to Elizabeth Bowen, Le Petit Bois, July 13, 1938.

"She is the most": MS to GS and EMS, Le Petit Bois, April 29, 1938.

"Perhaps I shall": MS to S. S. Koteliansky, Sunday [April 30, 1938].

"I must work": MS to GS and EMS, Le Petit Bois, May 8, 1938.

"No more emotional": MS to Elizabeth Bowen, Le Petit Bois, May 26, 1938.

122: "Kot, I really": MS to S. S. Koteliansky, Le Petit Bois, May 17, 1938.

"The wind which swept": published in *IL.*

"I am determined": MS to GS and EMS, 35 Rosslyn Hill, London NW3, June 27, 1938.

123: "If you slept": Grace Eliot Dudley to MS, July 1, 1938.

"I think I can help": MS to S. S. Koteliansky, Wed. morning [July 13, 1938].

"I have decided": MS to S. S. Koteliansky, Le Petit Bois, July 18, 1938.

"I feel that I": MS to GS and EMS, 35 Rosslyn Hill, London NW3, August 3, 1938.

124: "no chance that": MS to Juliette Huxley, aboard the *American Importer,* August 14 [1938].

"I wish you": EMS to S. S. Koteliansky, October 3, 1938.

"intelligent, nice": MS to S. S. Koteliansky, October 9, 1938.

The Waterfall: MS describes this unpublished novel in a letter to Elizabeth Bowen [October 9, 1938]: "I think perhaps I did do more or less what I wanted—to forsake the obvious poetic *style* and incorporate a poetic method into the work itself. . . ." The novel is about Miranda: the waterfall stood for her family; the island, for her escape from reality; the story describes her growing out of both these immature states.

"I feel very far": MS to S. S. Koteliansky, December 18, 1938.

"There are too many": unpublished poem, "We Are the Young," dated December 16, 1938.

125: "crashed through": MS to S. S. Koteliansky, January 1, 1939.

"he ever see" . . . "I dread so" . . . "intoxication and pleasure": MS to S. S. Koteliansky, January 22, 1939.

"an excess of love": MS to S. S. Koteliansky, March 12, 1939.

"You are wonderful": MS to S. S. Koteliansky, April 9, 1939.

"If her verses": Basil de Selincourt's three-column review in the *Observer* (April 9, 1939). It should be noted that de Selincourt was a conservative who hated T. S. Eliot, as well as a friend of MS.

125: "I believe": Ralph Abercrombie, *Time and Tide,* April 22, 1939; "Miss Sarton's language": Desmond Hawkins, *Spectator,* May 11, 1939; "It is not": Dudley Fitts, *Saturday Review,* August 26, 1939. MS's reaction to Abercrombie's criticisms was typical: "As always there is a grain of truth," she wrote Koteliansky on May 7, 1939, "and that I shall take to myself and forget the rest."

126: "forget your love" . . . "seek for sterner": MS, "A Letter to James Stephens," in *IL.*

"the central nerve": MS, "Architectural Image," in *IL.*

127: "almost drowning": MS to S. S. Koteliansky, April 1, 1939.

"a kind of illness": MS to S. S. Koteliansky, May 7, 1939.

"However something will": MS to S. S. Koteliansky, April 27, 1939.

"nice peaceful times": MS to GS and EMS, *Normandie,* June 18 [1939].

128: "not frightfully taken": MS to GS and EMS, 35 Rosslyn Hill, London NW3, June 22, 1939.

"I just can't" . . . "It is so dark": MS to EMS, June 27 [1939]. EMS commented on Ernesta Greene's remote, statuelike beauty, her silence. There was speculation that she felt an outsider in the family, not as bright as her three sisters, a failure; or that she took her family's gloomy discussions of world affairs too much to heart. Rather, her remoteness, commented upon for many years by MS and EMS, seems to indicate a severe personality disorder.

"sad, kind and *final*": MS to S. S. Koteliansky, *Normandie,* August 23 [1939].

129: "Please do not" . . . "I do love": MS to Juliette Huxley, Rockport, Mass., September 10 [1939] and 16 avenue Lequime, Brussels, August 12, 1939.

Chapter 10   My America: 1940–1944

130: "fears and doubts" . . . "an illness": Diary, St. Petersburg, Florida, December 27, 1939. MS frequently mentions this third novel, *F[ire] in a M[irror]*—unpublished, apparently discarded—in letters between 1939 and 1944. Marion, Alice, and John are characters; one theme is "What to do with living passion that has no outlet?" MS said in 1994 that the novel undoubtedly sprang from her frustrated passion for Edith Forbes Kennedy.

"I really felt": MS to Juliette Huxley, December 15, 1939. MS saw Julian two days in December, then flew to New York to see him January 6 and 7, 1940.

"absolutely enclosed": MS to S. S. Koteliansky, January 13, 1940.

131: "a fat boy": MS to S. S. Koteliansky, January 13, 1940.

"I haven't *touched*": Diary, March 15, 1940.

"An interesting idea": Diary, March 15, 1940.

"I have been going": MS to S. S. Koteliansky, March 17, 1940.

"like rayon": Diary, March 30, 1940.

"It is really": MS to S. S. Koteliansky, April 20, 1940.

"queer out of the way": MS to Juliette Huxley, Rockport, July 1, 1940.

"dead and unreal": MS to S. S. Koteliansky, June 9, 1940.

131: "inner *core*": Diary, May 14, 1940.

"with Spanish compliments": MS to S. S. Koteliansky, June 9, 1940.

132: "Yesterday I woke": Diary, August 12, 1940.

"Darling" . . . "strangely exalted state": MS to Margaret Hawley, August 16 and August 29 [1940].

"Mummy would adore": MS to Margaret Hawley, September 11, 1940.

"secret life-giving river": MS's unpublished "Letter to a Painter—For M.H.," dated August 1940.

"I suppose" . . . "We might have": MS to Margaret Hawley, postmark September 15, 1940; September 5, 1940. May's two days with Margaret Hawley in New York are a good example of the hectic pace she deliberately established: lunch with Roswell Hawley in Hartford on the way to New York; dinner with Margaret alone, but then a concert, after which Geoffrey Parsons, a *Herald Tribune* editor and former lover of Hawley's, came back to the studio and talked politics until 3:30 a.m.; on Sunday the zoo in Central Park for lunch, a drive, people for tea. "After that I felt quite ill with tiredness": MS to GS and EMS, October 1, 1940.

133: "I have been dead": MS to S. S. Koteliansky, November 1, 1940. An example of MS's indomitable spirit was her stay at Bethany College, where she arrived just after a winning football game had sent the campus into a celebratory frenzy. "Poetry," said May, "seemed like a very still small voice" (to GS and EMS, October 8, 1940). Undaunted, May composed a victory poem with which she began her lecture.

134: "I have saved" . . . "It must be spent": MS to Margaret Hawley, Limestone College, Gaffney, South Carolina, October 24, 1940.

"I'm afraid of what" . . . "I never really": MS to Margaret Hawley, Black Mountain College, Black Mountain, North Carolina, October 28 and 31, 1940.

135: "absurdly like a dove": MS, "Alice and Haniel Long," *AWOL*, 125. MS's portraits in *AWOL* were generally softened. To her parents she described Alice Long as "a dumpy woman with a vague blue eye, apparently no mind, a high vague voice and an incredible intuitive wisdom": December 17, 1940.

"camellia-white face": MS to Margaret Hawley, December 19, 1940.

"My only booking": MS to GS and EMS, December 17, 1940.

"It reminds me": MS to GS and EMS, December 30, 1940.

"*un coeur multiple*": MS, quoting Juliette, to Polly Thayer Starr, August 12 [1937].

136: "My heart beats" . . . "I am very": MS to Margaret Hawley, December 1940 and January 13, 1941.

137: "Dearest Daddy": MS to GS, January 21, 1941. "Beginning with March 1941," GS had written [January 20, 1941], "I'll give you $6 less each month and decrease by the same amount mother's allowance and the housekeeping expenses thus saving $18 a month or $180 for the remaining 10 months of 1941. My own expenditures will be decreased far more drastically. I trust you will do all you can to cooperate with Mother and me. To economize willingly in view of the future is not necessarily unpleasant; while to refrain from needed expenditures because there is no way out (neither reserve nor credit) is always painful, and sometimes very much so. Lovingly, George Sarton."

137: "see the landscape": MS to EMS, January 22, 1941.

"It matters": MS to S. S. Koteliansky, Allerton Hotel, Chicago, Easter Sunday [April 13, 1941].

138: "This has been": MS to S. S. Koteliansky, Straitsmouth Inn, Rockport, July 13, 1941.

"I say unfortunately": Diary, copy of a letter to Edith Forbes Kennedy, June 1941.

"forever of impatience" . . . "I am at peace" . . . "I cannot explain": MS to S. S. Koteliansky, Straitsmouth Inn, Rockport, August 24, 1941.

"all the waifs" . . . "I really had": MS to Juliette Huxley, December 29, 1941.

139: "queer pain" . . . "I really think": MS to Juliette Huxley, February 1, 1942.

"For me it is": MS to Juliette Huxley, March 4, 1942.

"your physical attractions": quoted in a letter from Gertrude Macy to MS, April 6, 1942.

"We layed": Gertrude Macy to MS, [April 20?] 1940.

"Near to tears": Diary, June 17, 1942.

140: "I have been worrying": GS to MS, June 21, 1942.

"The difficulty": MS to GS, June 24, 1942. MS did not stay at Anne Thorp's neocolonial Sudbury house continuously; she returned to Cambridge, for example, where five days of seeing people reduced her again to near nervous collapse. There was also a trip to Annisquam. Off and on she stayed at Sudbury through September.

"It is clear": MS to S. S. Koteliansky, July 19 [1942].

"She was the touchstone": MS to Juliette Huxley, September 19, 1942.

"a great large *sun*" . . . "something dangerous": MS to Juliette Huxley, January 29, 1943.

"It is very peaceful": MS to EMS, November 28, 1942.

141: "a great dynamic" . . . "It has been": MS to Juliette Huxley, January 29, 1943.

"white wonderful flaming": Muriel Rukeyser to MS [April 5, 1944].

"that delicate wiry": Muriel Rukeyser to MS, Wednesday, 1940.

"That was a brief": Muriel Rukeyser to MS, December 11, 1942.

"I can see" . . . "at the root": MS to Juliette Huxley, January 29, 1943.

"We do not need": MS to GS, January [4], 1943.

143: "Everyone is amazed": MS to GS and EMS, April 11, 1943. MS spent four days in Tennessee talking with the TVA staff in Knoxville, inspecting the Fontana and Watts Bar dams, inspecting demonstration farms.

"I like more": MS to GS and EMS, May 4, 1943. Son of the famed Irish-American humorist Finley Peter Dunne ("Mr. Dooley"), Philip Dunne was a founder of the Writers Guild of America, a Hollywood scriptwriter (*How Green Was My Valley*), director, and activist for liberal causes. MS later became disenchanted with Dunne's belief that they could combine her poetic with his "18th-century" style to produce a coherent script.

"The two things": MS to GS and EMS, 22 East Tenth Street, New York City, September 23 [1943].

144: "Do forgive me": EMS to MS, September 26, 1943.

"a shame for both": MS to GS and EMS, October 20, 1943.

144: "nervous, a bit": MS to GS and EMS, October 27, 1943.

145: "I love you": Muriel Rukeyser to MS [April 24, 1941].

"I am going to use": MS to Juliette Huxley, January 1, 1944.

"I wanted to live": MS to GS and EMS, quoting a San Francisco newspaper account of Tatlock's suicide, January 19, 1944. MS could not tell her parents the probable reason for Jean's death—another example of the secrecy her lesbianism forced her to adopt.

"Now it only remains": MS to GS and EMS, February 13, 1944.

"It occurred to me": GS to MS, February 27, 1944.

146: "Phil [Dunne] praised": MS to GS and EMS [March 3?10? 1943].

"so human": MS to Bill Brown, March 24, 1944.

"very beautiful" . . . "no better, deeper": MS to Bill Brown, April 23, 1944.

147: "be free in bed": Muriel Rukeyser to MS, quoting MS, February 8, 1945.

"I wish that": MS to Juliette Huxley, September 25, 1944.

Chapter 11   Judy: 1945–1947

148: "It is extraordinary": Céline Limbosch to EMS, April 8, 1940.

"the city died": "Letter from Chicago, for Virginia Woolf," written March 6 or 7, 1945, published in *The Land of Silence*. MS stayed with Marion Strobel, an editor of *Poetry,* in Chicago. "It was suddenly spring the day I came and I thought so much about Virginia Woolf. . . . And then I left Marion's and lived for a day on the 24th floor of the Stevens and wrote the poem" (MS to Bill Brown, March 11, 1945).

149: "a very nice": MS to GS and EMS, March 11, 1945.

"I have seen": MS to GS and EMS, March 12, 1945.

"poems are coming": MS to GS and EMS, March 12, 1945.

"in real *full tide*": MS to GS and EMS, 1945. The play was *The Underground River.* MS eventually sent it to Le Gallienne, who declined it but told her she should write plays, and to Katharine Cornell. It was not performed.

"simply on fire": MS to Bill Brown, March 22, 1945.

150: "Last summer": Muriel Rukeyser to MS, February 8, 1945.

"We are going" . . . "I feel sad": MS to Bill Brown, April 8, 1945, and April 27, 1946.

151: "It always seems": MS to MP, April 28, 1992.

"my own love": note added by Judith Matlack to MS to GS and EMS, May 2, 1945.

"I see all": MS to Bill Brown, June 24, 1945.

152: "I could never feel" . . . "We love each other": Diary, Taos, May 29, 1945. "Conversation last night—*Purity* of this," MS noted. MS and Judy had gone to Taos to be alone.

"I do occasionally": MS to Bill Brown, September 14, 1945.

"I feel like": MS to Juliette Huxley, November 26, 1945.

153: "It means quite a lot": MS to Juliette Huxley, January 20, 1946.

153: "this mixture": quoted by MS to Bill Brown, April 27, 1946. "The Lim-bosch[es] are really exactly the people in the book except that Paul [Raymond] is a poet and not a philosopher (but a very metaphysical and obscure poet who should have been a philosopher!)." MS omitted Jacques, the son who was killed moun-taineering, from *The Bridge of Years* because he didn't fit the story, but also because she felt including him would have been cruel. Professor Michel Thiery kindly lent me Céline's copy of *The Bridge of Years,* inscribed by MS, "For Aunty Lino and Oncle Raymond—This mixture of memory and inspiration, in which I hope they will find occasionally the gleam of truth—with love and homage—May, April 15, 1946." Céline has made astringent marginal notes, chiefly correcting factual matters: the Germans did *not* requisition the food off the table; Japanese cherry is not the same as nasturtiums; the Limbosches drank beer, not port; she *sowed* beans during lettuce time, not put up the poles; the mailman blew a whistle, not a horn. She also deleted phrases and lines.

"Its style is": *New York Herald Tribune,* April 21, 1946.

154: "abrupt, teasing meeting" . . . "*petite flame bleue*" . . . "nervousness and speed" . . . "I do love": MS to Juliette Huxley, July 13, 1946.

"buried in the heart": MS to Bill Brown [June 10, 1946].

"Here in the center": from "Poet in Residence" in *The Lion and the Rose* (1938–1948).

"You have made": MS to GS and EMS, July 3, 1946.

155: "oneself and one's family's": MS to Bill Brown, August 25, 1946.

"have them for consolation": MS to Bill Brown, November 7, 1946.

"a drama between" . . . "Nothing happens": MS to Bill Brown, December 10, 1946. MS makes diary notes (August 1946) for this novel (called *The Astounding Air*), which is obviously about Judy. "What N.E. [New England] qualities are exposed in her? The terrific sense of guilt (what kind of guilt? where from? about what?) Driv-ing her to 1) good works which really do not nourish 2) the fear of happiness as sin 3) to conceal her real feelings. . . ." She expanded further on this Santa Fe novel to Koteliansky on September 7, 1947: "The theme is really the effect upon a troubled and self-imprisoned New England woman of the landscape of the desert and high mountains of Santa Fe—the release of the self. But what has to be done now is to find the equivalent in *action* for this inward process."

"a large crowd": MS to GS, March 14, 1947.

"At nearly seventy": MS to GS, March 18, 1947.

156: "He was a little": MS to MP, March 14, 1992.

"a small wizened": MS to GS and EMS, April 18, 1947.

"I do not need": S. S. Koteliansky to MS, May 8, 1947.

157: "a ruin of what": MS to Bill Brown, May 5, 1947.

"The darkness crowds": MS to S. S. Koteliansky, May 11 [1947].

158: "Juliette has become": MS to S. S. Koteliansky, June 2, 1947.

"I am having": MS to GS and EMS, June 8, 1947.

"You should be": MS to MP, quoting Juliette, April 21, 1993.

"simply tie it": MS to Juliette Huxley, Saturday afternoon [June 14?, 1947].

158: "I remember everything": MS to Juliette Huxley [June 14?, 1947]. Socrates was Juliette's milliner; MS used him in "The Paris Hat" (*Cosmopolitan,* September 1948). "The David leaves" refers to an exhibition of Flemish art at which MS admired Gerard David's (c. 1460–1523) painting "of a wood with a stream, just leaves and trees but painted so that each leaf seemed a treasure" (MS to GS and EMS, June 13, 1947). Later MS and Juliette sat in chairs on the avenue Foch, looking up at the Arc de Triomphe. "The glittering leaves . . ." is the first stanza of an unpublished poem for Juliette.

159: "I do so wonder": MS to Juliette Huxley, June 16, 1947, and Sunday morning [June 15?, 1947].

160: "And on your part" . . . "You can say *no*": MS to Juliette Huxley, Sunday morning [June 15?, 1947].

"I bet you forget": MS to Juliette Huxley, June 20 [1947].

"frightfully quick" . . . "truly renounced": MS to Juliette Huxley, Sunday morning [June 22, 1947].

"I have invented": MS to Juliette Huxley, Hanswert, Zeeland, Wednesday, June 25 [1947].

"The boat was": MS to GS and EMS, June 28, 1947.

"I am much too": MS to S. S. Koteliansky, June 22, 1947.

"to fly over": MS to Juliette Huxley, July 2, 1947.

161: "rage of absence" . . . "could not receive" . . . "Darling": MS to Juliette Huxley, July 5, 1947.

"I shall not": MS to Juliette Huxley [July 8?, 1947].

"no pressure": MS to Juliette Huxley, July 13, 1947.

"the only flight": MS to Juliette Huxley, July 11, 1947.

"I think perhaps": MS to GS and EMS, July 18, 1947.

162: "I wear you": MS to Juliette Huxley [July 21, 1947].

"You have seen me in Hell": Juliette Huxley to MS [n.d], quoted in Diary, August 12–17 [1947]. Though perhaps written after MS's letter of July 24, 1947, it was undoubtedly typical of Juliette's replies that summer, and is one of the few fragments of her side of the correspondence to survive.

"But do not": MS to Juliette Huxley, Thursday afternoon [July 24?, 1947].

"I miss you": Judith Matlack to MS, June 12 [1948].

"endless bonds": Diary, quoting a letter of EMS to Elsie Masson, May 12, 1947, expressing her condolences to Mme Masson on the death of her son Yves and speculating that May's death would instill in her "the *habit of grief.*"

163: "I do not know": MS to Judith Matlack, June 10, 1947.

Chapter 12   Cast Out: 1947–1948

164: "that great monster": MS to S. S. Koteliansky, August 1, 1947.

"Of course I": MS to Juliette Huxley, Sunday morning, August 3 [1947].

"Love really does": MS to Juliette Huxley, August 1, 1947.

164: "May, your PUNCTUATION!" . . . "if a poem": MS to S. S. Koteliansky, September 18, 1947.

165: "I have to keep": MS to Juliette Huxley, September 17, 1947.

"very angry": MS to Juliette Huxley, September 27 [1947].

"*Perhaps* she will": MS to Juliette Huxley, September 27 [1947].

"fabulous news": MS to Bill Brown, November 20, 1947.

"My life seems": MS to Bill Brown, December 7, 1947.

166: "What hell!": MS to Juliette Huxley, February 16 [1948].

"It is really": MS quoting GS to MP, March 14, 1992.

"Men are terrible" . . . "Women are always": MS to Juliette Huxley, January 12, 1948, and April 16 [1948].

"It seems to me": Judith Matlack to MS, Valentine's Day, 1948.

"the sinew of" . . . "Of course Benét": MS to Bill Brown, January 26, 1948.

"an achievement": Martha Bacon in *Saturday Review,* April 17, 1948.

"troubling beauty" . . . "alchemical translation": Ray Smith in *Poetry* 73 (February 1949).

167: "In Texas the lid" . . . "The time must": "In Texas" and "Monticello" both appear in *The Lion and the Rose.* MS dropped this last stanza of "Monticello" for Norton's publication of *Collected Poems: 1930–1973* in 1974.

"You teachers, mothers": Unpublished "New Year Letter, 1944."

"One boy came": MS to Bill Brown, March 8, 1947.

168: "really heard": MS to GS and EMS, Fredericksburg, Virginia, March 2 [1948].

"The Negroes here": MS to GS and EMS, Durham, North Carolina, March 18 [1948].

"I do not dare" . . . "Thank God you": MS to Juliette Huxley, February 16 [1948] and February 22, 1948.

"In some ways": MS to Bill Brown, March 29, 1948.

169: "Now, my love": MS to Juliette Huxley, R.M.S. *Queen Mary,* April 11 [1948].

"Your daughter": S. S. Koteliansky to MS, March 28 [1948]—Kot's last preserved letter to MS.

"a wise old God": MS to Bill Brown, Kingham, Oxon, April 20, 1948.

"three unbelievably passionate": MS to Bill Brown, 18 avenue Lequime, Rhode-St.-Genèse, May 5, 1948.

"*wonderful* peaceful time": MS to EMS, May 4, 1948.

"I understand now": MS to Bill Brown, May 5, 1948.

"Now the storm" . . . "which exploits itself": MS to Juliette Huxley, Tuesday morning [May 4, 1948].

170: "a state of perpetual": MS to Bill Brown, May 19 [1948].

"full of bitter wisdom": MS to Judith Matlack, July 28, 1948.

"Apparently Juliette": MS to S. S. Koteliansky, May 12, 1948.

"Let me know": MS to Juliette Huxley, Friday night [May 7, 1948].

"which makes this": MS to Judith Matlack, May 26, 1948.

"I am getting over": MS to S. S. Koteliansky, June 10, 1948.

171: "Julian just wanted": MS to MP, March 29, 1994.

171: "swan and love and star": a second version, unpublished, of "The Swans," in *TLOTT.*

"I am very tempted": MS to Juliette Huxley, July 13 [1948] and July 14 [1948].

"three days of sheer Hell": MS to Judith Matlack, July 23, 1948. MS had arrived in Paris in an overwrought state due to a telegram from Juliette, "Situation sans controle," which she interpreted in the direst sense; it turned out that the garbled telegram had originally read, "Situation sous controle"—*under* control.

"It is dangerous": MS to Bill Brown, 18 avenue Lequime, August 4, 1948.

"the too-muchness": MS to Juliette Huxley, July 30 [1948].

172: "Just because": MS to Juliette Huxley, Kingham, August 13 [1948].

173: "Let us forget": MS to S. S. Koteliansky, August 21, 1948. MS was staying in London at Ruth Pitter's at 55A Old Church Street, since Kot would not have her.

"I think it made": MS to Juliette Huxley, Rockbrook House, Rockfarnham, Ireland, September 4, 1948.

"I felt I had": Beatrice Glenavy to MS, September 17, 1948.

174: "Anyway I am": MS to Bill Brown, *Britannia,* September 16, 1948.

"I think you are": Beatrice Glenavy to MS, September 25, 1948.

"I saw that you": Beatrice Glenavy to MS, October 21 [1948].

"The crying": Beatrice Glenavy to MS, December 14, 1948, quoting Juliette.

175: "Juliette got together": MS to Bill Brown, December 2, 1948. MS did destroy Juliette's letters written from May 1947 to November 1948. All of Julian Huxley's 388 letters to MS and the remainder of Juliette's are in the Berg Collection of the NYPL.

"You see, what happened": Juliette Huxley to MS, July 14, 1976. Juliette and MS began writing with some frequency again when Juliette went through MS's letters to Julian and herself after Julian's death. She sent MS's letters back, saying she thought the ones to her might eventually be published. Since MS told me several times that Juliette and Kot dropped her because she flirted with Beatrice Glenavy, it is probable that she had forgotten Juliette's damning revelation when she gave me her later letters to read.

177: "I wish you": MS to Juliette Huxley, 940 Acequia Madre, Santa Fe, April 15, 1945.

Chapter 13   Loss: 1949–1950

178: "You know, I" . . . "No, I can't": MS to MP, March 14, 1992, quoting EMS.

"total lack of": MS to Juliette Huxley, October 28, 1948.

179: "I think men": MS in the video *She Knew a Phoenix,* produced in 1980. MS had held this view most of her professional life.

"There is just no doubt": MS to Bill Brown, February 15, 1949.

180: "There is now" . . . "I do not wish" . . . "Please don't send": Juliette Huxley to MS, February 1949; February 10, 1949; April 26 [1949?].

"I feel just as I did": MS to Bill Brown, February 15, 1949.

"colossal check": MS to GS and EMS, May 5, 1949.

180: "Now she is 37": unpublished, undated poem in MS's diary, probably written in London in May 1949.

181: "All this love": MS to GS and EMS, May 13, 1949.

"Dearest Tata": MS to GS and EMS, May 25, 1949.

182: "I'm sure he is": MS to GS and EMS, May 29, 1949.

"One must expect": MS to GS and EMS, June 4, 1949.

"The fact is": MS to GS and EMS, June 8, 1949.

"So, dearest Daddums": MS to GS and EMS, June 17, 1949.

183: "a big, simple kind": MS to GS and EMS, July 24, 1949.

"Judy is happy" . . . "I do not deserve": MS to GS and EMS, July 20 and July 16, 1949.

"in a perpetual state": MS to GS and EMS, July 29, 1949.

"a heavenly afternoon" . . . "The evil spell": MS to GS and EMS, August 9, 1949.

"I really had" . . . "All I want": MS to Bill Brown, September 3 and 10, 1949. That fall MS continued to send Julian Huxley "non-committal but amusing post-cards," eliciting "a frigid letter from Juliette to stop bothering her." Bill Brown strongly advised MS to stop writing Juliette, advice she followed to a point.

184: "I am not really": MS to Bill Brown, October 2, 1949.

"I really have a pain": MS to GS and EMS, November 15, 1949.

"I am absolutely": MS to Bill Brown, January 15, 1950.

"feeling old, strange": "On a Winter Night," published in *TLOS* (1950–1953) and also in *Now I Become Myself* (1992), a collection in honor of MS's eightieth birthday.

185: "wonderful, kind": MS to Bill Brown, March 25, 1950.

186: "a dismal failure": MS to Bill Brown, October 14, 1950.

"with gardens springing": MS to Polly Thayer Starr, Wednesday, Stonehaven, Rockport [n.d.].

"I must say": MS to Bill Brown, September 23, 1950.

"What is this?": MS to MP, October 10, 1992.

"I cannot reach": EMS to MS, Mon. night [fall 1948], *Letters to May,* 71–72.

187: "She was beautiful": MS to Bill Brown, November 20, 1950.

"Perhaps she imagines": MS to GS, November 26, 1950.

188: "I failed her" . . . "The reader must": GS's unpublished notes for a biography of EMS (York).

"I saw my mother": unpublished "New Year Poem, 1950."

"Everything is perfect": MS to Juliette Huxley, writing about EMS's death [December 1950].

Chapter 14   New Novels, New Poems, New Lovers: 1951–1955

189: "You can give": MS to Judith Matlack, August 6 [1950]. Having given up the Oxford Street apartment, Judy was on a western trip that included Santa Fe. Perhaps her description of the tremendously warm welcome given her in Santa Fe annoyed May.

189: "You write too many": Judith Matlack to MS, June 5, 1951.

"I send you": MS to S. S. Koteliansky, January 7, 1951.

190: "I shall never" . . . "Vite!": Diary, quoting Eugénie [July 1951].

"Eugénie under the trees": Diary [July 1951].

"All that has happened": Eugénie Dubois to MS, July 20 and 28, 1951.

191: "old flame": MS referred to Méta as EMS's "old flame" in letters to Juliette Huxley and Bill Brown. As she said in the film *World of Light,* EMS had passionate friendships with women; probably they were not actually sexual.

"I like to think": Eugénie Dubois to MS, August 23, 1951.

"I was starving": Eugénie Dubois to MS, August 21, 1951.

192: "*cannot* leave off": Eugénie Dubois to MS, October 22, 1951.

"There you are": Eugénie Dubois to MS, June 5, 1952.

193: "Damned sentimental friends" . . . "and there I found": MS to Bill Brown, Satigny, Geneva, Switzerland, August 5 [1952].

"the vulnerable, thin-skinned": Eugénie Dubois to MS, August 8, 1952.

"It is queer": MS to Bill Brown, August 5 [1952]. Jean Dominique died July 19, 1952.

"I simply this time" . . . "I hope that": MS to Bill Brown, August 5 [1952].

194: "cut off again": MS to Bill Brown, September 21, 1952.

"like a neurotic rat": MS to Bill Brown, October 12, 1952.

"to regard teaching": Diary [October 1952].

"The values which": MS to Bill Brown, January 31, 1953.

"feminine sensitive": MS to S. S. Koteliansky, November 15, 1953.

195: "I get terrified": MS to Bill Brown, November 23 [1952].

"looking up": MS to Bill Brown, January 31, 1953.

"Now I become": "Now I Become Myself," in *TLOS* (1950–1953).

"Do not expect": GS to MS, June 24, 1952.

"like a metal image": MS to Juliette Huxley, December 15, 1939.

"this terrible division": MS to S. S. Koteliansky, May 19, 1940.

"Nothing, I suppose": Louise Bogan to MS, April 24, 1940.

196: "rather mean": MS to Bill Brown, February 15, 1953.

"fearfully attracted" . . . "great self restraint": MS to Bill Brown, October 4, 1953.

"Does she know": Eugénie Dubois to MS [1953].

"Even when here": Eugénie Dubois to MS, November 9, 1953.

"strange and terrifying": MS to Louise Bogan, June 27, 1954. MS would eventually forget Beth's last name, but at this writing Beth was visiting Wright Street during a week that Judy was away. "Nothing is solved," MS wrote Bogan, "or ever will be, but we have perhaps reached a place where love at least can flow through now and no recriminations. She is quite a remarkable person and has handled what, especially for her, was a devastating thing, with courage and wisdom."

"full of faults": MS to Bill Brown, October 27, 1953.

"the two most interesting": MS to Bill Brown, November 22 [1953].

197: "May, perhaps because": Richard Wilbur to Marilyn Kallet, quoted in *A House of Gathering: Poets on May Sarton's Poetry,* 16.

"I think the one": John Ciardi to John Holmes, October 26, 1955, in *The Selected Letters of John Ciardi,* ed. Edward M. Cifelli (Fayetteville: University of Arkansas Press, 1991).

"high-pitched" . . . "absolutely, fiercely": John Ciardi, *The Nation,* February 13, 1954, 184.

"What he does . . . into salt": MS to Bill Brown, January 3, 1954. There is a large gap in MS's correspondence with Bill Brown from this letter until October 24, 1966.

"this queer sensation": MS to Louise Bogan, May 20, 1954.

"The New Yorker": MS to Louise Bogan, January 30 [1954].

"happy and full": MS to S. S. Koteliansky, January 31, 1954.

"that robin's egg": MS to Louise Bogan, January 24, 1954.

198: "So far as" . . . "Be happy": Louise Bogan to MS, January 28 and February 16, 1954.

"Darling, darling, darling": MS to Louise Bogan [February or March 1954].

"The critical power": MS to Louise Bogan, March 21, 1954.

"You *do* drive": Louise Bogan to MS, April 16, 1954.

"The great and unexpected": Louise Bogan to MS, June 18, 1954.

"indignant essay" . . . "There are times": MS to Louise Bogan, March 12, 1955.

199: "Of course, everything": Louise Bogan to MS, March 17, 1955.

200: "inhuman, monstrous": MS to S. S. Koteliansky, April 3, 1954. With the exception of a postcard from Switzerland and her 1954 Christmas poem, "Nativity: Piero della Francesca," this is MS's last communication with Kot, who had stopped writing her in March 1948.

"I keep thinking": Louise Bogan to MS, May 11, 1953.

"at bottom she" . . . "because she is": MS to GS, August 11 and 14, 1954.

201: "pagan" Italy: MS to GS, September 12 [1954]: "The Italians do have a simple kind of pagan charm. . . . It is, I feel a pagan land, in spite of all its Christian surface."

"completely immobile" . . . "I love you" . . . "Do not agonize": Eugénie Dubois to MS, September 20, 1954.

"I do love": Eugénie Dubois to MS, October 3, 1954.

"I really have": MS to S. S. Koteliansky, September 22 [1954].

"How courageous!": Eugénie Dubois to MS, November 24, 1954.

202: "So many thoughts": Diary, passages headed "Kot, January 25 [1955].

"Maylume" . . . "I am so fond": From S. S. Koteliansky's letters to MS, June 1937–October 1939 (Berg).

"three beautiful dreams . . . Where is the": Diary, February 2 and January 8 [1955].

"I am a little": Eugénie Dubois to MS, April 4, 1955.

203: "It may interest": Harry Levin to MS, August 7, 1955, in reply to a letter from MS of July 20, 1955, defending her novel. Despite MS's claim that she was "forever barred" from Harvard, she taught at Radcliffe 1956–1958 and was invited to speak at the Harvard Signet Club (the first woman to do so) on April 15, 1967. Professor W. J. Bate believes that MS perhaps did not understand that the Briggs-Copeland appointments never led to tenure at Harvard, not even when held by Wallace Stegner, Mark Schorer, or Richard Ellmann.

203: "I did not feel": MS to Professor Katharine C. Turner, March 17, 1958. Turner had questioned MS's blend of fact and fiction in *Faithful* on a theoretical level.

"And I'd never": MS to MP, April 28, 1992.

204: "Oh, I know": Cora DuBois to MS, August 12, 1956.

"I curse it": Sonnet 6, *EIA* (1937).

"How to turn": Diary, December [1955].

"I loved my mother": Passages taken from two unpublished statements to Dr. Pederson-Krag, dated September 12 and 29, 1955.

206: "Never look straight": "The Furies," in *ITLA* (1958).

"So you really": Eugénie Dubois to MS, October 3, 1955.

"Poor Judy": Eugénie Dubois to MS, December 20, 1955.

Chapter 15   "No Longer Child": 1956–1958

207: "No Longer Child": From "My Father's Death," *ITLA* (1958).

"Daddy dear": MS to GS, March 20, 1956.

"My prayer is": MS to Judith Matlack, March 26 [1957]. MS's diary gives the time of GS's death as 7:30 a.m. He would have been seventy-two on August 31, the age of EMS when she died. MS's diary is also the source for the memorial service at the Harvard Chapel. She has said elsewhere that about one hundred people attended the service. The poor attendance bothered her the rest of her life.

"was not appropriate": MS to MP, April 8, 1993.

208: "I need neither hope": Diary, quoting a letter of September 10, 1935, to GS from Richard Cabot, who calls GS's motto "one of the most satisfying I have ever heard"— "Je n'ai pas besoin d'espérer pour entreprendre, ni de réussir pour persévérer."

"*We were talking*": MS to MP, April 8, 1993.

"thin smoke": "Burial" in *ADF.*

"I never saw": "A Celebration," printed as MS's 1956 Christmas poem, later published in *ITLA* as "A Celebration of George Sarton."

209: "the arch-neurotic": Diary, May 3 [1956]: "Mother—the arch-neurotic as *life-giver.*"

"lay down their deaths": Paraphrase of "How to lay down her death," "After Four Years," *ITLA.*

210: "As far as I can see": MS to MP, April 28, 1992.

"I told [a writer friend]": MS to Louise Bogan, Tuesday [February 2, 1954].

211: "My honey bunny": MS to Judith Matlack, May 22, 1956.

212: "drowning and uprootedness": MS to Eugénie Dubois, July 11, 1956.

"the earth under": Diary, December 25, 1953.

"My darling lamb": MS to Judith Matlack [March 11?, 1957].

"There is no point": Judith Matlack to MS, April 2, 1957.

"I most deeply": Judith Matlack to MS [after 1957]. About her psychoanalysis, Judith continues, "I have found no answers, I have only found some light in dark places."

212: "rich with spoils" . . . "power in reserve": Diary, March 28 [1957].

"the poet and the hero": MS's terms in "Dichotomy," an unpublished poem, February 1957.

213: "so sneering": MS to Kay Martin, May 31, 1957.

"I keep thinking": MS to Judith Matlack, June 6 [1957].

"An awful lot" . . . "I always imagine": MS to Kay Martin, June 16, 1957.

"follows me here . . . hard and clear": MS to Louise Bogan, June 17 [1957].

"locked into rage" . . . "I'll be glad": MS to Kay Martin, June 22, 1957.

214: "Everybody knows": MS to MP, May 1, 1992. See notes to chapter 1. The question of whether the Van Halmés were Jewish was still not resolved in MS's mind in 1992 (in 1994 her biographer obtained a report from Belgium indicating that they were Catholic). "I tried very hard to find out," MS told MP, "and I wasn't able to find out. . . . I even have a poem, which is probably in those poems which haven't been published, called 'If I Forget the Old Jerusalem.' I was tremendously moved at the idea of this; and I think being a quarter Jewish would be ideal. I mean, I'd rather not be all Jewish maybe, but a quarter would be *fine*."

"I have always": MS to Kay Martin, La Roselle, Geneva, July 24, 1957.

"would always have": MS to Kay Martin, August 4, 1957.

215: "You are so buoyant": Cora DuBois to MS, August 20, 1958.

"crude, corny": Granville Hicks, *New Leader,* October 7, 1957.

"My own private feeling": MS to Kay Martin, September 12, 1957.

"with infinite labor": MS to Kay Martin, September 12, 1957.

"this sense of despair": Diary, September 10 [1957].

216: "I am trying": MS to Kay Martin, September 12, 1957.

"I am in a bad low": MS to Kay Martin, October 4, 1957.

"the best kind": Raymond Holden, reviewing also Richard Aldrich's *An Apology Both Ways* and Evelyn Ames's *The Hawk from Heaven,* in *New York Times Book Review,* December 22, 1957.

"the ease" . . . "civilized and intricate": Robert Hazel in *Poetry,* August 1959.

217: "I did it for Cora": MS to MP, April 8, 1993.

218: "a beautiful green tree": Eleanor Newman Hutchens to MP, February 5, 1995.

"delicate as a leaf": "Inscription, for Ellen Douglas [sic]," unpublished poem, written April 19, 1958, on the flight from Decatur to Boston: "I feel your profile carve, / Delicate as a leaf, / Itself into my nerve."

"All the beauty": Ellen Douglass Leyburn to MS, April 21, 1958.

219: "In the evening": "The Light Left On," in *TLOS.*

"This letter comes": Draft of letter from Judith Matlack to MS, n.d., apparently written while MS was in Europe in 1957.

220: "Judy was a darling!": Eleanor Blair to MP, April 25, 1992. Eleanor Blair died at the age of ninety-seven on May 7, 1992, two weeks after I spoke with her. In 1943 she had been fired from Dana Hall ("driven out," in MS's words); she continued to live in Wellesley on Cottage Street, doing free-lance editing for publishing houses. Over the years she took hundreds of photographs of MS and Nelson, now in the archives of Wellesley College.

Chapter 16   Nelson: 1958–1960

221: "I moved into": "Moving In," in *CSSV*.

"Here at Nelson": Diary [May 1959].

222: "part of that whole": MS to Ellen Douglass Leyburn, July 21, 1958, quoting from a letter to Cora DuBois.

"I did a terrible thing": MS to MP, April 26, 1992.

"Darling, I cannot": MS to Cora DuBois, Wright Street, October 7, 1958.

223: "I *seem* to be": "Louise Bogan," in *AWOL,* 225.

"a dear true friend": MS to Kay Martin, February 10 [1959].

225: "Oh, all that book": MS to Kay Martin, May 12 [1959].

226: "an only child": Diary, Greenings Island, August 1958: "Notes for a Novel."

"inward depletion": MS to Kay Martin, in hospital, December 16 [1958].

"Do not grieve": Ellen Douglass Leyburn to MS, October 26, 1958.

227: "this awful expense": Ellen Douglass Leyburn to MS, January 4, 1959.

"claggy": Bowen's term for anything maudlin, sentimental, or hyperintense. Victoria Glendinning, *Elizabeth Bowen: A Biography* (New York: Alfred A. Knopf, 1978), 241.

"I shall get well": MS to Cora DuBois, April 8, 1959.

"I do love you": MS to Cora DuBois, April 14 [1959].

"I love you": MS to Kay Martin, May 12 [1959], quoting a letter from Cora.

228: "What is your *need*" . . . "What I can't": Diary, May 5 [1959].

"I have found" . . . "invisible walls": MS to Kay Martin, August 7 and 10 [1959].

"only relief": MS to Kay Martin, August 25, 1959.

229: "I see that far more": MS to Kay Martin, July 4 [1959].

"the dread of arriving": MS to Cora DuBois, May 3, 1959.

"If I were you" . . . "Let's eat": MS to Kay Martin, September 17 and 8, 1959.

"She did make": MS to Kay Martin, September 17 [1959].

"She will never love": MS to Kay Martin, September 17 [1959].

230: "Here is the room": Published in *CSSV.*

231: "going back": MS to Kay Martin, 20 Coolidge Hill, October 4, 1959.

"I saw Cora" . . . "Now you leave": MS to Kay Martin, October 30 [1959].

"There is no doubt": MS to Cora DuBois, December 5, 1959. Cora DuBois evidently did destroy MS's letters; passages of letters to Cora quoted in this and other chapters are taken from carbon copies made by MS.

Chapter 17   Wellesley: 1960–1968

234: "The ashtrays" . . . "so young and eager": MS to Kay Martin, February 17, 1960.

"sensitive to": MS to Cora DuBois, December 5 [1959]. MS paid Dr. Hall $200 a month from her $500 monthly salary.

"dwindle and pine": MS to Bill Brown, January 9, 1946.

"I can confess": MS to Kay Martin, April 4, 1960.

235: "feeling like a" . . . "I know it is": MS to Kay Martin, April 4, 1960.

"The cat sleeps": Sonnet 16, "A Divorce of Lovers," in *CSSV.*

"like a gentle" . . . "like very fine steel": MS to Kay Martin, June 6, 1960.

"Nell . . . is here": MS to Kay Martin, July 19, 1960.

236: "no one important": MS to MP, May 1, 1992. I had found three folders of letters from Kay Martin in MS's files and spent the day on the first two before MS told me not to bother.

237: "with such conviction": MS to Kay Martin, November 3, 1960. The collection MS made of GS's essays was never published.

"quite thrilling": MS to Kay Martin, January 1, 1961.

238: "I feel as if": MS to Kay Martin, January 24, 1961.

"Lover of ceremony": "Death of a Painter," published in the *Keene Sentinel,* January 26, 1961.

"ga-ga" over Dietrich: MS to Kay Martin, January 29, 1961.

239: "My big question": Carbon of April 16, 1961, letter.

"T'aint in character": Cora DuBois to MS, October 8, 1961.

"Which check" . . . "I've never" . . . "Next time": MS to Kay Martin, October 28, 1961.

240: "Great teachers": Diary, Greenings Island, August 1958: "Notes for a Novel."

"I almost never": MS to Kay Martin, October 28, 1961.

"mean review" . . . "I think they": MS to Kay Martin, October 14 [1961].

241: "I just quiver": MS to Kay Martin, October 28, 1961.

"My objection": Louise Bogan to MS, October 31, 1961.

243: "The hardest thing": MS to Louise Bogan, September 4, 1962, quoting from an apparently lost letter to Bogan of December 1960 or January 1961.

"I had her take": Louise Bogan to Ruth Limmer, September 28, 1960, in *What the Woman Lived: Selected Letters of Louise Bogan, 1920–1970,* 325. For MS's reaction to Bogan's stricture, see Chapter 26.

"There is something": Kay Martin to MS, February 25, 1966, on the occasion of MS's bewailing that she was "a failed, elderly writer."

"a little in love": "A Child's Japan," in *APM.*

"Rushing into the house": "A Country House, for Shio Sakanishi," in *APM.*

244: "She seems like" . . . "thank god!" . . . "There seems": MS to Kay Martin, Bhubaneswar, April 6, 1962.

245: "I have just been": MS to Kay Martin, September 4 [1962].

"*Noli me tangere*" . . . "I shall not bore": MS to Louise Bogan, September 4, 1962.

246: "two major and longish": MS to Kay Martin, Wright Street, September 25, 1962.

"Who listens so": "Death of a Psychiatrist," in *APM.* MS sent the poem to Dr. Hall's widow and was very hurt when she did not receive a reply. Two years later, however, Mrs. Hall wrote to say how much the poem had moved her.

"quite preposterous": MS to Kay Martin, Scripps College, Claremont, California, April 30, 1963. *Joanna and Ulysses* appeared in the September 1963 issue of *Ladies' Home Journal;* Norton published it that year.

246: "all the wild parts" . . . "being a woman": MS to Kay Martin, Cambridge, October 27 [1963].

247: "an idle lunch": from a series MS called "Letters to a Silence," fourteen poems written during December 1963 and January and February 1964. Nine of them were published in the *Virginia Quarterly,* winning second prize ($250) in a *VQ* poetry contest; six in *TSN* under "Letters to an Administrator."

248: "I think, on the whole": MS to Margaret Clapp, February 18, 1964.

"Margaret, there's" . . . "Miss Sarton": MS to MP, May 1, 1992.

"As usual the person": MS to Rosalind Greene, February 23, 1964.

"Margaret, I've sent": MS to MP, May 1, 1992.

249: "If we must do him in": "Interview," from "Letters to a Silence," published as "Moment of Truth" in *TSN.*

"It destroyed": MS to MP, May 1, 1992.

"It was because": MS to MP, edited from conversations of May 1, 1992, and July 20, 1993.

250: "I have thought": MS to Margaret Clapp, Yaddo, November 29 [1964].

251: "Everything is in order": MS to Margaret Clapp, January 26, 1966.

"filled with mystery" . . . "For a little while": MS to Margaret Clapp, June 25, 1966.

252: "tremendous scene" . . . "It was like": MS to MP, May 1, 1992. After the unsuccessful visit to Tyringham, May wrote on April 24, 1968: "I want to see you. . . . I still hope you will come to Nelson." It is the last of the carbon copies of MS's letters to Margaret Clapp in the York files.

Chapter 18   Mrs. Stevens Dreams Deep: 1965–1968

254: "People want to": MS to MP in a note of July 28, 1993, correcting a comment in an interview of July 20, 1993.

255: "horrendous gut-destroying": MS to Kay Martin, February 12, 1965. MS feared that Norton would not take *Mrs. Stevens,* but heard in mid-January 1965 that they would offer her a $3,000 advance.

"I suppose this": MS to Kay Martin, quoting Cora, February 12, 1965.

256: "I wake up": MS to Kay Martin, April 23, 1965.

"It is really wonderful": MS to Kay Martin, August 5, 1965.

257: "a sort of saint": MS to Kay Martin, October 5, 1965.

"that rat, Virginia Kirkus": MS to Kay Martin, August 5, 1965.

"a posturing, self-pitying": John Gardiner, "An Invective Against Mere Fiction," *Southern Review,* 3 (Spring 1967): 444–67.

"What hurts" . . . "not only the best": MS to Eleanor Blair, October 24, 1965.

258: "sheer Hell because": MS to Eleanor Blair, October 29, 1965.

"I sense that": MS to Eleanor Blair [early November? 1965].

259: "For Margaret": MS to Eleanor Blair, quoting, February 7, 1966.

260: "Meanwhile Ellen Douglass": MS to Kay Martin, March 15, 1966.

260: "Well, your face": MS to Eleanor Blair, quoting Céline, London, May 18, 1966.

"stealing the soul": MS to Eleanor Blair, May 3, 1966. According to MS, a lawyer, hoping to get money out of her, since *Joanna and Ulysses* had been optioned as a movie, persuaded Joanna Carayanni to sue. MS instructed Eleanor:

> It might be worth your going up to the files and taking a look in the bottom drawers of the tall *wooden files.* I have not kept Joanna's letters usually but I think there may be one or two there in a folder marked Joanna Carayanni. If you find them, read them all. Make copies of any that you think might be useful and send them to Eric Swenson and W. W. Norton. . . . There is one long letter or perhaps two that *may be* in the open file on the shelf to left of my desk either under "Business pending" *or* under "To File." Third possible, look in the bound copy of *J. and U.* in case there is a letter there. Also in the bottom section of the *new* grand file to left of door in the file room where I have folders containing letters concerned with specific books. I think the *J. and U.* folder is there and I think there is at least one letter from her in it. Quite a sleuthing job!

The suit was eventually dropped.

"Every time May's" . . . "The general atmosphere" . . . "Of course, my own": Judith Matlack to Eleanor Blair, May 8, 13, and 18, 1966.

"I have to be": MS to Eleanor Blair, May 3, 1966. Judy's purse contained all her money, her passport, and her return ticket. May drove back to the police station at Chartres, where a lost bag had been reported by an old woman who ran a café. They retrieved the purse miraculously at the café, giving the woman twenty dollars as a reward.

261: "I know that you": MS to Eleanor Blair, June 21, 1966.

"Miss Sarton has taken": William Pritchard, *Hudson Review,* Summer 1967, 307.

"savage brilliance" . . . "wrathful commitment": Joseph Bennett, *New York Times Book Review,* November 13, 1966.

262: "beyond beautiful": MS to Eleanor Blair, quoting Perley Cole, October 6, 1966.

"Just read over": MS to Eleanor Blair, October 17, 1966.

"small name-droppings": MS to Eleanor Blair, October 22, 1966.

"The real problem": MS to Eleanor Blair, November 2, 1966.

263: "Darling, I can": MS to Eleanor Blair, February 20, 1967.

"I did not sleep": MS to Eleanor Blair, Saturday morning [March? 1967].

"kind but extremely enervating": MS to Beverly Hallam, March 13 [1967].

"the whole book": MS to Eleanor Blair, April 4 [1967].

"a glorious revelation": MS to Eleanor Blair, February 28, 1967.

264: "snubbed and humiliated": MS to Bill Brown, May 30, 1967.

"I am really worried": MS to Eleanor Blair, May 29, 1967.

"I can only say" . . . "good animals": MS to Beverly Hallam, December 3, 1966, and October 31, 1967.

265: "the awful things": MS to Beverly Hallam, May 29, 1967.

"Let's go make": Joan Cobleigh Gerbis to MP, interview, October 17, 1992.

"I know only too well": MS to Eleanor Blair, August 2 [1967].

266: "What a sensitive" . . . "Don't ever feel": Katharine Taylor to MS, May 3, 1959, and July 9, 1965.

"fire engine": MS to Bill Brown, October 7 [1967].

"Of course I knew": MS to Bill Brown, Bussum, Holland, October 7 [1967].

267: "She was a lioness": MS to MP, May 1, 1992.

"caught up in the eye": MS to Eleanor Blair, Bussum, Holland, October 4, 1967.

"any major love affair": MS to Bill Brown, November 2, 1967. MS's report to Kay Martin of Hannie Van Till's letter-writing capacities differs: "Hannie writes such dear nourishing letters—it seems almost unbelievable to harried and wounded old me, to have this balm." Judging from the Van Till letters in MS's files, MS's description of Hannie as "non-verbal" is the truth.

"I now look": MS to Eleanor Blair, October 24, 1967.

"gather the grapes": written in 1967 after the Hannie Van Till affair; published as "Myself to Me" in *ADF* (1972).

"I am in a laocoon": MS to Bill Brown, November 8, 1967.

268: "That lovely, *lovely*": Katharine Taylor to MS, February 2, 1968.

Chapter 19   "Time of Burning": 1968–1970

270: "into a final hour": MS to Eleanor Blair, February 21, 1967.

"I appreciate all": MS to Eleanor Blair, July 18 [1968].

271: "Personne ne m'intéresse": Quoted in Eugénie Dubois to MS, November 24, 1977; "tes propres paroles"—"your own words."

"As to those": Eugénie Dubois to MS, April 24, 1969.

"just babble on": MS to Beverly Hallam, February 18 [1968]. MS's column, "Homeward," included such titles as "The Silent Ones," "Memorable Gifts," "Riches Beyond Measure," "The Mowing, Before and After," and "A Quiet Summer Night."

"What luck": Joan Cobleigh Gerbis to MP, interview, October 17, 1992.

"I am now getting": MS to Beverly Hallam, April 9 [1968]. MS told Bill Brown about buying Tammy Quigley a car; "Monica," however, said MS gave Tammy her old car, which she was planning to turn in.

"I had to": MS to Beverly Hallam, May 29, 1968.

"Thank God two": MS to Beverly Hallam, April 22, 1968. MS lectured at the College of Notre Dame of Maryland in Baltimore; Salisbury State College, Maryland; and Trinity College, Washington, D.C. She stayed in D.C. with Margaret Boughton, a curator at the National Gallery, and then joined Judy in Cambridge, where they visited a Boston showing of Beverly Hallam's monotypes.

"I called her" . . . "will I ever": MS to Eleanor Blair, May 17, 1968.

272: "She lay down": MS to Eleanor Blair, June 4 [1968].

"I am too old": MS to Beverly Hallam, July 11 [1968].

273: "an angel": MS to Beverly Hallam, July 23, 1968. Esmeralda also inspired a long free-verse poem, "The Donkey as Muse," published in a revised form as "The Muse as Donkey" in *TSN*.

273: "You are a fat": MS to Beverly Hallam, July 11, 1968.

"my ideal life": MS to Eleanor Blair, July 25, 1969—the following summer, but true of 1968, and of all summers.

"an ornery nut": MS to Beverly Hallam [March 4, 1968].

"more distinguished": MS to Eleanor Blair, January 13, 1969. "I read over the mss full of gratitude for all you have done to make it more distinguished, as to style."

274: "As long as it is not": Eugénie Dubois to MS, April 25, 1969.

"I decided I was": MS to MP, October 10, 1992.

275: "It is a miracle": MS to Rosalind Greene, May 28, 1969. Again, the supposedly homophobic Rosalind seems an unlikely confidante.

"intoxicated" . . . "stimulating": "Monica" to MP, interview of April 2, 1993, and letter of June 26, 1992.

"There will be no conflict": MS to Beverly Hallam, May 17 [1969].

"Now that poetry": MS to Eleanor Blair, quoting Eleanor Blair, Mon Eve [June 9, 1969].

"I have been useful" . . . "God knows you have": MS to Eleanor Blair, September 28 [1969].

276: "inward journey" . . . "about solitude": MS to Beverly Hallam, August 15 [1969]. MS's original title for *Journal of a Solitude* was *Inner Space*.

"Love is glorious": MS to Beverly Hallam, August 15 [1969].

277: "Never has anyone": MS to Beverly Hallam, November 20, 1969.

"mid-life madness": "Monica" to MP, April 2, 1993.

"You must be" . . . "hit the ceiling": MS to Beverly Hallam, February 8, 1969.

"My best Christmas": MS to Beverly Hallam, January 6, 1970.

"turtle-like progress": MS to Bill Brown, February 13, 1970. Eleanor's help could thoroughly exasperate MS. In February 1970, MS suggested that she pay to have part 4 of *Kinds of Love* typed for Eleanor, and that she also pay an accountant to do Eleanor's taxes, which were complicated by her work for MS. This seems to indicate that, contrary to MS's statement to Bill Brown, Eleanor did accept payment for her work.

"I cannot be put": MS to Beverly Hallam, March 2, 1969, suggesting that friends write in protest to *Family Circle* for cancelling her column.

"alone in her N.Y. apt." . . . "Yet what remains": MS to Bill Brown, February 13 [1970].

278: "Listen to this" . . . "*I don't need*": "Monica" to MP, April 2, 1993.

"But after all": MS to Bill Brown, April 5 [1970].

"a rich bourgeois": MS to Bill Brown, April 22 [1970].

"Céline has always" . . . "I hated Belgium": MS to Beverly Hallam, May 5, 1970. In letters to Bill Brown and Eleanor Blair, MS considerably ameliorated the Brussels visit, though obviously it was a disappointment.

279: "a tearful magnificent": MS to Beverly Hallam, May 5, 1970.

"a lyrical year" . . . "I came to see": MS to Bill Brown, June 24, 1970.

"The point is": MS to Beverly Hallam, June 27, 1970.

"stuttered staccato scream": "A Parrot," in *AGOMS* (1971).

280: "Any ideas?": MS to Eleanor Blair, June 29 [1970]. Again (October 19 [1970]), MS wrote, "I have changed the last line of the first poem, 'Ballad of the Sixties,' to 'Our love has withered away' instead of '*Where* love . . .' etc. The line has bothered me and I think this makes it end on more of a final chord. Hope you agree." EB's assistance, however, was chiefly technical: punctuation, italicization, indentation, double-spacing, brackets, etc.

"It came flowing": MS to Eleanor Blair, July 8 [1970].

"The quality": MS to Eleanor Blair, quoting Eric Swenson [August 2, 1970].

281: "the time of burning": "Invocation to Kali," *AGOMS*.

"I do feel sure": MS to Bill Brown, September 20 [1970].

"How much rage": First stanzas of "Hoping to Live," enclosed in MS to Bill Brown, December 4, 1970, eventually cut from the ms. of *ADF*.

282: "I am back": MS to Bill Brown, September 20 [1970]. I am indebted to Dr. John Houpis and Dr. Felix Sommer, both of Brattleboro, for their informative comments on their colleague the late Marynia Farnham.

"a dialogue": From a series of poems to Marynia Farnham, "Letters to a Psychiatrist," partially published in *ADF*.

Chapter 20   Chaos: 1970–1972

283: "a good face": Eric Swenson to MS, May 25, 1970. Carol Houck Smith, a Norton editor, loved *Kinds of Love;* didn't want it to end; had only minor suggestions, chiefly about the repetition of words like "gently," "shy," and "lair" and of actions like Christina kissing the top of Cornelius's head.

"I am drunk": MS to Bill Brown, December 3, 1970.

284: "a complete success": *New Yorker,* December 19, 1970.

"smoting" . . . "powerful" . . . "beautiful": letters to MS about *Kinds of Love*.

"that awful review" . . . "If I got" . . . "The journal": MS to Bill Brown, January 27 [1971].

285: loved Monica "wholly": MS to Bill Brown, February 16 [1971].

"madness" . . . "My father" . . . "My greatest": "Monica" to MP, telephone interview, July 22, 1992.

"that great genius" . . . "I am afraid": MS to Beverly Hallam, March 2, 1971.

"Yesterday I saw": MS to Bill Brown, February 16 [1971]. MS lectured in Norfolk, Virginia, and Washington, returning to Nelson February 21, 1971.

286: "with amused homage" . . . "no woman ever": MS to Bill Brown, March 24 [1971].

"quite ill": MS to Eleanor Blair, February 22, 1971.

"no sense of privacy": "Monica" to MP, April 2, 1993.

287: "It's far too large!": Mary-Leigh Smart to MP, October 14, 1992.

288: "I honor you": Carolyn Heilbrun to MS, March 8, 1968.

"If any of these": MS to Eleanor Blair [July 22, 1971].

"now appears to understand": MS to Beverly Hallam, July 25, 1971.

289: "immense radiant meadow": MS to Beverly Hallam, August 6 [1971].

"I'm leaving" . . . "Good, because": "Monica" to MP, April 2, 1993.

"I finally said": MS to MP, October 10, 1992.

"the destructiveness implied": "The Writing of a Poem," Scripps College pamphlet (1957); reprinted in *Writings on Writing* (1980).

"We fought an awful lot": MS to MP, October 10, 1992.

"the angel and the fury": MS's poem "The Angels and the Furies," in *ADF.*

290: "The investment": MS to Eleanor Blair, November 7 [1971].

"We hold it": "Fulfillment," *ADF.* When MP first spoke with "Monica," she had forgotten (or said she had forgotten) that she was the Muse of *ADF.*

"grieving fury" . . . "infant anguish": "The Autumn Sonnets," 1, *ADF.*

"made rather a pest": MS to MP, March 29, 1994.

"a deep friend": MS, "The Imaginary Psychiatrist: A Journal," unpublished.

"I am very tired" . . . "pathetic": MS to Bill Brown, September 2 and 12 [1971].

"a grotesque cartoon": MS's own observation in *JOAS,* 203.

291: "For me, it was not": MS to Bill Brown, Halloween 1971.

"and we spent": MS to Bill Brown, December 17, 1971.

292: "If I did": MS to Bill Brown, February 3 [1972], quoting Marynia.

"a cry of anguish" . . . "Woman, who are you?": MS to Bill Brown, December 17, 1972, enclosing the poem "The Gift," dated December 15 [1971].

"My Hell": MS to Bill Brown, February 3 [1972].

293: "I must leave": MS to Eleanor Blair, April 20 [1972], quoting Marynia.

"hundreds of long distance": MS to Bill Brown, April 5 [1972].

"I do not really fit": MS to Kay Martin, April 16 [1972], one of the last letters MS wrote to Martin—or that Martin kept.

"a dream of a car": MS to Eleanor Blair, April 23 [1972].

"There is no doubt": MS to Eleanor Blair, April 23 [1972].

"There are still" . . . "has given an entirely false": MS to Eleanor Blair, May 13 [1972].

294: "I am glad": MS to Beverly Hallam, May 13 [1972].

295: "I simply cannot talk": MS to Eleanor Blair, June 26, 1972.

"the failure of a style": *Parnassus,* Spring–Summer 1973; "May Sarton in this volume": Charles Willig, *Chronicle Herald,* August 13, 1972.

296: "From the start": MS to Eleanor Blair, July 4, 1972.

297: "Tamas was very *good*": Mary-Leigh Smart to MP, March 22, 1992.

"an earthquake of woe": MS, "The Imaginary Psychiatrist" (unpublished), the source of quotations through page 299. Speculation is always perilous, but May's lifelong behavior resembles what psychiatrists since the 1970s have called borderline personality disorder. Persons with BPD are more disturbed than neurotics, less than psychotics. As the term suggests, persons suffering from BPD vary considerably in the degree to which they are afflicted. Yet one recognizes May's behavior in descriptions like: "The borderline often makes unrealistic demands of others, appearing to observers as spoiled. . . . Suicidal threats or gestures are often used to obtain attention and rescue. . . . The borderline may use seduction as a manipulative strategy, even with someone known to be inappropriate and inaccessible, such as a therapist or minister"—or college president. "Though very sensitive to others the borderline lacks true empathy. . . . Both borderlines and narcissists display hypersensitivity to criticism.": Jerold J. Kreisman, M.D., and Hal Straus, *I Hate You—Don't Leave Me: Understanding the Borderline Personality* (Los Angeles: Body Press, 1989). There is even some evidence that homosexuality or bisexuality is more prevalent in borderline individuals. And women are more vulnerable to BPD than men. I am grateful to Dr. Eric Berger, a psychiatrist in New Haven, Connecticut, who suggested to me the possibility that MS suffered from borderline personality disorder.

299: "It all went off": MS to Bill Brown, August 18 [1972].

"One by one": Joan Cobleigh Gerbis to MP, October 17, 1992.

300: "Nelson has been": MS to Beverly Hallam, July 2, 1972.

"I feel that coming": MS to Beverly Hallam, May 13, 1972. Both this and the above quote are out of sequence by some months, but express MS's feelings until she left Nelson the following spring.

Chapter 21   Guru: 1973–1975

301: "the great influences": MS to MP, an undated note [1993]: "These are books I have lived with . . . for 40 years or more."

"a noble feast" . . . "Even the sky" . . . "How strange": MS to Bill Brown, May 14 [1973].

302: "terrible nursing home" . . . "Why can't I": MS to Bill Brown, May 14 [1973].

"a poor pathetic" . . . "with contempt and loathing" . . . "I bid you": MS to Mary-Leigh Smart, April 8, 1973.

303: "tension in equilibrium": "The School of Babylon," in *The Moment of Poetry,* ed. Don Cameron Allen (Baltimore: Johns Hopkins Press, 1962), a collection of essays on poetic creation by John Holmes, Richard Eberhart, Richard Wilbur, Randall Jarrell, and MS.

"a fabulous cook": Mary-Leigh Smart to MP, March 22, 1992.

"Never feel I can't": MS to Beverly Hallam, June 30 [1973].

304: "It was a terrible": Mary-Leigh Smart to MP, March 22, 1992.

"is my one true": MS to Bill Brown, December 30 [1973].

305: "peeling of the onion": MS to Bill Brown, September 6 [1973].

"like lifting a corpse": MS to Bill Brown, February 10, 1974.

"a bad blow" . . . "has decimated": MS to Bill Brown, November 10 [1973]. MS refers to the letter from Bogan of September 28, 1960, to Ruth Limmer, published in *What the Woman Lived: Selected Letters of Louise Bogan, 1920–1970,* 325.

"She had painted": MS to Bill Brown, December 7 [1974].

"the professors of English" . . . "Anyone interested": The incident is related in MS to Bill Brown, December 30 [1973].

306: "the audience were": MS to Eleanor Blair, January 24 [1974].

306: "The fact is": MS to Bill Brown, February 10, 1974. Bill's niece had wanted May's advice about coming out as a lesbian; MS only reluctantly answered her letter.

"I feel eaten": MS to Bill Brown, March 31, 1974.

"Went. Had strong bourbon": Morgan Mead to MP, December 27, 1991.

307: "beautiful to look upon": MS to Bill Brown, September 13, 1974.

"the last I shall ever": MS to Bill Brown, September 13, 1974. Heilbrun had written MS December 7, 1970: "Your next novel must *not* make use of a narrative voice. . . . You see—I have got to write you this—the two autobiographical books are superb because of the voice you have found. . . . I am overjoyed you are going to write a journal of solitude, because that is the perfect form for you, I am certain. But when you write your next novel, make technical use of the single consciousness. . . . At any rate, don't let one syllable of comment unassigned to a character slip into the work. Are you sorry you ever answered my letter?"

308: "Sarton has not avoided": Introduction to *Mrs. Stevens* (reprint, 1974), xii.

"Everybody thinks": Carolyn Heilbrun to MP, January 4, 1994. CH did not leave Wild Knoll after MS argued that she would have difficulty with directions in the dark, but she left the next morning without speaking to May.

309: "suddenly grown tiny" . . . "quietly and well" . . . "bitter mischance" . . . "simply crowded out": MS to Bill Brown, October 30, 1974.

"Francis was there": MS to Bill Brown, October 30, 1974.

"I feel . . . that": MS to Bill Brown, December 7, 1974.

310: "Tell me a little": MS to MP, March 27, 1993.

"The fact is": MS to Bill Brown, January 15, 1975.

"I became quite enraged": MS to Beverly Hallam and Mary-Leigh Smart, December 30, 1974.

"It has been an earthquake": MS to Bill Brown, January 15, 1975.

312: "Yes, the grandchildren": Quoted in *THBTS*, 84.

"pale smug profs": MS to Bill Brown, March 5, 1975.

"I DON'T like it": MS to Bill Brown, March 5, 1975.

"Not one single ad": MS to Eric Swenson [May 12, 1975].

"Hell, if you didn't": Eric Swenson to MS, May 20, 1975.

"undue admiration": Introduction to *Mrs. Stevens* (reprint, 1974), xxi. Without notifying Heilbrun, MS had Norton omit her introduction from a later printing.

"The trouble is": Christopher Lehmann-Haupt, *New York Times,* June 16, 1975, comparing *Crucial Conversations* to Christina Stead's *The Little Hotel,* in which the characters are "so embedded in European history that their creator can barely keep control of them."

313: "It's such a dirty world": MS to Bill Brown, November 21, 1975.

"I stand on": MS to Richard Henry, a Unitarian minister, May 29, 1975.

"The whole imposed criteria": MS to Morgan Mead, January 12, 1975.

"*Kinds of Love*": Katharine Taylor to MS, November 8, 1970.

"a frighteningly thin": *THBTS,* 86.

314: "But who—who": MS to Bill Brown, April 1, 1975, quoting Juliette Huxley's letter of March 1975.

"I do not think": *JOAS,* 142–43.

Chapter 22   Poetry Again: 1976–1978

315: "I am making": MS to Bill Brown, August 26 [1975].

"A hippie girl": MS to Bill Brown, January 24, 1976.

316: "After another day": *THBTS,* 202.

"a little dry" . . . "that this champagne": MS to Bill Brown, March 17, 1976.

"simply terrible" . . . "terribly loath": MS to Bill Brown, fragment, but written in April 1976 after her visit to Vassar.

"a singularly happy": *THBTS,* 242.

"it does just what": MS to Bill Brown, May 7, 1976.

"This is the material": Carolyn Heilbrun to MS, August 16, 1976.

317: "Only I wonder": MS to Bill Brown, September 18, 1976.

"I'm already quaking": MS to Bill Brown, October 12 [1976].

318: "a warm sweet vulgar": MS to Bill Brown, September 18, 1976.

"as usual was mean": MS to Bill Brown, October 12 [1976].

"keen talent": *New York Times Book Review,* October 3, 1976.

"The critic turns out": MS to Bill Brown, October 12 [1976].

319: "It was *sad*" . . . "I did not": MS to Bill Brown, January 10, 1977.

"people have got used": MS to Bill Brown, January 10, 1977.

"I had forgotten": MS to Bill Brown, January 10, 1977.

"a quicksand of despair": MS to Bill Brown, February 14, 1977.

"A big piece": MS to Bill Brown, January 10, 1977.

320: "fell into a trance": MS to Bill Brown, April 4, 1977.

"She has a great head": MS to Bill Brown, April 4, 1977.

"that poetry has come": MS to Bill Brown, June 1, 1977.

"absurdly reserved letters": MS to Bill Brown, April 16, 1977.

"four acolytes brought": MS to Bill Brown, May 12, 1977, quoting Lola Szladits.

"What a performer!": Interview with Deborah Pease, December 22, 1991.

321: "I do have some" . . . "hundreds of calls": MS to Bill Brown, June 1, 1977, quoting the opinion of the interviewer, Sukey Howe, Mark and Molly Howe's daughter.

"so the nights progressed": MS to Bill Brown, May 12, 1977.

"Then the bliss": MS to Bill Brown, June 19, 1977.

"has been such" . . . "It is about": MS to Eleanor Blair, June 19, 1977.

322: "Nous sommes sur des chemins": "We are on different paths"—Eugénie Dubois to MS, November 11, 1977. MS sent Eleanor Blair her itinerary: July 25–August 2 with the Duboises at Linkebeek; August 2–8 at the Mandeville Hotel, London; August 8–12 with a Brazilian friend, Eugenie Huneeus, in Suffolk; August 13–20 at the Hôtel Aval du Creux, Sark; August 20–23 with Molly Howe, Dublin.

"One day you must": Juliette Huxley to MS, January 5, 1976.

"survived himself": Juliette Huxley to MS, October 12, 1977.

323: "Two hours" . . . "charming, bright-eyed" . . . "but never a word" . . . "More than splendid": MS to Bill Brown, August 18, 1977, on Sark. Alice Dorling, Mabel Sarton's first cousin, had seven children, among them Janet (Mann), May (Pipe), and Ivy (Eastaugh). May's second cousins. Alan Eastaugh was Ivy's son.

324: "But I made": MS to MP, October 13, 1992.

324: "I think this whole": MS to Bill Brown, September 20 [1977].

"I feel it is": MS to Bill Brown, October 6, 1977.

"Two thirds": MS to Bill Brown, September 20 [1977].

325: "with her chatter": Roy Larson, *Chicago Sun-Times,* November 6, 1977.

"Sarton is": Doris Grumbach in the *Los Angeles Times,* November 27, 1977.

"a well that": MS to Bill Brown, January 31 [1978].

326: "She betrayed herself": Interview with Anne Woodson and Barbara Barton, April 29, 1992.

"in the midst": MS's experiences in Madison and Chicago are related in MS to Bill Brown, October 31, 1977.

327: "a marvellous cementing": MS to Bill Brown, January 31 [1978].

"It's good to let go" . . . "secret, passionate": MS to "Dinah," March 14, 1978.

"reached a place": MS to Bill Brown, January 31 [1978].

"full of love" . . . "What I have come": MS to "Dinah," April 30 [1978].

328: "somehow we felt": MS to Bill Brown, June 9, 1978.

"rather scared": MS to Bill Brown, June 9, 1978.

"I have no doubt": Interview with Joy Greene Sweet, May 4, 1992.

"very difficult" . . . "I was afraid": daughter and granddaughter of "Dinah" to MP, October 11, 1992.

"We had a bad scene": MS to Bill Brown, August 4 [1978]. The quotes following are from August and September letters to Bill Brown, "Dinah," and Eleanor Blair. May admitted that she "had elicited" Dinah's anger before she arrived, apparently by asking a neighbor of Dinah's to deliver the message in person (Dinah's phone was out of order) that May was suffering with bursitis—a move that Dinah interpreted as selfish and begging for sympathy.

329: "I'm learning all the time": MS to "Dinah" [August 18, 1978].

"What it all" . . . "in a homosexual" . . . "I sometimes think": MS to Bill Brown, August 4, 1978.

330: "I don't dare": All quotes are from the unpublished *We Aren't Getting Anywhere,* not dated but obviously written fairly soon after her two-week stay at Dinah's.

"Control," "The Lady of the Lake," and "At the Black Rock" are all published in *HTS.*

331: "It's so sad": MS to MP, October 12, 1992.

"This morning I couldn't": MS to Bill Brown, November 25, 1978.

332: "It may be": MS to "Dinah," December 7, 1978. MS wrote two letters to Dinah that day, one recalling past happiness and concluding that she was never meant to be happy; that the only light she shed was "from a wound." MS kept carbons of her letters to Dinah during this period.

Chapter 23   Intimations of Mortality: 1978–1982

333: "scurrilous review": MS to Bill Brown, November 25, 1978.

"which tends toward": Lore Dickstein, *New York Times Book Review,* November 12, 1978.

333: "*very bad*": MS to Morgan Mead, April 5, 1977: "I am still frightened about the novel—now 235 pages long, but *very bad,* I think." Previously to Morgan Mead, March 29, 1978: "Sometimes I think it is just awful mush."

"I had put too much": MS to "Dinah," November 12, 1978.

335: "simply excruciating": MS to Bill Brown, February 8, 1979.

"For me, sex": MS to "Dinah," January 12, 1979.

336: "Things are very good": MS to Bill Brown, February 8, 1979.

"One book a year": Juliette Huxley to MS, February 5, 1979.

"a sense of meaning": *R,* 9.

"hostages to fortune": MS to Bill Brown, January 11, 1979.

"a low form": *R,* 45.

"usual reaction": MS to Bill Brown, misdated Sunday, April 28, actually Saturday, April 28, 1979.

337: "How can I help": *R,* 95–96.

"as tender and loving": MS to Morgan Mead, June 5, 1979.

"Remembering my mother": MS to Bill Brown, June 8, 1979.

"Martha and Marita": *R,* 111. The text of the film *World of Light* was published in *May Sarton: A Self-Portrait* (1982), along with a selection of poems, in honor of May's seventieth birthday.

"the insoluble enigma": MS to Bill Brown, July 2, 1979.

338: "I'll go into the operation": MS to "Dinah," June 29 [1979].

"I'll spare you" . . . "I felt like" . . . "very weak": MS to Bill Brown, July 2, 1979.

"curious behavior" . . . "Of course I may": a composite of two carbon copies of letters to "Dinah" written June 29 [1979]. Since the originals of the letters were not available, it is uncertain which MS sent—or if she sent both or neither. MS kept carbons of numerous letters to Dinah, often two versions of a letter written the same day, an indication of her frustration and anger.

"If you're the lover": MS to MP, interview May 1, 1992.

"great fun": MS to Bill Brown, January 12, 1980.

"the heightened consciousness": MS to Bill Brown, February 17, 1980.

"I feel she is": MS to Bill Brown, October 25 [1979].

339: "Then the boy": From "Apple Tree in May," in *ADNH.*

"I certainly give": MS to Bill Brown, October 25 [1979].

"I feel devalued" . . . "I have been badly": *R,* 122, 245.

"a hard letter": MS to Bill Brown, June 10, 1980.

340: "never talk[ed]": MS to Polly Thayer Starr, July 28, 1942. Though the statement was made thirty-eight years before MS began the novel, their relationship had not altered: Anne Thorp continued to be reticent about personal matters.

"shock like having shit": MS to Bill Brown, February 17, 1980. The *Times Literary Supplement* review appeared February 8, 1980.

"darling new friend": MS to Bill Brown, April 3, 1980.

"And after two years": "The Seed," enclosed in a letter to Bill Brown, April 3, 1980, published in *LFM,* the first line altered from "Once more lay hurt aside" to "Once more I lay hurt aside."

"It's a beautiful": MS to Bill Brown, quoting "Dinah," April 26, 1980.

342: "I did truly love": MS to "Dinah," July 15, 1980. Again, May accused Dinah of never loving her, of not being able to love anyone. And "how can we ever be friends when our fundamental values are at opposite poles?"

"tremendously moving" . . . "because I believe" . . . "loving fellowship" . . . "in a state": MS to Bill Brown, August 31, 1980.

343: "I fear it will" . . . "could have benefited": MS to Bill Brown, quoting Anne Woodson, October 10, 1980.

"I am in a strange": MS to Bill Brown, December 8, 1980.

"but Karen and": MS to Bill Brown, December 8, 1980.

"She treated me": Karen Saum to MP, March 31, 1993.

344: "Be at my house": This and the following quotes from an interview with Janice Oberacker, March 29, 1993.

"I'm an important": Interview with "Monica," April 2, 1993.

345: "Dearest [Dinah]: I": MS to "Dinah" [n.d. but typical of the letters MS was writing Dinah during 1980–1981].

346: "hot versus cold": MS to Bill Brown, January 31, 1981.

"I was unbearably": Karen Saum to MP, interview March 31, 1993.

"most delicate" . . . "a little family" . . . "never led": MS to Bill Brown, February 1981.

"ugly and useless": MS to Bill Brown, March 21, 1981.

"[Dinah] is totally": MS to Bill Brown, March 21, 1981.

347: "a little harsh" . . . "Europe did the trick": MS to Bill Brown, July 16, 1981.

"What threw me": MS to Bill Brown, August 15, 1981.

348: "in a tight knot" . . . "Of course": MS to Bill Brown, November 21, 1981.

"huge anarchic dogs" . . . "the last straw": MS to Bill Brown, October 10, 1981.

"too many presents" . . . "It is quite absurd": MS to Bill Brown, January 1, 1982.

349: "marvelous letter": MS to Bill Brown, January 1, 1982.

"Impossible in 1982!": Carolyn Heilbrun to MP, January 4, 1994.

"The salesmen made": MS to Bill Brown, March 1, 1982.

"I found I chiefly": MS to Bill Brown, February 6, 1982.

"You had to make": MS to "Dinah," February 6, 1982.

"At least I left": MS to Bill Brown, April 9, 1982.

"I once thought": "Dinah" to MP, October 11, 1992.

Chapter 24   Last Muse: 1982–1984

350: "Such a peaceful" . . . "This is the best": *AS,* 9–10.

"incredible 70th" . . . "May taught me" . . . "Most moving because": MS to Bill Brown, May 15, 1982, quoting Lee Blair.

351: "they got tight" . . . "Be careful": Janice Oberacker to MP, October 15, 1992.

352: "People pour in" . . . "young women and men" . . . "This is my present": MS to Bill Brown, July 5, 1982.

"2000 people" . . . "your courage" . . . "for an old lesbian" . . . "But I am happy": MS to Bill Brown, July 5, 1982.

353: "after all the only": MS to Bill Brown, September 22, 1982.

"a sitting duck": MS to Bill Brown, October 6, 1982.

"an evasion": Sheila Ballantyne, *New York Times Book Review,* October 17, 1982. In an interview by Marcie Hershman in *Ms. Magazine,* October 1982, May amplified on her choice of heterosexual lovers in *Anger:* "And I didn't make the main characters two women because then people would have said: 'Oh, that's what women do together, they fight.' Now people can say: 'Oh, a man, a woman, and anger—it's universal.'"

"at least I was": MS to Bill Brown, November 7 [1982].

"It is a poor" . . . "written to a thesis": *R,* 75, 159.

354: "I can't stand": Kay Martin to MS, December 3, 1972.

"and fell madly": MS to Bill Brown, November 7 [1982].

"I'm in love": Janice Oberacker to MP, October 15, 1992.

"And there she is": MS to Bill Brown, November 1 [1982].

355: "Yes, I am home": "Letters from Maine: 1" in *LFM.*

"the blood withering": MS to Bill Brown, December 6, 1982. May used the phrase in "Letters from Maine": "When I heard you say in a brisk voice/'Perhaps we should never meet again'/The sun turned black, the tide froze/I could feel the blood withering in my veins."

"I want to know": MS to "Elspeth," Thursday, December 2 [1982].

"My muse": MS to Bill Brown, January 3, 1983.

"not up to the production": MS to Bill Brown, December 6, 1982. All the poems of *A Winter Garland* were eventually published in *LFM.*

"simply collapsed" . . . "You will never" . . . "like a plant": MS to Bill Brown, January 3, 1983.

356: "Judy is dead": "Mourning to Do," in *LFM.* Judy had asked her nephew Timothy Warren to give MS a hardbound manuscript book of her poems. Many are precise evocations of the sights, smells, and sounds of her childhood; many are full of pain; many are cryptic. Timothy Warren was also Judy's executor. "The trust which Judith established some time ago directs bequests of $1,000 each to sisters, nieces, nephews, colleges and you. (Yours is the first named bequest)," Timothy wrote MS January 13, 1983. "Then the balance of the estate goes to Willard [nephew], Patricia [niece], Joanna [daughter of niece], you and me. I don't know how long it will take to settle but my guess is that when it is done you might anticipate something like $5,000."

"I am very bad": MS to Bill Brown, February 22, 1983.

"I have been so": MS to Bill Brown, February 22, 1983.

"life and lovers(!)": MS to Bill Brown, May 13, 1983.

357: "It was a long": MS to Bill Brown, February 22, 1983.

"the autumn muse": *AS,* 311.

"Too expensive": MS to Bill Brown, May 13, 1983.

"who had provided": *AS,* 333.

"In spite of": *AS,* 334.

"What a nice lunch" . . . "With Janice" . . . "You are incapable" . . . "48 icy hours" . . . "I certainly did": MS to Bill Brown, June 10 [1983].

358: "You are my Muse" . . . "The Muse is not": Telephone interview with "Elspeth," February 20, 1993. A psychologist, "Elspeth" came to believe that MS suffered from histrionic personality disorder, a pervasive pattern of excess emotionalism and attention-seeking.

358: "No doubt": MS to "Elspeth," Saturday in the rain [1983].

"The muse is here": "Letters from Maine: 10," in *LFM*.

"I saw you once": "The Muse as Medusa" in *AGOMS*.

"it may be a little": MS to Bill Brown, May 13, 1983.

"Tim, I'm afraid": MS to Timothy Matlack Warren, June 9, 1983.

359: "after the disaster": MS to Bill Brown, July 9 [1983].

"dull and lonely": MS to Bill Brown, September 23, 1983.

"for my horrible muse" . . . "I am sad" . . . "black with rage": MS to Bill Brown, November 21, 1983.

"Of course I'll feel": MS to Bill Brown, November 21, 1983.

"You must learn" . . . "He should have": MS to Bill Brown, December 13, 1983.

"buried alive": MS to Bill Brown, January 28, 1984.

"scene of torture" . . . "just plain *boring*": MS to Bill Brown, February 25, 1984.

360: "irritating requests": MS to Bill Brown, November 21, 1983.

"She *had* to get": Mary-Leigh Smart to MP, March 22, 1992.

"a really triumphal": MS to Bill Brown, April 26, 1984.

"I think we should": Bill Brown to MP, April 17, 1994.

"Dearest Bill": MS to Bill Brown, August 27, 1984.

"Farewell—but fare": MS to Bill Brown [n.d.], adding, "It struck me with full force. I have been ill for so long—"

"It was sinister": Bill Brown to MP, April 17, 1994.

361: "true brother": MS to Bill Brown, April 26, 1984.

362: "passionate poet": Elaine Kendall, *Los Angeles Times,* April 2, 1984.

"May I please": MS to MP, May 1, 1992.

"*so* egotistic . . . always in the background": Michel Thiery to MP, September 11, 1993. As chair of the Sarton Society, Thiery would help establish the Sarton Chair of the History of Science at Ghent and the scholarly journal *Sartoniana*.

"George Sarton's European Roots": pamphlet of the exhibition, November 14–18, 1984, published by the Archives of the State University of Ghent: Communication and Cognition. The journal *Sartoniana* was first published in 1988.

363: "is mostly easy going": Ursula K. Le Guin, *Book World,* February 17, 1985.

"Because every day": in *Oblique Prayers: New Poems with 14 Translations from Jean Joubert* (New York: New Directions, 1984).

364: "Must we lose": "Absence," printed by William B. Ewart, publisher, Concord, New Hampshire; first edition limited to 336 copies, 36 numbered and signed by MS. Ewert printed and published MS's Christmas poems as well as small collections of poems such as *Coming into Eighty* (1992).

Chapter 25   Guardian Angel: 1985–1990

366: "such edgy writers": Stacey D'Erasmo, *New York Native,* January 20–26, 1986.

"the world of women": *TMS,* 160.

366: "a quintessential fantasy": Stacey D'Erasmo, *New York Native,* January 20–26, 1986.

367: "as a bridge": "The Art of Poetry XXXII: May Sarton," *Paris Review,* Fall 1983.

"I've had a stroke": Janice Oberacker to MP, October 15, 1992.

368: "macho kitten": MS to Jean Burden, July 9, 1986.

"I am a practical": "The Muse as Donkey," in *TSN.*

369: "only Janice": *ATS,* 42.

"Why do I trust" . . . "myself again" . . . "that rapid descent": *ATS,* 64–65, 108, 111.

370: "I have never": Telephone interview with Irene Morgan, November 13, 1993. MS's account of her relationship with Irene is rather different: "I've known Rene now, I think, for fifty years. . . . We've become what I might call root-friends. . . . A root-friend goes back a long way and therefore a great many things never have to be explained because they are already known" (*E,* 64–65).

"May weaves": Telephone interview with Lee Blair, June 3, 1992.

"I think it is best": *ATS,* 188.

371: "in some deep way": *ATS,* 223.

"I kept feeling": *ATS,* 226.

"I feel unable": *ATS,* 227.

"Cats, yes" and following passages: *ATS,* 228–9. Louise Bogan mentions the poem in question to Ruth Limmer, September 28, 1960. It begins: "The two sick kittens, round-eyed, stare/As if I were the one to be tamed/Or give them what they ask by being there."

372: "a sort of posthumous": Juliette Huxley to MS, December 12, 1979.

"curiously impersonal": Juliette Huxley to MS, February 25, 1986.

"our strange ghost": Juliette Huxley to MS, February 8, 1984.

"And why do you": Juliette Huxley to MS, January 17, 1986.

"How I feel": Juliette Huxley to MS, July 28, 1986.

"glittering plan": Juliette Huxley to MS, April 5, 1986.

373: "One reason I do not": *ATS,* 279, 271.

"Such a *stupid* person": MS to Jean Burden, July 27, 1987.

"angry and self-pitying": *Chicago Tribune,* May 1, 1988.

"Thank you, May": Nancy Mairs, *New York Times,* March 27, 1988.

"She borrowed": Morgan Mead to MP, April 25, 1992.

"a wildly accelerated": MS to Jean Burden, August 20, 1988.

374: "Inside my mother's": "New Year Resolve," in *TSN.*

"clear-as-crystal": *Publishers Weekly,* October 21, 1988.

"I fear I am": MS to Jean Burden, January 2, 1988.

"clear time": "Dream," in *TSN.*

375: "All right, if you": Janice Oberacker to MP, October 15, 1992.

"I had her": MS to Jean Burden, May 11, 1989.

"God knows whether": MS to Jean Burden, May 11, 1989.

376: "irremedial woes": Alfred Corn, *New York Times Book Review,* July 2, 1989.

376: "repetitive language": Katherine V. Forrest, *Los Angeles Times Book Review,* July 9, 1989.

"Her editor should": Marcie Hershman to MP, April 26, 1992.

"Sarton has called": Katherine V. Forrest, *Los Angeles Times Book Review,* July 9, 1989.

"several hours each": MS to Jean Burden [October 25, 1989].

377: "Don't leave me alone": Francis Huxley to MP, April 11, 1995.

"only your heart": *E,* 14.

"It's hard to believe": *E,* 13.

"I am to settle": *E,* 14.

378: "which is what I fear": *E,* 56.

"I think I am dying": MS to MP, September 17, 1991.

Chapter 26   Dying, and Beyond: 1991–1995

379: "The time Susan": *E,* 151.

"May shamelessly uses": Telephone interview with Lee Blair, June 3, 1992.

"take charge of": Margaret Whalen, quoting MS, May 1993.

380: "I don't have enough": Janice Oberacker to MP, October 15, 1992.

"You can glue": Telephone interview with Lee Blair, June 3, 1992.

"Susan changed May": Janice Oberacker to MP, October 15, 1992.

"I'll enjoy resuming": *E,* 225.

"*hideously* painful": *E,* 226.

381: "I'm Helena": *E,* 247, 249.

"abandoned by the": *E,* 332.

382: "I'm read by": *E,* 194–95.

383: "squalls": Eric Swenson to MP, December 30, 1995. "May's emotional eruptions . . . never worried me much. Well . . . *after* I learned how quickly the squalls passed and how little damage they left in their wake." MS's comment on Swenson's editing in *Endgame* is circumspect: "He was not an editor in the sense of asking for a great many changes. In fact, he perhaps bent over backwards to respect me and my style and to ask very little. Sometimes I wanted a little more editing than I got from him. But it is surely infinitely better to be underedited than to be overedited, as sometimes happens" (319–20).

"As Ms. Sarton's health": Nancy Mairs, "When Bad Things Happen to Good Writers," *New York Times Book Review,* February 21, 1993.

384: "Dear Margot Peters": MS to MP, May 14 [1991].

"All I ask": MS to MP, February 9, 1992.

385: "I want to get": MS to MP [postmark March 2, 1992].

"Dear ornery May": MP to MS, March 9, 1992.

"When someone tells": MS to MP [March 1992].

387: "burning sprite": "On a Winter Night," in *TLOS.*

388: "The best thing": MS to "Dinah" [n.d. but late June/early July 1992].

388: "Without writing letters": Last two stanzas of "Best Friend—for Barbara Hawthorne, In Memoriam," September 1992.

389: "You're so kind": MS to MP, March 5, 1993.

"as though this justified": Francis Huxley to MP, April 11, 1995.

"an eccentric poet" . . . "I never counted" . . . "because she has" . . . "It's such a happy thing": MS to MP, March 3, 1993.

"I don't know": Quotations from a journal Margaret Whalen kept from June 1992 to June 1993.

390: "I won't treat": MS to MP, telephone conversation, December 9, 1992.

391: "In the end": Edith Milton, *Women's Review of Books* 11 (December 1993): 8–9.

"I want to die": MS to MP, December 23, 1993.

392: "Fortunately, you had" . . . "Must I accept": MS to MP, July 20, 1994.

393: "One book a year": From Juliette Huxley's letters; MS's responses to MP on phone, November 1, 1994.

"Ô ô oh ô": Juliette Huxley to MS, November 24, 1991.

394: "This is to say": Juliette Huxley to MS, March 8 [1986].

"We have an aura": Maggie Vaughan to MP, July 26, 1995.

"Juliette *was* ambivalent": MS to MP, April 25, 1995.

396: "This time for sure": I am grateful to Margaret Whalen for notes she took during the week MS was in the hospital.

398: "a commanding stoical figure": obituary, *New York Times,* July 18, 1995.

"lacking nuance, ambiguity": *Times* (London), July 21, 1995.

Selected Bibliography

Works by May Sarton

A Durable Fire. New York: W. W. Norton, 1972.

After the Stroke: A Journal. New York: W. W. Norton, 1988.

Among the Usual Days: A Portrait. Edited by Susan Sherman. New York: W. W. Norton, 1993.

Anger. New York: W. W. Norton, 1982.

"The Art of Poetry XXXII: May Sarton." In *Paris Review,* Fall 1983.

As Does New Hampshire. Concord, N.H.: Richard R. Smith, Publisher, 1967.

As We Are Now. New York: W. W. Norton, 1973.

At Eighty-Two. New York: W. W. Norton, 1995.

At Seventy: A Journal. New York: W. W. Norton, 1984.

The Birth of a Grandfather. New York: Rinehart, 1957.

The Bridge of Years. New York: Doubleday, 1946.

Cloud, Stone, Sun, Vine. New York: W. W. Norton, 1961.

Collected Poems: 1930–1973. New York: W. W. Norton, 1974.

Collected Poems 1930–1993. New York: W. W. Norton, 1993.

Coming into Eighty: Poems. New York: W. W. Norton, 1994.

Crucial Conversations. New York: W. W. Norton, 1974.

The Education of Harriet Hatfield. New York: W. W. Norton, 1987.

Encore. New York: W. W. Norton, 1993.

Encounter in April. New York: Houghton Mifflin, 1937.

Endgame. New York: W. W. Norton, 1992.

Faithful Are the Wounds. New York: Rinehart, 1955.

The Fur Person. New York: Rinehart, 1956.

A Grain of Mustard Seed. New York: W. W. Norton, 1971.

Halfway to Silence. New York: W. W. Norton, 1980.

Honey in the Hive: Judith Matlack, 1898–1982. Boston: Warren Publishing, 1988.

The House By the Sea. New York: W. W. Norton, 1977.

I Knew a Phoenix. New York: Rinehart, 1959.

Inner Landscape. Boston: Houghton Mifflin, 1939.

In Time Like Air. New York: Rinehart, 1957.

Joanna and Ulysses. New York: W. W. Norton, 1963.

Journal of a Solitude. New York: W. W. Norton, 1973.

Kinds of Love. New York: W. W. Norton, 1970.

The Land of Silence. New York: Rinehart, 1953.

The Leaves of the Tree. Mount Vernon, Iowa: Cornell College Chapbooks, 1950.

Letters from Maine. New York: W. W. Norton, 1984.

The Lion and the Rose. New York: Rinehart, 1948.

The Magnificent Spinster. New York: W. W. Norton, 1985.

Miss Pickthorn and Mr. Hare. New York: W. W. Norton, 1966.

Mrs. Stevens Hears the Mermaids Singing. New York: W. W. Norton, 1965.

Now I Become Myself. Burlington, Vt.: Rumble Press, 1992.

The Phoenix Again: New Poems. Concord, N.H.: William B. Ewert, 1987.

Plant Dreaming Deep. New York: W. W. Norton, 1968.

The Poet and the Donkey. New York: W. W. Norton, 1968.

A Private Mythology. New York: W. W. Norton, 1966.

Punch's Secret. New York: Harper & Row, 1974.

A Reckoning. New York: W. W. Norton, 1978.

Recovering: A Journal. New York: W. W. Norton, 1980.

Sarton Selected: An Anthology of the Journals, Novels and Poems of May Sarton. Edited by Bradford Dudley Daziel. New York: W. W. Norton, 1991.

"The School of Babylon," in *The Moment of Poetry,* ed. Don Cameron Allen. Baltimore: Johns Hopkins Press, 1962.

Selected Poems of May Sarton. Edited by Serena Sue Hilsinger and Lois Brynes. New York: W. W. Norton, 1978.

Shadow of a Man. New York: Rinehart, 1950.

The Single Hound. New York: Houghton Mifflin, 1938.

A Shower of Summer Days. New York: Rinehart, 1952.

The Silence Now. New York: W. W. Norton, 1988.

The Small Room. New York: W. W. Norton, 1961.

A Walk Through the Woods. New York: Harper & Row, 1976.

A Winter Garland. Concord, N.H.: William B. Ewert, 1982.

A World of Light. New York: W. W. Norton, 1976.

Writings on Writing. Orono, Me.: Puckerbrush Press, 1980.

Works About May Sarton

Anderson, Dawn Holt. "May Sarton's Women." In *Images of Women in Fiction,* ed. Susan Koppelman Cornillon. Bowling Green, Ohio: Bowling Green University Popular Press, 1972.

Ascher, Carol, et al., eds. *Between Women.* New York: Routledge, 1993.

Blouin, Lenora. *May Sarton: A Bibliography.* Metuchen, N.J.: Scarecrow Press, 1978.

DeShazar, Mary. *Inspiring Women: Reimagining the Muse.* New York: Pergamon Press, 1986.

Evans, Elizabeth. *May Sarton Revisited.* Boston: Twayne Publishers, 1989.

Hunting, Constance, ed. *May Sarton, Woman and Poet.* Orono, Me.: National Poetry Foundation, 1982.

————, ed. *A Celebration for May Sarton.* Orono, Me.: Puckerbrush Press, 1994.

Ingersoll, Earl G., ed. *Conversations with May Sarton.* Jackson: University Press of Mississippi, 1991.

Kallet, Marilyn. *A House of Gathering: Poets on May Sarton's Poetry.* Knoxville: University of Tennessee Press, 1993.

Rule, Jane. "May Sarton," in *Lesbian Images.* New York: Doubleday, 1979.

Sarton, Eleanor Mabel. *Letters to May.* Orono, Me.: Puckerbrush Press, 1986.

Saum, Karen. *She Knew a Phoenix* (video). Women's Media Network, 1980.

Schade, Edith Royce, ed. and photographer. *From May Sarton's Well: Writings of May Sarton.* Watsonville, Calif.: Papier-Mache Press, 1994.

Sherman, Susan, ed. *Forward Into the Past: For May Sarton on Her Eightieth Birthday.* Concord, N.H.: William B. Ewert, 1992.

Sibley, Agnes. *May Sarton.* New York: Twayne Publishers, 1972.

Swartzlander, Susan, and Marilyn R. Mumford, eds. *That Great Sanity: Critical Essays on May Sarton.* Ann Arbor: University of Michigan Press, 1992.

Wheelock, Martha, and Marita Simpson. *World of Light* (video), 1979.

———. *May Sarton: A Self Portrait.* New York: W. W. Norton, 1982.

Related Works

Bloom, Harold, ed. *American Poetry, 1915–1945.* New York: Chelsea House Publishers, 1987.

Bogan, Louise. *What the Woman Lived: Selected Letters of Louise Bogan, 1920–1970.* Edited by Ruth Limmer. New York: Harcourt Brace Jovanovich, 1973.

Brodzki, Bella, and Celeste Schenck. *Life Lines: Theorizing Women's Biography.* Ithaca, N.Y.: Cornell University Press, 1988.

Clark, Ronald W. *The Huxleys.* London: Heinemann, 1968.

Clarke, Suzanne. *Sentimental Modernism: Women Writers and the Revolution of the Word.* Bloomington: Indiana University Press, 1991.

Faderman, Lillian. *Surpassing the Love of Men: Romantic Friendship and Love Between Women from the Renaissance to the Present.* London: Junction Books, 1981.

Frank, Elizabeth. *Louise Bogan: A Portrait.* New York: Alfred A. Knopf, 1985.

George Sarton's European Roots. Catalog of an exhibition organized by the Archives of the State University of Ghent, 14–18 November 1984. Ghent: Communication and Cognition, 1984.

Gilbert, Sandra, and Susan Gubar. *No Man's Land: The Place of the Woman Writer in the Twentieth Century.* New Haven: Yale University Press, 1989.

Glendinning, Victoria. *Elizabeth Bowen: A Biography.* New York: Alfred A. Knopf, 1978.

Guest, Barbara. *Herself Defined: The Poet H.D. and Her World.* New York: Quill, 1984.

Heilbrun, Carolyn. *Hamlet's Mother and Other Women.* New York: Columbia University Press, 1990.

———. *Toward a Recognition of Androgyny.* New York: W. W. Norton, 1982.

———. *Writing a Woman's Life.* New York: W. W. Norton, 1988.

Kertesz, Louise. *The Poetic Vision of Muriel Rukeyser.* Baton Rouge: Louisiana State University Press, 1980.

Lloyd, Norman. *Stages,* interviewed by Francine Parker. Metuchen, N.J.: Scarecrow Press, 1990.

Mansfield, Katherine. *The Letters of Katherine Mansfield.* 2 vols. Edited by J. Middleton Murry. London: Constable, 1928.

Miller, Jean Baker. *Toward a New Psychology of Women.* Boston: Beacon Press, 1986.

Ostriker, Alicia. *Stealing the Language: The Emergence of Women's Poetry in America.* Boston: Beacon Press, 1986.

Rexroth, Kenneth. *American Poetry in the Twentieth Century.* New York: Herder and Herder, 1971.

Rosenthal, M. L. *The New Poets: American and British Poetry Since World War II.* New York: Oxford University Press, 1967.

Schanke, Robert A. *Shattered Applause: The Lives of Eva Le Gallienne.* Foreword by May Sarton. Carbondale: Southern Illinois University Press, 1992.

Sheehy, Helen. *Eva Le Gallienne.* New York: Alfred A. Knopf, 1996.

Showalter, Elaine, ed. *The New Feminist Criticism: Essays on Women, Literature, and Theory.* New York: Pantheon, 1985.

Smith, Sidonie. *A Poetics of Women's Autobiography: Marginality and the Fictions of Self-Representation.* Bloomington: Indiana University Press, 1987.

Tomalin, Claire. *Katherine Mansfield: A Secret Life.* London: Viking, 1987.

Williams, Juanita H. *Psychology of Women.* New York: W. W. Norton, 1987.

Woolf, Virginia. *The Letters of Virginia Woolf.* Vol. 6. Edited by Nigel Nicolson and Joanne Trautmann. New York: Harcourt Brace Jovanovich, 1982.

Index

Italicized page numbers indicate photographs.

PHOTOGRAPHIC CREDITS

The photographs in this book are used by permission and courtesy of the following:

Eric Dubois: p. 191

Hermann Field: p. 40

Beverly Hallam (photographs by Beverly Hallam): pp. 272, 274, 322, 361

Lotte Jacobi Archives, University of New Hampshire, Durham: pp. 224, 255, 287

Jean Taylor Kroeber: p. 37

Norman Lloyd: pp. 82, 93

Barbara Martin (photographs by Barbara Martin): pp. 377, 395

Janice Oberacker: p. 353

Billy Rose Collection, New York Public Library at Lincoln Center: p. 71

May Sarton: pp. 8, 12, 25, 27, 33, 39, 43, 46, 50, 57, 60, 70, 77, 88, 90, 98, 100, 101, 108, 110, 114, 117, 119, 134, 140, 146, 150, 159, 172, 176, 199, 218, 220 (left), 220 (right), 230, 256, 264, 265, 307, 308, 323, 369, 381

Polly Thayer Starr: pp. 91, 185

University of New Hampshire: p. 317

Wellesley College Library: p. 247

Mrs. D. Bradford Wetherell Jr.: p. 258

My gratitude to Robert Huessner of Studio Victoria in Lake Mills, Wisconsin, who rephotographed the many old photographs (often of poor quality) that May Sarton lent me.